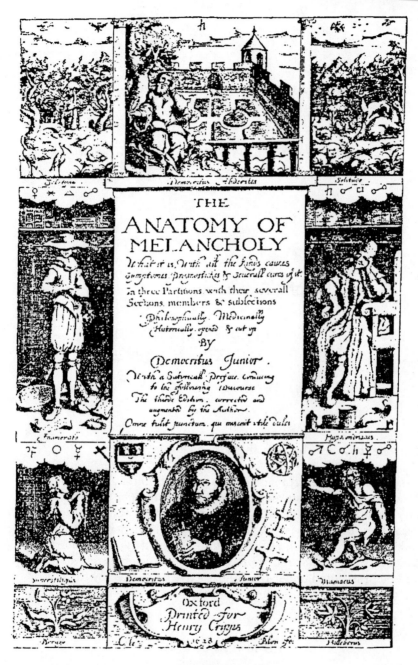

ISBN 1-56459-003-8

AAZ4656

We Publish and Purchase

Rare and Out-of-Print Metaphysical Books

For information, write to:

Kessinger Publishing Company
P.O. Box 160, Kila, MT 59920

Printed in U. S. A.

SECTION 3 MEMBER 1

A Consolatory Digression containing the Remedies of all manner of Discontents

ECAUSE, in the precedent Section, I have made mention of good counsel, comfortable speeches, persuasion, how necessarily they are required to the cure of a discontented or troubled mind, how present a remedy they yield, and many times a sole sufficient cure of themselves; I have thought fit, in this following Section, a little to digress, (if at least it be to digress in this subject), to collect and glean a few remedies, and comfortable speeches out of our best Orators, Philosophers, Divines, and Fathers of the Church, tending to this purpose. I confess, many have copiously written of this subject, Plato, Seneca, Plutarch, Xenophon, Epictetus, Theophrastus, Xenocrates, Crantor, Lucian, Boethius: and some of late, Sadoletus, Cardan, Budæus, Stella, Petrarch, Erasmus, besides Austin, Cyprian, Bernard, &c., and they so well, that, as Hierome in like case said, if our barren wits were dried up, they might be copiously irrigated from those well-springs: and I shall but repeat what has been done; yet, because these Tracts are not so obvious and common, I will epitomize, and briefly insert some of their divine precepts, reducing their voluminous and vast Treatises to my small scale; for it were otherwise impossible to bring so great vessels into so little a creek. And although (as Cardan said of his book): I know beforehand, this tract of mine many will contemn and reject; they that are fortunate, happy, and in flourishing estate, have no need of such consolatory speeches; they that are miserable and unhappy, think them unsufficient to ease their grieved minds, and comfort their misery: ————— yet I will go on; for this must needs do some good to such as are happy to bring them to a moderation, and make them reflect and know themselves, by seeing the unconstancy of human felicity, others' misery, and to such as are distressed, if they will but attend and consider of this, it cannot choose but give some content and comfort. 'Tis true, no medicine

can cure all diseases; some affections of the mind are altogether incurable; yet these helps of Art, Physick, and Philosophy, must not be contemned. Arrianus and Plotinus are stiff in the contrary opinion, that such precepts can do little good. Boethius himself cannot comfort in some cases, they will reject such speeches like bread of stones: these are the mad consolations of a doting mind.   .

Words add no courage, (which Catiline once said to his soldiers), a Captain's Oration doth not make a coward a valiant man: and, as Job feelingly said to his friends, you are but miserable comforters all. 'Tis to no purpose, in that vulgar phrase, to use a company of obsolete sentences, and familiar sayings: as Plinius Secundus, being now sorrowful and heavy for the departure of his dear friend, Cornelius Rufus, a Roman Senator, wrote to his fellow Tiro in like case: Comfort me, but supply me with new arguments that are resistless, that neither the writings nor the speeches of the philosophers can teach me; all these are by far too weak to support me under so heavy an affliction; — either say something that I never read nor heard of before, or else hold thy peace. Most men will here except trivial consolations, ordinary speeches, and known persuasions in this behalf will be of small force; what can any man say that hath not been said? To what end are such parænetical discourses? You may as soon remove mount Caucasus as alter some men's affections. Yet sure I think they cannot choose but do some good, comfort and ease a little: though it be the same again, I will say it, and upon that hope I will adventure. 'Tis not my speech this, but of Seneca, Plutarch, Epictetus, Austin, Bernard, Christ, and His Apostles. If I make nothing, as Montaigne said in like case, I will mar nothing; 'tis not my doctrine but by study, I hope I shall do no body wrong to speak what I think, and deserve not blame in imparting my mind. If it be not for thy ease, it may for mine own; so Tully, Cardan, and Boethius wrote their Consolations as well to help themselves as others. Be it as it may, I will essay.

Discontents and grievances are either general or particular; general are wars, plagues, dearths, famine, fires, inundations, unseasonable weather, epidemical diseases, which afflict whole Kingdoms, Territories, Cities: or peculiar to private men, as cares, crosses, losses, death of friends, poverty, want, sickness, orbities,* injuries, abuses, &c., generally all discontent; we men are battered by fortune's blasts; no condition free; each undergoes his own suffering. Even in the midst of our mirth and jollity, there is some grudging, some complaint; as he

* Bereavements.

saith, our whole life is a *glucupicron*, a bitter sweet passion, honey and gall mixt together, we are all miserable and discontent; who can deny it? If all, and that it be a common calamity, an inevitable necessity, all distressed, then as Cardan infers, who art thou that hopest to go free? Why dost thou not grieve thou art a mortal man, and not governor of the world? To bear the lot which all endure none can refuse! If it be common to all, why should one man be more disquieted than another? If thou alone wert distressed, it were indeed more irksome, and less to be endured; but, when the calamity is common, comfort thyself with this, thou hast more fellows, partners in woe, 'tis not thy sole case, & why shouldst thou be so impatient? " Ay, but, alas! we are more miserable than others: what shall we do? Besides private miseries, we live in perpetual fear, and danger of common enemies; we have Bellona's whips, and pitiful outcries, for Epithalamiums; for pleasant Musick, that fearful noise of Ordnance, Drums, and warlike Trumpets, still sounding in our ears; instead of nuptial Torches, we have firing of Towns & Cities; for triumphs, lamentations; for joy, tears." * *So it is, & so it was, and ever will be. He that refuseth to see and hear, to suffer this, is not fit to live in this world, and knows not the common condition of all men, to whom, so long as they live, with a reciprocal course, joys and sorrows are annexed, and succeed one another.* It is inevitable, it may not be avoided, and why then should'st thou be so much troubled? As Tully deems out of an old Poet, that which is necessary cannot be grievous. If it be so, then comfort thyself in this, that, whether thou wilt or no, it must be endured: make a virtue of necessity, and conform thyself to undergo it. If it be long, 'tis light; if grievous, it cannot last; it will away, and if nought else, yet time will wear it out, custom will ease it; oblivion is a common medicine for all losses, injuries, griefs, and detriments whatsoever, and when they are once past, this commodity comes of infelicity, it makes the rest of our life sweeter unto us: and one day it will be pleasant to remember these sufferings; the privation and want of a thing many times makes it more pleasant and delightsome than before it was. We must not think, the happiest of us all, to escape here without some misfortunes,

> *So true it is no pleasure is complete,*
> *Grief twines with joy; bitter is mix't with sweet.*   (OVID)

Heaven and earth are much unlike; those heavenly bodies indeed are freely carried in their orbs without any impediment or interruption, to continue their course for innumerable ages, and make their conversions:

* Lorchan: Gallobelgicus: 1598, of the Low Countries.

but men are urged with many difficulties, and have divers hindrances, oppositions, still crossing, interrupting their endeavours and desires; and no mortal man is free from this law of nature. We must not therefore hope to have all things answer our own expectation, to have a continuance of good success and fortunes. And as Minucius Felix, the Roman Consul, told that insulting Coriolanus, drunk with his good fortunes, " look not for that success thou hast hitherto had "; it never yet happened to any man since the beginning of the world, nor ever will, to have all things according to his desire, or to whom fortune was never opposite and adverse. Even so it fell out to him as he foretold. And so to others, even to that happiness of Augustus; though he were Jupiter's Almoner, Pluto's Treasurer, Neptune's Admiral, it could not secure him. Such was Alcibiades' fortune, Narses', that great Gonsalvo's, and most famous men's, that, as Jovius concludes, it is almost fatal to great Princes, through their own default, or otherwise circumvented with envy and malice, to lose their honours, and die contumeliously. 'Tis so, still hath been, and ever will be, there's nothing happy on its every side,

> *There's no perfection is so absolute,*
> *That some impurity doth not pollute.*

Whatsoever is under the Moon is subject to corruption, alteration; and, so long as thou livest upon the earth, look not for other. Thou shalt not here find peaceable and cheerful days, quiet times, but rather clouds, storms, calumnies; such is our fate. And as those errant planets, in their distinct orbs, have their several motions, sometimes direct, stationary, retrograde, in Apogee, Perigee, oriental, occidental, combust, feral, free, and, as our Astrologers will, have their fortitudes and debilities, by reason of those good and bad irradiations, conferred to each other's site in the heavens, in their terms, houses, case, detriments, &c., so we rise and fall in this world, ebb and flow, in and out, reared and dejected, lead a troublesome life, subject to many accidents and casualties of fortunes, variety of passions, infirmities, as well from ourselves as others.

Yea, but thou thinkest thou art more miserable than the rest, other men are happy in respect of thee, their miseries are but flea-bitings to thine, thou alone art unhappy, none so bad as thyself. Yet if, as Socrates said: all the men in the world should come and bring their grievances together, of body, mind, fortune, sores, ulcers, madness, epilepsies, agues, and all those common calamities of beggary, want, servitude, imprisonment, and lay them on a heap to be equally divided, wouldst thou share alike, and take thy portion, or be as thou art? Without question thou wouldst be as thou art. ———— If some Jupiter should say, to give us all content,

> *Well, be't so then: you, master soldier,*
> *Shall be a merchant; you, sir lawyer,*
> *A country gentleman; go you to this,*
> *That side you; why stand ye? It's well as 'tis.* (HORACE)

Every man knows his own, but not others' defects and miseries; and 'tis the nature of all men still to reflect upon themselves, their own misfortunes, not to examine or consider other men's, not to confer themselves with others: to recount their miseries, but not their good gifts, fortunes, benefits, which they have, to ruminate on their adversity, but not once to think on their prosperity, not what they have, but what they want: to look still on them that go before, but not on those infinite numbers that come after. Whereas many a man would think himself in heaven, a petty Prince, if he had but the lest part of that fortune which thou so much repinest at, abhorrest, and accountest a most vile and wretched estate. How many thousands want that which thou hast! how many myriads of poor slaves, captives, of such as work day and night in coal-pits, tin-mines, with sore toil to maintain a poor living, of such as labour in body and mind, live in extreme anguish, and pain, all which thou art free from! Thou art most happy if thou couldst be content, and acknowledge thy happiness. We know the value of a thing from the wanting more than from the enjoying; when thou shalt hereafter come to want, that which thou now loathest, abhorrest, and art weary of, and tired with, when 'tis past, thou wilt say thou werest most happy: and, after a little miss, wish with all thine heart thou hadst the same content again, might'st lead but such a life, a world for such a life: the remembrance of it is pleasant. Be silent then, rest satisfied, comfort thyself with other men's misfortunes, and, as the mouldwarp [mole] in Æsop told the fox, complaining for want of a tail, and the rest of his companions: " You complain of toys, but I am blind, be quiet "; I say to thee be thou satisfied. It is recorded of the hares, that, with a general consent, they went to drown themselves, out of a feeling of their misery; but when they saw a company of frogs more fearful than they were, they began to take courage and comfort again. Confer thine estate with others. Consider the like calamities of other men; thou wilt then bear thine own the better. Be content and rest satisfied, for thou art well in respect of others; be thankful for that thou hast, that God hath done for thee; he hath not made thee a monster, a beast, a base creature, as he might, but a man, a Christian, such a man; consider aright of it, thou art full well as thou art. No man can have what he will, he may choose whether he will desire that which he hath not: thy lot is fallen, make the best of it. If we should all sleep at all times, (as Endymion is said to have done), who then were happier than his fellow? Our life is but short, a very dream, and, while we look about, eternity is at hand: our life is a pilgrimage on earth, which wise men pass with great alacrity. If thou be in woe, sorrow, want, distress, in pain, or sickness, think of that of our Apostle, *God chastiseth them whom he loveth. They that sow in teares shall reap in joy. As the furnace proveth the potter's vessel, so doth temptation try men's thoughts;* 'tis for thy good; hadst thou not been so visited, thou hadst been utterly undone; as gold in the fire, so men are tried in adversity. Tribulation maketh rich: and, which Camerarius hath well shadowed in an Emblem of a thresher and corn,

> *As threshing separates from straw the corn,*
> *By crosses from the world's chaff are we born.*

'Tis the very same which Chrysostom comments: Corn is not separated but by threshing, nor men from worldly impediments but by tribulation. 'Tis that which Cyprian ingeminates. 'Tis that which Hierom, which all the Fathers, inculcate; so we are catechised for eternity. 'Tis that which the proverb insinuates: Harming's warning,—What hurteth teacheth; 'tis that which all the world rings into our ears. God, saith Austin, hath one son without sin, none without correction. An expert sea-man is tried in a tempest, a runner in a race, a Captain in a battle, a valiant man in adversity, a Christian in tentation and misery. We are sent as so many soldiers into this world, to strive with it, the flesh, the devil; our life is a warfare, and who knows it not? There is no easy path from earth to stars: and therefore, peradventure, this world here is made troublesome unto us, that, as Gregory notes, we should not be delighted by the way, and forget whither we are going.

> *Go now, brave men, pursue the path of high renown,*
> *Turn not your backs as dolts that fly;*
> *O'ercome the earth, as she the sky,*
> *Then you the stars shall crown.* (BOETHIUS)

Go on then merrily to heaven. If the way be troublesome, and you in misery, in many grievances, on the other side you have many pleasant sports, objects, sweet smells, delightsome tastes, musick, meats, herbs, flowers, &c., to recreate your senses. Or put case thou art now forsaken of the world, dejected, contemned, yet comfort thyself, as it was said to Hagar in the wilderness, *God sees thee, he takes notice of thee:*

there is a God above that can vindicate thy cause, that can relieve thee. And surely, Seneca thinks, he takes delight in seeing thee. The gods are well pleased when they see great men contending with adversity, as we are to see men fight, or a man with a beast. But these are toys in respect. Behold, saith he, a spectacle worthy of God: a good man contented with his estate. A tyrant is the best sacrifice to Jupiter, as the ancients held, and his best object a contented mind. For thy part then rest satisfied, *cast all thy care on him, thy burden on him, rely on him, trust on him, and he shall nourish thee, care for thee, give thee thine heart's desire;* say with David, *God is our hope and strength, in troubles ready to be found. For they that trust in the Lord shall be as mount Sion, which cannot be removed. As the mountains are about Jerusalem, so is the Lord about his people, from henceforth and for ever.*

MEMBER 2

Deformity of Body, Sickness, Baseness of Birth, Peculiar Discontents

PARTICULAR discontents and grievances are either of body, mind, or fortune, which, as they wound the soul of man, produce this melancholy, and many great inconveniences, by that antidote of good counsel and persuasion may be eased or expelled. Deformities & imperfections of our bodies, as lameness, crookedness, deafness, blindness, be they innate or accidental, torture many men: yet this may comfort them, that those imperfections of the body do not a whit blemish the soul, or hinder the operations of it, but rather help and much increase it. Thou art lame of body, deformed to the eye; yet this hinders not but that thou mayst be a good, a wise, upright, honest man. Seldom, saith Plutarch, honesty and beauty dwell together; and oftentimes under a threadbare coat lies an excellent understanding. Cornelius Mussus, that famous Preacher in Italy, when he came first into the Pulpit in Venice, was so much contemned by reason of his outside, a little, lean, poor, dejected person, they were all ready to leave the Church; but when they heard his voice they did admire him, and happy was that Senator could enjoy his company, or invite him first to his house. A silly fellow to look to may have more wit, learning, honesty, than he that struts it out, talks bombast, and is admired in the world's opinion. The best wine comes out of an old vessel. How many deformed Princes, Kings, Emperors, could I reckon up, Philosophers, Orators! Hannibal had but one eye, Appius Claudius, Timoleon, blind, Muley Hassan, King of Tunis, John, King of Bohemia, and Tiresias the Prophet. The night hath his pleasure; and for the loss of that one sense such men are commonly recompensed in the rest; they have excellent memories, other good parts, musick, and many recreations; much happiness, great wisdom, as Tully well discourseth in his Tusculan Questions. Homer was blind, yet who (saith he) made more accurate, lively, or better descriptions, with both his eyes? Democritus was blind, yet, as Laertius writes of him, he saw more than all Greece besides; as Plato concludes, when our bodily eyes are at worst, generally the eyes of our soul see best. Some Philosophers and Divines have evirated [or castrated] themselves, and cut out their eyes voluntarily, the better to contemplate. Angelus Politianus had a tetter in his nose continually running, fulsome in company, yet no man so eloquent and pleasing in his works. Aesop was crooked, Socrates pur-blind, long-legged, hairy, Democritus withered, Seneca lean and harsh, ugly to behold; yet shew me so many flourishing wits, such divine spirits! Horace a little blear-eyed contemptible fellow, yet who so sententious and wise? Marcilius Ficinus, Faber Stapulensis, a couple of dwarfs, Melancthon a short hard-favored man (little was he, yet great), yet of incomparable parts all three. Ignatius Loyola, the founder of the Jesuits, by reason of an hurt he received in his leg at the siege of Pampeluna, the chief town of Navarre in Spain, unfit for wars, and less serviceable at court, upon that accident betook himself to his beads, and by those means got more honour than ever he should have done with the use of his limbs, and properness of person: a wound hurts not the soul. Galba the Emperor was crook-backed, Epictetus lame; that great Alexander a little man of stature, Augustus Caesar of the same pitch; Agesilaus of despicable figure; Boccharis a most deformed Prince as ever Egypt had, yet, as Diodorus Siculus records of him, in wisdom and knowledge far beyond his predecessors. In the year of our Lord 1306, Uladeslaus Cubitalis, that pigmy King of Poland, reigned and fought more victorious battles than any of his long-shanked predecessors. Virtue refuseth no stature; and commonly your great vast bodies, and fine features, are sottish, dull, and leaden spirits. What's in them?

> *What, save sluggish weight, that's join'd*
> *With dull ferocity of mind?* (OVID)

What in Otus and Ephialtes (Neptune's sons in Homer) nine acres long?

> *Like tall Orion stalking o'er the flood,*
> *When with his brawny breast he cuts the waves,*
> *His shoulder scarce the topmost billow laves.* (VIRGIL)

What in Maximinus, Ajax, Caligula, and the rest of those great Zan-zummins, or gigantical Anakims, heavy, vast, barbarous lubbers?

> *If the Fates give thee a giant body,*
> *Wits they withhold, and thou'rt a noddy.*

Their body, saith Lemnius, is a burden to them, and their spirits not so lively, nor they so erect and merry. In a big body there's not a grain of wit. A little diamond is more worth than a rocky mountain; which made Alexander of Aphrodisias positively conclude, the lesser the wiser, because the soul was more contracted in such a body. Let Bodine in the fifth chapter of his Way to the Easy Understanding of History plead the rest: the lesser they are, as in Asia, Greece, they have generally the finest wits. And for bodily stature, which some so much admire, and goodly presence, 'tis true, to say the best of them, great men are proper and tall, I grant that they hide their heads in the clouds; but little men are pretty.

> *The best men of all men,*
> *Cotta, are the small men.*   (MARTIAL)

Sickness, diseases, trouble many, but without a cause. It may be 'tis for the good of their souls: 'tis parcel of their destiny: the flesh rebels against the spirit; that which hurts the one must needs help the other. Sickness is the mother of modesty, putteth us in mind of our mortality; and when we are in the full career of worldly pomp and jollity, she pulleth us by the ear, and maketh us know ourselves. Pliny calls it the sum of philosophy, if we could but perform that in our health, which we promise in our sickness. 'Tis when we are sick that we are most virtuous; for what sick man (as Secundus expostulates with Maximus) was ever lascivious, covetous, or ambitious? he envies no man, admires no man, flatters no man, despiseth no man, listens not after lies and tales, &c. And were it not for such gentle remembrances, men would have no moderation of themselves; they would be worse than tigers, wolves, and lions: who should keep them in awe? Princes, Masters, Parents, Magistrates, Judges, friends, enemies, fair or foul means, cannot contain us, but a little sickness (as Chrysostom observes) will correct and amend us. And therefore, with good discretion, Jovianus Pontanus caused this short sentence to be engraven on his tomb in Naples: Labor, sorrow, grief, sickness, want and woe, to serve proud masters, bear that superstitious yoke, and bury your dearest friends, &c., are the sauces of our life. ———— If thy disease be continuate and painful to thee, it will not surely last: *and a light affliction, which is but for a moment, causeth unto us a far more excellent and eternal weight of glory*. Bear it with patience: women endure much sorrow in child-bed, and yet they will not contain [or restrain themselves from it] ; and those that are barren, wish for this pain: be courageous, there is as much valour to be shewed in thy bed, as in an army, or at a sea-fight: thou shalt conquer or be conquered, thou shalt be rid at last. In the mean time, let it take his course, thy mind is not any way disabled. Bilibaldus Pirckheemerus, Senator to Charles V. ruled all Germany, lying most part of his days sick of the gout upon his bed. The more violent thy torture is, the less it will continue: and, though it be severe and hideous for the time, comfort thyself, as martyrs do, with honour and immortality. That famous philosopher, Epicurus, being in as miser-able pain of stone and colick as a man might endure, solaced himself with a conceit of immortality; the joy of his soul for his rare inven-tions repelled the pain of his bodily torments.

Baseness of birth is a great disparagement to some men, especially if they be wealthy, bear office, and come to promotion in a Common-wealth; then (as Boethius observes) if their birth be not answerable to their calling, and to their fellows, they are much abashed and ashamed of themselves. Some scorn their own father and mother, deny brothers and sisters, with the rest of their kindred and friends, and will not suffer them to come near them, when they are in their pomp, accounting it a scandal to their greatness to have such beggarly beginnings. Simon in Lucian, having now got a little wealth, changed his name from Simon to Simonides, for that there were so many beggars of his kin, and set the house on fire where he was born, because no body should point at it. Others buy titles, coats of arms, and by all means screw themselves into ancient families, falsifying pedigrees, usurping scutcheons, and all because they would not seem to be base. The reason is, for that this gentility is so much admired by a company of outsides, and such honour attributed to it, as amongst Germans, Frenchmen, and Venetians, the Gentry scorn the commonalty, and will not suffer them to match with them; they depress, and make them as so many asses to carry burdens. In our ordinary talk and fallings out, the most opprobrious and scur-rile name we can fasten upon a man, or first give, is to call him base rogue, beggarly rascal, and the like: whereas, in my judgement, this ought of all other grievances to trouble men least. Of all vanities and fopperies, to brag of Gentility is the greatest; for what is it they crack so much of, and challenge such superiority, as if they were demi-gods? Birth?

Didst thou so much rely upon thy birth?   (VIRGIL)

It is a nonentity, a mere flash, a ceremony, a toy, a thing of nought. Consider the beginning, present estate, progress, ending, of Gentry, and then tell me what it is. Oppression, fraud, cozening, usury, knavery, bawdry, murder, and tyranny, are the beginning of many ancient families. One hath been a blood-sucker, a parricide, the death of many a silly soul in some unjust quarrels, seditions, made many an orphan and poor widow: and for that he is made a Lord or an Earl, and his posterity Gentlemen for ever after. Another hath been a bawd, a pander to some great man, a parasite, a slave, prostituted himself, his wife, daughter, to some lascivious Prince, and for that he is exalted. Tiberius preferred many to honours in his time, because they were famous whore-masters and sturdy drinkers; many come into this parchment-row (so Varro calls it) by flattery or cozening; search your old families, and you shall scarce find of a multitude (as Æneas Sylvius [Pope Pius II., in his Boccacian novel] observes) any that have not had a wicked beginning; as that Plebeian in Machiavel in a set oration proved to his fellows, that do not rise by knavery, force, foolery, villainy, or such indirect means. They are commonly able that are wealthy; virtue and riches seldom settle on one man: who then sees not the base beginning of nobility? spoils enrich one, usury another, treason a third, witchcraft a fourth, flattery a fifth, lying, stealing, bearing false witness a sixth, adultery the seventh, &c. One makes a fool of himself to make his Lord merry, another dandles my young Master, bestows a little nag on him, a third marries a crackt piece, &c. Now may it please your good Worship, your Lordship, who was the first founder of your family? The poet answers,

> *Herding sheep, his humble lot;*
> *Or else, I'd rather not say what!* (JUVENAL)

Are he or you the better Gentleman? If he, then we have traced him to his form [or lair]. If you, what is it of which thou boastest so much? That thou art his son. It may be his heir, his reputed son, and yet indeed a Priest or a serving-man may be the true father of him; but we will not controvert that now; married women are all honest; thou art his son's son's son, begotten & born within the four seas,* &c. Thy great great great grandfather was a rich citizen, and then in all likelihood a usurer, a lawyer, and then a ———— a courtier, & then a ———— a Country

---

* The presumption in English Law is in favour of the legitimacy of any child of a married woman, and it was in Burton's time held by Sir Edward Coke that "if the husband be within the four seas, *i.e.*, within the jurisdiction of the king of England, and the wife hath issue, no proof shall be admitted to prove the child a bastard unless the husband hath an apparent impossibility of procreation."

Gentleman, and then he scraped it out of sheep, &c. And you are the heir of all his virtues, fortunes, titles; so then, what is your Gentry, but, as Hierom saith, riches grown old, ancient wealth? that is the definition of Gentility. The father goes often to the Devil to make his son a Gentleman. For the present, what is it? It began (saith Agrippa) with strong impiety, with tyranny, oppression, &c.; and so it is maintained: wealth began it (no matter how got), wealth continueth and increaseth it. Those Roman knights were so called, if they could dispend annually so much. In the kingdom of Naples and France, he that buys such lands buys the honour, title, Barony, together with it; and they that can dispend so much amongst us must be called to bear office, to be knights, or fine for it; as one observes, our nobles are measured by their means. And what now is the object of honour? What maintains our Gentry but wealth? Without means, Gentry is naught worth; nothing so contemptible and base: cheaper than seaweed. Saith Nevisanus the lawyer, to dispute of Gentry without wealth, is (saving your reverence) to discuss the original of a mard. So that it is wealth alone that denominates, money which maintains it, gives being to it, for which every man may have it. And what is their ordinary exercise? *sit to eat, drink, lie down to sleep, and rise to play:* wherein lies their worth and sufficiency? in a few coats of arms, eagles, lions, serpents, bears, tigers, dogs, crosses, bends, fesses and such like baubles, which they commonly set up in their galleries, porches, windows, on bowls, platters, coaches, in tombs, churches, men's sleeves, &c. If he can hawk and hunt, ride an horse, play at cards and dice, swagger, drink, swear, take tobacco with a grace, sing, dance, wear his clothes in fashion, court and please his mistress, talk big fustian, insult, scorn, strut, contemn others, and use a little mimical and apish compliment above the rest, he is a complete, (O illustrious praise!) a well-qualified gentleman; these are most of their employments, this their greatest commendation. What is Gentry, this parchment Nobility then, but, as Agrippa defines it, a sanctuary of knavery and naughtiness, a cloke for wickedness and execrable vices, of pride, fraud, contempt, boasting, oppression, dissimulation, lust, gluttony, malice, fornication, adultery, ignorance, impiety? A nobleman therefore, in some likelihood, as he concludes, is an atheist, an oppressor, an epicure, a gull, a dizzard, an illiterate idiot, an outside, a glow-worm, a proud fool, an arrant ass: a slave to his lust & belly, strong only in wantonness. And, as Salvianus observed of his countrymen the Aquitaines in France, first in high places, first too in the vices; and Cabinet du Roy, their own writer, distinctly of the rest: the Nobles

of Berry are most part lechers, they of Touraine thieves, they of Narbonne covetous, they of Guienne coiners, they of Provence atheists, they
of Rheims superstitious, they of Lyons treacherous, of Normandy
proud, of Picardy insolent, &c. We may generally conclude, the greater
men, the more vicious. In fine, as Æneas Sylvius adds, they are most
part miserable, sottish and filthy fellows, like the walls of their houses,
fair without, foul within. What dost thou vaunt of now? What dost
thou gape and wonder at? admire him for his brave apparel, horses,
dogs, fine houses, manors, orchards, gardens, walks? Why, a fool may
be possessor of this as well as he; and he that accounts him a better
man, a Nobleman, for having of it, he is a fool himself. Now go and brag
of thy Gentility. This is it belike, which makes the Turks at this day
scorn Nobility, and all those huffing bombast titles, which so much
elevate their poles: except it be such as have got it at first, maintain it
by some supereminent quality, or excellent worth. And for this cause,
the Ragusian Commonwealth, Switzers, and the United Provinces, in
all their Aristocracies, or Democratical Monarchies (if I may so call
them), exclude all these degrees of hereditary honours, and will admit of none to bear office but such as are learned, like those Athenian
Areopagites, wise, discreet, and well brought up. The Chinenses observe
the same custom, no man amongst them Noble by birth; out of their
Philosophers and Doctors they choose Magistrates; their politick
Nobles are taken from such as be virtuous noble: nobility is from office,
not from birth, as in Israel of old, and their office was to defend and
govern their Country, in war and peace, not to hawk, hunt, eat, drink,
game alone, as too many do. Their Lau-sie,* Mandarins, Literates [or
Scholars], Licentiates, and such as have raised themselves by their
worth, are their noblemen only, thought fit to govern a state; and why
then should any that is otherwise of worth be ashamed of his birth?
why should not he be as much respected that leaves a noble posterity, as
he that hath had noble ancestors? nay, why not more? for we adore the
rising sun most part; and how much better is it to say, I have outshone
my ancestors in goodness, to boast himself of his virtues, than of his
birth? Cathesbius, Sultan of Egypt and Syria, was by his condition a
slave, but for worth, valour, and manhood, second to no King, and for
that cause (as Jovius writes) elected Emperor of the Mamelukes. That

---

* Lau-ye, or Lau-sie, signifying Sir or Father, an honorific title given to Chinese
magistrates, their official title in Chinese being Quon-fu, according to the Jesuit missionary Matteo Ricci, whose history of the Christian Campaign in China in the 16th
century was the source of Burton's information. Ricci adds: "The Portuguese call
these magistrates Mandarins, perchance because they give mandates."

poor Spanish Pizarro, for his valour made by Charles the Fifth Marquess of Anatillo; the Turkey Pashas are all such. Pertinax, Phillipus Arabs, Maximinus, Probus, Aurelius, &c., from common soldiers became Emperors; Cato, Cincinnatus, &c., Consuls; Pius Secundus, Sixtus Quintus, Johannes Secundus, Nicholas Quintus, &c., Popes. Socrates, Virgil, Horace, born of a freedman father. The Kings of Denmark fetch their pedigree, as some say, from one Ulfo, that was the son of a bear. Many a worthy man comes out of a poor cottage. Hercules, Romulus, Alexander, (by Olympia's confession), Themistocles, Jugurtha, King Arthur, William the Conqueror, Homer, Demosthenes, P. Lombard, Peter Comestor, Bartholus, Pope Adrian the Fourth, &c., bastards; and almost in every Kingdom the most ancient families have been at first Princes' bastards; their worthiest captains, best wits, greatest scholars, bravest spirits, in all our Annals, have been base. Cardan, in his Subtilties, gives a reason why they are most part better able than others in body and mind, and so consequently more fortunate. Castruccius Castracanus, a poor child, found in the field, exposed to misery, became Prince of Lucca and Senes in Italy, a most complete soldier, and worthy captain; Machiavel compares him to Scipio or Alexander. And 'tis a wonderful thing (saith he) to him that shall consider of it, that all those, or the greatest part of them, that have done the bravest exploits here upon earth, and excelled the rest of the nobles of their time, have been still born in some abject, obscure place, or of base and obscure abject parents. A most memorable observation, Scaliger accounts it, and not to be overlooked, that most great men came of unknown fathers, and unchaste mothers. I could recite a great catalogue of them, every Kingdom, every Province, will yield innumerable examples: and why then should baseness of birth be objected to any man? Who thinks worse of Tully for being a provincial, an upstart, or Agathocles, that Sicilian King, for being a potter's son? Iphicrates and Marius were meanly born.

What wise man thinks better of any person for his nobility? As he said in Machiavel, we are all born from one ancestor, Adam's sons, conceived all and born in sin, &c. We are by nature all as one, all alike, if you see us naked; let us wear theirs and they our clothes, and what's the difference? To speak truth, as Bale did of P. Schalichius, I more esteem thy worth, learning, honesty, than thy nobility; honour thee more that thou art a writer, a Doctor of Divinity, than Earl of the Huns, Baron of Skradine, or hast title to such and such provinces, &c. Thou art more fortunate and great (so Jovius writes to Cosmo de

Medici, then Duke of Florence) for thy virtues than for thy lovely wife, and happy children, friends, fortunes, or great Duchy of Tuscany.
———— So I account thee, and who doth not so indeed? Abdolonymus was a gardener, and yet by Alexander for his virtues made King of Syria. How much better is it to be born of mean parentage, and to excel in worth, to be morally noble (which is preferred before that natural nobility, by divines, philosophers and politicians), to be learned, honest, discreet, well qualified, to be fit for any manner of employment, in country and commonwealth, war and peace, than to be degenerate Neoptolemuses, as many brave nobles are, only wise because rich, otherwise idiots, illiterate, unfit for any manner of service! Udalricus, Earl of Cilia, upbraided John Huniades with the baseness of his birth; but he replied, Thine Earldom is consumed with riot, mine begins with honor and renown. ———— Thou hast had so many noble ancestors; what is that to thee? Call not these thine own, when thou art a dizzard thyself:

Why, tell me, Ponticus, are we assessed
As to whose genealogy's longest and best? (JUVENAL)

I conclude, hast thou a sound body, and a good soul, good bringing up? art thou virtuous, honest, learned, well qualified, religious, are thy conditions good? thou art a true Nobleman, perfectly noble, although born of Thersites — (*if only thou be like Achilles*); not born but made noble, supereminent: for neither sword, nor fire, nor water, nor sickness, nor outward violence, nor the Devil himself, can take thy good parts from thee. Be not ashamed of thy birth then, thou art a Gentleman all the world over, and shalt be honored; whenas he, strip him of his fine clothes, dispossess him of his wealth, is a funge [or dolt] (which Polynices in his banishment found true by experience, Gentry was not esteemed), like a piece of coin in another country, that no man will take, and shall be contemned. Once more, though thou be a Barbarian, born at Tontonteac, a villain, a slave, a Saldanian Negro, or a rude Virginian in Dasamonquepeuc, he a French Monsieur, a Spanish Don, a Seignior of Italy, I care not how descended, of what family, of what order, Baron, Count, Prince, if thou be well qualified, and he not, but a degenerate Neoptolemus, I tell thee in a word, thou art a man, and he is a beast.

Let no son of the earth, or upstart, insult at this which I have said, no worthy Gentleman take offence. I speak it not to detract from such as are well deserving, truly virtuous and noble: I do much respect and honor true Gentry and Nobility; I was born of worshipful parents myself, in an ancient family, but I am a younger brother, it concerns me not: or had I been some great heir, richly endowed, so minded as I am, I should not have been elevated at all, but so esteemed of it, as of all other human happiness, honours, &c., they have their period, are brittle and unconstant. As Stuckius said of that great river Danube, it riseth from a small fountain, a little brook at first, sometimes broad, sometimes narrow, now slow, then swift, increased at last to an incredible greatness by the confluence of 60 navigable rivers, it vanisheth in conclusion, loseth his name, and is suddenly swallowed up of the Euxine Sea: I may say of our greatest families, they were mean at first, augmented by rich marriages, purchases, offices, they continue for some ages, with some little alteration of circumstances, fortunes, places, &c., by some prodigal son, for some default, or for want of issue, they are defaced in an instant, and their memory blotted out.

So much in the mean time I do attribute to Gentility, that, if he be well descended, of worshipful or noble parentage, he will express it in his conditions:

> *Nor, indeed are doves*
> *Begot from the fierce loves*
> *Of eagles.* (HORACE)

And although the nobility of our times be much like our coins, more in number and value, but less in weight and goodness, with finer stamps, cuts, or outsides, than of old: yet if he retain those ancient characters of true Gentry, he will be more affable, courteous, gently disposed, of fairer carriage, better temper, of a more magnanimous, heroical, and generous spirit than that common man, those ordinary boors and peasants, who are, as one observes of them, a rude, brutish, uncivil, wild, a currish generation, cruel, and malicious, uncapable of discipline and such as have scarce common sense. And it may be generally spoken of all, which Lemnius the Physician said of his travel into England, the common people were silly, sullen, dogged clowns, but the Gentlemen were courteous and civil. If it so fall out (as often it doth) that such peasants are preferred by reason of their wealth, chance, error, or otherwise, yet as the cat in the fable, when she was turned to a fair maid, would play with mice; a cur will be a cur, a clown will be a clown, he will likely favour of the stock whence he came, and that innate rusticity can hardly be shaken off.

> *Purse-proud, he struts as though he owned the earth,*
> *But still betrays the record of his birth.* (HORACE)

And though by their education such men may be better qualified, & more refined, yet there be many symptoms, by which they may likely be descried, an affected phantastical carriage, a tailor-like spruceness, a peculiar garb in all their proceedings, choicer than ordinary in his diet, and, as Hierome well describes such a one to his Nepotian: an upstart born in a base cottage, that scarce at first had coarse bread to fill his hungry guts, must now feed on kickshaws and made dishes, will have all variety of flesh and fish, the best oysters, &c. A beggar's brat will be commonly more scornful, imperious, insulting, insolent, than another man of his rank: nothing so intolerable as a fortunate fool, as Tully found long since out of his experience. Nothing ruder than a base-born one climbed above his station: set a beggar on horseback, and he will ride a-gallop, a-gallop, &c.

> *Who is this doth rage and rave?*
> *One that lately was a slave.*
> *Ah, the wild beasts gentler be*
> *Than a slave at length set free!* (CLAUDIAN)

He forgets what he was, domineers, and many such other symptoms he hath, by which you may know him from a true Gentleman. Many errors & obliquities are on both sides, noble, ignoble, made, born: yet still in all callings, as some degenerate, some are well deserving, and most worthy of their honours. And as Busbequius said of Solyman the Magnificent, he was worthy of that great Empire: many meanly descended are most worthy of their honour, politick nobles, and well deserve it. Many of our Nobility so born (which one said of Hephaestion, Ptolemaeus, Seleucus, Antigonus, and the rest of Alexander's followers, they were all worthy to be Monarchs and Generals of Armies) deserve to be Princes. And I am so far forth of Sesellius his mind, that they ought to be preferred (if capable) before others, as being nobly born, ingeniously brought up, and from their infancy trained to all manner of civility. For learning & virtue in a Nobleman is more eminent, and, as a jewel set in gold is more precious, and much to be respected, such a man deserves better than others, and is as great an honour to his family as his Noble family to him. In a word, many Noblemen are an ornament to their order; many poor men's sons are singularly well endowed, most eminent and well deserving for their worth, wisdom, learning, virtue, valour, integrity; excellent members and pillars of a Commonwealth. And, therefore, to conclude that which I first intended, to be base by birth, meanly born, is no such disparagement. And thus have I proved what I had to prove.

MEMBER 3

Against Poverty and Want, with such other Adversities

ONE of the greatest miseries that can befal a man, in the world's esteem, is poverty or want, which makes men steal, bear false witness, swear, forswear, contend, murder and rebel, which breaketh sleep, and causeth death itself. No burden (saith Menander) so intolerable as poverty: it makes men desperate, it erects and dejects: wealth gives honours, and friendships too; money makes, but poverty mars, &c., and all this in the world's esteem: yet, if considered aright, it is a great blessing in itself, an happy estate, and yields no such cause of discontent, or that men should therefore account themselves vile, hated of God, forsaken, miserable, unfortunate. Christ himself was poor, born in a manger, and had not a house to hide his head in all his life, lest any man should make poverty a judgement of God, or an odious estate. And as he was himself, so he informed his Apostles and Disciples, they were all poor, Prophets poor, Apostles poor (*Silver and gold have I none*). *As sorrowing* (saith Paul) *and yet always rejoicing; as having nothing, and yet possessing all things.* Your great Philosophers have been voluntarily poor, not only Christians, but many others. Crates Thebanus was adored for a god in Athens: a nobleman by birth, many servants he had, an honorable attendance, much wealth, many Manors, fine apparel; but when he saw this, that all the wealth of the world was but brittle, uncertain, and no whit availing to live well, he flung his burden into the sea, and renounced his estate. Those Curiuses and Fabriciuses will be ever renowned for contempt of these fopperies, wherewith the world is so much affected. Among Christians I could reckon up many Kings and Queens, that have forsaken their Crowns and fortunes, and wilfully abdicated themselves from these so much esteemed toys; many that have refused honours, titles, and all this vain pomp and happiness, which others so ambitiously seek, and carefully study to compass and attain. Riches, I deny not, are God's good gifts, and blessings; and honour is in being honoured, honours are from God; both rewards of virtue, and fit to be sought after, sued for, and may well be possessed: yet no such great happiness in having, or misery in wanting of them. Saith Austin, good men have wealth that we should not think it evil; and bad men that we * should not rely on or hold it so good; as the rain falls on both sorts, so are riches given to good and bad, but they are good only to the godly. But confer both estates, for natural parts they

---

* An emendation for the " they " of the text.

are not unlike; and a beggar's child, as Cardan well observes, is no whit inferior to a Prince's, most part better; and for those accidents of fortune, it will easily appear there is no such odds, no such extraordinary happiness in the one, or misery in the other. He is rich, wealthy, fat; what gets he by it: pride, insolency, lust, ambition, cares, fears, suspicion, trouble, anger, emulation and many filthy diseases of body and mind. He hath indeed variety of dishes, better fare, sweet wine, pleasant sauce, dainty musick, gay clothes, lords it bravely out, &c., and all that which Micyllus admired in Lucian, but with them he hath the gout, dropsies, apoplexies, palsies, stone, pox, rheums, catarrhes, crudities, oppilations, Melancholy, &c. Lust enters in, anger, ambition. According to Chrysostom, the sequel of riches is pride, riot, intemperance, arrogancy, fury, and all irrational courses.

> *Soft riches and luxurious ways*
> *Bring scandal to our present days,* (JUVENAL)

with their variety of dishes, many such maladies of body and mind get in, which the poor man knows not of. As Saturn, in Lucian, answered the discontented commonalty, (which because of their neglected Saturnal Feasts in Rome made a grievous complaint and exclamation against rich men), that they were much mistaken in supposing such happiness in riches; you see the best, (said he), but you know not their several gripings and discontents: they are like painted walls, fair without, rotten within: diseased, filthy, crazy, full of intemperate effects; and who can reckon half? if you but knew their fears, cares, anguish of mind, and vexation, to which they are subject, you would hereafter renounce all riches.

> *O that their breasts were but conspicuous,*
> *How full of fear within, how furious!*
> *The narrow seas are not so boisterous.* (SENECA)

Yea, but he hath the world at will that is rich, the good things of the earth; it is pleasant to draw from a great heap: he is a happy man, adored like a God, a Prince, every man seeks to him, applauds, honours, admires him. He hath honours indeed, abundance of all things: but (as I said) withal, pride, lust, anger, faction, emulation, fears, cares, suspicion, enter with his wealth; for his intemperance he hath aches, crudities, gouts, & as fruits of his idleness & fulness, lust, surfeiting, drunkenness, all manner of diseases: the wealthier, the more dishonest. He is exposed to hatred, envy, peril, and treason, fear of death, of degradation, &c.: 'tis a slippery position and close to a precipice, and the higher he climbs, the greater is his fall. The lightning commonly sets on fire the highest towers; in the more eminent place he is, the more subject to fall. As a tree that is heavy laden with fruit breaks her own boughs, with their own greatness they ruin themselves: which Joachimus Camerarius hath elegantly expressed. Plenty hath made me poor. Their means is their misery: though they do apply themselves to the times, to lie, dissemble, collogue, and flatter their lieges, obey, second his will and commands, as much as may be, yet too frequently they miscarry, they fat themselves like so many hogs, as Æneas Sylvius observes, that, when they are full fed, they may be devoured by their Princes, as Seneca by Nero was served, Sejanus by Tiberius, and Haman by Ahasuerus. I resolve with Gregory, honour is a tempest, the higher they are elevated, the more grievously depressed. For the rest of his prerogatives which wealth affords, as he hath more, his expenses are the greater. "When goods increase, they are increased that eat them; and what good cometh to the owners, but the beholding thereof with the eyes?"

You may thresh a hundred thousand bushels of grain,
But more than mine your belly will not contain. (HORACE)

An evil sickness, Solomon calls it, *and reserved to them for an evil. They that will be rich fall into many fears and temptations, into many foolish and noisome lusts, which drown men in perdition. Gold and silver hath destroyed many.* Worldly wealth is the devil's bait: so writes Bernard; and as the Moon, when she is fuller of light, is still farthest from the Sun, the more wealth they have, the farther they are commonly from God. (If I had said this of myself, rich men would have pulled me a-pieces, but hear who saith, & who seconds it, an Apostle) therefore St. James bids them *weep and howl for the miseries that shall come upon them, their gold shall rust and canker, and eat their flesh as fire.* I may then boldly conclude with Theodoret, as often as you see a man abounding in wealth, who drinks from golden cups and sleeps on down, and naught withal, I beseech you call him not happy, but esteem him unfortunate, because he hath many occasions offered to live unjustly: on the other side, a poor man is not miserable, if he be good, but therefore happy, that those evil occasions are taken from him.

He is not happy that is rich,
And hath the world at will,
But he that wisely can God's gifts
Possess and use them still:
That suffers and with patience
Abides hard poverty,
And chooseth rather for to die
Than do such villainy. (HORACE)

Wherein now consists his happiness? What privileges hath he more than other men? Or rather what miseries, what cares and discontents, hath he not more than other men?

Nor treasures, nor mayors' officers remove
The miserable tumults of the mind:
Or cares that lie about, or fly above
Their high-roofed houses, with huge beams combined. (HORACE)

'Tis not his wealth that can vindicate him, let him have Job's inventory; let who will be Crœsus or Crassus, the golden waves of Pactolus will not wash away a single one of their miseries: Crœsus or rich Crassus cannot now command health, or get himself a stomack. His Worship, as Apuleius describes him, in all his plenty and great provision, is forbidden to eat, or else hath no appetite (sick in bed, can take no rest, sore grieved with some chronick disease, contracted with full diet and ease, or troubled in mind) when as, in the mean time, all his household are merry, and the poorest servant that he keeps doth continually feast. 'Tis gilt happiness, as Seneca terms it, tin-foil'd happiness, an unhappy kind of happiness, if it be happiness at all. His gold, guard, clattering of harness, and fortifications against outward enemies, cannot free him from inward fears and cares.

*Indeed, men's * still attending fears and cares,*
Nor armours clashing, nor fierce weapons fears:
With kings converse they boldly, and king's peers,
Fearing no flashing that from gold appears. (LUCRETIUS)

Look how many servants he hath, and so many enemies he suspects; for liberty, he entertains ambition; his pleasures are no pleasures; and that which is worst, he cannot be private or enjoy himself as other men do, his state is a servitude. A countryman may travel from kingdom to kingdom, province to province, city to city, and glut his eyes with delightful objects, hawk, hunt, and use those ordinary disports, without any notice taken, all which a Prince or a great man cannot do. He keeps in for state, not to cheapen the dignity of majesty, as our China Kings, of Borneo, and Tartarian Chams, those golden slaves, are said to do, seldom or never seen abroad, that men may note him the more when he does, which the Persian Kings so precisely observed of old. A poor man takes more delight in an ordinary meal's meat, which he hath but seldom, than they do with all their exotick dainties, and continual viands:

Our very sports by repetition tire,
But rare delight breeds ever new desire. (JUVENAL)

'Tis the rarity and necessity that makes a thing acceptable and pleasant.

* An emendation for the " men " in Burton's text.

Darius, put to flight by Alexander, drank puddle water to quench his thirst, and it was pleasanter, he swore, than any wine or mead. All excess, as Epictetus argues, will cause a dislike; sweet will be sour, which made that temperate Epicurus sometimes voluntarily fast. But they, being always accustomed to the same dishes (which [as Tully hath said in his Tusculan Questions] are nastily dressed by slovenly cooks, that after their obscenities never wash their bawdy hands), be they fish, flesh, compounded, made dishes, or whatsoever else, are therefore cloyed: nectar's self grows loathsome to them, they are weary of all their fine palaces, they are to them as so many prisons. A poor man drinks in a wooden dish, and eats his meat in wooden spoons, wooden platters, earthen vessels, and such homely stuff; the other in gold, silver, and precious stones; but with what success? Fear of poison in the one, security in the other. A poor man is able to write, to speak his mind, to do his own business himself; saith Philostratus, a rich man employs a parasite, and, as the Mayor of a City, speaks by the Town-clerk, or by Mr. Recorder, when he cannot express himself. Nonius the Senator hath a purple coat as stiff with Jewels, as his mind is full of vices, rings on his fingers worth 20,000 sesterces, and as Perozes, the Persian King, an union [or pearl] in his ear worth 100 pound weight of gold: Cleopatra hath whole boars and sheep served up to her table at once, drinks jewels dissolved, 40,000 sesterces in value; but to what end? Doth a man that is a-dry, desire to drink in gold? Doth not a cloth suit become him as well, and keep him as warm, as all their silks, satins, damasks, taffeties and tissues? Is not home-spun cloth as great a preservative against cold, as a coat of Tartar Lambs' wool, dyed in grain, or a gown of Giants' beards? Nero, saith Suetonius, never put on one garment twice, and thou hast scarce one to put on; what's the difference? one's sick, the other sound: such is the whole tenor of their lives, and that which is the consummation and upshot of all, death itself, makes the greatest difference. One like an hen feeds on the dunghill all his days, but is served up at last to his Lord's table; the other as a Falcon is fed with Partridge and Pigeons, and carried on his master's fist, but when he dies, is flung to the muckhill, and there lies. The rich man lives, like Dives, jovially here on earth, drunk with money, makes the best of it; and *boasts himself in the multitude of his riches, he thinks his house, called after his own name, shall continue for ever; but he perisheth like a beast, his way utters his folly:* evilly got, evilly spent: *like sheep they lie in the grave. They spend their days in wealth, and go suddenly down to Hell.* For all Physicians and medicines enforcing nature, a swooning wife, family's complaints, friends' tears, Dirges, Masses, funeral-songs, funerals, for all Orations, counterfeit hired acclamations, Elogiums, Epitaphs, hearses, heralds, black mourners, solemnities, obelisks, and Mausolean tombs, if he have them at least, he like a hog goes to Hell with a guilty conscience (*Hell opens its mouth for them*) and a poor man's curse: his memory stinks like the snuff of a candle when it is put out; scurrile libels, and infamous obloquies accompany him; when as poor Lazarus is the Temple of God, lives and dies in true devotion, hath no more attendants but his own innocency, the Heaven a tomb, desires to be dissolved, buried in his Mother's lap, and hath a company of Angels ready to convey his soul into Abraham's bosom, he leaves an everlasting and a sweet memory behind him. Crassus and Sulla are indeed still recorded, but not so much for their wealth, as for their victories: Crœsus for his end, Solomon for his wisdom. In a word, to get wealth is a great trouble, anxiety to keep, grief to lose it.

> *I pray for those of doltish mind:*
> *To wealth and place let them aspire;*
> *What the true blessings are, they'll find*
> *When they of these false burdens tire.* (BOETHIUS)

But consider all those other unknown, concealed happinesses, which a poor man hath, (I call them unknown, because they be not acknowledged in the world's esteem, or so taken): happy are they in the mean time, if they would take notice of it, make use or apply it to themselves. *A poor man wise is better than a foolish King.* Poverty is the way to heaven, the mistress of philosophy, the mother of religion, virtue, sobriety, sister of innocency, and an upright mind. How many such encomiums might I add out of the Fathers, Philosophers, Orators! It troubles many that they are poor, they account of it as a great plague, curse, a sign of God's hatred, damn'd villainy itself, a disgrace, shame and reproach; but to whom, or why? If fortune hath envied me wealth, thieves have robbed me, my father have not left me such revenues as others have, that I am a younger brother, basely born, of mean parentage, a dirt-dauber's son, am I therefore to be blamed? an Eagle, a Bull, a Lion, is not rejected for his poverty, and why should a man? 'tis fortune's fault, not mine. Good Sir, I am a servant, (to use Seneca's words), howsoever your poor friend; a servant, and yet your chamber-fellow, and if you consider better of it, your fellow-servant. ———— I am thy drudge in the world's eyes, yet in God's sight peradventure thy better, my soul is more precious, and I dearer unto him. As Evangelus at large proves in Macrobius, the meanest servant is most precious in his

sight. Thou art an Epicure, I am a good Christian; thou art many
parasangs before me in means, favour, wealth, honour, Claudius his Narcissus, Nero's Massa, Domitian's Parthenius, a favourite, a golden slave;
thou coverest thy floors with marble, thy roofs with gold, thy walls with
statues, fine pictures, curious hangings, &c., thou dost tread upon riches,
&c., what of all this? what's all this to true happiness? I live and breathe
under that glorious Heaven, that august Capitol of nature, enjoy the
brightness of Stars, that clear light of Sun and Moon, those infinite
creatures, plants, birds, beasts, fishes, herbs, all that sea and land affords,
far surpassing all that art and opulence can give. I am free, and, which
Seneca said of Rome, a thatched roof sheltered free men, but slavery
afterward dwelt amidst marble and gold: thou hast Amalthea's horn
[of nectar and ambrosia], plenty, pleasure, the world at will, I am
despicable and poor; but a word over-shot, a blow in choler, a game at
tables, a loss at Sea, a sudden fire, the Prince's dislike, a little sickness,
&c., may make us equal in an instant; howsoever, take thy time, triumph
and insult a while: as Alphonsus said, death will equalize us all at last. I
live sparingly in the mean time, am clad homely, fare hardly; is this a
reproach? am I the worse for it? am I contemptible for it? am I to be
reprehended? A learned man in Nevisanus [the Lawyer, his book of
The Nuptial Grove] was taken down for sitting amongst Gentlemen,
but he replied, " my nobility is about the head, yours declines to the
tail," & they were silent. Let them mock, scoff and revile, 'tis not thy
scorn, but his that made thee so; *he that mocketh the poor reproacheth
him that made him*, and *he that rejoiceth at affliction, shall not be un-
punished*. For the rest, the poorer thou art, the happier thou art: saith
Epictetus, he is richer, not better, than thou art, not so free from lust,
envy, hatred, ambition.

> *Happy the man who, far from worldly moil,*
> *With his own oxen tills the paternal soil.*   (HORACE)

Happy he, in that he is freed from the tumults of the world, he seeks no
honours, gapes after no preferment, flatters not, envies not, temporizeth
not, but lives privately, and well contented with his estate;

> *Not hungry with untimely wishes,*
> *Nor fed upon care's empty dishes,*
> *Heeding little or not at all*
> *What in the great world may befal.*

He is not troubled with state matters, whether Kingdoms thrive better
by succession or election; whether Monarchies should be mixt, temperate, or absolute; the house of Ottomon's and Austria is all one to

him; he enquires not after Colonies or new discoveries; whether Peter were at Rome, or Constantine's donation be of force; what comets or new stars signify, whether the earth stand or move, there be a new world in the Moon, or infinite worlds, &c. He is not touched with fear of invasions, factions or emulations.

> *A happy soul, and like to God himself,*
> *Whom not vain glory macerates or strife,*
> *Or wicked joys of that proud swelling pelf,*
> *But leads a still, poor, and contented life.* (POLITIANUS)

A secure, quiet, blissful state he hath, if he could acknowledge it. But here is the misery, that he will not take notice of it; he repines at rich men's wealth, brave hangings, dainty fare, as Simonides objecteth to Hiero: he hath all the pleasures of the world; *he knows not the affliction of Joseph, stretching himself on ivory beds, and singing to the sound of the viol.* And it troubles him that hath not the like; there is a difference (he grumbles) between Laplolly [or Loblolly] and Pheasants, to tumble i'th'straw and lie in a down-bed, betwixt wine and water, a cottage and a palace. He hates nature (as Pliny characterizeth him) that she hath made him lower than a God, and is angry with the Gods that any man goes before him; and although he hath received much, yet (as Seneca follows it) he thinks it an injury that he hath no more, and is so far from giving thanks for his Tribuneship, that he complains he is not Praetor; neither doth that please him, except he may be Consul. Why is he not a Prince, why not a Monarch, why not an Emperor? Why should one man have so much more than his fellows, one have all, another nothing? Why should one man be a drudge or slave to another? one surfeit, another starve, one live at ease, another labour, without any hope of better fortune? Thus they grumble, mutter, and repine: not considering that inconstancy of human affairs, judicially conferring one condition with another, or well weighing their own present estate. What they are now, thou mayest shortly be; and what thou art, they shall likely be. Expect a little, confer future and times past with the present, see the event, and comfort thyself with it. It is as well to be discerned in Commonwealths, Cities, Families, as in private men's estates. Italy was once Lord of the world, Rome, the Queen of Cities, vaunted herself of two myriads of Inhabitants; now that all-commanding Country is possessed by petty Princes, Rome, a small village in respect. Greece, of old the seat of civility, mother of sciences and humanity; now forlorn, the nurse of barbarism, a den of thieves. Germany then, saith Tacitus, was incult and horrid; now full of magnificent Cities. Athens, Corinth,

Carthage, how flourishing Cities! now buried in their own ruins: the haunt of ravens and wild hogs, like so many wildernesses, a receptacle of wild beasts. Venice, a poor fisher-town, Paris, London, small Cottages in Cæsar's time; now most noble Emporiums. Valois, Plantagenet, and Scaliger, how fortunate families! how likely to continue! now quite extinguished and rooted out. He stands aloft to-day, full of favour, wealth, honour, and prosperity, in the top of fortune's wheel: to-morrow in prison, worse than nothing, his son's a beggar. Thou art a poor servile drudge. the dregs of the people, a very slave, thy son may come to be a Prince, with Maximinus, Agathocles, &c., a Senator, a General of an Army. Thou standest bare to him now, workest for him, drudgest for him and his, takest an alms of him: stay but a little, and his next heir peradventure shall consume all with riot, be degraded, thou exalted, and he shall beg of thee. Thou shalt be his most honourable Patron, he thy devout servant, his posterity shall run, ride, and do as much for thine, as it was with Frescobald and Cromwell, it may be for thee. Citizens devour country Gentlemen, and settle in their seats; after two or three descents, they consume all in riot, it returns to the City again.

> *Comes a new dweller now; for Nature planned*
> *None as perpetual owner of the land,*
> *Not he nor me; but he who me expels*
> *Must in his turn yet yield to some one else.* (HORACE)

A Lawyer buys out his poor Client, after a while his Client's posterity buy out him and his; so things go round, ebb and flow.

> *Umbrenus calls this land his own,*
> *As once Ofellus; be it known,*
> *No man can own it: we or they*
> *Use and enjoy it while we may.* (HORACE)

As he said then, Whose field are you, that have so many masters? so say I of land, houses, movables & money, mine to-day, his anon, whose to-morrow? In fine, (as Machiavel observes), virtue and prosperity beget rest, rest idleness, idleness riot, riot destruction, from which we come again to good Laws; good Laws engender virtuous actions, virtue glory, and prosperity; and it is no dishonour then (as Guicciardine adds) for a flourishing man, City, or State, to come to ruin, nor infelicity to be subject to the Law of nature. Therefore (I say) scorn this transitory state, look up to Heaven, think not what others are, but what thou art: what's thy place in the world: and what thou shalt be, what thou mayest be. Do (I say) as Christ himself did, when he lived here on earth, imitate him as much as in thee lies. How many great Cæsars, mighty Monarchs, Tetrarchs, Dynasts, Princes, lived in his days, in what plenty, what delicacy, how bravely attended, what a deal of gold and silver, what treasure, how many sumptuous palaces had they, what Provinces and Cities, ample territories, fields, rivers, fountains, parks, forests, lawns, woods, cells, &c.!

Yet Christ had none of all this, he would have none of this, he voluntarily rejected all this, he could not be ignorant, he could not err in his choice, he contemned all this, he chose that which was safer, better,. & more certain, and less to be repented, a mean estate, even poverty itself; and why dost thou then doubt to follow him, to imitate him, and his Apostles, to imitate all good men? So do thou tread in his divine steps, and thou shalt not err eternally, as too many worldlings do, that run on in their own dissolute courses, to their confusion and ruin, thou shalt not do amiss. Whatsoever thy fortune is, be contented with it, trust in him, rely on him, refer thyself wholly to him. For know this, in conclusion, *it is not as men, but as God will. The Lord maketh poor, and maketh rich, bringeth low, and exalteth, he lifteth the poor from the dust, and raiseth the beggar from the dunghill, to set them amongst Princes, and make them inherit the seat of glory;* 'tis all as he pleaseth, how, and when, and whom; he that appoints the end (though to us unknown) appoints the means likewise subordinate to the end.

Yea, but their present estate crucifies and torments most mortal men, they have no such forecast to see what may be, what shall likely be, but what is, though not wherefore, or from whom: thus it hurts, their present misfortunes grind their souls, and an envious eye which they cast upon other men's prosperities: their neighbor's flock is fatter: how rich, how fortunate, how happy is he! But in the mean time he doth not consider the other's miseries, his infirmities of body and mind, that accompany his estate, but still reflects upon his own false conceived woes and wants, whereas, if the matter were duly examined, he is in no distress at all, he hath no cause to complain.

> *Cease to complain; not poor, indeed,*
> *Is he who hath what fills his need.* (HORACE)

He is not poor, he is not in need. Nature is content with bread and water; and he that can rest satisfied with that, may contend with Jupiter himself for happiness. In that golden age, the trees gave wholesome shade to sleep under, and the clear rivers drink. The Israelites drank water in the wilderness; Sampson, David, Saul, Abraham's servant when he went for Isaac's wife, the Samaritan woman, and how many besides might I reckon up, Egypt, Palestine, whole countries in the

Indies, that drink pure water all their lives. The Persian Kings themselves drank no other drink than the water of Choaspes that runs by Susa, which was carried in bottles after them, whithersoever they went. Jacob desired no more of God, but bread to eat, and clothes to put on in his journey. Happy is he to whom with sparing hand God hath given sufficiency; bread is enough to strengthen the heart. And if you study philosophy aright, saith Madaurensis, whatever is beyond this moderation, is not useful, but troublesome. A. Gellius, out of Euripides, accounts bread and water enough to satisfy nature: of which there is no surfeit; the rest is not a feast, but riot. S. Hierome esteems him rich that hath bread to eat, and a potent man that is not compelled to be a slave: hunger is not ambitious, so that it have to eat, and thirst doth not prefer a cup of gold. It was no Epicurean speech of an Epicure, He that is not satisfied with a little will never have enough; and very good counsel of him in the Poet, O my son, mediocrity of means agrees best with men; too much is pernicious.

> *He who with a mind content*
> *Lives on little, is opulent.* (LUCRETIUS)

And if thou canst be content, thou hast abundance: thou hast little, thou wantest nothing. 'Tis all one to be hanged in a chain of gold, or in a rope; to be filled with dainties, or coarser meat.

> *If belly, sides, and feet be well at ease,*
> *A Prince's pleasure can thee no more please.* (HORACE)

Socrates in a Fair, seeing so many things bought and sold, such a multitude of people convened to that purpose, exclaimed forthwith, O ye Gods, what a sight of things do not I want! It is thy want alone that keeps thee in health of body and mind, and that which thou persecutest and abhorrest as a feral plague is thy Physician and chiefest friend, which makes thee a good man, an healthful, a sound, a virtuous, an honest, and happy man. For when Virtue came from Heaven, (as the Poet feigns), rich men kicked her up, wicked men abhorred her, Courtiers scoffed at her, Citizens hated her, and that she was thrust out of doors in every place, she came at last to her sister Poverty, where she had found good entertainment. Poverty and Virtue dwell together.

> *Ah, safe the poor man's narrow hearth:*
> *God's gift, not taken at its worth!* (LUCAN)

How happy art thou if thou couldst be content! "Godliness is great gain, if a man can be content with that which he hath"; and all true happiness is in a mean estate. I have little wealth, as he [Lipsius] said, but what the mind makes great, a Kingdom in conceit: —

I ask no more, O son of Maia, save
That I may keep these gifts that now I have. (HORACE)
I have enough, and desire no more.
———— *The Gods were kind*
In giving me a meek and modest mind. (HORACE)
'Tis very well, and to my content. Let my fortune and my garments be
both alike fit for me. And which Sebastian Foscarinus, sometime Duke
of Venice, caused to be engraven on his Tomb in St. Mark's Church,
Hear, O ye Venetians, and I will tell you which is the best thing in the
world: to contemn it. ———— I will engrave it in my heart, it shall be
my whole study to contemn it. Let them take wealth, let the mard love
mards, so that I may have security; who has been well hidden has lived
well; though I live obscure, yet I live clean and honest; and when as
the lofty oak is blown down, the silly reed may stand. Let them take
glory, for that's their misery; let them take honour, so that I may have
heart's ease. Lead me, O God, whither thou wilt, I am ready to follow;
command, I will obey. I do not envy at their wealth, titles, offices;
Let who will, in his might,
Stand on power's slippery height,
let me live quiet and at ease. Peradventure we shall be, (as Puteanus
comforted himself), when they are not; when they are dead and gone,
and all their pomp vanished, our memory may flourish:
The immortal Muses to a name
Give imperishable fame. (MARULLUS)
Let him be my Lord, Patron, Baron, Earl, and possess so many goodly
Castles, it is well for me that I have a poor house, and a little wood, and
a well by it, &c.
With which I feel myself more truly blest
Than if my sires the quaestor's power possess'd. (HORACE)
I live, thank God, as merrily as he, and triumph as much in this my
mean estate, as if my Father and Uncle had been Lord Treasurer, or my
Lord Mayor. He feeds of many dishes, I of one; I care for Christ [saith
S. Hierome], what care I of what stuff my excrements be made? ————
He that lives according to nature cannot be poor, and he that exceeds can
never have enough: the whole world cannot give him content. A small
thing that the righteous hath, is better than the riches of the ungodly.
And better is a poor morsel with quietness than abundance with strife.
Be content then, enjoy thyself, and, as Chrysostom adviseth, be not
angry for what thou hast not, but give God hearty thanks for what thou
hast received.

> *If scanty herbs thou canst with peace enjoy,*
> *Seek not for richer cates mixed with annoy.*

But what wantest thou, to expostulate the matter? or what hast thou not better than a rich man? Health, competent wealth, children, security, sleep, friends, liberty, diet, apparel, and what not, or at least mayest have (the means being so obvious, easy and well known) for as he inculcated to himself,

> *Merry Martial, make thy state*
> *By these means more fortunate,*
> *Toil no more to lay up treasure,*
> *Banish strife and welcome pleasure.*

I say again thou hast, or at least mayest have it, if thou wilt thyself, and that which I am sure he wants, a merry heart. Passing by a village in the territory of Milan, (saith S. Austin), I saw a poor beggar that had got, belike, his belly full of meat, jesting and merry; I sighed, and said to some of my friends that were then with me, What a deal of trouble, madness, pain and grief do we sustain and exaggerate unto ourselves, to get that secure happiness, which this poor beggar hath prevented us of, and which we peradventure shall never have! For that which he hath now attained with the begging of some small pieces of silver, a temporal happiness, and present heart's ease, I cannot compass with all my careful windings, and running in and out. And surely the beggar was very merry, but I was heavy: he was secure, but I was timorous. And if any man should ask me now, whether I had rather be merry, or still so solicitous and sad, I should say, Merry. If he should ask me again, Whether I had rather be as I am, or as this beggar was, I should sure choose to be as I am, tortured still with cares and fears; but out of peevishness, and not out of truth. ———— That which S. Austin said of himself here in this place, I may truly say to thee; thou discontented wretch, thou covetous niggard, thou churl, thou ambitious and swelling toad, 'tis not want, but peevishness, which is the cause of thy woes; settle thine affection, thou hast enough.

> *What thou didst covet, thou hast got;*
> *Rest, then, from thine laborious lot.* (HORACE)

Make an end of scraping, purchasing this Manor, this field, that house, for this and that child; thou hast enough for thyself and them:

> *Far from Ulubræ thou needst not to roam,*
> *All thou desirest can be found at home.* (HORACE)

'Tis at hand, at home already, which thou so earnestly seekest. But O that I had but one nook of ground, that field there, that pasture! O that

I could but find a poet of money now, to purchase, &c., to build me a new house, to marry my daughter, place my son, &c. O if I might but live a while longer to see all things settled, some two or three years, I would pay my debts, make all my reckonings even; but they are come and past, and thou hast more business than before. O madness! to think [as Cardan saith in his Book on Diversities] to settle that in thine old age when thou hast more, which in thy youth thou canst not now compose, having but a little. Pyrrhus [in Plutarch] would first conquer Africa, and then Asia, and then live merrily, and take his ease: but when Cineas the Orator told him he might do that already, rested satisfied, contemning his own folly. Comparing little things to great, thou mayest do the like, and therefore be composed in thy fortune. Thou hast enough; he that is wet in a bath can be no more wet if he be flung into Tiber, or into the Ocean itself; and if thou hadst all the world, or a solid mass of gold, as big as the world, thou canst not have more than enough; enjoy thyself at length, and that which thou hast; the mind is all; be content, thou art not poor, but rich, and so much the richer, as Censorinus well writ to Cerellius, in wishing less, not having more. I say then, ('tis Epicurus' advice), add no more wealth, but diminish thy desires; and, as Chrysostom well seconds him, if virtue is to be enriched, spurn wealth; that's true plenty, not to have, but not to want riches; 'tis more glory to contemn, than to possess; and to desire nothing is godlike. How many deaf, dumb, halt, lame, blind, miserable persons, could I reckon up that are poor, and withal distressed, in imprisonment, banishment, galley slaves, condemned to the mines, quarries, to gyves, in dungeons, perpetual thraldom, than all which thou art richer, thou art more happy, to whom thou art able to give an alms, a Lord, in respect, a petty Prince! Be contented then, I say, repine and mutter no more, for thou art not poor indeed, but in opinion.

Yea, but this is very good counsel, and rightly applied to such as have it, and will not use it, that have a competency, that are able to work and get their living by the sweat of their brows, by their trade, that have something yet; he that hath birds may catch birds; but what shall we do that are slaves by nature, impotent, and unable to help ourselves, mere beggars, than languish and pine away, that have no means at all, no hope of means, no trust of delivery, or of better success? as those old Britons complained to their Lords and Masters the Romans, oppressed by the Picts, the Barbarians drove them to the sea, the sea drove them back to the Barbarians; our present misery compels us to cry out and howl, to make our moan to rich men; they turn us back with a scornful answer to our misfortune again, and will take no pity of us; they commonly overlook their poor friends in adversity; if they chance to meet them, they voluntarily forget, and will take no notice of them; they will not, they cannot help us. Instead of comfort, they threaten us, miscall, scoff at us, to aggravate our misery, give us bad language, or, if they do give good words, what's that to relieve us? According to that of Thales, easy it is to advise others; who cannot give good counsel? 'tis cheap, it costs them nothing. It is an easy matter when one's belly is full to declaim against feasting. *Doth the wild Ass bray when he hath grass, or loweth the Ox when he hath fodder?* No men living so jocund, so merry, as the people of Rome when they had plenty; but when they came to want, to be hunger-starved, neither shame, nor laws, nor arms, nor Magistrates could keep them in obedience. Seneca pleaded hard for poverty, and so did those lazy Philosophers: but in the mean time he was rich, they had wherewithal to maintain themselves; but doth any poor man extol it? There are those (saith Bernard) that approve of a mean estate, but on that condition they never want themselves; and some again are meek, so long as they may say or do what they list; but if occasion be offered, how far are they from all patience! I would to God (as he said) no man should commend poverty, but he that is poor; or he that so much admires it, would relieve, help, or ease others.

Now if thou hear'st us, and art a good man,
Tell him that wants, to get means, if you can.   (PETRONIUS)

But no man hears us, we are most miserably dejected, the scum of the world,

On our hides there's scarce at all
Room for another blow to fall.   (OVID)

We can get no relief, no comfort, no succour. We have tried all means, yet find no remedy: no man living can express the anguish and bitterness of our souls, but we that endure it; we are distressed, forsaken, in torture of body and mind, in another Hell: and what shall we do? When Crassus, the Roman Consul, warred against the Parthians, after an unlucky battle fought, he fled away in the night, and left four thousand men, sore sick and wounded in his tents, to the fury of the enemy, which when the poor men perceived, they made lamentable moan, and roared down-right, as loud as Homer's Mars when he was hurt, which the noise of 10,000 men could not drown, and all for fear of present death. But our estate is far more tragical and miserable, much more to be deplored, and far greater cause have we to lament; the Devil and the world persecute us, all good fortune hath forsaken us, we are left to the rage of

beggary, cold, hunger, thirst, nastiness, sickness, irksomeness, to continual torment, labour and pain, to derision and contempt, bitter enemies
all, and far worse than any death; death alone we desire, death we seek,
yet cannot have it, and what shall we do?

> ————— *What's bad, 'tis sure*
> *Thou canst by custom well endure.* (OVID)

Accustom thyself to it, and it will be tolerable at last. Yea, but I may
not, I cannot, I am in the extremity of human adversity; and, as a
shadow leaves the body when the Sun is gone, I am now left and lost,
and quite forsaken of the world. Who's stretched on earth need fear no
fall; comfort thyself with this yet, thou art at the worst, and, before
it be long, it will either overcome thee, or thou it. If it be violent, it
cannot endure, 'twill end, or make an end: let the Devil himself and all
the plagues of Egypt come upon thee at once,

> *Yield not thou to any woe,*
> *Against it the more boldly go.* (VIRGIL)

Be of good courage; misery is virtue's whetstone. As Cato told his
soldiers marching in the deserts of Libya, thirst, heat, sands, serpents,
were pleasant to a valiant man; honorable enterprises are accompanied
with dangers and damages, as experience evinceth; they will make the
rest of thy life relish the better. But put case they continue, thou art not
so poor as thou wast born, and, as some hold, ['tis] much better to be
pitied than envied. But be it so thou hast lost all, poor thou art, dejected,
in pain of body, grief of mind, thine enemies insult over thee, thou art
as bad as Job; yet tell me (saith Chrysostom) was Job or the Devil the
greater conqueror? surely Job. The Devil had his goods, he sate on the
muck-hill, and kept his good name; he lost his children, health, friends,
but he kept his innocency; he lost his money, but he kept his confidence
in God, which was better than any treasure. Do thou then, as Job did,
triumph as Job did, and be not molested as every fool is. But how shall
this be done? Chrysostom answers, with great facility, if thou shalt but
meditate on Heaven. Hannah wept sore, and, troubled in mind, could
not eat; *but, why weepest thou?* said Elkanah her husband, *and why
eatest thou not? why is thine heart troubled? am not I better to thee
than ten sons?* and she was quiet. Thou art here vexed in this world; but
say to thyself, Why art thou troubled, O my soul? Is not God better to
thee than all temporalities, and momentary pleasures of the world? be
then pacified. And though thou beest now peradventure in extreme want,
it may be 'tis for thy further good, to try thy patience, as it did Job's,
and exercise thee in this life: trust in God, and rely upon Him, and thou

shalt be crowned in the end. What's this life to eternity? The world hath forsaken thee, thy friends and fortunes all are gone: yet know this, that the very hairs of thine head are numbered, that God is a spectator of all thy miseries, He sees thy wrongs, woes and wants. 'Tis His good will and pleasure it should be so, and He knows better what is for thy good than thou thyself. His providence is over all, at all times; *he hath set a guard of Angels over us, and keeps us as the apple of his eye.* Some he doth exalt, prefer, bless with worldly riches, honours, offices and preferments, as so many glistering stars he makes to shine above the rest: some he doth miraculously protect from thieves, incursions, sword, fire, and all violent mischances, and, as the Poet feigns of that Lycian Pandarus, Lycaon's son, when he shot at Menelaus the Grecian with a strong arm, and deadly arrow, Pallas, as a good mother keeps flies from her child's face asleep, turned by the shaft, and made it hit on the buckle of his girdle; so some he solicitously defends, others he exposeth to danger, poverty, sickness, want, misery, he chastiseth and corrects, as to him seems best, in his deep, unsearchable and secret judgement, and all for our good. The Tyrant took the City, (saith Chrysostom), God did not hinder it; led them away captives, so God would have it; he bound them, God yielded to it; flung them into the furnace, God permitted it; heated the Oven hotter, it was granted: and when the Tyrant had done his worst, God shewed his power, and the children's patience,——— he freed them: so can he thee, and can help in an instant, when it seems to him good. Rejoice not against me, O my enemy; for though I fall, I shall rise: when I sit in darkness, the Lord shall lighten me. Remember all those Martyrs, what they have endured, the utmost that human rage and fury could invent, with what patience they have borne, with what willingness embraced it. Though he kill me, saith Job, I will trust in him. As Chrysostom holds, a just man is impregnable, and not to be overcome. The gout may hurt his hands, lameness his feet, convulsions may torture his joints, but not his upright mind, his soul is free.

> *Take then my flock, my gold, my goods, my land,*
> *Put me in prison, bind me foot and hand.*   (HORACE)

Take away his money, his treasure is in Heaven; banish him his Country, he is an inhabitant of that heavenly Jerusalem; cast him into bonds, his conscience is free; kill his body, it shall rise again; he fights with a shadow, that contends with an upright man: he will not be moved. Though Heaven itself should fall on his head, he will not be offended. He is impenetrable, as an anvil hard, as constant as Job.

> *God can deliver me when he will, I ween.*   (HORACE)

Be thou such a one; let thy misery be what it will, what it can, with patience endure it, thou mayest be restored as he was. When the earth is forbidden thee, Heaven is thine; when deserted by men, flee to God. *The poor shall not always be forgotten, the patient abiding of the meek shall not perish for ever. The Lord will be a refuge of the oppressed, and a defence in the time of trouble.*

> *Lame was Epictetus, and poor Irus,*
> *Yet to them both God was propitious.*

Lodovicus Vertomannus, that famous traveller, endured much misery, yet surely, saith Scaliger, he was a favourite of God, in that he did escape so many dangers, God especially protected him, he was dear unto him. Thou art now in the vale of misery, in poverty, in agony, in temptation; rest, eternity, happiness, immortality, shall be thy reward, as Chrysostom pleads, if thou trust in God, and keep thine innocency. Though 'tis ill with thee now, 'twill not be always so; a good hour may come upon a sudden; expect a little.

Yea, but this expectation is it which tortures me in the mean time; future hope makes present hunger; whilst the grass grows, the horse starves; despair not, but hope well:

> *Think, Battus, that to-morrow may bring scope*
> *For better things; while there is life there's hope.* (THEOCRITUS)

Cheer up, I say, be not dismayed; the farmer lives on hope: he that sows in tears shall reap in joy.

> *When fortune torments me,*
> *Then hope contents me.*

Hope refresheth, as much as misery depresseth; hard beginnings have many times prosperous events, and that may happen at last, which never was yet. A desire accomplished delights the soul.

> *Which makes m' enjoy my joys long wished at last,*
> *Welcome that hour shall come when hope is past.* (HORACE)

A lowering morning may turn to a fair afternoon. *The hope that is deferred is the fainting of the heart, but when the desire cometh it is a tree of life.* Many men are both wretched and miserable at first, but afterwards most happy; and oftentimes it so falls out, as Machiavel relates of Cosimo de Medici, that fortunate and renowned Citizen of Europe, that all his youth was full of perplexity, danger and misery, till forty years were past, and then upon a sudden the Sun of his honour brake out as through a cloud. Hunniades was fetched out of prison, and Henry the Third of Portugal out of a poor Monastery, to be crowned Kings.

> *There's many a slip*
> *'Twixt cup and lip.* (ERASMUS)

Beyond all hope and expectation many things fall out, and who knows what may happen? As Phillippus said, all the Suns are not yet set, a day may come to make amends for all. *Though my father and mother forsake me, yet the Lord will gather me up. Wait patiently on the Lord and hope in him. Be strong, hope and trust in the Lord, and he will comfort thee and give thee thine heart's desire.*

> *Hope, and reserve thyself for better days.* (VIRGIL)

Fret not thyself because thou art poor, contemned, or not so well for the present as thou wouldst be, not respected as thou oughtest to be, by birth, place, worth; or that which is a double corrosive, thou hast been happy, honourable and rich, art now distressed and poor, a scorn of men, a burden to the world, irksome to thyself and others, thou hast lost all. Misery it is to have once been happy, and, as Boethius calls it, the worst kind of ill fortune; this made Timon half mad with melancholy, to think of his former fortunes and present misfortunes; this alone makes many miserable wretches discontent. I confess it is a great misery to have been happy, the quintessence of infelicity, to have been honourable and rich, but yet easily to be endured; security succeeds, and to a judicious man a far better estate. The loss of thy goods and money is no loss; thou hast lost them, they would otherwise have lost thee. If thy money be gone, thou art so much the lighter; and, as Saint Hierome persuades Rusticus the Monk to forsake all and follow Christ: gold and silver are too heavy metals for him to carry that seeks Heaven.

> *There in the sea now let us cast*
> *The gems and gold we have amassed, —*
> *If truly we repent our sins;*
> *For in these all vice begins.* (HORACE)

Zeno the Philosopher lost all his goods by shipwrack, he made light of it, fortune had done him a good turn: she can take away my means, but not my mind. He set her at defiance ever after, for she could not rob him that had nought to lose: for he was able to contemn more than they could possess or desire. Alexander sent an hundred talents of gold to Phocion of Athens for a present, because he heard he was a good man: but Phocion returned his talents back again with a " Permit me to be a good man still; let me be as I am. I ask not gold, nor any reward." That Theban Crates flung of his own accord his money into the Sea, " I had rather drown you, than you should drown me." Can

Stoicks and Epicures thus contemn wealth, and shall not we that are Christians? It was a generous speech of Cotta in Sallust, Many miseries have happened unto me at home, and in the wars abroad, of which, by the help of God, some I have endured, some I have repelled and by mine own valour overcome: courage was never wanting to my designs, nor industry to my intents: prosperity or adversity could never alter my disposition. A wise man's mind, as Seneca holds, is like the state of the world above the Moon, ever serene. Come then what can come, befall what may befall, meet it with an unbroken and unconquerable courage: 'tis in adversity that one should be bold. Hope and patience are two sovereign remedies for all, the surest reposals, the softest cushions to lean on in adversity. What can't be cured must be endured. If it cannot be helped, or amended, make the best of it; he is wise that suits himself to the time. As at a game at tables, so do by all such inevitable accidents. If thou canst not fling what thou wouldest, play thy cast as well as thou canst. Every thing, saith Epictetus, hath two handles, the one to be held by, the other not: 'tis in our choice to take and leave whether we will (all which Simplicius, his Commentator, hath illustrated by many examples); and 'tis in our own power, as they say, to make or mar ourselves. Conform thyself then to thy present fortune, and cut thy coat according to thy cloth: be contented with thy lot, state, and calling, whatsoever it is, and rest as well satisfied with thy present condition in this life.

> Be as thou art; and as they are, so let
> Others be still; what is and may be, covet.

And as he that is invited to a feast eats what is set before him and looks for no other, enjoy that thou hast, and ask no more of God than what he thinks fit to bestow upon thee.

> Not all of us such fortune gain
> As that Corinth we attain. (HORACE)

We may not be all Gentlemen, all Catos, or Læliuses, as Tully telleth us, all honourable, illustrious and serene, all rich; but because mortal men want many things, therefore, saith Theodoret, hath God diversely distributed his gifts, wealth to one, skill to another, that rich men might encourage and set poor men a-work, poor men might learn several trades to the common good. As a piece of arras is composed of several parcels, some wrought of silk, some of gold, silver, crewel of divers colours, all to serve for the exornation [or embellishment] of the whole; [as] Musick is made of divers discords and keys, a total sum of many small numbers: so is a Commonwealth of several inequal trades and callings. If all should be Crœsuses and Dariuses, all idle, all in fortunes equal, who should till the land? as Menenius Agrippa well satisfied the tumultuous rout of Rome in his elegant Apologue of the belly and the rest of the members. Who should build houses, make our several stuffs for raiments? We should all be starved for company, as Poverty declared at large in Aristophanes' Plutus, and sue at last to be as we were at first. And therefore God hath appointed this inequality of States, orders and degrees, a subordination, as in all other things. The earth yields nourishment to vegetals, sensible creatures feed on vegetals, both are substitutes to reasonable souls, and men are subject amongst themselves, and all to higher powers: so God would have it.

All things then being rightly examined, and duly considered as they ought, there is no such cause of so general discontent, 'tis not in the matter itself, but in our mind, as we moderate our passions, and esteem of things. Saith Cardan, Let thy fortune be what it will, 'tis thy mind alone that makes thee poor or rich, miserable or happy. Saith divine Seneca, I have seen men miserably dejected in a pleasant village, and some again well occupied and at good ease in a solitary desert; 'tis the mind, not the place, causeth tranquillity, and that gives true content. I will yet add a word or two for a corollary. Many rich men, I dare boldly say it, that lie on down-beds, with delicacies pampered every day, in their well furnished houses, live at less heart's ease, with more anguish, more bodily pain, and through their intemperance more bitter hours, than many a prisoner or galley-slave. Mæcenas sleeps no better on down than Regulus in his barrel. Those poor starved Hollanders, whom Bartison their Captain left in Nova Zembla in the year 1596, or those eight miserable Englishmen that were lately left behind to winter in a stove in Greenland in 77 degrees of latitude, 1630, so pitifully forsaken and forced to shift for themselves in a vast dark and desert place, to strive and struggle with hunger, cold, desperation, and death itself. 'Tis a patient and quiet mind (I say it again and again) gives true peace and content. So for all other things, they are, as old Chremes told us, as we use them. Parents, friends, fortunes, country, birth, alliance, &c., ebb and flow with our conceit; please or displease, as we accept and construe them, or apply them to ourselves. Everyone is the builder of his own fortune, and in some sort I may truly say prosperity and adversity are in our own hands. No one is hurt except by himself; and, which Seneca confirms out of his judgment and experience, every man's mind is stronger than fortune, and leads him to what side he will; a cause to himself each one is of his good or bad life. But, will we, or nill we, make the worst of it, and suppose a

man in the greatest extremity, 'tis a fortune which some infinitely * prefer before prosperity; of two extremes, it is the best. Pride runs riot in
prosperity; men in prosperity forget God and themselves, they are
besotted with their wealth, as birds with henbane: miserable, if fortune forsake them, but more miserable if she tarry and overwhelm
them: for when they come to be in great place, rich, they that were most
temperate, sober and discreet, in their private fortunes, as Nero, Otho,
Vitellius, Heliogabalus (excellent rulers, had they never ruled) degenerate on a sudden into brute beasts, so prodigious in lust, such tyrannical oppressors, &c., they cannot moderate themselves, they become
Monsters, odious, Harpies, what not? When they have achieved triumphs, riches, honours, then they give themselves up to revelling and
indolence; 'twas Cato's note, they cannot contain. For that cause belike,

> *Eutrapelus, when he would hurt a knave,*
> *Gave him gay clothes and wealth to make him brave:*
> *Because now rich he would quite change his mind,*
> *Keep whores, fly out, set honesty behind.* (HORACE)

On the other side, in adversity many mutter and repine, despair, &c.,
both bad I confess, as a shoe too big, or too little, one pincheth, the
other sets the foot awry; but of evils choose the least. If adversity hath
killed his thousand, prosperity hath killed his ten thousand: therefore
adversity is to be preferred; the one deceives, the other instructs: the
one miserably happy, the other happily miserable: and therefore many
Philosophers have voluntarily sought adversity, and so much commend
it in their precepts. Demetrius, in Seneca, esteemed it a great infelicity,
that in his lifetime he had no misfortune. Adversity then is not so
heavily to be taken, and we ought not in such cases so much to macerate
ourselves: there is no such odds in poverty and riches. To conclude in
Hierom's words, I will ask our Magnificoes that build with Marble, and
bestow a whole Manor on a thread, what difference betwixt them and
Paul the Eremite, that bare old man? they drink in jewels, he in [or
out of] his hand: he is poor and goes to Heaven, they are rich and go
to Hell.

MEMBER 4

Against Servitude, Loss of Liberty, Imprisonment, Banishment

SERVITUDE, loss of liberty, imprisonment, are no such miseries as they
are held to be: we are slaves & servants, the best of us all: as we do reverence our masters, so do our masters their superiors: Gentlemen serve

* "Indefinitely," in the text.

Nobles, & Nobles subordinate to Kings, every ruler under a harder ruler, Princes themselves are God's servants. They are subject to their own Laws, and, as the Kings of China, endure more than slavish imprisonment, to maintain their state and greatness, they never come abroad. Alexander was a slave to fear, Cæsar of pride, Vespasian to his money (it matters little whether we be enslaved by men or things), Heliogabalus to his gut, and so of the rest. Lovers are slaves to their Mistresses, rich men to their Gold, Courtiers generally to lust and ambition, and all slaves to our affections, as Evangelus well discourseth in Macrobius, and Seneca the Philosopher, an extreme and inescapable servitude, he calls it, a continual slavery, to be so captivated by vices, and who is free? Why then dost thou repine? He is master enough, Hierom saith, who is not forced to serve. Thou carriest no burdens, thou art no prisoner, no drudge, and thousands want that liberty, those pleasures, which thou hast. Thou art not sick, and what wouldest thou have? But we must all eat of the forbidden fruit. Were we enjoined to go to such and such places, we would not willingly go: but being barred of our liberty, this alone torments our wandering soul that we may not go. A Citizen of ours, saith Cardan, was sixty years of age, and had never been forth of the walls of the City Milan; the Prince hearing of it, commanded him not to stir out: being now forbidden that which all his life he had neglected, he earnestly desired, and being denied, he died for grief.

What I have said of servitude, I say again of imprisonment. We are all prisoners. What's our life but a prison? We are all imprisoned in an Island. The world itself to some men is a prison, our narrow seas as so many ditches, and when they have compassed the Globe of the earth, they would fain go see what is done in the Moon. In Muscovy, and many other Northern parts, all over Scandia, they are imprisoned half the year in stoves,* they dare not peep out for cold. At Aden in Arabia they are penned in all day long with that other extreme of heat, and keep their markets in the night. What is a ship but a prison? and so many Cities are but as so many hives of Bees, Ant-hills. But that which thou abhorrest, many seek: women keep in all the Winter, and most part of Summer, to preserve their beauties; some for love of study: Demosthenes shaved his beard, because he would cut off all occasion from going abroad: how many Monks and Friars, Anchorites, abandon the world! A monk in town is a fish out of water. Art in prison? Make right use of it, and mortify thyself. Where may a man contemplate

* Herbastein. See Index.

better than in solitariness, or study more than in quietness? Many worthy men have been imprisoned all their lives, and it hath been occasion of great honour and glory to them, much publick good by their excellent meditation. Ptolemæus, King of Egypt, now being taken with a grievous infirmity of body, that he could not stir abroad, became Strato's scholar, fell hard to his book, and gave himself wholly to contemplation, and upon that occasion (as mine Author adds) to his great honour built that renowned Library at Alexandria, wherein were 40,-000 volumes. Severinus Boethius never writ so elegantly as in prison, Paul so devoutly, for most of his Epistles were dictated in his bonds: Joseph, saith Austin, got more credit in prison than when he distributed corn and was Lord of Pharaoh's house. It brings many a lewd riotous fellow home, many wandering rogues it settles, that would otherwise have been like raving Tigers, ruined themselves and others.

Banishment is no grievance at all, every land is the brave man's land, and that's a man's country where he is well at ease. Many travel for pleasure to that city, saith Seneca, to which thou art banished, and what a great part of the citizens are strangers born in other places! 'Tis their country that are born in it, and they would think themselves banished to go to the place which thou leavest, and from which thou art so loth to depart. 'Tis no disparagement to be a stranger, or so irksome to be an exile. The rain is a stranger to the earth, rivers to the Sea, Jupiter in Egypt, the Sun to us all. The Soul is an alien to the Body, a Nightingale to the air, a Swallow in an house, and Ganymede in Heaven, an Elephant at Rome, a Phœnix in India; and such things commonly please us best which are most strange, and come farthest off. Those old Hebrews esteemed the whole world Gentiles; the Greeks held all Barbarians but themselves; our modern Italians account of us as dull Transalpines by way of reproach, they scorn thee and thy country, which thou so much admirest. 'Tis a childish humour to hone * after home, to be discontent at that which others seek; to prefer, as base Icelanders and Norwegians do, their own ragged Island before Italy or Greece, the Gardens of the world. There is a base Nation in the north, saith Pliny, called Chauci, that live amongst rocks and sands by the sea side, feed on fish, drink water: and yet these base people account themselves slaves in respect, when they come to Rome; (as he concludes), so it is, Fortune favours some to live at home to their further punishment: 'tis want of judgement. All places are distant from Heaven alike, the Sun shines happily as warm in one city as in another, and to a

* Yearn.

wise man there is no difference of climes; friends are every where to him that behaves himself well, and a Prophet is not esteemed in his own Country. Alexander, Cæsar, Trajan, Adrian, were as so many land-leapers [or vagrants], now in the East, now in the West, little at home, and Paulus Venetus, Lodovicus Vertomannus, Pinzonus, Cadamustus, Columbus, Americus Vespuccius, Vascus Gama, Drake, Candish, Oliver á Nort, Schouten, got all their honour by voluntary expeditions. But you say such men's travel is voluntary; we are compelled, and as malefactors must depart: yet know this of Plato to be true, God hath an especial care of strangers, and when he wants friends and allies, he shall deserve better and find more favour with God and men. Besides the pleasure of peregrination, variety of objects will make amends; and so many nobles, Tully, Aristides, Themistocles, Theseus, Codrus, &c., as have been banished, will give sufficient credit unto it. Read Peter Alcionius his two books of this subject.

MEMBER 5

Against Sorrow for Death of Friends or otherwise, vain Fear, &c.

DEATH and departure of friends are things generally grievous; the most austere and bitter accidents that can happen to a man in this life, to part for ever, to forsake the world and all our friends, 'tis the last and the greatest terror, most irksome and troublesome unto us; a man dies as often as he loses his friends. And though we hope for a better life, eternal happiness, after these painful and miserable days, yet we cannot compose ourselves willingly to die; the remembrance of it is most grievous unto us, especially to such who are fortunate and rich: they start at the name of death, as an horse at a rotten post. Say what you can of that other world, with Metezuma that Indian prince, they had rather be here. Nay, many generous spirits, and grave staid men otherwise, are so tender in this, that at the loss of a dear friend, they will cry out, roar, and tear their hair, lamenting some months after, howling O Hone, as those Irish women and Greeks at their graves, commit many undecent actions, and almost go beside themselves. My dear father, my sweet husband, mine only brother's dead, to whom shall I make my moan? O miserable me! What fountains of tears shall I shed, &c. What shall I do?

> *My brother's death my study hath undone,*
> *Woe's me! alas! my brother he is gone!*   (CATULLUS)

Mezentius would not live after his son:

> *Now mid my kind I linger still,*
> *And live: but leave the light I will.*   (VIRGIL)

And Pompey's wife cried out at the news of her husband's death,

> *Ah, 'twould be too base of me*
> *Not to die for love of thee,*   (LUCAN)

as Tacitus of Agrippina, not able to moderate her passions. So, when she heard her son was slain, she abruptly broke off her work, changed countenance and colour, tore her hair, and fell a roaring downright.

> *Her cheek at once the colour fled,*
> *She dropped the distaff and the thread,*
> *And with dishevelled locks she sped,*
> *Loud wailing in her womanhead.*   (VIRGIL)

Another would needs run upon the sword's point after Euryalus' departure:

> *O Rutules, your mercy shew,*
> *And pierce me with your arrows too!*   (VIRGIL)

O let me die, some good man or other make an end of me! How did Achilles take on for Patroclus' departure! A black cloud of sorrows overshadowed him, saith Homer. Jacob rent his clothes, put sack-cloth about his loins, sorrowed for his son a long season, and could not be comforted, but would needs go down into the grave unto his son. Many years after, the remembrance of such friends, of such accidents, is most grievous unto us, to see or hear of it, though it concern not ourselves, but others. Scaliger saith of himself, that he never read Socrates' death, in Plato's Phædo, but he wept. Austin shed tears when he read the destruction of Troy. But howsoever this passion of sorrow be violent, bitter, and seizeth familiarly on wise, valiant, discreet men, yet it may surely be withstood, it may be diverted. For what is there in this life, that it should be so dear unto us? or that we should so much deplore the departure of a friend? The greatest pleasures are common society, to enjoy one another's presence, feasting, hawking, hunting, brooks, woods, hills, musick, dancing, &c., all this is but vanity and loss of time, as I have sufficiently declared.

> *Whilst we drink, prank ourselves, with wenches dally,*
> *Old age upon 's at unawares doth sally.*   (JUVENAL)

As Alchemists spend that small modicum they have to get gold, and never find it, we lose and neglect eternity, for a little momentary pleasure which we cannot enjoy; nor shall ever attain to in this life. We abhor death, pain, & grief, all, & yet we will do nothing of that which should vindicate us from, but rather voluntarily thrust ourselves upon it. The lascivious prefers his whore before his life, or good estate; an angry man his revenge: a parasite his gut; ambitious, honours; covetous, wealth; a thief his booty; a soldier his spoil; we abhor diseases, and yet we pull them upon us. We are never better or freer from cares than when we sleep, and yet, which we so much avoid and lament, death is but a perpetual sleep; and why should it, as Epicurus argues, so much affright us? When we are, death is not: but when death is, then we are not: our life is tedious and troublesome unto him that lives best; 'tis a misery to be born, a pain to live, a trouble to die: death makes an end to our miseries, and yet we cannot consider of it. A little before Socrates drank his potion of hemlock, he bid the Citizens of Athens cheerfully farewell, and concluded his speech with this short sentence, My time is now come to be gone, I to my death, you to live on; but which of these is best, God alone knows. ———— For there is no pleasure here but sorrow is annexed to it, repentance follows it. If I feed liberally, I am likely sick or surfeit; if I live sparingly, my hunger and thirst is not allayed; I am well neither full nor fasting; if I live honest, I burn in lust; if I take my pleasure, I tire and starve myself, and do injury to my body and soul. Of so small a quantity of mirth, how much sorrow! after so little pleasure, how great misery! 'Tis both ways troublesome to me, to rise and go to bed, to eat and provide my meat; cares and contentions attend me all day long, fears and suspicions all my life. I am discontented, and why should I desire so much to live? But an happy death will make an end of all our woes and miseries; 'tis the certain cure for all our troubles; why shouldst not thou then say with old Simeon, since thou art so well affected, *Lord now let thy servant depart in peace:* or with Paul, *I desire to be dissolved, and to be with Christ?* 'Tis a blessed hour that leads us to a blessed life, and blessed are they that die in the Lord. But life is sweet, and death is not so terrible in itself as the concomitants of it, a loathsome disease, pain, horror, &c., and many times the manner of it, to be hanged, to be broken on the wheel, to be burned alive. Servetus the heretick, that suffered in Geneva, when he was brought to the stake, and saw the executioner come with fire in his hand, roared so loud that he terrified the people. An old Stoick would have scorned this. It troubles some to be unburied, or so:

> *Thy gentle parents shall not bury thee,*
> *Amongst thine ancestors entomb'd to be,*
> *But feral fowl thy carcass shall devour,*
> *Or drowned corpse hungry fish-maws shall scour.*   (VIRGIL)

As Socrates told Crito, it concerns me not what is done with me when I am dead; easy is the loss of burial: I care not so long as I feel it not; let them set mine head on the pike of Teneriffe, and my quarters in the four parts of the world; you shall, on a cross, feed crows; let wolves or bears devour me; the canopy of heaven covers him that hath no tomb. So likewise for our friends, why should their departure so much trouble us? They are better, as we hope, and for what then dost thou lament, as those do whom Paul taxed in his time, *that have no hope.* 'Tis fit there should be some solemnity.

> *After one day for grief we ought*
> *To bury our dead with steadfast thought.* (HOMER)

Job's friends said not a word to him the first seven days, but let sorrow and discontent take their course, themselves sitting sad and silent by him. When Jupiter himself wept for Sarpedon, what else did the Poet insinuate, but that some sorrow is good? Who can blame a tender mother, if she weep for her children? Beside, as Plutarch holds, 'tis not in our power not to lament, it takes away mercy and pity, not to be sad; 'tis a natural passion to weep for our friends, an irresistible passion to lament and grieve. I know not how (saith Seneca), but sometimes 'tis good to be miserable in misery: and for the most part all grief evacuates itself by tears.

> *'Tis a kind of pleasure so*
> *To glut thyself upon thy woe,*
> *Raining out thy grief in tears.* (OVID)

Yet after a day's mourning or two, comfort thyself for thy heaviness. 'Tis unbecoming idly to mourn the dead; 'twas Germanicus's advice of old, that we should not dwell too long upon our passions, to be desperately sad, immoderate grievers, to let them tyrannize, there's an art of not being too unhappy, a medium to be kept: we do not (saith Austin) forbid men to grieve, but to grieve overmuch: I forbid not a man to be angry, but I ask for what cause he is so? not to be sad, but why is he sad? not to fear, but wherefore is he afraid? —————— I require a moderation as well as a just reason. The Romans and most civil Commonwealths have set a time to such solemnities, they must not mourn after a set day, or if in a family a child be born, a daughter or son married, some state or honour be conferred, a brother be redeemed from his bands [or chains], a friend from his enemies, or the like, they must lament no more. And 'tis fit it should be so; to what end is all their funeral pomp, complaints, and tears? When Socrates was dying, his friends Apollodorus and Crito, with some others, were weeping by him, which he perceiving, asked them what they meant: for that very cause

he put all the women out of the room; upon which words of his they
were abashed, and ceased from their tears. Lodovicus Cortesius, a rich
lawyer of Padua (as Bernardinus Scardeonius relates) commanded by
his last will, and a great mulct if otherwise to his heir, that no funeral
should be kept for him, no man should lament: but as at a wedding,
music and minstrels to be provided; and instead of black mourners, he
took order, that twelve virgins clad in green should carry him to the
Church. His will and testament was accordingly performed, and he
buried in S. Sophia's Church. Tully was much grieved for his daughter
Tulliola's death at first, until such time that he had confirmed his mind
with some Philosophical precepts, then he began to triumph over fortune and grief, and for her reception into Heaven to be much more
joyed than before he was troubled for her loss. If an Heathen man could
so fortify himself from Philosophy, what shall a Christian from Divinity? Why dost thou so macerate thyself? 'Tis an inevitable chance,
the first statute in Magna Charta, an everlasting Act of Parliament, all
must die. It cannot be revoked, we are all mortal, and these all commanding Gods and Princes die like men: the proud as well as the lowly
head is hidden, the last is equalled with the first. O weak condition of
human estate! Sylvius exclaims: Ladislaus, King of Bohemia, 18 years
of age, in the flower of his youth, so potent, rich, fortunate and happy,
in the midst of all his friends, amongst so many Physicians, now ready
to be married, in 36 hours sickened and died. We must so be gone sooner
or later all, and as Calliopius in the Comedy took his leave of his spectators and auditors, must we bid the world farewell (Exit Calliopius),
and having now played our parts, for ever be gone. Tombs and monuments have the like fate, since even to sepulchres themselves are dooms
assigned; Kingdoms, Provinces, Towns and cities, have their periods,
and are consumed. In those flourishing times of Troy, Mycenæ was the
fairest city in Greece, ruled all Greece, but it, alas, and that Assyrian
Nineveh are quite overthrown. The like fate hath that Egyptian and
Bœotian Thebes, Delos, the common council-house of Greece, and
Babylon, the greatest city that ever the sun shone on, hath now nothing
but walls and rubbish left.

What of old Athens but the name remains? (OVID)

Thus Pausanias complained in his times. And where is Troy itself now,
Persepolis, Carthage, Cyzicum, Sparta, Argos, and all those Grecian
cities? Syracuse and Agrigentum, the fairest towns in Sicily, which had
sometime 700,000 inhabitants, are now decayed: the names of Hiero,
Empedocles, &c., of those mighty numbers of people, only left. One

Anacharsis is remembered amongst the Scythians; the world itself must have an end, and every part of it. All other towns are mortal, as Peter Gillius concludes of Constantinople, this city alone shall last as long as the world; but 'tis not so: nor site, nor strength, nor sea, nor land, can vindicate a city, but it and all must vanish at last. And as to a traveller, great mountains seem plains afar off, at last are not discerned at all, cities, men, monuments decay, nor can its fabrick preserve the solid globe; the names are only left, those at length forgotten, and are involved in perpetual night.

Returning out of Asia, when I sailed from Ægina towards Megara, I began (saith Servius Sulpicius, in a consolatory epistle of his to Tully) to view the country round about. Ægina was behind me, Megara before, Piræus on the right hand, Corinth on the left, what flourishing towns heretofore, now prostrate and overwhelmed before mine eyes! I began to think with myself, alas, why are we men so much disquieted with the departure of a friend, whose life is much shorter, when so many goodly cities lie buried before us? Remember, O Servius, thou art a man; and with that I was much confirmed, and corrected myself. ————— Correct then likewise, and comfort thyself in this, that we must necessarily die, and all die, that we shall rise again: as Tully held, our second meeting shall be much more pleasant than our departure was grievous.

Ay, but he was my most dear and loving friend, my sole friend,

And who can blame my woe? (HORACE)

Thou mayest be ashamed, I say with Seneca, to confess it, in such a tempest as this to have but one anchor, go seek another; and for his part thou dost him great injury to desire his longer life. Wilt thou have him crazed and sickly still (like a tired traveller that comes weary to his Inn, begin his journey afresh), or to be freed from his miseries? thou hadst more need rejoice that he is gone. Another complains of a most sweet young wife,

Not yet had Proserpine cut her golden hair, (VIRGIL) ·

such a wife as no mortal man ever had, so good a wife, but she is now dead and gone, and lies low in the tomb. I reply to him in Seneca's words, if such a woman at least ever was to be had, he did either so find or make her; if he found her, he may as happily find another; if he made her, as Critobulus in Xenophon did by his, he may as good cheap inform another, and the second will be as good as the first; he need not despair, so long as the same Master is to be had. But was she good? Had she been so tried peradventure, as that Ephesian widow in

Petronius, by some swaggering soldier, she might not have held out. Many a man would have been willingly rid of his: before thou wast bound, now thou art free; and 'tis but a folly to love thy fetters, though they be of gold. Come into a third place, you shall have an aged Father sighing for a Son, a pretty Child;

> —— *He now lies asleep,*
> *Would make an impious Thracian weep,*   (HORACE)

or some fine daughter that died young, not having ever yet known the joys of the bridal bed: or a forlorn Son for his deceased Father. But why? He came first, and he must go first. Vainly pious, alas, &c. What, wouldst thou have the Laws of Nature altered, and him to live always? Julius Cæsar, Augustus, Alcibiades, Galen, Aristotle, lost their Fathers young. And why on the other side shouldst thou so heavily take the death of thy little Son?

> *Neither by destiny nor desert, but pitifully too soon,*   (VIRGIL)

he died before his time, perhaps, not yet come to the solstice of his age, yet was he not mortal? Hear that divine Epictetus, If thou covet thy wife, friends, children should live always, thou art a fool. He was a fine Child indeed, worthy of Apollonian tears, a sweet, a loving, a fair, a witty Child, of great hope, another Eteoneus, whom Pindar the Poet, and Aristides the Rhetorician, so much lament; but who can tell whether he would have been an honest man? He might have proved a thief, a rogue, a spendthrift, a disobedient son, vexed and galled thee more than all the world beside, he might have wrangled with thee and disagreed, or with his brothers, as Eteocles and Polynices, and broke thy heart; he is now gone to eternity, as another Ganymede, in the flower of his youth, as if he had risen, saith Plutarch, from the midst of a feast before he was drunk; the longer he had lived, the worse he would have been (Ambrose thinks) more sinful, more to answer he would have had. If he was naught [or bad], thou mayest be glad he is gone; if good, be glad thou hadst such a son. Or art thou sure he was good? It may be he was an hypocrite, as many are, and howsoever he spake thee fair, per-adventure he prayed, amongst the rest that Icaromenippus heard at Jupiter's whispering place in Lucian, for his Father's death, because he now kept him short, he was to inherit much goods, and many fair Manors after his decease. Or put case he was very good, suppose the best, may not thy dead son expostulate with thee, as he did in the same Lucian, Why dost thou lament my death, or call me miserable that am much more happy than thyself? what misfortune is befallen me? is it because I am not bald, crooked, old, rotten, as thou art? what have I lost? some of your good cheer, gay clothes, musick, singing, dancing, kissing, merry meetings, happy beddings, &c., is that it? is it not much better not to hunger at all than to eat? not to thirst than to drink to satisfy thirst? not to be cold than to put on clothes to drive away cold? You had more need rejoice that I am freed from diseases, agues, cares, anxieties, livor [or spite], love, covetousness, hatred, envy, malice, that I fear no more thieves, tyrants, enemies, as you do. ————

> *Dost think for these things passing fair*
> *The ashes or the shades do care?*   (VIRGIL)

Do they concern us at all, think you, when we are once dead? Condole not others then overmuch, wish not or fear their death: 'tis to no purpose.

> *I left this irksome life with all mine heart,*
> *Lest worse than death should happen to my part.*

Cardinal Brundusinus caused this Epitaph in Rome to be inscribed on his tomb, to show his willingness to die, and tax those that were so loth to depart. Weep and howl no more then, 'tis to small purpose; and as Tully adviseth us in the like case, think what we do, not whom we have lost. So David did, *While the child was yet alive, I fasted and wept; but being now dead, why should I fast? Can I bring him again? I shall go to him, but he cannot return to me.* He that doth otherwise is an intemperate, a weak, a silly, and undiscreet man. Though Aristotle deny any part of intemperance to be conversant about sorrow, I am of Seneca's mind, he that is wise is temperate, and he that is temperate is constant, free from passion, and he that is such a one, is without sorrow: as all wise men should be. The Thracians wept still when a child was born, feasted and made mirth when any man was buried: and so should we rather be glad for such as die well, that they are so happily freed from the miseries of this life. When Eteoneus, that noble young Greek, was so generally lamented by his friends, Pindar the Poet feigns some God saying, be quiet, good folks, this young man is not so miserable as you think; he is neither gone to Styx nor Acheron, but he lives for ever in the Elysian Fields. He now enjoys that happiness which your great Kings so earnestly seek, and wears that garland for which ye contend. If our present weakness is such, we cannot moderate our passions in this behalf, we must divert them by all means, by doing something else, thinking of another subject. The Italians most part sleep away care and grief, if it unseasonably seize upon them; Danes, Dutchmen, Polanders and Bohemians drink it down, our countrymen go to Plays. Do something or other, let it not transpose thee; or by premeditation make such accidents familiar, as Ulysses that wept for his dog, but not for his wife, being prepared with steadfast mind: accustom thyself, and harden beforehand, by seeing other men's calamities, and applying them to thy present estate. The evil is lighter which we anticipate. I will conclude with Epictetus, If thou lovest a pot, remember 'tis but a pot thou lovest, and thou wilt not be troubled when 'tis broken: if thou lovest a son or wife, remember they were mortal, and thou wilt not be so impatient. ———— And for false fears and all other fortuitous inconveniences, mischances, calamities, to resist and prepare ourselves, not to faint is best: 'tis a folly to fear that which cannot be avoided, or to be discouraged at all. For he that so faints or fears, and yields to his passion, flings away his own weapons, makes a cord to bind himself, and pulls a beam upon his own head.

MEMBER 6

Against Envy, Livor, Emulation, Hatred, Ambition, Self-love, and all other Affections

AGAINST those other passions and affections, there is no better remedy than as Mariners when they go to Sea provide all things necessary to resist a tempest: to furnish ourselves with Philosophical and Divine Precepts, other men's examples, from the dangers of others take benefits for ourselves: to balance our hearts with love, charity, meekness, patience, and counterpoise those irregular motions of envy, livor, spleen, hatred, with their opposite virtues, as we bend a crooked staff another way, to oppose sufferance to labour, patience to reproach, bounty to covetousness, fortitude to pusillanimity, meekness to anger, humility to pride, to examine ourselves for what cause we are so much disquieted, on what ground, what occasion, is it just or feigned? And then either to pacify ourselves by reason, to divert by some other object, contrary passion, or premeditation. 'Tis fitting to meditate, like an exile returning home, what manner of misfortune may befall thee, as a son in mischief, a wife dead, a daughter afflicted, and such like, so as not to be anyways surprised; to make them familiar, even all kind of calamities, that when they happen they may be less troublesome unto us; or out of mature judgement to avoid the effect, or disannul the cause, as they do that are troubled with toothache, pull them quite out.

The beaver bites off's stones to save the rest:
Do thou the like with that thou art opprest. (ALCIATI)

Or as they that play at wasters [or fencing], exercise themselves by a few cudgels how to avoid an enemy's blows: let us arm ourselves against all such violent incursions, which may invade our minds. A little experience and practice will inure us to it; as the Proverb saith, an old fox is not so easily taken in a snare; an old soldier in the world methinks should not be disquieted, but ready to receive all fortunes, encounters, and with that resolute Captain, come what may come, to make answer,

> *No labour comes at unawares to me,*
> *For I have long before cast what may be.* (VIRGIL)
> *'Tis not the first, this wound so sore;*
> *I have suffered worse before!* (SENECA)

The Commonwealth of Venice in their Armoury have this inscription, *Happy is that city which in time of peace thinks of war;* a fit Motto for every man's private house, happy is the man that provides for a future assault. But many times we complain, repine and mutter, without a cause, we give way to passions we may resist, and will not. Socrates was bad by nature, envious, as he confessed to Zopirus the Physiognomer, accusing him of it, froward and lascivious: but as he was Socrates, he did correct and amend himself. Thou art malicious, envious, covetous, impatient, no doubt, and lascivious, yet as thou art a Christian, correct and moderate thyself. 'Tis something, I confess, and able to move any man, to see himself contemned, obscure, neglected, disgraced, undervalued, left behind; some cannot endure it, no, not constant Lipsius, a man discreet otherwise, yet too weak and passionate in this, as his words express, *Not without indignation can I see my old colleagues, nobodies then, now Mæcenases and Agrippas, at the top of the tree.* But he was much to blame for it: to a wise staid man this is nothing, we cannot all be honoured and rich, all Cæsars; if we will be content, our present state is good, and in some men's opinion to be preferred. Let them go on, get wealth, offices, titles, honours, preferments, and what they will themselves, by chance, fraud, imposture, Simony, and indirect means, as too many do, by bribery, flattery, and parasitical insinuation, by impudence and time-serving, let them climb up to advancement in despite of virtue, let them go before, cross me on every side; as he said, correcting his former error, they do not offend me so long as they run not into mine eyes. I am inglorious and poor, but I live secure and quiet: they are dignified, have great means, pomp, and state, they are glorious; but what have they with it? Envy, trouble, anxiety, as much labour to maintain their place with credit, as to get it at first. I am contented with my fortunes, a looker-on from a distance, and love to see the raging ocean from safe land: he is ambitious, and not satisfied with his: but what gets he by it? to have all his life laid open, his reproaches seen: not one of a thousand but he hath done more worthy of dispraise and animadversion than commendation; no better means to help this than to be private. Let them run, ride, strive as so many fishes for a crumb, scrape, climb, catch, snatch, cozen, collogue, temporize and fleer, take all amongst them, wealth, honour, and get what they can, it offends me not: my plot of land affords me a safe and sheltered home. I am well pleased with my fortunes; I reign a king without the things you praise.

I have learned in what state soever I am, therewith to be contented. Come what can come, I am prepared. Be it in a great ship or a tiny boat, nevertheless I sail on. I am the same. I was once so mad to bustle abroad, and seek about for preferment, tire myself, and trouble all my friends, but all my labour was unprofitable; for while death took off some of my friends, to others I remain unknown, or little liked, and these deceive me with false promises. Whilst I am canvassing one party, captivating another, making myself known to a third, my age increases, years glide away, I am put off, and now, tired of the world, and surfeited with human worthlessness, I rest content. And so I say still; although I may not deny but that I have had some bountiful patrons and noble benefactors; let me not now be ungrateful, and I do thankfully acknowledge it, I have received some kindness (which may God repay, if not by their wishes, yet according to their merits), more peradventure than I deserve, though not to my desire, more of them than I did expect, yet not of others to my desert; neither am I ambitious or covetous, all this while, or a Suffenus to myself; what I have said, without prejudice or alteration shall stand. And now as a mired horse that struggles at first with all his might and main to get out, but when he sees no remedy, that his beating will not serve, lies still, I have laboured in vain, rest satisfied, and if I may usurp that of Prudentius,

> *Mine haven's found, fortune and hope adieu,*
> *Mock others now, for I have done with you.*

MEMBER 7

Against Repulse, Abuses, Injuries, Contempts, Disgraces, Contumelies, Slanders, Scoffs, &c.

I MAY not yet conclude, think to appease passions, or quiet the mind, till such time as I have likewise removed some other of their more eminent and ordinary causes, which produce so grievous tortures and discontents: to divert all, I cannot hope; to point alone at some few of the chiefest, is that which I aim at.

Repulse and *disgrace* are two main causes of discontent, but to an understanding man not so hardly to be taken. Cæsar himself hath been denied, and when two stand equal in fortune, birth, and all other qualities alike, one of necessity must lose. Why shouldest thou take it so grievously? It hath been a familiar thing for thee thyself to deny others. If every man might have what he would, we should all be Deified, Emperors, Kings, Princes; if whatsoever vain hope suggests, insatiable appetite affects, our preposterous judgment thinks fit were granted, we should have another Chaos in an instant, a mere confusion. It is some satisfaction to him that is repelled, that dignities, honours, offices, are not always given by desert or worth, but for love, affinity, friendship, affection, great men's letters, or as commonly they are bought and sold. Honours in Court are bestowed not according to men's virtues and good conditions (as an old Courtier observes), but as every man hath means, or more potent friends, so he is preferred. With us in France (for so their own Countryman relates) most part the matter is carried by favour and grace; he that can get a great man to be his mediator, runs away with all the preferment. The most unworthy is oftenest preferred, a Vatinius to a Cato, a nobody to a somebody. Slaves govern; asses are decked with trappings, horses have none. An illiterate fool sits in a man's seat, and the common people hold him learned, grave and wise. One professeth (Cardan well notes) for a thousand Crowns, but he deserves not ten, when as he that deserves a thousand cannot get ten. His salary will scarce pay for his salt. As good horses draw in carts, as coaches. And oftentimes, which Machiavel seconds, those are not Princes who for eminence of virtue deserve to be such; he that is most worthy wants employment; he that hath skill to be a Pilot wants a Ship, and he that could govern a Commonwealth, a world itself, a King in conceit, wants means to exercise his worth, hath not a poor office to manage, and yet all this while he is a better man that is fit to reign, though he want a kingdom, than he that hath one, and knows not how to rule it. A Lion serves not always his Keeper, but oftentimes the Keeper the Lion, and as Polydore Virgil hath it: Kings a many, wards through ignorance, rule not but are ruled. Hiero of Syracuse was a brave King, but wanted a Kingdom; Perseus of Macedon had nothing of a King, but the bare name and title, for he could not govern it: so great places are often ill bestowed, worthy persons unrespected. Many times, too, the servants have more means than the masters whom they serve, which Epictetus counts an eye-sore and inconvenient. But who can help it? It is an ordinary thing in these days to see a base impudent ass, illiterate, unworthy, insufficient, to be preferred before his betters, because he can put himself forward, because he looks big, can bustle in the world, hath a fair outside, can temporise, collogue, insinuate, or hath good store of friends and money, whereas a more discreet, modest, and better-deserving man shall lie hid or have a repulse. 'Twas so of old, and ever will be, and which Tiresias advised Ulysses in the poet, how to grow rich, &c., is still in use; lie, flatter, and dissemble: if not, as he concludes, then go like a beggar as thou art. Erasmus, Melancthon, Lipsius, Budæus, Cardan, lived and died poor. Gesner was a silly old man, plodding with 's staff, amongst all those huffing Cardinals, swelling Bishops, that flourished in his time, & rode on foot-clothes [trappings]. It is not honesty, learning, worth, wisdom, that prefers men. The race is not to the swift, nor the battle to the strong, but as the wise man said, chance, and sometimes a ridiculous chance. 'Tis fortune's doings, as they say, which made Brutus now dying exclaim: O wretched virtue, you are nothing but a name, and while I have all this time looked upon you as a reality, you are yourself but the slave of fortune! ——— Believe it hereafter, O my friends! virtue serves fortune. Yet be not discouraged (O my well deserving spirits) with this which I have said, it may be otherwise, though seldom I confess, yet sometimes it is. But to your further content, I'll tell you a tale. In Moronia Pia, or Moronia Felix, I know not whether, nor how long since, nor in what Cathedral Church, a fat Prebend fell void. The carcass scarce cold, many suitors were up in an instant. The first had rich friends, a good purse, and he was resolved to outbid any man before he would lose it, every man supposed he should carry it. The second was my Lord Bishop's Chaplain (in whose gift it was), and he thought it his due to have it. The third was nobly born, and he meant to get it by his great parents, patrons, and allies. The fourth stood upon his worth, he had newly found out strange mysteries in Chemistry, and other rare inventions, which he would detect to the publick good. The fifth was a painful Preacher, and he was commended by the whole parish where he dwelt, he had all their hands to his certificate. The sixth was the Prebendary's son lately deceased, his Father died in debt (for it, as they say), left a wife and many poor children. The seventh stood upon fair promises, which to him and his noble friends had been formerly made for the next place in his Lordship's gift. The eighth pretended [that is, asserted as his reason] great losses, and what he had suffered for the Church, what pains he had taken at home and abroad, and besides he brought Noblemen's letters. The ninth had married a kinswoman, and he sent his wife to sue for him. The tenth was a foreign Doctor, a late convert, and wanted means. The eleventh would exchange for another, he did not like the former's site, could not agree with his neighbours and fellows upon any terms, he would be gone. The twelfth and last was (a suitor in conceit) a right honest, civil, sober man, an excellent scholar, and such a one as lived private in the University, but he had neither means nor money to compass it; besides he hated all such courses, he could not speak for himself, neither had he any friends to solicit his cause, and therefore made no suit, could not expect, neither did he hope for, or look after it. The good Bishop, amongst a jury of competitors thus perplexed, and not yet resolved what to do, or on whom to bestow it, at the last, of his own accord, mere motion and bountiful nature, gave it freely to the University student, altogether unknown to him but by fame; and to be brief, the Academical Scholar had the Prebend sent him for a present. The news was no sooner published abroad, but all good students rejoiced, and were much cheered up with it, though some would not believe it; others, as men amazed, said it was a miracle; but one amongst the rest thanked God for it, and said, at last there is some advantage in being studious, and in serving God with integrity! You have heard my tale: but alas! it is but a tale, a mere fiction, 'twas never so, never like to be, and so let it rest. Well, be it so then, they have wealth and honour, fortune and preferment, every man (there's no remedy) must scramble as he may, and shift as he can; yet Cardan comforted himself with this, the star Fomalhaut would make him immortal, and that after his decease his books should be found in Ladies' studies:

> *The Muse forbids the name to die*
> *That's worthy immortality.* (HORACE)

But why shouldest thou take thy neglect, thy canvas, so to heart? It may be thou art not fit, but, as a child that puts on his father's shoes, hat, headpiece, breastplate, breeches, or holds his spear, but is neither able to wield the one, or wear the other, so wouldest thou do by such an office, place, or Magistracy: thou art unfit. And what is dignity to an unworthy man but (as Salvianus holds) a gold ring in a swine's snout? Thou art a brute. Like a bad actor (so Plutarch compares such men) in a Tragedy, that wears a crown, yet cannot be heard: thou wouldest play a King's part, but actest a Clown, speakest like an ass. You ask too much, Phaeton, and for things beyond your powers, &c.; as James and John, the sons of Zebedee, did ask they knew not what; thou dost, as another Suffenus, overween thyself; thou art wise in thine own conceit, but in other more mature judgments altogether unfit to manage such a business. Or be it thou art more deserving than any of thy rank, God in his providence hath reserved thee for some other fortunes, thus divinely foreseen. Thou art humble as thou art, it may be; hadst thou been preferred, thou wouldest have forgotten God and thyself, insulted over others, contemned thy friends, been a block, a tyrant, or a demi-god; pride goeth with beauty. Therefore, saith Chrysostom, good men do not always find grace and favour, lest they should be puffed up with turgent titles, grow insolent and proud.

Injuries, abuses, are very offensive, and so much the more in that they think by taking one they provoke another; but it is an erroneous opinion: for if that were true, there would be no end of abusing each other; strife breeds strife; 'tis much better with patience to bear, or quietly put it up. "If an ass kick me," saith Socrates, "shall I strike him again?" & when his wife Xanthippe struck & misused him, to some friends that would have had him strike her again, he replied, that he would not make them sport, or that they should stand by and say "Go it, Socrates! Go it, Xanthippe!" as we do when dogs fight, animate them the more by clapping of hands. Many men spend themselves, their goods, friends, fortunes, upon small quarrels, and sometimes at other men's procurements, with much vexation of spirit and anguish of mind, all which with good advice, or mediation of friends, might have been happily composed, or if patience had taken place. Patience in such cases is a most sovereign remedy, to put up, conceal, or dissemble it, to forget and forgive, *not seven, but seventy-seven times, as often as he repents forgive him;* as our Saviour enjoins us, stricken, *to turn the other side:* as our Apostle persuades us, *to recompence no man evil for evil, but as much as is possible to have peace with all men: not to avenge ourselves, and we shall heap burning coals upon our adversary's head.* For if you put up wrong (as Chrysostom comments), you get the victory; he that loseth his money, loseth not the conquest in this our philosophy. If he contend with thee, submit thyself unto him first, yield to him. *Pull and haul build no wall*, as the diverb is, two refractory spirits will never agree, the only means to overcome is to relent, conquer by yielding. Euclid in Plutarch, when his brother had angered him, swore he would be revenged; but he gently replied, Let me not live if I do not make thee to love me again, upon which meek answer he was pacified.

> *A branch if easily bended yields to thee,*
> *Pull hard it breaks: the difference you see.* (CAMERARIUS)

The noble family of the Colonnas in Rome, when they were expelled the city by that furious Alexander the Sixth, gave the bending branch therefore as an impress, with this motto, Bend it may, break it cannot, to signify that he might break them by force, but so never make them stoop, for they fled in the midst of their hard usage to the Kingdom of Naples, and were honourably entertained by Frederick the King, according to their callings. Gentleness in this case might have done much more, and let thine adversary be never so perverse, it may be by that means thou mayest win him; soft words pacify wrath, and the fiercest spirits are so soonest overcome; a generous Lion will not hurt a beast that lies prostrate, nor an Elephant an innocuous creature, but is a terror and scourge alone to such as are stubborn, and make resistance. It was the symbol of Emanuel Philibert, Duke of Savoy, and he was not mistaken in it, for

> *A greater man is soonest pacified,*
> *A noble spirit quickly satisfied.* (OVID)

It is reported by Gualter Mapes, an old Historiographer of ours (who lived 400 years since), that King Edward Senior, and Leolin, Prince of Wales, being at an interview near Aust upon Severn, in Gloucestershire, and the Prince sent for, refused to come to the King; he would needs go over to him; which Leolin perceiving, went up to the arms in water, and embracing his boat, would have carried him out upon his shoulders, adding that his humility and wisdom had triumphed over his pride and folly, and thereupon he was reconciled unto him and did his homage. If thou canst not so win him, put it up, if thou beest a true Christian, a good Divine, an Imitator of Christ, (for he was reviled and put it up, whipped and sought no revenge,) thou wilt pray for thine enemies, *and bless them that persecute thee;* be patient, meek, humble, &c. An honest man will not offer thee injury, if he were a brangling knave, 'tis his fashion so to do; where is least heart is most tongue; the more sottish he is, still the more insolent: *Do not answer a fool according to his folly.* If he be thy superior, bear it by all means, grieve not at it, let him take his course; Anytus and Meletus may kill me, they cannot hurt me, as that generous Socrates made answer in like case. The mind remains steadfast; though the body be torn in pieces with wild horses, broken on the wheel, pinched with fiery tongs, the soul cannot be distracted. 'Tis an ordinary thing for great men to vilify and insult, oppress, injure, tyrannise, to take what liberty they list, and who dare speak against? A miserable thing 'tis to be injured of him, from whom is no appeal: and not safe to write against him that can proscribe and punish a man at his pleasure, which Asinius Pollio was aware of, when Octavianus provoked him. 'Tis hard, I confess, to be so injured; one of Chilo's three difficult things: to keep counsel; spend his time well; put up injuries; but be thou patient, and leave revenge unto the Lord. *Vengeance is mine and I will repay*, saith the Lord. *I know the Lord*, saith David, *will avenge the afflicted and judge the poor*. No man (as Plato farther adds) can so severely punish his adversary, as God will such as oppress miserable men. He gives a new judgement and a worse punishment. If there be any Religion, any God, and that God be just, it shall be so; if thou believest the one, believe the other: it shall be so. Nemesis comes after, late but terrible; stay but a little and thou shalt see God's just judgement overtake him.

> *Yet with sure steps, though lame and slow,*
> *Vengeance o'ertakes the trembling villain's speed.*   (HORACE)

Thou shalt perceive that verified of Samuel to Agag: *Thy sword hath made many women childless, so shall thy mother be childless amongst other women.* It shall be done to them, as they have done to others. Conradinus, that brave Suevian Prince, came with a well prepared army into the Kingdom of Naples, was taken prisoner by King Charles, and put to death in the flower of his youth; a little after (Nemesis for the death of Conrad, Pandulphus Collinutius, in his Neapolitan History, calls it) King Charles his own son, with 200 Nobles, was so taken prisoner, and beheaded in like sort. Not in this only, but in all other offences, they shall be punished in the same kind, in the same part, like nature, eye with or in the eye, head with or in the head, persecution with persecution, lust with effects of lust; let them march on with ensigns displayed, let drums beat on, trumpets sound taratantara, let them sack Cities, take the spoil of Countries, murder infants, deflower Virgins, destroy, burn, persecute, and tyrannize, they shall be fully rewarded at last in the same measure, they and theirs, and that to their desert.

> *Few tyrants in their beds do die,*
> *But stabb'd or maim'd to hell they hie.*   (JUVENAL)

Oftentimes too a base contemptible fellow is the instrument of God's justice to punish, to torture, to vex them, as an ichneumon doth a crocodile. They shall be recompenced according to the works of their hands, as Haman was hanged on the gallows he provided for Mordecai. *They shall have sorrow of heart, and be destroyed from under the Heaven.* Only be thou patient; who endures, conquers; and in the end thou shalt be crowned. Yea, but 'tis a hard matter to do this, flesh and blood may not abide it; 'tis hard, hard! No, (Chrysostom replies) 'tis not hard, man! 'tis not so grievous; neither had God commanded it, if it had been so difficult. But how shall it be done? Easily, as he follows it, if thou shalt look to Heaven, behold the beauty of it, and what God hath promised to such as put up injuries. But if thou resist, and go about to meet force with force, as the custom of the world is, to right thyself, or hast given just cause of offence, 'tis no injury then, but a condign punishment, thou hast deserved as much: 'tis thy fault, be silent, as Ambrose expostulates with Cain. Dionysius of Syracuse, in his exile, was made stand without door, he wisely put it up, and laid the fault where it was, on his own pride and scorn, which in his prosperity he had formerly shewed others. 'Tis Tully's axiom, men ought not to be vexed with what they have brought upon themselves; self do, self have, as the saying is, they may thank themselves. For he that doth wrong, must look to be wronged again; the least fly hath a spleen, and a little bee a sting. An ass overwhelmed a thisselwarp's nest, the little bird pecked his gall'd back in revenge; and the humble-bee in the fable flung down the eagle's eggs out of Jupiter's lap. Brasidas, in Plutarch, put his hand into a mouse-nest, and hurt her young ones, she bit him by the finger: I see now (saith he), there is no creature so contemptible, that will not be revenged. 'Tis the law of like for like, and the nature of all things so to do. If thou wilt live quietly thyself, do no wrong to others; if any be done thee, put it up, with patience endure it. For *this is thankworthy*, saith our Apostle, *if a man for conscience towards God endure grief, and suffer wrong undeserved: for what praise is it, if, when ye be buffeted for your faults, ye take it patiently? but if when ye do well, ye suffer wrong, and take it patiently, there is thanks with God; for hereunto verily we are called.* He that cannot bear injuries witnesseth against himself that he is no good man, as Gregory holds. 'Tis the nature of wicked men to do injuries, as it is the property of all honest men patiently to bear them. Wickedness is never turned aside by indulgence. The wolf in the Emblem sucked the goat, (so the shepherd would have it), but he kept nevertheless a wolf's nature; a knave will be a knave. Injury is on the other side a good man's foot-boy, his faithful Achates, and as a lackey follows him wheresoever he goes. Besides, he is in a miserable estate that wants enemies: it is a thing not to be avoided, and therefore with more patience to be endured. Cato Censorius, that upright Cato, of whom Paterculus gives that honourable elogium, he did well because he could not do otherwise, was 50 times indicted and accused by his fellow-citizens, and, as Ammianus well hath it, if it be sufficient to accuse a man openly or in private, who shall be free? If there were no other respect than that of Christianity, Religion, and the like, to induce men to be long-suffering and patient, yet methinks the nature of injury itself is sufficient to keep them quiet, the tumults, uproars, miseries, discontents, anguish, loss, dangers, that attend upon it, might restrain the calamities of contention: for, as it is with ordinary gamesters, the gains go to the box, so falls it out to such as contend, the Lawyers get all; and therefore, if they would consider of it, other men's misfortunes in this kind, and common experience, might detain them. The more they contend, the more they are involved in a Labyrinth of woes, and the Catastrophe is to consume one another, like the elephant and dragon's conflict in Pliny; the dragon got under the elephant's belly, and sucked his blood so long, till he fell down dead upon the dragon, and killed him with the fall; so both were ruin'd. 'Tis an Hydra's head, contention; the more they strive, the more they may: and, as Praxiteles did by his glass, when he saw a scurvy face in it, break it in pieces: but for that one, he saw many more as bad in a moment: for one injury done, they provoke another with interest, and twenty enemies for one. Do not stir up hornets, oppose not thyself to a multitude: but if thou hast received a wrong, wisely consider of it, and if thou canst possibly, compose thyself with patience to bear it. This is the safest course, and thou shalt find greatest ease to be quiet.

I say the same of scoffs, slanders, contumelies, obloquies, defamations, detractions, pasquilling libels, and the like, which may tend any way to our disgrace: 'tis but opinion: if we could neglect, contemn, or with patience digest them, they would reflect on them that offered them at first. A wise Citizen, I know not whence, had a scold to his wife: when she brawled, he played on his drum, and by that means madded her more, because she saw that he would not be moved. Diogenes in a crowd, when one called him back, and told him how the boys laughed him to scorn: I, he said, am not laughed at, took no notice of it. Socrates was brought upon the stage by Aristophanes, and misused to his face, but he laughed, as if it concerned him not: and, as Ælian relates of him, whatsoever good or bad accident or fortune befell him, going in, or coming out, Socrates still kept the same countenance. Even so should a Christian soldier do, as Hierom describes him, march on through good and bad reports to immortality, not to be moved: for honesty is a sufficient reward, and in our time the sole recompence to do well is to do well: but naughtiness will punish itself at last. As the diverb is, —

They that do well, shall have reward at last;
But they that ill, shall suffer for that's past.

Yea, but I am ashamed, disgraced, dishonoured, degraded, exploded: my notorious crimes and villainies are come to light ('tis bad to be found out), my filthy lust, abominable oppression, and avarice, lies open, my good name's lost, my fortune's gone, I have been stigmatized, whipt at post, arraigned, and condemned, I am a common obloquy, I have lost my ears: odious, execrable, abhorred of God and men. Be content, 'tis but a nine days' wonder, and as one sorrow drives out another, one passion another, one cloud another, one rumour is expelled by another; every day almost come new news unto our ears, as how the Sun was eclipsed, meteors seen i'th' air, monsters born, prodigies, how the Turks were overthrown in Persia, an Earthquake in Helvetia, Calabria, Japan, or China, an inundation in Holland, a great plague in Constantinople, a fire at Prague, a dearth in Germany, such a man is made a Lord, a Bishop, another hanged, deposed, pressed to death, for some murder, treason, rape, theft, oppression, all which we do hear at first with a kind of admiration, detestation, consternation, but by and by they are buried in silence: thy father's dead, thy brother robb'd, wife runs mad, neighbour hath kill'd himself; 'tis heavy, ghastly, fearful news at first, in every man's mouth, table talk; but after a while who speaks or thinks of it? It will be so with thee and thine offence, it will be forgotten in an instant, be it theft, rape, sodomy, murder, incest, treason, &c., thou art not the first offender, nor shalt thou be the last, 'tis no wonder; every hour such malefactors are called in question, nothing so common,

In every nation, under every sky. (JUVENAL)

Comfort thyself, thou art not the sole man. If he that were guiltless himself should fling the first stone at thee, and he alone should accuse thee that were faultless, how many executioners, how many accusers, wouldst thou have! If every man's sins were written in his forehead, and secret thoughts known, how many thousands would parallel, if not exceed, thine offence! It may be the Judge that gave sentence, the Jury that condemned thee, the spectators that gazed on thee, deserved much more, and were far more guilty than thou thyself. But it is thine infelicity to be taken, to be made a publick example of justice, to be a terror to the rest; yet should every man have his desert, thou wouldest peradventure be a Saint in comparison; doves are brought to judgement, poor souls are punished, the great ones do twenty thousand times worse, and are not so much as spoken of.

The net's not laid for kites or birds of prey,
But for the harmless still our gins we lay. (TERENCE)

Be not dismayed then, to err is human, we are all sinners, daily and hourly subject to temptations, the best of us is an hypocrite, a grievous offender in God's sight; Noah, Lot, David, Peter, &c., how many mortal sins do we commit! Shall I say, be penitent, ask forgiveness, and make amends, by the sequel of thy life, for that foul offence thou hast committed? recover thy credit by some noble exploit, as Themistocles did, for he was a most debauched and vicious youth, but made the world amends by brave exploits; at last become a new man, and seek to be reformed. He that runs away in a battle, as Demosthenes said, may fight again; and he that hath a fall, may stand as upright as ever he did before. None need despair of a better day: a wicked liver may be reclaimed, and prove an honest man; he that is odious in present, hissed out, an exile, may be received again with all men's favours, and singular applause; so Tully was in Rome, Alcibiades in Athens. Let thy disgrace then be what it will, that which is past cannot be recalled; trouble not thyself, vex and grieve thyself no more, be it obloquy, disgrace, &c. No better way than to neglect, contemn, or seem not to regard it, to make no reckoning of it; much speaking means small strength; if thou be guiltless, it concerns thee not. Regard not the harmless shafts of an idle tongue. Doth the Moon care for the barking of a dog? They detract, scoff and rail, saith one, and bark at me on every side, but I, like that Albanian dog sometime given to Alexander for a present, I lie still and sleep, vindicate myself by contempt alone. Free from fear as Achilles in his armour, as a tortoise in his shell, I wrap myself in my virtue, or an urchin [or hedgehog] round, I care not for their blows, a lizard in camomile [a plant which the more it was trodden on grew the more], I decline their fury, and am safe.

Virtue and integrity are their own fence,
Care not for envy or what comes from thence.

Let them rail then, scoff, and slander, a wise man, Seneca thinks, is not moved, because he knows there is no remedy for it: Kings and Princes, wise, grave, prudent, holy, good men, divine, all are so served alike. Thou only, two-faced Janus, hast no derisive finger pointed behind thy back! Antevorta and Postvorta,* Jupiter's guardians, may not help in this case, they cannot protect; Moses had a Dathan, a Corah, David a Shimei, God himself is blasphemed: thou art not yet happy, if the crowd hath not yet mocked thee. It is an ordinary thing so to be misused; the chiefest men, and most understanding, are so vilified; let him take his course. And, as that lusty courser in Æsop, that contemned the poor ass, came by and by after with his bowels burst, a pack on his back, and was derided of the same ass: they shall be contemned and laughed to scorn of those whom they have formerly derided. Let them contemn, defame, or undervalue, insult, oppress, scoff, slander, abuse, wrong, curse and swear, feign and lie, do thou comfort thyself with a good conscience, rejoice at heart when they have all done, a good conscience is a continual feast, innocency will vindicate itself. And which the Poet gave out of Hercules, *he enjoys the anger of the gods,* enjoy thyself, though all the world be set against thee, contemn and say with him, *My posy is, not to be moved,* that my Palladium, my breast-plate, my buckler, with which I ward all injuries, offences, lies, slanders; I lean upon that stake of modesty, so receive and break asunder all that foolish force of livor and spleen. And whosoever he is that shall observe these short instructions, without all question he shall much ease and benefit himself.

In fine, if Princes would do justice, Judges be upright, Clergymen truly devout, and so live as they teach, if great men would not be so insolent, if soldiers would quietly defend us, the poor would be patient, rich men would be liberal and humble, Citizens honest, Magistrates meek, Superiors would give good example, subjects peaceable, young men would stand in awe: if Parents would be kind to their children, and they again obedient to their Parents, brethren agree amongst themselves, enemies be reconciled, servants trusty to their Masters, Virgins chaste, Wives modest, Husbands would be loving, and less jealous: if we could imitate Christ and his Apostles, live after God's laws, these mischiefs would not so frequently happen amongst us; but being most part so irreconcileable as we are, perverse, proud, insolent, factious, and malicious, prone to contention, anger and revenge, of such fiery spirits, so captious, impious, irreligious, so opposite to virtue, void of grace, how should it otherwise be? Many men are very testy by nature, apt to mistake, apt to quarrel, apt to provoke, and misinterpret to the worst every thing that is said or done, and thereupon heap unto their selves

* Antevorta was the goddess who presided over childbirth, Postvorta the goddess who reminded men of things past.

a great deal of trouble, and disquietness to others, smatterers in other men's matters, tale-bearers, whisperers, liars, they cannot speak in season, or hold their tongues when they should, they will speak more than comes to their share in all companies, and by those bad courses accumulate much evil to their own souls, (who begins by arguing, will end in quarrelling), their life is a perpetual brawl, they snarl, like so many dogs, with their wives, children, servants, neighbours, and all the rest of their friends, they can agree with nobody. But to such as are judicious, meek, submiss, and quiet, these matters are easily remedied: they will forbear upon all such occasions, neglect, contemn, or take no notice of them, dissemble, or wisely turn it off. If it be a natural impediment, as a red nose, squint eyes, crooked legs, or any such imperfection, infirmity, disgrace, reproach, the best way is to speak of it first thyself, and so thou shalt surely take away all occasions from others to jest at, or contemn, that they may perceive thee to be careless of it. Vatinius was wont to scoff at his own deformed feet, to prevent his enemies' obloquies and sarcasms in that kind; or else by prevention, as Cotys, King of Thrace, that brake a company of fine glasses presented to him, with his own hands, lest he should be overmuch moved when they were broken by chance. And sometimes again, so that it be discreetly and moderately done, it shall not be amiss to make resistance, to take down such a saucy companion; no better means to vindicate himself to purchase final peace: for he that suffers himself to be ridden, or through pusillanimity or sottishness will let every man baffle him, shall be a common laughing stock for all to flout at. As a cur that goes through a Village, if he clap his tail between his legs, and run away, every cur will insult over him, but if he bristle up himself, and stand to it, give but a counter-snarl, there's not a dog dares meddle with him. Much is in a man's courage and discreet carriage of himself.

Many other grievances there are, which happen to mortals in this life, from friends, wives, children, servants, masters, companions, neighbours, our own defaults, ignorance, errors, intemperance, indiscretion, infirmities, &c., and many good remedies to mitigate and oppose them, many divine precepts to counterpoise our hearts, special antidotes both in Scripture and human Authors, which whoso will observe shall purchase much ease and quietness unto himself. I will point at a few. Those Prophetical, Apostolical admonitions, are well known to all; what Solomon, Siracides, our Saviour Christ himself, hath said tending to this purpose, as, Fear God: obey the Prince: be sober and watch: pray continually: be angry, but sin not: remember thy last: fashion not yourselves to this world, &c., apply yourselves to the times: strive not with a mighty man: recompence good for evil: let nothing be done through contention or vain-glory, but with meekness of mind, every man esteeming of others better than himself: love one another; or that Epitome of the Law and the Prophets, which our Saviour inculcates, *love God above all, thy neighbour as thyself*. And *whatsoever you would that men should do unto you, so do unto them*, which Alexander Severus writ in letters of gold, and used as a motto; Hierom commends to Celantia as an excellent way, amongst so many enticements and worldly provocations, to rectify her life. Out of human Authors take these few cautions: Know thyself. Be contented with thy lot. Trust not wealth, beauty, nor parasites; they will bring thee to destruction. Have peace with all men, war with vice. Be not idle. Look before you leap. Beware of, Had I wist. Honour thy parents, speak well of friends. Be temperate in four things, talking, spending, looking and drinking. Watch thine eye. Moderate thine expences. Hear much, speak little. Bear and forbear. If thou seest ought amiss in another, mend it in thyself. Keep thine own counsel, reveal not thy secrets, be silent in thine intentions. Give not ear to tale-tellers, babblers, be not scurrilous in conversation. Jest without bitterness: give no man cause of offence: set thine house in order: take heed of suretyship. Trust and distrust: as a fox on the ice, take heed whom you trust. Live not beyond thy means. Give cheerfully. Pay thy dues willingly. Be not a slave to thy money. Omit not occasion, embrace opportunity, lose no time. Be humble to thy superiors, respective to thine equals, affable to all, but not familiar: flatter no man. Lie not, dissemble not. Keep thy word and promise, be constant in a good resolution. Speak truth. Be not opinionative, maintain no factions. Lay no wagers, make no comparisons. Find no faults, meddle not with other men's matters. Admire not thyself. Be not proud or popular. Insult not. Stand in awe of fortune. Fear not that which cannot be avoided. Grieve not for that which cannot be recalled. Undervalue not thyself. Accuse no man, commend no man, rashly. Go not to law without great cause. Strive not with a greater man. Cast not off an old friend. Take heed of a reconciled enemy. If thou come as a guest, stay not too long. Be not unthankful. Be meek, merciful, and patient. Do good to all. Be not fond of fair words. Be not a neuter in a faction. Moderate thy passions. Think no place without a witness. Admonish thy friend in secret, commend him in publick. Keep good company. Love others, to be beloved thyself. Love what you would be hating. Be slow to become a friend. Provide for a tempest. Stir not up hornets.

Do not prostitute thy soul for gain. Make not a fool of thyself to make others merry. Marry not an old crone or a fool for money. Be not over solicitous or curious. Seek that which may be found. Seem not greater than thou art. Take thy pleasure soberly. Thresh not the basil-weed [which by its smell breeds scorpions in men's brains]. Live merrily as thou canst. Take heed by other men's examples. Go as thou wouldst be met, sit as thou wouldst be found, yield to the time, follow the stream. Wilt thou live free from fears and cares? Live innocently, keep thyself upright, thou needest no other keeper, &c. Look for more in Isocrates, Seneca, Plutarch, Epictetus, &c., and for defect, consult with cheese-trenchers and painted clothes.*

MEMBER 8

Against Melancholy itself

EVERY man, saith Seneca, thinks his own burthen the heaviest, and a melancholy man above all others complains most; weariness of life, abhorring all company and light, fear, sorrow, suspicion, anguish of mind, bashfulness, and those other dread symptoms of body and mind, must needs aggravate this misery; yet, conferred to other maladies, they are not so heinous as they be taken. For first, this disease is either in habit, or disposition, curable, or incurable. If new and in disposition, 'tis commonly pleasant, and it may be helped. If inveterate, or an habit, yet they have lucid intervals, sometimes well, and sometimes ill; or if more continuate, as the Veientes were to the Romans, 'tis a more durable enemy than dangerous: and, amongst many inconveniences, some comforts are annexed to it. First, it is not catching, and, as Erasmus comforted himself, when he was grievously sick of the stone, though it was most troublesome, and an intolerable pain to him, yet it was no whit offensive to others, not loathsome to the spectators, ghastly, fulsome, terrible, as plagues, apoplexies, leprosies, wounds, sores, tetters, pox, pestilent agues are, which either admit of no company, terrify or offend those that are present. In this malady, that which is, is wholly to themselves, and those symptoms not so dreadful, if they be compared to the opposite extremes. They are most part bashful, suspicious, solitary, &c.,

* Cheese-trenchers, wooden platters to cut cheese on, had mottoes sometimes round the edge. Painted cloths, or painted clothes, were a cheap substitute for tapestry as a hanging for rooms; they were of canvas, adorned with heraldic devices, mottoes, texts, verses & proverbs.

therefore no such ambitious, impudent intruders, as some are, no sharkers, no cony-catchers. no prowlers, no smell-feasts, praters, panders, parasites, bawds, drunkards, whoremasters: necessity and defect compels them to be honest; as Micio told Demea in the comedy, if we be honest, 'twas poverty made us so: if we melancholy men be not as bad as he that is worst, 'tis our Dame Melancholy kept us so: 'twas not the will but the way that was wanting.

Besides, they are freed in this from many other infirmities, solitariness makes them more apt to contemplate, suspicion wary, which is a necessary humour in these times; for, truly, he that takes most heed is often circumvented and overtaken. Fear and sorrow keep them temperate and sober, and free them from many dissolute acts, which jollity and boldness thrust men upon: they are therefore no cut-throats, roaring boys, thieves, or assassinates. As they are soon dejected, so they are as soon by soft words and good persuasions reared. Wearisomeness of life makes them they are not so besotted on the transitory vain pleasures of the world. If they dote in one thing, they are wise and well understanding in most other. If it be inveterate, they are, most part doting, or quite mad, insensible to any wrongs, ridiculous to others, but most happy and secure to themselves. Dotage is a state which many much magnify and commend: so is simplicity and folly, as he said, may this madness, O gods, be with me for ever! Some think fools and dizzards live the merriest lives, as Ajax in Sophocles, 'tis the pleasantest life to know nothing: ignorance is a down-right remedy of evils. These curious Arts, and laborious Sciences, Galen's, Tully's, Aristotle's, Justinian's, do but trouble the world, some think; we might live better with that illiterate Virginian simplicity and gross ignorance; entire idiots do best; they are not macerated with cares, tormented with fears, and anxiety, as other wise men are: for, as he said, if folly were a pain, you should hear them howl, roar, and cry out in every house, as you go by in the street, but they are most free, jocund and merry, and in some Countries, as amongst the Turks, honoured for Saints, and abundantly maintained out of the common stock. They are no dissemblers, liars, hypocrites, for fools and mad men tell commonly truth. In a word, as they are distressed, so are they pitied, which some hold better than to be envied, better to be sad than merry, better to be foolish and quiet than to be wise, and still vexed; better to be miserable than happy; of two extremes it is the best.

SECTION 4 MEMBER 1

SUBSECTION 1 — *Of Physick which cureth with Medicines*

AFTER a long and tedious discourse of these six non-natural things, and their several rectifications, all which are comprehended in Diet, I am come now at last to Pharmaceutics, or that kind of Physick which cureth by Medicines, which Apothecaries most part make, mingle, or sell in their shops. Many cavil at this kind of Physick, and hold it unnecessary, unprofitable to this or any other disease, because those Countries which use it least live longest, and are best in health, as Hector Boethius relates of the Isles of Orcades, the people are still sound of body and mind without any use of Physick, they live commonly 120 years; and Ortelius, in his Itinerary of the Inhabitants of the Forest of Arden, they are very painful, long-lived, sound, &c. Martianus Capella, speaking of the Indians of his time, saith, they were (much like our western Indians now) bigger than ordinary men, bred coarsely, very long-lived, insomuch that he that died at an hundred years of age went before his time, &c. Damianus A-Goes, Saxo Grammaticus, Aubanus Bohemus, say the like of them that live in Norway, Lapland, Finmark, Biarmia, Corelia, all over Scandia, and those Northern Countries, they are most healthful and very long-lived, in which places there is no use at all of Physick, the name of it is not once heard. Dithmarus Bleskenius, in his accurate description of Iceland, 1607, makes mention amongst other matters of the inhabitants, and their manner of living, which is dried fish instead of bread, butter, cheese, and salt-meats, most part they drink water and whey, and yet without Physick or Physician they live many of them 250 years. I find the same relation by Lerius, and some other Writers, of Indians in America. Paulus Jovius, in his description of Britain, and Levinus Lemnius, observe as much of this our Island, that there was of old no use of Physick amongst us, and but little at this day, except it be for a few nice idle Citizens, surfeiting Courtiers, and stall-fed Gentlemen lubbers. The country people use kitchen Physick, and common experience tells us that they live freest from all manner of infirmities that make least use of Apothecaries' Physick. Many are overthrown by preposterous use of it, and thereby get their bane, that might otherwise have escaped; some think Physicians kill as many as they save, and who can tell how many murders they make in a year, that may freely kill folks, and have a reward for it? and, according to the Dutch proverb, a new Physician must have a

new Church-yard; and who daily observes it not? Many that did ill under Physicians' hands have happily escaped when they have been given
over by them, left to God and Nature and themselves. 'Twas Pliny's dilemma of old, Every disease is either curable or incurable, a man recov-
ers of it or is killed by it; both ways Physick is to be rejected. If it be
deadly, it cannot be cured; if it may be helped, it requires no Physician;
Nature will expel it of itself. Plato made it a great sign of an intemperate and corrupt Commonwealth, where Lawyers and Physicians did
abound; and the Romans distasted them so much, that they were often
banished out of their City, as Pliny and Celsus relate, for 600 years not
admitted. It is no Art at all, as some hold, no not worthy the name of a
liberal science (nor Law neither) as Pet. And. Canonherius, a Patrician
of Rome, and a great Doctor himself, one of their own tribe, proves by
16 Arguments, because it is mercenary as now used, base, and as Fiddlers play for a reward. Lawyers and doctors on the publick live, 'tis a
corrupt Trade, no Science, Art, no Profession; the beginning, practice
and progress of it, all is naught, full of imposture, incertainty and doth
generally more harm than good. The Devil himself was the first inventor of it: Medicine is my invention, said Apollo: and what was Apollo,
but the Devil? The Greeks first made an Art of it, and they were all deluded by Apollo's Sons, Priests, Oracles. If we may believe Varro, Pliny,
Columella, most of their best medicines were derived from his Oracles.
Æsculapius his son had his Temples erected to his Deity, and did many
famous cures, but, as Lactantius holds, he was a Magician, a mere
Impostor, and as his successors, Phaon, Podalirius, Melampius, Menecrates (another God) by charms, spells, and ministry of bad spirits, performed most of their cures. The first that ever wrote in Physick to any
purpose was Hippocrates, and his Disciple and Commentator Galen,
whom Scaliger calls a mere ravelling of Hippocrates, but, as Cardan
censures them, both immethodical and obscure, as all those old ones
are, their precepts confused, their medicines obsolete, and now most
part rejected. Those cures which they did, Paracelsus holds, were rather
done out of their Patients' confidence, and good opinion they had of
them, than out of any skill of theirs, which was very small, he saith,
they themselves idiots and infants, as are all their Academical followers.
The Arabians received it from the Greeks, and so the Latins, adding
new precepts and medicines of their own, but so imperfect still, that
through ignorance of Professors, Impostors, Mountebanks, Empiricks,
disagreeing of Sectaries, (which are as many almost as there be diseases), envy, covetousness, and the like, they do much harm amongst

us. They are so different in their consultations, prescriptions, mistaking many times the parties' constitution, disease, and causes of it, they give quite contrary Physick. One saith this, another that, out of singularity or opposition, as he said of Adrian, a multitude of Physicians hath killed the Emperor; more danger there is from the Physician than from the disease. Besides, there is much imposture and malice amongst them. All Arts (saith Cardan) admit of cozening, Physick amongst the rest doth appropriate it to herself; and tells a story of one Curtius, a Physician in Venice, because he was a stranger, and practised among them, the rest of the Physicians did still cross him in all his precepts. If he prescribed hot medicines, they would prescribe cold, binders for purgatives, they changed everything about. If the party miscarried, they blamed Curtius, Curtius killed him, that disagreed from them: if he recovered, then they cured him themselves. Much emulation, imposture, malice, there is amongst them: if they be honest, and mean well, yet a knave Apothecary that administers the Physick, and makes the medicine, may do infinite harm, by his old obsolete doses, adulterine drugs, bad mixtures, substitutions, &c. See Fuchsius, Cordus' Dispensatory, and Brassivola. But it is their ignorance that doth more harm than rashness, their Art is wholly conjectural, if it be an Art, uncertain, imperfect, and got by killing of men, they are a kind of butchers, leeches, men-slayers; Chirurgeons, and Apothecaries especially, that are indeed the Physicians' hangmen, torturers, and common executioners; though, to say truth, Physicians themselves come not far behind; for according to that witty Epigram of Maximilianus Urentius, what's the difference? How (he asks) does the Surgeon differ from the Physician? One kills by hand, the other by drugs; and both differ from the hangman only in that they do slowly what he does quickly. But I return to their skill. Many diseases they cannot cure at all, as Apoplexy, Epilepsy, Stone, Stranguary, Gout.

Medicine cannot cure the knotty gout. (OVID)

Quartan Agues, a common Ague sometimes stumbles them all; they cannot so much as ease, they know not how to judge of it. If by pulses, that doctrine, some hold, is wholly superstitious, and I dare boldly say with Andrew Dudeth, that variety of pulses, described by Galen, is neither observed, nor understood of any. And for urine, that is the Physicians' strumpet, the most deceitful thing of all, as Forestus and some other Physicians have proved at large: I say nothing of critick days, errors in indications, &c. The most rational of them, and skilful, are so often deceived, that as Tholosanus infers, I had rather believe and commit myself to a mere Empirick than to a mere Doctor, and I cannot sufficiently commend that custom of the Babylonians, that have no professed Physicians, but bring all their patients to the market to be cured: which Herodotus relates of the Egyptians, Strabo, Sardus, and Aubanus Bohemus of many other Nations. And those that prescribed Physick amongst them, did not so arrogantly take upon them to cure all diseases as our professors do, but some one, some another, as their skill and experience did serve. One cured the eyes, a second the teeth, a third the head, another the lower parts, &c., not for gain, but in charity, to do good; they made neither art, profession, nor trade of it, which in other places was accustomed: and therefore Cambyses, in Xenophon, told Cyrus, that to his thinking Physicians were like Tailors and Cobblers, the one mended our sick bodies, as the other did our clothes. But I will urge these cavelling and contumelious arguments no farther, lest some Physician should mistake me, and deny me Physick when I am sick: for my part, I am well persuaded of Physick: I can distinguish the abuse from the use in this and many other Arts and Sciences; wine and drunkenness are two distinct things. I acknowledge it a most noble and divine science, insomuch that Apollo, Æsculapius, and the first founders of it, were worthily counted Gods by succeeding ages, for the excellency of their invention. And whereas Apollo at Delos, Venus at Cyprus, Diana at Ephesus, and those other Gods, were confined and adored alone in some peculiar places, Æsculapius had his Temple and Altars everywhere, in Corinth, Lacedæmon, Athens, Thebes, Epidaurus, &c., (Pausanias records), for the latitude of his art, Deity, worth and necessity. With all virtuous and wise men, therefore, I honour the name, and calling, as I am enjoined to *honour the Physician for necessity's sake. The knowledge of the Physician lifted up his head, and in the sight of great men he shall be admired. The Lord hath created medicines of the earth, and he that is wise will not abhor them.* But of this noble subject how many panegyricks are worthily written! For my part, as Sallust said of Carthage, 'tis better to be silent than to say little. I have said, yet one thing I will add, that this kind of Physick is very moderately and advisedly to be used, upon good occasion, when the former of diet will not take place. And 'tis no other which I say than that which Arnoldus prescribes in his 8th Aphorism: A discreet and godly Physician doth first endeavour to expel a disease by medicinal diet, then by pure medicine; and in his ninth, he that may be cured by diet must not meddle with Physick. So in the 11th Aphorism: A modest and wise Physician will never hasten to use medicines, but upon urgent necessity, and that sparingly too; because (as he adds in his 13th Aphorism) : Whosoever takes much Physick in his youth shall soon bewail it in his old age; purgative Physick especially, which doth much debilitate nature. For which causes some Physicians refrain from the use of Purgatives, or else sparingly use them. Henricus Ayrerus, in a consultation for a melancholy person, would have him take as few purges as he could, because there be no such medicines which do not steal away some of our strength, and rob the parts of our body, weaken Nature, and cause that Cacochymia, which Celsus and others observe, or ill digestion, and bad juice through all the parts of it. Galen himself confesseth that purgative Physick is contrary to Nature, takes away some of our best spirits, and consumes the very substance of our bodies. But this without question is to be understood of such purges as are unseasonably or immoderately taken; they have their excellent use in this as well as most other infirmities. Of Alteratives and Cordials no man doubts, be they simples or compounds. I will, amongst that infinite variety of medicines which I find in every Pharmacopœia, every Physician, Herbalist, &c., single out some of the chiefest.

SUBSECTION 2 — *Simples proper to Melancholy, against Exotick Simples*

MEDICINES properly applied to Melancholy are either *Simple* or *Compound. Simples* are *Alterative* or *Purgative. Alterative* are such as correct, strengthen Nature, alter, any way hinder or resist the disease; and they be herbs, stones, minerals, &c., all proper to this humour. For as there be divers distinct infirmities, continually vexing us,

> *Diseases steal both day and night on men,*
> *For Jupiter hath taken voice from them,* (HESIOD)

so there be several remedies, as he saith, for each disease a medicine, for every humour; and, as some hold, every clime, every country, and more than that, every private place, hath his proper remedies growing in it, peculiar almost to the domineering and most frequent maladies of it. As one discourseth, wormwood grows sparingly in Italy, because most part there they be misaffected with hot diseases; but henbane, poppy, and such cold herbs: with us in Germany and Poland great store of it in every waste. Baracellus and Baptista Porta give many instances and examples of it, and bring many other proofs. For that cause, belike, that learned Fuchsius of Nuremberg, when he came into a village, considered always what herbs did grow most frequently about it, and those he distilled in a silver limbeck, making use of others amongst them as occa-

sion served. I know that many are of opinion our Northern simples are
weak, unperfect, not so well concocted, of such force, as those in the
Southern parts, not so fit to be used in Physick, and will therefore fetch
their drugs afar off: Senna, Cassia out of Egypt, Rhubarb from Barbary, Aloes from Zocotora, Turbith [or Turpeth, a cathartick root],
Agarick, Mirabolanes [or Indian Plums], Hermodactils [or Wild Saf-
fron] from the East Indies, Tobacco from the West, and some as far as
China, Hellebore from the Anticyræ, or that of Austria which bears the
purple flower, which Mathiolus so much approves, and so of the rest.
In the Kingdom of Valencia in Spain, Maginus commends two mountains, Mariola and Renagolosa, famous for simples; Leander Albertus,
Baldus, a mountain near the lake Benacus, in the territory of Verona, to
which all the herbalists in the Country continually flock: Ortelius one
in Apulia, Munster mons Major in Histria: others Montpelier in France.
Prosper Alpinus prefers Egyptian simples, Garcias ab Horto [prefers]
Indian before the rest, another those of Italy, Crete, &c. Many times
they are overcurious in this kind, whom Fuchsius taxeth, that they think
they do nothing except they rake all over India, Arabia, Æthiopia, for
remedies, and fetch their Physick from the three quarters of the World,
and from beyond the Garamantes. Many an old wife or country woman
doth often more good with a few known and common garden herbs than
our bombast Physicians with all their prodigious, sumptuous, far-
fetched, rare, conjectural medicines. Without all question, if we have not
these rare Exotick simples, we hold that at home which is in virtue
equivalent unto them; ours will serve as well as theirs, if they be taken
in proportionable quantity, fitted and qualified aright, if not much
better, and more proper to our constitutions. But so 'tis for the most
part, as Pliny writes to Gallus, we are careless of that which is near us,
and follow that which is afar off, to know which we will travel and sail
beyond the Seas, wholly neglecting that which is under our eyes. Opium
in Turkey doth scarce offend, with us in a small quantity it stupifies;
cicuta (or hemlock) is a strong poison in Greece, but with us it hath
no such violent effects. I conclude with J. Voschius, who, as he much
inveighs against those exotick medicines, so he promiseth by our Euro-
pean a full cure, and absolute, of all diseases; from beginning to end,
our own simples agree best with us. It was a thing that Fernelius much
laboured in his French practice, to reduce all his cure to our proper and
domestick Physick: so did Janus Cornarius, and Martin Rulandus, in
Germany, T. B.* with us, as appeareth by a treatise of his divulged in

* Timothy Bright.

our tongue 1615, to prove the sufficiency of English medicines to the cure of all manner of diseases. If our simples be not altogether of such force, or so apposite, it may be, if like industry were used, those far fetched drugs would prosper as well with us as in those Countries whence now we have them, as well as Cherries, Artichokes, Tobacco, and many such. There have been divers worthy Physicians, which have tried excellent conclusions in this kind, and many diligent, painful, Apothecaries, as Gesner, Besler, Gerard, &c., but amongst the rest, those famous publick Gardens of Padua in Italy, Nuremberg in Germany, Leyden in Holland, Montpelier in France, (and ours in Oxford now being constructed at the cost and charges of the Right Honourable the Lord Danvers, Earl of Danby), are much to be commended, wherein all exotick plants almost are to be seen, and liberal allowance yearly made for their better maintenance, that young students may be the sooner informed in the knowledge of them: which, as Fuchsius holds, is most necessary for that exquisite manner of curing, and as great a shame for a Physician not to observe them as for a workman not to know his axe, saw, square, or any other tool which he must of necessity use.

SUBSECTION 3 — *Alteratives, Herbs, other Vegetals, &c.*

AMONGST those 800 simples, which Galeottus reckons up, and many exquisite Herbalists have written of, these few following alone I find appropriated to this humour: of which some be Alteratives; which by a secret force, saith Renodeus, and special quality, expel future diseases, perfectly cure those which are, and many such incurable effects. This is as well observed in other plants, stones, minerals, and creatures, as in herbs, in other maladies, as in this. How many things are related of a man's skull! What several virtues of corns in a horse's leg, of a wolf's liver, &c., of divers excrements of beasts, all good against several diseases! What extraordinary virtues are ascribed unto plants! Priest pintle and rocket [or ragwort and colewort] enliven the member; the chaste-tree [or Abraham's balm] and waterlily quench the sperm; some herbs provoke lust; some again, as chaste-lamb, waterlily, quite extinguish seed; poppy causeth sleep, cabbage resisteth drunkenness, &c. and that which is more to be admired, that such and such plants should have a peculiar virtue to such particular parts, as to the head, Aniseeds, Foalfoot, Betony, Calamint, Eye-bright, Lavender, Bays, Roses, Rue, Sage, Marjoram, Peony, &c.; for the lungs, Calamint, Liquorice, Enula Campana, Hyssop, Horehound, Water Germander, &c.; for the heart, Borage, Bugloss, Saffron, Balm, Basil, Rosemary, Violet, Roses, &c.;

for the stomack, Wormwood, Mints, Betony, Balm, Centaury, Sorel,
Purslain; for the liver, Darthspine, Germander, Agrimony, Fennel, Endive, Succory, Liverwort, Barberries; for the spleen, Maidenhair,
Finger-fern, Dodder of Thyme, Hop, the rind of Ash, Betony; for the
kidnies, Grumel, Parsley, Saxifrage, Plantain, Mallow; for the womb,
Mugwort, Pennyroyal, Fetherfew, Savine, &c.; for the joints, Camomile, S. John's wort, Organ, Rue, Cowslips, Centaury the less, &c., and
so to peculiar diseases. To this of Melancholy you shall find a Catalogue
of Herbs proper, and that in every part. See more in Wecker, Renodeus,
Heurnius, &c. I will briefly speak of them, as first of Alteratives, which
Galen, in his third book of diseased parts, prefers before diminutives,
and Trallianus brags that he hath done more cures on melancholy men
by moistening than by purging of them.

In this Catalogue, Borage and Bugloss may challenge the chiefest
place, whether in substance, juice, roots, seeds, flowers, leaves, decoctions, distilled waters, extracts, oils, &c., for such kind of herbs be diversely varied. Bugloss is hot and moist, and therefore worthily
reckoned up amongst those herbs which expel melancholy, and exhilarate the heart (Galen saith, & Dioscorides). Pliny much magnifies this
plant. It may be diversely used; as in Broth, in Wine, in Conserves,
Syrops, &c. It is an excellent cordial, and against this malady most frequently prescribed: an herb indeed of such sovereignty that, as Diodorus, Pliny, Plutarch, &c., suppose, it was that famous Nepenthes of
Homer, which Polydamna, Thonis's wife, (then King of Thebes in
Ægypt), sent Helen for a token, of such rare virtue, that, if taken steept
in wine, if wife and children, father and mother, brother and sister,
and all thy dearest friends, should die before thy face, thou couldst not
grieve or shed a tear for them. Helen's commended bowl to exhilarate
the heart had no other ingredient, as most of our criticks conjecture,
than this of Borage.

Honeyleaf Balm hath an admirable virtue to alter Melancholy, be
it steeped in our ordinary drink, extracted, or otherwise taken. Cardan
much admires this herb. It heats and dries, saith Heurnius, in the second degree, with a wonderful virtue comforts the heart, and purgeth all
melancholy vapours from the spirits (Matthiolus). Besides they ascribe
other virtues to it, as to help concoction, to cleanse the brain, expel all
careful thoughts and anxious imaginations. The same words in effect
are in Avicenna, Pliny, Simon Sethi, Fuchsius, Leobel, Dèlacampius,
and every Herbalist. Nothing better for him that is melancholy than to
steep this and Borage in his ordinary drink.

Matthiolus, in his fifth book of Medicinal Epistles, reckons up Scorzonera, not against poison only, falling sickness, and such as are vertiginous, but to this malady; the root of it taken by itself expels sorrow, causeth mirth and lightness of heart.

Antonius Musa, that renowned Physician to Cæsar Augustus, in his book which he writ of the virtues of Betony, wonderfully commends that herb, it preserves both body and mind from fears, cares, griefs, cures falling-sickness, this and many other diseases; to whom Galen subscribes.

Marigold is much approved against Melancholy, and often used therefore in our ordinary broth, as good against this and many other diseases.

Hop is a sovereign remedy; Fuchsius much extols it; it purgeth all choler, and purifies the blood. Matthiolus wonders the Physicians of his time made no more use of it, because it rarefies and cleanseth: we use it to this purpose in our ordinary beer, which before was thick and fulsome.

Wormwood, Centaury [a species of aster whose medicinal properties were said to have been discovered by the Centaur Chiron], Pennyroyal, are likewise magnified and much prescribed (as I shall after shew) especially in Hypochondriack Melancholy, daily to be used, sod [or seethed] in whey: and, as Ruffus Ephesius, Aretæus, relate, by breaking wind, and helping concoction, many melancholy men have been cured with frequent use of them alone.

And because the spleen and blood are often misaffected in Melancholy, I may not omit Endive, Succory, Dandelion, Fumitory, &c., which cleanse the blood; Scolopendria [Ferns], Cuscuta [or Dodders], Ceterach [or Miltwaste], Mugwort, Liverwort, Ash, Tamarisk, Genist [or Spanish Broom], Maidenhair, &c., which much help and ease the spleen.

To these I may add Roses, Violets, Capers, Fetherfew [or Feverfew], Scordium [or Water Germander], Stœchas [or French Lavender], Rosemary, Ros Solis [or Sun-Dew], Saffron, Ocyme [or Basil], sweet Apples, Wine, Tobacco, Sanders [or Sandalwood], &c., that Peruvian Chamico [or Wild Cane], of monstrous powers, Linshcosteus Datura; and to such as are cold the decoction of Guiacum, China [Roots], Sarsaparilla, Sassafras, the flowers of the Benedictus Thistle, which I find much used by Montanus in his consultations, Julius Alexandrinus, Lælius Eugubinus, and others. Bernardus Penottus prefers his Sun-Dew, or Dutch-Sindaw, before all the rest in this disease, and will admit of no herb upon the earth to be comparable to it. It excels Homer's Moly, cures this, falling-sickness, and almost all other infirmities. The same Penottus speaks of an excellent Balm out of Apponensis, which, taken to the quantity of three drops in a cup of wine, will cause a sudden alteration, drive away dumps, and cheer up the heart. Guianerius, in his Antidotary, hath many such. Jacobus de Dondis, the Aggregator, repeats Ambergrease, Nutmegs, and Allspice amongst the rest. But that cannot be general. Amber and Spice will make a hot brain mad, good for cold and moist. Garcias ab Horto hath many Indian Plants, whose virtues he much magnifies in this disease. Lemnius admires Rue, and commends it to have excellent virtue, to expel vain imaginations, Devils, and to ease afflicted souls. Other things are much magnified by writers, as an old Cock, a Ram's head, a Wolf's heart borne or eaten, which Mercurialis approves; Prosper Alpinus the water of Nilus, Gomesius all Sea water, and at seasonable times to be sea-sick: Goat's milk, Whey, &c.

SUBSECTION 4 — *Precious Stones, Metals, Minerals, Alteratives*

PRECIOUS Stones are diversely censured; many explode the use of them or any Minerals in Physick, of whom Thomas Erastus is the chief, in his Tract against Paracelsus, and in an Epistle of his to Peter Monavius: " That stones can work any wonders let them believe that list; no man shall persuade me, for my part I have found by experience there is no virtue in them." But Matthiolus, in his Comment upon Dioscorides, is as profuse on the other side in their commendation; so is Cardan, Renodeus, Alardus, Rueus, Encelius, Marbodeus, &c. Matthiolus specifies in Coral, and Oswaldus Crollius prefers the salt of Coral. Encelius will have them to be as so many several medicines against melancholy, sorrow, fear, dulness, and the like. Renodeus admires them, besides they adorn Kings' Crowns, grace the fingers, enrich our household-stuff, defend us from enchantments, preserve health, cure diseases, they drive away grief, cares, and exhilarate the mind. The particulars be these.

Granatus, a precious stone so called, because it is like the kernels of a Pomegranate, an unperfect kind of Ruby, it comes from Calicut; if hung about the neck, or taken in drink, it much resisteth sorrow, and recreates the heart. The same properties I find ascribed to the Jacinth and Topaz, they allay anger, grief, diminish madness, much delight and exhilarate the mind. If it be either carried about, or taken in a potion, it will increase wisdom, saith Cardan, expel fear; he brags that he hath cured many mad men with it, which, when they laid by the stone, were as mad again as ever they were at first. Petrus Bayerus and Fran.

Rueus, say as much of the Chrysolite, a friend of wisdom, an enemy to folly (Pliny, Solinus, Albertus, Cardan). Encelius highly magnifies the virtue of the Beryl, it much avails to a good understanding, represseth vain conceits, evil thoughts, causeth mirth, &c. In the belly of a swallow there is a stone found called Chelidonius [or Swallow-stone], which, if it be lapped in a fair cloth, and tied to the right arm, will cure lunaticks, mad men, make them amiable and merry.

There is a kind of Onyx, called a Chalcedony, which hath the same qualities, avails much against phantastick illusions which proceed from melancholy, preserves the vigour and good estate of the whole body.

The Eban stone, which Goldsmiths use to sleeken their gold with, borne about, or given to drink, hath the same properties, or not much unlike.

Lævinus Lemnius, amongst other Jewels makes mention of two more notable, Carbuncle and Coral, which drive away childish fears, Devils, overcome sorrow, and hung about the neck, repress troublesome dreams, which properties almost Cardan gives to that green coloured Emmetris, if it be carried about, or worn in a Ring; Rueus to the Diamond.

Nicholas Cabeus, a Jesuit of Ferrara, in the first book of his Magnetical Philosophy, speaking of the virtues of a loadstone, recites many several opinions; some say that, if it be taken in parcels inward, it will, like viper's wine, restore one to his youth, and yet, if carried about them, others will have it to cause melancholy; let experience determine.

Mercurialis admires the Emerald for his virtues in pacifying all affections of the mind; others the Sapphire, which is the fairest of all precious stones, of sky-colour, and a great enemy to black choler, frees the mind, mends manners, &c. Jacobus de Dondis, in his Catalogue of Simples, hath Ambergrease, the bone in a Stag's heart, a Monocerot's [or Unicorn's] horn, Bezoar's stone, (of which elsewhere), it is found in the belly of a little beast in the East Indies, brought into Europe by Hollanders and our Countrymen Merchants. Renodeus saith he saw two of these beasts alive in the Castle of the Lord of Vitry at Coubert.

Lapis Lazuli and Armenus, because they purge, shall be mentioned in their place.

Of the rest in brief thus much I will add out of Cardan, Renodeus, Rondoletius, &c., that almost all Jewels and precious stones have excellent virtues to pacify the affections of the mind, for which cause rich men so much covet to have them: and those smaller Unions [or Pearls] which are found in shells amongst the Persians and Indians, by the consent of all writers, are very cordial, and most part avail to the exhilaration of the heart.

Most men say as much of Gold, and some other Minerals, as these have done of precious stones. Erastus still maintains the opposite part. In his disputation against Paracelsus, he confesseth of Gold that it makes the heart merry, but in no other sense but as it is in a miser's chest: I am well content with myself at home, looking at my money in my strong-box, as he said in the Poet; it so revives the spirits, and is an excellent receipt against Melancholy.

> For gold in phisik is a cordial,
> Therefore he loved gold in special.*

Potable [or drinkable] gold he discommends and inveighs against it, by reason of the corrosive waters which are used in it, which arguments our Dr. Guin urgeth against Dr. Antonius. Erastus concludes their Philosophical stones and potable gold, &c., to be no better than poison, a mere imposture, a nothing; digg'd out of that broody hill, belike, this goodly golden stone is, where the ridiculous mouse was brought to birth. Paracelsus and his Chemistical followers, as so many Prometheuses, will fetch fire from Heaven, will cure all manner of diseases with minerals, accounting them the only Physick on the other side. Paracelsus calls Galen, Hippocrates, and all their adherents, infants, idiots, Sophisters, &c. Away (he says) with those who jeer at Vulcanian metamorphoses, ignorant sprouts, backward and stubborn nurslings, &c., not worthy the name of Physicians, for want of these remedies; and brags that by them he can make a man live 160 years, or to the world's end; with their Alexipharmacums [or Antidotes], Panaceas, Mummias [Powdered Mummy?], Weapon Salve, and such Magnetical cures, Lamps of Life and Death, Balsams, Baths of Diana, Magico-Physical Electrum [or Amber], Martian Amulets, &c. What will not he and his followers effect? He brags moreover that he was the First of Physicians, and did more famous cures than all the Physicians in Europe besides; a drop of his preparations should go further than a dram or ounce of theirs, those loathsome and fulsome filthy potions, heteroclitical pills (so he calls them), horse medicines, at the sight of which the Cyclops Polyphemus would shudder. And, though some condemn their skill, and Magnetical cures, as tending to Magical superstition, witchery, charms, &c., yet they admire, stiffly vindicate nevertheless, and infinitely prefer them. But these are both in extremes, the middle sort approve of Min-

---

* Chaucer.

erals, though not in so high a degree. Lemnius commends Gold inwardly and outwardly used, as in Rings, excellent good in medicines, and such mixtures as are made for melancholy men, saith Wecker, to whom Renodeus subscribes, and many others. Matthiolus approves of Potable Gold, Mercury, with many such Chemical Confections, and goes so far in approbation of them, that he holds no man can be an excellent Physician that hath not some skill in Chemistical Distillations, and that chronick diseases can hardly be cured without mineral medicines. Look for Antimony among purgers.

SUBSECTION 5 — *Compound Alteratives; censure of Compounds, and mixt Physick*

PLINY bitterly taxeth all compound medicines: Men's knavery, imposture, and captious wits, have invented these shops, in which every man's life is set to sale: and by and by came in those compositions and inexplicable mixtures, far fetcht out of India and Arabia; a medicine for a botch must be had as far as the Red Sea, &c. And 'tis not without cause which he saith, for out of question they are much to blame in their compositions, whilst they make infinite variety of mixtures, as Fuchsius notes: They think they get themselves great credit, excel others, and to be more learned than the rest, because they make many variations; but he accounts them fools; and whilst they brag of their skill, and think to get themselves a name, they become ridiculous, bewray their ignorance and error. A few simples, well prepared and understood, are better than such an heap of nonsense, confused compounds, which are in Apothecaries' shops ordinarily sold; in which many vain, superfluous, corrupt, exolete things out of date, are to be had (saith Cornarius) a company of barbarous names given to Syrops, Julips, an unnecessary company of mixt medicines; a rude & undigested mass. Many times (as Agrippa taxeth) there is by this means more danger from the medicine than from the disease, when they put together they know not what, or leave it to an illiterate Apothecary to be made, they cause death and horror for health. Those old Physicians had no such mixtures; a simple potion of Hellebore in Hippocrates' time was the ordinary purge; and at this day, saith Mat. Riccius, in that flourishing Commonwealth of China, their Physicians give precepts quite opposite to ours, not unhappy in their Physick: they use altogether roots, herbs, and simples, in their medicines, and all their Physick in a manner is comprehended in an Herbal: no science, no school, no art, no degree; but, like a trade, every man in private is instructed of his Master. Cardan cracks that he can cure all diseases with water alone, as Hippocrates of old did most infirmities with one medicine. Let the best of our rational Physicians demonstrate and give a sufficient reason for those intricate mixtures, why just so many simples in Mithridate or Treacle,* why such and such quantity; may they not be reduced to half or a quarter? 'Tis vain to do with much, (as the saying is) what can be done with a little; 300 simples in a Julip, Potion, or a little Pill, to what end or purpose? I know not what Alkindus, Capivaccius, Montagna, and Simon Eitover, the best of them all and most rational have said in this kind; but neither he, they, nor any one of them, gives his reader, to my judgement, that satisfaction which he ought; why such, so many simples? Roger Bacon hath taxed many errors in his tract Concerning Measurements, explained some things, but not cleared. Mercurialis, in his book on the Composition of Medicine, gives instance in Hamech, and Philonium Romanum, which Hamech, an Arabian, and Philonius, a Roman, long since composed, but dully as the rest. If they be so exact, as by him it seems they were, and those mixtures so perfect, why doth Fernelius alter the one, and why is the other obsolete? Cardan taxeth Galen for presuming out of his ambition to correct Theriacum Andromachi [an Antidote for Poison], and we as justly may carp at all the rest. Galen's medicines are now exploded and rejected; what Nicholas Meripsa, Mesue, Celsus, Scribanius, Actuarius, &c., writ of old, are most part contemned. Mellichius, Cordus, Wecker, Quercetan, Renodeus, the Venetian, Florentine states, have their several receipts and magistrals [or Sovereign Recipes], they of Nuremberg have theirs, and Augustana Pharmacopœia, peculiar medicines to the meridian of the City: London hers, every City, Town, almost every private man, hath his own mixtures, compositions, receipts, magistrals, precepts, as if he scorned antiquity and all others, in respect of himself. But each man must correct and alter, to shew his skill, every opinionative fellow must maintain his own paradox, be it what it will; the Kings rage, the Greeks suffer: they dote, and in the mean time the poor patients pay for their new experiments, the Commonalty rue it. ·

* Mithridate or Treacle: the famous King Mithridates of Pontus, afraid of being poisoned, took small doses of poison every day to inure himself to their effects, and invented an antidote containing opium. This was elaborated into a prescription containing 55 ingredients by Damocrates, Nero's physician, and called Mithridatum Damocratis. It was again elaborated by Andromachus, another of Nero's physicians, the flesh of the poisonous snake Tyrus being added, and the number of ingredients increased; it was now called Theriaca Andromachi. The name Treacle, or Mithridate, was commonly applied to it; and because of its syrupy nature the word treacle has come down to us with its familiar meaning.

Thus others object, thus I may conceive out of the weakness of my apprehension; but, to say truth, there is no such fault, no such ambition, no novelty, or ostentation, as some suppose: but as one answers, this of compound medicines is a most noble and profitable invention, found out, and brought into Physick with great judgement, wisdom, counsel, and discretion. Mixt diseases must have mixt remedies, and such simples are commonly mixt, as have reference to the part affected, some to qualify, the rest to comfort, some one part, some another. Cardan and Brassavola both hold that no simple medicine is without hurt or offence; and, although Hippocrates, Erasistratus, Diocles, of old, in the infancy of this Art, were content with ordinary simples, yet now, saith Aëtius, necessity compelleth to seek for new remedies, and to make compounds of simples, as well to correct their harms if cold, dry, hot, thick, thin, insipid, noisome to smell, to make them savoury to the palate, pleasant to taste and take, and to preserve them for continuance by admixtion of sugar, honey, to make them last months and years for several uses. In such cases compound medicines may be approved, and Arnoldus in his 18th Aphorism doth allow of it. If simples cannot, necessity compels us to use compounds; so for receipts and magistrals, one day teacheth another, and they are as so many words or phrases, which come in and go out of fashion again, ebb and flow with the season, and, as wits vary, so they may be infinitely varied. Every man as he likes; so many men, so many minds; and yet all tending to good purpose, though not the same way. As arts and sciences, so Physick is still perfected amongst the rest. Time nourisheth knowledge, and experience teacheth us every day many things which our predecessors knew not of. Nature is not effete, as he saith, or so lavish, to bestow all her gifts upon an age, but hath reserved some for posterity, to shew her power, that she is still the same, and not old or consumed. Birds and beasts can cure themselves by nature, but men must use much labour and industry to find it out. But I digress.

Compound medicines are inwardly taken, or outwardly applied. Inwardly taken be either liquid or solid: liquid are fluid or consisting. Fluid, as Wines and Syrups. The wines ordinarily used to this disease are Wormwood-wine, Tamarisk, and Buglossatum, wine made of Borage and Bugloss; the composition of which is specified in Arnoldus Villanovanus, in his book On Wines, of Borage, Balm, Bugloss, Cinnamon, &c., and highly commended for its virtues. It drives away Leprosy, Scabs, clears the blood, recreates the spirits, exhilarates the mind, purgeth the

brain of those anxious black melancholy fumes, and cleanseth the whole
body of that black humour by urine. To which I add, saith Villanovanus,
that " it will bring mad men, and such raging Bedlams as are tied in
chains, to the use of their reason again ; my conscience bears me witness,
that I do not lie, I saw a grave matron helped by this means, she was so
cholerick, and so furious sometimes, that she was almost mad, and beside herself, she said and did she knew not what, scolded, beat her maids,
and was now ready to be bound, till she drank of this Borage wine, and
by this excellent remedy was cured, which a poor foreigner, a silly beggar, taught her by chance, that came to crave an alms from door to
door." — The juice of Borage, if it be clarified, and drunk in wine, will
do as much, the roots sliced and steeped, &c., saith Ant. Mizaldus, who
cites this story word for word out of Villanovanus, and so doth Magninus, a Physician of Milan, in his regimen of health. Such another excellent compound water I find in Rubeus, which he highly magnifies, out of
Savanarola, for such as are solitary, dull, heavy or sad without a cause,
or be troubled with trembling of heart. Other excellent compound waters
for melancholy he cites in the same place, if their melancholy be not
inflamed, or their temperature over hot. Euonymus hath a precious
Aquavitae [or water of Life] to this purpose for such as are cold. But
he and most commend Potable Gold, and every writer prescribes clarified whey, with Borage, Bugloss, Endive, Succory, &c., of Goat's milk
especially, some indefinitely at all times, some thirty days together in
the Spring, every morning fasting, a good draught. Syrups are very good,
and often used to digest this humour in the heart, spleen, liver, &c., as
Syrup of Borage, (there is a famous Syrup of Borage highly commended
by Laurentius to this purpose in his Tract of Melancholy), of the Fruit
of King Sabor, now obsolete, of Thyme and Epithyme, Hops, Scolopendria, Fumitory, Maidenhair, Bizantine, &c. These are most used for
preparatives to other Physick, mixt with distilled waters of like nature,
or in Julips otherwise.

Consisting are conserves or confections : conserves of Borage, Bugloss,
Balm, Fumitory, Succory, Maidenhair, Violets, Roses, Wormwood, &c.;
confections, Treacle, Mithridate, Eclegms, or Linctures, &c.; Solid,
as Aromatical confections; hot, of Amber, Hot Pearls [concoctions
of medicinal seeds], Flowers, Sweet Musk, the Electuary of Gems,
the Gladdening Galen & Rhasis Electuary, Galingale, Cummin, Anise,
Pepper, Ginger, Capers, Cinnamon; cold as Cold Pearls [certain medicinal seeds], Petals, Abbas Roses, Poppies, &c., as every Pharmaco-

pœia will shew you, with tablets or losings [lozenges] that are made out of them; with Condites [or Preserves] and the like.*

Outwardly used as occasion serves, as Amulets, Oils hot and cold, as of Camomile, Stæchados, Violets, Roses, Almonds, Poppy, Nymphæa, Mandrake, &c., to be used after bathing, or to procure sleep.

Ointments composed of the said species, Oils and Wax, &c., as Poplar-Alabaster, some hot, some cold, to moisten, procure sleep, and correct other accidents.

Liniments are made of the same matter to the like purpose: emplasters of herbs, flowers, roots, &c., with oils and other liquors mixt and boiled together.

Cataplasms, salves, or poultices, made of green herbs, pounded, or sod in water till they be soft, which are applied to the Hypochondries [the Belly], and other parts, when the body is empty.

Cerotes [or plasters] are applied to several parts, and Frontals, to take away pain, grief, heat, procure sleep. Fomentations or sponges, wet in some decoctions, &c., epithemata, or those moist medicines, laid on linen, to bathe and cool several parts misaffected.

Sacculi, or little bags, of herbs, flowers, seeds, roots, and the like, applied to the head, heart, stomack, &c., odoraments, balls, perfumes, posies to smell to, all which have their several uses in melancholy, as shall be shewed, when I treat of the cure of the distinct species by themselves.

MEMBER 2

SUBSECTION 1 — *Purging Simples upward*

MELANAGOGA, or melancholy purging medicines, are either Simple or Compound, and that gently, or violently, purging upwards or downwards. These following purge upward. Asarum, or Asarabacca [Wildspikenard], which, as Mesue saith, is hot in the second degree, and dry in the third; it is commonly taken in wine, whey, or, as with us, the juice of two or three leaves, or more sometimes, pounded in posset-drink, qualified with a little Liquorice, or Aniseed, to avoid the fulsomeness of the taste, or as Fernelius' Mixture. Brassivola, On Cathartics, reckons it

---

* But since these were elaborate compounds, it is perhaps better to repeat, for the list of hot confections, their actual names: Diambra, Diamargaritum calidum, Dianthus, Diamoschum dulce, Electuarium de gemmis, lætificans Galen et Rhasis, Diagalinga, Diacimynum, Dianisum, Diatrion piperion, Diazinziber, Diacapers, Diacinnamonum; and for the cold: Diamargaritum frigidum, Diacorolli, Diarrhodon Abbatis, Diacodion.

up among those simples that only purge melancholy, and Ruellius confirms as much out of his experience, that it purgeth black choler, like Hellebore itself. Galen and Matthiolus ascribe other virtues to it, and will have it purge other humours as well as this.

Laurel, by Heurnius, is put amongst the strong purgers of melancholy; it is hot and dry in the fourth degree. Dioscorides adds other effects to it. Pliny sets down 15 berries in drink for a sufficient potion: it is commonly corrected with his opposites, cold and moist, as juice of Endive, Purslane, and is taken in a potion to seven grains and a half. But this, and Asarabacca, every Gentlewoman in the Country knows how to give, they are two common vomits.

Scilla, or Sea-Onion, is hot and dry in the third degree. Brassivola, out of Mesue, others, and his own experience, will have this simple to purge melancholy alone. It is an ordinary vomit, wine with squills, mixt with Rubel in a little white wine.

White Hellebore, which some call sneezing-powder, a strong purger upward, which many reject, as being too violent: Mesue and Averroes will not admit of it, by reason of danger of suffocation, great pain and trouble it puts the poor patient to, saith Dodonæus. Yet Galen and Dioscorides allow of it. It was indeed terrible in former times, as Pliny notes, but now familiar, insomuch that many took it in those days, that were students, to quicken their wits, which Persius objects to Accius the Poet, that he was drunk on Hellebore. It helps melancholy, the falling-sickness, madness, gout, &c., but not to be taken of old men, youths, such as are weaklings, nice, or effeminate, troubled with headache, high-coloured, or fear strangling, saith Dioscorides. Oribasius, an old Physician, hath written very copiously, and approves of it, in such affections, which can otherwise hardly be cured. Heurnius will not have it used but with great caution, by reason of its strength, and then when Antimony will do no good, which caused Hermophilus to compare it to a stout captain (as Codronchus observes) that will see all his soldiers go before him, and come, like the bragging soldier, last himself. When other helps fail in inveterate melancholy, in a desperate case, this vomit is to be taken. And yet for all this, if it be well prepared, it may be securely given at first. Matthiolus brags that he hath often, to the good of many, made use of it, and Heurnius, that he hath happily used it, prepared after his own prescript, and with good success. Christophorus à Vega is of the same opinion, that it may be lawfully given; and our Country Gentlewomen find it by their common practice that there is no such great danger in it. Dr. Turner, speaking of this plant in his Herbal, telleth us that in his time it was an ordinary receipt among good wives to give Hellebore in powder to two penny weight, and he is not much against it. But they do commonly exceed, for who so bold as blind Bayard? and prescribe it by pennyworths, and such irrational ways, as I have heard myself market folk ask for it in an Apothecary's shop: but with what success God knows; they smart often for their rash boldness and folly, break a vein, make their eyes ready to start out of their heads, or kill themselves. So that the fault is not in the Physick, but in the rude and undiscreet handling of it. He that will know therefore when to use, how to prepare it aright, and in what dose, let him read Heurnius, Brassivola, Godefridus Stegius, the Emperor Rodolphus' Physician, Matthiolus, and that excellent Commentary of Baptista Codronchus, which is worth them all, On White Hellebore, where he shall find great diversity of examples and receipts.

Antimony or Stibium, which our Chemists so much magnify, is either taken in substance, or infusion, &c., and frequently prescribed in this disease. It helps all infirmities, saith Matthiolus, which proceed from black choler, falling-sickness, and hypochondriacal passions; and for further proof of his assertion he gives several instances of such as have been freed with it: one of Andrew Gallus, a Physician of Trent, that, after many other essays, imputes the recovery of his health, next after God, to this remedy alone; another of George Handshius, that, in like sort, when other medicines failed, was by this restored to his former health, and which, of his knowledge, others have likewise tried, and by the help of this admirable medicine been recovered; a third of a Parish Priest at Prague in Bohemia, that was so far gone with melancholy, that he doted, and spake he knew not what, but after he had taken 12 grains of Stibium, (as I myself saw, and can witness [he saith] for I was called to see this miraculous accident), he was purged of a deal of black choler, like little gobbets of flesh, and all his excrements were as black blood (a Medicine fitter for a Horse than a Man): yet it did him so much good, that the next day he was perfectly cured. This very story of the Bohemian Priest Sckenkius relates word for word, with great approbation of it. Hercules de Saxoniâ calls it a profitable medicine, if it be taken after meat to 6 or 8 grains, of such as are apt to vomit. Rodericus à Fonseca, the Spaniard, and late Professor of Padua in Italy, extols it to this disease; so doth Lodovicus Mercatus, with many others. Jacobus Gervinus, a French Physician, on the other side, explodes all this, and saith he took three grains only, upon Matthiolus' and some others' commendation, but it almost killed him; whereupon he concludes, antimony is rather poison than a medicine. Th. Erastus concurs with him in his opinion, and so doth Ælian Montaltus. But what do I talk? 'tis the subject of whole books, I might cite a century of Authors pro and con. I will conclude with Zuinger, antimony is like Scanderbeg's sword, which is either good or bad, strong or weak, as the party is that prescribes or useth it; a worthy medicine, if it be rightly applied to a strong man, otherwise poison. For the preparing of it look in the Treasury of Euonymus, Quercetan, Oswaldus Crollius, Basilius Valentinus, &c.

Tobacco, divine, rare, superexcellent Tobacco, which goes far beyond all their panaceas, potable gold, and philosopher's stones, a sovereign remedy to all diseases. A good vomit, I confess, a virtuous herb, if it be well qualified, opportunely taken, and medicinally used, but, as it is commonly abused by most men, which take it as Tinkers do Ale, 'tis a plague, a mischief, a violent purger of goods, land, health, hellish, devilish, and damned Tobacco, the ruin and overthrow of body and soul.

SUBSECTION 2 — *Simples Purging Melancholy downward*

POLYPODY [Ferns], and Epithyme are, without all exceptions, gentle purgers of melancholy. Dioscorides will have them void flegm; but Brassivola, out of his experience, averreth that they purge this humour; they are used in decoction, infusion, &c., simple, mixt, &c.

Mirabolanes, all five kinds, are happily prescribed against melancholy and quartan agues, Brassivola speaks out of a thousand experiences; he gave them in pills, decoction, &c. Look for peculiar receipts in him.

Stœchas, Fumitory, Dodder, herb Mercury, roots of Capers, Genista or broom, Pennyroyal, and half-boiled Cabbage, I find in this Catalogue of purgers of black choler, Origan, Fetherfew, Ammoniack Salt, Saltpetre. But these are very gentle, Alypus, Dragon root, Centaury, Ditany, Colutea, which Fuchsius and others take for Senna, but most distinguish. Senna is in the middle of violent and gentle purgers downward, hot in the second degree, dry in the first. Brassivola calls it a wonderful herb against melancholy, it scours the blood, illightens the spirits, shakes off sorrow; a most profitable medicine, as Dodonæus terms it, invented by the Arabians, and not heard of before. It is taken divers ways, in powder, infusion, but most commonly in the infusion, with Ginger, or some cordial flowers added to correct it. Actuarius commends it sod in broth, with an old Cock, or in whey, which is the common conveyor of all such things as purge black choler; or steeped in wine, which Heurnius accounts sufficient, without any further correction.

Aloes by most is said to purge choler, but Aurelianus, Arculanus,

Julius Alexandrinus, Crato, prescribe it to this disease, as good for the stomack, and to open the Hæmrods, out of Mesue, Rhasis, Serapio, Avicenna. Menardus opposeth it: Aloes doth not open the veins, or move the Hæmrods, which Leonhartus Fuchsius likewise affirms; but Brassivola and Dodonæus defend Mesue out of their experience; let Valesius end the controversy.

Armenian Stone and Lapis Lazuli are much magnified by Alexander, Avicenna, Aëtius, and Actuarius, if they be well washed, that the water be no more coloured, fifty times, some say. That good Alexander (saith Guianerius) puts such confidence in this one medicine, that he thought all melancholy passions might be cured by it; and I, for my part, have oftentimes happily used it, and was never deceived in the operation of it [saith he].

The like may be said of Lapis Lazuli, though it be somewhat weaker than the other. Garcias ab Horto relates that the Physicians of the Moors familiarly prescribe it to all melancholy passions, and Matthiolus brags of that happy success which he still had in the administration of it. Nicholas Meripsa puts it amongst the best remedies; and if this will not serve (saith Rhasis) then there remains nothing but Armenian Stone and Hellebore itself. Valescus and Jason Pratensis much commend Hali's Powder,* which is made of it. James Damascen., Hercules de Saxoniâ, &c., speak well of it. Crato will not approve this; it and both Hellebores, he saith, are no better than poison. Victor Trincavellius found it, in his experience, to be very noisome, to trouble the stomack, and hurt their bodies that take it overmuch.

Black Hellebore, that most renowned plant, and famous purger of melancholy, which all antiquity so much used and admired, was first found out by Melampus, a Shepherd, (as Pliny records), who, seeing it to purge his Goats when they raved, practised it upon Elige and Calene, King Prœtus' daughters, that ruled in Arcadia, near the fountain Clitorius, and restored them to their former health. In Hippocrates' time it was in only request, insomuch that he writ a book of it, a fragment of which remains yet. Theophrastus, Galen, Pliny, Cælius Aurelianus, as ancient as Galen, Aretæus, Oribasius, a famous Greek, Aëtius, P. Ægineta, Galen's Ape, Actuarius, Trallianus, Cornelius Celsus, only remaining of the old Latins, extol and admire this excellent plant, and it was generally so much esteemed of the ancients for this disease amongst the rest, that they sent all such as were crazed, or that doted, to the Anticyrians, or to Phocis in Achaia, to be purged, where this plant was in abundance

* Pulvus Hali.

to be had. In Strabo's time it was an ordinary voyage; Sail to Anticyra, a common proverb among the Greeks and Latins to bid a dizzard or a mad man go take Hellebore; as in Lucian, Menippus to Tantalus: " thou art out of thy little wit, O Tantalus, and must needs drink Hellebore, and that without mixture "; Aristophanes in Vespis, " Drink Hellebore," &c., and Harpax, in the Comedian, told Simo and Ballio, two doting fellows, that they had need to be purged with this plant. When that proud Menecrates had writ an arrogant letter to Philip of Macedon, he sent back no other answer but this, I advise you to take yourself off to Anticyra, noting thereby that he was crazed, and had much need of a good purge. Lilius Geraldus saith that Hercules, after all his mad pranks upon his wife and children, was perfectly cured by a purge of Hellebore, which an Anticyrian administered unto him. They that were sound commonly took it to quicken their wits (as Ennius of old, who never sallied forth to write of arms, but when well whittled himself, and as our Poets drink Sack to improve their inventions). I find it so registered by A. Gellius. Carneades, the Academick, when he was to write against Zeno the Stoick, purged himself with Hellebore first, which Petronius puts upon Chrysippus. In such esteem it continued for many ages, till at length Mesue and some other Arabians began to reject and reprehend it, upon whose authority for many following lustres it was much debased and quite out of request, held to be poison, and no medicine; and is still oppugned to this day by Crato and some Junior Physicians. Their reasons are because Aristotle said Henbane and Hellebore were poison; and Alexander Aphrodisiæus, in the Preface of his Problems, gave out that (speaking of Hellebore) quails fed on that which was poison to men. Galen confirms as much: Constantine the Emperor, in his Geoponicks, attributes no other virtue to it than to kill mice and rats, flies and mouldwarps, and so Mizaldus. Nicander of old, Gervinus, Sckenkius, and some other Neotericks that have written of poisons, speak of Hellebore in a chief place. Nicholas Leonicus hath a story of Solon, that, besieging I know not what City, steeped Hellebore in a spring of water, which by pipes was conveyed into the middle of the Town, and so either poisoned, or else made them so feeble and weak by purging, that they were not able to bear arms. Notwithstanding all these cavils and objections, most of our late writers do much approve of it. Gariopontus, Codronchus, & others, so that it be opportunely given. Jacobus de Dondis and all our Herbalists subscribe. Fernelius confesseth it to be a terrible purge, and hard to take, yet well given to strong men, and such as have able bodies. P. Forestus and Capivaccius forbid it to be taken in substance, but allow it in decoction or infusion, both which ways P. Monavius approves above all others: Jacchinus commends a receipt of his own preparing; Penottus another of his chemically prepared, Euonymus another. Hildesheim hath many examples how it should be used, with diversity of receipts. Heurnius calls it an innocent medicine howsoever, if it be well prepared. The root of it is only in use, which may be kept many years, and by some given in substance, as by Fallopius, and Brassavola amongst the rest, who brags that he was the first that restored it again to his use, and tells a story how he cured one Melatasta a mad man, that was thought to be possessed, in the Duke of Ferrara's Court, with one purge of black Hellebore in substance: the receipt is there to be seen; his excrements were like ink, he perfectly healed at once; Vidus Vidius, a Dutch Physician, will not admit of it in substance, to whom most subscribe, but, as before in the decoction, infusion, or which is all in all, in the extract, which he prefers before the rest, and calls a sweet medicine, an easy, that may be securely given to women, children, and weaklings. Baracellus terms it a medicine of great worth and note. Quercetan (and many others) tells wonders of the extract. Paracelsus above all the rest is the greatest admirer of this plant, and especially the extract; he calls it another Treacle, a terrestrial Balm, all in all, the sole and last refuge to cure this malady, the Gout, Epilepsy, Leprosy, &c. If this will not help, no Physick in the world can but mineral, it is the upshot of all. Matthiolus laughs at those that except against it, and though some abhor it out of the authority of Mesue, and dare not adventure to prescribe it, yet I (saith he) have happily used it six hundred times without offence, and communicated it to divers worthy Physicians, who have given me great thanks for it. Look for receipts, dose, preparation, and other cautions concerning this simple in him, Brassivola, Baracellus, Codronchus, and the rest.

SUBSECTION 3 — *Compound Purgers*

COMPOUND medicines which purge melancholy are either taken in the superior or inferior parts: superior at mouth or nostrils. At the mouth swallowed or not swallowed: if swallowed, liquid or solid: liquid, as compound wine of Hellebore, Scilla, or Sea-Onion, Senna, Wine with Squills, Helleboratum [a mixture containing chiefly Hellebore], which Quercetan so much applauds for melancholy and madness, either inwardly taken, or outwardly applied to the head, with little pieces of linen dipped warm in it. Oxymel Scillicum [a mixture of vinegar, honey,

&c., with squills], Syrupus Helleboratus major and minor in Quercetan, and Syrupus Genistae [Syrup of Broom] for Hypochondriacal Melancholy in the same Author, compound Syrup of Succory [or Chicory], of Fumitory, Polypody, &c., [and] Heurnius his purging Cock-broth. Some except against these Syrups, as appears by Udalrinus Leonorus his Epistle to Matthiolus, as most pernicious, and that out of Hippocrates, no raw things to be used in Physick; but this in the following Epistle is exploded, and soundly confuted by Matthiolus; many julips, potions, receipts, are composed of these, as you shall find in Hildesheim, Huernius, George Sckenkius, &c.

Solid purgers are confections, electuaries, pills by themselves, or compound with others, as of Lapis Lazuli, Red Armenian Earth, Indian Pills, of Fumitory, &c., confection of Hamech, which though most approve, Solenander bitterly inveighs against, so doth Rondoletius, Fernelius and others; confections of Senna, Polypody, Cassia, the Diacatholicon [purging all humours], Wecker's Electuary of Epithyme, Ptolemy's Hierologodium, of which divers receipts are daily made.

Aëtius commends Ruffus' Medicine [Rufus' Pills, of aloes and myrrh]. Trincavellius approves of Hiera; I find no better medicine, he saith. Heurnius adds pills of Epithyme, Indian pills. Mesue describes in the Florentine Antidotary, pills one would not wish to be without. Cochia with Hellebore, Arabian Pills, Fœtida [or Assafœtida], of five kinds of Myrobalans [or Indian Plums], &c. More proper to melancholy, not excluding, in the mean time, Turbith, Manna, Rhubarb, Agarick, Elescophe, &c. which are not so proper to this humour. For, as Montaltus holds, and Montanus, choler is to be purged, because it feeds the other: and some are of an opinion, as Erasistratus and Asclepiades maintained of old, against whom Galen disputes, that no Physick doth purge one humour alone, but all alike, or what is next. Most therefore in their receipts and magistrals which are coined here, make a mixture of several simples and compounds to purge all humours in general as well as this. Some rather use potions than pills to purge this humour because that, as Heurnius and Crato observe, this juice is not so easily drawn by dry remedies; and, as Montanus adviseth, all drying medicines are to be repelled, as Aloe, Hiera, and all pills whatsoever, because the disease is dry of itself.

I might here insert many receipts of prescribed potions, boles, &c. the doses of these, but that they are common in every good Physician, and that I am loth to incur the censure of Forestus, against those that divulge and publish medicines in their mother tongue, and lest I should give occasion thereby to some ignorant Reader to practise on himself, without the consent of a good Physician.

Such as are not swallowed, but only kept in the mouth, are Gargarisms [or Gargles], used commonly after a purge, when the body is soluble and loose. Or Apophlegmatisms, Masticatories, to be held and chewed in the mouth, which are gentle, as Hyssop, Origan, Pennyroyal, Thyme, Mustard; strong, as Pellitory, Pepper, Ginger, &c.

Such as are taken into the nostrils, Errhina [or Nose Medicines] are liquid, or dry, juice of Pimpernel, Onions, &c., Castor, Pepper, white Hellebore, &c. To these you may add odoraments, perfumes, and suffumigations, &c.

Taken into the inferior parts are Clysters strong or weak, Suppositories of Castilian soap, honey boiled to a consistence; or stronger of Scammony, Hellebore, &c.

These are all used, and prescribed to this malady upon several occasions, as shall be shewed in his place.

MEMBER 3

Chirurgical Remedies

IN letting of blood, three main circumstances are to be considered, *who, how much, when?* That is, that it be done to such a one as may endure it, or to whom it may belong, that he be of a competent age, not too young, nor too old, overweak, fat, or lean, sore laboured, but to such as have need, and are full of bad blood, noxious humours, and may be eased by it.

The quantity depends upon the party's habit of body, as he is strong or weak, full or empty, may spare more or less.

In the morning is the fittest time: some doubt whether it be best fasting, or full, whether the Moon's motion or aspect of Planets be to be observed, some affirm, some deny, some grant in acute, but not in chronick diseases, whether before or after Physic. 'Tis Heurnius' Aphorism, you must begin with blood-letting and not Physick; some except this peculiar malady. But what do I? Horatius Augenius, a Physician of Padua, hath lately writ 17 books of this subject, Jobertus, &c.

Particular kinds of blood-letting in use are three, first is that opening a Vein in the arm with a sharp knife, or in the head, knees, or any other part, as shall be thought fit.

Cupping-glasses, with or without scarification, saith Fernelius, they work presently, and are applied to several parts, to divert humours, aches, wind, &c.

Horse-leeches are much used in melancholy, applied especially to the Hæmrods. Horatius Augenius, Platerus, Altomarus, Piso, and many others, prefer them before any evacuations in this kind.

Cauteries or searing with hot irons, combustions, borings, lancings, which, because they are terrible, Dropax and Sinapismus are invented, by plasters to raise blisters, and eating medicines of pitch, mustard-seed, and the like.

Issues still to be kept open, made as the former, and applied in and to several parts, have their use here on divers occasions, as shall be shewed.

SECTION 5 MEMBER 1

SUBSECTION 1 — *Particular Cure of the three several kinds of Head-Melancholy*

THE general cures thus briefly examined and discussed, it remains now to apply these medicines to the three particular species or kinds, that, according to the several parts affected, each man may tell in some sort how to help or ease himself. I will treat of head-melancholy first, in which, as in all other good cures, we must begin with Diet, as a matter of most moment, able oftentimes of itself to work this effect. I have read, saith Laurentius, that in old diseases which have gotten the upper hand or an habit, the manner of living is to more purpose than what-soever can be drawn out of the most precious boxes of the Apothecaries. This diet, as I have said, is not only in choice of meat and drink, but of all those other non-natural things. Let air be clear and moist most part: diet moistening, of good juice, easy of digestion, and not windy: drink clear, and well brewed, not too strong, nor too small. Make a melancholy man fat, as Rhasis saith, and thou hast finished the cure. Exercise not too remiss, nor too violent. Sleep a little more than ordinary. Excrements daily to be voided by art or nature; and, which Fernelius enjoins his Patient, above the rest, to avoid all passions and perturbations of the mind. Let him not be alone or idle (in any kind of melancholy); but still accompanied with such friends and familiars he most affects, neatly dressed, washed and combed, according to his ability at least, in clean sweet linen, spruce, handsome, decent, and good apparel; for nothing sooner dejects a man than want, squalor, nastiness. foul or old cloaths out of fashion. Concerning the medicinal part, he that will satisfy himself at large (in this precedent of diet) and see all at once the whole cure and manner of it in every distinct species, let him consult with Gordonius, Valescus, with Prosper Calenus, Laurentius, Ælian Montaltus, Donatus ab Altomari, Hercules de Saxoniâ, Savanarola, Sckenkius, Heurnius, Victorius Faventinus, Hildesheim, Felix Plater, Stockerus, Bruel, Petrus Bayerus, Forestus, Fuchsius, Cappivaccius, Rondoletius, Jason Pratensis, Sallustius Salvianus, Jacchinus, Lodovicus Mercatus, Alexander Messaria, Piso, Hollerius, &c., that have culled out of those old Greeks, Arabians, and Latins, whatsoever is observeable or fit to be used. Or let him read those counsels and consultations of Hugo Senensis, Renerus Solinander, Crato, Montanus, Lælius â Fonte Eugubinus, Fernelius, Julius Cæsar Claudinus, Mercurialis, Frambesarius, Sennertus, &c., wherein he shall find particular receipts, the whole method, preparatives, purgers, correctors, averters, cordials, in great variety and abundance : out of which, because every man cannot attend to read or peruse them, I will collect, for the benefit of the Reader, some few more notable medicines.

SUBSECTION 2 — *Blood-letting*

PHLEBOTOMY is promiscuously used before and after Physick, commonly before, and upon occasion is often reiterated, if there be any need at least of it. For Galen, and many others, make a doubt of bleeding at all in this kind of head-melancholy. If the malady, saith Piso, likewise Altomarus, Fuchsius, shall proceed primarily from the misaffected brain, the Patient in such case shall not need at all to bleed, except the blood otherwise abound; the veins be full, inflamed blood, and the party ready to run mad. In immaterial melancholy, which especially comes from a cold distemperature of spirits, Hercules de Saxoniâ will not admit of Phlebotomy; Laurentius approves it out of the authority of the Arabians; but as Mesue, Rhasis, Alexander appoint, especially in the head, to open the veins of the fore-head, nose, and ears, is good. They commonly set cupping-glasses on the party's shoulders, having first scarified the place; they apply horse-leeches on the head, and in all melancholy diseases, whether essential or accidental, they cause the Hæmrods to be opened, having the eleventh Aphorism of the 6th book of Hippocrates for their ground and warrant, which saith that in melancholy and mad men the varicous tumour or hœmorrhoides appearing doth heal the same. Valescus prescribes blood-letting in all three kinds, whom Sallustius Salvianus follows. If the blood abound, which is discerned by the fulness of the veins, his precedent diet, the party's laughter, age, &c., begin with the median or middle vein of the arm: if the blood be ruddy and clear, stop it; but if black in the spring time, or a good season, or thick, let it run, according to the party's strength: and some eight or twelve days after, open the head vein, and the veins in the forehead, or provoke it out of the nostrils, or cupping-glasses, &c. Trallianus allows of this, if there have been any suppression or stopping of blood at nose, or hemrods, or women's months, then to open a vein in the head or about the ankles. Yet he doth hardly approve of this course, if melancholy be sited in the head alone, or in any other dotage, except it primarily proceed from blood, or that the malady be increased by it; for blood-letting refrigerates and dries up, except the body be very full of blood, and a kind of ruddiness in the face. Therefore I conclude with Aretæus, before you let blood, deliberate of it, and well consider all circumstances belonging to it.

SUBSECTION 3 — *Preparatives and Purgers*

AFTER blood-letting we must proceed to other medicines; first prepare, and then purge, cleanse the Augean stables, make the body clean, before we hope to do any good. Gualter Bruel would have a practitioner begin first with a clyster of his, which he prescribes before blood-letting: the common sort, as Mercurialis, Montaltus, &c., proceed from lenitives to preparatives, and so to purgers. Lenitives are well known, the Lenitive Electuary, the Diaphænicum, the Diacatholicon, &c. Preparatives are usually Syrups of Borage, Bugloss, Apples, Fumitory, Thyme and Epithyme, with double as much of the same decoction or distilled water, or of the waters of Bugloss, Balm, Hops, Endive, Scolopendry, Fumitory, &c., or these sod in whey, which must be reiterated and used for many days together. Purges come last, which must not be used at all, if the malady may be otherwise helped, because they weaken nature, and dry so much; and in giving of them we must begin with the gentlest first. Some forbid all hot medicines, as Alexander, and Salvianus, &c.; hot medicines increase the disease by drying too much. Purge downward rather than upward, use potions rather than pills, and, when you begin Physick, persevere and continue in a course; for, as one observes, to stir up the humour (as one purge commonly doth) and not to prosecute doth more harm than good. They must continue in a course of Physick, yet not so that they tire and oppress nature, they must now and then remit, and let nature have some rest. The most gentle purges to begin with, are Senna, Cassia, Epithyme, Myrobalans, the Catholicon: if these prevail not, we may proceed to stronger, as the confection of Hamech, Indian Pills, Fumitories, of Assaieret, of Armenian Stone, and Lazuli, Senna Medicine. Or, if pills be too dry, some prescribe both Hellebores in the last place, amongst the rest Aretæus, because this disease will resist a gentle medicine. Laurentius and Hercules de Saxoniâ would have Antimony tried last, if the party be strong, and it warily given. Trincavellius prefers Hierologodium, to whom Francis Alexander subscribes, a very good medicine they account it. But Crato, in a counsel of his for the Duke of Bavaria's Chancellor, wholly rejects it.

I find a vast Chaos of medicines, a confusion of receipts and magistrals [or Sovereign Recipes], amongst writers, appropriated to this disease; some of the chiefest I will rehearse. To be sea-sick, first, is very good at seasonable times. The Helleborism of Matthiolus, with which he vaunts and boasts he did so many several cures: I never gave it (saith he) but, after once or .twice, by the help of God they were happily cured. The manner of making it he sets down at large in his third book of Epistles to George Hankshius, a Physician. Gualter Bruel and Heurnius make mention of it with great approbation; so doth Sckenkius in his memorable cures, and experimental medicines. That famous Helleborism of Montanus which he so often repeats in his consultations and counsels, and cracks to be a most sovereign remedy for all melancholy persons, which he hath often given without offence, and found by long experience and observation to be such.

Quercetan prefers a Syrup of Hellebore in his Chemical Pharmacopœia, and Hellebore's Extract, of his invention likewise (a most safe medicine, and not unfit to be given children) before all remedies whatsoever.

Paracelsus, in his book.of black Hellebore, admits this medicine, but as it is prepared by him. It is most certain (saith he) that the virtue of this herb is great, and admirable in effect, and little differing from Balm itself, and he that knows well how to make use hath more art than all their books contain, or all the doctors in Germany can show.

Ælianus Montaltus in his exquisite work on Diseases of the Head, sets a special receipt of his own, which in his practice he fortunately used; because it is but short I will set it down.

Take syrup of apples, 2 ounces; borage water, 4 ounces; black hellebore, steeped all night in a binding,* 6 or 8 grains; to be compounded by hand.

Other receipts of the same to this purpose you shall find in him. Valescus admires Hali's Powder, and Jason Pratensis after him: the confection of which our new London Pharmacopœia hath lately revived. Put case (saith he) all other medicines fail, by the help of God this alone shall do it, and 'tis a crowned medicine which must be kept in secret.

Take epithyme, one-half ounce; lapis lazuli and agarick, each 2 ounces; scammony, one drachm; cloves, 20; pulverize all, and of the powder make separate portions of 4 scruples each.†

To these I may add Arnold's Borage wine before mentioned, which Mizaldus calls a wonderful wine, and Stockerus vouchsafes to repeat word for word amongst other receipts. Rubeus his compound water out of Savanarola; Pinetus his balm; Cardan's Jacinth Powder, with which, in his book On Wonderful Cures, he boasts that he had cured many melancholy persons in eight days, which Sckenkius puts amongst his observeable medicines; Altomarus his syrup, with which he calls God so solemnly to witness, he hath in his kind done many excellent cures, and which Sckenkius mentioneth, Daniel Sennertus so much commends; Rulandus' admirable water for melancholy, which he names Golden Spirit of Life, Panacea, what not, and his absolute medicine of 50 Eggs, to be taken three in a morning, with a powder of his. Faventinus doubles this number of Eggs, and will have a hundred and one to be taken by three and three in like sort, which Sallustius Salvianus approves, with some of the same powder, till all be spent, a most excellent remedy for all melancholy and madmen.

Take epithyme, thyme, each, 2 drachms; white sugar, 1 ounce; saffron, 3 grains; cinnamon, 1 drachm; mix, and make powder.‡

---

* The recipe says " *Ellebori nigri per noctem infusi in ligatura.*" This appears to mean that the herbs were tied together in a cloth bag & infused (dipped in hot water). Perhaps it should be emphasised that the chief ingredient of this recipe is a drastic hydragogic cathartic, producing in overdoses gastric and intestinal inflammation, violent vomiting, vertigo, cramp, convulsions, and sometimes death. It is nowadays employed in veterinary surgery — as Burton elsewhere quotes Paracelsus, a medicine " fitter for a horse than a man."

† Scammony is now used to cure worms in children; in large doses it is a violent gastro-intestinal irritant.

‡ Epithyme is the flower of thyme. The chief ingredient in this recipe is saffron, made from the autumnal crocus, about four thousand flowers being required to make an ounce; it was once highly valued as a medicine, so much so that pharmacists were

All these yet are nothing to those Chemical preparatives of Cheledony Water, quintessence of Hellebore, salts, extracts, distillations, oils, Potable Gold, &c. Dr. Anthony, in his book On Potable Gold, 1600, is all in all for it: And though all the schools of Galenists, with a wicked and unthankful pride and scorn, detest it in their practice, yet in more grievous diseases, when their vegetals will do no good, they are compelled to seek the help of minerals, though they use them rashly, unprofitably, slackly, and [saith he] to no purpose. Rhenanus, a Dutch Chemist, takes upon him to apologize for Anthony, and sets light by all that speak against him. But what do I meddle with this great Controversy, which is the subject of many volumes? Let Paracelsus, Quercetan, Crollius, and the brethren of the Rosy Cross defend themselves as they may. Crato, Erastus, and the Galenists oppugn Paracelsus. He brags on the other side he did more famous cures by this means than all the Galenists in Europe, and calls himself a Monarch, Galen, Hippocrates, infants, illiterate, &c. As Thessalus of old railed against those ancient Asclepiadean writers, he condemns others, insults, triumphs, overcomes all antiquity (saith Galen, as if he spake to him) declares himself a conqueror, and crowns his own doings. One drop of their Chemical preparatives shall do more good than all their fulsome potions. Erastus and the rest of the Galenists vilify them, on the other side, as Hereticks in Physick; Paracelsus did that in Physick which Luther in Divinity. A drunken rogue he was, a base fellow, a Magician, he had the Devil for his master, Devils his familiar companions, and what he did was done by the help of the Devil. Thus they contend and rail, and every Mart write books pro and con, and the matter is not settled yet; let them agree as they will, I proceed.

SUBSECTION 4 — *Averters*

AVERTERS and Purgers must go together, as tending all to the same purpose, to divert this rebellious humour, and turn it another way. In this range Clysters and Suppositories challenge a chief place, to draw this humour from the brain and heart to the more ignoble parts. Some would have them still used a few days between, and those to be made with the boiled seeds of Anise, Fennel, and bastard Saffron, Hops, Thyme, Epithyme, Mallows, Fumitory, Bugloss, Polypody, Senna,

---

burned, and others buried alive, in Nuremberg, in the fifteenth century, for adulterating it. But its value (it was supposed to be stimulant, antispasmodic, or narcotic) was traditional and largely fictitious, as modern experiments have shown that it possesses little activity. It was also used as a golden dye-stuff.

Diasene, Hamech, Cassia, Diacatholicon, Hierologodium, Oil of Violets, sweet Almonds, &c. For without question a Clyster, opportunely used, cannot choose in this, as most other maladies, but to do very much good; sometimes Clysters nourish, as they may be prepared. as I was informed not long since by a learned Lecture of our Natural Philosophy Reader, which he handled by way of discourse, out of some other noted Physicians. Such things as provoke urine most commend, but not sweat. Trincavellius in head melancholy forbids it. P. Bayerus and others approve frictions of the outward parts, and to bathe them with warm water. Instead of ordinary frictions, Cardan prescribes rubbing with Nettles till they blister the skin, which likewise Basardus Visontinus so much magnifies.

Sneezing, masticatories, and nasals, are generally received. Montaltus, Hildesheim, give several receipts of all three. Hercules de Saxoniâ relates of an Empirick in Venice, that he had a strong water to purge by the mouth and nostrils, which he still used in head-melancholy, and would sell for no gold.

To open months and Hemroids is very good Physick, if they have been formerly stopped. Faventinus would have them opened with horse-leeches, so would Hercules de Saxoniâ. Julius Alexandrinus thinks Aloes fitter: most approve horse-leeches in this case, to be applied to the fore-head, nostrils, and other places.

Montaltus, out of Alexander and others, prescribes cupping-glasses, and issues in the left thigh. Aretæus, Paulus Regolinus, Sylvius, will have them without scarification, applied to the shoulders and back, thighs and feet. Montaltus bids open an issue in the arms, or hinder part of the head. Piso enjoins ligatures, frictions, suppositories, and cupping-glasses, still without scarification, and the rest.

Cauteries and hot irons are to be used in the suture of the crown, and the seared or ulcerated place suffered to run a good while. 'Tis not amiss to bore the skull with an instrument, to let out the fuliginous vapours. Sallustus Salvianus, because this humour hardly yields to other Physick, would have the leg cauterized, or the left leg below the knee, and the head bored in two or three places, for that it much avails to the exhalation of the vapours. I saw (saith he) a melancholy man at Rome, that by no remedies could be healed, but when by chance he was wounded in the head, and the skull broken, he was excellently cured. Another, to the admiration of the beholders, breaking his head with a fall from on high, was instantly recovered of his dotage. Gordonius, would have these cauteries tried last, when no other Physick will serve:

The head to be shaved and bored to let out fumes, which without doubt will do much good; " I saw a melancholy man wounded in the head with a sword, his brain-pan broken; so long as the wound was open, he was well, but when his wound was healed, his dotage returned again." But Alexander Messaria, a Professor in Padua, will allow no cauteries at all; 'tis too stiff an humour, and too thick, as he holds, to be so evaporated.

Guianerius cured a Nobleman in Savoy, by boring alone, leaving the hole open a month together, by means of which, after two years' melancholy and madness, he was delivered. All approve of this remedy in the suture of the Crown; but Arculanus would have the cautery to be made with gold. In many other parts these cauteries are prescribed for melancholy men, as in the thighs, (Mercurialis), arms, legs: Montanus, Rodericus à Fonseca, &c. but most in the head, if other Physick will do no good.

SUBSECTION 5 — *Alteratives and Cordials, corroborating, resolving the Reliques, and mending the Temperament*

BECAUSE this Humour is so malign of itself, and so hard to be removed, the reliques are to be cleansed, by Alteratives, Cordials, and such means; the temper is to be altered and amended, with such things as fortify and strengthen the heart and brain, which are commonly both affected in this malady, and do mutually misaffect one another: which are still to be given every other day, or some few days inserted after a purge or like Physick, as occasion serves, and are of such force that many times they help alone, and as Arnoldus holds in his Aphorisms, are to be preferred before all other medicines, in what kind soever.

Amongst this number of Cordials and Alteratives I do not find a more present remedy than a cup of wine or strong drink, if it be soberly and opportunely used. It makes a man bold, hardy, courageous, whetteth the wit, if moderately taken, (and, as Plutarch saith,) it makes those, which are otherwise dull, to exhale and evaporate like frankincense, or quicken (Xenophon adds) as oil doth fire. A famous cordial Matthiolus calls it, an excellent nutriment to refresh the body, it makes a good colour, a flourishing age, helps concoction, fortifies the stomack, takes away obstructions, provokes urine, drives out excrements, procures sleep, clears the blood, expels wind and cold poisons, attenuates, concocts, dissipates, all thick vapours, and fuliginous humours. And that which is all in all to my purpose, it takes away fear and sorrow.

Bacchus drives away fierce cares. (HORACE)

It glads the heart of man; the sweet school of mirth. Helen's bowl, the sole Nectar of the Gods, or that true Nepenthes in Homer, which puts away care and grief, as Oribasius and some others will, was naught else but a cup of good wine. *It makes the mind of the King and of the fatherless both one, of the bond and free-man, poor and rich; it turneth all his thoughts to joy and mirth, makes him remember no sorrow or debt, but enricheth his heart, and makes him speak by talents.* It gives life itself, spirits, wit, &c. For which cause the Antients called Bacchus, Liber Pater, Releaser, and sacrificed to Bacchus and Pallas still upon an Altar. *Wine measurably drunk, and in time, brings gladness and cheerfulness of mind, it cheereth God and men:* Bacchus, giver of joy, &c.; it makes an old wife dance, and such as are in misery to forget evil, and be merry.

> *Wine makes a troubled soul to rest,*
> *Though feet with fetters be opprest.* (TIBULLUS)

Demetrius in Plutarch, when he fell into Seleucus' hands, and was prisoner in Syria, spent his time with dice and drink, that he might so ease his discontented mind, and avoid those continual cogitations of his present condition wherewith he was tormented. Therefore Solomon *bids wine be given to him that is ready to perish, and to him that hath grief of heart; let him drink that he forget his poverty, and remember his misery no more.* It easeth a burdened soul, nothing speedier, nothing better: which the Prophet Zachary perceived, when he said, *that in the time of Messias they of Ephraim should be glad, and their heart should rejoice as through wine.* All which makes me very well approve of that pretty description of a feast in Bartholomæus Anglicus, when grace was said, their hands washed, and the Guests sufficiently exhilarated, with good discourse, sweet musick, dainty fare, as a Corollary to conclude the feast, and continue their mirth, a grace cup came in to cheer their hearts, and they drank healths to one another again and again. Which (as J. Fredericus Matenesius) was an old custom in all ages in every Commonwealth, so as they be not enforced to drink by coercion, but as in that Royal Feast of Assuerus which lasted 180 days, *without compulsion they drank by order in golden vessels,* when and what they would themselves. This of drink is a most easy and parable remedy, a common, a cheap, still ready against fear, sorrow, and such troublesome thoughts, that molest the mind; as brimstone with fire, the spirits on a sudden are enlightened by it. No better Physick (saith Rhasis) for a melancholy man: and he that can keep company, and carouse, needs no other medicines, 'tis enough. His Country-man, Avicenna, proceeds further yet,

and will have him that is troubled in mind, or melancholy, not to drink
only, but now and then to be drunk: excellent good Physick it is for
this and many other diseases. Magninus will have them to be so once
a month at least, and gives his reasons for it, because it scours the
body by vomit, urine, sweat, of all manner of superfluities, and keeps
it clean. Of the same mind is Seneca the Philosopher in his book On
Tranquillity, it is good sometimes to be drunk, it helps sorrow, depresseth cares, and so concludes his Tract with a cup of wine: Take, dearest
Serenus, what conduces to tranquillity of mind. But these are Epicureal
tenents, tending to looseness of life, Luxury and Atheism, maintained
alone by some Heathens, dissolute Arabians, profane Christians, and
are exploded by Rabbi Moses, Gulielmus Placentius, Valescus de
Taranta, and most accurately ventilated by Jo. Sylvaticus, a late writer
and Physician of Milan, where you shall find this tenent copiously confuted.

Howsoever you say, if this be true that wine and strong drink have
such virtue to expel fear and sorrow, and to exhilarate the mind, ever
hereafter let's drink and be merry.

> *Come, lusty Lydia, fill's a cup of sack,*
> *And, sirrah drawer, bigger pots we lack,*
> *And Scio wines that have so good a smack.*   (HORACE)

I say with him in A. Gellius, let us maintain the vigour of our souls
with a moderate cup of wine, (cups made to give gladness, &c.), and
drink to refresh our mind; if there be any cold sorrow in it, or torpid
bashfulness, let's wash it all away. — Now drown your cares in wine,
so saith Horace, so saith Anacreon,

> *Drink, then, while we may,*
> *For Death is on his way.*

Let's drive down care with a cup of wine: and so say I too (though I
drink none myself), for all this may be done, so that it be modestly,
soberly, opportunely used; so that they be not drunk with wine, wherein
is excess, which our Apostle forewarns; for, as Chrysostom well comments on that place, 'tis for mirth, wine, but not for madness: and will
you know where, when, and how, that is to be understood? Would you
know where wine is good? hear the Scriptures, *Give Wine to them that
are in sorrow*, or, as Paul bid Timothy drink wine for his stomack's
sake, for concoction, health, or some such honest occasion. Otherwise,
as Pliny telleth us, if singular moderation be not had, nothing so pernicious, 'tis mere Vinegar, a flattering demon, poison itself. But hear
a more fearful doom: *Woe be to him that makes his neighbour drunk,*

shameful spewing shall be upon his glory. Let not good fellows triumph therefore, (saith Matthiolus), that I have so much commended wine; if it be immoderately taken, instead of making glad, it confounds both body and soul, it makes a giddy head, a sorrowful heart. And 'twas well said of the Poet of old, Wine causeth mirth and grief; nothing so good for some, so bad for others, especially as one observes, that are hot or inflamed. And so of spices, they alone, as I have shewed, cause head-melancholy themselves, they must not use wine as an ordinary drink, or in their diet. But to determine with Laurentius, wine is bad for mad men, and such as are troubled with heat in their inner parts or brains; but to melancholy, which is cold (as most is), Wine soberly used may be very good.

I may say the same of the decoction of China roots, Sassafras, Sarsaparilla, Guaiacum. China, saith Manardus, makes a good colour in the face, takes away melancholy, and all infirmities proceeding from cold; even so Sarsaparilla provokes sweat mightily, Guaiacum dries. Claudinus. Montanus, Cappivaccius, make frequent and good use of Guaiacum, and China, so that the liver be not incensed, good for such as are cold, as most melancholy men are, but by no means to be mentioned in hot.

The Turks have a drink called Coffee (for they use no wine), so named of a berry as black as soot, and as bitter, (like that black drink which was in use amongst the Lacedæmonians, and perhaps the same), which they sip still off, and sup as warm as they can suffer; they spend much time in those Coffee-houses, which are somewhat like our Alehouses or Taverns, and there they sit chatting and drinking to drive away the time, and to be merry together, because they find by experience that kind of drink so used helpeth digestion, and procureth alacrity. Some of them take Opium to this purpose.

Borage, Balm, Saffron, Gold, I have spoken of; Montaltus commends Scorzonera roots condite [or preserved]. Garcias ab Horto makes mention of an herb called Datura, which, if it be eaten, for 24 hours following takes away all sense of grief, makes them incline to laughter and mirth: and another called bang, like in effect to Opium, which puts them for a time into a kind of Extasis, and makes them gently to laugh. One of the Roman Emperors had a seed, which he did ordinarily eat to exhilarate himself. Christophorus Ayrerus prefers Bezoar's stone, and the confection of Alkermes, before other cordials, and Amber in some cases. Alkermes comforts the inner parts; and Bezoar stone hath an especial virtue against all melancholy affections, it refresheth the heart, and corroborates the whole body. Amber provokes urine, helps the body, breaks wind, &c. After a purge, three or four grains of Bezoar stone, and three grains of Ambergrease drunk, or taken in Borage, or Bugloss water, in which gold hot hath been quenched, will do much good, and the purge shall diminish less (the heart so refreshed) of the strength and substance of the body.

> *Take Alkermes confection, half an ounce; Bezoar stone,*
> *1 scruple; powdered finest white Amber, 2 scruples, with*
> *syrup of citron rind; make an electuary.**

To Bezoar's stone most subscribe, Manardus, and many others; it takes away sadness, and makes merry him that useth it (saith Garcias ab Horto) : " I have seen some that have been much diseased with faintness, swooning, and melancholy, that, taking the weight of three grains of this stone in the water of Oxtongue, have been cured." Garcias ab Horto brags how many desperate cures he hath done upon melancholy men by this alone, when all Physicians had forsaken them. But Alchermes many except against; in some cases it may help, if it be good and of the best, such as that of Montpelier in France, which Jodocus Sincerus so much magnifies, and would have no traveller omit to see it made. But it is not so general a medicine as the other. Fernelius suspects Alchermes, by reason of its heat; nothing (saith he) sooner exasperates this disease than the use of hot working meats and medicines, and would have them for that cause warily taken. I conclude therefore of this and all other medicines, as Thucydides of the plague at Athens, no remedy could be prescribed for it, there is no Catholick medicine to be had: that which helps one is pernicious to another.

Medicine of Cold Pearls [certain medicinal seeds], of Amber, of Borage, the Gladdening Electuary of Galen & Rhasis, of Gems, of Sweet and Bitter Musk, the Conciliator Electuary, Syrup of Cydonian Apples, conserves of Roses, Violets, Fumitory, Enula campana, Satyrion, Lemons, Orange-pills condite, &c., have their good use.

> *Take musk and sweet marjoram, each, 2 drachms;*
> *bugloss, borage, sweet violets, each 1 ounce; to mix*
> *with syrup of apples.*

Every Physician is full of such receipts; one only I will add for the rareness of it, which I find recorded by many learned Authors, as an

---

* Alkermes, a compound cordial made of cider, rose-water, sugar, fragrantly flavored, and colored red by kermes, a dyestuff made from a Mediterranean insect. Bezoar stone, certain calculi or concretions found in the stomachs of animals, once esteemed as an antidote for poison.

approved medicine against dotage, head-melancholy, and such diseases of the brain. Take a Ram's head that never meddled with an Ewe, cut off at a blow, and, the horns only taken away, boil it well skin and wool together, after it is well sod, take out the brains, and put these spices to it. Cinnamon, Ginger, Nutmeg, Mace, Cloves, in equal parts of half an ounce, mingle the powder of these spices with it, and heat them in a platter upon a chafing-dish of coals together, stirring them well, that they do not burn; take heed it be not overmuch dried, or dryer than a Calves brains ready to be eaten. Keep it so prepared, and for three days give it the patient fasting, so that he fast two hours after it. It may be eaten with bread in an egg, or broth, or any way, so it be taken. For fourteen days let him use this diet, drink no wine, &c. Gesner, Caricterius, mention this medicine, though with some variation; he that list may try it, and many such.

Odoraments to smell to, of Rose-water, Violet flowers, Balm, Rosecakes, Vinegar, &c. do much recreate the brains and spirits, according to Solomon, *they rejoice the heart*, and, as some say, nourish: 'tis a question commonly controverted in our schools, whether odors nourish; let Ficinus decide it, many arguments he brings to prove it: as of Democritus, that lived by the smell of bread alone, applied to his nostrils, for some few days, when for old age he could eat no meat. Ferrerius speaks of an excellent confection of his making, of wine, saffron, &c., which he prescribed to dull, weak, feeble, and dying men, to smell to, and by it to have done very much good, as if he had given them drink. Our noble and learned Lord Verulam, in his book Concerning Life and Death, commends therefore all such cold smells as any way serve to refrigerate the spirits. Montanus prescribes a form which he would have his melancholy Patient never to have out of his hands. If you will have them spagirically [or chemically] prepared, look in Oswaldus Crollius.

Irrigation of the head shaven, of the flowers of water-lillies, lettuce, violets, camomile, wild mallows, wether's head, &c., must be used many mornings together. Montanus would have the head so washed once a week. Lælius à Fonte Eugubinus, for an Italian Count troubled with head-melancholy, repeats many medicines which he tried, but two alone which did the cure; use of whey made of goat's milk, with the extract of Hellebore, and irrigations of the head with water-lillies, lettuce, violets, camomile, &c., upon the suture of the crown. Piso commends a ram's lungs applied hot to the fore part of the head, or a young lamb divided in the back, exenterated, [disembowelled], &c. All acknowledge the chief cure to consist in moistening throughout. Some, saith Laurentius, use powders, and caps to the brain, but, forasmuch as such aromatical things are hot and dry, they must be sparingly administered.

Unto the heart we may do well to apply bags, epithemes, ointments, of which Laurentius gives examples. Bruel prescribes an epitheme for the heart, of bugloss, borage, water-lily, violet waters, sweet wine, balm leaves, nutmegs, cloves, &c.

For the Belly, make a Fomentation of oil, in which the seeds of cummin, rue, carrots, dill, have been boiled.

Baths are of wonderful great force in this malady, much admired by Galen, Aëtius, Rhasis, &c., of sweet water, in which is boiled the leaves of mallows, roses, violets, water-lilies, wether's head, flowers of Bugloss, Camomile, Melilot, &c. Guianerius would have them used twice a day, and when they come forth of the Baths, their back bones to be anointed with oil of Almonds, Violets, Nymphæa, fresh Capon-grease, &c.

Amulets and things to be borne about I find prescribed, taxed by some, approved by Renodeus, Platerus, (amulets, he saith, are not to be neglected), and others; look for them in Mizaldus, Porta, Albertus, &c. Bassardus Visontinus commends Hypericon, or S. John's Wort, gathered on a Friday in the hour of Jupiter, when it comes to his effectual operation (that is about the full Moon in July): so gathered, and borne or hung about the neck, it mightily helps this affection, and drives away all phantastical spirits. Philes, a Greek Author that flourished in the time of Michael Palæologus, writes that a Sheep or Kid's skin, whom a Wolf worried, ought not at all to be worn about a man, because it causeth palpitation of the heart, not for any fear, but a secret virtue which Amulets have. A ring made of the hoof of an ass's right fore-foot carried about, &c. I say with Renodeus, they are not altogether to be rejected. Peony doth cure Epilepsy, precious stones most diseases, a Wolf's dung borne with one helps the Cholick, a Spider an Ague, &c. Being in the Country in the vacation time not many years since at Lindley in Leicestershire, my Father's house, I first observed this Amulet of a Spider in a nut-shell lapped in silk, &c., so applied for an Ague by my Mother *; whom, although I knew to have excellent Skill in Chirurgery, sore eyes, aches, &c., and such experimental medicines, as all the country where she dwelt can witness, to have done many famous and good cures upon divers poor folks, that were otherwise destitute of help, yet, among all other experiments, this methought was most absurd and ridiculous, I could see no warrant for it. Why a Spider

* Mistress Dorothy Burton, she died 1629. — Burton's note.

for a fever? For what Antipathy? till at length, rambling amongst authors (as often I do) I found this very medicine in Dioscorides, approved by Matthiolus, repeated by Aldrovandus, in his chapter on Spiders, in his book on Insects, I began to have a better opinion of it, and to give more credit to Amulets, when I saw it in some parties answer to experience. Such medicines are to be exploded that consist of words, characters, spells, and charms, which can do no good at all, but out of a strong conceit, as Pomponatius proves; or the Devil's policy, who is the first founder and teacher of them.

SUBSECTION 6 — *Correctors of Accidents to procure Sleep. Against fearful Dreams, Redness, &c.*

WHEN you have used all good means and helps of alteratives, averters, diminutives, yet there will be still certain accidents to be corrected and amended, as waking, fearful dreams, flushing in the face to some, ruddiness, &c.

Waking, by reason of their continual cares, fears, sorrows, dry brains, is a symptom that much crucifies melancholy men, and must therefore be speedily helped, and sleep by all means procured, which sometimes is a sufficient remedy of itself without any other Physick. Sckenkius, in his observations, hath an example of a woman that was so cured. The means to procure it are inward or outward. Inwardly taken, are simples, or compounds; simples, as Poppy, Nymphæa, Violets, Roses, Lettuce, Mandrake, Henbane, Nightshade, or Solanum, Saffron, Hemp-seed, Nutmegs, Willows with their seeds, juice, decoctions, distilled waters, &c. Compounds are syrups, or Opiates, syrup of Poppy, Violets, Verbasco, which are commonly taken with distilled waters.

> *Take diacodium, 1 ounce; diascordium, one-half drachm;*
> *lettuce water, 3 and a half ounces; make a mingled potion;*
> *to be taken at bed-time.**

Nicholas' Rest, Philonium Romanum,† Triphera Magna [a gentle caustick], Pills of Cynoglossa [or Borage], Diascordium, Laudanum of Paracelsus, Opium, are in use, &c. Country folks commonly make a posset of hemp-seed, which Fuchsius in his Herbal so much discommends, yet I have seen the good effect, and it may be used where better medicines are not to be had.

* Diacodium, a syrup made of poppies; diascordium, a medicine invented by Fracastorius as a remedy for plague, containing water-germander (or perhaps garlic).

† Philonium Romanum, a medicine invented by Philon, of Tarsus, an ancient physician: it was composed of opium, saffron, pyrethrum, euphorbium, pepper, henbane, spikenard, honey, and other ingredients.

Laudanum of Paracelsus is prescribed in two or three grains, with a dram of Dioscordium, which Oswaldus Crollius commends. Opium itself is most part used outwardly, to smell to in a ball, though commonly so taken by the Turks to the same quantity for a cordial, and at Goa in the Indies; the dose 40 or 50 grains.

Rulandus calls Nicholas' Rest the last refuge, but of this and the rest look for peculiar receipts in Victorius Faventinus, Heurnius, Hildesheim, &c. Outwardly used, as oil of Nutmegs by extraction or expression, with Rose-water to anoint the temples, oils of Poppy, Nenuphar, Mandrake, Purslain, Violets, all to the same purpose.

Montanus much commends odoraments of Opium, Vinegar, and Rosewater. Laurentius prescribes Pomanders and nodules; see the receipts in him; Codronchus, wormwood to smell to.

Poplar-alabaster Ointments are used to anoint the temples, nostrils, or, if they be too weak, they mix Saffron and Opium. Take a grain or two of Opium, and dissolve it with three or four drops of Rose-water in a spoon, and after mingle with it as much Poplar Ointment as a nut, use it as before: or else take half a dram of Opium, Poplar Ointment, oil of Nenuphar, Rose-water, Rose-vinegar, of each half an ounce, with as much virgin wax as a nut; anoint your temples with some of it, at bed-time.

Sacks of Wormwood, Mandrake, Henbane, Roses, made like pillows and laid under the Patient's head, are mentioned by Cardan and Mizaldus, to anoint the soles of the feet with the fat of a dormouse, the teeth with ear-wax of a dog,* swine's gall, hare's ears: charms, &c.

Frontlets are well known to every good wife, Rose-water and Vinegar, with a little woman's milk, and Nutmegs grated upon a Rose-cake applied to both temples.

For an Emplaister, take of Castorium a dram and half, of Opium half a scruple, mixt both together with a little water of life, make two small plaisters thereof, and apply them to the temples.

Rulandus prescribes Epithemes, and lotions of the head, with the decoction of flowers of Nymphæa, Violet-leaves, Mandrake roots, Henbane, white Poppy. Hercules de Saxoniâ, rainwater, or droppings, &c. Lotions of the feet do much avail of the said herbs: by these means, saith Laurentius, I think you may procure sleep to the most melancholy men in the world. Some use horse-leeches behind the ears, and apply Opium to the place.

Bayerus sets down some remedies against fearful dreams, and such as walk and talk in their sleep. Baptista Porta, to procure pleasant

* Scarcely possible to believe, says Burton's Latin footnote.

dreams and quiet rest, would have you take Hippoglossa, or the herb
Horse-tongue, Balm, to use them or their distilled waters after supper,
&c. Such men must not eat Beans, Pease, Garlick, Onions, Cabbage,
Venison, Hare, use black wines, or any meat hard of digestion at supper,
or lie on their backs, &c.

Boorish shyness, bashfulness, flushing in the face, high colour. ruddiness, are common grievances, which much torture many melancholy
men, when they meet a man, or come in company of their betters,
strangers, after a meal, or if they drink a cup of wine or strong drink,
they are as red and fleckt, and sweat, as if they had been at a Mayor's
Feast; particularly if fear overcomes them, it [that is to say, bashful-
ness] exceeds, they think every man observes, takes notice of it: and
fear alone will effect it, suspicion without any other cause. Sckenkius
speaks of a waiting Gentlewoman in the Duke of Savoy's Court. that
was so much offended with it, that she kneeled down to him, and offered
Biarus, a Physician, all that she had to be cured of it. And 'tis most
true that Antony Lodovicus saith in his book On Shame, bashfulness
either hurts or helps; such men I am sure it hurts. If it proceed from
suspicion or fear, Felix Plater prescribes no other remedy but to reject
and contemn it: he is shielded by the crowd, as a worthy Physician in
our town said to a friend of mine in like case, complaining without a
cause, suppose one looked red, what matter is it? make light of it,
who observes it?

If it trouble at or after meals, (as Jobertus observes) after a little
exercise or stirring, for many are then hot and red in the face, or if they
do nothing at all, especially women; he would have them let blood in
both arms, first one, then another, two or three days between, if blood
abound, to use frictions of the other parts, feet especially, and washing
of them, because of that consent which is betwixt the head and the feet.
And withal to refrigerate the face, by washing it often with Rose,
Violet, Nenuphar, Lettuce, Lovage waters, and the like: but the best
of all is that Virgin Milk, or strained liquor of Litharge [Protoxide of
Lead]. It is diversely prepared; by Jobertus thus: Take litharge, 1
ounce; white lead, 3 drachms; camphire, 2 scruples; to be dissolved in
water of nightshade, lettuce, nenuphar, each, 3 ounces, white wine vinegar 2 ounces; let it settle for several hours, then put through a philter;
keep in a glass vessel, and moisten the face twice or thrice a day.
Quercetan commends the water of frogs' spawn for ruddiness in the
face. Crato would fain have them use all Summer the condite flowers
of Succory, Strawberry-water, Roses, (cupping-glasses are good for the
time), and to defecate impure blood with the infusion of Senna, Savory,

Balm-water. Hollerius knew one cured alone with the use of Succory boiled, and drunk for five months, every morning in the Summer.

It is good overnight to anoint the face with Hare's blood, and in the morning to wash it with strawberry and cowslip-water, the juice of distill'd Lemons, juice of cowcumbers, or to use the seeds of Melons, or kernels of Peaches beaten small, or the roots of arum, and mixt with wheat bran to bake it in an oven, and to crumble it in strawberry-water, or to put fresh cheese curds to a red face.

Take kernels of Persian melon-seeds, to
each ounce a half-scruple; strawberry-
water, 2 pounds; mix; apply by hand.

If it trouble them at meal times that flushing, as oft it doth, with sweating or the like, they must avoid all violent passions and actions, as laughing, &c., strong drink, and drink very little, one draught saith Crato, and that about the midst of their meal; avoid at all times indurate salt, and especially spice and windy meat.

Crato prescribes the condite fruit of wild rose to a Nobleman his Patient, to be taken before dinner or supper, to the quantity of a chestnut. It is made of sugar, as that of Quinces. The decoction of the roots of sow-thistle before meat by the same Author is much approved. To eat of a baked Apple some advise, or of a preserved Quince, Cumminseed prepared with meat instead of salt, to keep down fumes: not to study, or to be intentive after meals.

To apply cupping-glasses to the shoulders is very good. For the other kind of ruddiness which is settled in the face with pimples, &c., because it pertains not to my subject, I will not meddle with it. I refer you to Crato's Counsels, Arnoldus, Ruland, Peter Forestus on redness, to Platerus, Mercurialis, Ulmus, Randoletius, Heurnius, Menadous, and others, that have written largely of it.

Those other grievances and symptoms of head-ache, palpitation of heart, vertigo, deliquium, &c., which trouble many melancholy men, because they are copiously handled apart in every Physician, I do voluntarily omit.

MEMBER 2

Cure of Melancholy over all the Body

WHERE the melancholy blood possesseth the whole body with the Brain, it is best to begin with blood-letting. The Greeks prescribe the Median, or middle vein, to be opened, and so much blood to be taken away as the Patient may well spare, and the cut that is made must be wide enough. The Arabians hold it fittest to be taken from that arm on which side there is more pain and heaviness in the head: if black blood issue forth, bleed on, if it be clear and good, let it be instantly suppressed, because the malice of melancholy is much corrected by the goodness of the blood. If the party's strength will not admit much evacuation in this kind at once, it must be assayed again and again: if it may not be conveniently taken from the arm, it must be taken from the knees and ancles, especially to such men or women whose hemrods or months have been stopped. If the malady continue, it is not amiss to evacuate in a part, in the forehead, & to virgins in the ancles, which are melancholy for love-matters; so to widows that are much grieved and troubled with sorrow and cares: for bad blood flows in the heart, and so crucifies the mind. The hemrods are to be opened with an instrument, or horse-leeches, &c. See more in Montaltus. Sckenkius hath an example of one that was cured by an accidental wound in his thigh, much bleeding freed him from melancholy. Diet, Diminutives, Alteratives, Cordials, Correctors, as before, intermixt as occasion serves; all their study must be to make a melancholy man fat, and then the cure is ended. Diuretica, or medicines to procure urine, are prescribed by some in this kind, hot and cold: hot where the heat of the liver doth not forbid; cold where the heat of the liver is very great. Amongst hot are Parsley roots, Lovage, Fennel, &c. cold, Melon-seeds, &c., with whey of Goat's-milk, which is the common conveyer.

To purge and purify the blood use Sowthistle, Succory, Senna, Endive, Carduus Benedictus, Dandelion, Hop, Maidenhair, Fumitory, Bugloss, Borage, &c., with their juice, decoctions, distilled waters, syrups, &c.

Oswaldus Crollius much admires salt of Corals in this case, and Aëtius, Hieram Archigenis [Archigenes' Medicine], which is an excellent medicine to purify the blood for all melancholy affections, falling sickness, none to be compared to it.

MEMBER 3

SUBSECTION 1 — *Cure of Hypochondriacal Melancholy*

IN this cure, as in the rest, is especially required the rectification of those six non-natural things above all, as good diet, which Montanus enjoins a French Nobleman, to have an especial care of it, without which all other remedies are in vain. Blood-letting is not to be used, except the Patient's body be very full of blood, and that it be derived from the liver and spleen to the stomack and his vessels, then to draw it back, to cut the inner vein of either arm, some say the salvatella, [a vein between the ring finger and the little finger], and, if the malady be continuate, to open a vein in the forehead.

Preparatives and Alteratives may be used as before, saving that there must be respect had as well to the Liver, Spleen, Stomack, Hypochondries, as to the heart and brain. To comfort the Stomack and inner parts against wind and obstructions, by Aretæus, Galen, Aëtius, Aurelianus, &c., and many latter writers, are still prescribed the decoctions of Wormwood, Centaury, Pennyroyal, Betony sod in whey, and daily drunk: many have been cured by this medicine alone.

Prosper Alpinus and some others as much magnify the water of Nilus against this malady, an especial good remedy for windy melancholy. For which reason belike Ptolemæus Philadelphus, when he married his daughter Berenice to the King of Assyria (as Celsus records) to his great charge caused the water of Nilus to be carried with her, and gave command that during her life she should use no other drink. I find those that commend use of Apples in splenetick and this kind of melancholy, (Lambswool some call it), which, howsoever approved, must certainly be corrected of cold rawness and wind.

Codronchus magnifies the oil and salt of Wormwood above all other remedies, which works better and speedier than any simple whatsoever, and much to be preferred before all those fulsome decoctions, and infusions, which much offend by reason of their quantity; this alone, in a small measure taken, expels wind, and that most forcibly, moves urine, cleanseth the stomack of all gross humours, crudities, helps appetite, &c. Arnoldus hath a Wormwood wine which he would have used, which every Pharmacopœia speaks of.

Diminutives and purgers may be taken as before, of hiera, manna, cassia, which Montanus in this kind prefers before all other simples, and these must be often used, still abstaining from those which are more violent, lest they do exasperate the stomack, &c., and the mischief by that means be increased; though in some Physicians I find very strong purgers, Hellebore itself, prescribed in this affection. If it long continue, vomits may be taken after meat, or otherwise gently procured with warm water, oxymel, &c., now and then. Fuchsius prescribes Hellebore; but still take heed in this malady, which I have often warned, of hot medicines, because, (as Salvianus adds), drought follows heat,

which increaseth the disease: and yet Baptista Sylvaticus forbids cold
medicines, because they increase obstructions, and other bad symptoms.
But this varies as the parties do. and 'tis not easy to determine which
to use. The stomack most part in this infirmity is cold, the liver hot;
scarce therefore (which Montanus insinuates) can you help the one,
and not hurt the other: much discretion must be used; take no Physick
at all, he concludes. without great need. Lælius Eugubinus, for an hypochondriacal German Prince, used many medicines, but it was after
signified to him in letters, that the decoction of China and Sassafras,
and salt of Sassafras, wrought him an incredible good. In his 108th
consultation, he used as happily the same remedies; this to a third
might have been poison, by overheating his liver and blood.

For the other parts look for remedies in Savanarola, Gordonius, Mas-
saria, Mercatus, Johnson, &c. One for the spleen, amongst many other,
I will not omit, cited by Hildesheim. prescribed by Matthiolus Flaccius,
and out of the authority of Benevenius. Antony Benevenius in an
hypochondriacal passion cured an exceeding great swelling of the spleen
with Capers alone, a meat befitting that infirmity, and frequent use of
the water of a Smith's Forge; by this Physick he helped a sick man
whom all other Physicians had forsaken, that for seven years had been
Splenetick. And of such force is this water, that those creatures that
drink of it have commonly little or no spleen. See more excellent medicines for the Spleen in him and Lodovicus Mercatus, who is a great
magnifier of this medicine. This steel-drink is much likewise commended to this disease by Daniel Sennertus, and admired by J. Cæsar
Claudinus, he calls steel the proper Alexipharmacum of this malady,
and much magnifies it; look for receipts in them. Averters must be
used to the liver and spleen, and to scour the Meseraick Veins; and
they are either to open, or provoke urine. You can open no place better
than the Hemrods, which if by horse-leeches they be made to flow, there
may be again such an excellent remedy, as Plater holds. Sallustus
Salvianus will admit no other phlebotomy but this; and by his experience in an hospital which he kept he found all mad and melancholy
men worse for other blood-letting. Laurentius calls this of horse-leeches
a sure remedy to empty the spleen and Meseraick Membrane. Only
Montanus is against it; to other men (saith he) this opening of the
hæmrods seems to be a profitable remedy; for my part I do not approve
of it, because it draws away the thinnest blood, and leaves the thickest
behind.

Aëtius, Vidus Vidius, Mercurialis, Fuchsius, recommend Diureticks, or such things as provoke urine, as Aniseeds, Dill, Fennel, Germander, ground Pine, sod [seethed] in water, drunk in powder; and yet P. Bayerus is against them, and so is Hollerius; all melancholy men (saith he) must avoid such things as provoke urine, because by them the subtle or thinnest is evacuated, the thicker matter remains.

Clysters are in good request. Trincavellius esteems of them in the first place, and Hercules de Saxoniâ is a greater approver of them. I have found (saith he) by experience that many hypochondriacal melancholy men have been cured by the sole use of Clysters, receipts are to be had in him.

Besides those fomentations, irrigations, inunctions, odoraments, prescribed for the head, there must be the like used for the Liver, Spleen, Stomack, Hypochondries, &c. In crudity (saith Piso) 'tis good to bind the stomack hard, to hinder wind, and to help concoction.

Of inward medicines I need not speak; use the same Cordials as before. In this kind of melancholy some prescribe Treacle in Winter, especially before or after purges, or in the Spring, as Avicenna; Trincavellius, Mithridate: Montaltus, Peony seeds, Unicorn's horn, bone of the heart of a stag, &c.

Amongst Topicks, or outward medicines, none are more precious than Baths, but of them I have spoken. Fomentations to the Hypochondries are very good of wine and water, in which are sod [seethed] Southernwood, Melilot, Epithyme, Mugwort, Senna, Polypody, as also Plaisters, Liniments, Ointments for the Spleen, Liver, and Hypochondries, of which look for examples in Laurentius, Jobertus, Montanus, Montaltus, Hercules de Saxoniâ, Faventinus. And so of Epithemes, digestive powders, bags, oils. Octavius Horatianus prescribes chalastick [or laxative] Cataplasms, or dry purging medicines: Piso, Dropaces of pitch, and oil of Rue, applied at certain times to the stomack, to the metaphrene, or part of the back which is over against the heart; Aëtius, sinapisms; Montaltus would have the thighs to be cauterised, Mercurialis prescribes beneath the knees; Lælius Eugubinus will have the cautery made in the right thigh, and so Montanus. The same Montanus approves of issues in the arms or hinder part of the head. Bernardus Paternus, would have issues made in both the thighs: Lodovicus Mercatus prescribes them near the Spleen, or near the region of the belly, or in either of the thighs. Ligatures, Frictions, and Cupping-glasses above or about the belly, without scarification, which Felix Platerus so much approves, may be used as before.

SUBSECTION 2 — *Correctors to expel Wind. Against Costiveness, &c.*

In this kind of Melancholy one of the most offensive symptoms is wind, which, as in the other species, so in this, hath great need to be corrected and expelled.

The medicines to expel it are either inwardly taken or outwardly. Inwardly to expel wind, are simples or compounds: simples are herbs, roots, &c. as Galanga, Gentian, Angelica, Enula, Calamus Aromaticus, Valerian, Zeodoti, Iris, condite Ginger, Aristolochy, Cicliminus, China [Roots], Dittander, Pennyroyal, Rue, Calamint, Bay-berries and Bay-leaves, Betony, Rosemary, Hyssop, Sabine, Centaury, Mint, Camomile, French Lavender, Chaste-lamb, Broom-flowers, Origan, Orange-pills, &c., Spices, as Saffron, Cinnamon, Bezoar Stone, Myrrh, Mace, Nut-megs, Pepper, Cloves, Ginger, seeds of Anise, Fennel, Amni, Cary, Nettle, Rue, &c., Juniper berries, grana Paradisi; Compounds, of Anise, Galingale, Cinnamon, Calaminth, the Electuary of Laurel, the Blessed Laxative, the Powder Against Flatulence, the Florentian Antidote, the Charming Powder, Aromatick Rose Wine,* Treacle, Mithridate, &c. This one caution of Gualter Bruel is to be observed in the administering of these hot medicines and dry, that, whilst they covet to expel wind, they do not inflame the blood and increase the disease. Sometimes (as he saith) medicines must more decline to heat, sometimes more to cold, as the circumstances require, and as the parties are inclined to heat or cold.

Outwardly taken to expel winds, are oils, as of Camomile, Rue, Bays, &c. fomentations of the Hypochondries, with the decoctions of Dill, Pennyroyal, Rue, Bay-leaves, Cummin, &c., bags of Camomile-flowers, Aniseed, Cummin, Bays, Rue, Wormwood, Ointments of the Oil of Spikenard, Wormwood, Rue, &c. Aretæus prescribes Cataplasms of Camomile-flowers, Fennel, Aniseeds, Cummin, Rosemary, Worm-wood-leaves, &c.

Cupping-glasses applied to the Hypochondries, without scarification, do wonderfully resolve wind. Fernelius much approves of them at the lower end of the belly; Lodovicus Mercatus calls them a powerful remedy, and testifieth moreover out of his own knowledge how many he hath seen suddenly eased by them. Julius Cæsar Claudinus admires

---

* The Compounds, by their own names, run: Dianisum, Diagalanga, Diaciminum, Diacalaminth, Electuarium de Baccis Lauri, Benedicta Laxativa, Pulvis ad Flatus, Antid. Florent, Pulvis Carminativus, Aromaticum Rosatum, &c. The " Florentian Anti-dote " may be simply a reference to the Florentine Antidotary.

these Cupping-glasses, which he calls (out of Galen) a kind of enchantment, they cause such present help.

Empiricks have a myriad of medicines, as to swallow a bullet of lead, &c., which I voluntarily omit. Amatus Lusitanus for an Hypochondriacal person that was extremely tormented with wind, prescribes a strange remedy. Put a pair of bellows' end into a Clyster pipe, and applying it into the fundament, open the bowels, so draw forth the wind; nature abhors a vacuum. He vaunts he was the first invented this remedy, and by means of it speedily eased a melancholy man. Of the cure of this flatuous melancholy read more in Fienus.

Against Head-ache, Vertigo, Vapours which ascend forth of the stomack to molest the head, read Hercules de Saxoniâ and others.

If Costiveness offend in this, or in any other of the three species, it is to be corrected with suppositories, clysters, or lenitives, powder of Senna, condite [or preserved] Prunes, &c.

Make lenitive electuaries of
juice of roses, each 1 ounce.

Take as much as a Nutmeg at a time, half an hour before dinner or supper, or Mastic pills, 1 oz. in 6 pills, a pill or two at a time. See more in Montanus, Hildesheim. P. Cnemander and Montanus commend Cyprian Turpentine, which they would have familiarly taken, to the quantity of a small Nut, two or three hours before dinner and supper, twice or thrice a week, if need be; for, besides that it keeps the belly soluble, it clears the stomack, opens obstructions, cleanseth the liver, provokes urine.

These in brief are the ordinary medicines which belong to the cure of melancholy, which, if they be used aright, no doubt may do much good. Saith Bessardus, a good choice of particular receipts must needs ease, if not quite cure, not one, but all or most, as occasion serves.

Where one thing by itself may fail,
The many serve to cure our ail. (OVID)

THE THIRD PARTITION

Love and love melancholy, Memb. 1. Sect. 1.

Preface or Introduction. *Subsect.* 1.
Love's definition, pedigree, object, fair, amiable, gracious, and pleasant, from which comes beauty, grace, which all desire and love, parts affected.

Division or kinds, *Subs.* 2.

or

Natural, in things without life, as love and hatred of elements; and with life, as vegetable, vine and elm, sympathy, antipathy, &c.

Sensible, as of beasts, for pleasure, preservation of kind, mutual agreement, custom, bringing up together, &c.

Rational,

Simple, which hath three objects, as *M.* 1.

- Profitable, *Subs.* 1. — Health, wealth, honour, we love our benefactors: nothing so amiable as profit, or that which hath a show of commodity.
- Pleasant, *Subs.* 2. — Things without life, made by art, pictures, sports, games, sensible objects, as hawks, hounds, horses: or men themselves, for similitude of manners, natural affection, as to friends, children, kinsmen, &c., for glory such as commend us.
  - Of women, as — Before marriage, as *Heroical Mel.* Sect. 2, *vide* ♈ / Or after marriage, as *Jealousy*, Sect. 3, *vide* ♉
- Honest, *Subs.* 3. — Fucate in show, by some error or hypocrisy; some seem and are not; or truly for virtue, honesty, good parts, learning, eloquence, &c.

Mixed of all three, which extends to *M.* 3.

Common good, our neighbour, country, friends, which is charity; the defect of which is cause of much discontent and melancholy.

or

God, *Sect.* 4. { In excess, *vide* II. / In defect, *vide* ♑.

φ Heroical or Love-Melancholy, in which consider,

Memb. 1.
His pedigree, power, extent to vegetables and sensible creatures, as well as men, to spirits, devils, &c.
His name, definition, object, part affected, tyranny.

Causes, *Memb.* 2.
- Stars, temperature, full diet, place, country, clime, condition, idleness, S. 1.
- Natural allurements, and causes of love, as beauty, its praise, how it allureth.
- Comeliness, grace, resulting from the whole or some parts, as face, eyes, hair, hands, &c. *Subs.* 2.
- Artificial allurements, and provocations of lust and love, gestures, apparel, dowry, money, &c.
- *Quest.* Whether beauty owe more to Art or Nature? *Subs.* 3.
- Opportunity of time and place, conference, discourse, music, singing, dancing, amorous tales, lascivious objects, familiarity, gifts, promises, &c. *Subs.* 4.
- Bawds and Philters. *Subs.* 5.

Symptoms or signs, *Memb.* 3.
- Of body { Dryness, paleness, leanness, waking, sighing, &c. / *Quest. An detur pulsus amatorius?*
- or
- Of mind.
  - Bad, as { Fear, sorrow, suspicion, anxiety, &c. / A hell, torment, fire, blindness, &c. / Dotage, slavery, neglect of business.
  - or
  - Good, as { Spruceness, neatness, courage, aptness to learn music, singing, dancing, poetry, &c.

Prognostics: despair, madness, phrensy, death, *Memb.* 4.

Cures, *Memb.* 5.
- By labour, diet, physic, abstinence, *Subs.* 1.
- To withstand the beginnings, avoid occasions, fair and foul means, change of place, contrary passion, witty inventions, discommend the former, bring in another, *Subs.* 2.
- By good counsel, persuasion, from future miseries, inconveniences, &c., *Subs.* 3.
- By philters, magical, and poetical cures, *Subs.* 4.
- To let them have their desire disputed *pro* and *con.* Impediments removed, reasons for it, *Subs.* 5.

His name, definition, extent, power, tyranny, *Memb.* 1.

8 Jealousy, *Sect.* 3.

Division, Equivocations, kinds, *Subs.* 1.
- Improper or
  - To many beasts, as swans, cocks, bulls.
  - To kings and princes, of their subjects, successors.
  - To friends, parents, tutors over their children, or otherwise.
  - Before marriage, corrivals, &c.
- Proper
  - After, as in this place or present subject.

Causes, *Sect.* 2.
- In the parties themselves, or
  - Idleness, impotency in one party, melancholy, long absence.
  - They have been naught themselves. Hard usage, unkindness, wantonness, inequality of years, persons, fortunes, &c.
- from others. Outward enticements and provocations of others.

Symptoms, *Memb.* 2. Fear, sorrow, suspicion, anguish of mind, strange actions, gestures, looks, speeches, locking up, outrages, severe laws, prodigious trials, &c.

Prognostics, *Memb.* 3. Despair, madness, to make away themselves, and others.

Cures, *Memb.* 4.
- By avoiding occasions, always busy, never to be idle.
- By good counsel, advice of friends, to contemn or dissemble it. *Subs.* 1.
- By prevention before marriage. Plato's communion.
- To marry such as are equal in years, birth, fortunes, beauty, of like conditions, &c.
- Of a good family, good education. To use them well.

Religious melancholy, *Sect.* 4.

A proof that there is such a species of melancholy, name, object God, what his beauty is, how it allureth, part and parties affected, superstitious, idolaters, prophets, heretics, &c., *Subs.* 1.

II In excess of such as do that which is not required. *Memb.* 1.

Causes, *Subs.* 2.
- From others, or
  - The devil's allurements, false miracles, priests for their gain. Politicians, to keep men in obedience, bad instructors, blind guides.
- from themselves.
  - Simplicity, fear, ignorance, solitariness, melancholy, curiosity, pride, vain-glory, decayed image of God.

Symptoms, *Subs.* 3.
- General or
  - Zeal without knowledge, obstinacy, superstition, strange devotion, stupidity, confidence, stiff defence of their tenets, mutual love & hate of other sects, belief of incredibilities, impossibilities.
  - Of heretics, pride, contumacy, contempt of others, wilfulness, vain-glory, singularity, prodigious paradoxes.
- Particular.
  - In superstitious blind zeal, obedience, strange works, fasting, sacrifices, oblations, prayers, vows, pseudo-martyrdom, mad and ridiculous customs, ceremonies, observations.
  - In pseudo-prophets, visions, revelations, dreams, prophecies, new doctrines, &c., of Jews, Gentiles, Mahometans, &c.

Prognostics, *Subs.* 4. New doctrines, paradoxes, blasphemies, madness, stupidity, despair, damnation.

Cures, *Subs.* 5. By physic, if need be, conference, good counsel, persuasion, compulsion, correction, punishment. *Quæritur an cogi debent? Affir.*

In defect, as *Memb.* 2.

Secure, void of grace and fears. Epicures, atheists, magicians, hypocrites, such as have cauterised consciences, or else are in a reprobate sense, worldly-secure, some philosophers, impenitent sinners, *Subs.* 1.

or

Distrustful, or too timorous, as desperate. In despair consider,

Causes, *Subs.* 2.
- The devil and his allurements, rigid preachers, that wound their consciences, melancholy, contemplation, solitariness.
- How melancholy and despair differ. Distrust, weakness of faith. Guilty conscience for offence committed, misunderstanding Scr.

Symptoms, *Subs.* 3. Fear, sorrow, anguish of mind, extreme tortures and horror of conscience, fearful dreams, conceits, visions, &c.

Prognostics. Blasphemy, violent death, *Subs.* 4.

Cures, *S.* 5. Physic, as occasion serves, conference, not to be idle or alone. Good counsel, good company, all comforts and contents, &c.

THE THIRD PARTITION

LOVE–MELANCHOLY

THE FIRST SECTION, MEMBER, SUBSECTION

The Preface

HERE will not be wanting, I presume, one or other that will much discommend some part of this Treatise of Love-Melancholy, and object (which Erasmus in his Preface to Sir Thomas More suspects of his) that it is too light for a Divine, too Comical a subject, to speak of Love-Symptoms, too phantastical, and fit alone for a wanton Poet, a feeling young love-sick gallant, an effeminate Courtier, or some such idle person. And 'tis true they say: for by the naughtiness of men it is so come to pass, as Caussinus observes, that the very name of Love is odious to chaster ears. And therefore some again out of an affected gravity, will dislike all for the name's sake before they read a word; dissembling with him in Petronius, and seem to be angry that their ears are violated with such obscene speeches, that so they may be admired for grave Philosophers, and staid carriage. They cannot abide to hear talk of Love-toys, or amorous discourses; in mien and gesture, what strikes the eye, in their outward actions averse; and yet in their cogitations they are all out as bad, if not worse than others.

> *To read my book, the virgin shy*
> *May blush, while Brutus standeth by;*
> *But when he's gone, read through what's writ,*
> *And never stain a cheek for it.* (MARTIAL)

But let these cavillers and counterfeit Catos know that, as the Lord John answered the Queen in that Italian Guazzo, an old, a grave, discreet man is fittest to discourse of Love matters, because he hath likely more experience, observed more, hath a more staid judgement, can better discern, resolve, discuss, advise, give better cautions and more solid precepts, better inform his auditors in such a subject, and by reason of his riper years sooner divert. Besides, there is nothing here to be excepted at; Love is a species of melancholy, and a necessary part

of this my Treatise, which I may not omit; so Jacob Mycillus pleadeth
for himself in his translation of Lucian's Dialogues, and so do I; I must
and will perform my task. And that short excuse of Mercerus for his
edition of Aristænetus shall be mine: If I have spent my time ill to
write, let them not be so idle as to read. — But I am persuaded that it
is not so ill spent. I ought not to excuse or repent myself of this subject,
on which many grave and worthy men have written whole volumes:
Plato, Plutarch, Plotinus, Maximus Tyrius, Alcinous, Avicenna, Leon
Hebræus, in three large Dialogues, Xenophon in his Symposium, Theophrastus (if we may believe Athenaeus), Picus Mirandula, Marius
Aequicola, both in Italian, Kornmannus, in his Outline of Love, Petrus
Godefridus hath handled in three books, P. Hædus, and which almost
every Physician, as Arnoldus Villanovanus, Valleriola in his Medical
Observations, Aelian Montaltus and Laurentius in their Treatises of
Melancholy, Jason Pratensis, Valescus de Taranta, Gordonius, Hercules de Saxoniâ, Savanarola, Langius, &c., have treated of apart, and
in their works. I excuse myself therefore with Peter Godefridus, Valleriola, Ficinus, and in Langius' words: Cadmus Milesius writ fourteen
books of Love, and why should I be ashamed to write an Epistle in
favour of young men, of this subject? A company of stern Readers dislike the second of the Æneids, & tax Virgil's gravity for inserting such
amorous passages in an heroical subject; but Servius, his commentator,
justly vindicates the Poet's worth, wisdom, and discretion in doing as
he did. Castalio would not have young men read the Canticles, because
to his thinking it was too light and amorous a tract, a Ballad of Ballads, as our old English translation hath it. He might as well forbid
the reading of Genesis, because of the loves of Jacob and Rachel, the
stories of Shechem and Dinah, Judah and Tamar: reject the book of
Numbers, for the fornications of the people of Israel with the Moabites:
that of Judges, for Samson and Delilah's embracings: that of the
Kings, for David and Bathsheba's adulteries, the incest of Ammon and
Tamar, Solomon's Concubines, &c., the stories of Esther, Judith, Susanna, and many such. Dicaearchus, and some other, carp at Plato's
majesty, that he would vouchsafe to indite such Love toys; amongst
the rest, for that dalliance with Agathon:

> When Agathon I kissed,
> My very soul, I wist,
> Was on my lips; yet sick,
> It must return so quick.*

* This Plato, of course, was the Comic Poet, not Plato the Philosopher as is implied.

For my part, saith Maximus Tyrias, a great Platonist himself, I do not only admire but stand amazed to read that Plato and Socrates both should expel Homer from their City, because he writ of such light and wanton subjects, because he brought in Juno cohabiting with Jove on Ida, covered with an immortal cloud, Vulcan's net, Mars' and Venus' fopperies before all the Gods, because Apollo fled when he was persecuted by Achilles, the Gods were wounded and ran whining away, as Mars that roared louder than Stentor, and covered nine acres of ground with his fall; Vulcan was a Summer's day falling down from Heaven, and in Lemnos Isle brake his leg, with such ridiculous passages; when as both Socrates and Plato by his testimony writ lighter themselves: (as he follows it) what can be more absurd than for grave Philosophers to treat of such fooleries, to admire Autolycus, Alcibiades, for their beauties as they did, to run after, to gaze, to dote on fair Phædrus, delicate Agathon, young Lysis, fine Charmides? Doth this become grave Philosophers? Thus peradventure Callias, Thrasymachus, Polus, Aristophanes, or some of his adversaries and emulators might object; but neither they nor Anytus and Meletus, his bitter enemies, that condemned him for teaching Critias to tyrannize, his impiety for swearing by dogs and plane trees, for his juggling sophistry, &c., never so much as upbraided him with impure Love, writing or speaking of that subject; and therefore without question, as he concludes, both Socrates and Plato in this are justly to be excused. But suppose they had been a little over-seen, should divine Plato be defamed? No, rather, as he said of Cato's drunkenness, if Cato were drunk, it should be no vice at all to be drunk. They reprove Plato then, but without cause, (as Ficinus pleads), for all Love is honest and good, and they are worthy to be loved that speak well of Love. Being to speak of this admirable affection of Love, (saith Valleriolla), there lies open a vast and philosophical field to my discourse, by which many lovers become mad: let me leave my more serious meditations, wander in these Philosophical fields, and look into those pleasant Groves of the Muses, where with unspeakable variety of flowers we may make Garlands to ourselves, not to adorn us only, but with their pleasant smell and juice to nourish our souls, and fill our minds desirous of knowledge, &c. After an harsh and unpleasing discourse of Melancholy, which hath hitherto molested your patience, and tired the author, give him leave with Godefridus the lawyer and Laurentius to recreate himself in this kind after his laborious studies, since so many grave Divines and worthy men have without offence to manners, to help themselves and others, voluntarily written of it. Heliodorus, a Bishop, penned a Love story of Theagenes and Chariclea, and when some Catos of his time reprehended him for it, chose rather, saith Nicephorus, to leave his Bishoprick than his book. Æneas Sylvius, an ancient Divine, and past 40 years of age (as he confesseth himself), afterwards Pope Pius Secundus, indited that wanton history of Euryalus and Lucretia. And how many Superintendents of learning could I reckon up, that have written of light Phantastical subjects! Beroaldus, Erasmus, Alpheratius, twenty-four times printed in Spanish, &c. Give me leave then to refresh my Muse a little, and my weary Readers, to expatiate in this delightsome field, as Fonseca terms it, to season a surly discourse with a more pleasant aspersion of Love matters. As the Poet invites us, 'tis good to sweeten our life with some pleasing toys to relish it; and, as Pliny tells us, most of our students love such pleasant subjects. Though Macrobius teach us otherwise, that those old sages banished all such light tracts from their studies to nurses' cradles, to please only the ear, yet out of Apuleius I will oppose as honorable Patrons, Solon, Plato, Xenophon, Adrian, &c., that as highly approve of these Treatises. On the other side methinks they are not to be disliked, they are not so unfit. I will not peremptorily say as Aretine did, I will tell you such pretty stories, that foul befall him that is not pleased with them; neither will I say, may these things be agreeable to hear and pleasant to remember, with that confidence, as Beroaldus doth his enarrations on Propertius. I will not expect or hope for that approbation which Lipsius gives to his Epictetus: the more I read, the more shall I covet to read. I will not press you with my pamphlets, or beg attention, but if you like them you may. Pliny holds it expedient, and most fit, to season our works with some pleasant discourse; Synesius approves it, a pause for play is permitted, the Poet admires it:

> Profit and pleasure, then, to mix with art,
> T' inform the judgement, not offend the heart,
> Shall gain all votes. (HORACE)

And there be those, without question, that are more willing to read such toys than I am to write. Let me not live, saith Aretine's Antonia, if I had not rather hear thy discourse than see a play! No doubt but there be more of her mind, ever have been, ever will be, as Hierome bears me witness. A far greater part had rather read Apuleius than Plato: Tully himself confesseth he could not understand Plato's Timaeus, and therefore cared less for it; but every school-boy hath that famous testament of Grunnius Corocotta Porcellus at his finger's ends. The Comical Poet made this his only care and sole study, to please the people, tickle the ear, and to delight:

> *I care not, so I am able*
> *To please the audience with my fable.*   (TERENCE)

But mine earnest intent is as much to profit as to please; and these my writings, I hope, shall take like gilded pills, which are so composed as well to tempt the appetite and deceive the palate, as to help and medicinally work upon the whole body; my lines shall not only recreate but rectify the mind. I think I have said enough; if not, let him that is otherwise minded remember that of Apuleius Maudaurensis, he was in his life a Philosopher, (as Ausonius apologizeth for him), in his Epigrams a Lover, in his precepts most severe, in his Epistle to Caerellia a wanton. Annianus, Sulpicius, Evenus, Menander, and many old Poets besides, did write Fescennines [or wanton verses], Atellanes [or droll comedies], and lascivious songs, jocose things; yet they had virtuous ways, they were chaste, severe, and upright livers.

> *Be the poet free from smutch,*
> *But his verses far from such;*
> *For the Muse is at her best*
> *When she's laughing and undressed.*   (CATULLUS)

I am of Catullus' opinion, and make the same apology in mine own behalf. This that I write depends much on the opinion and authority of others; nor perchance am I mad myself, I only follow in the steps of those that are. Yet I may be a little off; we have all been mad at one time or another; you yourself, I think, are touched, and this man, and that man, so I must be, too.

> *I am a man; and naught in man can be*
> *That I can reckon wholly strange to me.*   (TERENCE)

And, which Martial urgeth for himself, accused of the like fault, I as justly plead:

> *Wanton though my pages seem*
> *Do not my own life so deem.*

Howsoever my lines err, my life is honest:

> *Jocund my Muse is, but my life is chaste.*   (OVID)

But I presume I need no such apologies. I need not, as Socrates in Plato, cover his face when he spake of Love, or blush and hide mine eyes, as Pallas did in her hood, when she was consulted by Jupiter about Mercury's marriage; it is no such lascivious, obscene, or wanton discourse; I have not offended your chaster ears with any thing that is here written, as many French and Italian Authors in their modern language of late have done, nay some of our Latin Pontifical writers, Zanchius, Asorius, Abulensis, Burchardus, &c., whom Rivet accuseth to be more lascivious than Virgil in his Priapian verses, Petronius in his Catalectics, Aristophanes in his Lysistrata, Martial, or any other Pagan profane writer, who have so badly sinned (Barthius notes), in this kind of writing, that chaste minds abhor for their obscenities many most ingenious works. 'Tis not scurrile, this, but chaste, honest, most part serious, and even of religion itself. Incensed (as Ficinus said) with the love of finding love, we have sought it, and found it. More yet, I have augmented and added something to this light Treatise (if light) which was not in the former Editions; I am not ashamed to confess it, with a good Author, that overborne by the importunity of friends, who asked me to enlarge and better my book, I have addressed my otherwise reluctant mind to the work; and now for the sixth time have I taken pen in hand and devoted myself to writings foreign enough to my studies and profession, stealing a few hours from serious occupations and giving them if you please to refreshment and play:

> *I trim my sails, and trace once more*
> *The same course that was mine before,*   (HORACE)

though I was hardly ignorant that new detractors would not be wanting to blame my additions.

And thus much I have thought good to say by way of preface, lest any man (which Godefridus feared in his book) should blame in me lightness, wantonness, rashness, in speaking of Love's causes, enticements, remedies, lawful and unlawful loves, and lust itself. I speak it only to tax and deter others from it, not to teach, but to show the vanities and fopperies of this heroical or Herculean Love, and to apply remedies unto it. I will treat of this with like liberty as of the rest.

> *I will tell all, that you in turn*
> *May tell all those who wish to learn;*
> *And when this writing is antique,*
> *Still in its pages may men seek.*   (CATULLUS)

Condemn me not, good Reader, then, or censure me too hardly, if some part of this Treatise to thy thinking as yet be too light, but consider better of it. To the pure all things are pure; a naked man to a modest woman is no otherwise than a picture, as Augusta Livia truly said; and evil mind, evil thoughts, 'tis as 'tis taken. If in thy censure it be too light, I advise thee, as Lipsius did his reader for some places of Plautus, avoid them then, as if they were the rocks of the Sirens; if they like thee not, let them pass; or oppose that which is good to that which is bad, and reject not therefore all. For to invert that verse of Martial, and with Hierom Wolfius to apply it to my present purpose, some is good, some bad, some is indifferent. I say farther with him yet, I have inserted foolish trifles that I might not be too oppressive, and jests from the market-place, the theatres, the streets, nay even the cook-shops, some things more homely, light or comical, the offering of Gratius,* &c., which I would request every man to interpret to the best, and, as Julius Cæsar Scaliger besought Cardan, *though you should prefer a somewhat more polite amusement, by the immortal Gods, Hieronymus Cardan, take me not badly amiss;* I beseech thee, good reader, not to mistake me, or misconstrue what is here written; by the Muses and Charities, and by the grace of all the Poets, gentle reader, do not take me ill. 'Tis a Comical subject; in sober sadness I crave pardon of what is amiss, and desire thee to suspend thy judgement, wink at small faults, or to be silent at least; but if thou likest, speak well of it, and wish me good success.

> *O Arethusa, one last time*
> *Give inspiration to my rhyme!*   (VIRGIL)

I am resolved howsoever, willy nilly, to go fearlessly into the arena, in the Olympics, with those Elean wrestlers in Philostratus, boldly to shew myself in this common Stage, and in this Tragi-Comedy of Love to act several parts, some Satirically, some Comically, some in a mixt tone, as the subject I have in hand gives occasion, and present Scene shall require or offer itself.

SUBSECTION 2 — *Love's Beginning, Object, Definition, Division*

LOVE'S limits are ample and great, and a spacious walk it hath, beset with thorns, and for that cause, which Scaliger reprehends in Cardan, not lightly to be passed over. Lest I incur the same censure, I will examine all the kinds of Love, his nature, beginning, difference, objects, how it is honest or dishonest, a virtue or vice, a natural passion or a disease, his power and effects, how far it extends: of which, although something hath been said in the first Partition, in those Sections of Perturbations (for Love and hatred are the first and most common passions, from which all the rest arise, and are attendant, as Piccolomineus holds, or, as Caussinus, the Primum Mobile of all other affections, which carry them all about them), I will now more copiously dilate, through all his parts and several branches, that so it may better appear what Love is, and how it varies with the objects, how in defect, or

---

* Gratius, a Latin poet who wrote of dogs and hunting.

(which is most ordinary and common) immoderate, and in excess, causeth melancholy.

Love, universally taken, is defined to be a Desire, as a word of more ample signification: and though Leon Hebræus, the most copious writer of this subject, in his third Dialogue make no difference, yet in his first he distinguisheth them again, and defines Love by desire. Love is a voluntary affection, and desire to enjoy that which is good. Desire wisheth, Love enjoys: the end of the one is the beginning of the other: that which we love is present; that which we desire is absent. It is worth the labour, saith Plotinus, to consider well of Love, whether it be a God or a Devil, or passion of the mind, or partly God, partly Devil, partly passion. He concludes Love to participate of all three, to arise from desire of that which is beautiful and fair, and defines it to be an action of the mind desiring that which is good. Plato calls it the great Devil, for its vehemency, and sovereignty over all other passions, and defines it an appetite, by which we desire some good to be present. Ficinus in his comment adds the word fair to this definition, Love is a desire of enjoying that which is good and fair. Austin dilates this common definition, and will have love to be a delectation of the heart for something which we seek to win, or joy to have, coveting by desire, resting in joy. Scaliger taxeth these former definitions, and will not have love to be defined by Desire or Appetite: for when we enjoy the things we desire, there remains no more appetite: as he defines it, Love is an affection by which we are either united to the thing we love, or perpetuate our union; which agrees in part with Leon Hebræus.

Now this Love varies as its object varies, which is always good, amiable, fair, gracious, and pleasant. All things desire that which is good, as we are taught in the Ethicks, or at least that which to them seems to be good; as Austin well infers, thou wilt wish no harm I suppose, no ill in all thine actions, thoughts or desires, wish ill to none; thou wilt not have bad corn, bad soil, a naughty tree, but all good; a good servant, a good horse, a good son, a good friend, a good neighbour, a good wife. From this goodness comes Beauty; from Beauty, Grace, and Comeliness, which result as so many rays from their good parts, make us to love, and so to covet it: for were it not pleasing and gracious in our eyes, we should not seek. No man loves, saith Aristotle, but he that was first delighted with comeliness and beauty. As this fair object varies, so doth our Love; for, as Proclus holds, every fair thing is amiable, and what we love is fair and gracious in our eyes, or at least we do so apprehend and still esteem of it. Amiableness is the object of

Love, the scope and end is to obtain it, for whose sake we love, and
which our mind covets to enjoy. And it seems to us especially fair and
good: for good, fair, and unity, cannot be separated. Beauty shines,
Plato saith, and by reason of its splendour and shining causeth admiration: and the fairer the object is, the more eagerly it is sought. For, as
the same Plato defines it, Beauty is a lively shining or glittering brightness, resulting from effused good, by ideas, seeds, reasons, shadows,
stirring up our minds, that by this good they may be united and made
one.

Others will have beauty to be the perfection of the whole composition, caused out of the congruous symmetry, measure, order and manner of parts; and that comeliness which proceeds from this beauty is
called grace, and from thence all fair things are gracious. For grace
and beauty are so wonderfully annexed, so sweetly and gently win our
souls, and strongly allure, that they confound our judgement and cannot be distinguished. Beauty and Grace are like those beams and
shinings that come from the glorious and divine Sun, which are diverse,
as they proceed from the diverse objects, to please and affect our several senses. As the species of beauty are taken at our eyes, ears, or conceived in our inner soul, as Plato disputes at large in his Dialogue on
Beauty, Phædrus, Hippias, and, after many sophistical errors confuted,
concludes that beauty is a grace in all things, delighting the eyes, ears
and soul itself; so that, as Valesius infers hence, whatsoever pleaseth
our ears, eyes, and soul, must needs be beautiful, fair, and delightsome
to us. And nothing can more please our ears than musick, or pacify our
minds. Fair houses, pictures, orchards, gardens, fields, a fair hawk, a
fair horse is most acceptable unto us; whatsoever pleaseth our eyes
and ears, we call beautiful and fair; pleasure belongeth to the rest of
the senses, but grace and beauty to these two alone. As the objects vary
and are diverse, so they diversely affect our eyes, ears, and soul itself;
which gives occasion to some to make so many several kinds of Love
as there be objects: one beauty ariseth from God, of which and divine
Love S. Dionysius, with many Fathers and Neotericks, have written
just volumes, On the Love of God, as they term it, many parænetical
discourses; another from his creatures; there is a beauty of the body, a
beauty of the soul, a beauty from virtue, a beauty of martyrs, Austin
calls it, which we see with the eyes of our mind; which beauty, as
Tully saith, if we could discern with these corporeal eyes, would cause
admirable affections, and ravish our souls. This other beauty, which
ariseth from those extreme parts, and graces which proceed from ges-

tures, speeches, several motions, and proportions of creatures, men and women (especially from women, which made those old Poets put the three Graces still in Venus' company, as attending on her, and holding up her train) are infinite almost, and vary their names with their objects, as love of money, covetousness, love of beauty, lust, immoderate desire of any pleasure, concupiscence, friendship, love, good will, &c., and is either virtue or vice, honest, dishonest, in excess, defect, as shall be shewed in his place; heroical love, religious love, &c. which may be reduced to a twofold division, according to the principal parts which are affected, the brain and liver: love and friendship, which Scaliger, Valesius and Melancthon, warrant out of Plato, from that speech of Pausanias, belike, that makes two Venuses and two loves: One Venus is ancient, without a mother, and descended from heaven, whom we call celestial; the younger begotten of Jupiter and Dione, whom commonly we call Venus.

Ficinus in his comment upon this place, following Plato, calls these two loves two Devils, or good and bad Angels according to us, which are still hovering about our souls: The one rears to heaven, the other depresseth us to hell; the one good, which stirs us up to the contemplation of that divine beauty, for whose sake we perform Justice, and all godly offices, study Philosophy, &c., the other base, and, though bad, yet to be respected; for indeed both are good in their own natures; procreation of children is as necessary as that finding out of truth, but therefore called bad because it is abused, and withdraws our soul from the speculation of that other to viler objects; so far Ficinus. S. Austin hath delivered as much in effect. Every creature is good, and may be loved well or ill: and two Cities make two Loves, Jerusalem and Babylon, the Love of God the one, the Love of the world the other; of these two cities we all are Citizens, as by examination of ourselves we may soon find, and of which: the one Love is the root of all mischief, the other of all good. So he will have those four cardinal virtues to be nought else but Love rightly composed; he calls virtue the order of Love, whom Thomas following, confirms as much, and amplifies in many words. Lucian to the same purpose hath a division of his own, one love was born in the sea, which is as various and raging in young men's breasts as the sea itself, and causeth burning lust: the other is that golden chain which was let down from heaven, and with a divine Fury ravisheth our souls, made to the image of God, and stirs us up to comprehend the innate and incorruptible beauty, to which we were once created. Beroaldus hath expressed all this in an Epigram of his.

If divine Plato's tenents they be true,
  Two Veneres, two loves there be;
The one from heaven, unbegotten still,
  Which knits our souls in unity.
The other famous over all the world,
  Binding the hearts of gods and men;
Dishonest, wanton, and seducing, she
  Rules whom she will, both where and when.

This twofold division of Love, Origen likewise follows in his Comment on the Canticles, one from God, the other from the Devil, as he holds, (understanding it in the worser sense) which many others repeat and imitate. Both which (to omit all subdivisions) in excess or defect, as they are abused, or degenerate, cause melancholy in a particular kind, as shall be shewed in his place. Austin, in another Tract, makes a threefold division of this Love, which we may use well or ill: God, our neighbour, and the world: God above us, our neighbour next us, the world beneath us. In the course of our desires God hath three things, the world one, our neighbour two. Our desire to God is either from God, with God, or to God, and ordinarily so runs. From God, when it receives from him, whence, and for which it should love him: with God, when it contradicts his will in nothing: to God, when it seeks to him, and rests itself in him. Our Love to our neighbour may proceed from him, and run with him, not to him; from him, as when we rejoice of his good safety, and well doing; with him when we desire to have him a fellow and companion of our journey in the way of the Lord; not in him, because there is no aid, hope, or confidence, in man. From the world our Love comes, when we begin to admire the Creator in his works, and glorify God in his creatures; with the world it should run, if, according to the mutability of all temporalities, it should be dejected in adversity, or over elevated in prosperity; to the world, if it would settle itself in its vain delights and studies. — Many such partitions of Love I could repeat, and Subdivisions, but lest (which Scaliger objects to Cardan) I confound filthy burning lust with pure and divine Love, I will follow that accurate Division of Leon Hebræus, in the Dialogue, betwixt Sophia and Philo, where he speaks of Natural, Sensible, and Rational Love, and handleth each apart. Natural Love or Hatred is that Sympathy or Antipathy which is to be seen in animate and inanimate creatures, in the four Elements, Metals, Stones, heavy things go downward, as a Stone to his Centre, Fire upward, and rivers to the Sea. The Sun, Moon, and Stars go still round, performing gladly their natural tasks, for love of perfection. This Love is manifest, I say, in inanimate creatures. How comes a load-stone to draw iron to it? jet, chaff? the ground to covet showers, but for Love? No creature, S. Hierom concludes, is to be found, that doth not love something, no stock, no stone, that hath not some feeling of love. 'Tis more eminent in Plants, Herbs, and is especially observed in vegetals; as betwixt the Vine and Elm a great Sympathy, betwixt the Vine and the Cabbage, betwixt the Vine and Olive,

The Virgin Goddess flees from Bacchus,   (ALCIATI)

betwixt the Vine and Bays a great antipathy, the Vine loves not the Bay nor his smell, and will kill him, if he grow near him; the Burr and the Lintle cannot endure one another, the Olive and the Myrtle embrace each other, in roots and branches, if they grow near. Read more of this in Piccolomineus, Crescentius, Baptista Porta, Fracastorius. Of the Love and Hatred of Planets consult with every Astrologer: Leon Hebræus gives many fabulous reasons, and moralizeth them withal. Sensible Love is that of brute beasts, of which the same Leon Hebræus, assigns these causes. First for the pleasure they take in the Act of Generation, male and female love one another. Secondly for the preservation of the species, and desire of young brood. Thirdly for the mutual agreement, as being of the same kind: the Pig is regarded by the Pig as the most beautiful thing in the world, the Dog by the Dog, the Cow by the Cow, the Ass by the Ass, as Epicharmus held, and according to that Adage of Diogenianus,

Jackdaw percheth beside Jackdaw,

they much delight in one another's company,

The grasshopper loves the grasshopper aye,
Likewise the ant the ant, they say,   (THEOCRITUS)

and birds of a feather will flock together. Fourthly for custom, use, and familiarity, as if a dog be trained up with a Lion and a Bear, contrary to their natures, they will love each other. Hawks, dogs, horses, love their masters and keepers: many stories I could relate in this kind, but see Gillius, those two Epistles of Lipsius, of dogs and horses, A. Gellius, &c. Fifthly, for bringing up, as if a bitch bring up a kid, a hen ducklings, an hedge-sparrow a cuckoo; &c.

The third kind is Cognitive Love, as Leo calls it, Rational Love, Intellectual Love, and is proper to men, on which I must insist. This appears in God, Angels, Men. God is love itself, the fountain of Love, the Disciple of love, as Plato styles him; the servant of peace, the God of love and peace; have peace with all men, and God is with you.   .

By this Love (saith Gerson) we purchase Heaven, and buy the Kingdom of God. This Love is either in the Trinity itself, for the Holy Ghost is the Love of the Father and the Son, &c., or towards us his creatures, as in making the world. Love made the world, Love built Cities, is the soul of the world, invented Arts, Sciences, and all good things, incites us to virtue and humanity, combines and quickens: keeps peace on earth, quietness by sea, mirth in the winds and elements, expels all fear, anger, and rusticity: is a round circle still from good to good; for Love is the beginner and end of all our actions, the efficient and instrumental cause, as our Poets in their Symbols, Impresses, Emblems of rings, squares, &c., shadow unto us.

> *If first and last of any thing you wit,*
> *Cease; love's the sole and only cause of it.*

Love, saith Leo, made the world, and afterwards, in redeeming of it, " God so loved the world, that he gave his only begotten son for it." " Behold what love the Father hath shewed on us, that we should be called the sons of God." Or by his sweet providence, in protecting of it; either all in general, or his Saints elect and Church in particular, whom he keeps as the apple of his eye, whom he loves freely, as Hosea speaks, and dearly respects. Dearer to the gods than to himself is man. Not that we are fair, nor for any merit or grace of ours, for we are most vile and base; but out of his incomparable love and goodness, out of his divine Nature. And this is that Homer's golden chain, which reacheth down from Heaven to Earth, by which every creature is annexed, and depends on his Creator. He made all, saith Moses, " and it was good," and he loves it as good.

The love of Angels and living souls, is mutual amongst themselves, towards us militant in the Church, and all such as love God; as the Sun beams irradiate the Earth from those celestial Thrones, they by their well-wishes reflect on us; eager are they in good will to men, constant in guidance, there is joy in Heaven for every sinner that repenteth; they pray for us, are solicitous for our good, pure spirits. Where charity reigns, sweet desire, joy and love of God are there also. Love proper to mortal men is the third Member of this subdivision, and the subject of my following discourse.

MEMBER 2

SUBSECTION 1 — *Love of Men, which varies as his objects, profitable,*
pleasant, honest

VALESIUS defines this love which is in men, to be an affection of both
powers, Appetite, and Reason. The rational resides in the Brain, the
other in the Liver (as before hath been said out of Plato and others)
the heart is diversely affected of both, and carried a thousand ways by
consent. The sensitive faculty most part over-rules reason, the Soul is
carried hood-winkt, and the understanding captive like a beast. The
heart is variously inclined, sometimes they are merry, sometimes sad,
and from Love arise Hope and Fear, Jealousy, Fury, Desperation. Now
this Love of men is diverse, and varies, as the object varies, by which
they are enticed, as virtue, wisdom, eloquence, profit, wealth, money,
fame, honour, or comeliness of person, &c. Leon Hebræus, in his first
Dialogue, reduceth them all to these three, Profitable, Pleasant, Honest,
(out of Aristotle, belike), of which he discourseth at large; and whatsoever is beautiful and fair, is referred to them, or any way to be desired. To profitable, is ascribed health, wealth, honour, &c., which is
rather Ambition, Desire, Covetousness, than Love. Friends, Children,
Love of women, all delightful and pleasant objects, are referred to the
second. The love of honest things consists in virtue and wisdom, and is
preferred before that which is profitable and pleasant: Intellectual
about that which is honest. St. Austin calls profitable, worldly; pleasant,
carnal; honest, spiritual. Of and from all three result Charity, Friendship and true Love, which respects God and our neighbour. Of each of
these I will briefly dilate, and shew in what sort they cause melancholy.

Amongst all these fair enticing objects, which procure Love, and
bewitch the Soul of man, there is none so moving, so forcible, as profit;
and that which carrieth with it a shew of commodity. Health indeed is
a precious thing, to recover and preserve which we will undergo any
misery, drink bitter potions, freely give our goods: restore a man to his
health, his purse lies open to thee, bountiful he is, thankful and beholding to thee; but give him wealth and honour, give him gold, or
what shall be for his advantage and preferment, and thou shalt command his affections, oblige him eternally to thee, heart, hand, life and
all, is at thy service, thou art his dear and loving friend, good and
gracious Lord and Master, his Mæcenas; he is thy slave, thy vassal,

most devote, affectioned, and bound in all duty: tell him good tidings in this kind, there spoke an Angel, a blessed hour that brings in gain, he is thy creature, and thou his creator, he hugs and admires thee; he is thine for ever. No Loadstone so attractive as that of profit, none so fair an object as this of gold: nothing wins a man sooner than a good turn; bounty and liberality command body and soul.

Good turns doth pacify both God and men,
And Jupiter himself is won by them. (OVID)

Gold of all other is a most delicious object, a sweet light, a goodly lustre it hath; and, saith Austin, we had rather see it than the Sun. Sweet and pleasant in getting, in keeping; it seasons all our labours, intolerable pains we take for it, base employments, endure bitter flouts and taunts, long journeys, heavy burdens, all are made light and easy by this hope of gain;

At home I think I have what's best,
Counting the money in my chest. (HORACE)

The sight of gold refresheth our spirits, and ravisheth our hearts, as that Babylonian garment and golden wedge did Achan in the camp, the very sight and hearing sets on fire his soul with desire of it. It will make a man run to the Antipodes, or tarry at home and turn parasite, lie, flatter, prostitute himself, swear and bear false witness; he will venture his body, kill a king, murder his father, and damn his soul to come at it. As he well observed, the mass of gold is fairer than all your Grecian pictures, that Apelles, Phidias, or any doting painter could ever make: we are enamoured with it.

The promptest prayer, to all the temples known,
Is, Let increase of riches be my own: (JUVENAL)

All our labours, studies, endeavours, vows, prayers and wishes, are to get, how to compass it. This is the great Goddess we adore and worship, this is the sole object of our desire. If we have it, as we think, we are made for ever, thrice happy, Princes, Lords, &c. If we lose it, we are dull, heavy, dejected, discontent, miserable, desperate, and mad. Our estate and well being ebbs and flows with our commodity; and, as we are endowed or enriched, so are we beloved and esteemed: it lasts no longer than our wealth; when that is gone, and the object removed, farewell friendship: as long as bounty, good cheer, and rewards were to be hoped, friends enough; they were tied to thee by the teeth, and would follow thee as Crows do a Carcass: but when thy goods are gone and spent, the lamp of their Love is out, and thou shalt be contemned, scorned, hated, injured. Lucian's Timon, when he lived in prosperity, was the sole spectacle of Greece, only admired; who but Timon? Everybody loved, honoured, applauded him, each man offered him his service, and sought to be kin to him; but when his gold was spent, his fair possessions gone, farewell Timon: none so ugly, none so deformed, so odious an object as Timon, no man so ridiculous on a sudden, they gave him a penny to buy a rope; no man would know him.

'Tis the general humour of the world, commodity steers our affections throughout, we love those that are fortunate and rich, that thrive, or by whom we may receive mutual kindness, hope for like courtesies, get any good, gain, or profit: hate those, and abhor, on the other side, which are poor and miserable, or by whom we may sustain loss or inconvenience. And even those that were now familiar and dear unto us, our loving and long friends, neighbours, kinsmen, allies, with whom we have conversed and lived as so many Geryons for some years past, striving still to give one another all good content and entertainment, with mutual invitations, feastings, disports, offices, for whom we would ride, run, spend ourselves, and of whom we have so freely and honourably spoken, to whom we have given all those turgent titles, and magnificent elogiums, most excellent and most noble, worthy, wise, grave, learned, valiant, &c., and magnified beyond measure: if any controversy arise betwixt us, some trespass, injury, abuse, some part of our goods be detained, a piece of Land come to be litigious, if they cross us in our suit, or touch the string of our commodity, we detest and depress them upon a sudden: neither affinity, consanguinity, or old acquaintance, can contain us, but the vainglorious avoid the wretched. A golden apple sets all together by the ears, as if a marrow-bone, or honeycomb, were flung amongst Bears: Father and Son, Brother and Sister, kinsmen are at odds: and look what malice, deadly hatred can invent, that shall be done, dreadful, ill-omened, pestilential, savage, beastly, mutual injuries, desire of revenge, and how to hurt them, him and his, are all our studies. If our pleasures be interrupt, we can tolerate it: our bodies hurt, we can put it up and be reconciled: but touch our commodities, we are most impatient: fair becomes foul, the Graces are turned to Harpies, friendly salutations to bitter imprecations, mutual feastings to plotting villainies, minings, and counterminings; good words to Satires and invectives, we revile against him, nought but his imperfections are in our eyes, he is a base knave, a Devil, a Monster, a Caterpillar, a Viper, an Hog-rubber, &c. What began as a lovely woman turns out to have a fish's tail. The Scene is altered on a sudden, Love is turned to hate, mirth to melancholy: so furiously are we most part bent, our affections fixed, upon this object of commodity, and upon money, the desire of which in excess is covetousness. Ambition tyrannizeth over our souls, as I have shewed, and in defect crucifies as much, as if a man by negligence, ill husbandry, improvidence, prodigality, waste and consume his goods and fortunes, beggary follows, and melancholy, he becomes an abject, odious and worse than an Infidel, in not providing for his family.

SUBSECTION 2 — *Pleasant Objects of Love*

PLEASANT Objects are infinite, whether they be such as have life, or be without life. Inanimate are Countries, Provinces, Towers, Towns, Cities, as he said, we see a fair Island by description when we see it not. The Sun never saw a fairer City, 'tis as charming as Tempe in Thessaly, Orchards, Gardens, pleasant walks, Groves, Fountains, &c. The heaven itself is said to be fair or foul: fair buildings, fair pictures, all artificial, elaborate and curious works, clothes, give an admirable lustre: we admire, and gaze upon them, as children do on a Peacock: a fair Dog, a fair Horse and Hawk, &c. The Thessalian loves a colt, the Egyptian a bullock, the Lacedaemonian a young dog, &c., such things we love, are most gracious in our sight, acceptable unto us, and whatsoever else may cause this passion, if it be superfluous or immoderately loved, as Guianerius observes. These things in themselves are pleasing and good, singular ornaments, necessary, comely, and fit to be had; but when we fix an immoderate eye, and dote on them over much, this pleasure may turn to pain, bring much sorrow, and discontent unto us, work our final overthrow, and cause melancholy in the end. Many are carried away with those bewitching sports of gaming, hawking, hunting, and such vain pleasures, as I have said: some with immoderate desire of fame, to be crowned in the Olympicks, knighted in the field, &c., and by these means ruinate themselves. The lascivious dotes on his fair mistress, the glutton on his dishes, which are infinitely varied to please the palate, the epicure on his several pleasures, the superstitious on his idol, and fats himself with future joys, as Turks feed themselves with an imaginary persuasion of a sensual Paradise: so several pleasant objects diversely affect divers men. But the fairest objects and enticings proceed from men themselves, which most frequently captivate, allure, and make them dote beyond all measure upon one another, and that for many respects. First, as some suppose, by that secret force of stars: (What star brings me to thee?) They do singularly dote on such a man, hate such again, and can give no reason for it. I do not love thee, Sir, &c. Alexander admired Hephæstion, Adrian Antinous, Nero Sporus, &c. The physicians refer this to their temperament, Astrologers to trine and sextile Aspects, or opposite of their several Ascendants, Lords of their genitures, love and hatred of Planets: Cicogna, to concord and discord of Spirits; but most to outward Graces. A merry companion is welcome and acceptable to all men, and therefore, saith Gomesius, Princes and great men entertain Jesters and players commonly in their Courts. But, 'tis similitude of manners which ties most men in an inseparable link, as if they be addicted to the same studies or disports, they delight in one another's companies, birds of a feather will gather together: if they be of diverse inclinations, or opposite in manners, they can seldom agree. Secondly, affability, custom, and familiarity, may convert nature many times, though they be different in manners, as if they be Country-men, fellow students, colleagues, or have been fellow-soldiers, brethren in affliction (for calamity joineth unlike men together), affinity, or some such accidental occasion, though they cannot agree amongst themselves, they will stick together like burrs, and hold against a third: so after some discontinuance, or death, enmity ceaseth; or in a foreign place.

> Envy feeds on the living, after death 'twill tire;
> Hatred rests in the grave, with grief and ire.   (ovid)

A third cause of Love and hate may be mutual offices, the receiving of benefits, commend him, use him kindly, take his part in a quarrel, relieve him in his misery, thou winnest him for ever; do the opposite, and be sure of a perpetual enemy. Praise and dispraise of each other do as much, though unknown, as Scioppius by Scaliger and Casaubonus: Mule scratcheth Mule, who but Scaliger with him? what Encomiums, Epithets, Elogiums! Master of Wisdom, perpetual dictator, ornament of literature, wonder of Europe, noble Scaliger, incredible excellence of genius, &c., in every respect more comparable to Gods than men, we venerate his writings on bended knees as like unto those [Roman] shields fallen from Heaven, &c., but when they began to vary, none so absurd as Scaliger, so vile and base, as his books, Concerning the Bordone Family,* & other Satirical invectives, may witness. Ovid in Ibis, Archil-

---

* Joseph Lustus Scaliger had asserted himself to be a scion of the ancient house of La Scala, princes and rulers of Verona; his son, Joseph Justus Scaliger, took him at his word and wrote a life of his father in which these claims were put forth. Scioppius wrote a sarcastic book, The Suppositious Scaliger, undertaking to show that he was really the son of a schoolmaster named Bordone. J. J. Scaliger replied with a Confutation of the Bordone Fable. But he was unable to prove his father's claims, and the calling in question of his lineage and his father's veracity is said to have hastened his death.

ochus himself, was not so bitter. Another great tie or cause of Love is
consanguinity; parents are dear to their children, children to their parents, brothers and sisters, cousins of all sorts, as an hen and chickens, all
of a knot: every crow thinks her own bird fairest. Many memorable
examples are in this kind, and 'tis monstrous, if they do not: a mother
cannot forget her child; Solomon so found out the true owner: love of
parents may not be concealed, 'tis natural, descends, and they that are
inhuman in this kind, are unworthy of that air they breathe, and of the
four elements; yet many unnatural examples we have in this rank, of
hard-hearted parents, disobedient children, of disagreeing brothers,
nothing so common. The love of kinsmen is grown cold, many kinsmen,
(as the saying is) few friends; if thine estate be good, and thou able
to requite their kindness, there will be mutual correspondence, otherwise thou art a burden, most odious to them above all others. The last
object that ties man and man, is comeliness of person, and beauty alone,
as men love women with a wanton eye: which, above all, is termed
Heroical, or Love-melancholy. Other Loves (saith Piccolomineus) are
so called with some contraction, as the Love of wine, gold, &c., but this
of women is predominant in an higher strain, whose part affected is the
liver, and this Love deserves a longer explication, and shall be dilated
apart in the next Section.

SUBSECTION 3 — *Honest objects of Love*

BEAUTY is the common object of all Love, as jet draws a straw, so doth
beauty love: virtue and honesty are great motives, and give as fair a
lustre as the rest, especially if they be sincere and right, not fucate, but
proceeding from true form, and an incorrupt judgement; those two
Venus twins, Eros and Anteros, are then most firm and fast. For many
times otherwise men are deceived by their flattering Gnathos, dissembling Chamæleons, out-sides, hypocrites, that make a shew of great love,
learning, pretend honesty, virtue, zeal, modesty, with affected looks and
counterfeit gestures: feigned protestations often steal away the hearts
and favours of men, and deceive them, the appearance and shadow of
virtue, when as in truth and indeed there is no worth or honesty at all
in them, no truth, but mere hypocrisy, subtilty, knavery, and the like.
As true friends they are, as he that Cælius Secundus met by the highway
side; and hard it is in this temporising age to distinguish such companions, or to find them out. Such Gnathos as these for the most part
belong to great men, and by this glozing flattery, affability, and such
like philters, so dive and insinuate into their favours, that they are

taken for men of excellent worth, wisdom, learning, demi-Gods, and so screw themselves into dignities, honours, offices : but these men cause harsh confusion often, and as many stirs as Rehoboam's Counsellors in a common-wealth, overthrow themselves and others. Tandlerus, and some authors, make a doubt whether Love and Hatred may be compelled by philters or characters ; Cardan, and Marbodius, by precious stones and amulets ; Astrologers by election of times, &c., as I shall elsewhere discuss. The true object of this honest Love is virtue, wisdom, honesty, real worth, inward beauty, and this Love cannot deceive or be compelled : may you be loved that are worthy of love ; Love itself is the most potent philter, virtue and wisdom, favour creating favour, the sole and only grace, not counterfeit, but open, honest, simple, naked, descending from heaven, as our Apostle hath it, an infused habit from God, which hath given several gifts, as wit, learning, tongues, for which they shall be amiable and gracious, as to Saul stature and a goodly presence. Joseph found favour in Pharaoh's court for his person ; and Daniel with the Princes of the Eunuchs. Christ was gracious with God and men. There is still some peculiar grace, as of good discourse, eloquence, wit, honesty, which is the first mover and a most forcible loadstone to draw the favours and good wills of men's eyes, ears, and affections, unto them. When Jesus spake, *they were all astonished at his answers, and wondered at his gracious words which proceeded from his mouth*. An Orator steals away the hearts of men, and as another Orpheus, he pulls them to him by speech alone : a sweet voice causeth admiration ; and he that can utter himself in good words, in our ordinary phrase, is called a proper man, a divine spirit. For which cause belike, our old Poets, the senate and populace of poets, made Mercury the Gentleman-usher to the Graces, Captain of eloquence, and those Charites to be Jupiter and Eurymone's daughters, descended from above. Though they be otherwise deformed, crooked, ugly to behold, those good parts of the mind denominate them fair. Plato commends the beauty of Socrates ; yet who was more grim of countenance, stern and ghastly to look upon ? So are and have been many great Philosophers, as Gregory Nazianzen observes, deformed most part in that which is to be seen with the eyes, but most elegant in that which is not to be seen. Often under a threadbare coat lies an excellent understanding. Æsop, Democritus, Aristotle, Politianus, Melancthon, Gesner, &c., withered old men, old Satyrs very harsh and impolite to the eye ; but who were so terse, polite, eloquent, generally learned, temperate and modest ? No man then living was so fair as Alcibiades, so lovely to the eye, as Boethius observes, but he had a most deformed soul.

Honesty, virtue, fair conditions, are great enticers to such as are well given, and much avail to get the favour and good will of men. Abdolonymus in Curtius, a poor man, (but, which mine Author notes, the cause of this poverty was his honesty), for his modesty and continency from a private person (for they found him digging in his garden) was saluted King, and preferred before all the Magnificoes of his time, a purple embroidered garment was put upon him, and they bade him wash himself, and, as he was worthy, take upon him the style and spirit of a King, continue his continency and the rest of his good parts. Titus Pomponius Atticus, that noble Citizen of Rome, was so fair conditioned, of so sweet a carriage, that he was generally beloved of all good men, of Cæsar, Pompey, Antony, Tully, of divers sects, &c., many estates (Cornelius Nepos writes) following him only for his worth. To hear of rich works, &c., it is worthy of your attention, Livy cries, you that scorn all but riches, and give no esteem to virtue, except they be wealthy withal. Q. Cincinnatus had but four acres, and by the consent of the Senate was chosen Dictator of Rome. Of such account were Cato, Fabricius, Aristides, Antonius, Probus, for their eminent worth: so Cæsar, Trajan, Alexander admired for valour, Hephæstio loved Alexander, but Parmenio the King: Titus, the delight of mankind, and which Aurelius Victor hath of Vespasian, the dilling [or darling] of his time, as Edgar Etheling was in England, for his excellent virtues: their memory is yet fresh, sweet, and we love them many ages after, though they be dead: he leaves behind a sweet memory of himself, saith Lipsius of his friend, living and dead they are all one. I have ever loved as thou knowest (so Tully wrote to Dolabella) Marcus Brutus for his great wit, singular honesty, constancy, sweet conditions; and believe it, there is nothing so amiable and fair as virtue. — I do mightily love Calvisinus (so Pliny writes to Sossius), a most industrious, eloquent, upright man, which is all in all with me: the affection came from his good parts. And, as S. Austin comments on the 84th Psalm, there is a peculiar beauty of justice, an inward beauty, which we see with the eyes of our hearts, love, and are enamoured with, as in Martyrs, though their bodies be torn in pieces with wild beasts, yet this beauty shines, and we love their virtues. The Stoicks are of opinion that a wise man is only fair; and Cato contends the same, that the lineaments of the mind are far fairer than those of the body, incomparably beyond them: wisdom and valour, according to Xenophon, especially deserve the name of beauty, & denominate one fair; and (as Austin holds) fairer is the truth of the Christians than the Helen of the Greeks. " Wine is strong, the king is strong, women are strong, but truth overcometh all things." " Blessed is the man that findeth wisdom, and getteth understanding: for the merchandise thereof is better than silver, and the gain thereof better than gold; it is more precious than pearls, and all the things thou canst desire are not to be compared to her." A wise, true, just, upright, and good man, I say it again, is only fair. It is reported of Magdalen, Queen of France, and wife to Lewis 11th, a Scottish woman by birth, that, walking forth in an evening with her Ladies, she spied M. Alanus, one of the King's Chaplains, a silly, old, hard-favoured man, fast asleep in a bower, and kissed him sweetly; when the young Ladies laughed at her for it, she replied, that it was not his person that she did embrace and reverence, but, with a Platonick love, the divine beauty of his soul. Thus in all ages virtue hath been adored, admired, a singular lustre hath proceeded from it: and the more virtuous he is, the more gracious, the more admired.

No man so much followed upon earth, as Christ himself; & as the Psalmist saith, *he was fairer than the sons of men.* Chrysostom, Bernard, Austin, Cassiodore, Hierome, interpret it of the beauty of his person; there was a divine Majesty in his looks, it shined like Lightning, and drew all men to it: but Basil, Cyril, Esay, Theodoret, Arnobius, &c., of the beauty of his divinity, justice, grace, eloquence, &c. Thomas of both; and so doth Baradius, and Peter Morales, adding as much of Joseph and the Virgin Mary, she excelled all others in beauty, according to that prediction of the Cumæan Sybil. Be they present or absent, near us, or afar off, this beauty shines, and will attract men many miles to come and visit it. Plato and Pythagoras left their Country to see those wise Egyptian Priests: Apollonius travelled into Æthiopia, Persia, to consult with the Magi, Brachymanes, Gymnosophists. The Queen of Sheba came to visit Solomon; and many, saith Hierom, went out of Spain and remote places a thousand miles, to behold that eloquent Livy; not to see the most beautiful of cities, nor the city-world of Octavian, but to see and hear this man. No beauty leaves such an impression, strikes so deep, or links the souls of men closer than virtue. No painter, no Graver, no Carver, can express virtue's lustre, or those admirable rays that come from it, those enchanting rays that enamour posterity, those everlasting rays that continue to the world's end. Many, saith Favorinus, that loved and admired Alcibiades in his youth, knew not, cared not, for Alcibiades a man; now seeking him they ask, where is Alcibiades: but the beauty of Socrates is still the same; virtue's lustre never fades, is ever fresh and green to all succeeding ages, and a most attractive loadstone, to draw and combine such as are present. For

that reason, belike, Homer feigns the three Graces to be linked and
tied hand in hand, because the hearts of men are so firmly united with
such graces. O sweet bands (Seneca exclaims) which so happily combine, that those which are bound by them love their binders, desiring
withal much more harder to be bound; and, as so many Geryons, to be
united into one. For the nature of true friendship is to combine, to be
like affected, of one mind;

> *To will and nill alike, and be*
> *Of the same mind eternally,*   (SILIUS ITALICUS)

as the Poet saith, still to continue one and the same. And where this
Love takes place, there is a peace and quietness, a true correspondence,
perfect amity, a Diapason of vows and wishes, the same opinions, as
betwixt David and Jonathan, Damon and Pythias, Pylades and Orestes,
Nisus and Euryalus, Theseus and Pirithous, they will live and die together, and prosecute one another with good turns (for those bound in
love put away evil), not only living, but when their friends are dead,
with Tombs and Monuments, Dirges, Epitaphs, Elegies, Inscriptions,
Pyramids, Obelisks, Statues, Images, Pictures, Histories, Poems, Annals, Feasts, Anniversaries, many ages after (as Plato's Scholars did),
they will make offerings to their spirits still, omit no good office that
may tend to the preservation of their names, honours, and eternal
memory. He did express his son in colours, in wax, in brass, in ivory,
in marble, gold and silver, (as Pliny reports of a Citizen in Rome)
and, in a great Auditory not long since, recited a just volume of his life.
In another place, speaking of an Epigram which Martial had composed
in praise of him: He gave me as much as he might, and would have done
more if he could; though what can a man give more than honour, glory,
and eternity? But that which he wrote, peradventure, will not continue;
yet he wrote it to continue. — 'Tis all the recompence a poor scholar
can make his well deserving Patron, Mæcenas, friend, to mention him
in his works, to dedicate a book to his name, to write his life, &c., as
all our Poets, Orators, Historiographers, have ever done, and the greatest revenge such men take of their adversaries, to persecute them with
Satires, Invectives, &c., and 'tis both ways of great moment, as Plato
gives us to understand. Paulus Jovius in the Fourth book of the Life
and Deeds of Pope Leo Decimus, his noble Patron, concludes in these
words: Because I cannot honour him as other rich men do, with like
endeavour, affection, and piety, I have undertaken to write his life;
since my fortunes will not give me leave to make a more sumptuous
monument, I will perform those rites to his sacred ashes which a small,

perhaps, but a liberal wit can afford. But I rove. Where this true love is wanting, there can be no firm peace, friendship from teeth outward, counterfeit, or from some by-respects, so long dissembled, till they have satisfied their own ends, which upon every small occasion breaks out into enmity, open war, defiance, heart-burnings, whispering, calumnies, contentions, and all manner of bitter melancholy discontents. And those men which have no other object of their Love than greatness, wealth, authority, &c., are rather feared than beloved; they neither love nor are loved; and howsoever borne with for a time, yet for their tyranny and oppression, griping, covetousness, currish hardness, folly, intemperance, imprudence, and such like vices, they are generally odious, abhorred of all, both God and men. Wife and children, friends, neighbours, all the world forsakes them, would fain be rid of them, and are compelled many times to lay violent hands on them, or else God's judgements overtake them: instead of graces come Furies. So when fair Abigail, a woman of singular wisdom, was acceptable to David, Nabal was churlish and evil-conditioned; and therefore Mordecai was received, when Haman was executed, Haman the favourite, " that had his seat above the other Princes, to whom all the King's servants that stood in the gates bowed their knees and reverenced." Though they flourish many times, such Hypocrites, such temporizing Foxes, and blear the world's eyes by flattery, bribery, dissembling their natures, or other men's weakness, that cannot so soon apprehend their tricks, yet in the end they will be discerned, and precipitated in a moment: " surely, saith David, thou hast set them in slippery places "; as so many Sejanuses, they will come down to the Gemonian steps; and, as Eusebius in Ammianus, that was in such authority, exalted to Imperial command, be cast down headlong on a sudden. Or put case they escape, and rest unmasked to their lives' end, yet, after their death, their memory stinks as a snuff of a candle put out, and those that durst not so much as mutter against them in their lives, will prosecute their name with Satires, Libels, and bitter imprecations, they shall have a bad name in all succeeding ages, and be odious to the world's end.

MEMBER 3

Charity composed of all three kinds, Pleasant, Profitable, Honest

BESIDES this Love that comes from Profit, pleasant, honest, (for one good turn asks another in equity) that which proceeds from the law of nature, or from discipline and Philosophy, there is yet another Love compounded of all these three, which is Charity, and includes piety, dilection, benevolence, friendship, even all those virtuous habits; for Love is the circle equant of all other affections, (of which Aristotle dilates at large in his Ethicks,) and is commanded by God, which no man can well perform, but he that is a Christian, and a true regenerate man. This is to love God above all, and our neighbour as ourself; for this Love is a communicating light, apt to illuminate itself as well as others. All other objects are fair, and very beautiful, I confess; kindred, alliance, friendship, the Love that we owe to our country, nature, wealth, pleasure, honour, and such moral respects, &c. of which read copious Aristotle in his Morals; a man is beloved of a man, in that he is a man; but all these are far more eminent and great, when they shall proceed from a sanctified spirit, that hath a true touch of Religion, and a reference to God. Nature binds all creatures to love their young ones: an Hen to preserve her brood will run upon a Lion, an Hind will fight with a Bull, a Sow with a Bear, a silly Sheep with a Fox. So the same nature urgeth a man to love his Parents,

————— *all the Gods would hate me, father,*
Did I not cherish thee more than my very eyes! (TERENCE)

and this Love cannot be dissolved, as Tully holds, without detestable offence: but much more God's commandment, which enjoins a filial Love, and an obedience in this kind. The Love of brethren is great, and like an arch of stones, where, if one be displaced, all comes down; no Love so forcible & strong, honest, to the combination of which nature, fortune, virtue, happily concur; yet this Love comes short of it.

Sweet and proper 'tis to die for one's country; (HORACE)

it cannot be expressed, what a deal of Charity that one name of Country contains.

Love of one's country serves instead of wages.

The Decii, Horatii, Curii, Scævola, Regulus, Codrus, did sacrifice themselves, for their Country's peace and good.

One day the Fabii stoutly warred,
One day the Fabii were destroyed. (OVID)

Fifty thousand Englishmen lost their lives willingly near Battle Abbey in defence of their Country. P. Æmilius speaks of six Senators of Calais, that came with halters in their hands to the King of England, to die for the rest. This love makes so many writers take such pains, so many Historiographers, Physicians, &c., or at least as they pretend, for common safety, and their country's benefit. Friendship is an holy name, and a sacred communion of friends. As the Sun is in the Firmament, so is friendship in the world, a most divine and heavenly band. As nuptial Love makes, this perfects mankind, and is to be preferred (if you will stand to the judgment of Cornelius Nepos) before affinity or consanguinity; the cords of Love bind faster than any other wreath whatsoever. Take this away, and take all pleasure, joy, comfort, happiness, and true content, out of the world; 'tis the greatest tie, the surest Indenture, strongest band. and, as our modern Maro decides it, is much to be preferred before the rest.

> *Hard is the doubt, and difficult to deem,*
>   *When all three kinds of Love together meet;*
>   *And do dispart the heart with power extreme,*
>   *Whether shall weigh the balance down; to wit,*
>   *The dear affection unto kindred sweet,*
>   *Or raging fire of Love to women kind,*
>   *Or zeal of friends, combin'd by virtues meet;*
>   *But of them all, the band of virtuous mind,*
> *Methinks the gentle heart should most assured bind.*
>
> *For natural affection soon doth cease,*
>   *And quenchèd is with Cupid's greater flame;*
>   *But faithful friendship doth them both suppress,*
>   *And them with mastering discipline doth tame,*
>   *Through thoughts aspiring to eternal fame.*
>   *For as the soul doth rule the earthly mass,*
>   *And all the service of the body frame,*
>   *So Love of soul doth Love of body pass,*
> *No less than perfect gold surmounts the meanest brass.*
>
>   (SPENSER)

A faithful friend is better than gold, a medicine or misery, an only possession; yet this Love of friends, nuptial, heroical, profitable, pleasant, honest, all three Loves put together, are little worth, if they proceed not from a true Christian illuminated soul, if it be not done for God's sake. *Though I had the gift of Prophecy, spake with the tongues of men and Angels, though I feed the poor with all my goods, give my body to be burned, and have not this love, it profiteth me nothing,* 'tis a glittering sin without charity. This is an all-apprehending love, a deifying love, a refined, pure, divine love, the quintessence of all love, the true Philosopher's stone; as Austin infers, he is no true friend that loves not God's truth. And therefore this is true Love indeed, the cause of all good to mortal men, that reconciles all creatures, and glues them together in perpetual amity and firm league, and can no more abide bitterness. hate, malice, than fair and foul weather, light, and darkness, sterility and plenty, may be together. As the Sun in the Firmament, (I say) so is Love in the world; and for this cause 'tis Love without an addition, Love pre-eminent, Love of God and Love of men. The Love of God begets the Love of man; and by this Love of our neighbour the Love of God is nourished and increased. By this happy union of Love all well governed families and Cities are combined, the heavens annexed, and divine souls complicated, the world itself composed, and all that is in it conjoined in God, and reduced to one. This Love causeth true and absolute virtues, the life, spirit and root of every virtuous action, it finisheth prosperity, easeth adversity, corrects all natural incumbrances, inconveniences, sustained by Faith and Hope, which with this our Love make an indissoluble twist, a Gordian knot, an Æquilateral Triangle, *and yet the greatest of them is Love,* which inflames our souls with a divine heat, and being so inflamed, purgeth, and so purged, elevates to God, makes an atonement, and reconciles us unto him. That other Love infects the soul of man, this cleanseth; that depresses, this rears: that causeth cares and troubles, this quietness of mind; this informs, that deforms, our life; that leads to repentance, this to heaven. For if once we be truly link'd and touched with this charity, we shall love God above all, *our neighbour as ourself,* as we are enjoined: perform those duties and exercises, even all the operations of a good Christian.

This Love suffereth long, it is bountiful, envieth not, boasteth not itself, it is not puffed up, it deceiveth not, it seeketh not his own things, it is not provoked to anger, it thinketh not evil, it rejoiceth not in iniquity, but in truth. It suffereth all things, believeth all things, hopeth all things, ———— *it covereth all trespasses,* ———— *a multitude of sins,* ———— as our Saviour told the woman in the Gospel, that washed his feet, *many sins were forgiven her, for she loved much,* ———— *it will defend the fatherless and the widow,* ———— *will seek no revenge, or be mindful of wrong,* ———— *will bring home his brother's ox if he go astray,* as 'tis commanded, ———— *will resist evil, give to him that asketh, and not turn from him that borroweth, bless them that curse him, love his enemy,* ———— *bear his brother's burden.* He that so loves will be hospitable, and distribute to the necessities of the Saints; he will, if it be possible, have peace with all men, *feed his enemy, if he be hungry, if he be athirst, give him drink,* he will perform those seven works of mercy, *he will make himself equal to them of the lower sort, rejoice with them that rejoice, weep with them that weep,* he will speak truth to his neighbour, be courteous and tender-hearted, *forgiving others*

for Christ's sake, as God forgave him, ———— *he will be like-minded,*
———— *of one judgement ; be humble, meek, long-suffering,* ————
forbear, forget and forgive, and what he doth, shall be heartily done to
God, and not to men; *be pitiful and courteous,* ———— *seek peace and
follow it.* He will love his brother *not in word and tongue, but in deed
and truth,* ———— *and he that loves God, Christ will love him that is
begotten of him,* &c.

Thus should we willingly do, if we had a true touch of this charity, of
this divine Love, if we would perform this which we are enjoined, forget and forgive, and compose ourselves to those Christian Laws of Love.
Angelical souls, how blessed, how happy should we be, so loving, how
might we triumph over the devil, and have another heaven upon earth !

But this we cannot do; and which is the cause of all our woes,
miseries, discontent, melancholy, want of this charity. We do press one
another by turns, insult, contemn, vex, torture, molest, and hold one
another's noses to the grind-stone hard, provoke, rail, scoff, calumniate,
challenge, hate, abuse (hard-hearted, implacable, malicious, peevish,
inexorable as we are) to satisfy our lust or private spleen, for toys,
trifles, and impertinent occasions, spend ourselves, goods, friends, fortunes, to be revenged on our adversary, to ruin him and his. 'Tis all our
study, practice, and business, how to plot mischief, mine, countermine,
defend and offend, ward ourselves, injure others, hurt all; as if we were
born to do mischief; and that with such eagerness and bitterness, with
such rancour, malice, rage and fury, we prosecute our intended designs,
that neither affinity or consanguinity, love or fear of God or men can
contain us: no satisfaction, no composition will be accepted, no offices
will serve, no submission; though he shall upon his knees, as Sarpedon
did to Glaucus in Homer, acknowledging his error, yield himself with
tears in his eyes, beg his pardon, we will not relent, forgive, or forget,
till we have confounded him and his, made dice of his bones, as they
say, see him rot in prison, banish his friends, followers, and the whole
hated stock, rooted him out and all his posterity. Monsters of men as
we are, Dogs, Wolves, Tigers, Fiends, incarnate Devils, we do not only
contend, oppress, and tyrannize ourselves, but, as so many fire-brands,
we set on, and animate others: our whole life is a perpetual combat, a
conflict, a set battle, a snarling fit: the goddess of discord is settled in our
tents, all are contaminated, opposing wit to wit, wealth to wealth,
strength to strength, fortunes to fortunes, friends to friends, as at a
sea-fight, we turn our broad sides, or two millstones with continual
attrition, we fire ourselves, or break one another's backs, and both are

ruined and consumed in the end. Miserable wretches, to fat and enrich ourselves, we care not how we get it, by what manner of means, how many thousands we undo, whom we oppress, by whose ruin and downfall we arise, whom we injure, fatherless children, widows, common societies, to satisfy our own private lust. Though we have myriads, abundance of wealth and treasure, (pitiless, merciless, remorseless, and uncharitable in the highest degree) and our poor brother in need, sickness, in great extremity, and now ready to be starved for want of food, we had rather, as the Fox told the Ape, his tail should sweep the ground still, than cover his buttocks; rather spend it idly, consume it with dogs, hawks, hounds, unnecessary buildings, in riotous apparel, ingurgitate, or let it be lost, than he should have part of it; rather take from him that little which he hath than relieve him.

Like the dog in the manger, we neither use it ourselves, let others make use of, or enjoy it; part with nothing while we live: for want of disposing our household, and setting things in order, set all the world together by the ears after our death. Poor Lazarus lies howling at his gates for a few crumbs, he only seeks chippings, offals; let him roar and howl, famish, and eat his own flesh, he respects him not. A poor decayed kinsman of his sets upon him by the way in all his jollity, and runs begging bareheaded by him, conjuring by those former bonds of friendship, alliance, consanguinity, &c., uncle, cousin, brother, father,

> *By these tears and by that hand of thine,*
> *If any wise I have deserved well of thee,*
> *If aught of mine hath ever been sweet to thee,*
> *Pity me!*   (VIRGIL)

Shew some pity for Christ's sake, pity a sick man, an old man, &c., he cares not, ride on: pretend [that is, assert] sickness, inevitable loss of limbs, goods, plead suretyship, or shipwrack, fires, common calamities, shew thy wants and imperfections,

> ———— *by holy Osiris swearing,*
> *Believe me, I deceive thee not, O help me!*   (HORACE)

Swear, protest, take God and all his Angels to witness,

> *Seek out some stranger!*   (HORACE)

thou art a counterfeit crank [or one who feigns phrenzy to get money], a cheater, he is not touched with it,

> *Everywhere is the poor man neglected,*   (OVID)

ride on, he takes no notice of it. Put up a supplication to him in the name of a thousand Orphans, an Hospital, a Spittle, a Prison as he goes by, they cry out to him for aid, ride on, you speak to a deaf man, he cares not, let them eat stones, devour themselves with vermin, rot in their own dung, he cares not. Shew him a decayed haven, a bridge, a school, a fortification, &c., or some publick work, ride on; good your Worship, your Honour, for God's sake, your country's sake, ride on. But shew him a roll wherein his name shall be registered in golden letters, and commended to all posterity, his arms set up, with his devices to be seen, and then peradventure he will stay and contribute; or if thou canst thunder upon him, as Papists do, with satisfactory and meritorious works, or persuade him by this means he shall save his soul out of Hell, and free it from Purgatory (if he be of any religion) then in all likelihood he will listen and stay; or that he have no children, no near kinsman, heir, he cares for at least, or cannot well tell otherwise how or where to bestow his possessions (for carry them with him he cannot) it may be then he will build some School or Hospital in his life, or be induced to give liberally to pious uses after his death. For, I dare boldly say, vain glory, that opinion of merit, and this enforced necessity, when they know not otherwise how to leave, or what better to do with them, is the main cause of most of our good works. I will not urge this to derogate from any man's charitable devotion, or bounty in this kind, to censure any good work; no doubt there be many sanctified, heroical, and worthy-minded men, that in true zeal, and for virtue's sake (divine spirits) that out of commiseration and pity extend their liberality, and, as much as in them lies, do good to all men, clothe the naked, feed the hungry, comfort the sick and needy, relieve all, forget and forgive injuries, as true charity requires; yet most part there is a deal of hypocrisy in this kind, much default and defect. Cosmo de Medici, that rich citizen of Florence, ingenuously confessed to a near friend of his, that would know of him why he built so many publick and magnificent palaces, and bestowed so liberally on Scholars, not that he loved learning more than others, but to eternize his own name, to be immortal by the benefit of Scholars; for when his friends were dead, walls decayed, and all Inscriptions gone, books would remain to the world's end. The lanthorn in Athens was built by Xenocles, the Theatre by Pericles, the famous port Piræus by Themicles, Pallas Palladium by Phidias, the Parthenon by Callicrates; but these brave monuments are decayed all, and ruined long since, their builders' names alone flourish by mediation of writers. And as he said of that Marian oak, now cut down and dead, no plant can grow so long as that which is set and manured by those everliving wits. Allon bacuth, that weeping oak, under which Deborah, Rebecca's nurse, died, and was buried, may not survive the memory of such everlasting monuments. Vain glory and emulation (as to most men) was the cause efficient, and to be a trumpeter of his own fame, Cosmo's sole intent so to do good, that all the world might take notice of it. Such for the most part is the charity of our times, such our Benefactors, Mæcenases and Patrons. Shew me, amongst so many myriads, a truly devout, a right, honest, upright, meek, humble, a patient, innocuous, innocent, a merciful, a loving, a charitable man! Lives there an honest man amongst us? Shew me a Caleb or a Joshua!

Sing for me, Muse, the man, &c.　(HORACE)

shew a virtuous woman, a constant wife, a good neighbour, a trusty servant, an obedient child, a true friend, &c. Crows in Africa are not so scant. He that shall examine this iron age wherein we live, where love is cold, Astræa gone from earth, Justice fled with her assistants, virtue expelled,

　　　　　　———— sister of Justice, unsullied Faith,
And naked Truth,　(HORACE)

all goodness gone, where vice abounds, the Devil is loose, & see one man vilify & insult over his brother, as if he were an innocent, or a block, oppress, tyrannize, prey upon, torture him, vex, gall, torment and crucify him, starve him, where is charity? He that shall see men swear and forswear, lie and bear false witness, to advantage themselves, prejudice others, hazard goods, lives, fortunes, credit, all, to be revenged on their enemies, men so unspeakable in their lusts, unnatural in malice, such bloody designments, Italian blaspheming, Spanish renouncing, &c., may well ask where is charity? He that shall observe so many law-suits, such endless contentions, such plotting, undermining, so much money spent with such eagerness and fury, every man for himself, his own ends, the Devil for all: so many distressed souls, such lamentable complaints, so many factions, conspiracies, seditions, oppressions, abuses, injuries, such grudging, repining, discontent, so much emulation, envy, so many brawls, quarrels, monomachies, &c., may well inquire what is become of charity? when we see and read of such cruel wars, tumults, uproars, bloody battles, so many men slain, so many cities ruinated, &c., (for what else is the subject of all our stories almost, but Bills, Bows, and Guns?) so many murders and massacres, &c., where is Charity? Or see men wholly devote to God, Churchmen, professed Divines, holy men, to make the trumpet of the gospel the trumpet of war, a company of Hell-born Jesuits, and fiery-spirited Friars, hold the torch to all seditions: as so many firebrands set all the world by the ears (I say nothing of their contentious and railing books, whole ages spent in writing one against another, and that with such virulency and bitterness, satires like Bion's and poisonous wit), and by their bloody inquisitions, that in thirty years Bale saith, consumed 39 Princes, 148 Earls, 235 Barons, 14,755 Commons, worse than those ten persecutions, may justly doubt where is Charity? For Heaven's sake, what sort of Christians are these? Are these Christians? I beseech you, tell me. He that shall observe and see these things, may say to them as Cato to Cæsar, sure I think thou art of opinion there is neither Heaven, nor Hell. Let them pretend religion. zeal, make what shews they will, give alms, [be] peace-makers, frequent sermons, if we may guess at the tree by the fruit, they are no better than Hypocrites, Epicures, Atheists, with the " fool in their hearts they say there is no God." 'Tis no marvel, then, if being so uncharitable, hardhearted as we are, we have so frequent and so many discontents, such melancholy fits, so many bitter pangs, mutual discords, all in a combustion, often complaints, so common grievances, general mischiefs, so many tragedies on earth, devastating mankind, so many pestilences, wars, uproars, losses, deluges, fires, inundations, God's vengeance, and all the plagues of Egypt, come not upon us, since we are so currish one towards another, so respectless of God and our neighbours, and by our crying sins pull these miseries upon our own heads. Nay more, 'tis justly to be feared, which Josephus once said of his Countrymen Jews, if the Romans had not come when they did to sack their City, surely it had been swallowed up with some earthquake, deluge, or fired from Heaven as Sodom and Gomorrah: their desperate malice, wickedness, and peevishness, was such. 'Tis to be suspected, if we continue these wretched ways, we may look for the like heavy visitations to come upon us. If we had any sense or feeling of these things, surely we should not go on as we do in such irregular courses, practise all manner of impieties; our whole carriage would not be so averse from God. If a man would but consider, when he is in the midst and full career of such prodigious and uncharitable actions, how displeasing they are in God's sight, how noxious to himself, as Solomon told Joab, *the Lord shall bring this blood upon their heads,* —— *sudden desolation and destruction shall come like a whirlwind upon them: affliction, anguish, the reward of his hand shall be given him,* &c., —— *they shall fall into the pit they have digged for others,* and when they are scraping, tyrannizing, getting, wallowing in their wealth, *this night, O fool, I will take away thy soul,* what a severe account they must make; and how gracious on the other side a charitable man is in God's eyes. *Blessed are the merciful, for they shall obtain mercy. He that lendeth to the poor,* gives to God; and how *it shall be restored to them again,* ———— how by their patience and long suffering they shall *heap coals on their enemies' heads,* ———— and *he that followeth after righteousness and mercy shall find righteousness and glory;* surely they would check their desires, curb in their unnatural, inordinate affections, agree amongst themselves, abstain from doing evil, amend their lives, and learn to do well. *Behold how comely and good a thing it is for brethren to live together in union: it is like the precious ointment, &c.* How odious to contend one with the other! Why do we contend and vex one another? behold death is over our heads, and we must shortly give an account of all our uncharitable words and actions: think upon it, and be wise!

SECTION 2 MEMBER 1

SUBSECTION 1 — *Heroical love causing Melancholy. His Pedigree, Power, and Extent*

IN the precedent Section mention was made, amongst other pleasant objects, of the comeliness and beauty which proceeds from women, that causeth Heroical, or Love-melancholy, is more eminent above the rest, and properly called Love. The part affected in men is the liver, and therefore called Heroical, because commonly Gallants, Noblemen, and the most generous spirits are possessed with it. His power and extent is very large, and in that twofold division of Love, Love and Friendship, those two Venuses, which Plato and some other make mention of, it is most eminent, and par excellence called Venus, as I have said, or Love itself. Which, although it be denominated from men, and most evident in them, yet it extends and shews itself in vegetal and sensible creatures, those incorporeal substances (as shall be specified) and hath a large dominion of sovereignty over them. His pedigree is very ancient, derived from the beginning of the world, as Phædrus contends, and his parentage of such antiquity, that no Poet could ever find it out. Hesiod makes Earth and Chaos to be Love's parents, before the Gods were born.

Love was created first, before the gods.

Some think it is the self same fire Prometheus fetched from heaven. Plutarch will have Love to be the son of Iris and Favonius, but Socrates in that pleasant Dialogue of Plato, when it came to his turn to speak of Love, (of which subject Agathon, the Rhetorician, the eloquent Agathon, that Chanter Agathon, had newly given occasion), in a poetical strain.

telleth this tale. When Venus was born, all the Gods were invited to a banquet, and, amongst the rest, Porus the God of bounty and wealth; Penia or poverty came a begging to the door; Porus, well whittled with Nectar, (for there was no wine in those days), walking in Jupiter's garden, in a Bower met with Penia, and in his drink got her with child, of whom was born Love; and, because he was begotten on Venus' birth day, Venus still attends upon him. The moral of this is in Ficinus. Another tale is there, borrowed out of Aristophanes. In the beginning of the world, men had four arms, and four feet, but for their pride, because they compared themselves with the Gods, were parted into halves, and now peradventure by love they hope to be united again and made one. Otherwise thus; Vulcan met two lovers, and bid them ask what they would, and they should have it; but they made answer, O Vulcan the Gods' great Smith, we beseech thee to work us anew in thy furnace, and of two make us one; which he presently did, and ever since true lovers are either all one, or else desire to be united. Many such tales you shall find in Leon Hebræus, and their moral to them. The reason why Love was still painted young, (as Phornutus and others will) is because young men are most apt to love; soft, fair, and fat, because such folks are soonest taken: naked, because all true affection is simple and open: he smiles, because merry and given to delights: hath a quiver, to shew, his power none can escape: is blind, because he sees not where he strikes, whom he hits, &c. His power and sovereignty is expressed by the poets, in that he is held to be a God, and a great commanding God, above Jupiter himself; the great Daimon, as Plato calls him, the strongest and merriest of all the Gods, according to Alcinous and Athenæus. As Euripides, Love is the God of Gods and governor of men; for we must do all homage to him, keep an holy day for his Deity, adore in his Temples, worship his image (a God divine, and no mere Shrine), sacrifice to his altar, that conquers all, and rules all. I had rather contend with Bulls, Lions, Bears, and Giants, than with Love; he is so powerful, enforceth all to pay tribute to him, domineers over all, and can make mad and sober whom he list; insomuch that Cæcilius, in Tully's Tusculans, holds him to be no better than a fool, or an idiot, that doth not acknowledge Love to be a great God, that can make sick and cure whom he list. Homer and Stesichorus were both made blind, if you will believe Leon Hebræus, for speaking against his god-head. And though Aristophanes degrade him, and say that he was scornfully rejected from the counsel of the Gods, had his wings clipped besides, that he might come no more amongst them, and to his farther disgrace banished heaven for ever, and confined to dwell on earth, yet he is of that power, majesty, omnipotency, and dominion, that no creature can withstand him.

Cupid rules with the power of the Gods,

And not great Jove himself can give him odds. (SOPHOCLES)

He is more than Quarter-Master with the Gods, he divides the empire of the Sea with Thetis, of the Shades with Æacus, of Heaven with Jupiter, and hath not so much possession as dominion. Jupiter himself was turned into a Satyr, a Shepherd, a Bull, a Swan, a golden shower, and what not, for love; that as Lucian's Juno right well objected to him, Thou art Cupid's whirligig: how did he insult over all the other Gods, Mars, Neptune, Pan, Mercury, Bacchus, and the rest! Lucian brings in Jupiter complaining of Cupid that he could not be quiet for him: and the Moon lamenting that she was so impotently besotted on Endymion, even Venus herself confessing as much, how rudely and in what sort her own son Cupid had used her, being his mother, now drawing her to mount Ida for the love of that Trojan Anchises, now to Libanus for that Assyrian youth's sake. And although she threatened to break his bow and arrows, to clip his wings, and whipped him besides on the bare buttocks with her pantophle, [or slipper] yet all would not serve, he was too head-strong and unruly. That monster-conquering Hercules was tamed by him:

Whom neither beasts nor enemies could tame,

Nor Juno's might subdue, Love quell'd the same. (OVID)

Your bravest soldiers and most generous spirits are enervated with it, when they surrender to feminine blandishments and defile themselves with embraces. Apollo, that took upon him to cure all diseases, could not help himself of this; and therefore Socrates calls Love a tyrant, and brings him triumphing in a Chariot, whom Petrarch imitates in his triumph of Love, and Fracastorius in an elegant Poem expresseth at large, Cupid riding, Mars and Apollo following his Chariot, Psyche weeping, &c.

In vegetal creatures what sovereignty Love hath by many pregnant proofs and familiar examples may be proved, especially of palm trees, which are both he and she, and express not a sympathy but a love-passion, as by many observations have been confirmed. Boughs live for love, and every flourishing tree in turn feels the passion: palms nod mutual vows, poplar sighs to poplar, plane to plane, and alder murmurs to alder. Constantine gives an instance out of Florentius his Georgicks, of a Palm-tree that loved most fervently, and would not be comforted until such time her Love applied himself unto her; you might see the two trees bend, and of their own accords stretch out their boughs to embrace and kiss each other: they will give manifest signs of mutual love. Ammianus Marcellinus reports that they marry one another, and fall in love if they grow in sight; and when the wind brings the smell to them, they are marvellously affected. Philostratus observes as much, and Galen, they will be sick for love, ready to die and pine away, which the husbandmen perceiving, saith Constantine, stroke many Palms that grow together, and so stroking again the Palm that is enamoured, they carry kisses from the one to the other: or tying the leaves and branches of the one to the stem of the other, will make them both flourish and prosper a great deal better: which are enamoured, they can perceive, by the bending of boughs, and inclination of their bodies. If any man think this which I say to be a tale, let him read that story of two palm trees in Italy, the male growing at Brundusium, the female at Otranto (related by Jovianus Pontanus in an excellent Poem, sometime Tutor to Alphonso Junior, King of Naples, his Secretary of State, and a great Philosopher), which were barren, and so continued a long time, till they came to see one another growing up higher, though many Stadiums asunder. Pierius in his Hieroglyphicks, and Melchior Guilandinus, in his Tract on Papyrus, cites this story of Pontanus for a truth. See more in Salmuth, Mizaldus, Sand's voyages, &c.

If such fury be in vegetals, what shall we think of sensible creatures? how much more violent and apparent shall it be in them!

> *All kind of creatures in the earth,*
> *And fishes of the sea,*
> *And painted birds do rage alike*
> *This love bears equal sway.*   (VIRGIL)
>
> *This God rules earth and the deep seas alike.*   (PROPERTIUS)

Common experience and our sense will inform us, how violently brute beasts are carried away with this passion, horses above the rest, the lust of mares is noted. Cupid, in Lucian, bids Venus his mother be of good cheer, for he was now familiar with Lions, and oftentimes did get on their backs, hold them by the mane, and ride them about like horses, and they would fawn upon him with their tails. Bulls, Bears, and Boars, are so furious in this kind, they kill one another: but especially Cocks, Lions, and Harts, which are so fierce that you may hear them fight half a mile off, saith Turberville, and many times kill each other, or compel them to abandon the rut, that they may remain masters in their places; and when one hath driven his corrival away, he raiseth his nose up into the air, and looks aloft, as though he gave thanks to nature, which affords him such great delight. How Birds are affected in this kind, appears out of Aristotle, he will have them to sing for joy or in hope of their venery which is to come.

> *First the birds of the air, O Goddess, of thee*
> *And thy coming aware, are smit to the heart by thy power.*
>
> (LUCRETIUS)

Fishes pine away for love and wax lean, if Gomesius's authority may be taken, and are rampant too, some of them. Peter Gellius tells wonders of a Triton in Epirus: there was a well not far from the shore, where the country wenches fetched water; they, the Tritons, to ravish them, would set upon them and carry them to the Sea, and there drown them, if they would not yield; so Love tyrannizeth in dumb creatures. Yet this is natural for one beast to dote upon another of the same kind; but what strange fury is that, when a Beast shall dote upon a man! Saxo Grammaticus hath a story of a Bear that loved a woman, kept her in his den a long time, and begot a son of her, out of whose loins proceeded many Northern Kings: this is the original belike of that common tale of Valentine and Orson. Ælian, Pliny, Peter Gellius are full of such relations. A Peacock in Leucadia loved a maid, and when she died the Peacock pined. A Dolphin loved a boy called Hernias, and when he died, the fish came on land, and so perished. The like, adds Gellius, out of Apion, a Dolphin at Puteoli loved a child, would come often to him, let him get on his back, and carry him about, and when by sickness the child was taken away, the Dolphin died. Every book is full (saith Busbequius, the Emperor's Orator, with the Grand Seignior not long since), and yields such instances, to believe which I was always afraid, lest I should be thought to give credit to fables, until I saw a Lynx, which I had from Assyria, so affected towards one of my men, that it cannot be denied but that he was in love with him. When my man was present, the beast would use many notable enticements, and pleasant motions, and when he was going, hold him back, and look after him when he was gone, very sad in his absence, but most jocund when he returned: and when my man went from me, the beast expressed his love with continual sickness, and after he had pined away some few days, died. — Such another story he hath of a Crane of Majorca, that loved a Spaniard, that would walk any way with him, and in his absence seek about for him, make a noise that he might hear her, and knock at his door, and when he took his last farewell, famished herself. Such pretty pranks can love play with Birds, Fishes, Beasts: Venus keeps the keys of the air, earth, and sea, and alone retains the rulership of all. And if all be certain that is credibly reported, with the Spirits of the Air, and Devils of Hell themselves, who are as much enamoured and dote (if I may use that word) as any other creatures whatsoever. For if those stories be true that are written of Incubi and Succubi, of Nymphs, lascivious Fauns, Satyrs, and those Heathen gods which were Devils, those lascivious Telchines [or Elves], of whom the Platonists tell so many fables; or those familiar meetings in our days, and company of Witches and Devils, there is some probability for it. I know that Biarmannus, Wierus, and some others stoutly deny it, that the Devil hath any carnal copulation with women, that the Devil takes no pleasure in such facts, they be mere phantasies, all such relations of Incubi, Succubi, lies and tales: but Austin doth acknowledge it; Erastus, on Lamias, Jacobus Sprenger and his colleagues, &c., Zanchius, Dandinus, Bodine, and Paracelsus, a great champion of this Tenent amongst the rest, which give sundry peculiar instances, by many testimonies, proofs, and confessions, evince it. Hector Boethius, in his Scottish History, hath three or four such examples, which Cardan confirms out of him, of such as have had familiar company many years with them, and that in the habit of men and women.

Philostratus, in his Fourth Book of his Life of Apollonius, hath a memorable instance in this kind, which I may not omit, of one Menippus Lycius, a young man 25 years of age, that going betwixt Cenchreæ and Corinth, met such a phantasm in the habit of a fair gentlewoman, which, taking him by the hand, carried him home to her house in the suburbs of Corinth, and told him she was a Phœnician by birth, and if he would tarry with her, he should hear her sing and play, and drink such wine as never any drank, and no man should molest him; but she being fair and lovely would live and die with him, that was fair and lovely to behold. The young man, a Philosopher, otherwise staid and discreet, able to moderate his passions, though not this of love, tarried with her a while to his great content, and at last married her, to whose wedding, among other guests, came Apollonius, who by some probable conjectures found her out to be a Serpent, a Lamia, and that all her furniture was like Tantalus' gold described by Homer, no substance, but mere illusions. When she saw herself descried, she wept, and desired Apollonius to be silent, but he would not be moved, and thereupon she, plate, house, and all that was in it, vanished in an instant: many thousands took notice of this fact, for it was done in the midst of Greece.

Sabine, in his Comment on the 10ᵗʰ. of Ovid's Metamorphoses, at the tale of Orpheus, telleth us of a Gentleman of Bavaria, that for many

months together bewailed the loss of his dear wife; at length the Devil
in her habit came and comforted him, and told him, because he was so
importunate for her, that she would come and live with him again, on
that condition he would be new married, never swear and blaspheme as
he used formerly to do; for if he did, she should be gone: he vowed it,
married, and lived with her, she brought him children, and governed his
house, but was still pale and sad, and so continued, till one day falling
out with him, he fell a swearing; she vanished thereupon, and was never
after seen. This I have heard, saith Sabine, from persons of good credit,
which told me that the Duke of Bavaria did tell it for a certainty to the
Duke of Saxony.

One more I will relate out of Florilegus, about the year 1058, an
honest Historian of our nation, because he telleth it so confidently, as a
thing in those days talked of all over Europe. A young Gentleman of
Rome, the same day that he was married, after dinner with the Bride
and his friends went a walking into the fields, and towards evening to
the Tennis Court to recreate himself; whilst he played, he put his ring
upon the finger of a statue of Venus, which was thereby, made in brass;
after he had sufficiently played, and now made an end of his sport, he
came to fetch his ring, but Venus had bowed her finger in, and he could
not get it off. Whereupon loath to make his company tarry at present,
there he left it, intending to fetch it the next day, or at some more convenient time, went thence to supper, and so to bed. In the night, when he
should come to perform those nuptial rites, Venus steps between him
and his wife, (unseen or felt of her) and told him that she was his wife,
that he had betrothed himself unto her by that ring, which he put upon
her finger: she troubled him for some following nights. He, not knowing how to help himself, made his moan to one Palumbus, a learned
Magician in those days, who gave him a letter, and bid him at such a
time of the night, in such a crossway, at the Town's end, where old
Saturn would pass by, with his associates in procession, as commonly
he did, deliver that script with his own hands to Saturn himself; the
young man, of a bold spirit, accordingly did it; and when the old fiend
had read it, he called Venus to him, who rode before him, and commanded her to deliver his ring, which forthwith she did, and so the
gentleman was freed.

Many such stories I find in several Authors to confirm this which I
have said: as that more notable among the rest, of Philinium and
Machates in Phlegon's Tract On Marvellous Things, and, though many
be against it, yet I for my part will subscribe to Lactantius, God sent

Angels to the tuition of men; but whilst they lived amongst us, that mischievous all-commander of the Earth, and hot in lust, enticed them by little and little to this vice, and defiled them with the company of women. And Anaxagoras: Many of those spiritual bodies overcome by the love of Maids, and lust, failed, of whom those were born we call Giants. Justin Martyr, Clemens Alexandrinus, Sulpicius Severus, Eusebius, &c., to this sense make a twofold fall of Angels, one from the beginning of the world, another a little before the deluge, as Moses teacheth us, openly professing that these Genii can beget, and have carnal copulation with women. At Japan in the East Indies, at this present (if we may believe the relation of travellers) there is an Idol called Teuchedy, to whom one of the fairest virgins in the country is monthly brought, and left in a private room, in the Fotoqui, or Church, where she sits alone to be deflowered. At certain times the Teuchedy (which is thought to be the Devil) appears to her, and knoweth her carnally. Every month a fair Virgin is taken in, but what becomes of the old, no man can tell. In that goodly temple of Jupiter Belus in Babylon, there was a fair Chapel, saith Herodotus, an eye-witness of it, in which was a brave bed, a table of gold, &c., into which no creature came but one only woman, which their God made choice of, as the Chaldæan Priests told him, and that their God lay with her himself, as at Thebes in Egypt was the like done of old. So that you see this is no news, the Devils themselves, or their juggling Priests, have played such pranks in all ages. Many Divines stiffly contradict this; but I will conclude with Lipsius, that since examples, testimonies, and confessions of those unhappy women are so manifest on the other side, and many, even in this our Town of Louvain, that it is likely to be so; one thing I will add, that I suppose that in no age past, I know not by what destiny of this unhappy time, there have never appeared or showed themselves so many lecherous Devils, Satyrs, and Genii, as in this of ours, as appears by the daily narrations, and judicial sentences upon record. - - Read more of this question in Plutarch, Austin, Wierus, Giraldus Cambrensis, the Hammer of Witches [by Jacob Sprenger, the Cologne Inquisitor], Jacobus Reussus, Godelman, Erastus, Valesius, John Nider, Delrio, Lipsius, Bodine, Pererius, King James, &c.

SUBSECTION 2 — *How Love tyrannizeth over men. Love, or Heroical Melancholy, his definition, part affected*

You have heard how this tyrant Love rageth with brute beasts and spirits; now let us consider what passions it causeth amongst men.

Naughty Love, to what dost thou not compel our mortal hearts? How it tickles the hearts of mortal men, I am almost afraid to relate, amazed, and ashamed, it hath wrought such stupend and prodigious effects, such foul offences. Love indeed (I may not deny) first united provinces, built Cities, and by a perpetual generation makes and preserves mankind, propagates the Church; but if it rage, it is no more Love, but burning Lust, a Disease, Phrensy, Madness, Hell. 'Tis death, 'tis an immedicable calamity, 'tis a raging madness; 'tis no virtuous habit this, but a vehement perturbation of the mind, a monster of nature, wit, and art; as Alexis in Athenæus sets it out, manfully rash, womanishly timid, furiously headlong, bitter sweet, a caressing blow, &c. It subverts kingdoms, overthrows cities, towns, families; mars, corrupts, and makes a massacre of men; thunder and lightning, wars, fires, plagues, have not done that mischief to mankind, as this burning lust, this brutish passion. Let Sodom and Gomorrah, Troy, (which Dares Phrygius, and Dictys Cretensis will make good) and I know not how many cities bear record. Helen was not the first petticoat that caused a war, &c., all succeeding ages will subscribe: Joan of Naples in Italy, Frédégunde and Brunhalt in France, all histories are full of these Basilisks. Besides those daily monomachies, murders, effusion of blood, rapes, riot, and immoderate expense, to satisfy their lust, beggary, shame, loss, torture, punishment, disgrace, loathsome diseases that proceed from thence, worse than calentures and pestilent fevers, those often Gouts, Pox, Arthritis, palsies, cramps, Sciatica, convulsions, aches, combustions, &c., which torment the body, that feral melancholy which crucifies the Soul in this life, and everlasting torments in the world to come.

Notwithstanding they know these and many such miseries, threats, tortures, will surely come upon them; rewards, exhortations, to the contrary; yet either out of their own weakness, a depraved nature, or love's tyranny, which so furiously rageth, they suffer themselves to be led " like an ox to the slaughter"; (easy the descent to Avernus), they go down headlong to their own perdition, they will commit folly with beasts, men " leaving the natural use of women," as Paul saith, " burned in lust one towards another, and man with man wrought filthiness."

Semiramis with a horse, Pasiphae with a bull, Aristo Ephesius with a she-ass, Fulvius with a mare, others with dogs, goats, &c., from such combinations in ancient days were sprung monsters, Centaurs, Silvanuses, and prodigious sights to affright mankind. And not with brutes only, but men among themselves, which sin is vulgarly called Sodomy; this vice was customary in old times with the Orientals, the Greeks without question, the Italians, Africans, Asiaticks: Hercules * had Hylas,

* Lilius Giraldus, his life. — Burton's note.

Polycletus, Dion, Pirithous, Abderus and the Phrygian, and 'tis given
out by some that Eurystheus even was his minion. Socrates used to frequent the Gymnasium because of the beauty of the youngsters, feeding
his hungry eyes on that spectacle, wherefore Philebus and Phædo were
corrivals, as Charmides and other Dialogues of Plato sufficiently show;
and in truth it was this very Socrates who said of Alcibiades: gladly
would I keep silent, and indeed I am averse, he offers too much in-
centive to wantonness. Theodoretus censures this. Plato himself delighted in Agathon, Xenophon in Clinias, Virgil in Alexis, Anacreon in
Bathyllus. But of the portentous lusts of Nero, Claudius and others
of infamous memory, assailed by Petronius, Suetonius, and others, exceeding all belief, how much more might be looked for here; but 'tis
an ancient ill. Among the Asiaticks, Turks, Italians, the vice is customary to this day; sodomy is [in a manner of speaking] the Diana of
the Romans; they make a practice of this everywhere among the Turks
— sowing seed among the rocks, as the poet saith, ploughing the sands;
nor are there lacking complaints of it even in the married state, where
an opposite part is used from that which is lawful; nothing a more
familiar sin among the Italians, who following Lucianus and Tatius,
defend themselves in many writings. Johannes de la Casa, Bishop Be-
ventius, calls it a holy act, the smug rascal, and goes so far as to say
that Venus should not otherwise be used. Nothing more common among
monks and priestlings, an inordinate passion even to death and madness.
Angelus Politianus, because of the love of boys, laid violent hands on
himself. And terrible to say, in our own country, within memory, how
much that detestable sin hath raged. For, indeed, in the year 1538,
the most prudent King Henry the Eighth, through the venerable Doctors of Laws, Thomas Lee and Richard Layton, inspected the cloisters
of cowls and companies of priests and votaries, and found among them
so great a number of wenchers, gelded youths, debauchees, catamites,
boy-things, pederasts, Sodomites, (as it saith in Bale), Ganymedes, &c.,
that in every one of them you may be certain of a new Gomorrah. But
see, if you please, the catalogue of these things in Bale: girls (he saith)
are not able to sleep in their beds because of necromantick Friars. If
'tis thus among monks, votaries, and such-like saintly rascals, what
may we not suspect in towns, in palaces? what among nobles, what in
cellars, how much nastiness, how much filth! I am silent meanwhile as
to the other uncleannesses of self-defiling monks, scarce to be named.
Rodericus a Castro tells that they take turns scourging each other with

whips, by way of incitation to Venus, that they have Spintrias [or those that seek out and invent new and monstrous actions of lust], Succubas, Ambubaias [or Dancing-Girls], and those wanton-loined womanlings, Tribadas, that fret each other by turns, and fulfil Venus, even among Eunuchs, with their so artful secrets. Nay, then, what wonder that a woman in Constantinople, being mad in love with another woman, dared an incredible thing, went through the ceremonial of marriage disguised as a man, and in short was married: but consult the author, Busbequius, yourself. I pass over those Egyptian Salinarios [or Dissectors] who couch with beautiful cadavers: and their insane lust, who are in love with idols and images: too well known is the fable of Pygmalion, in Ovid; or Mundus and Paulina, in Hegesippus, in that chapter of his Jewish Wars on Pontius, the legate of Cæsar (look in Pliny), the same that crucified Christ; of the picture of Atalanta and Helena, so inflaming to desire that one wanted to ravish them away, but that they were painted on a wall; another loved the statue of Good Fortune madly (saith Ælianus), another Bona Dea. And no part free from lewdness, no orifice not defiled and given over to shameful lust: Heliogabalus, saith Lampridius in his life of him, welcomed lust at every gateway of his body. Hostius made a looking-glass and so arranged it as to see his virility falsely magnified to his delight, acting both the man and woman at once, a nastiness and abomination even to speak of. 'Tis plain truth, what Plutarch's Gryllus objects to in Ulysses; moreover, he saith, we have not to this day, in the matter of men with men or women with women, so many sorts of vile actions as among your memorable and famous heroes, as Hercules following beardless comrades, mad for his friends, &c.; you are not able to confine your desires within their natural boundaries, but rather, like overflooding rivers, bring about violence, filthiness, turmoil, and confusion of nature in regard to love; for not only men go with goats, swine, and horses, but women are inflamed with mad passion for beasts, whence Minotaurs, Centaurs, Silvanuses, Sphynxes, &c. — Neither do I argue the contrary, nor bring things to the light which it is not proper for all to know, but for the learned only, for whose sake, like Rodericus, I would wish to have written; neither for light wits nor for depraved minds have I made note of these nasty sins, and I am unwilling to inquire any longer into such evils.

I come at last to that Heroical Love, which is proper to men and women, is a frequent cause of melancholy, and deserves much rather

to be called burning lust, than by such an honourable title. There is
an honest love, I confess, which is natural, a secret snare to captivate
the hearts of men, as Christopher Fonseca proves, a strong allurement,
of a most attractive, occult, adamantine property, and powerful virtue, and no man living can avoid it. He is not a man, but a block, a
very stone, and either a God or a Nebuchadnezzar, he hath a gourd for
his head, a pepon [or pumpkin] for his heart, that hath not felt the
power of it, and a rare creature to be found, one in an age,

*Whom no maiden's beauty ever inflamed,** (JUVENAL)

for once at least we have been mad. dote we either young or old, as he
[Chaucer] said, and none are excepted but Minerva and the Muses: so
Cupid in Lucian complains to his Mother Venus, that, amongst all the
rest, his arrows could not pierce them. But this nuptial love is a common passion, and honest, for men to love in the way of marriage; as
matter seeks form, so woman man. You know marriage is honourable,
a blessed calling, appointed by God himself in Paradise, it breeds true
peace, tranquillity, content and happiness, than which no holier union
exists or ever did, as Daphnæus in Plutarch could well prove (and
which gives immortality to human kind), when they live without jar-
ring, scolding, lovingly, as they should do.

Thrice happy they, and more than that,
Whom bond of love so firmly ties,
That without brawls till death them part,
'Tis undissolved and never dies. (HORACE)

As Seneca lived with his Paulina, Abraham and Sarah, Orpheus and
Eurydice, Arria and Pœtus, Artemisia and Mausolus, Rubenius Celer,
that would needs have it engraven on his tomb, he had led his life with
Ennea, his dear wife, forty three years eight months, and never fell
out. There is no pleasure in this world comparable to it, 'tis the height
of mortal good,

Delight of Gods and men, kind Venus. (LUCRETIUS)

As one holds, there's something in a woman beyond all human delight;
a magnetick virtue, a charming quality, an occult and powerful motive.
The husband rules her as head, but she again commands his heart, he
is her servant, she his only joy and content: no happiness is like unto
it, no love so great as this of man and wife, no such comfort, as a sweet
wife,

---

*The line is usually translated, "Who burned with lust for a girl he had never
seen," but the context calls for the meaning given above, and it has been so translated
by previous editors of Burton.

Mighty is love, but most in naked wedlock, (PROPERTIUS)
when they love at last as fresh as they did at first,

Growing old in love and years together, (SIMONIDES)
as Homer brings Paris kissing Helena, after they had been married ten
years, protesting withal that he loved her as dear as he did the first
hour that he was betrothed. And in their old age when they make much
of one another, saying as he did to his wife in the Poet,

Dear wife, let's live in love and die together,
As hitherto we have in all good will:
Let no day change or alter our affections,
But let's be young to one another still. (AUSONIUS)

Such should conjugal love be, still the same, and as they are one flesh,
so should they be of one mind, as in an Aristocratical government, one
consent, Geryon-like, join in one, have one heart in two bodies, will and
nill the same. A good wife, according to Plutarch, should be as a looking-glass, to represent her husband's face and passion. If he be pleasant,
she should be merry; if he laugh, she should smile; if he look sad, she
should participate of his sorrow, and bear a part with him, and so they
should continue in mutual love one towards another:

No age shall part my love from thee, sweet wife,
Though I live Nestor or Tithonus' life. (PROPERTIUS)

And she again to him, as the Bride saluted the Bridegroom of old in
Rome, Be thou still Caius, I'll be Caia.

'Tis an happy state this indeed, when the fountain is blessed (saith
Solomon) " and he rejoiceth with the wife of his youth, and she is to
him as the loving Hind, and pleasant Roe, and he delights in her continually."

But this love of ours is immoderate, inordinate, and not to be comprehended in any bounds. It will not contain itself within the union
of marriage, or apply to one object, but is a wandering, extravagant, a
domineering, a boundless, an irrefragable, a destructive passion: sometimes this burning lust rageth after marriage, and then it is properly
called Jealousy; sometimes before, and then it is called Heroical Melancholy; it extends sometimes to corrivals, &c., begets rapes, incests,
murders: Marcus Antonius embraced his sister Faustina, Caracalla his
stepmother Julia, Nero his mother, Caligula his sisters, Cinyras his
daughter Myrrha, &c. But it is confined within no terms of blood, years,
sex, or whatsoever else. Some furiously rage before they come to discretion or age. Quartilla in Petronius never remembered she was a maid:
and the wife of Bath in Chaucer cracks,

Since I was twelve years old, believe,
*Husbands at Kirk-door had I five.**

Aretine's Lucretia sold her Maiden-head a thousand times before she was twenty-four years old, nor were those lacking who could make it whole again. Rahab that harlot began to be a professed quean at ten years of age, and was but fifteen when she hid the spies, as Hugh Broughton proves, to whom Serrarius the Jesuit subscribes. Generally women begin to sprout hair, as they call it, or yearn for a male, as Julius Pollux cites, out of Aristophanes, at fourteen years old, then they do offer themselves, and some plainly rage. Leo Afer saith, that in Africa a man shall scarce find a Maid at fourteen years of age, they are so forward, and many amongst us after they come into the teens, do not live without husbands, but linger [or sicken]. What pranks in this kind the middle age have played, is not to be recorded.

Though I spoke with an hundred tongues, with an hundred mouths,
                                       (VIRGIL)

no tongue can sufficiently declare, every story is full of men and women's insatiable lust, Neros, Heliogabaluses, Bonoses, &c. Cœlius burned for Aufilenus, Quinctius for Aufilena, &c. They neigh after other men's wives (as Jeremiah complaineth) like fed horses, or range like Town Bulls, ravishers of virginity and widowhood, as many of our great ones do. Solomon's wisdom was extinguished in this fire of lust, Samson's strength enervated, piety in Lot's daughters quite forgot, gravity of Priesthood in Eli's sons, reverend old age in the Elders that would violate Susanna, filial duty in Absalom to his stepmothers, brotherly love in Amnon towards his sister. Human, divine laws, precepts, exhortations, fear of God and men, fair, foul means, fame, fortunes, shame, disgrace, honour, cannot oppose, stave off, or withstand the fury of it, love overcomes all, &c. No cord, nor cable, can so forcibly draw, or hold so fast, as Love can do with a twin'd thread. The scorching beams under the Æquinoctial, or extremity of cold within the circle Arctick, where the very Seas are frozen, cold or torrid zone cannot avoid, or expel this heat, fury and rage of mortal men.

Why vainly seek to flee? Love will pursue you
Even as far as Scythian Tanais. (PROPERTIUS)

Of women's unnatural, unsatiable lust, what Country, what Village

---

* Quoted from memory. The lines in Chaucer are:
    For, lordinges, sith I twelf yeer was of age,
    Thonked be god that is eterne on lyve,
    Housbondes at chirche-dore I have had fyve.

doth not complain? Mother and daughter sometimes dote on the same man, father and son, master and servant on one woman.

> *What have desire and lust unbridled left*
> *Chaste and inviolate upon the earth?*　(EURIPIDES)

What breach of vows and oaths, fury, dotage, madness, might I reckon up! Yet this is more tolerable in youth, and such as are still in their hot blood; but for an old fool to dote, to see an old lecher, what more odious, what can be more absurd? and yet what so common? Who so furious?

> *Those who love in age,*
> *All the more madly rage.*　(PLAUTUS)

Some dote then more than ever they did in their youth. How many decrepit, hoary, harsh, writhen, bursten-bellied, crooked, toothless, bald, blear-eyed, impotent, rotten, old men shall you see flickering still in every place! One gets him a young wife, another a courtisan, and when he can scarce lift his leg over a sill, and hath one foot already in Charon's boat, when he hath the trembling in his joints, the gout in his feet, a perpetual rheum in his head, a continuate cough, his sight fails him, thick of hearing, his breath stinks, all his moisture is dried up and gone, may not spit from him, a very child again, that cannot dress himself, or cut his own meat, yet he will be dreaming of, and honing after wenches, what can be more unseemly? Worse it is in women than in men, when she is in her declining years, an old widow, a mother so long since (in Pliny's opinion) she doth very unseemly seek to marry, yet whilst she is so old a crone, a beldam, she can neither see, nor hear, go nor stand, a mere carcass, a witch, and scarce feel; she catterwauls, and must have a stallion, a champion, she must and will marry again, and betroth herself to some young man, that hates to look on her but for her goods, abhors the sight of her, to the prejudice of her good name, her own undoing, grief of friends, and ruin of her children.

But to enlarge or illustrate this power and effects of love is to set a candle in the Sun. It rageth with all sorts and conditions of men, yet is most evident among such as are young and lusty, in the flower of their years, nobly descended, high fed, such as live idly, and at ease; and for that cause (which our Divines call burning lust) this mad and beastly passion, as I have said, is named by our Physicians Heroical Love, and a more honourable title put upon it, Noble Love, as Savanarola styles it, because Noble men and women make a common practice of it, and are so ordinarily affected with it. Avicenna calleth this passion Ilishi, and defines it to be a disease or melancholy vexation, or anguish of mind, in which a man continually meditates of the beauty, gesture, manners of his Mistress, and troubles himself about it: desiring (as Savanarola adds) with all intentions and eagerness of mind to compass or enjoy her, as commonly Hunters trouble themselves about their sports, the covetous about their gold and goods, so is he tormented still about his Mistress. Arnoldus Villanovanus, in his book of Heroical Love, defines it a continual cogitation of that which he desires, with a confidence or hope of compassing it: which definition his Commentator cavils at. For continual cogitation is not the kind, but a symptom, of Love; we continually think of that which we hate and abhor as well as that which we love; and many things we covet and desire without all hope of attaining. Carolus à Lorme, in his Questions, makes a doubt, whether this heroical love be a disease: Julius Pollux determines it. They that are in love are likewise sick; to be lustful, lecherous, wanton, to be raging in desire, is certainly to be sick. Arnoldus will have it improperly so called, and a malady rather of the body than mind. Tully in his Tusculans defines it a furious disease of the mind, Plato madness itself, Ficinus, his Commentator, a species of madness, " for many have run mad for women," but Rhasis a melancholy passion, and most Physicians make it a species or kind of melancholy (as will appear by the Symptoms) and treat of it apart: whom I mean to imitate, and to discuss it in all his kinds, to examine his several causes, to shew his symptoms, indications, prognosticks, effects, that so it may be with more facility cured.

The part affected in the mean time, as Arnoldus supposeth, is the former part of the head for want of moisture, which his Commentator rejects. Langius will have this passion sited in the liver, and to keep residence in the heart, to proceed first from the eyes, so carried by our spirits, and kindled with imagination in the liver and heart; the liver will compel one to love, as the saying is, He will strike through the liver, as Cupid in Anacreon. For some such cause belike Homer feigns Tityus' liver (who was enamoured on Latona) to be still gnawed by two Vultures day and night in Hell, for that young men's bowels thus enamoured, are so continually tormented by love. Gordonius will have the testicles an immediate subject or cause, the liver an antecedent. Fracastorius agrees in this with Gordonius, from thence originally come the images of desire, erection, &c.; it calls for an exceeding titillation of the part, adds Guastivinus, so that until the seed is put forth there is no end of frisking voluptuousness and continual remembrance of venery. But properly it is a passion of the brain, as all other melancholy, by reason of corrupt imagination, and so doth Jason Pratensis, (who writes copiously of this Erotical love), place and reckon it amongst the affections of the brain. Melancthon confutes those that make the liver a part affected, and Guianerius, though many put all the affections in the heart, refers it to the brain. Ficinus will have the blood to be the part affected. Jo. Frietagius supposeth all four affected, heart, liver, brain, blood; but the major part concur upon the brain, 'tis an injury, a lesion of the fancy, and both imagination and reason are misaffected; because of his corrupt judgement, and continual meditation of that which he desires, he may truly be said to be melancholy. If it be violent, or his disease inveterate, as I have determined in the precedent partitions, both imagination and reason are·mis-affected, first one, then the other.

MEMBER 2

SUBSECTION 1 — *Causes of Heroical Love, Temperature, full Diet, Idleness, Place, Climate, &c.*

OF all causes the remotest are stars. Ficinus saith they are most prone to this burning lust, that have Venus in Leo in their Horoscope, when the Moon and Venus be mutually aspected, or such as be of Venus' complexion. Plutarch interprets Astrologically that tale of Mars and Venus, in whose genitures Mars and Venus are in conjunction, they are commonly lascivious, and if women, queans; as the good wife of Bath confessed in Chaucer;

> I folwed ay myn inclinacioun
> By vertu of my constellacioun.

But of all those Astrological Aphorisms which I have ever read, that of Cardan is most memorable, for which, howsoever he be bitterly censured by Marinus Marcennus, a malapert Friar, and some others (which he himself suspected), yet methinks it is free, downright, plain and ingenuous. In his eighth Geniture or example, he hath these words of himself: When Venus and Mercury are in conjunction, Mercury in the ascendant, I am so urged with thoughts of love that I cannot rest. And a little after, he saith: The thought of the pleasures of love torments me perpetually, and inasmuch as it is not permissable to find satisfaction in deed, or at least shameful, I am continually sunk in the feigned pleasures of fancy. And again he saith: Because of the mingled dominion of the Moon and Mercury, I am deeply inclined toward wantonness, given over to foul and obscene lust. ———— So far Cardan of himself, confessing what use he made of the time allotted to study, and for this he is traduced by Marcennus whenas in effect he saith no more than what Gregory Nazianzen of old to Chilo his scholar, Visionary women offered themselves to me, by their surpassing grace and marvellous beauty making trial of my chastity; and though I escaped the sin of fornication, yet in my secret heart I ravished their virgin flowers. ———— But to the point. They are more apt to masculine venery, at whose birth Venus is in a masculine sign, and Saturn in other parts of the heaven or in opposition. Ptolemy, saith his commentator Cardan, knew of these things, proved them true, and wrote of them in his Aphorisms. Thomas Campanella, in his remonstrances against amatory madness in his book of Astrology, hath collected many previous aphorisms, which who will may consult. The Chiromanticks are full of conjectures concerning the girdle of Venus, the mount of Venus, as to which teachings you may look in Taisnerus, Johan. de Indagine, Goclenius, and others, if it please you. Physicians divine wholly from the temperature and complexion; phlegmatick persons are seldom taken, according to Ficinus, naturally melancholy less than they, but once taken they are never freed; though many are of opinion flatuous or hypochondriacal melancholy are most subject of all others to this infirmity. Valescus assigns their strong imagination for a cause, Bodine abundance of wind, Gordonius of seed, and spirits, or atomi in the seed, which cause their violent and furious passions. Sanguine thence are soon caught, young folks most apt to love, and by their good wills, saith Lucian, would have a bout with every one they see: the colt's evil is common to all complexions. Theomnestus, a young and lusty gallant, acknowledgeth (in the said Author) all this to be verified in him: I am so amorously given, you may sooner number the Sea sands, and Snow falling from the skies, than my several loves. Cupid hath shot all his arrows at me, I am deluded with various desires, one love succeeds another, and that so soon, that before one is ended, I begin with a second; she that is last is still fairest, and she that is present pleaseth me most: as an Hydra's head my loves increase, no Iolaus can help me. Mine eyes are so moist a refuge and sanctuary of love, that they draw all beauties to them, and are never satisfied. I am in a doubt what fury of Venus this should be. Alas, how have I offended her so to vex me, what Hippolytus am I! What Telchin is my Genius? Or is it a natural imperfection, an hereditary passion? — Another in Anacreon confesseth that he had twenty sweet-hearts in Athens at once, fifteen at Corinth, as many at Thebes, at Lesbos, and at Rhodes, twice as many in Ionia, thrice in Caria, twenty thousand in all: or in a word, as the leaves of the forest, &c.

> *Canst count the leaves in May,*
> *Or sands i' th' ocean sea?*
> *Then count my loves I pray.*

His eyes are like a balance, apt to propend each way, and to be weighed down with every wench's looks; his heart a weathercock, his affection tinder, or naptha itself, which every fair object, sweet smile, or mistress' favour sets on fire. Guianerius refers all this to the hot temperature of the testicles; Ferandus, a Frenchman, in his Erotique Melancholy, (which book came first to my hands after the Third Edition) to certain atomi in the seed, such as are very spermatick and full of seed. I find the same in Aristotle, if they cannot be rid of the seed, they cannot stop burning, for which cause these young men that be strong set, of able bodies, are so subject to it. Hercules de Saxoniâ hath the same words in effect. But most part, I say, such are aptest to love that are young and lusty, live at ease, stall-fed, free from cares, like cattle in a rank pasture, idle and solitary persons, they must needs be goatish, as Guastavinius recites out of Censorinus.

> *The mind is apt to lust, and hot or cold,*
> *As corn luxuriates in a better mould.*   (OVID)

The place itself makes much wherein we live, the clime, air, and discipline if they concur. In our Mysia, saith Galen, near to Pergamus, thou shalt scarce find an adulterer, but many at Rome, by reason of the delights of the seat. It was that plenty of all things which made Corinth so infamous of old, and the opportunity of the place to entertain those foreign comers; every day strangers came in at each gate from all quarters. In that one Temple of Venus a thousand whores did prostitute themselves, as Strabo writes, besides Lais and the rest of better note. All nations resorted thither as to a school of Venus. Your hot and Southern countries are prone to lust, and far more incontinent than those that live in the North, as Bodine discourseth at large. The Asiaticks are amorous; so are Turks, Greeks, Spaniards, Italians, even all that latitude: and in those Tracts such as are more fruitful, plentiful, and delicious, as Valentia in Spain, Capua in Italy, a luxurious abode, Tully terms it, and (which Hannibal's soldiers can witness) Canopus in Egypt, Sybaris, Phæacia, Baiæ, Cyprus, Lampsacus. In Naples the fruits of the soil and pleasant air enervate their bodies, and alter constitutions: insomuch, that Florus calls it a contest of Bacchus and Venus, but Foliet admires it. In Italy and Spain they have their

stews in every great City, as in Rome, Venice, Florence, wherein some
say dwell ninety thousand inhabitants of which ten thousand are Courtisans; and yet for all this, every Gentleman almost hath a peculiar
Mistress; fornications, adulteries are nowhere so common: the city is
one great bawdy house; how should a man live honest among so many
provocations? now if vigour of youth, greatness, liberty I mean, and
that impunity of sin which Grandees take unto themselves in this kind
shall meet, what a gap must it needs open to all manner of vice, with
what fury will it rage! For, as Maximus Tyrius the Platonist observes,
lewdness follows wherever there is a weak disposition, and precipitate
license, and unbridled rashness, &c.; what will not lust effect in such
persons? For commonly Princes and great men make no scruple at all
of such matters, but with that whore in Spartian, they think they may
do what they list, profess it publickly, and rather brag with Proculus
(that writ to a friend of his in Rome, what famous exploits he had
done in that kind) than any way be abashed at it. Nicholas Sanders
relates of Henry the 8th (I know not how truly) he saw very few
pretty maids that he did not desire, and desired fewer whom he did
not enjoy: nothing so familiar amongst them, 'tis most of their business. Sardanapalus, Messalina, and Joan of Naples, are not comparable
to meaner men and women; Solomon of old had a thousand Concubines, Ahasuerus his Eunuchs and keepers, Nero his Tigillinus, Pandars, and Bawds, the Turks, Muscovites, Mogors, Xeriffs of Barbary,
and Persian Sophies, are no whit inferior to them in our times. The
most beautiful girls are all brought (saith Jovius) before the Emperor;
and those he leaves, the Nobles have; they press and muster up wenches
as we do soldiers, and have their choice of the rarest beauties their
countries can afford, and yet all this cannot keep them from adultery,
incest, sodomy, buggery, and such prodigious lusts. We may conclude
that, if they be young, fortunate, rich, high-fed, and idle withal, it is
almost impossible they should live honest, not rage, and precipitate
themselves into those inconveniences of burning lust.

Such idleness hath kings and thriving towns
Ere now laid in the dust. (CATULLUS)

Idleness overthrows all, in the empty heart love reigns, love tyrannizeth in an idle person. Thou dost overflow with longing, Antipho.
If thou hast nothing to do, thou shalt be haled in pieces with envy, lust,
some passion or other. Those with nothing to do find something evil to
do. 'Tis Aristotle's Simile, as match or touchwood takes fire, so doth an
idle person love. Why was Ægisthus a whoremaster? You need not ask

a reason of it. Ismenadora stole Bacho, a woman forced a man as Aurora did Cephalus: no marvel, saith Plutarch, great riches make women behave like men: she was rich, fortunate and jolly, and doth but as men do in that case, as Jupiter did by Europa, Neptune by Amyone. The Poets therefore did well to feign all Shepherds Lovers, to give themselves to songs and dalliances, because they lived such idle lives. For love, as Theophrastus defines it, is an affection of an idle mind, or as Seneca describes it, youth begets it, riot maintains it, idleness nourisheth it, &c., which makes Gordonius the Physician call this disease the proper passion of Nobility. Now if a weak judgement and a strong apprehension do concur, how, saith Hercules de Saxoniâ, shall they resist? Savanarola appropriates it almost to Monks, Friars, and religious persons, because they live solitary, fare daintily, and do nothing: and well he may, for how should they otherwise choose?

Diet alone is able to cause it: a rare thing to see a young man or a woman that lives idly, and fares well, of what condition soever, not to be in love. Alcibiades was still dallying with wanton young women, immoderate in his expenses, effeminate in his apparel, ever in love, but why? he was over-delicate in his diet, too frequent and excessive in banquets. Lust and security domineer together, as S. Hierome averreth. All which the wife of Bath in Chaucer freely justifies, —

For al so siker as cold engendrith hayl,
A likerous mouth most han a likerous tayl.

Especially if they shall further it by choice Diet, as many times those Sybarites and Phæacians do, feed liberally, and by their good will eat nothing else but lascivious meats. Noble Wine first of all, Pulse, Beans, Roots of all sorts well preserved, and liberally sprinkled with Pepper, Garden Chard, Lettuces, Rocket, Rape, Scallions, Onions, Pistachio Nuts, Sweet Almonds, Electuaries, Syrups, Broths, Snails, Oysters, Fishes, richly prepared young Fowls, the Fries or testicular parts of animals, Condiments of divers kinds, assorted Sweets, Pigeon-pies, &c. And whatsoever Physicians may prescribe to those suffering from impotency in matters of love, they have as it were an Aphrodisiack in delicacies and sumptuous repasts: in Honey mixtures, exquisite and exotick Fruits, Allspices, Cakes, Meat-broths, smoothly powerful Wine, all that the Kitchen, the Pharmacopœia and the Shops are able to offer. And having stuffed themselves with all this victual, like those who made ready for Chrysis herself [a harlot in Terence], having medicined themselves with scallions and snails, so as to be capable of addressing themselves to Venus, and exerting themselves in the lists, who would not then exceedingly rage with lust, who would not run wholly mad? Inflammation of the belly is quickly worked off in venery, Hierome saith. After benching, then comes wenching. Who can then contain himself? Immoderate drinking foments lust, saith Augustine; a smooth devil, Bernardus; the milk of venery, Aristophanes. Not Ætna, nor Vesuvius, is so fiery as young bellies full of wine, adds Hierome. That the vines might prosper, Lampsacus was of old dedicated to Priapus; and Venus listened to Bacchus as well as to Orpheus. If the wine is unmixed, and is taken by itself before food (whither is Bacchus carrying me, full of his influence?) shall we not expect fury and madness? Gomesius puts salt among those things which are wont to provoke tempests of lust, and maintains that women are made wanton through being corroded by salt: 'twas from the Ocean, they say, that Venus rose.

> Why so many harlots stray
> In Venetia every day?
> 'Tis Venus risen from the sea.　(KORNMANNUS)

And from this Ocean goddess, in a word, peradventure, from salt comes salacity. So many Bacchic disorders disgraced the loves of old time that the statues of Bacchus were discrowned. Cubebs steeped in wine are used by the East Indians to incite to venery, and the Surax root by the Africans. China roots have the same effect, and others of the sort are mentioned. Baptista Porta brought some from India, of which he and Theophrastus made mention. (These are not only eaten, but applied to the parts, that they may have as much pleasure, and as many times, as possible; some succeeding twelve, others sixty times.) A multitude of like things are in Rhasis, Matthiolus, Mizaldus, and other medicos, always with the same warning, not to meddle with these things ignorantly, but beware of the dangerous reefs of such virility, lest you be destroyed.

SUBSECTION 2 — *Other Causes of Love-Melancholy, Sight, Beauty from the Face, Eyes, other parts, and how it pierceth*

MANY such causes may be reckoned up, but they cannot avail, except opportunity be offered of time, place, and those other beautiful objects, or artificial enticements, as kissing, conference, discourse, gestures concur, with such like lascivious provocations. Kornmannus, in his book, The Outline of Love, makes five degrees of lust, out of Lucian belike, which he handles in five Chapters: Sight, Speech, Company, Kissing, Handling. Sight, of all other, is the first step of this unruly love, though sometimes it be prevented by relation or hearing, or rather incensed. For there be those so apt, credulous and facile to love, that if they hear of a proper man, or woman, they are in love before they see them, and that merely by relation, as Achilles Tatius observes. Such is their intemperance and lust, that they are as much maimed by report as if they saw them. Callisthenes, a rich young Gentleman of Byzantium in Thrace, hearing of Leucippe, Sostratus' fair daughter, was far in love with her, and out of fame and common rumour so much incensed that he would needs have her to be his wife. And sometimes by reading they are so affected, as he in Lucian confesseth of himself: I never read that place of Panthea in Xenophon, but I am as much affected as if I were present with her. Such persons commonly feign a kind of beauty to themselves; and so did those three Gentlewomen, in Balthasar Castilio, fall in love with a young man, whom they never knew, but only heard him commended: or by reading of a letter; for there is a grace cometh from hearing, as a moral Philosopher informeth us, as well as from sight; and the species [or lineaments] of love are received into the phantasy by relation alone; both senses affect. Sometimes we love those that are absent, saith Philostratus, and gives instance in his friend Athenodorus, that loved a Maid at Corinth whom he never saw; we see with the eyes of our understanding.

But the most familiar and usual cause of Love is that which comes by sight, which conveys those admirable rays of beauty and pleasing graces to the heart. Plotinus derives love from sight, Eros as if 'twere ὁρασις [seeing]. The eyes are the harbingers of love, and the first step of love is sight, as Lilius Giraldus proves at large, they as two sluices let in the influences of that divine, powerful, soul-ravishing, and captivating beauty, which, as one saith, is sharper than any dart or needle, wounds deeper into the heart, and opens a gap through our eyes to that lovely wound, which pierceth the soul itself. " Through it love is kindled like a fire." This amazing, confounding, admirable, amiable Beauty, than which in all Nature's treasure (saith Isocrates) there is nothing so majestical and sacred, nothing so divine, lovely, precious, 'tis nature's Crown, gold and glory; good if not best, and often triumphing over the best, whose power hence may be discerned: we contemn and abhor generally such things as are foul and ugly to behold, account them filthy, but love and covet that which is fair. 'Tis beauty in all things, which pleaseth and allureth us, a fair hawk, a fine garment, a goodly building, a fair house, &c. That Persian Xerxes, when he destroyed all those Temples of the Gods in Greece, caused that of Diana to be spared alone for that excellent beauty and magnificence of it. Inanimate beauty can so command. 'Tis that which Painters, Artificers, Orators, all aim at, as Erixymachus, the Physician in Plato, contends: It was beauty first that ministered occasion to art, to find out the knowledge of carving, painting, building, to find out models, perspectives, rich furnitures, and so many rare inventions. Whiteness in the Lily, red in the Rose, purple in the Violet, a lustre in all things without life, the clear light of the Moon, the bright beams of the Sun, splendour of Gold, purple, sparkling Diamond, the excellent feature of the Horse, the Majesty of the Lion, the colour of Birds, Peacocks' tails, the silver scales of Fish, we behold with singular delight and admiration. And which is rich in plants, delightful in flowers, wonderful in beasts, but most glorious in men, doth make us affect and earnestly desire it, as when we hear any sweet harmony, an eloquent tongue, see any excellent quality, curious work of man, elaborate art, or ought that is exquisite, there ariseth instantly in us a longing for the same. We love such men, but most part for comeliness of person; we call them Gods and Goddesses, divine, serene, happy, &c. And of all mortal men they alone (Calcagninus holds) are free from calumny; we backbite, wrong, hate, renowned, rich, and happy men, we repine at their felicity, they are undeserving, we think, fortune is a stepmother to us, a parent to them. We envy (saith Isocrates) wise, just, honest men, except with mutual offices and kindnesses, some good turn or other, they extort this love from us; only fair persons we love at first sight, desire their acquaintance, and adore them as so many Gods: we had rather serve them than command others, and account ourselves the more beholding to them, the more service they enjoin us; though they be otherwise vicious, unhonest, we love them, favour them, and are ready to do them any good office for their beauty's sake, though they have no other good quality beside. As that eloquent Phavorinus breaks out in Stobæus: Speak, fair youth, speak Autolycus, thy words are sweeter than Nectar; speak O Telemachus, thou art more powerful than Ulysses; speak Alcibiades, though drunk, we will willingly hear thee as thou art. — Faults in such are no faults. For when the said Alcibiades had stolen Anytus his gold and silver plate, he was so far from prosecuting so foul a fact (though every man else condemned his impudence and insolency) that he wished it had been more, and much better (he loved him dearly) for his sweet sake. No worth is eminent in such lovely persons, all imperfections hid; for hearing, sight, touch, &c., our mind and all our senses are captivated. Many men have been preferred for their person alone, chosen Kings, as amongst the Indians, Persians, Æthiopians of old; the properest man of person the country could afford was elected their Sovereign Lord; virtue seems even lovelier in a lovely body; and so have many other nations thought and done, as Curtius observes; for there is a majestical presence in such men; and so far was beauty adored amongst them, that no man was thought fit to reign that was not in all parts complete and supereminent. Archidamus, King of Lacedæmon, had like to have been deposed, because he married a little wife; they would not have their royal issue degenerate. Who would ever have thought that Adrian the Fourth, an English Monk's Bastard (as Papirius Massovius writes in his life) a poor forsaken child, should ever come to be Pope of Rome? But why was it? As he follows it out of Nubrigensis, for he " ploughs with his heifer," he was wise, learned, eloquent, of a pleasant, a promising countenance, a goodly proper man; he had, in a word, a winning look of his own, and that carried it, for that he was especially advanced. So Saul was a goodly person and a fair. Maximinus elected Emperor, &c. Branchus the son of Apollo, whom he begot of Jance, Succron's daughter, (saith Lactantius), when he kept King Admetus' Herds in Thessaly, now grown a man, was an earnest suitor to his mother to know his father; the Nymph denied him, because Apollo had conjured her to the contrary; yet, overcome by his importunity, at last she sent him to his father; when he came into Apollo's presence, kissing reverently the god's cheeks, he carried himself so well, and was so fair a young man, that Apollo was infinitely taken with the beauty of his person, he could scarce look off him, and said he was worthy of such parents, gave him a crown of gold, the spirit of Divination, and in conclusion made him a Demi-god. A Goddess beauty is, whom the very Gods adore; she is love's mistress, love's harbinger, love's loadstone, a witch, a charm, &c. Beauty is a dower of itself, a sufficient patrimony, an ample commendation, an accurate epistle, as Lucian, Apuleius, Tiraquellus, and some others conclude. Beauty deserves a Kingdom, saith Abulensis, immortality, and more have got this honour and eternity for their beauty than for all other virtues besides: and such as are fair are worthy to be honoured of God and men. That Idalian Ganymedes was therefore fetched by Jupiter into Heaven, Hephæstion dear to Alexander, Antinous to Adrian. Plato calls beauty, for that cause, a privilege of Nature, nature's master-piece, a dumb comment; Theophrastus, a silent fraud; still rhetorick, Carneades, that persuades without speech, a kingdom without a guard, because beautiful persons command as so many Captains; Socrates, a tyranny, which tyrannizeth over tyrants themselves; which made Diogenes belike call proper women Queens, because men were so obedient to their commands. They will adore, cringe, compliment, and bow to a common wench (if she be fair) as if she were a Noble woman, a Countess, a Queen, or a Goddess. Those intemperate young men of Greece erected at Delphi a golden Image, with infinite cost, to the eternal memory of Phryne the Courtisan, as Ælian relates, for she was a most beautiful woman, in so much, saith Athenæus, that Apelles and Praxiteles drew Venus' picture from her. Thus young men will adore and honour beauty: nay, Kings themselves, I say, will do it, and voluntarily submit their sovereignty to a lovely woman. "Wine is strong, Kings are strong, but a woman strongest," as Zorobabel proved at large to King Darius, his Princes and Noblemen: "Kings sit still and command Sea and Land, &c., all pay tribute to the King; but women make Kings pay tribute, and have dominion over them. When they have got gold and silver, they submit all to a beautiful woman, give themselves wholly to her, gape and gaze on her, and all men desire her more than gold or silver, or any precious thing: they will leave Father and Mother, and venture their lives for her, labour and travail to get, and bring all their gains to women, steal, fight, and spoil, for their Mistress' sakes. And no King so strong, but a fair woman is stronger than he is. All things (as he proceeds) fear to touch the King; yet I saw him, and Apame his concubine, the Daughter of the famous Bartacus, sitting on the right hand of the King, and she took the Crown off his head, and put it on her own, and struck him with her left hand; yet the King gaped and gazed on her, and when she laughed, he laughed, and when she was angry, he flattered to be reconciled to her." So beauty commands even Kings themselves; nay whole Armies and Kingdoms are captivated together with their Kings. Beauty conquers arms, loveliness takes war itself captive; we are conquered by looks, who are not conquered in battle. And 'tis a great matter, saith Xenophon, and of which all fair persons may worthily brag, that a strong man must labour for his living, if he will have ought, a valiant man must fight and endanger himself for it, a wise man speak, shew himself, and toil; but a fair and beautiful person doth all with ease, he compasseth his desire without any painstaking; God and men, Heaven and Earth, conspire to honour him; every one pities him above other, if he be in need, and all the world is willing to do him good. Chariclea fell into the hands of Pirates, but when all the rest were put to the edge of the sword, she alone was preserved for her person. When Constantinople was sacked by the Turk,

Irene escaped, and was so far from being made a captive, that she even captivated the Grand Seignior himself. So did Rosamond insult over King Henry the Second:

——————— I was so fair an object,
Whom fortune made my king, my love made subject ;
He found by proof the privilege of beauty,
That it had power to countermand all duty. (DANIEL)

It captivates the very Gods themselves, even the severest of them,

The God of Gods, for beauty's sake of old,
Became a swan, a bull, a shower of gold. (STROZA FILIUS)

And those evil spirits are taken with it, as I have already proved. The Barbarians stand in awe of a fair woman, and at a beautiful aspect a fierce spirit is pacified. For when as Troy was taken, and the wars ended (as Clemens Alexandrinus quotes out of Euripides) angry Menelaus, with rage and fury armed, came with his sword drawn to have killed Helena with his own hands, as being the sole cause of all those wars and miseries: but when he saw her fair face, as one amazed at her divine beauty, he let his weapon fall, and embraced her besides, he had no power to strike so sweet a creature. The edge of a sharp sword (as the saying is) is dulled with a beautiful aspect, and severity itself is overcome. Hyperides the Orator, when Phryne his Client was accused at Athens for her lewdness, used no other defence in her cause, but tearing her upper garment, disclosed her naked breast to the Judges, with which comeliness of her body, and amiable gesture, they were so moved and astonished, that they did acquit her forthwith, and let her go. O noble piece of Justice! mine Author exclaims, and who is he that would not rather lose his seat and robes, forfeit his office, than give sentence against the majesty of beauty? Such prerogatives have fair persons, and they alone are free from danger. Parthenopæus was so lovely and fair, that when he fought in the Theban wars, if his face had been by chance bare, no enemy would offer to strike at, or hurt him. Such immunities hath beauty; beasts themselves are moved with it. Sinalda was a woman of such excellent feature, and a Queen, that when she was to be trodden on by wild horses for a punishment, the wild beasts stood in admiration of her person (Saxo Grammaticus) and would not hurt her. Wherefore did that royal Virgin in Apuleius, when she fled from the thieves' den, in a desert, make such an Apostrophe to her Ass on whom she rode: (for what knew she to the contrary but that he was an Ass?) If you will bring me back to my parents, and my beautiful lover, what thanks shall I not owe you, what honour, what provender shall I not supply you? She would comb him, dress him, feed him, and trick him every day herself, and he should work no more, toil no more, but rest and play, &c. And besides, she would have a dainty picture drawn, in perpetual remembrance, a Virgin riding upon an Ass's back with this motto, A captured fleeing royal Virgin riding on an Ass. Why said she all this? why did she make such promises to a dumb beast? but that she perceived the poor Ass to be taken with her beauty; for he did often kiss her feet as she rid, offer to give consent as much as in him was to her delicate speeches, and besides he had some feeling, as she conceived, of her misery. And why did Theagenes' horse in Heliodorus curvet, prance, and go so proudly, but that sure, as mine Author supposeth, he was in love with his Master? A fly lighted on Malthius' cheek as he lay asleep, but why? Not to hurt him, as a parasite of his standing by well perceived, but certainly to kiss him, as ravished with his divine looks. Inanimate creatures, I suppose, have a touch of this. When a drop of Psyche's Candle fell on Cupid's shoulder, I think, sure, it was to kiss it. When Venus ran to meet her rose-cheeked Adonis, as an elegant Poet of ours sets her out,

> ———— *the bushes in the way*
> *Some catch her by the neck, some kiss her face,*
> *Some twine about her legs to make her stay,*
> *And all did covet her for to embrace.*　(SHAKESPEARE)

As Heliodorus holds, the air itself is in love: for when Hero played upon her Lute,

> *The wanton air in twenty sweet forms danc't*
> *After her fingers.*　(CHAPMAN)

And those lascivious winds staid Daphne when she fled from Apollo:

> *The winds sought to undress her, and each gust*
> *Played with her garments as in wanton lust.*　(OVID)

The wind Boreas loved Hyacinthus, and Orithyia, Erectheus' daughter of Athens; he took her away by force, as she was playing with other wenches at Ilissus, and begat Zetes and Calais his two sons of her. That seas and waters are enamoured with this our beauty is all out as likely as that of the air and winds; for when Leander swimmed in the Hellespont, Neptune with his Trident did beat down the waves, but they

> *Still mounted up, intending to have kiss'd him,*
> *And fell in drops like tears because they missed him.*　(MARLOWE)

The River Alpheus was in love with Arethusa, as she tells the tale herself,

And having with her hand wrung dry her fair green hanging hair,
The River Alphey's ancient loves she thus began to tell:
I was (quoth she) a Nymph of them that in Achaia dwell, &c.　(OVID)
When our Thames and Isis meet,
The air resounds with kisses, pale their arms
With twining grow, their necks with mutual clasps.　(LELAND)
Inachus and Peneus, and how many loving rivers can I reckon up, whom
beauty hath enthrall'd! I say nothing all this while of Idols them-
selves that have committed Idolatry in this kind, of looking glasses
that have been rapt in love (if you will believe Poets) when their
Ladies and Mistresses looked on to dress them.

　　Though I no sense at all of feeling have,
　　Yet your sweet looks do animate and save;
　　And when your speaking eyes do this way turn,
　　Methinks my wounded members live and burn.　(ANGERIANUS)
I could tell you such another story of a spindle that was fired by a fair
Lady's looks, or fingers, some say, I know not well whether, but fired it
was, by report, and of a cold bath that suddenly smoked, and was very
hot, when naked Cælia came into it,
　　We marvel why it raises such a steam, &c.
But of all the tales in this kind, that is the most memorable of Death
himself, when he should have stroken a sweet young Virgin with his
dart, he fell in love with the object. Many more such could I relate,
which are to be believed with a poetical faith. So dumb and dead
creatures dote, but men are mad, stupefied many times at the first sight
of beauty, amazed, as that fisherman in Aristænetus, that espied a
Maid bathing herself by the Sea side, —
　　From head to foot my limbs seem'd paralys'd,
　　My spirits, as in a dream, were all bound up.　(STOBÆUS)
And as Lucian, in his Images, confesseth of himself, that he was at his
Mistress' presence void of all sense, immoveable, as if he had seen a
Gorgon's head: which was no such cruel monster (as Cælius interprets
it) but the very quintessence of beauty, some fair creature, as without
doubt the Poet understood in the first fiction of it, at which the spec-
tators were amazed. Poor wretches are compelled at the very sight of
her ravishing looks to run mad, or make away themselves.
　　They wait the sentence of her scornful eyes;
　　And whom she favours lives, the other dies.　(MARLOWE)
Heliodorus brings in Thyamis almost besides himself, when he saw
Chariclea first, and not daring to look upon her a second time, for he

thought it unpossible for any man living to see her, and contain himself. The very fame of beauty will fetch them to it many miles off (such an attractive power this loadstone hath) and they will seem but short, they will undertake any toil or trouble, long journeys, Penia or Atalanta shall not overgo them, through Seas, Deserts, Mountains, and dangerous places, as they did to gaze on Psyche: many mortal men came far and near to see that glorious object of her age, as Paris for Helena, Corœbus to Troy, —

> *Who in those days had come to windy Troy,*
> *Haply through violent passion for Cassandra.*　(VIRGIL)

King John of France, once prisoner in England, came to visit his old friends again, crossing the Seas; but the truth is, his coming was to see the Countess of Salisbury, the Non-pareil of those times, and his dear Mistress. That infernal God Plutus came from Hell itself, to steal Proserpine; Achilles left all his friends for Polyxena's sake, his enemy's daughter; and all the Grecian Gods forsook their heavenly mansions for that fair Lady, Philo Dioneus daughter's sake, the Paragon of Greece in those days; so graceful was she that all the gods were rivals for her favour.

The gods are conquered by a girl's loveliness.　(JOHANNES SECUNDUS)

They will not only come to see, but as a Falconer makes an hungry Hawk hover about, follow, give attendance and service, spend goods, lives, and all their fortunes to attain;

> *Were beauty under twenty locks kept fast,*
> *Yet love breaks through, and picks them all at last.*

When fair Hero came abroad, the eyes, hearts, and affections of her spectators were still attendant on her.

> *So far above the rest fair Hero shined,*
> *And stole away the enchanted gazer's mind.*　(MARLOWE)

When Peter Aretine's Lucretia came first to Rome, and that the fame of her beauty was spread abroad, they came in (as they say) thick and threefold to see her, and hovered about her gates, as they did of old to Lais of Corinth and Phryne of Thebes, —

> *At whose doors lay all Greece.*　(PROPERTIUS)

Every man sought to get her Love, some with gallant and costly apparel, some with an affected pace, some with musick, others with rich gifts, pleasant discourse, multitude of followers; others with letters, vows, and promises, to commend themselves, and to be gracious in her eyes. Happy was he that could see her, thrice happy that enjoyed her company. Charmides in Plato was a proper young man, in comeliness

of person, and all good qualities, far exceeding others; whensoever fair
Charmides came abroad, they seemed all to be in love with him (as
Critias describes their carriage) and were troubled at the very sight of
him; many came near him, many followed him wheresoever he went:
as those lovers of beauty did Acontius, if at any time he walked abroad:
the Athenian Lasses stared on Alcibiades; Sappho and the Miletian
women on Phaon the fair. Such lovely sights do not only please, entice,
but ravish & amaze. Cleonymus, a delicate & tender youth, present at a
feast which Androcles his uncle made in the Piræus at Athens, when
he sacrificed to Mercury, so stupified the guests, Dineas, Aristippus,
Agasthenes, and the rest (as Charidemus in Lucian relates it) that they
could not eat their meat, they sate all supper time gazing, glancing at
him, stealing looks, and admiring of his beauty. Many will condemn
these men that are so enamoured for fools; but some again commend
them for it: many reject Paris' judgement, and yet Lucian approves
of it; admiring Paris for his choice; he would have done as much himself, and by good desert in his mind; beauty is to be preferred before
wealth or wisdom. Athenæus holds it not such indignity for the Trojans and Greeks to contend ten years, to spend so much labour, lose so
many men's lives for Helen's sake, for so fair a Lady's sake;

> *Such a mistress, of so surpassing beauty,*
> *Scarcely mortal.* (HOMER)

That one woman was worth a kingdom, a hundred thousand other
women, a world itself. Well might Stesichorus be blind for carping at
so fair a creature; and a just punishment it was. The same testimony
gives Homer of the old men of Troy, that were spectators of that single
combat betwixt Paris and Menelaus at the Scæan [or Western] gate;
when Helena stood in presence, they said all, the war was worthily pro-
longed and undertaken for her sake. The very gods themselves (as
Homer and Isocrates record) fought more for Helena than they did
against the Giants. When Venus lost her son Cupid, she made proclamation by Mercury, that he that could bring tidings of him should have
seven kisses; a noble reward some say; and much better than so many
golden talents; seven such kisses to many men were more precious than
seven Cities, or so many Provinces. One such a kiss alone would
recover a man if he were a dying. Great Alexander married Roxane,
a poor man's child, only for her person. 'Twas well done of Alexander,
and heroically done, I admire him for it. Orlando was mad for Angelica,
and who doth not condole his mishap? Thisbe died for Pyramus, Dido
for Æneas; who doth not weep, as (before his conversion) Austin did

in commiseration of her estate? she died for him, methinks (as he said)
I could die for her!

But this is not the matter in hand, what prerogative this Beauty
hath, of what power and sovereignty it is, and how far such persons
that so much admire, and dote upon it, are to be justified; no man
doubts of these matters; the question is how and by what means Beauty
produceth this effect? By sight: the Eye betrays the soul, and is both
Active and Passive in this business; it wounds and is wounded, is an
especial cause and instrument, both in the subject, and in the object. As
tears, it begins in the eyes, descends to the breast, it conveys these beauteous rays, as I have said, unto the heart. I saw, I was undone. Mars sees
her, and would have her at first sight. Shechem saw Dinah, the daughter
of Leah, and defiled her; Jacob [loved] Rachel, for she was beautiful
and fair: David spied Bathsheba afar off; the Elders Susanna, as that
Orthomenian Strato saw fair Aristoclea, the daughter of Theophanes,
bathing herself at that Hercyne well in Lebadea; and were captivated
in an instant. Their eyes saw, their breasts were ravaged with flames.
Amnon fell sick for Tamar's sake. The beauty of Esther was such that
she found favour, not only in the sight of Ahasuerus, " but of all those
that looked upon her." Gerson, Origen, and some others, contended
that Christ himself was the fairest of the sons of men, and Joseph next
unto him, and they will have it literally taken; his very person was
such, that he found grace and favour of all those that looked upon
him. Joseph was so fair, that as the ordinary Gloss hath it, they ran to
the top of the walls and to the windows to gaze on him, as we do commonly to see some great personage go by: and so Matthew Paris describes Matilda the Empress going through Cologne. P. Morales the
Jesuit saith as much of the Virgin Mary. Antony no sooner saw Cleopatra, but, saith Appian, he was enamoured on her. Theseus at the first
sight of Helen was so besotted, that he esteemed himself the happiest
man in the world if he might enjoy her, and to that purpose kneeled
down, and made his pathetical prayers unto the gods. Charicles, by
chance espying that curious picture of smiling Venus naked in her
Temple, stood a great while gazing, as one amazed; at length he brake
into that mad passionate speech: O fortunate God Mars, that wast
bound in chains, and made ridiculous for her sake! He could not contain himself, but kissed her picture, I know not how oft, and heartily
desired to be so disgraced as Mars was. And what did he that his Betters
had not done before him?

The other gods desire the like disgrace.   (OVID)

When Venus came first to Heaven, her comeliness was such, that (as mine Author saith) all the gods came flocking about, and saluted her. each of them went to Jupiter, and desired he might have her to be his wife. When fair Autolycus came in presence, as a candle in the dark his beauty shined, all men's eyes (as Xenophon describes the manner of it) were instantly fixed on him, and moved at the sight, insomuch that they could not conceal themselves, but in gesture or looks it was discerned and expressed. Those other senses, hearing, touching, may much penetrate and affect, but none so much, none so forcible as sight. Achilles was moved in the midst of a battle by fair Briseis, Ajax by Tecmessa: Judith captivated that great Captain Holofernes; Delilah, Samson; Rosamund, Henry the Second, Roxalana, Solyman the Magnificent, &c. A fair woman overcomes fire and sword.

> *Nought under heaven so strongly doth allure*
> *The sense of man and all his mind possess,*
> *As beauty's loveliest bait, that doth procure*
> *Great warriors oft their rigour to suppress,*
> *And mighty hands forget their manliness,*
> *Drawne with the power of an heart-robbing eye,*
> *And wrapt in fetters of a golden tress,*
> *That can with melting pleasaunce mollify*
> *Their harden'd hearts enur'd to blood and cruelty.*　　(SPENSER)

Clitiphon ingenuously confesseth that he no sooner came in Leucippe's presence, but that he did tremble at heart and looked with desirous eyes; he was wounded at the first sight, his heart panted, and he could not possibly turn his eyes from her. So doth Calasiris in Heliodorus, Isis' Priest, a reverend old man, complain, who, by chance at Memphis seeing that Thracian Rhodophis, might not hold his eyes off her: I will not conceal it, she overcame me with her presence, and quite assaulted my continency, which I had kept unto mine old age; I resisted a long time my bodily eyes with the eyes of my understanding; at last I was conquered, and as in a tempest carried headlong. ———— Xenopeithes, a Philosopher, railed at women down-right for many years together, scorned, hated, scoffed at them: coming at last into Daphnis a fair maid's company (as he condoles his mishap to his friend Demaretus) though free before, was far in love, and quite overcome upon a sudden. I confess I am taken, she, only she, has touched my feelings, and shaken my mind. I could hold out no longer. Such another mishap, but worse, had Stratocles, the Physician, that blear-eyed old man, full of snivel (so Prodromus describes him); he was a severe woman-hater all

his life, a bitter persecutor of the whole sex, he called them asps and
vipers, he forswore them all still, and mocked them wheresoever he
came, in such vile terms, that, if thou hadst heard him, thou wouldest
have loathed thine own Mother and Sisters for his words' sake. Yet this
old doting fool was taken at last with that celestial and divine look of
Myrilla, the daughter of Anticles the gardener, that smirking wench,
that he shaved off his bushy beard, painted his face, curl'd his hair, wore
a Laurel Crown to cover his bald pate, and for her love besides was
ready to run mad. For the very day that he married, he was so furious,
(a terrible, a monstrous long day), he could not stay till it was night,
but, the meat scarce out of his mouth, without any leave taking, he
would needs go presently to bed. What young man therefore, if old men
be so intemperate, can secure himself? Who can say, I will not be
taken with a beautiful object, I can, I will contain? No, saith Lucian
of his Mistress, she is so fair, that if thou dost but see her, she will
stupify thee, kill thee straight, and, Medusa like, turn thee to a stone,
thou canst not pull thine eyes from her, but as an adamant doth iron;
she will carry thee bound headlong whither she will herself, infect thee
like a Basilisk. It holds both in men and women. Dido was amazed at
Æneas' presence: and, as he feelingly verified out of his experience,

> *I lov'd her not as others, soberly,*
>
>   *But as a madman rageth, so did I.*   (PLAUTUS)

So Musæus of Leander, he never takes his eyes from her; and Chaucer
of Palamon:

> *He caste his eyen upon Emelia,*
> *And therewithal he blent and cryed ah!*
> *As though he stongen were unto the herte.*

If you desire to know more particularly what this Beauty is, how it
doth influence, how it doth fascinate (for as all hold love is a fascination) thus in brief. This comeliness or beauty ariseth from the due
proportion of the whole, or from each several part. For an exact delinea-
tion of which, I refer you to Poets, Historiographers, and those amorous
Writers, to Lucian's Images and Charidemus, Xenophon's description
of Panthea, Petronius' Catalects, Heliodorus' Chariclea, Tatius' Leucippe, Longus Sophista's Daphnis and Chloe, Theodorus Prodromus
his Rhodanthe, Aristænetus' and Philostratus' Epistles, Balthasar Castilio, Laurentius, Æneas Sylvius his Lucretia, and every Poet almost,
which have most accurately described a perfect beauty, an absolute
feature, and that through every member, both in men and women. Each
part must concur to the perfection of it; for as Seneca saith, she is no

fair woman, whose arm, thigh, &c., are commended, except the face
and all the other parts be correspondent. And the face especially gives
a lustre to the rest: the Face is it that commonly denominates fair or
foul; the Face is Beauty's Tower; and though the other parts be deformed, yet a good face carries it, (the face and not the wife is loved),
that alone is most part respected, principally valued, and of itself able
to captivate.

Glycera's face, too fair to see!   (HORACE)

Glycera's too fair a face was it that set him on fire, too fine to be
beheld. When Chærea saw the singing wench's sweet looks, he was so
taken, that he cried out, O fair face, I'll never love any but her, look
on any other hereafter but her, I am weary of these ordinary beauties,
away with them. The more he sees her, the worse he is; the sight burns,
as in a burning-glass the Sun beams are recollected to a centre, the rays
of Love are projected from her eyes. It was Æneas' countenance
ravished Queen Dido, he had an Angelical face.

O sacred looks, befitting Majesty,
Which never mortal wight could safely see.   (PETRONIUS)

Although for the greater part this beauty be most eminent in the face,
yet many times those other members yield a most pleasing grace, and
are alone sufficient to enamour. An high brow like unto the bright heavens, white and smooth like the polished Alabaster; a pair of cheeks of
Vermilion colour, in which Love lodgeth; Love that basks all night on
a girl's soft cheeks; a coral lip, temple of delights, in which

A thousand kisses shalt thou find,
Yet still a thousand lurk behind,

the most pleasant seat of the graces, a sweet-smelling flower, from
which Bees may gather honey, a dell of thyme and roses, &c.

Come, bees, to my lady's lips,
There roses breathe, &c.   (JOHANNES SECUNDUS)

A white and round neck, that Milky Way, dimple in the chin, black
eyebrows, Cupid's bows, sweet breath, white and even teeth, which some
call the sale-piece, a fine soft round pap, gives an excellent grace,

What splendour of swelling breasts, as of Parian marble!   (LOCHÆUS)

and makes a pleasant valley, a milky vale, between two chalky hills,
sisterly little breasts, snowy companions, that merely to see them arouse
desire,

Beautiful breasts made perfect for caresses,   (OVID)

again

Those calm unyielding breasts inflame the sight.

A flaxen hair; golden hair was ever in great account, for which Virgil commends Dido,

> *Not yet had Proserpine clipped her golden hair,*   (VIRGIL)

and

> *All her yellow hair bound up in gold.*   (VIRGIL)

Apollonius will have Jason's golden hair to be the main cause of Medea's dotage on him. Castor and Pollux were both yellow-hair'd; Paris, Menelaus, and most amorous young men have been such in all ages, smooth and sweet, as Baptista Porta infers, lovely to behold. Homer so commends Helena, makes Patroclus and Achilles both yellow-hair'd: lovely-hair'd Venus, and Cupid himself, was yellow-hair'd, with crisp hair glittering like gold, like that neat picture of Narcissus in Callistratus; for so Psyche spied him asleep; Briseis, Polyxena, were all yellow-hair'd,

> ——— *and Hero the fair,*
>
> *Whom young Apollo courted for her hair.*   (MARLOWE)

Leland commends Guithera, King Arthur's wife, for a fair flaxen hair; so Paulus Æmilius sets out Clodoveus, that lovely King of France. Synesius holds every effeminate fellow or adulterer is fair hair'd: & Apuleius adds that Venus herself, Goddess of Love, cannot delight, though she come accompanied with the Graces, and all Cupid's train to attend upon her, girt with her own girdle, and smell of Cinnamon and Balm, yet if she be bald or bad hair'd, she cannot please her Vulcan. Which belike makes our Venetian Ladies at this day to counterfeit yellow hair so much, great women to calamistrate [with a curling-iron] and curl it up, with that glitter to take all captive, to adorn their head with spangles, pearls, and made flowers, and all Courtiers to affect a pleasing grace in this kind. In a word, the hairs are Cupid's nets, to catch all comers, a brushy wood, in which Cupid builds his nest, and under whose shadow all Loves a thousand several ways sport themselves.

A little soft hand, pretty little mouth, small, fine, long fingers, 'tis that which Apollo did admire in Daphne; a straight and slender body, a small foot, and well proportioned leg, hath an excellent lustre, bearing the body like the foundation of a temple. Clearchus vowed to his friend Amynander, in Aristænetus, that the most attractive part in his Mistress, to make him love and like her first, was her pretty leg and foot; a soft and white skin, &c., have their peculiar graces, a cloud is not softer, by Pollux, than the surface of her lovely breasts. Though in men these parts are not so much respected; a grim Saracen sometimes, a Pyracmon with naked limbs, a martial hirsute face pleaseth best; a black man is a pearl in a fair woman's eye, and is as acceptable as lame Vulcan was to Venus; for he being a sweaty fuliginous blacksmith, was dearly beloved of her, when fair Apollo, nimble Mercury, were rejected, and the rest of the sweet-fac'd gods forsaken. Many women (as Petronius observes) are hot after dirty ones, (as many men are more moved with kitchen-wenches, and a poor market-maid, than all these illustrious Court and City Dames) will sooner dote upon a slave, a servant, a Dirt-dauber, a Blacksmith, a Cook, a Player, if they see his naked legs or brawny arms, like that Huntsman Meleager in Philostratus, though he be all in rags, obscene and dirty, besmeared like a ruddle-man, [or digger of red clay], a gipsy, or a chimney-sweeper, than upon a Noble Gallant, Nireus, Hephæstion, Alcibiades, or those embroidered Courtiers full of silk and gold. Justine's wife, a Citizen of Rome, fell in love with Pylades, a Player, and was ready to run mad for him, had not Galen himself helped her by chance. Faustina the Empress doted on a Fencer.

Not one of a thousand falls in love, but there is some peculiar part or other which pleaseth most, and inflames him above the rest. A company of young Philosophers on a time fell at variance, which part of a woman was most desirable, and pleased best? some said the forehead, some the teeth, some the eyes, cheeks, lip, neck, chin, &c., the controversy was referred to Lais of Corinth to decide; but she, smiling, said they were a company of fools; for suppose they had her where they wished, what would they first seek? Yet, this notwithstanding, I do easily grant, nor, I think, would any of you contradict me, all parts are attractive, but especially the eyes, — sparkling and bright as stars, — which are Love's Fowlers; the shoeing-horns, the hooks of Love (as Arandus will) the guides, touchstone, judges, that in a moment cure mad men, and make sound folks mad, the watchmen of the body; what do they not? How vex they not? All this is true, and (which Athæneus and Tatius hold) they are the chief seats of Love, and as James Lernutius hath facetely expressed in an elegant Ode of his, —

> I saw Love sitting in my mistress' eyes
>   Sparkling, believe it, all posterity,
> And his attendants playing round about,
>   With bow and arrows ready for to fly.

Scaliger calls the eyes, Cupid's arrows; the tongue, the lightning of Love; the paps, the tents: Balthasar Castilio, the causes, the chariots, the lamps of Love,

> *Eyes emulating stars in light,*
> *Enticing gods at the first sight ;*

Love's Orators, Petronius.

> *O sweet and pretty speaking eyes,*
> *Where Venus, love, and pleasure lies.*

Love's Torches, Touch-box, Naptha, and Matches, Tibullus.

> *Tart Love, when he will set the gods on fire.*
> *Lightens the eyes as torches to desire.*

Leander, at the first sight of Hero's eyes, was incensed, saith Musæus.

> *Love's torches 'gan to burn first in her eyes,*
> *And set his heart on fire which never dies:*
> *For the fair beauty of a virgin pure*
> *Is sharper than a dart, and doth inure*
> *A deeper wound, which pierceth to the heart,*
> *By the eyes, and causeth such a cruel smart.*

A modern Poet brings in Amnon complaining of Tamar, —

> *It was thy beauty, 'twas thy pleasing smile,*
> *Thy grace and comeliness did me beguile ;*
> *Thy rose-like cheeks, and unto purple fair,*
> *Thy lovely eyes and golden knotted hair.* (JACOB CORNELIUS)

Philostratus Lemnius cries out on his Mistress' Basilisk eyes, those two burning-glasses, they had so inflamed his soul, that no water could quench it. What a tyranny (saith he) what a penetration of bodies is this! thou drawest with violence, and swallowest me up, as Charybdis doth Sailors, with thy rocky eyes; he that falls into this gulf of Love, can never get out. — Let this be the Corollary then, the strongest beams of beauty are still darted from the eyes.

> *For who such eyes with his can see,*
> *And not forthwith enamoured be?* (LOECHÆUS)

And as men catch dotterels [or plovers], by putting out a leg or an arm, with those mutual glances of the eyes they first inveigle one another.

> *'Twas Cynthia's eyes that first ensnared poor me.* (PROPERTIUS)

Of all eyes, (by the way), black are most amiable, enticing, and fairer, which the Poet observes in commending of his Mistress.

> *Wonderful black eyes and jet-black hair,*

which Hesiod admires in his Alcmena,

> *From her black eyes, and from her golden face:*
> *As if from Venus, came a lovely grace.*

and Triton in his Milane —

> *My black-eyed beauty.*

Homer useth that Epithet of Ox-eyed, in describing Juno, because a round black eye is the best, the Sun of Beauty, and farthest from black the worse: which Polydore Virgil taxeth in our Nation; we have grey eyes for the most part. Baptista Porta puts grey colour upon children. they be childish eyes, dull and heavy. Many commend on the other side Spanish Ladies, and those Greek Dames at this day, for the blackness of their eyes, as Porta doth his Neapolitan young wives. Suetonius describes Julius Cæsar to have been of a black quick sparkling eye: and although Averroes, in his Colliget, will have such persons timorous, yet without question they are most amorous.

Now, last of all, I will shew you by what means beauty doth fascinate, bewitch, as some hold, and work upon the soul of a man by the eye. For certainly I am of the Poet's mind, Love doth bewitch, and strangely change us.

> Love mocks our senses, curbs our liberties,
> And doth bewitch us with his art and rings,
> I think some devil gets into our entrails,
> And kindles coals, and heaves our souls from th' hinges.

Heliodorus proves at large that Love is witchcraft, it gets in at our eyes, pores, nostrils, ingenders the same qualities, and affections in us, as were in the party whence it came. The manner of the fascination, as Ficinus declares it, is thus: Mortal men are then especially bewitched, when as by often gazing one on the other, they direct sight to sight, join eye to eye, and so drink and suck in Love between them; for the beginning of this disease is the Eye; and therefore he that hath a clear Eye, though he be otherwise deformed, by often looking upon him, will make one mad, and tie him fast to him by the eye. — Leonard. Varius telleth us, that by this interview, the purer spirits are infected, the one Eye pierceth through the other with his rays, which he sends forth, and many men have those excellent piercing eyes, that, which Suetonius relates of Augustus, their brightness is such, they compel their spectators to look off, and can no more endure them than the Sun beams. Barradius reports as much of our Saviour Christ, and Peter Morales of the Virgin Mary, whom Nicephorus describes likewise to have been yellow-hair'd, of a wheat colour, but of a most amiable and piercing eye. The rays, as some think, sent from the eyes, carry certain spiritual vapours with them, and so infect the other party, and that in a moment. I know, they that hold that sight goes inward, will make a doubt of this; but Ficinus proves it from blear-eyes, that by sight alone, make others blear-eyed: and it is more than manifest, that the vapour of the corrupt blood doth get in together with the rays, and so by the contagion the spectators' eyes are infected. Other arguments there are of a Basilisk, that kills afar off by sight, as that Ephesian did of whom Philostratus speaks, of so pernicious an eye, he poisoned all he looked steadily on: and that other argument, of menstruous women, out of Aristotle's Problems: full of disease, Capivaccius adds, and Septalius the Commentator, that contaminate a looking-glass with beholding it. So the beams that come from the Agent's heart, by the eyes infect the spirits about the patients, inwardly wound, and thence the spirits infect the blood. To this effect she complained in Apuleius, Thou art the cause of my grief, thy eyes piercing through mine eyes to mine inner parts, have set my bowels on fire, and therefore pity me that am now ready to die for thy sake. Ficinus illustrates this with a familiar example of that Marrhusian Phædrus and Theban Lycias: Lycias he stares on Phædrus' face, and Phædrus fastens the balls of his eyes upon Lycias, and with those sparkling rays sends out his spirits. The beams of Phædrus' eyes are easily mingled with the beams of Lycias', and spirits are joined to spirits. This vapour begot in Phædrus' heart, enters into Lycias' bowels: and that which is a greater wonder, Phædrus' blood is in Lycias' heart, and thence come those ordinary love speeches, my sweetheart Phædrus, and mine own self, my dear bowels! And Phædrus again to Lycias, O my light, my joy, my soul, my life! Phædrus follows Lycias, because his heart would have his spirits; and Lycias follows Phædrus, because he loves the seat of his spirits; both follow, but Lycias the earnester of the two: the river hath more need of the fountain than the fountain of the river; as iron is drawn to that which is touched with a loadstone, but draws not it again: so Lycias draws Phædrus. But how comes it to pass then, that the blind man loves, that never saw? We read, in the Lives of the Fathers, a story of a child that was brought up in the wilderness, from his infancy, by an old Hermit: now come to man's estate, he saw by chance two comely women wandering in the woods: he asked the old man what creatures they were, he told him Fairies; after awhile talking casually, the Hermit demanded of him, which was the pleasantest sight that ever he saw in his life? he readily replied, the two Fairies he spied in the wilderness. So that, without doubt, there is some secret loadstone in a beautiful woman, a magnetick power, a natural inbred affection, which moves our concupiscence, as he sings,

Methinks I have a mistress yet to come,
And still I seek, I love, I know not whom.

'Tis true indeed of natural and chaste love, but not of this Heroical passion, or rather brutish burning lust of which we treat; we speak of wandering, wanton, adulterous eyes, which, as he saith, lie still in wait, as so many soldiers, and when they spy an innocent spectator fixed on them, shoot him through, and presently bewitch him: especially when they shall gaze and gloat, as wanton lovers do one upon another, and with a pleasant eye-conflict participate each other's souls. Hence you may perceive how easily, and how quickly, we may be taken in love, since at the twinkling of an eye Phædrus' spirits may so perniciously infect Lycias' blood. Neither is it any wonder, if we but consider how many other diseases closely and as suddenly, are caught by infection, Plague, Itch, Scabs, Flux, &c. The spirits taken in, will not let him rest that hath received them, but egg him on.

And the mind seeks the body whence came the love-wound.

(LUCRETIUS)

And we may manifestly perceive a strange eduction of spirits, by such as bleed at nose after they be dead, at the presence of their murderer; but read more of this in Lemnius, Valleriola, Valesius against Ficinus, Cardan, Libanius, &c.

SUBSECTION 3 — *Artificial Allurements of Love, Causes and Provocations to Lust, Gestures, Clothes, Dower, &c.*

NATURAL Beauty is a strong loadstone of itself, as you have heard, a great temptation, and pierceth to the very heart; a girl's modest beauty wounds my sight; but much more when those artificial enticements and provocations of Gestures, Clothes, Jewels, Pigments, Exornations, shall be annexed unto it; those other circumstances, opportunity of time and place, shall concur, which of themselves alone were all sufficient, each one in particular, to produce this effect. It is a question much controverted by some wise men, whether natural or artificial objects be more powerful? but not decided: for my part, I am of opinion, that, though Beauty itself be a great motive, and give an excellent lustre in beggary, as a Jewel on a dunghill will shine, and cast his rays, it cannot be suppressed, which Heliodorus feigns of Chariclea, though she were in beggar's weeds: yet, as it is used, artificial is of more force, and much to be preferred.

> *So toothless Ægle seems a pretty one,*
> *Set out with new-bought teeth of Indy bone:*
> *So foul Lycoris blacker than berry*
> *Herself admires, now finer than cherry.*   (MARTIAL)

John Lerius the Burgundian is altogether on my side. For whereas (saith he) at our coming to Brasil, we found both men and women naked as they were born, without any covering, so much as of their privities, and could not be persuaded, by our Frenchmen that lived a year with them, to wear any; many will think [saith he] that our so long commerce with naked women must needs be a great provocation to lust: but he concludes otherwise, that their nakedness did much less entice them to lasciviousness, than our women's clothes. And I dare boldly affirm (saith he) that those glittering attires, counterfeit colours, headgears, curled hairs, plaited coats, cloaks, gowns, costly stomachers, guarded and loose garments, and all those other accoutrements, wherewith our country-women counterfeit a beauty, and so curiously set out themselves, cause more inconvenience in this kind, than that barbarian homeliness, although they be no whit inferior unto them in beauty. I could evince the truth of this by many other arguments, but I appeal (saith he) to my companions at that present, which were all of the same mind. — His country-man Montaigne, in his Essays, is of the same opinion, and so are many others; out of whose assertions thus much in brief we may conclude: that beauty is more beholding to Art than Nature, and stronger provocations proceed from outward ornaments, than such as nature hath provided. It is true, that those fair sparkling eyes, white neck, coral lips, turgent paps, rose-coloured cheeks, &c., of themselves are potent enticers; but when a comely, artificial, well-composed look, pleasing gesture, an affected carriage shall be added, it must needs be far more forcible than it was, when those curious needle-works, variety of colours, purest dyes, jewels, spangles, pendants, lawn, lace, tiffanies, fair and fine linen, embroideries, calamistrations [or hair-curlings], ointments, &c., shall be added, they will make the veriest dowdy otherwise a Goddess, when nature shall be furthered by Art. For it is not the eye of itself that enticeth to lust, but an " adulterous eye," as Peter terms it, a wanton, a rolling, lascivious eye: a wandering eye, which Isaiah taxeth. Christ himself and the Virgin Mary had most beautiful eyes, as amiable eyes as any persons, saith Barzadius, that ever lived, but withal so modest, so chaste, that whosoever looked on them, was freed from that passion of burning lust; if we may believe Gerson and Bonaventure, there was no such Antidote against it, as the Virgin Mary's face. 'Tis not the eye, but carriage of it, as they use it, that causeth such effects. When Pallas, Juno, Venus, were to win Paris' favour for the golden Apple, as it is elegantly described in that pleasant interlude of Apuleius, Juno came with majesty upon the stage, Minerva with gravity, but Venus came in smiling with her gracious graces, and exquisite musick, as if she had danced, and which was the main matter of all, she danced with her rolling eyes: they were the Brokers and Harbingers of her suit. So she makes her brags in a modern Poet,

> Soon could I make my brow to tyrannise,
> And force the world do homage to mine eyes.   (DANIEL)

The eye is a secret Orator, the first bawd, the gateway of love, and with private looks, winking, glances and smiles, as so many dialogues, they make up the match many times, and understand one another's meanings, before they come to speak a word. Euryalus and Lucretia were so mutually enamoured by the eye, and prepared to give each other entertainment, before ever they had conference: he asked her good will with his eye; she did favour him, and gave consent with a pleasant look. That Thracian Rhodopis was so excellent at this dumb Rhetorick, that if she had but looked upon any one almost (saith Calasiris) she would have bewitched him, and he could not possibly escape it. For, as Salvianus observes, the eyes are the windows of our souls, by which as so many channels, all dishonest concupiscence gets into our hearts. They reveal our thoughts, and as they say, the face is the index of the mind, but the eye of the countenance, —

> Why look upon me with such wanton eyes?   (BUCHANAN)

I may say the same of smiling, gait, nakedness of parts, plausible gestures, &c. To laugh is the proper passion of a man, an ordinary thing to smile, but those counterfeit, composed, affected, artificial, and reciprocal, those counter-smiles are the dumb shews and prognosticks of greater matters, which they most part use, to inveigle and deceive; though many fond lovers again are so frequently mistaken, and led into a fool's paradise. For if they see but a fair Maid laugh, or shew a pleasant countenance, use some gracious words or gestures, they apply it all to themselves, as done in their favour, sure she loves them, she is willing, coming, &c.

> When a fool sees a fair maid for to smile,
> He thinks she loves him, 'tis but to beguile.

They make an Art of it, as the Poet telleth us,

> Who can believe? to laugh maids make an art,
> And seek a pleasant grace to that same part.   (OVID)

And 'tis as great an enticement as any of the rest. She makes thine heart leap with a pleasing gentle smile of hers. I love Lalage as much for smiling, as for discoursing; 'Twas delightful, as he said in Petronius of his Mistress, being well pleased, she gave so sweet a smile. It won

Ismenias, as he confesseth, Ismene smiled so lovingly the second time I saw her, that I could not choose but admire her: and Galla's sweet smile quite overcame Faustus the Shepherd. All other gestures of the body will enforce as much. Daphnis in Lucian was a poor tattered wench, when I knew her first, said Crobyle, but now she is a stately piece indeed, hath her Maids to attend her, brave attires, money in her purse, &c., and will you know how this came to pass? by setting out herself after the best fashion, by her pleasant carriage, affability, sweet smiling upon all, &c. Many women dote upon a man for his compliment only, and good behaviour, they are won in an instant; too credulous to believe that every light, wanton suitor, who sees or makes love to them, is instantly enamoured, he certainly dotes on, admires them, will surely marry, when as he means nothing less, 'tis his ordinary carriage in all such companies. So both delude each other, by such outward shews, and amongst the rest, an upright, a comely grace, courtesies, gentle salutations, cringes, a mincing gate, a decent and an affected pace, are most powerful enticers, and which the Prophet Esay, a Courtier himself, and a great observer, objected to the daughters of Sion, " they minced as they went, and made a tinkling with their feet." To say the truth, what can they not effect by such means?

> *Whilst nature decks them in their best attires*
> *Of youth and beauty which the world admires.*

She sets you all afire with her voice, her hand, her walk, her breast, her face, her eyes. When Art shall be annexed to Beauty, when wiles and guiles shall concur: for to speak as it is, Love is a kind of legerdemain, mere juggling, a fascination. When they shew their fair hand, fine foot and leg withal, saith Balthazar Castilio, they set us a longing, and so when they pull up their petticoats, and outward garments, as usually they do to shew their fine stockings, and those of purest silken dye, gold fringes, laces, embroiderings, (it shall go hard but when they go to Church, or to any other place, all shall be seen) 'tis but a springe to catch woodcocks; and as Chrysostom telleth them down-right, though they say nothing with their mouths, they speak in their gate, they speak with their eyes, they speak in the carriage of their bodies. And what shall we say otherwise of that baring of their necks, shoulders, naked breasts, arms and wrists, to what end are they but only to tempt men to lust?

> *Pray, why display those milk-white breasts and paps*
> *Without the modesty-piece? 'Tis but to say,*
> *" Ask me, and I surrender;" 'tis but to*
> *Invite your lovers to the field of Love.*   (JOVIANUS PONTANUS)

There needs no more, as Fredericus Matenesius well observes, but a
Crier to go before them so dressed, to bid us look out, a trumpet to
sound, or for defect, a sow-gelder to blow, —

> *Look out, look out and see*
> *What object this may be*
> *That doth perstringe mine eye;*
> *A gallant lady goes*
> *In rich and gaudy clothes,*
> *But whither away God knows,**

or to what end and purpose? But to leave all these phantastical raptures,
I'll prosecute mine intended Theme. Nakedness, as I have said, is an
odious thing of itself, an antidote to love, yet it may be so used, in part,
and at set times, that there can be no such enticement as it is:

> *Chaste Diana, and naked Venus, neither is quite to my mind,*
> *The one has nothing wanton about her, the other too much, I find.*
>
> (AUSONIUS)

David so espied Bathsheba, the Elders Susanna; Apelles was enamoured
with Campaspe, when he was to paint her naked. Tiberius supped with
Sestius Gallus, an old lecher, waited on by naked girls; some say as
much of Nero, and Pontus Heuter of Carolus Pugnax. Amongst the
Babylonians, it was the custom of some lascivious queans to dance frisking in that fashion, saith Curtius, and Sardus writes of others to that
effect. The Tuscans, at some set banquets, had naked women to attend
upon them, which Leonicus confirms of such other bawdy nations. Nero
would have filthy pictures still hanging in his chamber, which is too
commonly used in our times; and Heliogabalus had others perform
Venus in his presence that he might be aroused to the same. So things
may be abused. A servant maid in Aristænetus spied her Master and
Mistress through the key-hole merrily disposed; upon the sight she fell
in love with her Master. Antoninus Caracalla observed his mother-in-
law with her breasts amorously laid open, he was so much moved, that
he said, Oh that I might! which she by chance over-hearing, replied as
impudently, Thou mayest do what thou wilt. And upon that temptation
he married her: this object was not in cause, not the thing itself, but that
unseemly, undecent carriage of it.

When you have all done, the greatest provocations of lust are from
our apparel; God makes, they say, man shapes, and there is no motive
like unto it;

> *Which doth even beauty beautify,*
> *And most bewitch a wretched eye.*   (SIDNEY)

* If you can tell how, you may sing this to the tune a sow-gelder blows. — B's
note.

A filthy knave, a deformed quean, a crooked carkass, a maukin, a witch, a rotten post, an hedge-stake, may be so set out, and tricked up, that it shall make as fair a shew, as much enamour as the rest: many a silly fellow is so taken. One calls it the first snare of lust; Bossus, a fatal reed; the greatest bawd, saith Matenesius, and with tears of blood to be deplored. Not that comeliness of clothes is therefore to be condemned, and those usual ornaments: there is a decency and decorum in this, as well as in other things, fit to be used, becoming several persons, and befitting their estates; he is only phantastical, that is not in fashion, and like an old Image in Arras hangings, when a manner of Attire is generally received: but when they are so new-fangled, so unstaid, so prodigious in their Attires, beyond their means and fortunes, unbefitting their age, place, quality, condition, what should we otherwise think of them? Why do they adorn themselves with so many colours of herbs, fictitious flowers, curious needleworks, quaint devices, sweet-smelling odours, with those inestimable riches of precious stones, pearls, rubies, diamonds, emeralds, &c.? Why do they crown themselves with gold and silver, use coronets, and tires of several fashions, deck themselves with pendants, bracelets, ear-rings, chains, girdles, rings, pins, spangles, embroideries, shadows, rabatoes [or turned-down collars], versicolour ribbands? Why do they make such glorious shews with their scarfs, feathers, fans, masks, furs, laces, tiffanies, ruffs, falls, cauls [or hair-nets], cuffs, damasks, velvets, tinsels, cloth of gold, silver, tissue? with colours of heavens, stars, planets? the strength of metals, stones, odours, flowers, birds, beasts, fishes, and whatsoever Africa, Asia, America, sea, land, art, and industry of man can afford? Why do they use and covet such novelty of inventions, such new-fangled tires, and spend such inestimable sums on them? To what end are those crisped, false hairs, painted faces, as the Satirist observes, such a composed gate, not a step awry? Why are they like so many Sybarites, or Nero's Poppæa, Ahasuerus' Concubines, so costly, so long a dressing as Cæsar was marshalling his army, or an hawk in pruning? They take a year to trim and comb themselves; a gardener takes not so much delight and pains in his garden, an horseman to dress his horse, scour his armour, a mariner about his ship, a merchant his shop and shop-book, as they do about their faces, and all those other parts: such setting up with corks, straightening with whalebones, why is it but, as a day-net catcheth Larks, to make young men stoop unto them? Philocharus, a gallant in Aristænetus, advised his friend Polyænus to take heed of such enticements, for it was the sweet sound and motion of his Mistress' spangles and bracelets, the smell of her ointments, that captivated him first. Saith Lucian, to what use are pins, pots, glasses, ointments, irons, combs, bodkins, setting-sticks? Why bestow they all their patrimonies and husbands' yearly revenues on such fooleries? why use they dragons, wasps, snakes, for chains, enamelled jewels on their necks, ears? They had more need some of them be tied in Bedlam with iron chains, have a whip for a fan, and haircloths next to their skins, and instead of wrought smocks, have their cheeks stigmatised with a hot iron: I say, some of our Jezebels instead of painting, if they were well served. But why is all this labour, all this cost, preparation, riding, running, far-fetched, and dear bought stuff? Because forsooth they would be fair and fine, and where nature is defective, supply it by art.

> *Who blushes not by nature, doth by art,*   (OVID)

and to that purpose they anoint and paint their faces, to make Helen of Hecuba — a distorted dwarf an Europa. To this intent they crush in their feet and bodies, hurt and crucify themselves, some in lax clothes, an hundred yards I think in a gown, a sleeve; and sometimes again so close, as to show their naked shape. Now long tails and trains, and then short, up, down, high, low, thick, thin, &c., now little or no bands, then as big as cart wheels; now loose bodies, then great fardingales and close girt, &c. Why is all this, but with the whore in the Proverbs, to intoxicate some or other? A snare for the eyes, one therefore calls it, and the trap of lust, and sure token, as an Ivy-bush is to a Tavern.

> *O Glycere, in that you paint so much,*
> *Your hair is so bedeckt in order such,*
> *With rings on fingers, bracelets in your ear,*
> *Although no prophet, tell I can, I fear.*

To be admired, to be gazed on, to circumvent some novice, as many times they do, that instead of a Lady he loves a cap and a feather, instead of a maid that should have true color, a solid body, and plenty of juice, (as Chærea describes his mistress in the Poet), a painted face, a ruff-band, fair and fine linen, a coronet, a flower.

> *He thinks that nature which is due to art,*   (STROZA, FILIUS)

a wrought waistcoat he dotes on, or a pied petticoat, a pure dye instead of a proper woman. For generally, as with rich furred Conies, their cases are far better than their bodies, and like the bark of a Cinnamon tree which is dearer than the whole bulk, their outward accoutrements are far more precious than their inward endowments. 'Tis too commonly so.

> *With gold and jewels all is covered,*
> *And with a strange tire we are won,*
> *(While she's the least part of herself),*
> *And with such baubles quite undone.*   (OVID)

Why do they keep in so long together, a whole winter sometimes, and will not be seen but by torch or candle-light. and come abroad with all the preparation may be, when they have no business, but only to shew themselves?

> *They come to see, and to be seen, forsooth.*   (OVID)
> *For what is beauty if it be not seen.*
> *Or what is't to be seen, if not admir'd.*
> *And though admir'd, unless in love desir'd?*   (DANIEL)

Why do they go with such counterfeit gait. which Philo Judæus reprehends them for, and use (I say it again) such gestures, apish, ridiculous, undecent Attires, Sybaritical tricks. use those sweet perfumes, powders, and ointments, in publick, flock to hear sermons so frequent, is it for devotion? or rather, as Basil tells them, to meet their sweethearts, and see fashion; for, as he saith, commonly they come so provided to that place, with such curious compliments, with such gestures and tires, as if they should go to a dancing-school, a stage-play, or bawdy-house, fitter than a Church,

> *When such a she-priest comes her mass to say,*
> *Twenty to one they all forget to pray.*   (DRAYTON)

They make those holy Temples consecrated to godly Martyrs, and religious uses, the shops of impudence, dens of whores and thieves, and little better than brothel-houses. When we shall see these things daily done, their husbands bankrupts, if not cornutos, their wives light huswives, daughters dishonest; and hear of such dissolute acts, as daily we do, how should we think otherwise? what is their end, but to deceive and inveigle young men? As tow takes fire, such enticing objects produce their effect, how can it be altered? When Venus stood before Anchises (as Homer feigns in one of his Hymns) in her costly robes, he was instantly taken, —

> *When Venus stood before Anchises first,*
> *He was amazed to see her in her tires ;*
> *For she had on a hood as red as fire,*
> *And glittering chains, and ivy-twisted spires,*
> *About her tender neck were costly brooches,*
> *And necklaces of gold-enamell'd ouches.*

So when Medea came in presence of Jason first, attended by her Nymphs and Ladies, as she is described by Apollonius [Rhodius]:

> *A lustre followed them like flaming fire,*
> *And from their golden borders came such beams,*
> *Which in his eyes provok'd a sweet desire.*

Such a relation we have in Plutarch, when the Queens came and offered themselves to Antony, with divers presents, and enticing ornaments. Asiatick allurements, with such wonderful joy and festivity, they did so inveigle the Romans, that no man could contain himself, all was turned to delight and pleasure. The women transformed themselves to Bacchus shapes, the men-children to Satyrs and Pans; but Antony himself was quite besotted with Cleopatra's sweet speeches, philters. beauty, pleasing tires: for when she sailed along the River Cydnus. with such incredible pomp, in a gilded ship, herself dressed like Venus. her maids like the Graces, her Pages like so many Cupids, Antony was amazed. and rapt beyond himself. Heliodorus brings in Damæneta, Step-mother to Cnemon, whom she saw in his scarfs, rings, robes and coronet, quite mad for the love of him. It was Judith's Pantofles that ravished the eyes of Holofernes. And Cardan is not ashamed to confess, that, seeing his wife the first time all in white, he did admire, and instantly love her. If these outward ornaments were not of such force, why doth Naomi give Ruth counsel how to please Boaz? And Judith seeking to captivate Holofernes, washed and anointed herself with sweet ointments, dressed her hair, and put on costly attires. The riot in this kind hath been excessive in times past; no man almost came abroad, but curled and anointed, one spent as much as two funerals at once, and with perfumed hairs, — our grey hairs, saith Horace, made odorous with roses and Syrian nard. What strange things doth Suetonius relate in·this matter of Caligula's riot. And Pliny. Read more in Dioscorides, Ulmus, Arnoldus, Randoletius On Cosmetics and Adornments, for it is now an art, as it was of old, (so Seneca records), perfumery is a trade. Women are bad, and men worse, no difference at all betwixt their and our times. Good manners (as Seneca complains) are extinct with wantonness, in tricking up themselves men go beyond women, they wear harlot's colours, and do not walk, but jet and dance, he-women, she-men, more like Players, Butterflies, Baboons, Apes, Anticks, than men. So ridiculous moreover we are in our attires, and for cost so excessive, that, as Hierome said of old, the price of a villa goes into a fillet, ten sesterces into a garment; 'tis an ordinary thing to put a thousand oaks and an hundred oxen into a suit of apparel, to wear a whole Manor on his back. What with shoe-ties, hangers, points, caps and feathers, scarfs, bands, cuffs, &c., in a short space their whole patrimonies are consumed. Heliogabalus is taxed by Lampridius, and admired in his age, for wearing jewels in his shoes, a common thing in our times, not for Emperors and Princes, but almost for serving-men & tailors: all the flowers, stars, constellations, gold &

precious stones, do condescend to set out their shoes. To repress the
luxury of those Roman Matrons, there was the Valerian Law, & the Oppian, & a Cato to contradict; but no Laws will serve to repress the
pride and insolency of our days, the prodigious riot in this kind. Lucullus' wardrobe is put down by our ordinary Citizens; and a Cobbler's
wife in Venice, a Courtesan in Florence, is no whit inferior to a Queen,
if our Geographers say true: and why is all this? Why do they glory in
their jewels (as he saith) or exult and triumph in the beauty of clothes?
why is all this cost? to incite men the sooner to burning lust. They pretend decency and ornament; but let them take heed, lest, while they set
out their bodies, they do not damn their souls: 'tis Bernard's counsel:
shine in jewels, stink in conditions: have purple robes, and a torn conscience. Let them take heed of Esay's Prophecy, that their slippers and
tires be not taken from them, [their] sweet balls, bracelets, ear-rings,
veils, wimples, crisping-pins, glasses, fine linen, hoods, lawns, and sweet
savours, they become not bald, burnt, and stink upon a sudden. And let
Maids beware, as Cyprian adviseth, lest, while they wander too loosely
abroad, they lose not their virginities: and, like Egyptian Temples,
seem fair without, but prove rotten carkasses within. How much better
were it for them to follow that good counsel of Tertullian! To have their
eyes painted with chastity, the Word of God inserted into their ears,
Christ's yoke tied to the hair, to subject themselves to their husbands.
If they would do so, they should be comely enough, clothe themselves
with the silk of sanctity, damask of devotion, purple of piety and chastity, and so painted, they shall have God himself to be a suitor. Let
whores and queans prank up themselves, let them paint their faces with
minium and ceruse, they are but fuels of lust, and signs of a corrupt
soul: if ye be good, honest, virtuous, and religious Matrons, let sobriety,
modesty, and chastity, be your honour, and God himself your love and
desire. Then a woman smells best, when she hath no perfume at all; no
Crown, Chain, or Jewel (Guevarra adds) is such an ornament to a Virgin, or virtuous woman, as chastity is: more credit in a wise man's eye
and judgment they get by their plainness, and seem fairer than they
that are set out with baubles, as a Butcher's meat is with pricks [or
skewers], puffed up and adorned, like so many jays, with variety of
colours. It is reported of Cornelia, that virtuous Roman Lady, great
Scipio's daughter, Titus Sempronius' wife, and the Mother of the
Gracchi, that being by chance in company with a companion, a strange
gentlewoman (some light huswife belike, that was dressed like a May-
Lady, and as most of our gentlewomen are, was more solicitous of her

head-tire than of her health, that spent her time betwixt a comb and a glass, and had rather be fair than honest, as Cato said, and have the Commonwealth turned topsy turvy than her tires marred) and she did naught but brag of her fine Robes and Jewels, and provoked the Roman Matron to shew hers: Cornelia kept her in talk till her children came from school, and these, said she, are my Jewels, and so deluded and put off a proud, vain, phantastical huswife. How much better were it for our Matrons to do as she did, to go civilly and decently, to use gold as it is gold, and for that use it serves, and when they need it, than to consume it in riot, beggar their husbands, prostitute themselves, inveigle others, and peradventure damn their own souls! How much more would it be for their honour and credit! Thus doing, as Hierome said of Blæsilla, Furius did not so triumph over the Gauls, Papirius of the Samnites, Scipio of Numantia, as she did by her temperance; always clad soberly, &c. They should insult and domineer over lust, folly, vain-glory, all such inordinate, furious, and unruly passions.

But I am over tedious, I confess, and whilst I stand gaping after fine clothes, there is another great allurement (in the world's eye at least) which had like to have stolen out of sight, and that is money, 'tis from the dowry that love's arrows come, money makes the match; they look only to money, 'tis like sauce to their meat, a good dowry with a wife. Many men, if they do hear but of a great portion, a rich heir, are more mad, than if they had all the beauteous ornaments, and those good parts Art and Nature can afford, they care not for honesty, bringing up, birth, beauty, person, but for money.

> *Our dogs and horses still from the best breed*
> *We carefully seek, and well may they speed:*
> *But for our wives, so they prove wealthy,*
> *Fair or foul, we care not what they be.*   (THEOGNIS)

If she be rich, then she is fair, fine, absolute and perfect, then they burn like fire, they love her dearly, like pig and pie, and are ready to hang themselves if they may not have her. Nothing so familiar in these days, as for a young man to marry an old wife, as they say, for a piece of gold; an ass laden with money; and though she be an old crone, and have never a tooth in her head, neither good conditions, nor good face, a natural fool, but only rich, she shall have twenty young Gallants to be suitors in an instant. As she said in Suetonius, 'tis not for her sake, but for her lands or money; and an excellent match it were (as he added) if she were away. So, on the other side, many a young lovely Maid will cast away herself upon an old, doting, decrepit dizzard, that is rheumatick and gouty, hath some twenty diseases, perhaps but one eye, one leg, never a nose, no hair on his head, wit in his brains, nor honesty, if he have land or money, she will have him before all other suitors.

If only rich, a very barbarian pleases.   (OVID)

If he be rich, he is the man, fine man, and a proper man, she'll go to Jacaktres or Tidore with him: Galesimus of the golden mountain. Sir Giles Goosecap, Sʳ Amorous La-Fool, shall have her. And as Philematium in Aristænetus told Eumusus, hang him that hath no money, 'tis to no purpose to talk of marriage without means, trouble me not with such motions; let others do as they will, I'll be sure to have one shall maintain me fine and brave. Most are of her mind; the question of his qualities shall come last; for his conditions [or behaviours], she shall enquire after them another time, or when all is done, the match made, and every body gone home. Lucian's Lycia was a proper young Maid, and had many fine Gentlemen to her suitors; Ethecles, a Senator's son, Melissus, a Merchant, &c., but she forsook them all for one Passius, a base, hirsute, bald-pated knave; but why was it? His Father lately died, and left him sole heir of his goods and lands. This is not amongst your dust-worms alone, poor snakes that will prostitute their souls for money, but with this bait you may catch our most potent, puissant, and illustrious Princes. That proud upstart domineering Bishop of Ely, in the time of Richard the First, Viceroy in his absence, as Nubrigensis relates it, to fortify himself, and maintain his greatness, married his poor kinswomen (which came forth of Normandy by droves) to the chiefest Nobles of the land, and they were glad to accept of such matches, fair or foul, for themselves, their Sons, Nephews, &c. Who would not have done as much for money and preferment? as mine author adds. Vortigern, King of Britain, married Rowena the daughter of Hengist, the Saxon Prince, his mortal enemy; but wherefore? she had Kent for her dowry. Iagello the great Duke of Lithuania, 1386, was mightily enamoured on Hedenga, insomuch that he turned Christian from a Pagan, and was baptized himself by the name of Uladislaus, and all his subjects for her sake: but why was it? she was daughter and heir of Poland, and his desire was to have both Kingdoms incorporated into one. Charles the Great was an earnest suitor to Irene the Empress, but, saith Zonaras, for the sake of rulership, to annex the Empire of the East to that of the West. Yet what is the event of all such matches, that are so made for money, goods, by deceit, or for burning lust, what follows? they are almost mad at first, but 'tis a mere flash; as chaff and straw soon fired, burn vehemently for a while, yet out in a moment; so are all such matches made by those allurements of burning lust; where there is no respect of honesty, parentage, virtue, religion, education, and the like, they are extinguished in an instant, and instead of love, comes hate; for joy, repentance, and desperation itself. Franciscus Barbarus, in his first book On Uxoriousness, hath a story of one Philip of Padua, that fell in love with a common whore, and was now ready to run mad for her; his Father, having no more sons, let him enjoy her; but after a few days, the young man began to loathe, could not so much as endure the sight of her, and from one madness fell into another. Such event commonly have all these lovers; and he that so marries, or for such respects, let them look for no better success than Menelaus had with Helen, Vulcan with Venus, Theseus with Phædra, Minos with Pasiphæ, and Claudius with Messalina; shame, sorrow, misery, melancholy, discontent.

SUBSECTION 4 — *Importunity and opportunity of time, place, confer- ence, discourse, singing, dancing, musick, amorous tales, objects, kissing, familiarity, tokens, presents, bribes, promises, protesta- tions, tears, &c.*

ALL these allurements hitherto are afar off, and at a distance; I will come nearer to those other degrees of Love, which are conference, kiss- ing, dalliance, discourse, singing, dancing, amorous tales, objects, pres- ents, &c., which as so many Sirens steal away the hearts of men and women. For, as Tatius observes, It is no sufficient trial of a Maid's affection by her eyes alone, but you must say something that shall be more available, and use such other forcible engines; therefore take her by her hand, wring her fingers hard, and sigh withal; if she accept this in good part, and seem not to be much averse, then call her Mistress, take her about the neck and kiss her, &c. — But this cannot be done except they first get opportunity of living or coming together, ingress, egress, and regress; letters and commendations may do much, outward gestures and actions: but when they come to live near one another, in the same street, village, or together in an house, Love is kindled on a sudden. Many a Serving-man by reason of this opportunity and impor- tunity inveigles his Master's daughter, many a Gallant loves a Dowdy, many a Gentleman runs upon his Wife's Maids, many Ladies dote upon their [serving] men as the Queen in Ariosto did upon the Dwarf, many matches are so made in haste, and they compelled as it were by necessity so to love, which, had they been free, come in company of others, seen that variety which many places afford, or compared them to a third, would never have looked one upon another. (Hungry dogs will eat dirty puddings.) Or had not that opportunity of discourse & familiarity been offered. they would have loathed and contemned those, whom for want of better choice, and other objects, they are fatally driven on, and by reason of their hot blood, idle life, full diet, &c., are forced to dote upon them that come next. And many times those which at the first sight cannot fancy or affect each other, but are harsh and ready to disagree, offended with each other's carriage, like Benedick and Beatrice in the Comedy, and in whom they find many faults, by this living together in a house. conference, kissing, colling, and such like allurements, begin at last to dote insensibly one upon another.

It was the greatest motive that Potiphar's wife had to dote upon Joseph. and Clitophon upon Leucippe, his Uncle's Daughter, because the plague being at Byzantium, it was his fortune for a time to sojourn with her, to sit next her at the Table, as he telleth the tale himself in Tatius, (which though it be but a fiction, is grounded upon good observation, and doth well express the passions of lovers), he had opportunity to take her by the hand, and after a while to kiss and handle her paps, &c.; which made him almost mad. Ismenius the Orator makes the like confession in Eustathius, when he came first to Sosthenes' house, and sate at table with Cratisthenes his friend, Ismene, Sosthenes' daughter, waiting on them with her breasts open, arms half bare, after the Greek fashion in those times, naked armed, as Daphne was when she fled from Phœbus (which moved him much), was ever ready to give attendance on him, to fill him drink, her eyes were never off him, those speaking eyes, courting eyes, enchanting eyes; but she was still smiling on him, and when they were risen, that she had gotten a little opportunity, she came and drank to him, and withal trod upon his toes, and would come and go, and when she could not speak for the company, she would wring his hand, and blush when she met him : and by this means first she overcame him, she would kiss the cup and drink to him, and smile, and drink where he drank on that side of the cup, by which mutual compressions, kissings, wringing of hands, treading of feet, &c., I sipt and sipt, and sipt so long, till at length I was drunk in love upon a sudden. Philochorus, in Aristænetus, met a fair maid by chance, a mere stranger to him, he looked back at her, she looked back at him again, and smiled withal.

Of that day death and disaster came.   (VIRGIL)

It was the sole cause of his farther acquaintance and love, that undid him.

'Tis never safe to yield to blandishments.   (PROPERTIUS)

This opportunity of time and place, with their circumstances, are so forcible motives, that it is unpossible almost for two young folks, equal in years, to live together, and not be in love, especially in great houses, Princes' Courts, where they are idle in their eminence, fare well, live at ease, and cannot tell otherwise how to spend their time.

Put an Hippolytus there, he'd soon be a Priapus. (ovid)

Achilles was sent by his Mother Thetis to the Island of Scyros in the Ægean Sea (where Lycomedes then reigned) in his nonage to be brought up, to avoid that hard destiny of the Oracle (he should be slain at the siege of Troy): and for that cause was nurtured in the Gynecium [or women's side of the house], amongst the King's children in a woman's habit, but see the event; he comprest Deidamia, the King's fair daughter, and had a fine son, called Pyrrhus, by her. Peter Abelard the Philosopher, as he tells the tale himself, being set by Fulbert her Uncle to teach Heloise his lovely Niece, and to that purpose sojourned in his house, had committed his tender lamb to an hungry wolf, I use his own words, he soon got her good will, and he read her more of Love than any other Lecture; such pretty feats can opportunity plea; already under one roof, soon of one mind, &c. But when, as I say, youth, wine, and night, shall concur (night, conspirator with love and sleep), 'tis a wonder they be not all plunged over head and ears in love; for youth is benign to love, a favouring condition, a very combustible matter, naptha itself, the fuel of Love's fire, and most apt to kindle it. If there be seven servants in an ordinary house, you shall have three couples in some good liking at least, and amongst idle persons how should it be otherwise? Living at Rome, saith Aretine's Lucretia, in the flower of my fortunes, rich, fair, young, and so well brought up, my conversation, age, beauty, fortune, made all the world admire and love me.—Night alone, that one occasion is enough to set all on fire, and they are so cunning in great houses, that they make their best advantage of it. Many a Gentlewoman, that is guilty to herself of her imperfections, paintings, impostures, will not willingly be seen by day, but as Castilio noteth, in the night; she hates the day like a dor-mouse, and above all things loves torches and candle-light, and if she must come abroad in the day, she covets, as in a Mercer's shop, a very obfuscate and obscure light. And good reason she hath for it: blemishes are not seen at night, and many an amorous gull is fetched over by that means. Gomesius gives instance in a Florentine Gentleman, that was so deceived with a wife, she was so radiantly set out with rings and jewels, lawns, scarfs, laces, gold, spangles, and gaudy devices, that the young man took her to be a goddess (for he never saw her but by torch-light), but after the wedding solemnities, when as he viewed her the next morning without her tires, and in a clear day, she was so deformed, lean, yellow, riveld [or wrinkled], &c., such a beastly creature in his eyes, that he could not endure to look upon her. Such matches are frequently made in Italy, where they have no other opportunity to woo, but when they go to Church, or, as in Turkey, see them at a distance, they must interchange few or no words, till such time they come to be married, and then as Sardus and Bohemus relate of those old Lacedæmonians, the Bride is brought into the chamber, with her hair girt about her, the Bridegroom comes in, and unties the knot, and must not see her at all by day-light, till such time as he is made a Father by her. In those hotter Countries these are ordinary practices at this day ; but in our Northern parts, amongst Germans, Danes, French, and Britains, the continent of Scandia and the rest, we assume more liberty in such causes ; we allow them, as Bohemus saith, to kiss coming and going, to talk merrily, sport, play, sing, and dance, so that it be modestly done, go to the Ale-house and Tavern together. And 'tis not amiss, though Chrysostom, Cyprian, Hierome, and some other of the Fathers speak bitterly against it : but that is the abuse which is commonly seen at some drunken matches, dissolute meetings, or great unruly feasts. A young pickitivanted [or peak'd-bearded], trim-bearded fellow, saith Hierome, will come with a company of compliments, and hold you up by the arm as you go, and wringing your fingers, will so be enticed or entice : one drinks to you, another embraceth, a third kisseth, and all this while the Fiddler plays or sings a lascivious song ; a fourth singles you out to dance, one speaks by becks and signs, and that which he dares not say, signifies by passions ; amongst so many and so great provocations of pleasure, lust conquers the most hard and crabbed minds, and scarce can a man live honest amongst feastings, and sports, or at such great-meetings. For as he goes on, she walks along, and with the ruffling of her clothes makes men look at her, her shoes creak, her paps tied up, her waist pulled in to make her look small, she is straight girded, her hairs hang loose about her ears, her upper garment sometimes falls, and sometimes tarries, to shew her naked shoulders, and as if she would not be seen, she covers that in all haste which voluntarily she shewed. — And not [only] at Feasts, Plays, Pageants, and such assemblies, but as Chrysostom objects, these tricks are put in practice at Service-time in Churches, and at the Communion itself. If such dumb shews, signs, and more obscure significations of Love can so move, what shall they do that have full liberty to sing, dance, kiss, coll, to use all manner of discourse and dalliance? What shall he do that is beleaguered on all sides?

After whom so many rosy maids inquire,
Whom dainty dames and loving wights desire,
In every place, still, and at all times sue,
Whom gods and gentle goddesses do woo.   (JOVIANUS PONTANUS)

How shall he contain? The very tone of some of their voices, a pretty pleasing speech, an affected tone they use, is able of itself to captivate a young man; but when a good wit shall concur, art and eloquence, fascinating speech, pleasant discourse, sweet gestures, the Sirens themselves cannot so enchant. P. Jovius commends his Italian Countrywomen, to have an excellent faculty in this kind, above all other nations, and amongst them the Florentine Ladies: some prefer Roman and Venetian Courtesans, they have such pleasing tongues, and such elegancy of speech, that they are able to overcome a Saint.

Songs too have charms: let girls learn how to sing;
A charming voice will serve instead of looks.   (OVID)

Often a pleasing voice brings fame, saith Petronius in his fragment of pure impurities, I mean his Satyricon; she sang so sweetly, that she charmed the air, and thou wouldst have thought thou hadst heard a consort of Sirens. O good God, when Lais speaks, how sweet it is! Philocaus exclaims in Aristænetus. To hear a fair young Gentlewoman play upon the Virginals, Lute, Viol, and sing to it, which as Gellius observes, are the chief delight of Lovers, must needs be a great enticement. Parthenis was so taken.

Greedily my mind drinks in that lovely voice.

O sister Harpedona (she laments) I am undone, how sweetly he sings! I'll speak a bold word, he is the properest man that ever I saw in my life! O how sweetly he sings! I die for his sake, O that he would love me again! — If thou didst but hear her sing, saith Lucian, thou wouldst forget father and mother, forsake all thy friends, and follow her. Helen is highly commended by Theocritus the Poet for her sweet voice and musick, none could play so well as she, and Daphnis in the same Idyll:

How sweet a face hath Daphnis, how lovely a voice!
Honey itself is not so pleasant in my choice.

A sweet voice and musick are powerful enticers. Those Samian singing wenches, Aristonica, Oenanthe and Agathoclea, insulted over Kings themselves, as Plutarch contends. Argus had an hundred eyes, all so charmed by one silly pipe, that he lost his head. Clitiphon complains in Tatius of Leucippe's sweet tunes, he heard her play by chance upon the Lute, and sing a pretty song to it, in commendations of a Rose, out of old Anacreon belike;

> *Rose, the fairest of all flowers,*
> *Rose, delight of higher powers,*
> *Rose, the joy of mortal men,*
> *Rose, the pleasure of fine women,*
> *Rose, the Grace's ornament,*
> *Rose, Dione's sweet content.*

To this effect the lovely Virgin with a melodious Air upon her golden wired Harp or Lute, I know not well whether, played and sang, and that transported him beyond himself, and that ravished his heart. It was Jason's discourse as much as his beauty, or any other of his good parts, which delighted Medea so much.

> *Eloquence equally with beauty moves the heart.* (APOLLONIUS)

It was Cleopatra's sweet voice, and pleasant speech, which inveigled Antony, above the rest of her enticements. As a bull's horns are bound with ropes, so are men's hearts with pleasant words. Her words burn as fire. Roxalana bewitched Solyman the Magnificent; and Shore's wife by this engine overcame Edward the Fourth;

> *In her sole self the stolen charms of all.* (CATULLUS)

The wife of Bath in Chaucer confesseth all this out of her experience.

> Thou sepst. some folk despre us for richesse,
> Som for our shap, and som for our fairness;
> And some, for she can outher singe or daunce,
> And som, for gentilesse and daliaunce.

Peter Aretine's Lucretia telleth as much and more of herself, I counterfeited honesty, as if I had been more than a Vestal virgin, I looked like a wife, I was so demure and chaste, I did add such gestures, tunes, speeches, signs and motions upon all occasions, that my spectators and auditors were stupified, enchanted, fastened all to their places, like so many stocks and stones.——— Many silly Gentlewomen are fetched over in like sort, by a company of gulls and swaggering companions, that frequently bely Noblemen's favours, rhyming Corybantiasmics, Thrasonian Rhodomonts or Bombomachides, that have nothing in them but a few players' ends, and compliments, vain braggadocians, impudent intruders, that can discourse at table of Knights and Lords' combats, like Lucian's Leontichus, of other men's travels, brave adventures, and such common trivial news, ride, dance, sing old ballet tunes, and wear their clothes in fashion, with a good grace; a fine sweet gentleman, a proper man, who could not love him? She will have him, though all her friends say no, though she beg with him! Some again are incensed by reading amorous toys, Amadis de Gaul, Palmerin de Oliva, the Knight of the Sun, &c., or hearing such tales of lovers, descriptions of their persons, lascivious discourses, such as Astyanassa, Helena's waiting-woman, by the report of Suidas, writ of old, of the various positions in love-making, and after her, Philænis and Elephantis; or those light tracts of Aristides Milesius (mentioned by Plutarch) and found by the Persians in Crassus' Army amongst the spoils, Aretine's Dialogues, with ditties, Love-songs, &c., must needs set them on fire, with such like pictures as those of Aretine, or wanton objects in what kind soever; no stronger engine than to hear or read of Love-toys, fables, and discourses, (one saith) and many by this means are quite mad. At Abdera in Thrace, (Andromeda, one of Euripides' Tragedies, being played), the spectators were so much moved with the object, and those pathetical Love-speeches of Perseus, amongst the rest, O Cupid, Prince of Gods and Men, &c., that every man almost a good while after spake pure Iambicks, and raved still on Perseus' speech, O Cupid, Prince of Gods and Men! As Car-men, Boys, and Prentices, when a new song is published with us, go singing that new tune still in the streets; they continually acted that Tragical part of Perseus, and in every man's mouth was, O Cupid, in every street, O Cupid, in every house almost, O Cupid, Prince of Gods and Men, pronouncing still like stage-players, O Cupid; they were so possessed all with that rapture, and thought of that pathetical Love-speech, they could not for a long time after forget, or drive it out of their minds, but, O Cupid, Prince of Gods and Men, was ever in their mouths. This belike made Aristotle forbid young men to see Comedies, or to hear amorous tales.

> *O therefore let not youths to girls*
> *Have easy access.* (MARTIAL)

Let not young folks meddle at all with such matters. And this made the Romans, as Vitruvius relates, put Venus' Temple in the Suburbs, that youths might not become accustomed to love-making, to avoid all occasions and objects. For what will not such an object do? Ismenius, as he walked in Sosthenes' garden, being now in love, when he saw so many lascivious pictures, Thetis' marriage, and I know not what, was almost beside himself. And to say truth, with a lascivious object who is not moved, to see others dally, kiss, dance? And much more when he shall come to be an Actor himself.

To kiss and to be kissed, which amongst other lascivious provocations, is as a burden in a song, and a most forcible battery, as infectious, Xenophon thinks, as the poison of a spider; a great allurement, a fire itself, the prologue of burning lust (as Apuleius adds), lust itself.

> *It hath the very quintessence of Venus's nectar.* (HORACE)

A strong assault, that conquers Captains, and those all-commanding forces,

>*You conquer with swords, but are conquered with a kiss.*
>
>   (HEINSIUS)

Aretine's Lucretia, when she would in kindness overcome a suitor of hers, and have her desire of him, took him about the neck, and kissed him again and again, and to that, which she could not otherwise effect, she made him so speedily and willingly condescend. And 'tis a continual assault,

>*Beginning ever, ending never,*   (PETRONIUS)

always fresh, and ready to begin as at first, a kiss that hath no close, yet is ever new, and hath a fiery touch with it.

>*The least touch of her body,*
>*And you're all ablaze already.*   (PETRONIUS)

Especially when they shall be lasciviously given, as he feelingly said, when Fotis gave him a hard kiss, laced in her arms, with lips twisted cunningly.

>*So sharply sweet her kiss,*
>*'Tis less a kiss than a wound;*
>*And at my lips, my soul*
>*Lies in a breathless swound.*   (In AULUS GELLIUS)

The soul and all is moved; with the shock of many kisses, saith Petronius, the lips ache, and breaths are mixt breathlessly, and in the stress of mutual embraces the soul is at its last gasp:

>——— *Hotly cleaving each to each,*
>*And by each other's eager lips transpierced,*
>*Your souls will stray: such lovers may ye be.*   (PETRONIUS)

They breathe out their souls and spirits together with their kisses, saith Balthasar Castilio, change hearts and spirits, and mingle affections, as they do kisses, and it is rather a connexion of the mind than of the body. And although these kisses be delightsome and pleasant, Ambrosial kisses, such as Ganymede gave Jupiter, sweeter than Nectar, Balsom, Honey, Love-dropping kisses; for

>*The Gilliflower, the Rose is not so sweet,*
>*As sugared kisses be when Lovers meet,*

yet they leave an irksome impression, like that of Aloes or Gall,

>*At first ambrose itself was not sweeter,*
>*At last black hellebore was not so bitter.*   (CATULLUS)

They are deceitful kisses,

>*Why dost within thine arms me lap,*
>*And with false kisses me entrap?*   (BUCHANAN)

They are destructive, and the more the worse:

A thousand kisses, that were my utter ruin.   (OVID)

They are the bane of these miserable Lovers. There be honest kisses I deny not, the respectful kiss, friendly kisses, modest kisses, Vestal-Virgin kisses, officious and ceremonial kisses, &c. Kissing and embracing are proper gifts of nature to a man: but these are too lascivious kisses,

With arms about my neck enfolded tight,   (OVID)

too continuate, and too violent; they cling like Ivy, close as an Oyster, bill as Doves, meretricious [or courtesan's] kisses, biting of lips, with other tricks, mouth-suckings (saith Lucian), such as the lips can scarce be withdrawn from, with bitings between, and with open mouth caressing the paps, &c., such kisses as she gave to Giton, in Petronius, innumerable kisses not unpleasing to the lad, assaulting the neck, &c. More than kisses, or too homely kisses: as those that he [Apuleius] spake of, having had from her the seven sweet kinds of love, with such other obscenities that vain Lovers use, which are abominable and pernicious. If, as Peter de Ledesmo holds, *every kiss a man gives his wife after marriage be a mortal sin,* or that of Hierome, *whoever is hotly in love with his own wife is an adulterer,* or that of Thomas Secundus, *handling and kissing is a mortal sin,* or that of Durandus, *married folks should abstain from caresses during the entire time when the nuptial deed is interdicted,* what shall become of all such immodest kisses, and obscene actions, the forerunners of brutish lust, if not lust itself? What shall become of them, that often abuse their own wives? But what have I to do with this?

That which I aim at, is to shew you the progress of this burning lust: to epitomize therefore all this which I have hitherto said, with a familiar example out of that elegant Musæus; observe but with me those amorous proceedings of Leander and Hero. They began first to look one on the other with a lascivious look,

With becks and nods he first began
  To try the wench's mind,
With becks and nods and smiles again
  An answer he did find.
And in the dark he took her by the hand,
And wrung it hard, and sighed grievously,
And kiss'd her too, and woo'd her as he might,
With Pity me, sweetheart, or else I die,
And with such words and gestures as there past,
He won his Mistress' favour at the last.

The same proceeding is elegantly described by Apollonius in his Argo-
nauticks, betwixt Jason and Medea, by Eustathius in the eleven
books of the loves of Ismenias and Ismene, Achilles Tatius betwixt his
Clitophon and Leucippe, Chaucer's neat poem of Troilus and Cresseide;
and in that notable tale in Petronius of a Soldier and a Gentlewoman
of Ephesus, that was so famous all over Asia for her chastity, and that
mourned for her husband: the Soldier wooed her with such Rhetorick
as Lovers use to do. — why struggle against love, &c., at last, breaking
down her resistance, he got her good will, not only to satisfy his lust,
but to hang her dead husband's body on the cross (which he watched
instead of the thieves) that was newly stolen away, whilst he wooed
her in her Cabin. These are tales you will say, but they have most
significant Morals, and do well express those ordinary proceedings of
doting Lovers.

Many such allurements there are, Nods, Jests, Winks, Smiles, Wrest-
lings, Tokens, Favours, Symbols, Letters, Valentines, &c. For which
cause belike Godefridus would not have women learn to write. Many
such provocations are used when they come in presence, they will and
will not.

> *My Mistress with an apple woos me,*
>   *And hastily to covert goes*
> *To hide herself, but would be seen*
>   *With all her heart before, God knows.*   (VIRGIL)

Hero so tripped away from Leander as one displeased,

> *Yet as she went full often lookt behind,*
> *And many poor excuses did she find*
>   *To linger by the way,* ——   (MARLOWE)

but if he chance to overtake her, she is most averse, nice and coy, —

> *She refuses, and struggles, but desires above all to be conquered.*
>   (BAPTISTA MANTUANUS)

> *She seems not won, but won she is at length,*
> *In such wars women use but half their strength.*   (MARLOWE)

Sometimes they lie open and are most tractable and coming, apt, yielding, & willing to embrace, to take a green gown, with that Shepherdess
in Theocritus, to let their Coats, &c., to play and dally, at such seasons,
and to some, as they spy their advantage; and then coy, close again, so
nice, so surly, so demure, you had much better tame a colt, catch or
ride a wild horse, than get her favour, or win her love, not a look, not a
smile, not a kiss for a kingdom. Aretine's Lucretia was an excellent
Artisan in this kind, as she tells her own tale: Though I was by nature

and art most beautiful and fair, yet by these tricks I seem'd to be far
more amiable than I was. For that which men earnestly seek and cannot attain, draws on their affection with a most furious desire. I had a
suitor lov'd me dearly (saith she) and the more he gave me, the more
eagerly he wooed me, the more I seemed to neglect, to scorn him, and
(which I commonly gave others), I would not let him see me, converse
with me, no not have a kiss. To gull him the more, and fetch him over
(for him only I aimed at) I personated mine own servant to bring in a
present from a Spanish Count, whilst he was in my company, as if he
had been the Count's servant, which he did excellently well perform : The
Count de monte Turco, my Lord and Master, hath sent your Ladyship
a small present, and part of his hunting, a piece of Venison, a Pheasant,
a few Partridges, &c., (all which she bought with her own money) commends his love and service to you. desiring you to accept of it in good
part, and he means very shortly to come and see you. Withal she shewed
him rings, gloves, scarfs, coronets, which others had sent her, when there
was no such matter, but only to circumvent him. By these means (as
she concludes) I made the poor Gentleman so mad, that he was ready
to spend himself, and venture his dearest blood for my sake. Philinna
in Lucian practised all this long before, as it shall appear unto you by
her discourse; for when Diphilus her sweetheart came to see her (as
his daily custom was) she frowned upon him, would not vouchsafe him
her company, but kissed Lamprias, his corrival, at the same time before his face : but why was it? To make him (as she telleth her mother
that chid her for it) more jealous; to whetten his love, to come with
a greater appetite, and to know that her favour was not so easy to be
had. Many other tricks she used besides this (as she there confesseth)
for she would fall out with, and anger him of set purpose, pick quarrels
upon no occasion, because she would be reconciled to him again. As
the old saying is, the falling out of lovers is the renewing of love; and
according to that of Aristænetus, love is increased by injuries, as the
Sunbeams are more gracious after a cloud. And surely this Aphorism
is most true; for as Ampelis informs Chrysis in the said Lucian, If a
lover be not jealous, angry, waspish, apt to fall out, sigh and swear, he
is no true lover. To kiss and coll, hang about her neck, protest, swear,
and wish, are but ordinary symptoms, signs of the beginning and growth
of love; but if he be jealous, angry, apt to mistake, &c., breathe easily,
sweet sister, he is thine own; yet if you let him alone, humour him,
please him, &c., and that he perceive once he hath you sure, without
any corrival, his love will languish, and he will not care so much for

you. Hitherto (saith she) can I speak out of experience; Demophantus,
a rich fellow, was a suitor of mine; I seem'd to neglect him, and gave
better entertainment to Callides the Painter before his face; at first
he went his way all in a chafe, cursing and swearing, but at last he
came submitting himself, vowing and protesting that he loved me most
dearly, I should have all he had, and that he would kill himself for my
sake. Therefore I advise thee (dear sister Chrysis) and all maids, not
to use your suitors over kindly; 'twill make them proud and insolent;
but now and then reject them, estrange thyself, and if you will list to me,
shut him out of doors once or twice, let him dance attendance; follow
my counsel, and by this means you shall make him mad, come off
roundly, stand to any conditions, and do whatsoever you will have him.
— These are the ordinary practices; yet, in the said Lucian, Melissa,
methinks, had a trick beyond all this; for when her suitor came coldly
on, to stir him up, she writ one of his corrival's names and her own in a
paper, Melissa loves Hermotimus, Hermotimus Melissa, causing it to
be stuck upon a post, for all gazers to behold, and lost it in the way
where he used to walk; which when the silly novice perceived, he instantly apprehended it was so, came raving to me, &c.: and so, when I
was in despair of his love, four months after I recovered him again. —
Eugenia drew Timocles for her Valentine, and wore his name a long time
after in her bosom; Camæna singled out Pamphilus to dance, at Myson's
wedding (some say) for there she saw him first; Felicianus overtook
Cælia by the high-way side, offered his service, thence came further acquaintance, and thence came love. But who can repeat half their devices; what Aretine experienced, what conceited Lucian, or wanton
Aristænetus? They will deny and take, stiffly refuse, and yet earnestly
seek the same, repel to make them come with more eagerness, fly from if
you follow, but if averse, as a shadow they will follow you again; with
a regaining retrait, a gentle reluctancy, a smiling threat, a pretty pleasant peevishness, they will put you off, and have a thousand such several
enticements. For as he saith,

> 'Tis not enough though she be fair of hue,
> For her to use this vulgar compliment:
> But pretty toys and jests, and saws and smiles,
> Are far beyond what beauty can attempt. (PETRONIUS)

For this cause, belike, Philostratus, in his Images, makes divers Loves,
some young, some of one age, some of another, some winged, some of
one sex, some of another, some with torches, some with golden apples,
some with darts, gins, snares, and other engines in their hands, as

Propertius hath prettily painted them out, and which some interpret, divers enticements, or divers affections of Lovers, which if not alone, yet jointly may batter and overcome the strongest constitutions.

It is reported of Decius and Valerianus, those two notorious persecutors of the Church, that when they could enforce a young Christian by no means (as Hierome records) to sacrifice to their idols, by no torments or promises, they took another course to tempt them: they put him into a fair Garden, and set a young Courtesan to dally with him; she took him about the neck and kissed him, and that which is not to be named, fondled with the hands, &c., and all those enticements which might be used, that whom Torments could not, Love might batter and beleaguer. But such was his constancy, she could not overcome, and when this last engine would take no place, they left him to his own ways. At Berkeley in Gloucestershire, there was in times past a Nunnery (saith Gualterus Mapes, an old Historiographer, that lived 400 years since) of which there was a noble and a fair Lady Abbess: Godwin, that subtil Earl of Kent travelling that way (seeking not her but hers) leaves a Nephew of his, a proper young Gallant (as if he had been sick) with her, till he came back again, and gives the young man charge so long to counterfeit, till he had deflowered the Abbess, and as many besides of the Nuns as he could, and leaves him withal rings, jewels, girdles, and such toys to give them still, when they came to visit him. The young man, willing to undergo such a business, played his part so well, that in short space he got up most of their bellies, and when he had done, told his Lord how he had sped; his Lord makes instantly to the Court, tells the King how such a Nunnery was become a bawdy house, procures a visitation, gets them to be turned out, and begs the lands to his own use. This story I do therefore repeat, that you may see of what force these enticements are, if they be opportunely used, and how hard it is even for the most averse and sanctified souls to resist such allurements. John Major, in the life of John the Monk, that lived in the days of Theodosius, commends the Hermit to have been a man of singular continency, and of a most austere life; but one night by chance the Devil came to his Cell in the habit of a young market wench that had lost her way, and desired for God's sake some lodging with him. The old man let her in, and after some common conference of her mishap, she began to inveigle him with lascivious talk and jests, to play with his beard, to kiss him, and do worse, till at last she overcame him. As he went to address himself to that business, she vanished on a sudden, and the Devils in the air laughed him to scorn. Whether this be a true story, or a tale, I will not much contend, it serves to illustrate this which I have said.

Yet were it so, that these of which I have hitherto spoken, and such like enticing baits be not sufficient, there be many others, which will of themselves intend this passion of burning lust, amongst which, dancing is none of the least; and it is an engine of such force, I may not omit it. Petrarch calls it the spur of lust, a circle of which the Devil himself is the centre. Many women that use it have come dishonest home, most indifferent, none better. Another terms it, the companion of all filthy delights and enticements, and 'tis not easily told what inconveniences come by it, what scurrile talk, obscene actions, and many times such monstrous gestures, such lascivious motions, such wanton tunes, meretricious kisses, homely embracings, —

> *Comes now some Gaditanian with his troop*
> *Of naughty singers, and the wanton pranks*
> *Of much applauded dancing girls that stoop*
> *And rouse desire with undulating flanks —*
>
> (JUVENAL)

that it will make the spectators mad. When that Epitomizer of Trogus had to the full described and set out King Ptolemy's riot, as a chief engine and instrument of his overthrow, he adds fiddling and dancing; the King was not a spectator only, but a principal actor himself. A thing nevertheless frequently used, and part of a Gentlewoman's bringing up, to sing, dance, and play on the Lute, or some such instrument, before she can say her Pater Noster, or ten Commandments. 'Tis the next way their Parents think to get them husbands, they are compelled to learn, and by that means, from earliest years their thoughts run to wantonness. 'Tis a great allurement as it is often used, and many are undone by it. Thais, in Lucian, inveigled Lamprias in a dance. Herodias so far pleased Herod, that she made him swear to give her what she would ask, John Baptist's head in a platter. Robert, Duke of Normandy, riding by Falais, spied Arletta a fair maid, as she danced on a green, and was so much enamoured with the object, that he must needs lie with her that night, (of whom he begat William the Conqueror; by the same token she tore her smock down, saying, &c.). Owen Tudor won Queen Katherine's affection in a dance, falling by chance with his head in her lap. Who cannot parallel these stories out of his experience? Speucippus, a noble gallant in that Greek Aristænetus, seeing Panareta a fair young Gentlewoman dancing by accident, was so far in love with her, that for a long time after he could think of nothing but Panareta: he

came raving home full of Panareta. Who would not admire her, who
would not love her, that should but see her dance as I did? O admirable,
O divine Panareta! I have seen old and new Rome, many fair Cities,
many proper women, but never any like to Panareta, they are dross,
dowdies all to Panareta! O how she danced, how she tript, how she
turn'd, with what a grace! happy is that man that shall enjoy her! O
most incomparable, only Panareta! — When Xenophon in the Symposium or Banquet, had discoursed of love, and used all the engines that
might be devised, to move Socrates amongst the rest, to stir him the
more, he shuts up all with a pleasant interlude or dance of Dionysus
and Ariadne: First Ariadne dressed like a bride came in and took her
place; by and by Dionysus entered. dancing to the Musick. The spectators did all admire the young man's carriage; and Ariadne herself
was so much affected with the sight, that she could scarce sit. After a
while Dionysus beholding Ariadne, and incensed with love, bowing to
her knees, embraced her first, and kissed her with a grace; she embraced him again, and kissed him with like affection, &c., as the dance
required: but they that stood by and saw this, did much applaud and
commend them both for it. And when Dionysus rose up, he raised her
up with him, and many pretty gestures, embraces, kisses, and love compliments passed between them; which when they saw fair Bacchus and
beautiful Ariadne so sweetly and so unfeignedly kissing each other, so
really embracing, they swore they loved indeed, and were so inflamed
with the object, that they began to rouse up themselves, as if they would
have flown. At the last when they saw them still so willing embracing,
and now ready to go to the Bride-chamber, they were so ravished with
it, that they that were unmarried swore they would forthwith marry,
and those that were married, called instantly for their horses, and gal-
loped home to their wives. What greater motive can there be than this
burning lust? What so violent an oppugner? Not without good cause
therefore so many general Councils condemn it, so many Fathers abhor
it, so many grave men speak against it. Use not the company of a
woman, saith Siracides, that is a singer or a dancer; neither hear, lest
you be taken in her craftiness. Hædus holds, lust in Theatres is not
seen, but learned. Gregory Nazianzen, that eloquent Divine (as he
relates the story himself), when a noble friend of his solemnly invited
him, with other Bishops, to his daughter Olympia's wedding, refused
to come: for it is absurd to see an old gouty Bishop sit amongst dancers,
he held it unfit to be a spectator, much less an actor. Tully writes, he
is not a sober man that danceth; for some such reason (belike) Domi-

tian forbade the Roman Senators to dance, and for that fact removed many of them from the Senate. But these, you will say, are lascivious and Pagan dances, 'tis the abuse that causeth such inconvenience, and I do not well therefore to condemn, speak against, or innocently to accuse the best and pleasantest thing (so Lucian calls it) that belongs to mortal men. You mis-interpret, I condemn it not; I hold it notwithstanding an honest disport, a lawful recreation, if it be opportune, moderately and soberly used: I am of Plutarch's mind, that which respects pleasure alone, honest recreation, or bodily exercise, ought not to be rejected and contemned; I subscribe to Lucian, 'tis an elegant thing, which cheereth up the mind, exerciseth the body, delights the spectators, which teacheth many comely gestures, equally affecting the ears, eyes, and soul itself. Sallust discommends singing and dancing in Sempronia, not that she did sing and dance, but that she did it in excess, 'tis the abuse of it: and Gregory's refusal doth not simply condemn it, but in some folks. Many will not allow men and women to dance together, because it is a provocation to lust: they may as well, with Lycurgus and Mahomet, cut down all Vines, forbid the drinking of wine, for that it makes some men drunk.

> *There's nothing good that cannot evil be.*
> *Fire is good, yet evil too, we see.*   (OVID)

I say of this, as of all other honest recreations, they are like fire, good and bad, and I see no such inconvenience, but that they may so dance, if it be done at due times, and by fit persons: and conclude with Wolfongus Hider, and most of our modern divines: If the dancing is decorous, sober, modest, and in the plain view of good men and honest matrons, and at fitting times, it may and should be approved. "There is a time to mourn, a time to dance." Let them take their pleasures then, and as Apuleius said of old, young men and maids flourishing in their age, fair and lovely to behold, well attired, and of comely carriage, dancing a Greek galliard, and as their dance required, kept their time, now turning, now tracing, now apart, now altogether, now a courtesy, then a caper, &c.; and it was a pleasant sight, to see those pretty knots, and swimming figures. The Sun and Moon (some say) dance about the earth, the three upper Planets about the Sun as their centre, now stationary, now direct, now retrograde, now in apogee then in perigee, now swift, then slow, occidental, oriental, they turn round, jump and trace, Venus and Mercury about the Sun with those thirty three Maculæ or Bourbonian planets, dancers about the harping Sun, saith Fromundus. Four Medicean stars dance about Jupiter, two Austrian about

Saturn, &c., and all (belike) to the musick of the Spheres. Our greatest Councillors, and staid Senators, at some times dance, as David before the Ark, Miriam, Judith, (though the Devil hence perhaps hath brought in those bawdy Bacchanals), and well may they do it. The greatest Soldiers, as Quintilianus, Æmilius Probus, Cælius Rhodiginus, have proved at large, still use it in Greece, Rome, and the most worthy Senators, sing, and dance. Lucian, Macrobius, Libanius, Plutarch, Julius Pollux, Athenæus, have written just tracts in commendation of it. In this our age it is in much request in those Countries, as in all civil Commonwealths, as Alexander ab Alexandro hath proved at large, amongst the Barbarians themselves nothing so precious; all the World allows it.

> Croesus, I despise your gold,
> All your Asia I'd have sold,
> Traded, given, or thrown away,
> For sweet-limb'd dancers young and gay.
>
> (EROTOPÆDIA OF ANGERIANUS)

Plato, in his Common-wealth, will have dancing-schools to be maintained, that young folks might meet, be acquainted, see one another, and be seen; nay more, he would have them dance naked, and scoffs at them that laugh at it. But Eusebius, and Theodoret, worthily lash him for it; and well they might: for as one saith, the very sight of naked parts causeth enormous, exceeding concupiscences, and stirs up both men and women to burning lust. There is a mean in all things: this is my censure in brief; dancing is a pleasant recreation of body and mind, if sober and modest (such as our Christian dances are) if tempestively [or timely] used; a furious motive to burning lust, if, as by Pagans heretofore, unchastely abused. But I proceed.

If these allurements do not take place, for Simierus, that great master of dalliance, shall not behave himself better, the more effectually to move others, and satisfy their lust, they will swear and lie, promise, protest, forge, counterfeit, brag, bribe, flatter and dissemble of all sides. 'Twas Lucretia's counsel in Aretine, if you would profit from your admirers, promise, pretend, swear and forswear, lie and cheat, and they put it well in practice, as Apollo to Daphne, —

> Delphos, Claros, and Tenedos serve me,
> And Jupiter is known my sire to be. (OVID)

The poorest swains will do as much: I have a thousand sheep, good store of cattle, and they are all at her command; house, land, goods, are at her service, as he is himself. Dinomachus, a Senator's Son in

Lucian, in love with a wench inferior to him in birth and fortunes, the sooner to accomplish his desire, wept unto her, and swore he loved her with all his heart, and her alone, and that as soon as ever his Father died, (a very rich man, and almost decrepit), he would make her his wife. The Maid by chance made her Mother acquainted with the business, who being an old Fox, well experienced in such matters, told her daughter, now ready to yield to his desire, that he meant nothing less, for dost thou think he will ever care for thee, being a poor wench, that may have his choice of all the beauties in the City, one Noble by birth, with so many talents, as young, better qualified, and fairer than thyself? Daughter, believe him not: the Maid was abasht, and so the matter broke off. When Jupiter wooed Juno first (Lilius Giraldus relates it out of an old Comment on Theocritus) the better to effect his suit, he turned himself into a Cuckoo, and spying her one day walking alone, separated from the other Goddesses, caused a tempest suddenly to arise, for fear of which she fled to shelter: Jupiter to avoid the storm likewise flew into her lap, whom Juno for pity covered in her Apron. But he turned himself forthwith into his own shape, began to embrace and offer violence unto her, but she by no means would yield, till he vowed and swore to marry her, and then she gave consent. This fact was done at Thornax hill, which ever after was called Cuckoo hill, and in perpetual remembrance there was a Temple erected to Juno Teleia in the same place. So powerful are fair promises, vows, oaths, and protestations. It is an ordinary thing too in this case to belie their age, which widows usually do, that mean to marry again, and bachelors too sometimes, coming on to forty, to say they are younger than they are. Charmides, in the said Lucian, loved Philematium, an old Maid of five and forty years, she swore to him she was but two and thirty next December. But to dissemble in this kind is familiar of all sides, and often it takes.

> *'Tis no great thing so to deceive*
> *One who cannot but believe,*   (OVID)

'tis soon done, no such great mastery,

> *Vast, in all truth, the renown, and ample the spoils,*   (VIRGIL)

and nothing so frequent as to belie their estates, to prefer their suits, and to advance themselves. Many men, to fetch over a young woman, widows, or whom they love, will not stick to crack, forge, and feign, anything comes next, bid his boy fetch his cloak, rapier, gloves, jewels, &c., in such a chest, scarlet, golden, tissue breeches, &c., when there is no such matter; or make any scruple to give out, as he did in Petronius, that he was Master of a Ship, kept so many servants, and to personate their part the better, take upon them to be gentlemen of good houses, well descended and allied, hire apparel at brokers, some Scavenger or pricklouse Tailors to attend upon them for the time, swear they have great possessions, bribe, lie, cog, and foist, how dearly they love, how bravely they will maintain her, like any Lady, Countess, Duchess, or Queen: they shall have gowns, tires, jewels, coaches, and caroches, choice diet, —

> *The heads of Parrots, tongues of Nightingales,*
> *The brains of Peacocks, and of Ostriches,*
> *Their bath shall be the juice of Gilliflowers,*
> *Spirit of Roses and of Violets,*
> *The milk of Unicorns, &c.*

as old Volpone courted Cælia in the Comedy, when as they are no such men, not worth a groat, but mere sharkers, to make a fortune, to get their desire, or else pretend love to spend their idle hours, to be more welcome, and for better entertainment. The conclusion is, they mean nothing less.

> *Oaths, vows, promises, are much protested;*
> *But when their mind and lust is satisfied,*
> *Oaths, vows, promises, are quite neglected.*   (CATULLUS)

Though he solemnly swear by the Genius of Cæsar, by Venus' shrine, Hymen's deity, by Jupiter, and all the other gods, give no credit to his words. For when Lovers swear, Venus laughs, Venus laughs at lovers' lies, Jupiter himself smiles, and pardons it withal; as grave Plato gives out, of all perjury, that alone for love matters is forgiven by the gods. If promises, lies, oaths, and protestations will not avail, they fall to bribes, tokens, gifts, and such like feats. 'Tis by gold that love is won; as Jupiter corrupted Danaë with a golden shower, and Liber Ariadne with a lovely Crown (which was afterwards translated into the Heavens, and there for ever shines); they will rain Chickens, Florins, Crowns, Angels, all manner of coins and stamps in her lap. And so must he certainly do that will speed, make many feasts, banquets, invitations, send her some present or other every foot [of the way]. He must give feasts and presents galore, (saith Hædus), he must be very bountiful and liberal, seek and sue, not to her only, but to all her followers, friends, familiars, fiddlers, panders, parasites, and household-servants; he must insinuate himself, and surely will, to all, of all sorts, messengers, porters, carriers; no man must be unrewarded, or unrespected. I had a suitor (saith Aretine's Lucretia) that when he came to my house, flung gold and silver about as if it had been chaff. Another suitor I had was a very cholerick fellow, but I so handled him that for all his fuming, I brought him upon his knees. If there had been an excellent bit in the market, any novelty. fish, fruit, or fowl, muskadel, or malmsey, or a cup of neat wine in all the city, it was presented presently to me, though never so dear, hard to come by, yet I had it: the poor fellow was so fond at last, that I think, if I would, I might have had one of his eyes out of his head. A third suitor was a merchant of Rome, and his manner of wooing was with exquisite musick, costly banquets, poems, &c. I held him off till at length he protested, promised, and swore if I gave him my virginity, I should have all he had, house, goods and lands, only for lying with me. Neither was there ever any Conjurer, I think, to charm his spirits. that used such attention, or mighty words, as he did exquisite phrases: or General of any army, so many stratagems to win a city, as he did tricks and devices to get the love of me. Thus men are active and passive. and women not far behind them in this kind. Bold are women, both in love and hate.

> For half so boldely can ther no man
> Swere and lyen as a womman can.

They will crack, counterfeit, and collogue, as well as the best, with handkerchiefs, and wrought nightcaps, purses, posies, and such toys: as he justly complained,

> *Why dost thou send me violets, my dear?*
> *To make me burn more violent, I fear,*
> *With violets too violent thou art,*
>   *To violate and wound my gentle heart.*   (JOVIANUS PONTANUS)

When nothing else will serve, the last refuge is their tears. 'Twixt tears and sighs I write this (I take love to witness), saith Chelidonia to Philonius. Those burning torches are now turned to floods of tears. Aretine's Lucretia, when her sweetheart came to Town, wept in his bosom, that he might be persuaded those tears were shed for joy of his return. Quartilla, in Petronius, when nought would move, fell a weeping; and, as Balthazar Castilio paints them out, To these crocodile's tears, they will add sobs, fiery sighs, and sorrowful countenance, pale colour, leanness, and if you do but stir abroad, these fiends are ready to meet you at every turn, with such a sluttish, neglected habit, dejected look, as if they were now ready to die for your sake; and how saith he, shall a young novice thus beset, escape? But believe them not.

> *Trust not your hearts to girls, the sea's more certain*
>   *Than woman's faith.*   (PETRONIUS)

Thou thinkest peradventure because of her vows, tears, smiles, and protestations, she is solely thine, thou hast her heart, hand, and affection, when as indeed there is no such matter, as the Spanish Bawd said. she will have one sweetheart in bed, another in the gate, a third sighing at home, a fourth, &c. Every young man she sees and likes, hath as much interest, and shall as soon enjoy her as thyself. On the other side, which I have said, men are as false, let them swear, protect, and lie;

What they tell you, they've told a thousand girls.　(OVID)

They love some of them those eleven thousand Virgins at once, [of whom later], and make them believe each particular, he is besotted on her, or love one till they see another, and then her alone: like Milo's wife in Apuleius, who could not see a good looking youth without employing all her charms to corrupt him. 'Tis their common compliment in that case, they care not what they swear, say, or do. One while they slight them, care not for them, rail down right and scoff at them, and then again they will run mad, hang themselves, stab and kill, if they may not enjoy them. Henceforth therefore, let not Maids believe them. These tricks and counterfeit passions are more familiar with women; Today shall end my sorrow or my life, quoth Phædra to Hippolytus. Joessa, in Lucian, told Pythias, a young man, to move him the more, that if he would not have her, she was resolved to make away herself: There is a Nemesis, and it cannot choose but grieve and trouble thee, to hear that I have either strangled or drowned myself for thy sake. — Nothing so common to this sex, as oaths, vows, and protestations, and as I have already said, tears, which they have at command: for they can so weep, that one would think their very hearts were dissolved within them, and would come out in tears, their eyes are like rocks, which still drop water; saith Aristænetus, they wipe away their tears like sweat, weep with one eye, laugh with the other; or as children weep and cry, they can both together.

> *Care not for women's tears, I counsel thee,*
> *They teach their eyes as much to weep as see.*　(OVID)

And as much pity is to be taken of a woman weeping, as of a goose going barefoot. When Venus lost her son Cupid, she sent a Cryer about to bid every one that met him take heed.

> *Take heed of Cupid's tears, if cautelous,*
> *And of his smiles and kisses, I thee tell,*
> *If that he offer't, for they be noxious,*
> *And very poison in his lips doth dwell.*　(MOSCHUS)

A thousand years, as Castilio conceives, will scarce serve to reckon up those allurements and guiles, that men and women use to deceive one another with.

SUBSECTION 5 — *Bawds, Philters, Causes*

WHEN all other Engines fail, that they can proceed no further of
themselves, their last refuge is to fly to Bawds, Panders, Magical
Philters, and Receipts, rather than fail, to the Devil himself.

They will move Hell, if Heaven will not hear them. (VIRGIL)

And by those indirect means many a man is overcome, and precipitated
into this malady, if he take not good heed. For these Bawds first, they
are every where so common, and so many, that as he said of old Croton,
all here either inveigle, or be inveigled, we may say of most of our
Cities, there be so many professed, cunning bawds in them. Besides,
bawdry is become an art, or a liberal science, as Lucian calls it; and
there be such tricks and subtilties, so many nurses, old women, Pandars, letter-carriers, beggars, Physicians, Friars, Confessors, employed
about it, that no one pen could deal with it all,

Not even in three hundred verses
One your vileness rehearses. (PLAUTUS)

Such occult notes, Stenography, Polygraphy, mind reading, or magnetical telling of their minds, which Cabeus the Jesuit, by the way,
counts fabulous and false; cunning conveyances in this kind, that
neither Juno's jealousy, nor Danae's custody, nor Argo's vigilancy can
keep them safe. 'Tis the last and common refuge to use an assistant,
such as that Catanean Phillippa was to Joan Queen of Naples; a Bawd's
help, an old woman in the business, as Myrrha did when she doted
on Cinyras, and could not compass her desire, the old Jade her Nurse
was ready at a pinch, saying, Fear it not, if it be possible to be done,
I will effect it. There's no woman that a woman can't come over, as
Cælestina said, let him or her be never so honest, watched, and reserved,
'tis hard but one of these old women will get access: and scarce shall
you find, as Austin observes, in a Nunnery a maid alone; if she cannot
have egress, before her window you shall have an old woman, or some
prating Gossip tell her some tales of this Clerk, and that Monk, describing or commending some young Gentleman or other unto her. —
As I was walking in the street (saith a good fellow in Petronius) to
see the town served one evening, I spied an old woman in a corner selling of Cabbages and Roots (as our Hucksters do Plums, Apples, and
such like fruits); mother (quoth I), can you tell where I dwell? she
being well pleased with my foolish urbanity, replied, And why sir
should I not tell? with that she rose up and went before me; I took
her for a wise woman, and by and by she led me into a by-lane, and

told me there I should dwell; I replied again I knew not the house; but I perceived on a sudden by the naked queans, that I was now come into a bawdy-house, and then too late I began to curse the treachery of this old Jade. —————— Such tricks you shall have in many places, and among the rest it is ordinary in Venice, and in the Island of Zante, for a man to be Bawd to his own wife. No sooner shall you land or come on shore, but as the Comical Poet hath it,

> *The courtesans within the place are wont*
> *To send their slaves and girls down to the harbour,*
> *Whenever any strange ship comes in port;*
> *They ask the vessel's name, and where it comes from,*
> *Then swoop upon the officers and crew.*   (PLAUTUS)

These white Devils have their Panders, Bawds, and Factors, in every place, to seek about and bring in customers, to tempt and way-lay novices, and silly travellers. And when they have them once within their clutches, as Ægidius Maserius in his comment upon Valerius Flaccus describes them, with promises and pleasant discourse, with gifts, tokens, and taking their opportunities, they lay nets which Lucretia cannot avoid, and baits that Hippolytus himself would swallow; they make such strong assaults and batteries, that the Goddess of Virginity cannot withstand them: give gifts and bribes to move Penelope, and with threats able to terrify Susanna. How many Proserpinas with those catchpoles doth Pluto take! These are the sleepy rods with which their souls touched descend to hell; this the glew or lime with which the wings of the mind once taken cannot fly away; the Devil's ministers to allure, entice, &c. Many young men and maids without all question are inveigled by these Eumenides and their associates. But these are trivial and well known. The most sly, dangerous, and cunning bawds, are your knavish Physicians, Empiricks, Mass-Priests, Monks, Jesuits, and Friars. Though it be against Hippocrates' oath, some of them will give a dram, a promise to restore maidenheads, and do it without danger, make an abort if need be; keep down their paps, hinder conception, procure lust, make them able with Satyrions, and now and then step in themselves. No Monastery so close, house so private, or prison so well kept, but these honest men are admitted to censure and ask questions, to feel their pulse beat at their bed side, and all under pretence of giving Physick. Now as for Monks, Confessors, and Friars, as he said,

> *That Stygian Pluto dares not tempt or do,*
> *What an old hag or monk will undergo,*   (ÆNEAS SYLVIUS)

either for himself, to satisfy his own lust, for another. if he be hired thereto, or both at once, having such excellent means. For under colour of visitation, auricular confession, comfort, and penance, they have free egress and regress, and corrupt God knows how many. They can use trades some of them, practise Physick, use exorcisms, &c.

> For ther as wont to walken was an Elf,
> There walketh now the Limitour himself,
> In every bush, and under every tree,
> Ther is non other Incubus but he.

In the Mountains betwixt Dauphiné and Savoy, the Friars persuaded the good wives to counterfeit themselves possessed, that their husbands might give them free access, and were so familiar in those days with some of them, that, as one observes, wenches could not sleep in their beds for Necromantick Friars: and the good Abbess in Boccaccio may in some sort witness, that rising betimes mistook and put on the Friar's breeches instead of her veil or hat. You have heard the story, I presume, of Paulina, a chaste matron in Hegesippus, whom one of Isis' Priests did prostitute to Mundus, a young Knight, and made her believe it was their God Anubis. Many such pranks are played by our Jesuits, sometimes in their own habits, sometimes in others, like soldiers, courtiers, citizens, scholars, gallants, and women themselves. Proteus-like in all forms, and disguises, they go abroad in the night, to inescate [or allure] and beguile young women, or to have their pleasure of other men's wives: and if we may believe some relations, they have wardrobes of several suits in their Colleges for that purpose. Howsoever in publick they pretend much zeal, seem to be very holy men, and bitterly preach against adultery, fornication, there are no verier Bawds or whore-masters in a Country. Whose soul they should gain to God, they sacrifice to the Devil. But I spare these men for the present.

The last battering engines are Philters, Amulets, Spells, Charms, Images, and such unlawful means; if they cannot prevail of themselves by the help of Bawds, Panders, and their adherents, they will fly for succour to the Devil himself. I know there be those that deny the Devil can do any such thing, (Crato, and many Divines), there is no other fascination than that which comes by the eyes, of which I have formerly spoken; and if you desire to be better informed, read Camerarius. It was given out of old, that a Thessalian wench had bewitched King Philip to dote upon her, and by Philters enforced his love; but when Olympias, the Queen, saw the Maid of an excellent beauty, well brought up, and qualified: these, quoth she, were the Philters which inveigled King Philip; those the true charms, as Henry to Rosamund, —

One accent from thy lips the blood more warms
Than all their philters, exorcisms, and charms. (DRAYTON)

With this alone Lucretia brags, in Aretine, she could do more than
all Philosophers, Astrologers, Alchemists, Necromancers, Witches, and
the rest of the crew. As for herbs and Philters, [saith she,] I could
never skill of them, the sole Philter that ever I used was kissing and
embracing, by which alone I made men rave like beasts stupified, and
compelled them to worship me like an Idol. In our time 'tis a common
thing, saith Erastus in his book On Lamias, for witches to take upon
them the making of these Philters, to force men and women to love and
hate whom they will, to cause tempests, diseases, &c., by Charms,
Spells, Characters, Knots.

Love-potions from Thessaly he sells. (JUVENAL)

St. Hierome proves that they can do it, (as in Hilarion's life), he hath
a story of a young man that with a Philter made a Maid mad for the
love of him, which Maid was afterward cured by Hilarion. Such instances I find in John Nider. Plutarch records of Lucullus that he died of
a Philter, and that Cleopatra used Philters to inveigle Antony, amongst
other allurements. Eusebius reports as much of Lucretius the Poet.
Panormitan hath a story of one Stephen, a Neapolitan Knight, that
by a Philter was forced to run mad for love. But of all others, that which
Petrarch relates of Charles the Great, is most memorable. He foolishly
doted upon a woman of mean favour and condition, many years together, wholly delighting in her company, to the great grief and indignation of his friends and followers. When she was dead, he did embrace
her corpse, as Apollo did the bay-tree for his Daphne, and caused her
Coffin (richly embalmed and decked with Jewels) to be carried about
with him, over which he still lamented. At last a venerable Bishop that
followed his Court, prayed earnestly to God (commiserating his Lord
and Master's case) to know the true cause of this mad passion, and
whence it proceeded; it was revealed to him in fine, that the cause of
the Emperor's mad love lay under the dead woman's tongue. The
Bishop went hastily to the carkass, and took a small ring thence; upon
the removal the Emperor abhorred the Corpse, and instead of it fell as
furiously in love with the Bishop, he would not suffer him to be out of
his presence: which when the Bishop perceived, he flung the ring into
the midst of a great Lake, where the King then was. From that hour
the Emperor, neglecting all his other houses, dwelt at Aix, built a fair
house in the midst of the Marsh, to his infinite expense, and a Temple

by it, where after he was buried, and in which City all his posterity ever since use to be crowned. Marcus the Heretick is accused by Irenæus to have inveigled a young Maid by this means; and some writers speak hardly of the Lady Katherine Cobham, that by the same Art she circumvented Humphrey Duke of Gloucester to be her husband. Sicinius Æmilianus summoned Apuleius to come before Claudius Maximus, Proconsul of Africa, that he, being a poor fellow, had bewitched by Philters Pudentilla, an ancient rich Matron, to love him, and being worth so many thousand sesterces, to be his wife. Agrippa attributes much in this kind to Philters, Amulets, Images: and Salmuth saith, 'tis an ordinary practice at Fez, in Africa, there are many tricksters there, who bring lovers to bed together, as skilful all out as that Hyperborean Magician, of whom Cleodemus in Lucian tells so many fine feats, perform'd in this kind. But Erastus, Wierus, and others, are against it; they grant indeed such things may be done, but (as Wierus discourseth) not by Charms, Incantations, Philters, but the Devil himself; he contends as much; so doth Freitagius, Andreas Cisalpinus, and so much Sigismundus Schereczius proves at large. Unchaste women by the help of these witches, the Devil's kitchen-maids, have their Loves brought to them in the night, and carried back again by a phantasm flying in the Air in the likeness of a Goat. I have heard (saith he) divers confess that they have been so carried on a Goat's back to their sweet-hearts, many miles in a night. — Others are of opinion that these feats, which most suppose to be done by Charms and Philters, are merely effected by natural causes, as by man's blood chemically prepared, which much avails, saith Ernestus Burgravius, in a Revelatory Lamp of Life and Death, to procure love and hate (so huntsmen make their dogs love them and farmers their pullen [poultry]), 'tis an excellent Philter, as he holds, but not fit to be made common: and so be apples of madness, Mandrake roots, Mandrake apples, precious stones, dead men's clothes, candles, apples of drunkenness, swine's bread [the herb of cyclamen], Hippomanes [which is the venomus humour that comes from a mare in heat], a certain hair in a Wolf's tail, &c., of which Rhasis, Dioscorides, Porta, Wecker, Rubeus, Mizaldus, Albertus, treat: a swallow's heart, dust of a dove's heart, vipers' tongues are much valued, asses' brains, horses' pintles, cauls, the rope with which a man hath been hanged, a stone from an eagle's nest, &c. See more in Sckenkius, which are as forcible, and of as much virtue, as that fountain Salmacis in Vitruvius. Ovid, Strabo, that made all such mad for love that drank of it, or that hot bath at Aix in Germany, wherein Cupid once dipt his arrows, which ever since hath a peculiar virtue to make them lovers all that wash in it. But hear the Poet's own description of it.

> *Whence this heat of waters tost*
> *Bubbling upward from earth's frost?*
> *Cupid once his arrows hot*
> *Dipt in waters of this spot,*
> *And delighted with the sound*
> *Of waters steaming from the ground,*
> *' Lo,' he said, ' boil on for ever,*
> *Keeping memory of my quiver!'*
> *Since when 'tis a magick spring,*
> *And who dares bathe here feels love's sting.*

These above-named remedies have happily as much power as that bath of Aix, or Venus' enchanted girdle, in which, saith Natalis Comes, Love-toys and dalliance, pleasantness, sweetness, persuasions, subtilties, gentle speeches, and all witchcraft to enforce love, was contained. Read more of these in Agrippa's Occult Philosophy, the Hammer of Witches, Delrio, Wierus, Pomponatius on Incantations, Ficinus on the Theology of Plato, Calcagninus, &c.

MEMBER 3

Symptoms or signs of Love-Melancholy, in Body, Mind, good, bad, &c.

SYMPTOMS are either of Body or Mind; of body, Paleness, Leanness, dryness, &c. Let everyone that loves be pale, for lovers 'tis the proper hue, as the Poet [Ovid] describes lovers; love causeth leanness. Avicenna makes hollow eyes, dryness, symptoms of this disease, to go smiling to themselves, or acting as if they saw or heard some delectable object. Valleriola, Laurentius, Ælianus Montaltus, Langius, deliver as much, the body lean, pale,

> *Like one who hath trodden barefoot on a snake,*   (JUVENAL)

hollow-ey'd, their eyes are hidden in their heads, they pine away, and look ill with waking, cares, sighs, eyes that rivall'd the sunny locks of Phœbus lose their lustre, with groans, griefs, sadness, dulness, want of appetite, &c. A reason of all this, Jason Pratensis gives, because of the distraction of the spirits, the Liver doth not perform his part, nor turns the aliment into blood as it ought; and for that cause the members are weak for want of sustenance, they are lean and pine, as the herbs of my garden do this month of May, for want of rain. The Green-sickness therefore often happeneth to young women, a Cachexia, or an evil habit to men, besides their ordinary sighs, complaints and lamentations, which are too frequent. As drops from a Still, doth Cupid's fire provoke tears from a true Lover's eyes.

> *The mighty Mars did oft for Venus shriek,*
> *Privily moistening his horid cheek*
> *With womanish tears, ——* (SPENSER)

with many such like passions. When Chariclea was enamoured on Theagenes, as Heliodorus sets her out, she was half distracted, and spake she knew not what, sighed to herself, lay much awake, and was lean upon a sudden: and when she was besotted on her son-in-law, she had ugly paleness, hollow eyes, restless thoughts, short wind, &c. Euryalus, in an Epistle sent to Lucretia his Mistress, complains amongst other grievances, thou hast taken my stomack and my sleep from me. So he [Chaucer] describes it aright:

> His slepe, his mete, his drinke is him byraft,
> That lene he wex, and drie as is a shaft,
> His eyen holwe, and grisly to behold,
> His hewe falwe, and pale as ashen cold,
> And solitary he was and ever alone,
> And waking all the night, making his mone.

Theocritus makes a fair maid of Delphi, in love with a young man of Minda confess as much,

> *No sooner seen I had, than mad I was,*
> *My beauty fail'd, and I no more did care*
> *For any pomp, I knew not where I was,*
> *But sick I was, and evil I did fare;*
> *I lay upon my bed ten days and nights,*
> *A skeleton I was in all men's sights.*

All these passions are well expressed by that Heroical Poet in the person of Dido:

> *Unhappy Dido could not sleep at all,*
> *But lies awake, and takes no rest:*
> *And up she gets again, whilst care and grief,*
> *And raging love torments her breast.* (VIRGIL)

Accius Sannazarius in the same manner feigns his Lycoris tormenting herself for want of sleep, sighing, sobbing, and lamenting; and Eustathius his Ismenias much troubled, and panting at heart at the sight of his mistress, he could not sleep, his bed was thorns. All make leanness, want of appetite, want of sleep ordinary Symptoms, and by that means they are brought often so low, so much altered and changed, that as he

[Terence] jested in the Comedy, one can scarce know them to be the same men.

> *Let sleepless nights make thin the young men's bodies,*
> *Care, too, and the grief that comes from violent love.* (OVID)

Many such Symptoms there are of the body to discern lovers by,

> *For who is there can hide his love?* (OVID)

Can a man, said Solomon, carry fire in his bosom, and not burn? It will hardly be hid, though they do all they can to hide it, it must out; by more than a thousand Symptoms it may be descried.

> *The more concealed, the more it breaks to light.* (OVID)

'Twas Antiphanes the Comedian's observation of old, Love and Drunkenness cannot be concealed, words, looks, gestures, all will betray them: but two of the most notable signs are observed by the Pulse and Countenance. When Antiochus the son of Seleucus was sick for Stratonice his Mother-in-law, and would not confess his grief, or the cause of his disease, Erasistratus the Physician found him by his Pulse and Countenance to be in love with her, because that when she came in presence, or was named, his pulse varied, and he blushed besides. In this very sort was the love of Charicles, the son of Polycles, discovered by Panacius the Physician, as you may read the story at large in Aristænetus. By the same signs Galen brags that he found out Justa, Boëthius the Consul's wife, to dote on Pylades the Player, because at his name still she both altered Pulse and Countenance, as Poliarchus did at the name of Argenis. Franciscus Valesius denies there is any such pulse of love, or that love may be so discerned; but Avicenna confirms this of Galen out of his experience, and Gordonius; their pulse, he saith, is inordinate and swift, if she go by whom he loves; Langius, Nevisanus, Valescus de Taranta, Guianerius. Valleriola sets down this for a Symptom, difference of Pulse, neglect of business, want of sleep, often sighs, blushings, when there is any speech of their Mistress, are manifest signs. But amongst the rest, Josephus Struthius, that Polonian, in the fifth Book of his Doctrine of Pulses, holds that this, and all other passions of the mind, may be discovered by the Pulse. And if you will know, saith he, whether the men suspected be such or such, touch their arteries, &c. And in his fourth Book, he speaks of this particular Pulse, Love makes an unequal pulse, &c.; he gives instance of a Gentlewoman, a Patient of his, whom by this means he found to be much enamoured, and with whom: he named many persons, but at the last when his name came whom he suspected, her pulse began to vary, and to beat swifter, and so by often feeling her pulse, he perceived what the matter was. Apollonius, poetically setting down the meeting of Jason and Medea, makes them both to blush at one another's sight, and at the first they were not able to speak. " I'm all trembling & chill at the very sight of her, Parmeno " (Terence). Phædria trembled at the sight of Thais, others sweat, blow short, tremble in their knees, are troubled with palpitation of heart upon the like occasion, saith Aristænetus, their heart is at their mouth, leaps, these burn and freeze, (for love is fire, ice, hot, cold, itch, fever, phrenzy, pleurisy, what not?) they look pale, red, and commonly blush at their first congress; and sometimes, through violent agitation of spirits, bleed at nose, or when she is talked of; which very sign Eustathius makes an argument of Ismene's affection, that, when she met her Sweetheart by chance, she changed her countenance to a Maiden-blush. 'Tis a common thing amongst Lovers, as Arnulphus, that merry, conceited Bishop, hath well expressed in a facete Epigram of his,

> *Their faces answer, and by blushing say,*
> *How both affected are, they do bewray.*

But the best conjectures are taken from such symptoms as appear when they are both present; all their speeches, amorous glances, actions, lascivious gestures, will bewray them, they cannot contain themselves, but that they will be still kissing. Stratocles the Physician upon his Wedding day, when he was at dinner, could not eat his meat for kissing the Bride, &c. First a word, and then a kiss, then some other Compliment, and then a kiss, then an idle question, then a kiss, and when he had pumped his wits dry, can say no more, kissing and colling are never out of season.

> *Never ceasing, still beginning,* (PETRONIUS)

'tis never at an end, another kiss, and then another, another, and another, &c.

> *Come hither, O Thelayra!* (LŒCHEUS)

Come, kiss me, Corinna!

> *A hundred hundred kisses,*
> *A hundred thousand kisses,*
> *A thousand thousand kisses,*
> *Thousands of thousands altogether,*
> *As drops of water in the Sicilian Sea,*
> *As many as there are stars in the sky,*
> *Upon your rosy knees,*
> *Upon your swelling lips,*
> *Upon your speaking eyes,*
> *I fix with unceasing passion,*
> *O lovely Neæra!* (JOHANNES SECUNDUS)

As Catullus to Lesbia,

> ——— *first give a hundred,*
> *Then a thousand, then another*
> *Hundred, then unto the other*
> *Add a thousand, and so more, &c.**

Till you equal with the store all the grass, &c. So Venus did by her Adonis, the Moon with Endymion, they are still dallying and culling, as so many Doves, and that with alacrity and courage,

> *With indrawn breath, hungrily breast to breast,*
> *With mingling of spittle, and teeth against mouths hard pressed.*
>
> (LUCRETIUS)

With such hard kisses on the mouth that the lips can scarce be withdrawn, head thrown back, as Lamprias in Lucian kist Thais, Philippus her in Aristænetus, in a phrenzy of love cleaving so hotly that 'twas hard to free the lips, he bruised his whole mouth against her. Aretine's Lucretia, by a suitor of hers was so saluted, and 'tis their ordinary fashion,

> *With bitten lips, and clashing of mouth on mouth.* (LUCRETIUS)

They cannot, I say, contain themselves, they will be still not only joining hands, kissing, but embracing, treading on their toes, &c., diving into their bosoms, and that as a welcome pleasance, as Philostratus confesseth to his Mistress; and Lamprias in Lucian, with the hand secretly in the bosom, feeling their paps, and that scarce honestly sometimes; as the old man in the Comedy well observed of his son, Did not I see thee put thy hand into her bosom? Go to, with many such love tricks. Juno in Lucian, complains to Jupiter of Ixion, he looked so attentively on her, and sometimes would sigh and weep in her company: And when I drank by chance, and gave Ganymede the cup, he would desire to drink still in the very cup that I drank of, and in the same place where I drank, and would kiss the cup, and then look steadily on me, and sometimes sigh, and then again smile. If it be so they cannot come near to dally, have not that opportunity, familiarity, or acquaintance, to confer and talk together; yet, if they be in presence, their eyes will bewray them: as the common saying is, Where I look, I like; and where I like, I love; but they will lose themselves in her looks.

> *Each, with bright glances at the other's face,*
> *Demanded silently tidings of our love.* (OVID)

They cannot look off whom they love, they will deflower her with their eyes, be still gazing, staring, stealing faces, smiling, glancing at her, as

---

* Translated or imitated by M[r]. B. Johnson, our arch poet, in his 119th epigram. — Burton's note.

Apollo on Leucothöe, the Moon on her Endymion, when she stood still in Caria, and at Latmos caused her Chariot to be stayed. They must all stand and admire, or, if she go by, look after her as long as they can see her; she is the charioteer of the soul, as Anacreon calls her, they cannot go by her door or window, but, as an Adamant, she draws their eyes to it, though she be not there present, they must needs glance that way, and look back to it. Aristænetus of Euxitheus, Lucian in Images, of himself, and Tatius of Clitophon say as much, he never could turn his eyes away from Leucippe, and many Lovers confess, when they came in their Mistress' presence, they could not hold off their eyes, but looked wistly and steadfastly on her, with an unwinking glance, with much eagerness and greediness, as if they would look through, or should never have enough sight of her, —

> *Rooted motionless in one set gaze.*   (VIRGIL)

So she will do by him, drink to him with her eyes, nay drink him up, devour him, swallow him, as Martial's Mamurra is remembered to have done:

She looked at the sweet lads, eating them up with her eyes.   (MARTIAL)

There is a pleasant story to this purpose in Vertomannus. The Sultan of Sana's wife in Arabia, because Vertomannus was fair and white, could not look off him, from Sun-rising to Sun-setting she could not desist, she made him one day come into her chamber, for two hours' space she still gazed on him, averting not one glance of her eyes, observing him as though he were Cupid himself. A young man in Lucian fell in love with Venus' picture, he came every morning to her Temple, and there continued all day long from Sun-rising to Sun-set, unwilling to go home at night, sitting over against the Goddess' Picture, he did continually look upon her, and mutter to himself I know not what. If so be they cannot see them whom they love, they will still be walking and waiting about their Mistress' doors, taking all opportunity to see them; as in Longus Sophista, Daphnis and Chloe, two Lovers, were still hovering at one another's gates, he sought all occasions to be in her company, to hunt in Summer, and catch Birds in the Frost about her Father's house in the Winter, that she might see him, and he her. A King's Palace was not so diligently attended, saith Aretine's Lucretia, as my house was when I lay in Rome, the porch and street was ever full of some, walking or riding, on set purpose to see me, their eye was still upon my window as they passed by, they could not choose but look back to my house when they were past, and sometimes hem, or cough, or take some impertinent occasion to speak aloud, that I might look out and observe them. 'Tis

so in other places, 'tis common to every Lover, 'tis all his felicity to be
with her, to talk with her, he is never well but in her company, and will
walk seven or eight times in a day through the street where she dwells,
and make sleeveless [or idle] errands to see her, plotting still where,
when, and how to visit her,

> *Now let soft whispers in the dusk of evening*
> *Be renewed at the appointed hour.* (HORACE)

And when he is gone, he thinks every minute an hour, every hour as long
as a day, ten days a whole year, till he see her again —

> *If thou dost reckon the time, which we who love reckon so carefully.*
>
> (OVID)

And if thou be in love, thou wilt say so too, and at length, Farewell,
beautiful one, farewell, Sweetheart. Farewell, my dearest Argenis, once
more farewell, farewell. And though he is to meet her by compact, and
that very shortly, perchance to-morrow, yet loath to depart, he'll take
his leave again and again, and then come back again, look after, and
shake his hand, wave his hat afar off. Now gone, he thinks it long till
he see her again, and she him, the clocks are surely set back, the hour's
past.

> *I, thy hostess, I, thy Rhodopeian Phyllis,*
> *Wonder why beyond the promis'd time thou'rt absent.* (HORACE)

She looks out at window still to see whether he come, and by report
Phyllis went nine times to the Sea side that day, to see if her Demophoon
were approaching, and Troilus to the City gates, to look for his Creseid.
She is ill at ease, and sick till she see him again, peevish in the mean
time, discontent, heavy, sad, and why comes he not? where is he? why
breaks he promise? why tarries he so long? sure he is not well; sure he
hath some mischance, sure he forgets himself and me, with infinite such.
And then confident again, up she gets, out she looks, listens and enquires,
hearkens, kens [looks about]; every man afar off is sure he, every stirring
in the street, now he is there, that's he; an evil day, she says, the longest
day that ever was; so she raves, restless and impatient; for love brooks
no delays: the time's quickly gone that's spent in her company, the miles
short, the way pleasant, all weather is good whilst he goes to her house,
heat or cold, though his teeth chatter in his head, he moves not, wet or
dry, 'tis all one; wet to the skin, he feels it not, cares not at least for it,
but will easily endure it, and much more, because it is done with alacrity, and for his Mistress' sweet sake; let the burthen be never so heavy,
Love makes it light. Jacob served seven years for Rachel, and it was
quickly gone, because he loved her. None so merry, if he may happily

enjoy her company, he is in heaven for a time; and if he may not, dejected in an instant, solitary, silent, he departs weeping, lamenting, sighing, complaining.

But the Symptoms of the mind in Lovers are almost infinite, and so diverse, that no Art can comprehend them: though they be merry sometimes, and rapt beyond themselves for joy, yet most part, Love is a plague, a torture, an hell, a bitter-sweet passion at last. 'Tis a sweet bitterness, a delicious pain, a gay torment:

> *Sweeter than honey, it pleases me;*
> *More bitter than gall, it teases me.*

Like a Summer Fly, or Sphine's wings, or a Rainbow of all colours, fair, foul, and full of variation, though most part irksome and bad. For in a word, the Spanish Inquisition is not comparable to it; a torment and execution it is, as he calls it in the Poet, an unquenchable fire, and what not? From it, saith Austin, arise biting cares, perturbations, passions, sorrows, fears, suspicions, discontents, contentions, discords, wars, treacheries, enmities, flattery, cozening, riot, lust, impudence, cruelty, knavery, &c.

> *Pains and plaints, regrets and endless tears,*
> *Weariness and care, bitterness and fears,*   (MARULLUS)

these be the companions of lovers, and the ordinary symptoms, as the Poet repeats them.

> *In love these vices are: suspicions,*
> *Peace, war, and impudence, detractions,*
> *Dreams, cares, and errors, terrors and affrights,*
> *Immodest pranks, devices, sleights and flights,*
> *Heart-burnings, wants, neglects, desire of wrong,*
> *Loss continual, expense, and hurt among.*   (TERENCE)

Every Poet is full of such Catalogues of Love Symptoms; but fear and sorrow may justly challenge the chief place. Though Hercules de Saxoniâ will exclude fear from Love Melancholy, yet I am otherwise persuaded. 'Tis full of fear, anxiety, doubt, care, peevishness, suspicion, it turns a man into a woman, which made Hesiod, belike, put Fear and Paleness [as] Venus' daughters, because fear and love are still linked together. Moreover, they are apt to mistake, amplify, too credulous sometimes, too full of hope and confidence, and then again very jealous, unapt to believe or entertain any good news. The Comical Poet hath prettily painted out this passage amongst the rest, in a Dialogue betwixt Micio and Æschines, a gentle father and a love-sick son: M. *Be of good cheer, my son, thou shalt have her to wife.* Æ. *Ah father, do you mock*

me now? M. I mock thee, why? Æ. That which I so earnestly desire, I
more suspect and fear. M. Get you home, and send for her to be your
wife. Æ. What now, a wife, now father, &c. — These doubts, anxieties,
suspicions, are the least part of their torments; they break many times
from passions to actions, speak fair, and flatter, now most obsequious
and willing, by and by they are averse, wrangle, fight, swear, quarrel,
laugh, weep: and he that doth not so by fits, Lucian holds, is not thoroughly touched with this Loadstone of Love. So their actions and passions are intermixt, but of all other passions, Sorrow hath the greatest
share; Love to many is bitterness itself; Plato calls it a bitter potion, an
agony, a plague.

> *O take away this plague, this mischief from me,*
> *Which as a numbness over all my body,*
> *Expels my joys, and makes my soul so heavy.* (CATULLUS)

Phædria had a true touch of this, when he cried out,

> *O Thais, would thou hadst of these my pains a part,*
> *Or, as it doth me now, so it would make thee smart.*   (TERENCE)

So had that young man, when he roared again for discontent,

> *I am vext and toss'd, and rack'd on Love's wheel;*
> *Where not, I am; but where am, do not feel.* (PLAUTUS)

The Moon, in Lucian, made her moan to Venus, that she was almost
dead for love, and after a long tale, she broke off abruptly and wept, O
Venus, thou knowest my poor heart. Charmides, in Lucian, was so impatient, that he sobb'd and sighed, and tore his hair, and said he would
hang himself: I am undone, O sister Tryphæna, I cannot endure these
love pangs, what shall I do? — O ye Gods, free me from these cares and
miseries! out of the anguish of his Soul, Theocles prays. Shall I say,
most part of a Lover's life is full of agony, anxiety, fear, and grief, complaints, sighs, suspicions, and cares, (heigh-ho, my heart is wo), full of
silence and irksome solitariness?

> *Frequenting shady bowers in discontent,*
> *To the air his fruitless clamours he will vent,*

except at such times that he hath lucid intervals, pleasant gales, or sudden alterations; as, if his Mistress smile upon him, give him a good
look, a kiss, or that some comfortable message be brought him, his
service is accepted, &c.

He is then too confident, and rapt beyond himself, as if he had heard
the Nightingale in the Spring before the Cuckoo, or as Callisto was at
Meliboea's presence, Who ever saw so glorious a sight, what man ever
enjoyed such delight? More content cannot be given of the Gods, wished,

had, or hoped, of any mortal man. There is no happiness in the world
comparable to his; no content, no joy to this, no life to Love, he is in
Paradise.

> *Who lives so happy as myself? what bliss*
> *In this our life may be compared to this?*   (CATULLUS)

He will not change fortune in that case with a Prince. Whilst he is
pleasing to her, the Persian Kings are not so jovial as he is. O happy
day; so Chærea exclaims when he came from Pamphila, his Sweetheart,
well pleased; he could find in his heart to be killed instantly, lest, if he
live longer, some sorrow or sickness should contaminate his joys. A little
after, he was so merrily set upon the same occasion, that he could not
contain himself. Is't possible (O my Countrymen) for any living to be
so happy as myself! No, sure, it cannot be, for the Gods have shewed all
their power, all their goodness in me. Yet by and by, when this young
Gallant was crossed in his Wench, he laments, and cries, and roars down-
right. I am undone. The Virgin's gone, and I am gone; she's gone, she's
gone, and what shall I do? where shall I seek her, where shall I find her,
whom shall I ask? what way, what course shall I take? what will become of me? He was weary of his life, sick, mad and desperate. 'Tis not
Chærea's case this alone, but his, and his, and every Lover's in the like
state. If he hear ill news, have bad success in his suit, she frown upon
him, or that his Mistress in his presence respect another more, (as
Hædus observes), prefer another suitor, speak more familiarly to him, or
use more kindly than himself, if by nod, smile, message, she discloseth
herself to another, he is instantly tormented, none so dejected as he is,
utterly undone, a cast-away, a dead man, the scorn of fortune, a monster of fortune, worse than naught, the loss of a Kingdom had been less.
Aretine's Lucretia made very good proof of this, as she relates it herself: For when I made some of my suitors believe I would betake myself
to a Nunnery, they took on, as if they had lost Father and Mother, because they were for ever after to want my company. All other labour
was light; but this might not be endured, for I cannot be without thy
company, mournful Amyntas, painful Amyntas, careful Amyntas; better
a Metropolitan City were sackt, a Royal Army overcome, an Invincible
Armada sunk, and twenty thousand Kings should perish, than her little
finger ache, so zealous are they, and so tender of her good. They would
all turn Friars for my sake, as she follows it, in hope by that means to
meet, or see me again, as my Confessors, at stool-ball, or at barley-break.
And so afterwards, when an importunate suitor came, If I had bid my
Maid say that I was not at leisure, not within, busy, could not speak

with him, he was instantly astonished, and stood like a pillar of marble; another went swearing, chafing, cursing, foaming.

That voice was like the wrath of God,

the voice of a Mandrake had been sweeter musick; but he to whom I gave entertainment, was in the Elysian fields, ravished for joy, quite beyond himself. 'Tis the general humour of all Lovers, she is their stern, Pole-star, and guide,

The delight and desire of the soul.   (LOCHÆUS)

As a Tulipant to the Sun (which our Herbalists call Narcissus) when it shines, is a glorious Flower exposing itself; but when the Sun sets, or a tempest comes, it hides itself, pines away, and hath no pleasure left (which Carolus Gonzaga, Duke of Mantua, in a cause not unlike, sometimes used for an Impress) do all enamoratoes to their Mistress, she is their Sun, their prime mover or informing breath; this, one hath elegantly expressed by a windmill, still moved by the wind, which otherwise hath no motion of itself. He is wholly animated from her breath, his soul lives in her body, she keeps the keys of his life; his fortune ebbs and flows with her favour, a gracious or bad aspect turns him up or down,

The light of my mind, Lucia, at thy light is lit.

Howsoever his present state be pleasing or displeasing, 'tis continuate so long as he loves, he can do nothing, think of nothing but her; desire hath no rest, she is his Cynosure [or North Star], his Hesper and Vesper, his morning and evening Star, his Goddess, his Mistress, his life, his soul, his every thing, dreaming, waking, she is always in his mouth: his heart, eyes, ears, and all his thoughts are full of her. His Laura, his Victorina, his Columbina, Flavia, Flaminia, Cælia, Delia, or Isabella, (call her how you will), she is the sole object of his senses, the substance of his soul, he magnifies her above measure, he is full of her, can breathe nothing but her. I adore Melibœa, saith Love-sick Callisto, I believe in Melibœa, I honour, admire, and love, my Melibœa: his soul was sowced, imparadised, imprisoned in his Lady. When Thais took her leave of Phædria, Sweetheart (she said) will you command me any further service? He readily replied, and gave this in charge, —

> *Dost ask (my dear) what service I will have?*
> *To love me day and night is all I crave,*
> *To dream on me, to expect, to think on me,*
> *Depend and hope, still covet me to see,*
> *Delight thyself in me, be wholly mine,*
> *For know, my love, that I am wholly thine.*

But all this needed not, you will say, if she affect once, she will be his, settle her love on him, on him alone.

> *Seeing and hearing him, though they be parted,* (VIRGIL)

she can, she must think and dream of nought else but him, continually of him, as did Orpheus on his Eurydice.

> *On thee, sweet wife, was all my song,*
> *Morn, Evening, and all along.* (VIRGIL)

And Dido upon her Æneas:

> *And ever and anon she thinks upon the man*
> *That was so fine, so fair, so blythe, so debonair.* (VIRGIL)

Clitophon, in the first book of Achilles Tatius, complaineth how that his Mistress Leucippe tormented him much more in the night than in the day: For all day long he had some object or other to distract his senses, but in the night all ran upon her: all night long he lay awake and could think of nothing else but her, he could not get her out of his mind: towards morning, sleep took a little pity on him, he slumbered a while, but all his dreams were of her.

> *In the dark night I speak, embrace, and find*
> *That fading joys deceive my careful mind.* (BUCHANAN)

The same complaint Euryalus makes to his Lucretia, day and night I think of thee, I wish for thee, I talk of thee, call on thee, look for thee, hope for thee, delight myself in thee, day and night I love thee. Morning, Evening, all is alike with me, I have restless thoughts,

> *Thee with waking eyes and anxious mind I follow all night.*
> (PETRONIUS)

Still I think on thee. The soul is not where it lives, but where it loves. I live and breathe in thee, I wish for thee. O happy day that shall restore thee to my sight! In the mean time he raves on her; her sweet face, eyes, actions, gestures, hands, feet, speech, length, breadth, height, depth, and the rest of her dimensions, are so surveyed, measured, and taken, by that Astrolabe of Phantasy, and that so violently sometimes, with such earnestness and eagerness, such continuance, so strong an imagination, that at length he thinks he sees her indeed; he talks with her, he embraceth her, Ixion-like, a cloud for Juno, as he said, I see and meditate of nought but Leucippe. Be she present or absent, all is one;

> *Though her fair presence is wanting,*
> *The love which it kindled stays,* (OVID)

that impression of her beauty is still fixed in his mind; as he that is bitten with a mad dog, thinks all he sees dogs, dogs in his meat, dogs in his dish, dogs in his drink: his Mistress is in his eyes, ears, heart, in all

his senses. Valleriola had a Merchant his Patient in the same predicament: and Ulricus Molitor, out of Austin, hath a story of one, that
through vehemency of his love passion, still thought he saw his Mistress
present with him, she talked with him, still embracing him.

Now if this passion of Love can produce such effects, if it be pleas-
antly intended, what bitter torments shall it breed, when it is with fear
& continual sorrow, suspicion, care, agony, as commonly it is, still accompanied, what an intolerable pain must it be!

> *Mount Gargarus hath not so many stems,*
> *As Lover's breast hath grievous wounds,*
> *And linked cares, which love compounds.*

When the King of Babylon would have punished a Courtier of his, for
loving of a young Lady of the Royal blood, and far above his fortunes,
Apollonius in presence by all means persuaded to let him alone: for to
love, and not enjoy, was a most unspeakable torment, no tyrant could
invent the like punishment; as a gnat at a candle, in a short space he
would consume himself. For Love is a perpetual flux, an anguish of the
soul, a warfare, every lover a soldier, a grievous wound is love still, & a
Lover's heart is Cupid's quiver, a consuming fire, an inextinguishable
fire. As Ætna rageth, so doth Love, and more than Ætna, or any material
fire. Vulcan's flames are but smoke to this. For fire, saith Xenophon,
burns them alone that stand near it, or touch it; but this fire of Love
burneth and scorcheth afar off, and is more hot and vehement than any
material fire; 'tis a fire in a fire, the quintessence of fire. For when Nero
burnt Rome, as Callisto urgeth, he fired houses, consumed men's bodies
and goods; but this fire devours the soul itself, and one soul is worth
100,000 bodies. No water can quench this wild fire.

> *A fire he took into his breast,*
> *Which water could not quench,*
> *Nor Herb, nor Art, nor Magic spells*
> *Could quell, nor any drench,*   (MANTUAN)

except it be tears and sighs, for so they may chance find a little ease.

> *So thy white neck, Neæra, me, poor soul,*
> *Doth scorch, thy cheeks, thy wanton eyes that roll:*
> *Were it not for my dropping tears that hinder,*
> *I should be quite burnt up forthwith to cinder.*   (MARULLUS)

This fire strikes like lightning, which made those old Grecians paint
Cupid in many of their Temples with Jupiter's thunder-bolts in his
hands; for it wounds, and cannot be perceived how, whence it came,
where it pierced,

> *I burn, and my breast hath a secret wound,* (OVID)

and can hardly be discerned at first.

> *A gentle wound, an easy fire it was,*
> *And fly at first, and secretly did pass.* (VIRGIL)

But by and by it began to rage and burn amain;

> *This fiery vapour rageth in the veins,*
> *And scorcheth entrails as when fire burns*
> *An house, it nimbly runs along the beams,*
> *And at the last the whole it overturns.* (SENECA)

Abraham Hoffemannus relates out of Plato, how that Empedocles the Philosopher was present at the cutting up of one that died for love, his heart was combust, his liver smoky, his lungs dried up, insomuch that he verily believed his soul was either sod or roasted, through the vehemency of Love's fire. Which belike made a modern writer of amorous Emblems express Love's fury by a pot hanging over the fire, and Cupid blowing the coals. As the heat consumes the water, so doth Love dry up his radical moisture. Another compares Love to a melting torch, which stood too near the fire.

> *The nearer he unto his mistress is,*
> *The nearer he unto his ruin is.* (GROTIUS)

So that to say truth, as Castilio describes it, the beginning, middle, end of Love is nought else but sorrow, vexation, agony, torment, irksomeness, wearisomeness, so that to be squalid, ugly, miserable, solitary, discontent, dejected, to wish for death, to complain, rave, and to be peevish, are the certain signs, and ordinary actions of a Love-sick person. This continual pain and torture makes them forget themselves, if they be far gone with it, in doubt, despair of obtaining, or eagerly bent, to neglect all ordinary business.

> *The works unfinished hang, the threatening walls,*
> *And turrets mounting upward to the skies.* (VIRGIL)

Love-sick Dido left her works undone, so did Phædra,

> *The web of Pallas languishes, the work*
> *Even in Phædra's hands is left undone.*

Faustus, in Mantuan, took no pleasure in any thing he did,

> *No rest, no labor, pleased my love-sick breast,*
> *My faculties were asleep, my mind was dull,*
> *I lost my zest for poesy and song.*

And 'tis the humour of them all, to be careless of their persons, and their estates, as the shepherd in Theocritus, their beards flag, and they have no more care of pranking themselves, or of any business, they care not, as they say, which end goes forward.

> *Forgetting flocks of sheep and country farms,*
> *The silly shepherd always mourns and burns.*

Love-sick Chærea when he came from Pamphila's house, and had not so good welcome as he did expect, was all amort, Parmeno meets him, *Why art thou so sad, man? whence com'st, how dost?* but he sadly replies, *I have so forgotten myself, I neither know where I am, nor whence I come, nor whither I will, what I do.* P. *How so?* Ch. *I am in love.*

> *Living, I die, and know not what I do.* (TERENCE)

He that erst had his thoughts free (as Philostratus Lemnius, in an Epistle of his, describes this fiery passion) and spent his time like an hard student, in those delightsome philosophical precepts, he that with the Sun and Moon wandered all over the world, with Stars themselves ranged about, and left no secret or small mystery in Nature unsearched, since he was enamoured, can do nothing now but think and meditate of Love-matters, day and night composeth himself how to please his Mistress; all his study, endeavour, is to approve himself to his Mistress, to win his Mistress' favour, to compass his desire, to be counted her servant. When Peter Abelard, that great scholar of his age,

> *To whom alone was known whate'er is knowable,**

was now in love with Heloise, he had no mind to visit or frequent Schools and Scholars any more. Very tedious it was, (as he confesseth) to go to the disputations, or linger there, all his mind was on his new Mistress.

Now to this end and purpose, if there be any hope of obtaining his suit, to prosecute his cause, he will spend himself, goods, fortunes for her, and though he lose and alienate all his friends, be threatened, be cast off, and disinherited; for as the Poet saith, who can set bounds to love? though he be utterly undone by it, disgraced, go a begging, yet for her sweet sake, to enjoy her, he will willingly beg, hazard all he hath, goods, lands, shame, scandal, fame, and life itself.

> *I'll never rest or cease my suit,*
> *'Till she or death do make me mute.* (PLAUTUS)

Parthenis in Aristænetus was fully resolved to do as much. I may have better matches, I confess, but farewell shame, farewell honour, farewell honesty, farewell friends and fortune, &c. O Harpedona, keep my counsel, I will leave all for his sweet sake, I will have him, say no more, against all the world I am resolved, I will have him. Gobryas the Cap-

* His epitaph.

tain, when he had espied Rhodanthe, the fair captive Maid, fell upon his knees before Mystylus the General, with tears, vows, and all the Rhetorick he could, by the scars he had formerly received, the good service he had done, or whatsoever else was dear unto him besought his Governor he might have the captive Virgin to be his wife, as a reward of his worth and service: and moreover, he would forgive him the money which was owing, and all reckonings besides due unto him, I ask no more, no part of booty, no portion, but Rhodanthe to be my wife. And when as he could not compass her by fair means, he fell to treachery, force and villainy, and set his life at stake at last, to accomplish his desire. 'Tis a common humour this, a general passion of all Lovers, to be so affected, and which Æmilia told Aretinus a Courtier in Castilio's discourse, Surely, Aretinus, and if thou wert not so indeed, thou didst not love; ingenuously confess, for if thou hadst been thoroughly enamoured, thou wouldst have desired nothing more than to please thy Mistress. For that is the law of love, to will and nill the same.

Undoubtedly this may be pronounced of them all, they are very slaves, drudges for the time, mad-men, fools, dizzards, melancholy, beside themselves, and as blind as Beetles. Their dotage is most eminent; as Seneca holds, Jupiter himself cannot love and be wise both together; the very best of them, if once they be overtaken with this passion, the most staid, discreet, grave, generous and wise, otherwise able to govern themselves, in this commit many absurdities, many indecorums, unbefitting their gravity and persons.

> *Whoever loves is a slave, his beloved's captive,*
> *Wearing the yoke tamely upon his neck.*   (MANTUAN)

Samson, David, Solomon, Hercules, Socrates, &c., are justly taxed of indiscretion in this point; the middle sort are betwixt hawk and buzzard; and although they do perceive and acknowledge their own dotage, weakness, fury, yet they cannot withstand it: as well may witness those expostulations, and confessions of Dido in Virgil:

> *She began to speak, but silent became in mid-utterance.*

Phædra in Seneca:

> *Reason is overcome and sway'd by passion,*
> *The potent god of love reigns in her soul.*

Myrrha in Ovid:

> *She sees and knows her fault, and doth resist,*
> *Against her filthy lust she doth contend.*
> *And whither go I, what am I about?*
> *And God forbid! yet doth it in the end.*

Again:

> *With raging lust she burns, and now recalls*
> *Her vow, and then despairs, and when 'tis past,*
> *Her former thoughts she'll prosecute in haste,*
> *And what to do she knows not at the last.*

She will and will not, abhors, and yet, as Medea did, doth it:

> *Reason pulls one way, burning lust another,*
> *She sees and knows what's good, but she doth neither.*　(OVID)

> *Beguiling love, and passion, what a gate*
> *You've led me!*　(BUCHANAN)

The major part of Lovers are carried headlong like so many brute beasts, reason counsels one way, thy friends, fortunes, shame, disgrace, danger and an ocean of cares that will certainly follow; yet this furious lust precipitates, counterpoiseth, weighs down on the other; though it be their utter undoing, perpetual infamy, loss, yet they will do it, and become at last void of sense; degenerate into dogs, hogs, asses, brutes; as Jupiter into a Bull, Apuleius an Ass, Lycaon a Wolf, Tereus a Lapwing, Callisto a Bear,* Elpenor and Gryllus into Swine by Circe. For what else may we think those ingenious Poets to have shadowed in their witty fictions and Poems, but that a man once given over to his lust (as Fulgentius interprets that of Apuleius, Alciati of Tereus) is no better than a beast.

> *I was a King, my Crown a witness is,*
> *But by my filthiness am come to this.*　(ALCIATI)

Their blindness is all out as great, as manifest as their weakness and dotage, or rather an inseparable companion, an ordinary sign of it. Love is blind, as the saying is, Cupid's blind, and so are all his followers.

> *Who loves a frog, thinks the frog as fair as Diana.*

Every Lover admires his Mistress, though she be very deformed of her self, ill-favoured, wrinkled, pimpled, pale, red, yellow, tanned, tallow-faced, have a swollen Juggler's platter-face, or a thin, lean, chitty-face, have clouds in her face, be crooked, dry, bald, goggle-ey'd, blear-ey'd, or with staring eyes, she looks like a squis'd [or squeez'd] cat, hold her head still awry, heavy, dull, hollow-eyed, black or yellow about the eyes, or squint-eyed, sparrow-mouthed, Persean hook-nosed, have a sharp Fox nose, a red nose, China flat great nose, snub-nose with wide nostrils, a nose like a promontory, gubber-tushed, rotten teeth, black, uneven, brown teeth, beetle-browed, a Witch's beard, her breath stink all over the room, her nose drop winter and summer, with a Bavarian poke [or

---

* An immodest woman is like a bear. — Burton's note.

pouch] under her chin, a sharp chin, lave eared [or big-eared], with a long crane's neck, which stands awry too, with hanging breasts, her dugs like two double jugs, or else no dugs, in the other extreme, bloody-faln [or chilblain'd] fingers, she have filthy long unpared nails, scabbed hands or wrists, a tanned skin, a rotten carkass, crooked back, she stoops, is lame, splay-footed, as slender in the middle as a Cow in the waist, gouty legs, her ankles hang over her shoes, her feet stink, she breeds lice, a mere changeling, a very monster, an auf [or oaf, or elf], imperfect, her whole complexion savours, an harsh voice, incondite gesture, vile gait, a vast virago, or an ugly Tit, a slug, a fat fustilugs, a truss, a long lean rawbone, a skeleton, a sneaker, (suppose, as the poet saith, her unseen beauties somewhat better), and to thy judgement looks like a merd in a lanthorn, whom thou couldest not fancy for a world, but hatest, loathest, and wouldest have spit in her face, or blow thy nose in her bosom, the very antidote of love to another man, a dowdy, a slut, a scold, a nasty, rank, rammy, filthy, beastly quean, dishonest peradventure, obscene, base, beggarly, rude, foolish, untaught, peevish, Irus' daughter, Thersites' sister, Grobian's scholar, if he love her once, he admires her for all this, he takes no notice of any such errors, or imperfections of body or mind.

> *These very things enchant him then,*
> *As upon Agna's nose the wen*
> *Charms poor Balbinus,* (HORACE)

he had rather have her than any woman in the world. If he were a King, she alone should be his Queen, his Empress. O that he had but the wealth and treasure of both the Indies to endow her with, a carrack [or great ship] of Diamonds, a chain of Pearl, a cascanet of Jewels (a pair of calf-skin gloves of four pence a pair were fitter) or some such toy, to send her for a token, she should have it with all his heart; he would spend myriads of crowns for her sake. Venus herself, Panthea, Cleopatra, Tarquin's Tanaquil, Herod's Mariamne, or Mary of Burgundy, if she were alive, would not match her,

> *Her beauty beats Helen's, who did inspire*
> *The Trojan War,*

(let Paris himself be Judge), renowned Helena comes short, that Rhodopeian Phyllis, Larissæan Coronis, Babylonian Thisbe, Polyxena, Laura, Lesbia, &c., your counterfeit Ladies were never so fair as she is.

> *Whate'er is pretty, pleasant, facete, well,*
> *Whate'er Pandora had, she doth excel.* (LOECHAEUS)

Diana was not to be compared to her, nor Juno, nor Minerva, nor any Goddess. Thetis' feet were as bright as silver, the ancles of Hebe clearer than Crystal, the arms of Aurora as ruddy as the Rose, Juno's breasts as white as Snow, Minerva wise, Venus fair; but what of this? Dainty, come thou to me! She is all in all.

> *Fairest of fair, that fairness doth excel.* (SPENSER)

Euemerus, in Aristænetus, so far admireth his Mistress' good parts, that he makes proclamation of them, and challengeth all comers in her behalf. Who ever saw the beauties of the East, or of the West, let them come from all quarters, all, and tell truth, if ever they saw such an excellent feature, as this is! A good fellow in Petronius cries out, no tongue can tell his Lady's fine feature, or express it,

> *No tongue can her perfections tell,*
> *In whose each part all tongues may dwell.* (SIDNEY)

Most of your Lovers are of his humour and opinion. She is second to none, a rare creature, a Phœnix, the sole commandress of his thoughts, Queen of his desires, his only delight: as Triton now feelingly sings, that Love-sick Sea-God.

> *Fair Leucothoe, black Melæne please me well,*
> *But Galatea doth by odds the rest excel.*
>
> > (CALCAGNINUS)

All the gracious Eulogies, Metaphors, Hyperbolical comparisons of the best things in the world, the most glorious names; whatsoever, I say, is pleasant, amiable, sweet, grateful, and delicious, are too little for her.

> *His Phœbe is so fair, she is so bright,*
> *She dims the Sun's lustre, and the Moon's light.*

Stars, Suns, Moons, Metals, sweet-smelling Flowers, Odours, Perfumes, Colours, Gold, Silver, Ivory, Pearls, Precious Stones, Snow, painted Birds, Doves, Honey, Sugar, Spice, cannot express her, so soft, so tender, so radiant, sweet, so fair is she: softer than a coney's fur, &c.

> *Fine Lydia, my Mistress, white and fair,*
> *The milk, the Lily do not thee come near;*
> *The Rose so white, the Rose so red to see,*
> *And Indian Ivory comes short of thee.* (PETRONIUS)

Such a description our English Homer makes of a fair Lady:

> That Emelie, that fairer was to sene,
> Than is the lilie upon his stalke grene:
> And fresher than the May with floures newe,
> For with the rose-colour strofe hire hewe;
> I no't which was the finer of hem two.

In this very phrase Polyphemus courts Galatea:

Whiter Galatea than the white withy-wind,
Fresher than a field, higher than a tree,
Brighter than glass, more wanton than a kid,
Softer than swan's down, or ought that may be. (OVID)

So she admires him again in that conceited Dialogue of Lucian, which Joannes Secundus, an Elegant Dutch modern Poet, hath translated into verse. When Doris, and those other Sea-Nymphs, upbraided her with her ugly mis-shapen Lover Polyphemus; she replies, they speak out of envy and malice:

Plainly 'tis envy prompts, since he
Doth not love you as he doth me.

Say what they could, he was a proper man. And as Heloise writ to her Sweetheart Peter Abelard, she had rather be his vassal, his Quean, than the world's Empress or Queen, she would not change her love for Jupiter himself.

To thy thinking she is a most loathsome creature, and as when a country-fellow discommended once that exquisite picture of Helena, made by Zeuxis, for he saw no such beauty in it; Nicomachus, a love-sick spectator replied, Take mine eyes, and thou wilt think she is a Goddess; dote on her forthwith, count all her vices, virtues; her imperfections, infirmities, absolute and perfect. If she be flat-nosed, she is lovely; if hook-nosed, kingly; if dwarfish and little, pretty; if tall, proper and man-like, our brave British Boadicea; if crooked, wise; if monstrous, comely; her defects are no defects at all, she hath no deformities. Though she be nasty, fulsome, as Sostratus's bitch, or Parmeno's sow: thou hadst as lieve have a snake in thy bosom, a toad in thy dish, and callest her witch, devil, hag, with all the filthy names thou canst invent; he admires her, on the other side, she is his Idol, Lady, Mistress, Venerilla [or Little Venus], Queen, the quintessence of beauty, an Angel, a Star, a Goddess.

Thou art my Vesta, thou my Goddess art,
Thy hallowed Temple only is my heart. (DRAYTON)

The fragrancy of a thousand Courtesans is in her face: 'tis not Venus' picture that, nor the Spanish Infanta's as you suppose (good Sir) no Princess, or King's daughter; no, no, but his divine Mistress forsooth, his dainty Dulcinea, his dear Antiphila, to whose service he is wholly consecrate, whom he alone adores.

To whom conferr'd a Peacock's undecent,
A squirrel's harsh, a Phœnix too frequent. (MARTIAL)

All the Graces, veneries, elegances, pleasures, attend her. He prefers
her before a Myriad of Court-Ladies.

> *He that commends Phyllis or Neæra*
> *Or Amaryllis, or Galatea,*
> *Tityrus or Melibœa, by your leave,*
> *Let him be mute, his Love the praises have.* (ARIOSTO)

Nay, before all the Gods and Goddesses themselves. So Quintus Catulus
admired his squint-eyed friend Roscius.

> *By your leave, gentle Gods, this I'll say true,*
> *There's none of you that have so fair a hue.* (CICERO)

All the bombast Epithets, pathetical adjuncts, incomparably fair, curiously neat, divine. sweet, dainty, delicious, &c., pretty diminutives.
Little Heart, Little Kiss, &c., pleasant names may be invented. bird,
mouse, lamb, puss, pigeon, pigsney, kid, honey, love, dove, chicken. &c.,
he puts on her.

> *My honey, my heart, my sweetness,*
> *My rabbit, my little kiss,* (MARULLUS)

my life, my light. my jewel, my glory, my sweet Margaret, my sole
delight and darling! And as Rhodomant courted Isabella:

> *By all kind words and gestures that he might,*
> *He calls her his dear heart, his sole beloved,*
> *His joyful comfort, and his sweet delight,*
> *His Mistress, and his Goddess, and such names,*
> *As loving Knights apply to lovely Dames.* (ARIOSTO)

Every cloath she wears, every fashion, pleaseth him above measure;
her hand,

> *O such fingers on that hand of hers!*

pretty foot, pretty coronets, [or head-dresses], her sweet carriage, sweet
voice, tone, O that pretty tone, her divine and lovely looks, her every
thing, lovely, sweet, amiable and pretty, pretty, pretty! Her very name
(let it be what it will) is the most pretty pleasing name; I believe now
there is some secret power and virtue in names, every action, sight,
habit, gesture, he admires, whether she play, sing, or dance, in what tires
soever she goeth, how excellent it was, how well it became her, never
the like seen or heard.

> *She wears a thousand dresses*
> *In a thousand charming ways.* (TIBULLUS)

Let her wear what she will, do what she will, say what she will, 'tis all
becoming. He applauds and admires every thing she wears, saith, or
doth.

What e'er she doth, or whither e'er she go,
A sweet and pleasing grace attends forsooth;
Or loose, or bind her hair, or comb it up,
She's to be honoured in what she doth. (TIBULLUS)

Let her be dressed or undressed. all is one, she is excellent still, beautiful, fair, and lovely to behold. Women do as much by men, nay more, far fonder, weaker, and that by many parasangs. Come to me, my dear Lysias (saith Musarium in Aristænetus) come quickly Sweetheart, all other men are Satyrs, mere clowns, block-heads to thee, nobody to thee: thy looks, words, gestures, actions, &c., are incomparably beyond all others. Venus was never so much besotted on her Adonis, Phædra so delighted in Hippolytus, Ariadne in Theseus, Thisbe in her Pyramus, as she is enamoured on her Mopsus.

Be thou the Marigold, and I will be the Sun,
Be thou the Friar, and I will be the Nun.

I could repeat centuries of such. Now tell me what greater dotage, or blindness can there be than this in both sexes? and yet their slavery is more eminent, a greater sign of their folly than the rest.

They are commonly slaves, captives, voluntary servants, a lover is the slave of his beloved, as Castilio terms him, his Mistress' servant, her drudge, prisoner, bond-man, what not? He composeth himself wholly to her affections, to please her; and, as Æmilia said, makes himself her lackey; all his cares, actions, all his thoughts, are subordinate to her will and commandment; her most devote, obsequious, affectionate, servant and vassal. For Love (as Cyrus in Xenophon well observed) is a mere tyranny, worse than any disease, and they that are troubled with it, desire to be free, and cannot, but are harder bound than if they were in iron chains. What greater captivity or slavery can there be (as Tully expostulates) than to be in love? Is he a free man over whom a woman domineers, to whom she prescribes Laws, commands, forbids what she will herself? that dares deny nothing she demands; she asks, he gives; she calls, he comes; she threatens, he fears; I account this man a very drudge. And as he follows it, Is this no small servitude for an enamorite to be every hour combing his head, stiffening his beard, perfuming his hair, washing his face with sweet waters, painting, curling, and not to come abroad but sprucely crowned, decked and apparelled?

Yet these are but toys in respect, to go to the Barber, Baths, Theatres, &c., he must attend upon her wherever she goes, run along the streets by her doors and windows to see her, take all opportunities,

sleeveless errands, disguise, counterfeit shapes, and as many forms as
Jupiter himself ever took; and come every day to her house (as he will
surely do if he be truly enamoured) and offer her service, and follow
her up and down from room to room, as Lucretia's suitors did. he cannot
contain himself, but he will do it, he must and will be where she is, sit
next her, still talking with her. If I did but let my glove fall by chance
(as the said Aretine's Lucretia brags) I had one of my suitors, nay two
or three at once ready to stoop and take it up, and kiss it, and with a
low congee deliver it unto me: if I would walk, another was ready to
sustain me by the arm; a third to provide fruits, Pears, Plums, Cherries,
or whatsoever I would eat or drink. — All this and much more he doth
in her presence, and when he comes home, as Troilus to his Creseid, 'tis
all his meditation to recount with himself his actions, words, gestures,
what entertainment he had, how kindly she used him in such a place,
how she smiled, how she graced him, and that infinitely pleased him;
then he breaks out, O sweet Areusa, O my dearest Antiphila, O most
divine looks, O lovely graces, and thereupon instantly he makes an
Epigram, or a Sonnet to five or seven tunes, in her commendation, or
else he ruminates how she rejected his service, denied him a kiss, disgraced him, &c., and that as effectually torments him. And these are
his exercises betwixt comb and glass, Madrigals, Elegies, &c., these his
cogitations till he see her again. But all this is easy and gentle, and
the least part of his labour and bondage, no hunter will take such pains
for his Game, Fowler for his sport, or Soldier to sack a City, as he will
for his Mistress' favour.

I will be your companion, nought shall fright me,
Nor rugged rocks, nor tusk of savage boar,

as Phædra to Hippolytus. No danger shall affright; for if that be true
the Poets feign, Love is the son of Mars and Venus; as he hath delights, pleasures, elegancies from his Mother, so hath he hardness,
valour, and boldness, from his father. And 'tis true that Bernard hath:
nothing so boisterous, nothing so tender as Love. If once therefore
enamoured, he will go, run, ride many a mile to meet her, day and
night, in a very dark night, endure scorching heat, cold, wait in frost
and snow, rain, tempests, till his teeth chatter in his head, those Northern winds and showers cannot cool or quench his flames of love. By
unseasonable night he is not deterred, he will, take my word, he will
sustain hunger, thirst, penetrate all, overthrow all, love will find out a
way, through thick and thin he will go to her; he will swim through an
Ocean, ride post over the Alps, Apennines, or Pyrenean hills, fire, flood,

whirlpools, though it rain daggers with their points downwards, light or dark, all is one:

Dew-drenched through the darkness Faunus came to the grotto,
for her sweet sake he will undertake Hercules' twelve Labours, endure hazard, &c., he feels it not. What shall I say (saith Hædus) of their great dangers they undergo, single combats they undertake, how they will venture their lives, creep in at windows, gutters, climb over walls to come to their sweethearts, (anointing the doors and hinges with oil, because they should not creak, tread soft, swim, wade, watch, &c.), and if they be surprised, leap out at windows, cast themselves headlong down, bruising or breaking their legs or arms, and sometimes losing life itself, as Callisto did for his lovely Melibœa? Hear some of their own confessions, protestations, complaints, proffers, expostulations, wishes, brutish attempts, labours in this kind. Hercules served Omphale, put on an apron, took a distaff and spun; Thraso the soldier was so submissive to Thais, that he was resolved to do whatsoever she enjoined. I give myself to Thais, I am at her service. Philostratus, in an Epistle to his Mistress: I am ready to die, Sweetheart, if it be thy will; allay his thirst whom thy star has scorched and undone; the fountains and rivers deny no man drink that comes; the fountain doth not say, thou shalt not drink, nor the apple, thou shalt not eat, nor the fair meadow, walk not in me, but thou alone wilt not let me come near thee, or see thee, contemned and despised I die for grief. Polyænos, when his Mistress Circe did but frown upon him in Petronius, drew his sword, and bade her kill, stab, or whip him to death, he would strip himself naked, and not resist. Another will take a journey to Japan, uncaring for the troubles of a long voyage. A third (if she say it) will not speak a word for a twelve-month's space, her command shall be most inviolably kept. A fourth will take Hercules' club from him, and, with that Centurion in the Spanish Cælestina, will kill ten men for his Mistress Areusa, for a word of her mouth, he will cut bucklers in two like pippins, and flap down men like flies, saying to her, Choose how you will have him killed. Galeatus of Mantua did a little more, for when he was almost mad for love of a fair Maid in the City, she to try him, belike, what he would do for her sake, bade him, in jest, leap into the River Po, if he loved her; he forthwith did leap headlong off the bridge, and was drowned. Another at Ficinum in like passion, when his Mistress by chance (thinking no harm I dare sware) bade him go hang, the next night at her doors hanged himself. Money (saith Xenophon) is a very acceptable and welcome guest, yet I had rather give it my dear Cleinias, than take it of others, I had rather

serve him, than command others, I had rather be his drudge, than take my ease, undergo any danger for his sake, than live in security. For I had rather see Cleinias than all the world besides, and had rather want the sight of all other things, than him alone; I am angry with the night and sleep that I may not see him, and thank the light and Sun because they shew me my Cleinias; I will run into the fire for his sake, and if you did but see him, I know that you likewise would run with me. So Philostratus to his Mistress: Command me what you will, I will do it: bid me go to Sea, I am gone in an instant; take so many stripes, I am ready; run through the fire, and lay down my life and soul at thy feet, 'tis done. So did Æolus to Juno,

> *O Queen, it is thy pains to enjoin me still,*
> *And I am bound to execute thy will.*　(VIRGIL)

And Phædra to Hippolytus,

> *O call me sister, call me servant, choose,*
> *Or rather servant, I am thine to use.*
> *It shall not grieve me to the snowy hills,*
> *Or frozen Pindus' tops forthwith to climb,*
> *Or run through fire, or through an Army,*
> *Say but the word, for I am always thine.*　(SENECA)

Callicratides, in Lucian, breaks out in this passionate speech: O God of heaven, grant me this life for ever to sit over against my Mistress, and to hear her sweet voice, to go in and out with her, to have every other business common with her; I would labour when she labours, sail when she sails; he that hates her should hate me; and if a tyrant kill her, he should kill me; if she should die, I would not live, and one grave should hold us both.

> *When she dies, my love shall likewise be at rest in the tomb.*
>
> 　　　　　　　　　　　　　　　　(BUCHANAN)

Abrocomas in Aristænetus makes the like petition for his Delphis.

> *Gladly I'd live with thee, or gladly die.*　(HORACE)

'Tis the same strain which Theagenes used to his Chariclea: So that I may but enjoy thy love, let me die presently; Leander to his Hero, when he besought the Sea waves to let him go quietly to his Love, and kill him coming back.

> *Spare me while I go, o'erwhelm me returning.*　(MARTIAL)

'Tis the common humour of them all, to contemn death, to wish for death, to confront death in this case, caring neither for wild beasts, nor fire, nor precipices, nor straits, nor of weapons, nor of heavy seas: 'tis their desire (saith Tyrius) to die.

He fears not death, nay, he desires to run
Upon the very swords. (SENECA)

Though a thousand dragons or devils kept the gates, Cerberus himself, Sciron and Procrustes lay in wait, and the way as dangerous, as inaccessible as hell, through fiery flames and over burning coulters, he will adventure for all this. And as Peter Abelard lost his testicles for his Heloise, he will (I say) not venture an incision, but life itself. For how many gallants offered to lose their lives for a night's lodging with Cleopatra in those days! And in the hour and moment of death, 'tis their sole comfort to remember their dear Mistress, as Zerbino slain in France, and Brandimart in Barbary; as Arcite did his Emily:

> ————when he felte death,
> Dusked been his even two, faded his breath,
> But on his lady yet caste he his eye,
> His laste word was, mercy Emely.
> His spirit changed, and out wente there,
> Whither I cannot tell, ne where.

When Captain Gobrias by an unlucky accident had received his death's wound, miserable man that I am (instead of other devotions) he cries out, Shall I die before I see Rhodanthe my Sweetheart? Saith mine Author, so Love triumphs, contemns, insults over death itself. Thirteen proper young men lost their lives for that fair Hippodamia's sake, the daughter of Œnomaus, King of Elis: when that hard condition was proposed of death or victory, they made no account of it, but courageously for love died, till Pelops at last won her by a sleight. As many gallants desperately adventured their dearest blood for Atalanta the daughter of Schœneus, in hope of marriage, all vanquished and overcome, till Hippomenes by a few golden apples happily obtained his suit. Perseus of old fought with a Sea-monster for Andromeda's sake; and our S. George freed the King's daughter of Sabea, (the Golden Legend is mine Author), that was exposed to a Dragon, by a terrible Combat. Our Knights Errant, and the Sir Lancelots of these days, I hope will adventure as much for Ladies' favours, as the Squire of Dames, Knight of the Sun, Sir Bevis of Southampton, or that renowned Peer

Orlando, who long time had lovéd dear
Angelica the fair, and for her sake
About the world, in nations far and near,
Did high attempts perform and undertake. (ARIOSTO)

He is a very dastard, a coward, a block and a beast, that will not do as much, but they will sure, they will; for 'tis an ordinary thing for these inamoratos of our times, to say and do more, to stab their arms, carouse in blood, or as that Thessalian Thero, that bit off his own thumb, to make his Corrival do as much. 'Tis frequent with them to challenge the field for their Lady and Mistress' sake, to run a tilt,

> *That either bears (so furiously they meet)*
> *The other down under the horses' feet,*   (SPENSER)

and then up and to it again,

> *And with their axes both so sorely pour,*
> *That neither plate nor mail sustained the stour,*
> *But riveld wreak like rotten wood asunder,*
> *And fire did flash like lightning after thunder,*

and in her quarrel, to fight so long, till their head-piece, bucklers, be all broken, and swords hackt like so many saws; for they must not see her abused in any sort, 'tis blasphemy to speak against her, a dishonour without all good respect to name her. 'Tis common with these creatures, to drink healths upon their bare knees, though it were a mile to the bottom (no matter of what mixture) off it comes. If she bid them, they will go barefoot to Jerusalem, to the great Cham's Court, to the East Indies, to fetch her a bird to wear in her hat: and with Drake and Cavendish sail round about the world for her sweet sake, with adverse winds, serve twice seven years, as Jacob did for Rachel; do as much as Gismunda the daughter of Tancredus, Prince of Salerna, did for Guiscardus her true love, eat his heart when he died; or as Artemisia drank her husband's bones beaten to powder, and so bury him in herself, and endure more torments than Theseus or Paris. With such sacrifices as these (as Aristænetus holds) Venus is well pleased. Generally they undertake any pain, any labour, any toil, for their Mistress' sake, love and admire a servant, not to her alone, but to all her friends and followers, they hug and embrace them for her sake; her dog, picture, and every thing she wears, they adore it as a relique. If any man come from her, they feast him, reward him, will not be out of his company, do him all offices, still remembering, still talking of her:

> *For though the object of thy love be absent*
> *Her image stays, her sweet name rings in thine ears.*   (LUCRETIUS)

The very Carrier that comes from him to her is a most welcome guest, and if he bring a letter, she will read it twenty times over; and as Lucretia did by Euryalus, kiss the letter a thousand times together, and then read it: and Chelidonia by Philonius, after many sweet kisses, put the letter in her bosom,

And kiss again, and often look thereon,
   And stay the Messenger that would be gone, (ARISTÆNETUS)
and ask many pretty questions, over and over again, as how he looked,
what he did, and what he said? In a word,

He strives to please his Mistress and her maid,
   Her servants, and her dog, and's well apaid.   (PLAUTUS)

If he get any remnant of hers, a busk-point, a feather of her fan, a
shoe-tie, a lace, a ring, a bracelet of hair,

Some token snatched from her arm,
   Or hardly resisting finger,   (HORACE)

he wears it for a favour on his arm, in his hat, finger, or next his heart.
Her picture he adores twice a day, and for two hours together will not
look off it: as Laodomia did by Protesilaus, when he went to war, sit
at home with his picture before her; a garter or a bracelet of hers is
more precious than any Saint's Relique, he lays it up in his casket (O
blessed Relique) and every day will kiss it: if in her presence, his eye is
never off her, and drink he will where she drank, if it be possible, in
that very place, &c. If absent, he will walk in the walk, sit under that
tree where she did use to sit, in that bower, in that very seat,

And sadly prints his kisses on the doors,   (LUCRETIUS)

many years after sometimes, though she be far distant, and dwell many
miles off, he loves yet to walk that way still, to have his chamber
window look that way: to walk by that River's side which (though far
away) runs by the house where she dwells, he loves the wind blows
to that coast.

O happy Western winds that blow that way,
   For you shall see my love's fair face to-day.   (BUCHANAN)

He will send a message to her by the wind,

Ye Alpine breezes, mountain winds,
   Bear her these tidings.   (FRACASTORIUS)

He desires to confer with some of her acquaintance, for his heart is
still with her, to talk of her, admiring and commending her, lamenting,
moaning, wishing himself any thing for her sake, to have opportunity
to see her, O that he might but enjoy her presence! So did Philostratus
to his Mistress: O happy ground on which she treads, and happy were
I if she would tread upon me! I think her countenance would make the
Rivers stand, and when she comes abroad, birds will sing and come
about her.

The fields will laugh, the pleasant valleys burn,
And all the grass will into flowers turn.
All the air will breathe ambrosia.

When she is in the meadow, she is fairer than any flower, for that lasts but for a day; the river is pleasing, but it vanisheth on a sudden, but thy flower doth not fade, thy stream is greater than the Sea. If I look upon the Heaven. methinks, I see the Sun fallen down to shine below, and thee to shine in his place, whom I desire. If I look upon the night, methinks I see two more glorious Stars, Hesperus and thyself. A little after he thus courts his Mistress: If thou goest forth of the City, the protecting Gods that keep the town, will run after to gaze upon thee: if thou sail upon the Seas, as so many small boats, they will follow thee: what River would not run into the Sea? Another, he sighs and sobs, swears he hath an heart bruised to powder, dissolved and melted within him, or quite gone from him, to his Mistress' bosom belike; he is an Oven, a Salamander in the fire. so scorched with love's heat; he wisheth himself a saddle for her to sit on. a posy for her to smell to, and it would not grieve him to be hanged, if he might be strangled in her garters; he would willingly die to-morrow, so that she might kill him with her own hands. Ovid would be a Flea, a Gnat, a Ring, Catullus a Sparrow,

> O that I might thus play with thee
> And set my mind from sorrow free.

Anacreon, a glass, a gown, a chain, any thing:

> But I a looking-glass would be,
> Still to be lookt upon by thee,
> Or I, my Love, would be thy gown,
> By thee to be worn up and down;
> Or a pure well full to the brims,
> That I might wash thy purer limbs:
> Or, I'd be precious balm to 'noint,
> With choicest care each choicest joint;
> Or, if I might, I would be fain
> About thy neck thy happy chain,
> Or would it were my blessed hap
> To be the lawn o'er thy fair pap.
> Or would I were thy shoe, to be
> Daily trod upon by thee. (Englished by Mr. B. Holliday,

O thrice happy man that shall enjoy her: as they that saw Hero in Musæus, and Salmacis to Hermaphroditus,

> Happy thy mother, happy thy nurse,
> But happiest she, the bride that shares thy bed.   (OVID)

The same passion made her break out in the Comedy, happy are his bed-fellows; and as she said of Cyrus, blessed is that woman that shall be his wife, nay thrice happy she that shall enjoy him but a night. Such a night's lodging is worth Jupiter's Sceptre. O what a blissful night would it be, how soft, how sweet a bed! She will adventure all her estate for such a night, for a Nectarean, a balsam kiss alone.

> *Happy is he who sees thee,*
> *Happier he who hears thee,*
> *A demigod he who kisses thee,*
> *A god he who possesses thee.* (GREEK ANTHOLOGY)

The Sultan of Sana's wife in Arabia, when she had seen Vertomannus, that comely Traveller, lamented to herself in this manner, O God, thou hast made this man whiter than the Sun: but me, mine husband, and all my children black: I would to God he were mine husband, or that I had such a son; she fell a weeping, and so impatient for love at last, that (as Potiphar's wife did by Joseph) she would have had him gone in with her, she sent away Gazella, Tegeia, Galzerana, her waiting maids, loaded him with fair promises and gifts, and wooed him with all the Rhetorick she could,

> *Grant this last favour to your hapless lover.* (VIRGIL)

But when he gave not consent, she would have gone with him, and left all, to be his page, his servant, or his lackey, so that she might enjoy him; threatening moreover to kill herself, &c. Men will do as much and more for women, spend goods, lands, lives, fortunes; Kings will leave their Crowns, as King John for Matilda the Nun at Dunmow.

> *But kings in this yet privileg'd may be,*
> *I'll be a monk, so I may live with thee.* (DRAYTON)

The very Gods will endure any shame, be a spectacle as Mars and Venus were to all the rest; so did Lucian's Mercury wish, and peradventure so dost thou. They will adventure their lives with alacrity,

> *I would not fear to die for her,* (HORACE)

nay more, I will die twice, nay twenty times for her. If she die, there's no remedy, they must die with her, they cannot help it. A Lover, in Calcagninus, wrote this on his darling's Tomb:

> *Quincia my dear is dead, but not alone,*
> *For I am dead, and with her I am gone:*
> *Sweet smiles, mirth, graces, all with her do rest,*
> *And my soul, too, for 'tis not in my breast.*

How many doting Lovers upon the like occasion might say the same! But these are toys in respect, they will hazard their very souls for their Mistress' sake.

One said, to heaven would I not
Desire at all to go,
If that at mine own house I had
Such a fine wife as Hero. (MUSAEUS)

Venus forsook Heaven for Adonis' sake. Old January, in Chaucer, thought when he had his fair May, he should never go to heaven, he should live so merrily here on earth: had I such a Mistress, he protests,

I would not envy their prosperity,
The Gods should envy my felicity. (BUCHANAN)

Another as earnestly desires to behold his Sweetheart, he will adventure and leave all this, and more than this, to see her alone.

If all my mischiefs were recompensed,
And God would give me what I requested,
I would my Mistress' presence only seek,
Which doth my heart in prison captive keep. (PETRARCH)

But who can reckon up the dotage, madness, servitude and blindness, the foolish phantasms and vanities of Lovers, their torments, wishes, idle attempts?

Yet for all this, amongst so many irksome, absurd, troublesome symptoms, inconveniences, phantastical fits and passions, which are usually incident to such persons, there be some good and graceful qualities in Lovers, which this affection causeth. As it makes wise men fools, so many times it makes fools become wise; it makes base fellows become generous, cowards courageous, as Cardan notes out of Plutarch; covetous, liberal and magnificent; clowns, civil; cruel, gentle; wicked profane persons, to become religious; slovens, neat; churls, merciful; and dumb dogs, eloquent: your lazy drones, quick and nimble; love tames savage breasts; that fierce, cruel and rude Cyclops Polyphemus sighed, and shed many a salt tear, for Galatea's sake. No passion causeth greater alterations, or more vehement of joy or discontent. Plutarch saith that the soul of a man in love is full of perfumes and sweet odours, and all manner of pleasing tones and tunes, insomuch that it is hard to say (as he adds) whether love do mortal men more harm than good. It adds spirits, and makes them otherwise soft and silly, generous and courageous. Ariadne's love made Theseus so adventurous, and Medea's beauty Jason so victorious; love drives out fear. Plato is of opinion that the love of Venus made Mars so valorous. A young man will be much abashed to commit any foul offence that shall come to the hearing or sight of his Mistress. As he that desired of his enemy, now dying, to lay him with his face upward, lest his Sweetheart should say he was a

Coward. And if it were possible to have an Army consist of Lovers, such as love, or are beloved, they would be extraordinary valiant and wise in their Government, modesty would detain them from doing amiss, emulation incite them to do that which is good and honest, and a few of them would overcome a great company of others. There is no man so pusillanimous, so very a dastard, whom Love would not incense, make of a divine temper, and an heroical spirit. As he said in like case, though the heavens should fall, nothing can terrify, nothing can dismay them : but as Sir Blandamour and Paridell, those two brave Fairy Knights, fought for the love of fair Florimell in presence ——

> And drawing both their swords with rage anew,
> Like two mad mastives each other slew,
> And shields did share, and mailes did rash, and helms did hew :
> So furiously each other did assail,
> As if their souls at once they would have rent
> Out of their breasts, that streams of blood did trail
> Adown, as if their springs of life were spent,
> That all the ground with purple blood was sprent,
> And all their armour stained with bloody gore ;
> Yet scarcely once to breathe would they relent.
> So mortal was their malice and so sore,
> That both resolved (than yield) to die before.

Every base Swain in love will dare to do as much for his dear Mistress' sake. He will fight, and fetch that famous buckler of Argos, to do her service, adventure at all, undertake any enterprize. And as Serranus the Spaniard, then Governor of Sluys, made answer to Marquess Spinola, if the enemy brought 50.000 Devils against him, he would keep it. The nine Worthies, Oliver and Roland, and forty dozen of Peers are all in him, he is all metal, armour of proof, more than a man, and in this case improved beyond himself. For, as Agathon contends, a true Lover is wise, just, temperate and valiant. I doubt not therefore, but if a man had such an Army of Lovers (as Castilio supposeth) he might soon conquer all the world, except by chance he met with such another Army of Inamoratos to oppose it. For so perhaps they might fight as that fatal Dog, and fatal Hare in the Heavens, course one another round, and never make an end. Castilio thinks Ferdinand King of Spain would never have conquered Granada had not Queen Isabel and her Ladies been present at the siege : it cannot be expressed what courage the Spanish Knights took, when the Ladies were present, a few Spaniards overcame a multitude of Moors. They will undergo any danger whatsoever, as Sir Walter Manny in Edward the Third's time, stuck full of Ladies' favours, fought like a Dragon. For, as Plato holds, only Lovers will die for their friends, and in their Mistress' quarrel. And for that cause he would have women follow the Camp, to be spectators and encouragers of noble actions: upon such an occasion, the Squire of Dames himself, Sir Lancelot, or Sir Tristram, Cæsar, or Alexander, shall not be more resolute, or go beyond them.

Not courage only doth Love add, but, as I said, subtilty, wit, and many pretty devises,

For love inspires to stratagems and frauds. (MANTUAN)

Jupiter, in love with Leda, and not knowing how to compass his desire, turn'd himself into a Swan, and got Venus to pursue him in the likeness of an Eagle; which she doing, for shelter he fled to Leda's lap. Leda embraced him, and so fell fast asleep, but he took her asleep, by which means Jupiter had his will. Infinite such tricks can Love devise, such fine feats in abundance, with wisdom and wariness:

Who can deceive a lover?

All manner of civility, decency, compliment, and good behaviour, polite graces, and merry conceits. Boccaccio hath a pleasant tale to this purpose, which he borrowed from the Greeks, and which Beroaldus hath turned into Latin, Bebelius in verse, of Cimon and Iphigenia. This Cimon was a fool, a proper man of person, and the Governor of Cyprus' son, but a very ass; insomuch that his father, being ashamed of him, sent him to a Farm-house he had in the Country to be brought up; where by chance, as his manner was, walking alone, he espied a gallant young Gentlewoman named Iphigenia, a Burgomaster's daughter of Cyprus, with her maid, by a brook side in a little thicket, fast asleep in her smock, where she had newly bathed herself. When Cimon saw her, he stood leaning on his staff, gaping on her immoveable, and in a maze. At last he fell so far in love with the glorious object, that he began to rouse himself up, to bethink what he was, would needs follow her to the City, and for her sake began to be civil, to learn to sing and dance, to play on Instruments, and got all those Gentlemen-like qualities and compliments in a short space, which his friends were most glad of. In brief, he became, from an Idiot and a Clown, to be one of the most complete Gentlemen in Cyprus, did many valorous exploits, and all for the love of Mistress Iphigenia. In a word, I may say thus much of them all, let them be never so clownish, rude and horrid, Grobians [or slovens] and sluts, if once they be in love, they will be most neat and spruce; for love is foremost in the nicenesses of elegance, they will follow the fashion, begin to trick up, and to have a good opinion of themselves; for Venus is mother of the graces; a ship is not so long a-rigging, as a young Gentlewoman a-trimming up herself against her Sweetheart comes. A Painter's shop, a flowery Meadow, no so gracious aspect in Nature's storehouse as a young maid, a Novista or Venetian Bride, that looks for a husband, or a young man that is her suitor; composed looks, composed gait, clothes, gestures, actions, all composed; all the graces, elegancies in the world are in her face. Their best robes, ribbons, chains, Jewels, Lawns, Linnens, Laces, Spangles, must come on, before all things they must study to be elegant, they are beyond all measure coy, nice, and too curious on a sudden: 'tis all their study, all their business, how to wear their clothes neat, to be polite and terse, and to set out themselves. No sooner doth a young man see his Sweetheart coming, but he smugs up himself, pulls up his cloak now fallen about his shoulders, ties his garters, points, sets his band, cuffs, slicks his hair, twires his beard, &c. When Mercury was to come before his Mistress,

> *He put his cloak in order, that the lace,*
> *And hem, and gold-work all might have his grace.* (OVID)

Salmacis would not be seen of Hermophroditus, till she had spruced up herself first.

> *Nor did she come, although 'twas her desire,*
> *Till she composed herself, and trimm'd her tire,*
> *And set her looks to make him to admire.* (OVID)

Venus had so ordered the matter, that when her son Æneas was to appear before Queen Dido, he was like a God, for she was the tirewoman herself, to set him out with all natural and artificial impostures. As Mother Mamæa did her son Severus, new chosen Emperor, when he was to be seen of the people first. When the hirsute Cyclopical Polyphemus courted Galatea:

> *And then he did begin to prank himself,*
> *To plait and comb his head, and beard to shave,*
> *And look his face i' th' water as a glass,*
> *And to compose himself for to be brave.* (OVID)

He was upon a sudden now spruce and keen, as a new-ground hatchet. He now began to have a good opinion of his own feature, and good parts, now to be a gallant.

> *Come now, my Galatea, scorn me not,*
> *Nor my poor presents; for but yesterday*
> *I saw myself i' th' water, and methought*
> *Full fair I was, then scorn me not I say.* (OVID)

'Tis the common humour of all Suitors to trick up themselves, to be prodigal in apparel, faultless as a lotus, neat, comb'd and curl'd, with powdered hairs, with a long Love-lock, a flower in his ear, perfumed gloves, rings, scarfs, feathers, points, &c., as if he were a Prince's Ganymede, with every day new suits, as the fashion varies; going as if he trod upon eggs, and as Heinsius writ to Primerius, If once he be besotted on a Wench, he must lie awake a-nights, renounce his book, sigh and lament, now and then weep for his hard hap, and mark above all things what Hats, Bands, Doublets, Breeches, are in fashion, how to cut his beard, and wear his lock, to turn up his Mushatos, and curl his head, prune his pickitivant [or peaked beard], or if he wear it abroad, that the East side be correspondent to the West; he may be scoffed at otherwise, as Julian that Apostate Emperor was for wearing a long hirsute goatish beard, fit to make ropes with, as in his Misopogon, or that Apologetical Oration he made at Antioch to excuse himself, he doth ironically confess, it hindered his kissing; but he did not much esteem it [kissing], as it seems by the sequel, I do not exert myself, said he, in the giving and taking of kisses; yet (to follow mine Author) it may much concern a young lover, he must be more respectful in this behalf, he must be in league with an excellent Tailor, Barber, —

> *A barber boy, yet such an artist*
> *As Nero's Thalamus was,* (MARTIAL)

— have neat shoe-ties, points, garters, speak in Print, walk in Print, eat and drink in Print, and that which is all in all, he must be mad in Print.

Amongst other good qualities an amorous fellow is endowed with, he must learn to sing and dance, play upon some instrument or other, as without all doubt he will, if he be truly touched with this Loadstone of Love. For as Erasmus hath it, Love will make them Musicians, and to compose Ditties, Madrigals, Elegies, Love Sonnets, and sing them to several pretty tunes, to get all good qualities may be had. Jupiter perceived Mercury to be in love with Philologia, because he learned languages, polite speech, (for Suadela [the Goddess of Persuasion], herself was Venus' daughter, as some write), Arts and Sciences, all to ingratiate himself and please his Mistress. 'Tis their chiefest study to sing, dance; and without question, so many Gentlemen and Gentlewomen would not be so well qualified in this kind, if love did not incite them. Who, saith Castilio, would learn to play, or give his mind to Musick, learn to dance, or make so many rhymes, Love-songs, as most do, but for women's sake, because they hope by that means to purchase their good wills, and win their favour? We see this daily verified in our young women and wives, they that being maids took so much pains to sing,

play, and dance, with such cost and charge to their Parents, to get
those graceful qualities, now being married, will scarce touch an instrument, they care not for it. Constantine makes Cupid himself to be a
great dancer, by the same token as he was capering amongst the Gods,
he flung down a bowl of Nectar, which distilling upon the white Rose,
ever since made it red: and Callistratus, by the help of Dædalus, about
Cupid's Statue made a many of young Wenches still a dancing, to signify belike that Cupid was much affected with it, as without all doubt
he was. For at his and Psyche's wedding, the Gods being present to
grace the Feast, Ganymede filled Nectar in abundance (as Apuleius
describes it), Vulcan was the Cook, the Hours made all fine with
Roses and Flowers, Apollo played on the harp, the Muses sang to it,
but his Mother Venus danced to his and their sweet content. Witty
Lucian, in that Pathetical Love passage, or pleasant description of
Jupiter's stealing of Europa, and swimming from Phœnicia to Crete,
makes the Sea calm, the winds hush, Neptune and Amphitrite riding in
their Chariot to break the waves before them, the Tritons dancing
round about, with every one a Torch, the Sea-Nymphs half naked, keeping time on Dolphins' backs, and singing Hymenæus, Cupid nimbly
tripping on the top of the waters, and Venus herself coming after in a
shell, strewing Roses and Flowers on their heads. Praxiteles in all his
pictures of Love, feigns Cupid ever smiling, and looking upon dancers;
and in Saint Mark's Garden in Rome, (whose work I know not), one
of the most delicious pieces is a many of Satyrs dancing about a wench
asleep. So that dancing still is, as it were, a necessary appendix to love
matters. Young Lasses are never better pleased, than when as upon an
Holiday after Even-song, they may meet their Sweethearts, and dance
about a May-pole, or in a Town-Green under a shady Elm. Nothing so
familiar in France, as for Citizens' wives and maids to dance a round in
the streets, and often too, for want of better instruments, to make good
Musick of their own voices, and dance after it. Yea, many times this
Love will make old men and women, that have more toes than teeth,
dance, —— " John come kiss me now," mask and mum: for Comus and
Hymen love masks, and all such merriments above measure, will allow
men to put on women's apparel in some cases, and promiscuously to
dance, young and old, rich and poor, generous and base, of all sorts.
Paulus Jovius taxeth Augustine Niphus the Philosopher, for that being
an old man, and a publick Professor, a father of many children, he was
so mad for the love of a young maid (that which many of his friends
were ashamed to see), an old gouty fellow, yet would dance after

Fiddlers. Many laughed him to scorn for it, but this omnipotent love would have it so.

> Love hasty with his purple staff did make
> Me follow, and the dance to undertake.   (ANACREON)

And 'tis no news this, no indecorum: for why? a good reason may be given of it. Cupid and Death met both in an Inn, and being merrily disposed, they did exchange some arrows from either quiver; ever since young men die, and oftentimes old men dote.

> Therefore youth dies, therefore the near-dead love.   (BELLIUS)

And who can then withstand it? If once we be in love, young or old, though our teeth shake in our heads, like Virginal Jacks, or stand parallel asunder like the arches of a bridge, there's no remedy, we must dance trenchmore * for a need, over tables, chairs, and stools, &c. And princum prancum is a fine dance. Plutarch doth in some sort excuse it, and telleth us moreover in what sense, Love teacheth music, how Love makes them that had no skill before, learn to sing and dance; he concludes, 'tis only that power and prerogative Love hath over us. Love (as he holds) will make a silent man speak, a modest man most officious; dull, quick; slow, nimble: and that which is most to be admired, an hard, base, untractable churl, as fire doth iron in a Smith's forge, free, facile, gentle, and easy to be entreated. Nay, 'twill make him prodigal in the other extreme, and give an hundred sesterces for a night's lodging, as they did of old to Lais of Corinth, or two hundred drachmas for a single night, as Mundus to Paulina,† spend all his fortunes (as too many do in like case) to obtain his suit. For which cause many compare Love to wine, which makes men jovial and merry, frolick and sad, whine, sing, dance, and what not.

But above all the other Symptoms of Lovers, this is not lightly to be over-passed, that likely of what condition soever, if once they be in love, they turn to their ability, Rhymers, Ballet-makers, and Poets. For, as Plutarch saith, they will be Witnesses and Trumpeters of their Paramours' good parts, bedecking them with verses and commendatory songs, as we do statues with gold, that they may be remembered and admired of all. Ancient men will dote in this kind sometimes as well as the rest; the heat of love will thaw their frozen affections, dissolve the ice of age, and so far enable them, though they be sixty years of age above the girdle, to be scarce thirty beneath. Jovianus Pontanus makes an old fool rhyme, and turn Poetaster to please his Mistress.

* Trenchmore, a boisterous country dance.
† See page 718.

Sweet Marian, do not mine age disdain,
For thou canst make an old man young again.

They will be still singing amorous songs and ditties (if young especially) and cannot abstain, though it be when they go to, or should be at Church. We have a pretty story to this purpose in Westmonasteriensis, an old Writer of ours (if you will believe it). In the year 1012, at Colewiz, in Saxony, on Christmas Eve, a company of young men and maids, whilst the Priest was at Mass in the Church, were singing catches and love-songs in the Church-yard: he sent to them to make less noise, but they sung on still; and if you will, you shall have the very song itself:

A fellow rid by the greenwood side,
And fair Meswinde was his bride,
   Why stand we so, and do not go?

This they sung, he chaft, till at length, impatient as he was, he prayed to S. Magnus, Patron of the Church, they might all there sing and dance till that time twelvemonth, and so they did, without meat and drink, wearisomeness or giving over, till at year's end they ceased singing, and were absolved by Herebertus, Archbishop of Cologne. They will in all places be doing thus, young folks especially, reading love stories, talking of this or that young man, such a fair maid, singing, telling or hearing lascivious tales, scurrile tunes, such objects are their sole delight, their continual meditation; and as Guastavinius adds, of an abundance of seed comes much thought of love, continual memories, &c., an earnest longing comes hence, itching body, itching mind, amorous conceits, tickling thoughts, sweet and pleasant hopes: hence it is, they can think, discourse willingly, or speak almost of no other subject. 'Tis their only desire, if it may be done by Art, to see their husband's picture in a glass, they'll give any thing to know when they shall be married, how many husbands they shall have, by Cromnysmantia, a kind of Divination with Onions laid on the Altar on Christmas Eve, or by fasting on S. Agnes' Eve or Night, to know who shall be their first husband; or by Alphitomantia, by beans in a Cake, &c., to burn the same. This Love is the cause of all good conceits, neatness, exornations, plays, elegancies, delights, pleasant expressions, sweet motions, and gestures, joys, comforts, exultancies, and all the sweetness of our life, what would life be worth, or what pleasure without Venus? Let me live no longer than I may love, saith a mad merry fellow in Mimnermus. This Love is that salt that seasoneth our harsh and dull labours, and gives a pleasant relish to our other unsavoury proceedings; when love goes, the shadows gather, old age with its stiff joints, disease, &c. All our feasts almost, masques, mummings, banquets merry meetings, weddings, pleasing songs, fine tunes, Poems, Love-stories, Plays, Comedies, Atellanes [or Farces], Jigs, Fescennines, [or Facetious Verses], Elegies, Odes, &c., proceed hence. Danaus the son of Belus. at his daughter's wedding at Argos, instituted the first plays (some say) that ever were heard of, Symbols, Emblems, Impresses, Devices, if we shall believe Jovius, Contiles, Paradine, Camillus de Camillis, may be ascribed to it: most of our Arts and Sciences: painting amongst the rest, was first invented, saith Patritius, for love's sake. For when the daughter of Deburiades the Sicyonian, was to take leave of her Sweetheart, now going to wars, to comfort herself in his absence, she took his picture with coal upon a wall, as the candle gave the shadow, which her Father admiring perfected afterwards, and it was the first picture by report that ever was made. And long after, Sicyon for painting, carving, statuary, musick, and Philosophy, was preferred before all the Cities in Greece. Apollo was the first inventor of Physic, Divination, Oracles; Minerva found out weaving, Vulcan curious Ironwork, Mercury letters, but who prompted all this into their heads? Love. Never had they found out such things, had they not loved; they loved such things, or some party, for whose sake they were undertaken at first. 'Tis true, Vulcan made a most admirable Brooch or neck-lace, which long after Axion and Temenus, Phegeus' sons, for the singular worth of it, consecrated to Apollo at Delphi, but Pharyllus the Tyrant stole it away, and presented it to Aristo's wife, on whom he miserably doted (Parthenius tells the story out of Phylarchus); but why did Vulcan make this excellent ouch? to give Hermione, Cadmus' wife, whom he dearly loved. All our Tilts and Tournaments, Orders of the Garter, Golden Fleece, &c., owe their beginnings to love, and many of our histories. By this means, saith Jovius, they would express their loving minds to their Mistress, and to the beholders. 'Tis the sole object almost of Poetry, all our invention tends to it, all our songs, and therefore Hesiod makes the Muses and Graces still follow Cupid, and, as Plutarch holds, Menander and the rest of the Poets were Love's Priests, whatever those old Anacreons, all our Greek and Latin Epigrammatists, Love-writers, Antony Diogenes the most ancient, whose Epitome we find in Photius' Bibliotheca, Longus Sophista, Eustathius, Achilles Tatius, Aristænetus, Heliodorus, Plato, Plutarch, Lucian, Parthenius, Theodorus Prodromus, Ovid, Catullus, Tibullus, &c., our new Ariostos, Boiardos, Authors of Arcadia, Urania, Fairy Queen, &c., Marullus, Lotichius, Angerianus, Stroza,

Secundus, Capellanus, &c., with the rest of those facete modern Poets, have written in this kind, are but as so many Symptoms of Love. Their whole books are a Synopsis, or Breviary of Love, the Portuous [or Portesse, or Breviary] of Love, Legends of Lovers' lives and deaths, and of their memorable adventures, nay more, as Nevisanus the Lawyer holds, there never was any excellent Poet, that invented good fables, or made laudable verses, which was not in love himself; had he not taken a quill from Cupid's wings, he could never have written so amorously as he did.

> *Wanton Propertius and witty Gallus,*
> *Subtile Tibullus, and learned Catullus,*
> *It was Cynthia, Lesbia, Lycoris,*
> *That made you poets all; and if Alexis,*
> *Or Corinna chance my paramour to be,*
> *Virgil and Ovid shall not despise me.* (MARTIAL)
> *Not Thracian Orpheus shall vanquish me in song,*
> *Nor Linus.* (VIRGIL)

Petrarch's Laura made him so famous, Astrophel's Stella, and Jovianus Pontanus' Mistress was the cause of his Roses, Violets, Lilies, profligacies, flatteries, jests, elegance, Spikenard, Spring, Garland, Frankincense, Mars, Pallas, Venus, Grace, Saffron, Laurel, Perfume, Costum [the herb Zedoary], Tears, Myrrh, the Muses, and the rest of his Poems. Why are Italians at this day generally so good Poets and Painters? Because every man of any fashion amongst them hath his Mistress. The very rusticks and hog-rubbers, Menalcas and Corydon, stinking of horse-dirt, those fulsome knaves, if once they taste of this Love-liquor, are inspired in an instant. Instead of those accurate Emblems, curious Impresses, gaudy Masques, Tilts, Tournaments, &c., they have their Wakes, Whitsun-ales, Shepherds'-feasts, meetings on holy-days, country-dances, roundelays, writing their names on trees, true-lovers'-knots, pretty gifts.

> *With tokens, hearts divided, and half rings,*
> *Shepherds are in their Loves as coy as Kings.*

Choosing Lords, Ladies, Kings, Queens, and Valentines, &c., they go by couples,

> *Corydon's Phillis, Nysa and Mopsus,*
> *With dainty Dousibel and Sir Tophus.*

Instead of Odes, Epigrams, and Elegies, &c., they have their Ballads, Country-tunes, *O the Broom, the bonny bonny Broom,* Ditties and Songs, *Bess a Bell she doth excel,* — they must write likewise and indite all in rhyme.

Thou honeysuckle of the hawthorn hedge,
Vouchsafe in Cupid's cup my heart to pledge;
My heart's dear blood, sweet Cis, is thy carouse,
Worth all the ale in Gammer Gubbin's house.
I say no more, affairs call me away,
My father's horse for provender doth stay.
Be thou the Lady Cressetlight to me,
Sir Trolly Lolly will I prove to thee.
Written in haste, farewell, my Cowslip sweet,
Pray let's a Sunday at the alehouse meet. (ROWLANDS)

Your most grim Stoicks and severe Philosophers will melt away with
this passion, and if Athenæus bely them not, Aristippus, Apollodorus,
Antiphanes, &c., have made love-songs and Commentaries of their Mistress' praises, Orators wrote Epistles, Princes given Titles, Honours,
what not? Xerxes gave to Themistocles Lampsacus to find him wine,
Magnesia for bread, and Myus for the rest of his diet. The Persian Kings
allotted whole Cities to like use, one whole City served to dress her hair,
another her neck, a third her hood. Ahasuerus would have given Esther
half his Empire, and Herod bid Herodias ask what she would, she
should have it. Caligula gave an 100,000 sesterces to his Courtisan at
first word to buy her pins, and yet, when he was solicited by the Senate
to bestow something to repair the decayed walls of Rome for the
Commonwealth's good, he would give but 6,000 sesterces at most.
Dionysius, that Sicilian tyrant, rejected all his privy Councillors, and
was so besotted on Myrrha, his favourite and Mistress, that he would
bestow no office, or in the most weightiest business of the Kingdom do
ought, without her especial advice, prefer, depose, send, entertain no
man, though worthy and well-deserving, but by her consent; and he
again whom she commended, howsoever unfit, unworthy, was as highly
approved. Kings and Emperors, instead of Poems, build Cities; Adrian
built Antinoe in Egypt, besides Constellations, Temples, Altars, Statues,
Images, &c., in the honour of his Antinous. Alexander bestowed infinite
sums, to set out his Hephæstion to all eternity. Socrates professeth
himself Love's servant, ignorant in all arts and sciences, a Doctor alone
in love-matters, saith Maximus Tyrius, his sectator [or follower], a
teacher of these matters, &c., and this he spake openly, at home and
abroad, at publick feasts, in the Academy, in the Piraeus, the Lyceum,
under the plane trees, &c., the very blood-hound of beauty, as he is
styled by others. But I conclude there is no end of Love's Symptoms, 'tis
a bottomless pit. Love is subject to no dimensions; not to be surveyed
by any art or engine: and besides, I am of Hædus' mind, no man can

discourse of love-matters, or judge of them aright, that hath not made
trial in his own person, or, as Æneas Sylvius adds, hath not a little
doted, been mad or love-sick himself. I confess I am but a novice, a
Contemplator only,

I'm not in love, nor know what love may be.

I have a tincture; for why should I lie, dissemble or excuse it, yet I'm
a man, &c. not altogether inexpert in this subject, I am not a teacher of
love, and what I say is merely reading, the follies of others, by mine own
observation, and others' relation.

MEMBER 4

Prognosticks of Love-Melancholy

WHAT Fires, Torments, Cares, Jealousies, Suspicions, Fears, Griefs,
Anxieties, accompany such as are in love, I have sufficiently said: the
next question is, what will be the event of such miseries, what they
fore-tell. Some are of opinion that this love cannot be cured, there
flowers no balm to sain them, it accompanies them to the last.

The same love slays alike the sheep and the shepherd,   (VIRGIL)
and is so continuate, that by no persuasion almost it may be relieved.
Bid me not love, said Euryalus, bid the Mountains come down into
the plains, bid the Rivers run back to their fountains; I can as soon
leave to love, as the Sun leave his course.

First seas shall want their fish, the mountains shade,
Woods singing birds, the wind's murmur shall fade,
Than my fair Amaryllis' love allay'd.   (BUCHANAN)

Bid me not love, bid a deaf man hear, a blind man see, a dumb speak,
lame run, counsel can do no good, a sick man cannot relish, no Physick
can ease me.

Those arts help not their master which help all,
as Apollo confessed, and Jupiter himself could not be cured.

Physick can soon cure every disease,
Excepting love, that can it not appease.   (PROPERTIUS)

But whether love may be cured or no, and by what means, shall be
explained in his place; in the mean time, if it take his course, and be
not otherwise eased or amended, it breaks out often into outrageous and
prodigious events. As Tatius observes, Love and Bacchus are so violent
Gods, so furiously rage in our minds, that they make us forget all
honesty, shame, and common civility. For such men ordinarily as are

throughly possessed with this humour, become senseless and mad, for it is insane love as the Poet calls it, beside themselves, and as I have proved, no better than beasts, irrational, stupid, headstrong, void of fear of God or men, they frequently forswear themselves, spend, steal, commit incests, rapes, adulteries, murders, depopulate Towns, Cities, Countries, to satisfy their lust.

> *A Devil 'tis, and mischief such doth work,*
> *As never yet did Pagan, Jew, or Turk.* (R. T.)

The wars of Troy may be a sufficient witness; and as Appian saith of Antony and Cleopatra, their Love brought themselves and all Egypt into extreme and miserable calamities, the end of her is as bitter as worm-wood, and as sharp as a two-edged sword. *Her feet go down to death, her steps lead on to hell. She is more bitter than death, and the sinner shall be taken by her.* He that runs head-long from the top of a rock, is not in so bad a case, as he that falls into the gulf of love. For hence, saith Platina, comes Repentance, Dotage, they lose themselves, their wits, and make shipwrack of their fortunes altogether: madness, to make away themselves and others, violent death. Saith Gordonius, the prognostication is, they will either run mad or die. For if this passion continue, saith Ælian Montaltus, it makes the blood hot, thick, and black; and if the inflammation get into the brain, with continual meditation and waking, it so dries it up, that madness follows, or else they make away themselves.

O Corydon, Corydon, what madness hath seized upon you? (VIRGIL)

Now, as Arnoldus adds, it will speedily work these effects, if it be not presently helped; they will pine away, run mad, and die upon a sudden; saith Valescus, quickly mad, if good order be not taken.

> *Oh heavy yoke of love, which whoso bears,*
> *Is quite undone, and that at unawares.* (CALCAGNINUS)

So she confessed of herself in the Poet,

> *I shall be mad before it be perceived,*
> *A hair-breadth off scarce am I, now distracted.* (LUCIAN)

As mad as Orlando for his Angelica, or Hercules for his Hylas,

> *He went he car'd not whither, mad he was,*
> *The cruel God so tortur'd him, alas!* (THEOCRITUS)

At the sight of Hero I cannot tell how many ran mad,

> *And whilst he doth conceal his grief,*
> *Madness comes on him like a thief.* (MUSÆUS)

Go to Bedlam for examples. It is so well known in every village, how many have either died for love, or voluntarily made away themselves, that I need not much labour to prove it; Death is the common Catastrophe to such persons.

> *Would I were dead! for nought, God knows,*
> *But death can rid me of these woes.*   (ANACREON)

As soon as Euryalus departed from Siena, Lucretia, his Paramour, never looked up, no jests could exhilarate her sad mind, no joys comfort her wounded and distressed soul, but a little after she fell sick and died. But this is a gentle end, a natural death, such persons commonly make away themselves:

> *Gladly the impatient spirit*
> *Is effused upon the vacant air.*   (PRODROMUS)

So did Dido:

> *" O let me die," she said; " 'tis pleasant thus*
> *To journey to the shadows."*

Pyramus and Thisbe, Medea, Coresus and Callirhoe, Theagenes the Philosopher, and many Myriads besides, and so will ever do,

> *For this one dead I also have a hand that's brave,*
> *I too have love: twill gird me for the grave.*   (OVID)
> *Who ever heard a story of more woe,*
> *Than that of Juliet and her Romeo?*   (SHAKESPEARE)

Read Parthenius on Romances, and Plutarch's Love-stories, all tending almost to this purpose. Valleriola hath a lamentable narration of a Merchant his patient, that raving through impatience of love, had he not been watched, would every while have offered violence to himself. Amatus Lusitanus hath such another story, and Felix Plater a third of a young Gentleman that studied Physick, and for the love of a Doctor's daughter, having no hope to compass his desire, poisoned himself. In the year 1615, a Barber in Frankfort, because his wench was betrothed to another, cut his own throat. At Neuburg the same year a young man, because he could not get her parents' consent, killed his sweetheart, and afterwards himself, desiring this of the Magistrate, as he gave up the Ghost, that they might be buried in one grave, which Gismunda besought of Tancredus her Father, that she might be in like sort buried with Guiscardus her Lover, that so their bodies might lie together in the grave, as their souls wander about in the Elysian fields,

> *Whom relentless love consumed with wasting pain,*   (VIRGIL)

in a myrtle grove they dwell.

> *Even in death, the pang doth never leave them*   (VIRGIL)

You have not yet heard the worst, they do not offer violence to themselves in this rage of lust, but unto others, their nearest and dearest friends. Catiline killed his only Son, for the love of Aurelia Orestilla, because she would not marry him while his son yet lived. Laodice, the sister of Mithridates, poisoned her husband, to give content to a base fellow whom she loved. Alexander to please Thais, a Concubine of his, set Persepolis on fire. Nereus' wife, a widow and Lady of Athens, for the love of a Venetian Gentleman, betrayed the City; and he for her sake murthered his wife, the daughter of a Noble man in Venice. Constantine Despota made away Catherine his wife, turned his son Michael and his other children out of doors, for the love of a base Scrivener's daughter in Thessalonica, with whose beauty he was enamoured. Leucophrye betrayed the City where she dwelt, for her sweetheart's sake, that was in the enemy's Camp. Pithidice, the Governor's daughter of Methinia, for the love of Achilles, betrayed the whole Island to him, her Father's enemy. Diognetus did as much, in the city where he dwelt, for the love of Polycrite, Medea for the love of Jason; she taught him how to tame the fire-breathing, brass-feeted Bulls, and kill the mighty Dragon that kept the golden fleece; and tore her little brother Absyrtus in pieces, that her Father Aëetes might have something to detain him, while she ran away with her beloved Jason, &c. Such Acts and Scenes hath this Tragicomedy of love.

MEMBER 5

SUBSECTION 1 — *Cure of Love-Melancholy, by Labour, Diet, Physick,*
Fasting, &c.

ALTHOUGH it be controverted by some, whether Love-Melancholy may be cured, because it is so irresistible and violent a passion; for, as you know,

> *It is an easy passage down to hell,*
>
> *But to come back, once there, you cannot well.*　(VIRGIL)

Yet without question, if it be taken in time, it may be helped, and by many good remedies amended. Avicenna sets down seven compendious ways how this malady may be eased, altered and expelled. Savanarola, 9 principal observations, Jason Pratensis prescribes eight rules besides Physick, how this passion may be tamed, Laurentius 2 main precepts, Arnoldus, Valleriola, Montaltus, Hildesheim, Langius, and others inform us otherwise, and yet all tending to the same purpose. The sum of which I will briefly epitomize (for I light my Candle from their Torches) and enlarge again upon occasion, as shall seem best to me, and that after mine own method. The first rule to be observed in this stubborn and unbridled passion, is exercise and diet. It is an old and well known sentence. without Ceres and Bacchus, Venus grows cold. As an idle sedentary life, liberal feeding, are great causes of it, so the opposite, labour, slender and sparing diet, with continual business, are the best and most ordinary means to prevent it.

> *Take idleness away, and put to flight*
> *Are Cupid's arts, his torches. give no light.* (OVID)

Minerva, Diana. Vesta. and the nine Muses were not enamoured at all, because they never were idle.

> *In vain are all your flatteries,*
> *In vain are all your knaveries,*
> *Delights, deceits, procacities,*
> *Sighs, kisses, and conspiracies,*
> *And whate'er is done by Art,*
> *To bewitch a Lover's heart.* (BUCHANAN)

'Tis in vain to set upon those that are busy. 'Tis Savanarola's third rule, to be occupied with many and large affairs. and Avicenna's precept, —

> *Love yields to business ; be at work, you're safe.* (OVID)

To be busy still. and as Guianerius enjoins, about matters of great moment, if it may be. Magninus adds, never to be idle, but at the hours of sleep.

> *For if thou dost not ply thy book,*
> *By candle-light to study bent,*
> *Employ'd about some honest thing,*
> *Envy or Love shall thee torment.* (HORACE)

No better Physick than to be always occupied, seriously intent.

> *Why dost thou ask, poor folks are often free*
> *And dainty places still molested be?* (SENECA)

Because poor people fare coarsely, work hard, go wool-ward and bare.

> *Poverty hath not means to feed love fat.* (OVID)

Guianerius therefore prescribes his patient to go with hair-cloth next his skin, to go bare-footed, and bare-legged in cold weather, to whip himself now and then, as Monks do, but above all, to fast. Not with sweet wine, mutton and pottage, as many of those Tenterbellies [or Gluttons] do, howsoever they put on Lenten faces, and whatsoever they pretend, but from all manner of meat. Fasting is an all-sufficient remedy of itself, for, as Jason Pratensis holds, the bodies of such persons that feed liberally, and live at ease, are full of bad spirits and Devils, devilish thoughts; no better Physick for such parties, than to fast. Hildesheim, to this of hunger, adds often baths, much exercise and sweat, but hunger and fasting he prescribes before the rest. And 'tis indeed our Saviour's Oracle, " This kind of devil is not cast out but by fasting and prayer," which makes the Fathers so immoderate in commendation of fasting. As Hunger, saith Ambrose, is a friend of Virginity, so is it an enemy to lasciviousness, but fulness overthrows chastity, and fostereth all manner of provocations. If thine horse be too lusty, Hierome adviseth thee to take away some of his provender; by this means those Pauls, Hilaries, Antonies, and famous Anchorites, subdued the lust of the flesh; by this means Hilarion made his ass, as he called his own body, leave kicking, (so Hierome relates of him in his life) when the Devil tempted him to any such foul offence. By this means those Indian Brachmanes kept themselves continent, they lay upon the ground covered with skins, as the Redshanks [or Highlanders] do on Hadder [or Heather], and dieted themselves sparingly on one dish, which Guianerius would have all young men put in practice; and if that will not serve, Gordonius would have them soundly whipped, or, to cool their courage, kept in prison, and there be fed with bread and water, till they acknowledge their error, and become of another mind. If imprisonment and hunger will not take them down, according to the direction of that Theban Crates, time must wear it out; if time will not, the last refuge is an halter. But this, you will say, is comically spoken. Howsoever, Fasting by all means must be still used; and as they must refrain from such meats formerly mentioned, which cause venery, or provoke lust, so they must use an opposite diet. Wine must be altogether avoided of the younger sort. So Plato prescribes, and would have the Magistrates themselves abstain from it, for example's sake, highly commending the Carthaginians for their temperance in this kind. And 'twas a good edict, a commendable thing, so that it were not done for some sinister respect, as those old Egyptians abstained from Wine, because some fabulous Poets had given out, Wine sprang first from the blood of the Giants, or out of superstition, as our modern Turks, but for temperance, it being a poison to the mind and an encourager of faults, a plague itself if immoderately taken. Women of old for that cause, in hot Countries, were forbid the use of it; and as severely punished for drinking of wine, as for adultery, and young folks, as Leonicus hath recorded, out of Athenæus and others; and is still practised in Italy and some other Countries of Europe, and Asia, as Claudius Minos hath well illustrated in his Comment on the 23rd Emblem of Alciati. So choice is to be made of other diet.

Eringoes are not good for to be taken,
And all lascivious meats must be forsaken.   (OVID)

Those opposite meats which ought to be used are Cowcumbers, Melons, Purselan, Water-Lilies, Rue, Woodbine, Ammi, Lettice, which Lemnius so much commends, and Mizaldus, to this purpose; Vitex before the rest, which, saith Magninus, hath a wonderful virtue in it. Those Athenian women, in their solemn feasts called Thesmophoria, were to abstain nine days from the company of men, during which time, saith Ælian, they laid a certain herb named Hanea [agnos, agnus castus, or chaste-lamb], in their beds, which assuaged those ardent flames of love, and freed them from the torments of that violent passion. See more in Porta, Matthiolus, Crescentius, &c., and what every Herbalist almost and Physician hath written, in their chapters on Satyriasis and Priapism, Rhasis amongst the rest. In some cases again, if they be much dejected and brought low in body, and now ready to despair through anguish, grief, and too sensible a feeling of their misery, a cup of wine and full diet is not amiss, and, as Valescus adviseth, together with other worthy means, the frequent use of Venus, which Langius approves out of Rhasis (he urgeth to frequent indulgence), and Guianerius seconds it as a very profitable remedy.

When of Venus thou art fain,
And a serving-maid stands by,
Wouldst thou rather keep thy pain
Than take what's nearest? No, not I!   (HORACE)

Jason Pratensis subscribes to this counsel of the Poet, such voiding may be relied on to heal at once or at least mitigate the sickness. As it did the raging lust of Ahasuerus, who in the impatient assuaging of his passions deflowered new virgins each night. And to be drunk too by fits; but this is mad Physick, if it be at all to be permitted. If not, yet some pleasure is to be allowed, as that which Vives speaks of: A lover that hath as it were lost himself through impotency, impatience, must be called home as a traveller by musick, feasting, good wine, if need be, to drunkenness itself, which many so much commend for the easing of the mind, all kinds of sports and merriments, to see fair pictures, hangings, buildings, pleasant fields, Orchards, Gardens, Groves, Ponds, Pools, Rivers, fishing, fowling, hawking, hunting, to hear merry tales, and pleasant discourse, reading, to use exercise till he sweat, that new spirits may succeed, or by some vehement affection or contrary passion, to be diverted, till he be fully weaned from anger, suspicion, cares, fears, &c., and habituated into another course. Mayest thou (as Sempronius

adviseth Callisto his love-sick Master) still have a pleasant companion
to sing and tell merry tales, songs, and facete histories, sweet discourse,
&c. And as the melody of musick, merriment, singing, dancing, doth
augment the passion of some Lovers, as Avicenna notes, so it expelleth
it in others, and doth very much good. These things must be warily
applied, as the parties' Symptoms vary, and they shall stand variously
affected.

If there be any need of Physick, that the humours be altered, or any
new matter aggregated, they must be cured as melancholy men. Carolus
à Lorme, amongst other questions discussed for his degree at Montpelier
in France, hath this, Whether amantes (lovers) and amentes (mad men)
be cured by the same remedies? he affirms it; for love extended is
mere madness. Such Physick then as is prescribed, is either inward or
outward, as hath been formerly handled in the precedent partition in
the cure of Melancholy. Consult with Valleriola, Lodovicus Mercatus,
Daniel Sennertus, Jacobus Ferrandus, the Frenchman, in his Tract on
Erotick Love, Forestus, Jason Pratensis and others for peculiar receipts.
Amatus Lusitanus cured a young Jew that was almost mad for love,
with the syrup of Hellebore, and such other evacuations and purges,
which are usually prescribed to black choler; Avicenna confirms as
much, if need require, and blood-letting above the rest, which makes
amantes no more amentes, lovers come to themselves, and keep in their
right mind. 'Tis the same which the Salernitan school, Jason Pratensis,
Hildesheim, &c., prescribe, blood-letting to be used as a principal
remedy. Those old Scythians had a trick to cure all appetite of burning
lust, by letting themselves blood under the ears, and to make both men
and women barren, as Sabellicus in his Enneads relates of them. Which
Salmuth, out of Hippocrates and Benzo, say still is in use amongst the
Indians, a reason of which Langius gives.

Here they make medicines to allay lust, such as putting Camphor on
the parts, and carrying it in the breeches (one saith) keeps the pintle
flaccid. A noble virgin being sick with this affliction, a Physician prescribed for her, among other things, that she wear on her back for
twenty days a thin sheet of lead pierced with many holes; and for the
drying up of seed he ordered that she be very sparing of victual, and
chew frequently a preparation of coriander, lettuce-seed and vinegar,
and so freed her of the malady. Further, they hinder or prevent coitus
by a willow-leaf rubbed and drunk, and if frequently used, they cease
from it wholly. Topaz is likewise recommended, worn in a ring; the
right stone of a wolf, brayed; and oil or water of roses will cause weari-

ness of venery, writes Alexander Benedictus; buttermilk, Canabis seed, and Camphor are also commended. Carrying a Verbena herb extinguish-eth lust, and pulverized frog, beheaded and dried up. To extinguish coi-tus, anoint the genitals and belly and chest with water in which opium Thebaicum has been dissolved; Camphor is in the highest degree inimi-cal to lust, and dried coriander diminishes coitus and hinders erection; mustard drink does the same. Give verbena in a potion, and the pintle will not lift for six days; dried mint with vinegar in the uterus, the genitals smeared with juice of Henbane or Hemlock, quiets the appe-tite for coitus, &c. Take seeds of lettuce, purslain, coriander, each, 1 drachm; dried mint, one-half drachm; white sugar, 4 ounces: let all be pulverized very fine, then mixt with water of Nenuphar, and made into lozenges; take one in the morning on arising. Many similar re-ceipts are to be found in Hildesheim, Mizaldus, Porta, and the others.

SUBSECTION 2 — *Withstand the beginnings, avoid occasions, change his place: fair and foul means, contrary passions, with witty inven-tions: to bring in another, and discommend the former*

OTHER good rules and precepts are enjoined by our Physicians, which, if not alone, yet certainly conjoined may do much; the first of which is, to withstand the beginnings; he that will but resist at first, may easily be a conqueror at the last. Balthasar Castilio urgeth this pre-script above the rest, when he shall chance (saith he) to light upon a woman that hath good behaviour joined with her excellent person, and shall perceive his eyes with a kind of greediness to pull unto them this image of beauty, and carry it to the heart: shall observe himself to be somewhat incensed with this influence, which moveth within: when he shall discern those subtile spirits sparkling in her eyes to administer more fuel to the fire, he must wisely withstand the beginnings, rouse up reason, stupefied almost, fortify his heart by all means, and shut up all those passages, by which it may have entrance. — 'Tis a precept which all concur upon.

> *Thy quick disease, whilst it is fresh to-day,*
> *By all means crush, thy feet at first step stay.* (OVID)

Which cannot speedier be done, than if he confess his grief and passion to some judicious friend (the more he conceals, the greater is his pain) that by his good advice may happily ease him on a sudden; and withal to avoid occasions, or any circumstance that may aggravate his disease, to remove the object by all means; for who can stand by a fire and not burn?

Shoot back, ye bolts, and cast her out of doors,
That has drunk up the blood of me her lover. (PLAUTUS)

'Tis good therefore to keep quite out of her company, which Hierome so much labours to Paula, to Nepotian; Chrysostom so much inculcates, Cyprian, and many other Fathers of the Church. Siracides in his ninth chapter, Jason Pratensis, Savanarola, Arnoldus, Valleriola, &c., and every Physician that treats of this subject. Not only to avoid, as Gregory Tholosanus exhorts, kissing, dalliance, all speeches, tokens, love-letters, and the like, or as Castilio, to converse with them, hear them speak, or sing (thou hadst better hear, saith Cyprian, a serpent hiss), those amiable smiles, admirable graces, and sweet gestures, which their presence affords,

Let them not bend their heads to bite their wonted little kisses,
Nor press with gentle touches the nipples of their misses, (LIPSIUS)

but all talk, name, mention, or cogitation of them, and of any other women, persons, circumstance, amorous book or tale, that may administer any occasion of remembrance. Prosper adviseth young men not to read the Canticles, and some parts of Genesis at other times; but for such as are enamoured, they forbid, as before, the name mentioned, &c., especially all sight, they must not so much as come near, or look upon them.

'Tis best to shun the sight and food of love,
Turn the mind wholly from the thought thereof. (LUCRETIUS)

Gaze not on a Maid, saith Siracides, turn away thine eyes from a beautiful woman; " avert thine eyes," saith David, or if thou dost see them, as Ficinus adviseth, let not thine eye be intent on lust, do not intend [or attend to] her more than the rest: for, as Propertius holds, 'tis by this food that love grows fat, Love as a snow-ball inlargeth itself by sight: but as Hierome to Nepotian, either see all alike, or let all alone; make a league with thine eyes, as Job did, and that is the safest course, let all alone, see none of them. Nothing sooner revives, or waxeth sore again, as Petrarch holds, than Love doth by sight. As Pomp renews ambition; the sight of gold, covetousness, a beauteous object sets on fire this burning lust. The sight of drink makes one dry, and the sight of meat increaseth appetite. 'Tis dangerous therefore to see. A young Gentleman in merriment, would needs put on his Mistress' clothes, and walk abroad alone, which some of her suitors espying, stole him away for her that he represented. So much can sight enforce. Especially if he have been formerly enamoured, the sight of his Mistress strikes him into a new fit, and makes him rave many days after.

A sickly man a little thing offends,
  As brimstone doth a fire decayed renew,
And make it burn afresh, doth Love's dead flames,
  If that the former object it review. (OVID)

Or, as the Poet compares it to embers in ashes, which the wind blows, a scald head (as the saying is) is soon broken, dry wood quickly kindles, and when they have been formerly wounded with sight, how can they by seeing but be inflamed? Ismenias acknowledgeth as much of himself, when he had been long absent, and almost forgotten his Mistress, at the first sight of her, as straw in a fire, I burned afresh, and more than ever I did before. Chariclea was as much moved at the sight of her dear Theagenes, after he had been a great stranger. Myrtila in Aristænetus swore she would never love Pamphilus again, and did moderate her passion, so long as he was absent; but the next time he came in presence, she could not contain, she broke her vow, and did profusely embrace him. Hermotinus a young man (in the said Author) is all out as unstaid, he had forgot his Mistress quite, and by his friends was well weaned from her love, but seeing her by chance, he remembered his old flame, he raved amain, she did appear as a blazing-star, or an Angel, to his sight. And it is the common passion of all lovers to be overcome in this sort. For that cause, belike, Alexander discerning this inconvenience and danger that comes by seeing, when he heard Darius' wife so much commended for her beauty, would scarce admit her to come in his sight, foreknowing belike that of Plutarch, how full of danger it is to see a proper woman; and though he was intemperate in other things, yet in this he carried himself bravely. And so when as Araspes, in Xenophon, had so much magnified that divine face of Panthea to Cyrus, by how much she was fairer than ordinary, by so much he was the more unwilling to see her. Scipio, a young man of 23 years of age, and the most beautiful of the Romans, equal in person to that of Grecian Cleinias, or Homer's Nireus, at the siege of a City in Spain, when as a noble and a most fair young Gentlewoman was brought unto him, and he had heard she was betrothed to a Lord, rewarded her, and sent her back to her sweetheart. S. Austin, as Gregory reports of him, would not live in the house with his own sister. Xenocrates lay with Lais of Corinth all night, and would not touch her. Socrates, though all the City of Athens supposed him to dote upon fair Alcibiades, yet when he had an opportunity to lie in the chamber with him all to himself, and was wooed by him besides, as the said Alcibiades publickly confessed, he scornfully rejected him. Petrarch, that had so magnified his Laura in several Poems, when by the Pope's means she was offered unto him, would not accept of her. It is a good happiness to be free from this passion of Love, and great discretion it argues in such a man that he can so contain himself; but when thou art once in love, to moderate thyself (as Heliodorus saith) is a singular point of wisdom.

> To avoid such nets is no such mastery,
> But ta'en, to escape is all the victory.   (LUCRETIUS)

But forasmuch as few men are free, so discreet Lovers, or that can contain themselves, and moderate their passions, to curb their senses, as not to see them, not to look lasciviously, not to confer with them, such is the fury of this head-strong passion of raging lust, and their weakness, as Haedus terms it, such a furious desire nature hath inscribed, such unspeakable delight,

> The fury of holy Venus
> Brings madness among men,

which neither reason, counsel, poverty, pain, misery, drudgery, the throes of travail, &c., can deter them from; we must use some speedy means to correct and prevent that, and all other inconveniences, which come by conference and the like. The best, readiest, surest way, and which all approve, is, change of scene, to send them several ways, that they may neither hear of, see, nor have opportunity to send to one another again, or live together he alone with her alone, as so many Gilbertines.* Be long away from home, 'tis Savanarola's fourth rule, and Gordonius' precept, send him to travel. 'Tis that which most run upon, as so many hounds with full cry, Poets, Divines, Philosophers, Physicians, all; change country, saith Valesius; as a sick man, he must be cured by change of air, Tully. The best remedy is to get thee gone, Jason Pratensis; change air and soil, Laurentius.

> Flee the cherished shore.   (VIRGIL)
> 'Tis best to keep away from neighboring haunts.   (OVID)
> Go then and tread the long and distant ways,
> Safety is but in flight.

Travelling is an Antidote of Love. For this purpose, saith Propertius, my parents sent me to Athens; time and absence wear away pain and grief, as fire goes out for want of fuel.

> As far as eye can see, so far the soul can love.   (PROPERTIUS)

But so as they tarry out long enough: a whole year [Socrates in] Xenophon prescribes Critobulus: some will hardly be weaned under. All this

* Gilbertines, a double order comprising both monks and nuns, founded by St. Gilbert of Sempringham in England in the 12th century.

Heinsius merrily inculcates in an Epistle to his friend Primerius: first fast, then tarry, thirdly change thy place, fourthly think of an halter. If change of place, continuance of time, absence, will not wear it out, with those precedent remedies, it will hardly be removed: but these commonly are of force. Felix Plater had a baker to his patient, almost mad for the love of his maid, and desperate: by removing her from him, he was in a short space cured. Isæus, a Philosopher of Assyria, was a most dissolute liver in his youth, openly lustful, in love with all he met; but after he betook himself by his friend's advice to his study, and left women's company, he was so changed, that he cared no more for Plays, nor Feasts, nor Masks, nor Songs, nor Verses, fine clothes, nor no such love-toys; he became a new man upon a sudden, (saith mine Author) as if he had lost his former eyes. Peter Godefridus, in the last Chapter of his third Book, hath a story out of S. Ambrose, of a young man, that meeting his old love, after long absence, on whom he had extremely doted, would scarce take notice of her; she wondered at it, that he should so lightly esteem her, called him again, spoke persuasively, and told him who she was, I am So-and-so, she said: but he replied, he was not the same man: tore himself away, as Æneas fled from Dido, not vouchsafing her any farther parley, loathing his folly, and ashamed of that which formerly he had done.

I am not as foolish as I was, Neæra,   (BUCHANAN)

O Neæra, put your tricks, and practise hereafter upon some body else, you shall befool me no longer. Petrarch hath such another tale of a young Gallant, that loved a wench with one eye, and for that cause by his parents was sent to travel into far Countries; after some years he returned, and meeting the maid for whose sake he was sent abroad, asked her how, and by what chance she lost her eye? No, said she, I have lost none, but you have found yours: signifying thereby, that all Lovers were blind; as Fabius saith, Lovers cannot judge of beauty, nor scarce of anything else, as they will easily confess, after they return unto themselves, by some discontinuance or better advice, wonder at their own folly, madness, stupidity, blindness, be much abashed, and laugh at Love, and call't an idle thing, condemn themselves, that ever they should be so besotted or misled; and be heartily glad they have so happily escaped.

If so be (which is seldom) that change of place will not effect this alteration, then other remedies are to be annexed, fair and foul means, as to persuade, promise, threaten, terrify, or to divert by some contrary passion, rumour, tales, news, or some witty invention, to alter his affection: by some greater sorrow to drive out the less, saith Gordonius, as that his house is on fire, his best friends dead, his money stolen, that he is made some great Governor, or hath some honour, office, some inheritance is befallen him, he shall be a Knight, a Baron: or by some false accusation, as they do to such as have the hiccup, to make them forget it. Saint Hierome, in his epistle to Rusticus the Monk, hath an instance of a young man of Greece, that lived in a Monastery in Egypt, that by no labour, no continence, no persuasion, could be diverted, but at last by this trick he was delivered. The Abbot sets one of his Convent to quarrel with him, and with some scandalous reproach or other to defame him before company, and then to come and complain first, the witnesses were likewise suborned for the Plaintiff. The young man wept, and when all were against him, the Abbot cunningly took his part, lest he should be overcome with immoderate grief: but what need many words? By this invention he was cured, and alienated from his pristine love-thoughts. — Injuries, slanders, contempts, disgraces,

———— *the affront of slighted beauty,* (VIRGIL)

are very forcible means to withdraw men's affections; as Lucian saith, Lovers reviled or neglected, contemned or misused, turn love to hate. Comest thou back? Not for all thine entreaties, I'll never love thee more. What's she to me? So Zephyrus hated Hyacinthus because he scorned him and preferred his corrival Apollo; he will not come again though he be invited. Tell him but how he was scoffed at behind his back ('tis the counsel of Avicenna), that his Love is false, and entertains another, rejects him, cares not for him, or that she is a fool, a nasty quean, a slut, a vixen, a scold, a Devil; or which Italians commonly do, that he or she hath some loathsome filthy disease, gout, stone, strangury, falling-sickness, and they are hereditary, not to be avoided, he is subject to a Consumption, hath the Pox, that he hath three or four incurable tetters, issues: that she is bald, her breath stinks, she is mad by inheritance, and so are all the kindred, an hare-brain, with many other secret infirmities, which I will not so much as name, belonging to women. That he is an Hermaphrodite, an Eunuch, imperfect, impotent, a spendthrift, a gamester, a fool, a gull, a beggar, a whoremaster, far in debt, and not able to maintain her, a common drunkard, his mother was a witch, his father hang'd, that he hath a Wolf [or running sore] in his bosom, a sore leg, he is a Leper, hath some incurable disease, that he will surely beat her, he cannot hold his water, that he cries out or walks in the night, will stab his bed-fellow, tell all his secrets in his sleep, and that no body dare lie with him, his house is haunted with spirits, with such fearful and tragical things, able to avert and terrify any man or woman living. Gordonius adviseth in this manner; and having brought secretly a menstruous rag, if these things will not persuade, draw it forth of a sudden, flourish it before the face, crying out. Such is thy beloved; and if this will not cure him, he is not a man, but a devil incarnate. Avicenna saith the same: Let some old woman tell of filthy things concerning women. So Arculanus, Rhasis, &c.

Withal, as they do discommend the old, for the better affecting a more speedy alteration, they must commend another Paramour, set him or her to be wooed, or woo some other that shall be fairer, of better note, better fortune, birth, parentage, much to be preferred,

> *Thou'lt find another Alexis, if he disdain thee.* (VIRGIL)

by this means, which Jason Pratensis wisheth, to turn the stream of affection another way,

> *A new love thrusteth out the old,* (OVID)

or, as Valesius adviseth, by subdividing to diminish it, as a great River cut into many channels, runs low at last.

> *Take, I advise, two mistresses at once.* (OVID)

If you suspect to be taken, be sure, saith the Poet, to have two Mistresses at once, or go from one to another. As he that goes from a good fire in cold weather, is loath to depart from it, though in the next room there be a better, which will refresh him as much; there's as much difference of shes as fires; or bring him to some publick shews, plays, meetings, where he may see variety, and he shall likely loathe his first choice: carry him but to the next Town, yea, peradventure to the next house, and as Paris lost Ænone's love by seeing Helena, and Cressida forsook Troilus by conversing with Diomede, he will dislike his former Mistress, and leave her quite behind him, as Theseus left Ariadne fast asleep in the Island of Dia, to seek her fortune, that was erst his loving Mistress. As he said [in Petronius] Doris is but a dowdy to this. As he that looks himself in a glass, forgets his Physiognomy forthwith, this flattering glass of love will be diminished by remove; after a little absence, it will be remitted, the next fair object will likely alter it. A young man in Lucian was pitifully in love, he came to the Theatre by chance, and by seeing other fair objects there, was fully recovered, and went merrily home, as if he had taken a dram of oblivion. A Mouse (saith an Apologer) was brought up in a chest, there fed with fragments of bread and cheese, thought there could be no better meat, till coming forth at last, and feeding liberally of other variety of viands, loathed his former life: moralize this fable by thyself. Plato, in his seventh book of his Republic, hath a pretty fiction of a City under ground, to which by little holes some small store of light came; the inhabitants thought there could not be a better place, and at their first coming abroad they might not endure the light; but, after they were accustomed a little to it, they deplored their fellows' misery that lived under ground. A silly Lover is in like state, none so fair as his Mistress at first, he cares for none but her; yet after a while, when he hath compared her with others, he abhors her name, sight, and memory. 'Tis generally true: for as he observes, one fire drives out another, and such is women's weakness, that they love commonly him that is present. And so do many men (as he confesseth), he loved Amy till he saw Flora, and when he saw Cynthia, forgat them both: but fair Phyllis was incomparably beyond them all, Chloris surpassed her, and yet when he espied Amaryllis, she was his sole Mistress; O divine Amaryllis! &c. how lovely, how tall, how comely, she was (saith Polemius) till he saw another, and then she was the sole subject of his thoughts. In conclusion, her he loves best he saw last. Triton the Sea-God first loved Leucothoë, till he came in presence of Milæne, she was the Commandress of his heart, till he saw Galatea; but (as she complains) he loved another eftsoons, another, and another. 'Tis a thing which by Hierom's report, hath been usually practised. Heathen Philosophers drive out one love with another, as they do a peg, or pin with a pin. Which those seven Persian Princes did to Ahasuerus, that they might requite the desire of Queen Vashti with the love of others. Pausanias, in Eliacis, saith that therefore one Cupid was painted to contend with another, and to take the Garland from him, because one love drives out another.

One passion diminisheth another's power,   (OVID)

and Tully, disputing with C. Cotta, makes mention of three several Cupids, all differing in office. Felix Plater in the first book of his observations, boasts how he cured a widower in Basil, a Patient of his, by this stratagem alone, that doted upon a poor servant his maid, when friends, children, no persuasion could serve to alienate his mind: they motioned him to another honest man's daughter in the Town, whom he loved, and lived with, long after, abhorring the very name and sight of the first. After the death of Lucretia, Euryalus would admit of no comfort, till the Emperor Sigismund married him to a noble Lady of his Court, and so in short space he was freed.

SUBSECTION 3 — *By counsel and persuasion, foulness of the fact, men's, women's faults, miseries of marriage, events of lust, &c.*

As there be divers causes of this burning lust, or heroical love, so there be many good remedies to ease and help; amongst which, good counsel and persuasion, which I should have handled in the first place, are of great moment, and not to be omitted. Many are of opinion, that in this blind head-strong passion counsel can do no good.

> *Which thing hath neither judgment, or an end,*
> *How should advice or counsel it amend?* (TERENCE)
> *For what term shall be set to love?* (VIRGIL)

But without question, good counsel and advice must needs be of great force, especially if it shall proceed from a wise, fatherly, reverend, discreet person, a man of authority, whom the parties do respect, stand in awe of, or from a judicious friend, of itself alone, it is able to divert and suffice. Gordonius, the Physician, attributes so much to it, that he would have it by all means used in the first place: I counsel him that would not be poisoned to turn from her, pointing to mortal perils, the judgment of hell, the joys of Paradise. He would have some discreet men to dissuade them, after the fury of passion is a little spent, or by absence allayed; for it is as intempestive at first to give counsel, as to comfort parents when their children are in that instant departed: to no purpose to prescribe Narcoticks, Cordials, Nectarines, Potions, Homer's Nepenthes, or Helena's Bowl, &c. She will not cease to beat her breast, she will lament and howl for a season: let passion have his course a while, and then he may proceed, by fore-shewing the miserable events and dangers which will surely happen, the pains of Hell, joys of Paradise, and the like, which by their preposterous courses they shall forfeit or incur; and 'tis a fit method, a very good means. For what Seneca said of Vice, I say of Love, 'tis learned of itself, but hardly left without a Tutor. 'Tis not amiss therefore to have some such overseer, to expostulate and shew them such absurdities, inconveniences, imperfections, discontents, as usually follow; which their blindness, fury, madness, cannot apply unto themselves, or will not apprehend through weakness: and good for them to disclose themselves, to give ear to friendly admonitions. Tell me, Sweetheart (saith Tryphæna, to love-sick Charmides in Lucian) what is it that troubles thee: peradventure I can ease thy mind, and further thee in thy suit; and so without question she might, and so mayest thou, if the Patient be capable of good counsel, and will hear at least what may be said.

If he love at all, she is either an honest woman or a whore. If dishonest, let him read, or inculcate to him, that fifth of Solomon's Proverbs, Ecclesiastes 26, Ambrose in his book of Abel and Cain, Philo Judæus, Platina's Dialogue on Loves, Espencæus, and those three books of Peter Hædus On the Disdain of Love, Æneas Sylvius' tart Epistle, which he wrote to his friend Nicholas of Wartburg, which he calls a medicine for illicit love, &c. For what's an whore, as he saith, but a poller [or fleecer] of youth, ruin of men, a destruction, a devourer of patrimonies, a downfall of honour, fodder for the Devil, the gate of death, and supplement of hell? Such love is a snare to the soul, &c., a bitter honey, sweet poison, delicate destruction, a voluntary mischief, a defiling filth, a dung-pit. And as Peter Aretine's Lucretia, a notable quean, confesseth: gluttony, anger, envy, pride, sacrilege, theft, slaughter, were all born that day that a whore began her profession: for, as she follows it, her pride is greater than a rich churl's, she is more envious than the pox, as malicious, as melancholy, as covetous as Hell. If from the beginning of the world any were bad, worse, worst, bad in the superlative degree, 'tis a whore: how many have I undone, caused to be wounded, slain! O Antonia, thou seest what I am without, but within, God knows, a puddle of iniquity, a sink of sin, a pocky quean. — Let him now that so dotes meditate on this: let him see the event and success of others, Samson, Hercules, Holofernes, &c. Those infinite mischiefs attend it: if she be another man's wife he loves, 'tis abominable in the sight of God and men: adultery is expressly forbidden in God's Commandment, a mortal sin, able to endanger his soul: if he be such a one that fears God, or have any Religion, he will eschew it, and abhor the loathsomeness of his own fact. If he love an honest maid, 'tis to abuse, or marry her: if to abuse, 'tis fornication, a foul fact (though some make light of it) and almost equal to adultery itself. If to marry, let him seriously consider what he takes in hand, look before he leap, as the proverb is, or settle his affections, and examine first the party, and condition of his estate and hers, whether it be a fit match, for fortunes, years, parentage, and such other circumstances, whether it be of Venus herself: whether it be likely to proceed: if not, let him wisely stave himself off at the first, curb in his inordinate passion, and moderate his desire, by thinking of some other subject, divert his cogitations. Or if it be not for his good, as Æneas, forewarned by Mercury in a dream, left Dido's love, and in all haste got him to Sea,

> *Calling his comrades three,*
> *He bids them quietly*
> *Prepare the ships for sea,*

and although she did oppose with vows, tears, prayers, and imprecation,

> *He is not moved by sigh or tear,*
> *Her pleading voice he will not hear.*

Let thy Mercury, reason, rule thee against all allurements, seeming delights, pleasing inward or outward provocations. Thou mayst do this if thou wilt, a father dotes not on his own daughter, a brother on a sister: and why? because it is unnatural, unlawful, unfit. If he be sickly, soft, deformed, let him think of his deformities, vices, infirmities; if in debt, let him ruminate how to pay his debts: if he be in any danger, let him seek to avoid it: if he have any law-suit, or other business, he may do well to let his love matters alone, and follow it, labour in his vocation, whatever it is. But if he cannot so ease himself, yet let him wisely pre-meditate of both their estates: if they be unequal in years, she young and he old, what an unfit match must it needs be, an uneven yoke, how absurd and undecent a thing it is! as Lycinus in Lucian told Timolaus, for an old bald crook-nosed knave, to marry a young wench; how odious a thing it is to see an old Lecher! What should a bald fellow do with a comb, a dumb doter with a pipe, a blind man with a looking-glass, and thou with such a wife? How absurd is it for a young man to marry an old wife for a piece of good[s]! But put case she be equal in years, birth, fortunes, and other qualities correspondent, he doth desire to be coupled in marriage, which is an honourable estate, but for what respects? Her beauty belike, and comeliness of person, that is commonly the main object, she is a most absolute form in his eye at least, she hath the Paphian's beauty, the elegancies of the Graces, but do other men affirm as much? or is it an error in his judgement? our eyes and other senses will commonly deceive us; it may be, to thee thyself upon a more serious examination, or after a little absence, she is not so fair as she seems. Some things seem and are not so; compare her to another standing by, 'tis a touchstone to try. confer hand to hand, body to body, face to face, eye to eye, nose to nose. neck to neck, &c., examine every part by itself, then altogether, in all postures, several sites, and tell me how thou likest her. It may be not she that is so fair, but her coats, or put another in her clothes, and she will seem all out as fair; as the Poet then prescribes, separate her from her clothes: suppose thou saw her in a base beggar's weed, or else dressed in some old hirsute attires out of fashion, foul linen, coarse raiment, besmeared with soot, colly [or smut], perfumed with Opoponax, Sagapenum, Assafœtida, or some such filthy gums, dirty, about some undecent action or other; or in such a case as Brassivola the Physician found Malatasta, his patient, after a potion of Hellebore, which he had prescribed: with hands on the ground and hinder parts elevated to heaven (as that Socratic in Aristophanes, who while writing geometrick figures on the earth, seemed to be grubbing for truffles) blackening the white wall with bile, and what is worse, the whole room and himself defiled, &c., all to bewrayed, or worse; if thou saw'st her (I say), wouldst thou affect her as thou dost? Suppose thou beheldest her in a frosty morning, in cold weather, in some passion or perturbation of mind, weeping, chafing, &c. rivel'd and ill-favoured to behold. She many times that in a composed look seems so amiable and delicious, of so handsome a figure, if she do but laugh or smile, makes an ugly sparrow-mouthed face, and shews a pair of uneven, loathsome, rotten, foul teeth: she hath a black skin, gouty legs, a deformed crooked carkass under a fine coat. It may be for all her costly tires she is bald, and though she seem so fair by dark, by candle-light, or afar off at such a distance, as Callicratides observed in Lucian, if thou shouldst see her near, or in a morning, she would appear more ugly than a beast; if you but carefully consider what comes forth of mouth and nostrils and other bodily conduits, you ne'er saw viler stuff. Follow my counsel, see her undrest, see her, if it be possible, out of her attires, stripped of her borrowed feathers; it may be she is like Æsop's Jay, or Pliny's Cantharides,* she will be loathsome, ridiculous, thou wilt not endure her sight: or suppose thou saw'st her sick, pale, in a Consumption, on her death-bed, skin and bones, or now dead, the embrace of whom was most pleasant, as Bernard saith, will be horrible to see.

> *She that smelled so sweet of yore,*
> *Smelleth now, but sweet no more.†*

As a posy, she smells sweet, is most fresh and fair one day, but dried up, withered, and stinks another. Beautiful Nireus, by that Homer so much admired, once dead, is more deformed than Thersites, and Solomon deceased, as ugly as Marcolphus: thy lovely Mistress, that was erst dearer to thee than thine eyes, once sick or departed, is worse than any dirt or dunghill. Her embraces were not so acceptable, as now her looks be terrible: thou hadst better behold a Gorgon's head than Helena's carkass.

Some are of opinion, that to see a woman naked, is able of itself to alter his affection; and it is worthy of consideration, saith Montaigne the Frenchman in his Essays, that the skilfullest masters of amorous dalliance, appoint for a remedy of venereous passions, a full survey of the body; which the Poet insinuates,

> *The love stood still, that ran in full career,*
> *When once it saw those parts should not appear.* (OVID)

It is reported of Seleucus King of Syria, that seeing his wife Stratonice's

---

* A fly that hath golden wings but a poisoned body. — Burton's note.
† From the Epigram on Rosamund the Fair, mistress to Henry II. of England.

bald pate, as she was undressing her by chance, he could never affect her after. Raymond Lully, the Physician, spying an ulcer or canker in his Mistress' breast, whom he so dearly loved, from that day following abhorr'd the looks of her. Philip, the French King, as Nubrigensis relates it, married the King of Denmark's daughter, and after he had used her as a wife one night, because her breath stunk, they say, or for some other secret fault, sent her back again to her father. Peter Matthaeus in the life of Lewis the Eleventh, finds fault with our English Chronicles, for writing how Margaret the King of Scots' daughter, and wife to Lewis the XI. French King, was for bad breath rejected by her husband. Many such matches are made for by-respects, or some seemly comeliness, which, after honey-moon's past, turn to bitterness: for burning lust is but a flash, a Gunpowder passion; and hatred oft follows in the highest degree, dislike and contempt.

> *When the skin's no longer tight,*
> *And the teeth no longer white,*   (JUVENAL)

when they wax old, and ill-favoured, they may commonly no longer abide them.

> *Thou'rt offensive to me now,*   (JUVENAL)

be gone, they grow stale, fulsome, loathsome, odious, thou art a beastly, filthy quean, hast the face of one straining at stool, thou art Saturn's hind-end, withered and dry,

> *Now that wrinkles spoil thine airs,*
> *And the grey is in thy hairs.*   (OVID)

(I say) be gone, the door's open, off with you.

Yea, but you will infer, your Mistress is complete, of a most absolute form in all men's opinions, no exceptions can be taken at her, nothing may be added to her person, nothing detracted, she is the mirror of women for her beauty, comeliness, and pleasant grace, unimitable, of unmixt pleasures, unmixt charms, she is the Ointment-Box of Love, the Casket of Graces, a mere magazine of natural perfections, she hath all the Loves and Graces, a thousand aspects and forms, in each part absolute and complete,

> *Gladsome cheeks, rosy mouth, languishing eyes,*   (LOCHÆUS)

to be admired for her person, a most incomparable, unmatchable piece, a golden child, made in the image of the goddesses, a Phoenix, a blossoming little Venus, a Nymph, a Fairy, like Venus herself when she was a maid, second to none, a mere quintessence, a breathing flower, sweet marjoram, a feminine prodigy, put case she be, how long will she continue?

Each day weareth away the flower's beauty. (SENECA)

Each day detracts from her person, and this beauty is a fragile good, a mere flash, a Venice glass, quickly broken,

Beauty is a dubious boon
To mortals, and departeth soon, (SENECA)

it will not last. As that fair flower Adonis, which we call an Anemone, flourisheth but one month, this gracious, all-commanding beauty fades in an instant. It is a jewel soon lost, the Painter's Goddess, a false truth, a mere picture. " Favour is deceitful, and beauty is vanity," Proverbs.

A little gem, bubble, is beauty pale,
A rose, dew, snow, smoke, wind, air, naught at all. (BAUHUSIUS)

If she be fair, as the saying is, she is commonly a fool; if proud, scornful (arrogance follows beauty), or dishonest; rare is the union of beauty and modesty; can she be fair and honest too? Aristo, the son of Agasicles, married a Spartan Lass, the fairest Lady in all Greece next to Helen, but, for her conditions [or character] the most abominable and beastly creature of the world. So that I would wish thee to respect, with Seneca, not her person, but qualities. Will you say that's a good blade, which hath a gilded scabbard, embroidered with gold and jewels? No, but that which hath a good edge and point, well-tempered metal, able to resist. This beauty is of the body alone, and what is that, but as Gregory Nazianzen telleth us, a mock of time and sickness? or as Boethius, as mutable as a flower, and 'tis not nature so makes us, but most part the infirmity of the beholder. For ask another, he sees no such matter: I pray thee tell me how thou likest my Sweetheart, as she asked her sister in Aristænetus; whom I so much admire, methinks he is the sweetest Gentleman, the properest man that ever I saw: but I am in love, I confess, and cannot therefore well judge. But be she fair indeed, golden-haired, as Anacreon his Bathyllus, (to examine particulars), she have

Sparkling eyes and milky neck. (BRUGENSIS)

a pure sanguine complexion, little mouth, coral lips, white teeth, soft and plump neck, body, hands, feet, all fair and lovely to behold, composed of all graces, elegancies, an absolute piece,

Let my Melita's eyes like Juno's be,
Her hand Minerva's, Venus's her breasts,
And her leg Amphitrite's, &c. (BRUGENSIS)

Let her head be from Prague, paps out of Austria, belly from France, back from Brabant, hands out of England, feet from Rhine, buttocks from Switzerland, let her have the Spanish gait, the Venetian tire, Italian compliment and endowments;

Let her eyes shine as bright as stars, her neck
Bloom as the rose, her hair outshine pure gold,
Her honey lips display the ruddy blush,
Let her in all her glory outdo Venus
And all the goddesses, &c. (PETRONIUS)

Let her be such a one throughout, as Lucian deciphers in his Images;
as Euphranor of old painted Venus, Aristænetus describes Lais, another
Helen, Chariclea, Leucippe, Lucretia, Pandora: let her have a box of
beauty to repair herself still, such a one as Venus gave Phaon, when he
carried her over the Ford; let her use all helps Art and Nature can
yield; be like her, and her, and whom thou wilt, or all these in one; a
little sickness, a fever, small pox, wound, scar, loss of an eye, or limb, a
violent passion, a distemperature of heat or cold, mars all in an instant,
disfigures all; child-bearing, old age, that Tyrant Time, will turn Venus
to Erinnys; raging Time, care, rivels her upon a sudden; after she hath
been married a small while, and the black ox hath trodden on her toe,
she will be so much altered, and wax out of favour, thou wilt not know
her. One grows too fat, another too lean, &c., modest Matilda, pretty
pleasing Peg, sweet singing Susan, mincing merry Moll, dainty dancing
Doll, neat Nancy, jolly Joan, nimble Nell, kissing Kate, bouncing Bess
with black eyes, fair Phyllis with fine white hands, fiddling Frances, tall
Tib, slender Sib, &c., will quickly lose their grace, grow fulsome, stale,
sad, heavy, dull, sour, and all at last out of fashion. Where now the
speaking look, the pleasing pleasantries, the blandishing smiles? &c.
Those fair sparkling eyes will look dull, her soft coral lips, will be pale,
dry, cold, rough, and blue, her skin rugged, that soft and tender surface
will be hard and harsh, her whole complexion change in a moment, and
as Matilda writ to King John,

I am not now as when thou saw'st me last,
That favour soon is vanishèd and past:
That rosy blush lapt in a lilly vale,
Now is with morphew overgrown and pale. (DRAYTON)

'Tis so in the rest, their beauty fades as a tree in winter, which Deianira
hath elegantly expressed in the Poet:

And as a tree that in the green wood grows,
With fruit and leaves, and in the Summer blows,
In Winter like a stock deformèd shows:
Our beauty takes his race and journey goes,
And doth decrease, and lose, and come to nought,
Admir'd of old, to this by child-birth brought:

And mother hath bereft me of my grace,
And crooked old age coming on apace. (SENECA)

To conclude with Chrysostom, When thou seest a fair and beautiful person, (a brave Bonaroba, or well-dress'd woman, a beautiful Donna who'd make your mouth water, a merry girl and one not hard to love) * a comely woman, having bright eyes, a merry countenance, a shining lustre in her look, a pleasant grace, wringing thy soul, and increasing thy concupiscence: bethink with thyself that it is but earth thou lovest, a mere excrement, which so vexeth thee, which thou so admirest, and thy raging soul will be at rest. Take her skin from her face, and thou shalt see [saith Chrysostom] all loathsomeness under it, that beauty is a superficial skin and bones, nerves, sinews: suppose her sick, now rivel'd, hoary-headed, hollow-cheeked, old: within she is full of filthy fleam, stinking, putrid, excremental stuff: snot and snivel in her nostrils, spittle in her mouth, water in her eyes, what filth in her brains, &c. ———— Or take her at her best, and look narrowly upon her in the light, stand nearer her, nearer yet, thou shalt perceive almost as much, and love less; as Cardan well writes, they love less who see sharply, though Scaliger deride him for it: if he see her near, or look exactly at such a posture, whosoever he is, according to the true rules of symmetry and proportion, those I mean of Albert Durer, Lomatius, and Taisnier, examine him of her. If he be a good judge of fine faces, he shall find many faults in Physiognomy, and ill colour, ill form, one side of the face likely bigger than the other, or crooked nose, bad eyes, prominent veins, concavities about the eyes, wrinkles, pimples, red streaks, freckons [or freckles], hairs, warts, neves [or moles], inequalities, roughness, scabredity, paleness, yellowness, and as many colours as are in a Turkey-cock's neck, many indecorums in their other parts; what you wish is to lop something off, one leers, another frowns, a third gapes, squints, &c. And 'tis true that he [Cardan] saith, seldom shall you find an absolute face without fault, as I have often observed; not in the face alone is this defect or disproportion to be found, but in all the other parts, of body and mind; she is fair indeed, but foolish; pretty, comely, and decent, of a majestical presence, but peradventure imperious, unhonest, self-will'd: she is rich, but deformed; hath a sweet face, but bad carriage, no bringing up, a rude and wanton flirt; a neat body she hath, but it is a nasty quean otherwise, a very slut, of a bad kind. As flowers in a garden have colour some, but no smell, others have

* The words in parentheses are Burton's interjection into the celebrated passage on woman's beauty by the great Christian divine.

a fragrant smell, but are unseemly to the eye: one is unsavoury to the taste as rue, as bitter as wormwood, and yet a most medicinal cordial flower, most acceptable to the stomack; so are men and women, one is well qualified, but of ill proportion, poor and base: a good eye she hath, but a bad hand and foot, a fine leg, bad teeth, a vast body, &c. Examine all parts of body and mind, I advise thee to enquire of all. See her angry, merry, laugh, weep, hot, cold, sick, sullen, dressed, undressed, in all attires, sites, gestures, passions, eat her meals, &c., and in some of these you will surely dislike. Yea, not her only let them observe, but her parents, how they carry themselves: for what deformities, defects, incumbrances of body or mind be in them, at such an age, they will likely be subject to, be molested in like manner, they will take after their father or mother. And with all let him take notice of her companions, in publick gatherings (as Quiverra prescribes) and whom she converseth with. Show me your company, I'll tell you who you are. According to Thucydides, she is commonly the best, that is least talked of abroad. For if she be a noted reveller, a gadder, a singer, a pranker or dancer, then take heed of her. For what saith Theocritus?

> *Dance less, ye merry girls, the rakish goat*
> *Will lead you else another dance ere long!*

Young men will do it, when they come to it. Fauns and Satyrs will certainly play wreeks [pay them out] when they come in such wanton Bacchis' or Elenora's presence. Now when they shall perceive any such obliquity, indecency, disproportion, deformity, bad conditions, &c., let them still ruminate on that, and as Hædus adviseth out of Ovid, note their faults, vices, errors, and think of their imperfections; 'tis the next way to divert and mitigate Love's furious head-strong passions, as a Peacock's feet, and filthy comb, they say, make him forget his fine feathers, and pride of his tail; she is lovely, fair, well-favoured, well qualified, courteous and kind: But if she be not so to me, what care I how kind she be? I say with Philostratus, beautiful to others, she is a tyrant to me, and so let her go. Besides these outward neves, or open faults, errors, there be many inward infirmities, secret, some private (which I will omit), and some more common to the sex, sullen fits, evil qualities, filthy diseases, in this case fit to be considered; the filthiness of women, in the first place the menstrual dirtinesses, which Savanarola exposes, Platina censures at length, Lodovicus Boncialus, Pet. Hædus, Albertus, and many other Physicians touch on. A Lover, in Calcagninus' Apologies, wished with all his heart he were his Mistress' Ring, to hear, embrace, see, and do, I know not what: O thou fool, quoth the Ring, if thou wer'st in my room, thou shouldst hear, observe and see things abominable and shameful, that which would make thee loathe and hate her, yea, peradventure, all women for her sake.

I will say nothing of the vices of their minds, their pride, envy, inconstancy, weakness, malice, self-will, lightness, insatiable lust, jealousy. " No malice like to a woman's, no bitterness like to hers," and as the same Author urgeth, " Who shall find a virtuous woman ? " He makes a question of it. They know neither good nor bad, be it better or worse (as the Comical Poet hath it) beneficial or hurtful, they will do what they list.

> *Snares of the human race, torment of life,*
> *Spoils of the night, bitterest cares of the day,*
> *Torture of husbands, and the ruin of youths.*   (LOCHÆUS)

And to that purpose were they first made, as Jupiter insinuates in the Poet *;

> *The fire that bold Prometheus stole from me,*
> *With plagues call'd Women shall revengèd be,*
> *On whose alluring and enticing face*
> *Poor mortals doting, shall their death embrace.*   (HESIOD)

In fine, as Diogenes concludes in Nevisanus, they have all their faults.

> Eberiche of hem hath some bice.
> If one be full of billany,
> Another hath a likerous eye.
> If one be full of wantonness,
> Another is a chideress.

When Leander was drowned, the inhabitants of Sestos consecrated Hero's Lantern to Anteros, and he that had good success in his love, should light the candle : but never any man was found to light it ; which I can refer to nought, but the inconstancy and lightness of women.

> *For in a thousand, good there is not one ;*
> *All be so proud, unthankful, and unkind,*
> *With flinty hearts, careless of others' moan,*
> *In their own lusts carried most headlong blind,*
> *But more herein to speak I am forbidden :*
> *Sometime for speaking truth one may be chidden.*   (ARIOSTO)

I am not willing, you see, to prosecute the cause against them, and therefore take heed you mistake me not, I say nothing against any good woman, I honour the sex, with all good men, and as I ought to do, rather than displease them, I will voluntarily take the oath which Mercurius Britannicus took : Never have I, in word or act, borne malice

* See our English Tatius book 1 — Burton's note. [See Index.]

against that most noble sex, &c. Let Simonides, Mantuan, Platina, Peter Aretine, and such women-haters bear the blame, if ought be said amiss; I have not writ a tenth of that which might be urged out of them and others; a single book would not hold all the satire and invective that has been written against women. And that which I have said (to speak truth) no more concerns them than men, though women be more frequently named in this Tract; (to apologize once for all) I am neither partial against them, or therefore bitter: what is said of the one, change but the name, may most part be understood of the other. My words are like Pauso's picture in Lucian, of whom, when a good fellow had bespoke an horse to be painted with his heels upward, tumbling on his back, he made him passant [or walking, with three hoofs on the ground and the left fore-foot lifted], now when the fellow came for his piece, he was very angry, and said, it was quite opposite to his mind; but Pauso instantly turned the Picture upside down, shewed him the horse at that site which he requested, and so gave him satisfaction. If any man take exception at my words, let him alter the name, read him for her, and 'tis all one in effect.

But to my purpose. If women in general be so bad (and men worse than they) what a hazard is it to marry! where shall a man find a good wife, or a woman a good husband? A woman a man may eschew, but not a wife: wedding is undoing (as some say), marrying marring, wooing woeing: a wife is a fever hectick, as Scaliger calls her, and not to be cured but by death, as out of Menander; Athenæus adds,

> *Thou wadest into a sea itself of woes;*
> *In Libyck and Ægean each man knows*
> *Of thirty not three ships are cast away,*
> *But on this rock not one escapes, I say.*

The worldly cares, miseries, discontents, that accompany marriage, I pray you learn of them that have experience, for I have none; by books the mind is warned. For my part, I'll not dissemble with him,

> *Go away, girls, you're a deceitful lot,*
> *No married life for me,*

many married men exclaim at the miseries of it, and rail at wives down right; I never tried, but as I hear some of them say, an Irish Sea is not so turbulent and raging as a litigious wife.

> *Scylla and Charybdis are less dangerous,*
> *There is no beast that is so noxious.* (SENECA)

Which made the Devil, belike, as most interpreters hold, when he had taken away Job's goods, health, children, friends, to persecute him the more, leave his wicked wife, as Pineda proves out of Tertullian, Cyprian, Austin, Chrysostom, Prosper, Gaudentius, &c., to vex and gall him worse than all the fiends in hell, as knowing the conditions of a bad woman. Jupiter hath given man no more pestilential evil, saith Simonides. *Better dwell with a Dragon or a Lion, than keep house with a wicked wife. Better dwell in a wilderness. No wickedness like to her. She makes a sorry heart, an heavy countenance, a wounded mind, weak hands, and feeble knees.* A woman and death are two the bitterest things in the world.

> *Saying, You must wed today,*
> *Go hang yourself, he seem'd to say.*   (TERENCE)

And yet for all this we bachelors desire to be married; with that Vestal Virgin, we long for it.

> *Happy nuptials! let me die,*
> *Unless those wedded sweets I try.*   (SENECA)

'Tis the sweetest thing in the world, I would I had a wife, saith he,

> *For fain would I leave a single life,*
> *If I could get me a good wife.*

Heigh-ho for a husband, cries she, a bad husband, nay the worst that ever was, is better than none: O blissful marriage, O most welcome marriage, and happy are they that are so coupled: we do earnestly seek it, and are never well till we have effected it. But with what fate? like those birds in the Emblem, that fed about a cage, so long as they could fly away at their pleasure, liked well of it; but when they were taken, and might not get loose, though they had the same meat, pined away for sullenness, and would not eat. So we commend marriage, so long as we are wooers, may kiss and coll at our pleasure, nothing is so sweet, we are in heaven as we think: but when we are once tied, and have lost our liberty, marriage is an hell, give me my yellow hose again: a mouse in a trap lives as merrily, we are in a purgatory some of us, if not hell itself. As the proverb is, 'tis fine talking of war, and marriage sweet in contemplation, till it be tried: and then as wars are most dangerous, irksome, every minute at death's door, so is, &c. When those wild Irish Peers, saith Stanihurst, were feasted by King Henry the Second (at what time he kept his Christmas at Dublin) and had tasted of his Prince-like cheer, generous wines, dainty fare, had seen his massy plate of silver, gold, enamell'd, beset with jewels, golden candle-sticks, goodly rich hangings, brave furniture, heard his trumpets sound, Fifes, Drums, and his exquisite musick in all kinds: when they had observed his majestical presence as he sat in purple robes, crowned, with his sceptre,

&c., in his royal seat, the poor men were so amazed, enamoured, and taken with the object, that they were weary and ashamed of their own sordidity and manner of life. They would all be English forthwith: who but English! but when they had now submitted themselves, and lost their former liberty, they began to rebel some of them, others repent of what they had done, when it was too late. 'Tis so with us Bachelors, when we see and behold those sweet faces, those gaudy shews that women make, observe their pleasant gestures and graces, give ear to their Siren tunes, see them dance, &c., we think their conditions are as fine as their faces, we are taken with dumb signs, we rush to embrace them, we rave, we burn, and would fain be married. But when we feel the miseries, cares, woes, that accompany it, we make our moan many of us, cry out at length, and cannot be released. If this be true now, as some out of experience will inform us, farewell wiving for my part, and as the Comical Poet merrily saith,

Foul fall him that brought the second match to pass,
The first I wish no harm, poor man, alas!
He knew not what he did, nor what it was.*

What shall I say to him that marries again and again, who puts his neck into the halter a second time? I pity him not, for the first time he must do as he may, bear it out sometimes by the head and shoulders, and let his next neighbour ride, or else run away, or as that Syracusan in a tempest, when all ponderous things were to be exonerated out of the ship, because she was his heaviest burthen, fling his wife in the Sea. But this I confess is Comically spoken, and so I pray you take it. In sober sadness, marriage is a bondage, a thraldom, a yoke, an hindrance to all good enterprises, (" he hath married a wife and cannot come ") a stop to all preferments, a rock on which many are saved, many impinge, and are cast away: not that the thing is evil in itself, or troublesome, but full of all contentment and happiness, one of the three things which please God, " when a man and his wife agree together," an honourable and happy estate, who knows it not? If they be sober, wise, honest, as the Poet infers,

If fitly match'd be man and wife.
No pleasure's wanting to their life. (EURIPIDES)

But to undiscreet sensual persons, that as brutes are wholly led by sense, it is a fearful plague, many times an Hell itself, and can give little or no content, being that they are often so irregular and prodigious in their lusts, so diverse in their affections. As Aelius Verus said, a wife is a name of honour, not of pleasure: she is fit to bear the office,

* Translated [from Eubulus] by my brother, Ralph Burton. — Burton's note.

govern a family, to bring up children, sit at board's end and carve; as some carnal men think and say, they had rather go to the stews, or have now and then a snatch as they can come by it, borrow of their neighbours, than have wives of their own; except they may, as some Princes and great men do, keep as many Courtisans as they will themselves, fly out recklessly, meddling with others' wives; [they had rather] that polygamy of Turks, Lex Julia, which Cæsar once enforced in Rome (though Levinus Torrentius and others suspect it) that every great man might marry, and keep as many wives as he would, or Irish divorcement were in use: but as it is, 'tis hard, and gives not that satisfaction to these carnal men, beastly men as too many are. What still the same, to be tied * to one, be she never so fair, never so virtuous, is a thing they may not endure, to love one long. Say thy pleasure, and counterfeit as thou wilt, as Parmeno told Thais, one man will never please thee; nor one woman many men. But as Pan replied to his Father Mercury, when he asked whether he was married, No Father, no, I am a Lover still, and cannot be contented with one woman. Pitys, Echo, the Mænades, and I know not how many besides, were his Mistresses, he might not abide marriage. Variety delights; 'tis loathsome and tedious, what, one still? which the Satirist said of Iberina, is verified in most,

> 'Tis not one man will serve her by her will,
> As soon she'll have one eye as one man still.   (JUVENAL)

As capable of any impression as primal matter itself, that still desires new forms; like the Sea, their affections ebb and flow. Husband is a cloak for some to hide their villainy; once married she may fly out at her pleasure, the name of Husband is a sanctuary to make all good. It comes to this (saith Seneca) that they take a husband only to get a lover. They are right and straight, as true Trojans as mine host's daughter, that Spanish wench in Ariosto, as good wives as Messalina. Many men are as constant in their choice, and as good husbands as Nero himself, they must have their pleasure of all they see, and are in a word far more fickle than any woman.

> For either they be full of jealousye,
> Our masterfull, or loven noveltye.

Good men have often ill wives, as bad as Xanthippe was to Socrates, Elenora to St. Lewis † Isabella to our Edward the Second: and good wives are as often matched to ill husbands, as Mariamne to Herod, Serena to Diocletian, Theodora to Theophilus, and Thyra to Gurmunde.

---

* For better for worse, for richer for poorer, in sickness and in health, &c., 'tis a hard saying to a sensual man. — Burton's note.

† Should be Lewis the Seventh.

But I will say nothing of dissolute and bad husbands, of Bachelors and their vices; their good qualities are a fitter subject for a just volume, too well known already in every village, town and city, they need no blazon; and lest I should mar any matches, or dis-hearten loving Maids, for this present I will let them pass.

Being that men and women are so irreligious, depraved by nature, so wandering in their affections, so brutish, so subject to disagreement, so unobservant of marriage rites, what shall I say? If thou beest such a one, or thou light on such a wife, what concord can there be, what hope of agreement? 'tis not yoked with each other but provoked with each other, as the Reed and Fern in the Emblem, averse and opposite in nature: 'tis twenty to one thou wilt not marry to thy contentment: but as in a lottery forty blanks were drawn commonly for one prize, out of a multitude you shall hardly choose a good one: a small ease hence then, little comfort.

> *If he or she be such a one,*
> *Thou hadst much better be alone.* (SIMONIDES)

If she be barren, she is not ———— &c. If she have children, and thy state be not good, though thou be wary and circumspect, thy charge will undo thee, she will sink your whole establishment by her fecundity, thou wilt not be able to bring them up, and what greater misery can there be, than to beget children, to whom thou canst leave no other inheritance but hunger and thirst? when thou art oppressed by hunger, shrill voices cry for bread, piercing the father's heart: what so grievous as to turn them up to the wide world, to shift for themselves? No plague like to want: and when thou hast good means, and art very careful of their education, they will not be ruled. Think but of that old proverb, great men's sons seldom do well. Would that I had either remained single or not had children! Augustus exclaims in Suetonius. Jacob had his Reuben, Simeon, and Levi: David an Amnon, an Absalom, an Adonijah; wise men's sons are commonly fools, insomuch that Spartian concludes, they had been much better to have been childless. 'Tis too common in the middle sort; thy son's a drunkard, a gamester, a spendthrift; thy daughter a fool, a whore; thy servants lazy drones and thieves; thy neighbours devils, they will make thee weary of thy life. If thy wife be froward, when she may not have her will, thou hadst better be buried alive; she will be so impatient, raving still, and roaring like Juno in the Tragedy, there's nothing but tempests, all is in an uproar. If she be soft and foolish, thou wert better have a block, she will shame thee, and reveal thy secrets; if wise and learned, well qualified, there is

as much danger on the other side, saith Nevisanus, she will be too insolent and peevish,

> *Some simple rustick at Venusium bred,*
> *O let me, rather than Cornelia, wed,*
> *If to great virtues, greater pride she join,*
> *And count her ancestors as current coin.* (JUVENAL)

Take heed; if she be a slut, thou wilt loathe her; if proud, she'll beggar
thee, she'll spend thy patrimony in baubles, all Arabia will not serve to
perfume her hair, saith Lucian: if fair and wanton, she'll make thee
a Cornuto; if deformed, she will paint. If her face be filthy by nature,
she will mend it by art, which who can endure? If she do not paint, she
will look so filthy, thou canst not love her, and that peradventure will
make thee unhonest. Cromerus relates of Casimirus, that he was unchaste, because his wife Aleida the daughter of Henry, Landgrave of
Hesse, was so deformed. If she be poor, she brings beggary with her
(saith Nevisanus), misery and discontent. If you marry a maid, it is
uncertain how she proves, perhaps she will not suit you. If young, she
is likely wanton and untaught; if lusty, too lascivious; and if she be not
satisfied, you know where and when, nothing but quarrels, all is in an
uproar, and there is little quietness to be had: if an old maid, 'tis an
hazard she dies in child-bed; if a rich widow, thou dost halter thyself,
she will make all away before hand, to her other children, &c. Who can
endure a virago for a wife? she will hit thee still in the teeth with her
first husband: if a young widow, she is often unsatiable and immodest.
If she be rich, well descended, bring a great dowry, or be nobly allied,
thy wife's friends will eat thee out of house and home, she will be so
proud, so high-minded, so imperious. For

> *Sure, of all ills with which mankind are curst,*
> *A wife who brings you money is the worst.* (JUVENAL)

There's nothing so intolerable, thou shalt be as the Tassell of a Goss-
hawk, she will ride upon thee, domineer as she list, wear the breeches in
her oligarchical government, and beggar thee besides. Rich wives force
us into slavery, (as Seneca hits them), who accepts a dowry, loses
rulership. They will have sovereignty, they will have attendance, they
will do what they list. In taking a dowry thou losest thy liberty, hazard-
est thine estate.

> *These and others be the ills*
> *Of large dowries — frightful bills,* (PLAUTUS)

with many such inconveniences. Say the best, she is a commanding
servant; thou hadst better have taken a good housewife maid in her

smock. Since then there is such hazard. if thou be wise, keep thyself as
thou art, 'tis good to match, much better to be free. To be a father is
very pleasant, to be a free man is still more so. Art thou young? then
match not yet; if old, match not at all. And therefore, with that Philosopher, [Thales], still make answer to thy friends that importune thee
to marry, 'tis yet unseasonable, and ever will be.

Consider withal how free, how happy, how secure, how heavenly, in
respect, a single man is; as he said in the Comedy, And that which all
my neighbours admire and applaud me for, account so great an happiness, I never had a wife; consider how contentedly, quietly, neatly,
plentifully, sweetly and how merrily he lives! He hath no man to care
for but himself, none to please, no charge, none to control him, is tied
to no residence, no cure to serve, may go and come, when, whither, live
where he will, his own master, and do what he list himself. Consider the
excellency of Virgins, marriage replenisheth earth, but virginity Paradise; Elias, Eliseus, John Baptist, were Bachelors: Virginity is a
precious Jewel, a fair garland, a never-fading flower; for why was
Daphne turned to a green bay-tree, but to shew that virginity is immortal?

> *As the sequestered flower that grows within*
> *Some fenced-in garden, to the herd unknown,*
> *Ne'er turned up by the plough, fanned by the air,*
> *By the sun strengthened, by the shower reared,*
> *So is the virgin in her maiden state,*
> *Dear to her friends, but if her flower be ta'en,*
> *She is undone and meets no more regard.* (CATULLUS)

Virginity is a fine picture, as Bonaventure calls it, a blessed thing in
itself, and if you will believe a Papist, meritorious. And although there
be some inconveniences, irksomeness, solitariness, &c., incident to such
persons, want of those comforts, tending in sickness, &c., embracing,
dalliance, kissing, colling, &c., those furious motives and wanton pleasures a new married wife most part enjoys; yet they are but toys in
respect, easily to be endured, if conferred to those frequent incumbrances of marriage; solitariness may be otherwise avoided with mirth,
musick, good company, business, employment; in a word, he shall have
less of joy and less of sorrow; for their good nights he shall have good
days. And methinks sometime or other, amongst so many rich Bachelors, a benefactor should be found to build a monastical College for
old, decayed, deformed, or discontented maids to live together in, that
have lost their first loves, or otherwise miscarried, or else are willing

howsoever to lead a single life. The rest, I say, are toys in respect, and
sufficiently recompensed by those innumerable contents and incomparable privileges of Virginity. Think of these things, confer both lives,
and consider last of all these commodious prerogatives a Bachelor hath,
how well he is esteemed, how heartily welcome to all his friends, as
Tertullian observes, with what counterfeit courtesies they will adore
him, follow him, present him with gifts; it cannot be believed (saith
Ammianus) with what humble service he shall be worshipped, how
loved and respected: if he want children (and have means) he shall
be often invited, attended on by Princes, and have advocates to plead
his cause for nothing, as Plutarch adds. Wilt thou then be reverenced,
and had in estimation?

> ———— *If you'd have the Prince's friendship,*
> *Let there be no little son to sport in your hall,*
> *Nor daughter dearer still. 'Tis a barren wife*
> *That curries favour with your Noble friends.* (JUVENAL)

Live a single man, marry not, and thou shalt soon perceive how those
Succession-hunters, (for so they were called of old) will seek after thee,
bribe and flatter thee for thy favour, to be thine heir or executor: Ar-
runtius and Haterius, those famous parasites in this kind, as Tacitus
and Seneca have recorded, shall not go beyond them. Periplectomenes,
that good personate old man, well understood this in Plautus; for
when Pleusides exhorted him to marry, that he might have children of
his own, he readily replied in this sort,

> *Whilst I have kin, what need I brats to have?*
> *Now I live well, and as I will, most brave.*
> *And when I die, my goods I'll give away*
> *To them that do invite me every day,*
> *That visit me, and send me pretty toys,*
> *And strive who shall do me most courtesies.*

This respect thou shalt have in like manner, living as he did, a single
man.

But if thou marry once, bethink thyself what a slavery it is, what
an heavy burthen thou shalt undertake, how hard a task thou art
tied to (for as Hierome hath it, who hath a wife is a bondman, bound
to serve her), and how continuate, what squalor attends it, what irksomeness, what charges; for wife and children are a perpetual bill of
charges; besides a Myriad of cares, miseries, and troubles; for as that
Comical Plautus merrily and truly said, he that wants trouble must
get to be Master of a Ship, or marry a Wife; and as another seconds

him, wife and children have undone me: so many, and such infinite. incumbrances accompany this kind of life. Furthermore, a wife is a shrew, &c., or as he said, in the Comedy, I have married a wife, what misery it has brought me! sons were born, other cares followed.

All gifts and invitations cease, no friend will esteem thee, and thou shalt be compelled to lament thy misery, and make thy moan with Bartholomæus Scheræus, that famous Poet Laureate, and Professor of Hebrew in Witenberg: I had finished this work long since, but that (I use his own words) amongst many miseries which almost broke my back, a shrew to my wife, tormented my mind above measure, and beyond the rest. So shalt thou be compelled to complain, and to cry out at last, with Phoroneus the Lawyer, How happy had I been, if I had wanted a wife! If this which I have said will not suffice, see more in Lemnius, Espencæus, Kornmannus, Platina, Barbarus, Arnisæus, and him that is worth them all, Nevisanus, the Lawyer, almost in every page.

SUBSECTION 4 — *Philters, Magical, and Poetical cures*

WHERE persuasions and other remedies will not take place, many fly to unlawful means, Philters, Amulets, Magick Spells, Ligatures, Characters, Charms, which as a wound with a spear of Achilles, is so made and caused, must so be cured. If forced by Spells and Philters, saith Paracelsus, it must be eased by Characters, and by Incantations. See Fernelius. Sckenkius hath some examples of such as have been so magically caused and magically cured, and by witch-craft: so saith Baptista Codronchus. 'Tis not permitted to be done, I confess; yet often attempted: see more in Wierus on the Devil's Tricks, of Remedies through Philters, Delrio on Magick. Cardan reckons up many magnetical medicines, as to piss through a ring, &c. Mizaldus, Baptista Porta, Jason Pratensis, Lobelius, Matthiolus, &c., prescribe many absurd remedies: The root of a Mandrake drunk, parings from as Ass's hoof, the excrement of his beloved placed under his pillow without her knowledge, when he smells the foul odor, love is dissolved. Eating the egg of a night-owl causeth abstemiousness, according to Iarcha the Indian gymnosophist, as related by Philostratus; drinking the blood of the beloved taketh away all feeling of love; Faustina the wife of Marcus Aurelius, being seized by love for a gladiator, was completely set free by the axiom of the Chaldæans, as told by Julius Capitolinus. Some of our Astrologers will effect as much by Characteristical Images, Seals of

Hermes, or Solomon, of Chael,* &c., the seal of a woman with dishev-elled hair, &c. Our old Poets and Phantastical writers have many fab-ulous remedies for such as are love-sick, as that of Protesilaus' tomb in Philostratus, in his dialogue betwixt Phœnix and Vinitor. Vinitor upon occasion discoursing of the rare virtues of that shrine, telleth him, that Protesilaus' Altar and Tomb cures almost all manner of diseases, con-sumptions, dropsies, quartan agues, sore eyes, and amongst the rest, such as are love-sick shall there be helped. But the most famous is Leucata Petra, that renowned Rock in Greece, of which Strabo writes, not far from Saint Maura, saith Sands, from which rock if any Lover flung himself down headlong, he was instantly cured.† Venus, after the death of Adonis, when she could take no rest for love,

> *When hearts burn with raging flame,*   (CATULLUS)

came to the Temple of Apollo to know what she should do to be eased of her pain: Apollo sent her to Leucata Petra, where she precipitated herself, and was forthwith freed, and when she would needs know of him a reason of it, he told her again, that he had often observed Jupiter, when he was enamoured on Juno, thither go to ease and wash himself, and after him divers others. Cephalus for the love of Pelater, Desoneius' daughter, leapt down here, that Lesbian Sappho for Phaon, on whom she miserably doted;

> *Stricken by the gadfly of love, rushed headlong from the summit,*
> (MENANDER)

hoping thus to ease herself, and to be free of her love-pangs.

> *Hither Deucalion came, when Pyrrha's love*
> *Tormented him, and leapt down to the Sea,*
> *And had no harm at all, but by and by*
> *His Love was gone and chasèd quite away.*   (OVID)

This medicine Joseph Scaliger speaks of, Salmuth, and other writers. Pliny reports, that amongst the Cyziceni, there is a Well consecrated to Cupid, of which, if any Lover taste, his passion is mitigated: and Anthony Verdurius saith, that amongst the Antients there was Amor Lethes; he took burning torches, and extinguished them in the river; his statue was to be seen in the Temple of Venus Eleusina, of which Ovid makes mention, and saith, that all Lovers of old went thither on

---

* Chael, an ancient Hebrew physician, who is said to have made as many as thirty-two sigils for the cure of disease. See Marcus Antonius Zimara's *Antrum Magico-Medi-cum*, vol. I. p. 178 (Frankfort, 1625–6).

† The moral is, vehement fear expels love. — Burton's note.

pilgrimage, that would be rid of their love-pangs. Pausanias, in Phocicis, writes of a Temple dedicated to Venus in the vault, at Naupactus in Achaia (now Lepanto) in which your widows that would have second husbands made their supplications to the Goddess: all manner of suits concerning Lovers were commenced, and their grievances helped. The same Author, in Achaicis, tells as much of the river Selemnus in Greece: if any Lover washed himself in it, by a secret virtue of that water (by reason of the extreme coldness belike) he was healed of Love's torments, the cause and remedy of love being the same; which if it be so, that water, as he holds, is better than any gold. Where none of all these remedies will take place, I know no other, but that all Lovers must make an head, and rebel, as they did in Ausonius, and crucify Cupid, till he grant their request, or satisfy their desires.

SUBSECTION 5 — *The last and best Cure of Love-Melancholy is, to let them have their desire*

THE last refuge and surest remedy, to be put in practice in the utmost place, when no other means will take effect, is, to let them go together, and enjoy one another; so saith Guianerius. Æsculapius himself, to this malady, cannot invent a better remedy, (saith Jason Pratensis) than that a Lover have his desire.

> *And let them both be joinèd in a bed,*
> *And let Æneas fair Lavinia wed.*

'Tis the special cure, to let them bleed in the hymenean vein, for love is a pleurisy, and if it be possible, so let it be,

> *And the wished-for joy is taken.*

Arculanus holds it the speediest and the best cure, 'tis Savanarola's last precept, a principal infallible remedy, the last, sole, and safest refuge.

> *Julia alone can quench my desire,*
> *With neither ice nor snow, but with like fire.* (PETRONIUS)

When you have all done, saith Avicenna, there is no speedier or safer course, than to join the parties together according to their desires and wishes, the custom and form of law; and so we have seen him quickly restored to his former health, that was languished away to skin and bones; after his desire was satisfied, his discontent ceased, and we thought it strange; our opinion is therefore, that in such cases Nature is to be obeyed. Aretæus, an old Author, hath an instance of a young man, when no other means could prevail, was so speedily relieved. What remains then but to join them in marriage?

Give and take their ticklish kisses,
Urging on to newer blisses,
Tasting one another's charms,
Sporting in each other's arms.   (JOVIANUS PONTANUS)

They may then kiss and coll, lie and lock babies in one another's eyes, as their sires before them did, they may then satiate themselves with love's pleasures, which they have so long wished and expected;

In one slumber now held fast,
All their fevers sweetly past,
Quiet in one bed at last.

Yea, but 'tis hard, 'tis difficult, this cannot conveniently be done, by reason of many and several impediments. Sometimes both parties themselves are not agreed: Parents, Tutors, Masters, Guardians, will not give consent; Laws, Customs, Statutes hinder; poverty, superstition, fear and suspicion: many men dote on one woman, all at once and once for all: she dotes as much on him, or them, and in modesty must not, cannot woo, as unwilling to confess, as willing to love: she dares not make it known, shew her affection, or speak her mind. And hard is the choice (as it is in Euphues) when one is compelled either by silence to die with grief, or by speaking to live with shame. In this case almost was the fair Lady Elizabeth, Edward the Fourth his daughter, when she was enamoured on Henry the Seventh, that noble young Prince, and new saluted King, when she brake forth into that passionate speech, O that I were worthy of that comely Prince! but my father being dead, I want friends to motion such a matter. What shall I say? I am all alone, and dare not open my mind to any. What if I acquaint my mother with it? bashfulness forbids. What if some of the Lords? audacity wants. O that I might but confer with him, perhaps in discourse I might let slip such a word that might discover mine intention! How many modest maids may this concern, I am a poor servant, what shall I do? I am a fatherless child, and want means, I am blithe and buxom, young and lusty, but I have never a suitor; as she said [in the play], a company of silly fellows, [they] look belike that I should woo them and speak first: fain they would and cannot woo; how can I begin? Being merely passive they may not make suit, with many such lets and inconveniences, which I know not; what shall we do in such a case? sing Fortune my Foe? ——

Some are so curious in this behalf, as those old Romans, our modern Venetians, Dutch and French, that if two parties dearly love, the one noble, the other ignoble, they may not by their Laws match, though equal otherwise in years, fortunes, education, and all good affection. In Germany, except they can prove their gentility by three descents, they scorn to match with them. A noble man must marry a noble woman: a Baron, a Baron's daughter; a Knight, a Knight's; a Gentleman, a Gentleman's; as slaters sort their slates, do they degrees and families. If she be never so rich, fair, well-qualified otherwise, they will make him forsake her. The Spaniards abhor all widows; the Turks repute them old women, if past five and twenty. But these are too severe Laws, and strict Customs, we must make some concession to love, we are all the sons of Adam, 'tis opposite to Nature, it ought not to be so. Again, he loves her most impotently, she loves not him, and so on the other hand. Pan loved Echo, Echo Satyrus, Satyrus Lyda.

> *For each did hate a lover, yet each with love did burn,*
> *And as each hurt the other, so each was hurt in turn.*　(moschus)

They love and loath of all sorts, he loves her, she hates him; and is loathed of him on whom she dotes. Cupid hath two darts, one to force love, all of Gold, and that sharp, another blunt, of Lead, and that to hinder; this dispels, that creates love. This we see too often verified in our common experience. Coresus dearly loved that Virgin Callirrhoe, but the more he loved her, the more she hated him. Œnone loved Paris, but he rejected her; they are stiff of all sides, as if beauty were therefore created to undo, or be undone. I give her all attendance, all observance, I pray and intreat, fair Mistress pity me, I spend myself, my time, friends and fortunes to win her favour (as he complains in the Eclogue), I lament, sigh, weep, and make my moan to her, but she is hard as flint, as fair and hard as a Diamond, she will not respect or hear me; she has no compassion on my tears, flees from my prayers, is inflexible to my demands. What shall I do?

> *I wooed her as a young man should do,*
> *But Sir, she said, I love not you.*
> *Rock, marble, heart of oak with iron barr'd,*
> *Frost, flint or adamants are not so hard.*　(angerianus)

I give, I bribe, I send presents, but they are refused. [As Virgil hath it:] *Corydon, thou art but a yokel! thy beloved cares nothing for gifts.* I protest, I swear, I weep; she neglects me for all this, she derides me, contemns me, she hates me: Phillida flouts me: stiff, churlish, rocky still.

And 'tis most true, many Gentlewomen are so nice, they scorn all suitors, crucify their poor Paramours, and think nobody good enough for them, as dainty to please as Daphne herself,

Many did woo her, but she scorn'd them still,
And said she would not marry by her will.   (OVID)

One while they will not marry, as they say at least (when as they intend nothing less), another while not yet, when 'tis their only desire,
they rave upon it. She will marry at last, but not him: he is a proper
man indeed, and well qualified, but he wants means: another of her
suitors hath good means, but he wants wit; one is too old, another too
young, too deformed, she likes not his carriage: a third too loosely given,
he is rich, but base born: she will be a Gentlewoman, a Lady, as her
Sister is, as her Mother is: she is all out as fair, as well brought up,
hath as good a portion, and she looks for as good a match, as Matilda
or Dorinda: if not, she is resolved as yet to tarry; so apt are young
maids to boggle at every object, so soon won or lost with every toy, so
quickly diverted, so hard to be pleased. In the mean time, one suitor
pines away, languisheth in love, another sighs and grieves, she cares
not: and which Stroza objected to Ariadne,

Is no more mov'd with those sad sighs and tears,
Of her sweetheart, than raging sea with prayers:
Thou scorn'st the fairest youth in all our city,
And mak'st him almost mad for love to die.

They take a pride to prank up themselves, to make young men enamoured, to captivate the men but despise them when captive; to dote on
them, and to run mad for their sakes,

Whilst niggardly their favours they discover,
They love to be belov'd, yet scorn the Lover.   (VIRGIL)

All suit and service is too little for them, presents too base: they delight
in tormenting and fleecing their lovers. As Atalanta, they must be
over-run, or not won. Many young men are as obstinate, and as
curious in their choice, as tyrannically proud, insulting, deceitful,
false-hearted, as irrefragable and peevish on the other side, Narcissus-
like,

Young men and maids did to him sue,
But in his youth, so proud, so coy was he,
Young men and maids bade him adieu.   (OVID)

Echo wept and wooed him by all means above the rest, love me for
pity, or pity me for love, but he was obstinate, he would rather die
than give consent. Psyche ran whining after Cupid,

Fair Cupid, thy fair Psyche to thee sues,
A lovely lass a fine young gallant wooes,   (FRACASTORIUS)

but he rejected her nevertheless. Thus many Lovers do hold out so long,

doting on themselves, stand in their own light, till in the end they come
to be scorned and rejected, as Stroza's Gargiliana was,

> *Both young and old do hate thee scornèd now,*
> *That once was all their joy and comfort too,*

as Narcissus was himself,

> ——— *Who, despising many,*
> *Died ere he could enjoy the love of any.*

They begin to be contemned themselves of others, as he was of his
shadow, and take up with a poor curate, or an old serving-man at last,
that might have had their choice of right good matches in their youth,
like that generous Mare in Plutarch, which would admit of none but
great Horses, but when her tail was cut off, and mane shorn close, and
she now saw herself so deformed in the water, when she came to drink,
she was contented at last to be covered by an Ass. Yet this is a common
humour, will not be left, and cannot be helped.

> *I love a maid, she loves me not: full fain*
> *She would have me, but I not her again;*
> *So Love to crucify men's souls is bent:*
> *But seldom doth it please or give content.*   (AUSONIUS)

Their love danceth in a ring, and Cupid hunts them round about, he
dotes, is doted on again, their affection cannot be reconciled. Oftentimes
they may and will not, 'tis their own foolish proceeding that mars all,
they are too distrustful of themselves, too soon dejected: say she be
rich, thou poor; she young, thou old; she lovely and fair, thou most
ill-favoured and deformed; she noble, thou base; she spruce and fine,
but thou an ugly Clown: never despair, there's hope enough yet:
Mopsus takes Nysa! is there aught we lovers may not hope? — put
thyself forward once more, as unlikely matches have been and are
daily made, see what will be the event. Many leave roses and gather
thistles, loathe honey and love verjuice: our likings are as various as
our palates. But commonly they omit opportunities, taking a kiss, all
else they miss, &c., they neglect the usual means and times.

> *He that will not when he may,*
> *When he will he shall have nay.*

They look to be wooed, sought after, and sued to. Most part they will
and cannot, either for the above-named reasons, or for that there is a
multitude of suitors equally enamoured, doting all alike; and where
one alone must speed, what shall become of the rest? Hero was beloved
of many, but one did enjoy her; Penelope had a company of suitors,
yet all missed of their aim. In such cases he or they must wisely and

warily unwind themselves, unsettle his affections by those rules above
prescribed, shake off this senseless passion, divert his cogitations, or
else bravely bear it out, as Turnus did, Lavinia is thine to wed, when
he could not get her, with a kind of heroical scorn he bid Æneas take
her, or with a milder farewell, let her go, Take Phyllis for thyself, take
her to you, God give you joy, Sir. The Fox in the Emblem would eat
no grapes, but why? because he could not get them! care not thou for
that which may not be had.

    Many such inconveniences, lets and hindrances there are, which cross
their projects, and crucify poor Lovers, which sometimes may, sometimes again cannot, be so easily removed. But put case they be reconciled all, agreed hitherto, suppose this love or good liking be betwixt
two alone, both parties well pleased, there is mutual love and great
affection: yet their Parents, Guardians, Tutors, cannot agree, thence
all is dashed, the match is unequal: one rich, another poor: an hard-
hearted, unnatural, a covetous Father will not marry his son, except he
have so much money, all are mad for money, as Chrysostom notes, nor
join his daughter in marriage, to save her dowry, or for that he cannot
spare her for the service she doth him, and is resolved to part with
nothing whilst he lives, not a penny, though he may peradventure well
give it, he will not till he dies, and then as a pot of money broke, it is
divided amongst them that gaped after it so earnestly. Or else he wants
means to set her out, he hath no money, and though it be to the manifest prejudice of her body and soul's health, he cares not, he will take
no notice of it, she must and shall tarry. Many slack and careless
Parents measure their children's affections by their own, they are now
cold and decrepit themselves, past all such youthful conceits, and they
will therefore starve their children's Genius, have them with old heads
on young shoulders, they must not marry, as he said in the Comedy:
they will stifle nature, their young bloods must not participate of
youthful pleasures, but be as they are themselves, old on a sudden.
And 'tis a general fault amongst most Parents in bestowing of their
children, the Father wholly respects wealth, when through his own
folly, riot, indiscretion, he hath embezzled his estate, to recover himself,
he confines and prostitutes his eldest son's love and affection to some
fool, or ancient, or deformed piece for money; he shall marry the
daughter of rich parents, a red-hair'd, blear-eyed, big-mouth'd, crook-
nosed wench — and though his son utterly dislike, with Clitipho in
the Comedy [of Terence], I cannot, father: if she be rich (he replies), he must and shall have her, she is fair enough, young enough;

if he look or hope to inherit his lands, he shall marry, not when or whom he loves, but whom his Father commands, when and where he likes, his affection must dance attendance upon him. His daughter is in the same predicament forsooth, as an empty boat she must carry what, where, when, and whom, her Father will. So that in these businesses, the Father is still for the best advantage. Now the mother respects good kindred, most part the son a proper woman. All which Livy exemplifies: a Gentleman and a Yeoman woo'd a wench in Rome (contrary to that statute that the gentry and commonalty must not match together), the matter was controverted: the Gentleman was preferred by the Mother's voice, she wanted a richer marriage: the overseers stood for him that was most worth, &c. But parents ought not to be so strict in this behalf, Beauty is a dowry of itself all-sufficient; Rachel was so married by Jacob, and Bonaventure denies that he so much as venially sins, that marries a maid for comeliness of person. The Jews, if they saw amongst the captives a beautiful woman, some small circumstances observed, might take her to wife. They should not be too severe in that kind, especially if there be no such urgent occasion, or grievous impediment. 'Tis good for a commonwealth. Plato holds, that in their contracts young men should never avoid the affinity of poor folks, or seek after rich. Poverty and base parentage may be sufficiently recompensed by many other good qualities, modesty, virtue, religion, and choice bringing up. I am poor, I confess, but am I therefore contemptible, and an abject? Love itself is naked, the Graces, the Stars, and Hercules was clad in a Lion's skin. Give something to virtue, love, wisdom, favour, beauty, person; be not all for money. Besides, you must consider, that Love cannot be compelled, they must affect as they may: Fate rules even what the toga hides; as the saying is, marriage and hanging goes by destiny, matches are made in Heaven.

> *It lies not in our power to love or hate,*
> *For will in us is overrul'd by fate.* (MARLOWE)

A servant maid in Aristænetus loved her Mistress' Minion, which when her Dame perceived, in a jealous humour she dragg'd her about the house by the hair of the head, and vexed her sore. The wench cried out, O Mistress, fortune hath made my body your servant, but not my soul! Affections are free, not to be commanded. Moreover it may be to restrain their ambition, pride, and covetousness, to correct those hereditary diseases of a family, God in his just judgement assigns & permits such matches to be made. For I am of Plato and Bodine's mind, that Families have their bounds and periods as well as Kingdoms, beyond

which for extent or continuance they shall not exceed, six or seven
hundred years, as they there illustrate by a multitude of examples,
and which Peucer and Melancthon approve, but in a perpetual tenor
(as we see by many pedigrees of Knights, Gentlemen, Yeomen) continue as they began, for many descents with little alteration. Howsoever, let them I say, give something to youth, to love; they must not
think they can fancy whom they appoint. This is a free passion, as Pliny
said in a Panegyrick of his, and may not be forced. Love craves liking,
as the saying is, it requires mutual affections, a correspondency: it
cannot be given nor taken away; it may not be learned, Ovid himself
cannot teach us how to love, Solomon describe, Apelles paint, or Helena
express it. They must not therefore compel or intrude; for who (as
Fabius urgeth) can love with an estranged mind? but consider withal
the miseries of enforced marriages; take pity upon youth: and such
above the rest as have daughters to bestow, should be very careful and
provident to marry them in due time. Siracides calls it a weighty matter
to perform, so to marry a daughter to a man of understanding in due
time. As Lemnius admonisheth, virgins must be provided for in season,
to prevent many diseases, of which Rodericus a Castro, and Lod.
Mercatus, have both largely discoursed. And therefore as well to avoid
these feral maladies, 'tis good to get them husbands betimes, as to
prevent other gross inconveniences, and for a thing that I know besides;
when the time and age for marriage hath come, as Chrysostom adviseth,
let them not defer it; they perchance will marry themselves else, or
do worse. If Nevisanus the Lawyer do not impose, they may do it by
right: for as he proves out of Curtius, and some other Civilians, a Maid
past 25 years of age, against her parents' consent, may marry such a
one as is unworthy of, and inferior to her, and her Father by law must
be compelled to give her a competent dowry. Mistake me not in the
mean time, or think that I do apologize here for any headstrong unruly
wanton flirts. I do approve that of S. Ambrose which he hath written
touching Rebecca's spousals: A woman should give unto her parents
the choice of her husband, lest she be reputed to be malapert and
wanton, if she take upon her to make her own choice, for she should
rather seem to be desired by a man, than to desire a man herself.
To those hard parents alone I retort that of Curtius (in the behalf of
modester Maids) that are too remiss and careless of their due time and
riper years. For if they tarry longer, to say truth, they are past date,
and nobody will respect them. A woman with us in Italy (saith Aretine's
Lucretia) 24 years of age, is old already, past the best, of no account.

An old fellow, as Lysistrata confesseth in Aristophanes, though grey-haired, can have as wife a young maid, and 'tis no news for an old fellow to marry a young wench: but as he follows it, a woman's term is brief, and if 'tis not used in time, no one wants her for a wife; who cares for an old Maid? she may sit and wait. A virgin, as the Poet holds, a desirous and sportive girl, is like a flower, a Rose withered on a sudden.

> *She that was erst a Maid as fresh as May,*
> *Is now an old Crone, time so steals away.* (AUSONIUS)

Let them take time then while they may, make advantage of youth, and as he prescribes,

> *Fair Maids, go gather Roses in the prime,*
> *And think that as a flower so goes on time.* (AUSONIUS)

Let's all love, whiles we are in the flower of years, fit for Love-matters, and while time serves: for

> *Suns that set may rise again,*
> *But if once we lose this light,*
> *'Tis with us perpetual night.** (CATULLUS)

Time past cannot be recall'd. But we need no such exhortation, we are all commonly too forward: yet if there be any escape, and all be not as it should, as Diogenes struck the Father when the son swore, because he taught him no better; if a maid or young man miscarry, I think their Parents oftentimes, Guardians, Overseers, Governours, (saith Chrysostom) are in as much fault, and as severely to be punished, as their children, in providing for them no sooner.

Now for such as have free liberty to bestow themselves, I could wish that good counsel of the Comical old man were put in practice,

> *That rich men would marry poor maidens some,*
> *And that without dowry, and so bring them home,*
> *So would much concord be in our city,*
> *Less envy should we have, much more pity.* (PLAUTUS)

If they would care less for wealth, we should have much more content and quietness in a Common-wealth. Beauty, good bringing up, methinks, is a sufficient portion of itself; their beauty is girls' dowry, and he doth well that will accept of such a wife. Eubulides in Aristænetus married a poor man's child, of a merry countenance, and heavenly visage, in pity of her estate, and that quickly. Acontius, coming to Delos to sacrifice to Diana, fell in love with Cydippe, a noble lass, and wanting means to get her love, flung a golden apple into her lap, with this inscription upon it,

* Translated by Mr. B. Jonson. — Burton's note.

I swear by all the Rites of Diana,
I'll come and be thy husband if I may.

She considered of it, and upon some small enquiry of his person and
estate was married unto him.

Blessed is the wooing,
That is not long a doing,

as the saying is; when the parties are sufficiently known to each other,
what needs such scrupulosity, so many circumstances? dost thou know
her conditions, her bringing up, like her person? let her means be what
they will, take her without any more ado. Dido and Æneas were acci-
dently driven by a storm both into one cave, they made a match upon
it: Masinissa was married to that fair captive Sophonisba, King Syphax'
wife, the same day that he saw her first, to prevent Scipio and Lælius,
lest they should determine otherwise of her. If thou lovest the party,
do as much: good education and beauty is a competent dowry, stand
not upon money. Mens' hearts once were made of gold (saith Theocritus) and troth met troth, in days of old; in the golden world men did
so (in the reign of Ogyges belike, before staggering Ninus began to
domineer) if all be true that is reported: and some few nowadays will
do as much, here and there one; 'tis well done methinks, and all happiness befall them for so doing. Leontius, a Philosopher of Athens, had
a fair daughter called Athenais, (saith mine author) of a comely carriage, he gave her no portion but her bringing up, out of some secret fore-
knowledge of her fortune, bestowing that little which he had amongst
his other children. But she, thus qualified, was preferred by some
friends to Constantinople to serve Pulcheria, the Emperor's sister, of
whom she was baptized and called Eudocia. Theodosius the Emperor
in short space took notice of her excellent beauty and good parts, and a
little after, upon his sister's sole commendation, made her his wife:
'twas nobly done of Theodosius. Rhodope was the fairest Lady in
her days in all Egypt; she went to wash her, and by chance (her
maids meanwhile looking but carelessly to her clothes) an Eagle stole
away one of her shoes, and laid it in Psammetichus the King of Egypt's
lap at Memphis: he wondered at the excellency of the shoe, and pretty
foot, but more at the deed of the eagle, at the manner of the bringing
of it: and caused forthwith proclamation to be made, that she that
owned that shoe, should come presently to his Court; the Virgin came
and was forthwith married to the King. I say this was heroically done,
and like a Prince: I commend him for it, and all such as have means,
that will either do (as he did) themselves, or so for love, &c. marry

their children. If he be rich, let him take such a one as wants, if she be virtuously given; for as Siracides adviseth, Forego not a wife and good woman; for her grace is above gold. If she have fortunes of her own, let her take * a man. Danaus of Lacedæmon had a many daughters to bestow, and means enough for them all, he never stood enquiring after great matches, as others used to do, but sent for a company of brave young gallants home to his house, and bid his daughters choose every one one, whom she liked best, and take him for her husband, without any more ado. This act of his was much approved in those times. But in this Iron age of ours we respect riches alone (for a maid must buy her husband now, with a great dowry, if she will have him), covetousness and filthy lucre mars all good matches, or some such by-respects. Crales, a Servian Prince (as Nicephorus Gregoras relates it), was an earnest suitor to Eudocia the Emperor's sister; though her brother much desired it, yet she could not abide him, for he had three former wives, all basely abused; but the Emperor still, because he was a great Prince, and a troublesome neighbour, much desired his affinity, and to that end betrothed his own daughter Simonida to him, a little girl five years of age (he being forty-five) and five years elder than the Emperor himself: such disproportionable and unlikely matches can wealth and a fair fortune make. And yet not that alone, it is not only money, but sometimes vain-glory, pride, ambition, do as much harm as wretched covetousness itself in another extreme. If a Yeoman have one sole daughter, he must over-match her, above her birth and calling, to a Gentleman forsooth, because of her great portion, too good for one of her own rank, as he supposeth. A Gentleman's daughter and heir must be married to a Knight baronet's eldest son at least; and a Knight's only daughter to a Baron himself, or an Earl, and so upwards, her great dowry deserves it. And thus striving for more honour to their wealth, they undo their children, many discontents follow, and oftentimes they ruinate their Families. Paulus Jovius gives instance in Galeatius the second, that Heroical Duke of Milan, who sought foreign matrimonial alliances, honourable indeed and of royal state, but hurtful and almost fatal to him and his successors; he married his eldest son John Galeatius to Isabella, the King of France his sister, but she was so great a burden to her father-in-law, he spent two hundred thousand gold pieces on her appointments, her entertainment at Milan was so costly, that it almost undid him. His daughter Violanta was married to Lionel, Duke of Clarence, the youngest son to Edward the Third, King of England, but he was welcomed with such incredible magnificence, that a King's purse

✎ " Make," in text.

was scarce able to bear it; for besides many rich presents of horses, arms, plate, money, jewels, &c., he made one dinner for him and his company, in which were thirty-two messes, and as much provision left as would serve ten thousand men: but a little after Lionel died, devoting himself to his bride and untimely entertainments, and to the Duke's great loss, the solemnity was ended. So can titles, honours, ambition, make many brave, but unfortunate matches, of all sides, for by-respects, though both crazed in body and mind, most unwilling, averse, and often unfit: so love is banished, and we feel the smart of it in the end. But I am too lavish peradventure in this subject.

Another let or hindrance is strict and severe Discipline, Laws and rigorous customs that forbid men to marry at set times, and in some places: as Prentices, Servants, Collegiates, States of lives in Copy-holds, or in some base inferior Offices, *thou mayst crave*, in such cases, *thou canst not have*, as he * said. They see but as prisoners through a grate, they covet and catch but as Tantalus the waters that recede from his lips. Their love is lost, and vain it is in such an estate to attempt. 'Tis a grievous thing to love and not enjoy. They may indeed, I deny not, marry if they will, and have free choice some of them; but in the mean time their case is desperate, they hold a Wolf by the ears, they must either burn or starve. 'Tis a sophistical dilemma, hard to resolve. If they marry, they forfeit their estates, they are undone and starve themselves through beggary and want: if they do not marry, in this heroical passion they furiously rage, are tormented, and torn to pieces by their predominate affections.

Every man hath not the gift of continence, let him pray for it then, as Beza adviseth in his Tract on Divorce, because God hath so called him to a single life, in taking away the means of marriage: Paul would have gone from Mysia to Bithynia, but the Spirit suffered him not, and thou wouldst peradventure be a married man with all thy will, but that protecting Angel holds it not fit. The devil too sometimes may divert by his ill suggestions, and mar many good matches, as the same Paul was willing to see the Romans, but hindered of Satan, he could not.

There be those that think they are necessitated by Fate, their Stars have so decreed, and therefore they grumble at their hard fortune, they are well inclined to marry, but one rub or other is ever in the way: I know what Astrologers say in this behalf, what Ptolemy, Skoner, what Leovitius, in his first Example of Geniture, which Sextus ab Heminga takes to be the Horoscope of Hieronymus Wulfius, what Pezelius, Origanaus, and Leovitius his illustrator, Garceus, what Junc-

* Apuleius.

tine, Protanus, Campanella, what the rest (to omit those Arabian conjectures as to marriage, as to lasciviousness, the threefold Venus, &c.,
and those resolutions upon a question, whether he will obtain a mistress,
&c.) determine in this behalf, for example, whether he was born to have
a wife, whether he will win a spouse easily or hardly, how many marriages, when, what kind of wives, as to their mutual love, both in men's
and women's genitures, by the examination of the seventh house, the
Almutens [or prevailing planets in the horoscope], Lords and Planets
there, a Moon dominant and Sun ascendant, &c., by particular Aphorisms, whether the Lord of the Seventh, in the Seventh or the Second,
awards a better wife, a slave or one not noble in the Twelfth, if Venus
in the Twelfth ———— with many such, too tedious to relate. Yet let
no man be troubled, or find himself grieved with such Predictions, as
Hier. Wolfius well saith in his Astrological Dialogue, these are not decrees, they be but conjectures, the Stars incline, but not enforce. The
heavenly bodies have power over our bodies, these being but of vile
clay: but they bind not the rational mind, for that is under the dominion of God only. Wisdom, diligence, discretion, may mitigate, if not
quite alter, such decrees; everyone is the architect of his own fortune,
those who are cautious and prudent compass their desires. Let no man
then be terrified or molested with such Astrological Aphorisms, or be
much moved, either to vain hope or fear, from such predictions, but let
every man follow his own free will in this case, and do as he sees cause.
Better it is indeed to marry than burn for their soul's health, but for
their present fortunes by some other means to pacify themselves, and
divert the stream of this fiery torrent, to continue as they are, rest satisfied, lamenting the flower of virginity thus ungathered, deploring their
misery with that Eunuch in Libanius, since there is no help or remedy,
and with Jephthah's daughter to bewail their virginities.

Of like nature is superstition, those rash vows of Monks and Friars,
and such as live in religious Orders, but far more tyrannical and much
worse. Nature, youth, and his furious passion forcibly inclines, and
rageth on the one side: but their Order and Vow checks them on the
other.

Thy beauty doth such vows forbid. (OVID)

What Merits and Indulgences they heap unto themselves by it, what
commodities, I know not; but I am sure, from such rash vows, and
inhuman manner of life proceed many inconveniences, many diseases,
many vices, mastupration, satyriasis, priapism, melancholy, madness,

fornication, adultery, buggary, sodomy, theft, murder, and all manner of mischiefs: read but Bale's Catalogue of Sodomites at the Visitation of Abbies here in England, Henry Stephan his Apology for Herodotus, that which Ulricus writes in one of his Epistles, that Pope Gregory, when he saw 6,000 skulls and bones of infants taken out of a fish-pond near a Nunnery, thereupon retracted that decree of Priests' marriages, which was the cause of such a slaughter, was much grieved at it, and purged himself by repentance. Read many such, and then ask what is to be done, is this vow to be broke or not? No, saith Bellarmine, better burn or fly out than to break thy vow. And Coster saith it is absolutely a greater sin for a Priest to marry, than to keep a concubine at home. Gregory de Valence maintains the same, as those Essenes and Montanists of old. Insomuch that many Votaries, out of a false persuasion of merit and holiness in this kind, will sooner die than marry, though it be to the saving of their lives. In the year 1419, Pius 2, [being] Pope, James Rossa, Nephew to the King of Portugal, and then elect Archbishop of Lisbon, being very sick at Florence, when his Physicians told him that his disease was such he must either lie with a wench, marry, or die, cheerfully chose to die. Now they commended him for it: but S. Paul teacheth otherwise, Better marry than burn, and as S. Hierome gravely delivers it, There's a difference betwixt God's ordinances, and men's laws: and therefore Cyprian boldly denounceth, it is abominable, impious, adulterous, and sacrilegious, what men make and ordain after their own furies to cross God's laws. Georgius Wicelius, one of their own arch Divines, exclaims against it, and all such rash monastical vows, and would have such persons seriously to consider what they do, whom they admit, lest they repent it at last. For either, as he follows it, you must allow them Concubines, or suffer them to marry, for scarce shall you find three Priests of three thousand, in their prime that are not troubled with burning lust. Wherefore I conclude, it is an unnatural and impious thing to bar men of this Christian liberty, too severe and inhuman an edict.

> The silly wrenne, the titmouse also,
> The little redbrest have free election,
> To flyen p-fere and together gone,
> Whereas hem list, aboute environ,
> As they of kinde have inclination,
> And as Nature, empresse and guide,
> Of everything list to provide,
> But man alone, alas the hard stond,
> Full cruelly by kindes ordinance

Constrained is, and by statutes bound,
And debarred from all suche pleasance:
What meaneth this, what is this pretence
Of lawes, I wis, against all right of kinde,
Without a cause, so narrow men to binde? *

Many Lay-men repine still at Priests' marriages above the rest, and not at Clergymen only, but all of the meaner sort and condition, they would have none marry but such as are rich and able to maintain wives, because their parish belike shall be pestered with orphans, and the world full of beggars: but these are hard-hearted, unnatural, monsters of men, shallow politicians, they do not consider that a great part of the world is not yet inhabited as it ought, how many Colonies into America, Terra Australis Incognita, Africa, may be sent! Let them consult with Sir William Alexander's Book of Colonies, Orpheus Junior's Golden Fleece, Captain Whitburne, Mr. Hagthorpe, &c., and they shall surely be otherwise informed. Those politick Romans were of another mind, they thought their City and Country could never be too populous. Adrian the Emperor said he had rather have men than money. Augustus Cæsar made an oration in Rome to bachelors to persuade them to marry; some countries compelled them to marry of old, as Jews, Turks, Indians, Chinese, amongst the rest in these days, who much wonder at our discipline to suffer so many idle persons to live in Monasteries, and often marvel how they can live honest. In the Isle of Maragnan the Governor and petty King there did wonder at the Frenchmen, and admire how so many Friars, and the rest of their company could live without wives, they thought it a thing unpossible, and would not believe it. If these men should but survey our multitudes of religious houses, observe our numbers of Monasteries all over Europe, 18 Nunneries in Padua, in Venice 31 Cloisters of Monks, 28 of Nuns, &c., from the claw guessing what size the beast must be, 'tis to this proportion in all other Provinces and Cities, what would they think, do they live honest? Let them dissemble as they will, I am of Tertullian's mind, that few can contain but by compulsion. O chastity (saith he) thou art a rare Goddess in the world, not so easily got, seldom continuate: thou may'st now and then be compelled either for defect of nature, or if discipline persuade, decrees enforce; — or for some such by-respects, sullenness, discontent, they have lost their first loves, may not have whom they will themselves, want of means, rash vows, &c. But can he willingly contain? I think not. Therefore, either out of commiseration of human imbecility, in policy, or to prevent a far worse inconvenience, for they

* Lydgate.

hold it some of them as necessary as meat and drink, and because vigour of youth, the state and temper of most men's bodies, do so furiously desire it, they have heretofore in some Nations liberally admitted polygamy and stews, an hundred thousand Courtisans in grand Cairo in Egypt, as Radzivilius observes, are tolerated, besides boys: how many at Fessa, Rome, Naples, Florence, Venice, &c.? and still in many other Provinces and Cities of Europe they do as much, because they think young men, Church-men, and servants amongst the rest, can hardly live honest. The consideration of this belike made Vibius, the Spaniard, when his friend Crassus that rich Roman gallant lay hid in the Cave, to gratify him the more, send two lusty lasses to accompany him all the while he was there imprisoned: and Surenas the Parthian General, when he warred against the Romans, to carry about with him 200 Concubines, as the Swiss Soldiers do now commonly their wives. But because this course is not generally approved, but rather contradicted as unlawful, and abhorred, in most Countries they do much encourage them to marriage, give great rewards for such as have many children, and mulct those that will not marry; the Law of three children, and in A. Gellius, Ælian, Valerius, we read that three children freed the father from painful offices, and five from all contribution. "A woman shall be saved by bearing children." Epictetus would have all marry, and as Plato will, he that marrieth not before 35 years of his age must be compelled or punished, and the money consecrated to Juno's Temple, or applied to publick uses. They account him in some Countries unfortunate that dies without a wife, a most unhappy man, as Boethius infers, and if at all happy, yet unhappy in his supposed happiness. They commonly deplore his estate, and much lament him for it; O my sweet son! &c. See Lucian, Sands, &c.

Yet notwithstanding many with us are of the opposite part, they are married themselves, and for others, let them burn, fire, and flame, they care not, so they be not troubled with them. Some are too curious, and some too covetous, they may marry when they will, both for ability and means, but so nice, that except, as Theophilus, the Emperor, was presented, by his Mother Euphrosyne, with all the rarest beauties of the Empire in the Great Chamber of his Palace at once, and bid to give a golden apple to her he liked best. If they might so take and choose whom they list out of all the fair Maids their Nation affords, they could happily condescend to marry: otherwise, &c., why should a man marry, saith another Epicurean rout, what's matrimony but a matter of money? why should free nature be entrenched on, confined or obliged,

to this or that man or woman, with these manacles of body and goods?
&c. There are those too, that dearly love, admire and follow women, all
their lives long, like Penelope's suitors, never well but in their companies, wistly gazing on their beauties, observing close, hanging after
them, dallying still with them, and yet dare not, will not, marry. Many
poor people, and of the meaner sort, are too distrustful of God's providence, they will not, dare not for such worldly respects, fear of want,
woes, miseries, or that they shall light, as Lemnius saith, on a scold, a
slut, or a bad wife. And therefore turning away from Venus they spend
a joyless youth, they are resolved to live single, as Epaminondas
did, —

    There's nothing better than a single life,   (HORACE)

— and ready with Hippolytus to abjure all women, detest, abhor, flee,
execrate them all. But alas, poor Hippolytus, thou knowest not what
thou sayest, 'tis otherwise, Hippolytus. Some make a doubt whether a
Scholar should marry; if she be fair, she will bring him back from his
grammar to his horn-book, or else with kissing and dalliance she will
hinder his study; if foul, with scolding, he cannot well intend to both,
as Philippus Beroaldus, that great Bononian [or Bolognian] Doctor,
once writ, 'tis sure to hinder the study of letters; but he recanted at
last, and in a solemn sort with true conceived words he did ask the world
and all women forgiveness. But you shall have the story as he relates
himself, in his Commentaries on the sixth of Apuleius: For a long time
I lived a single life, I could not abide marriage, but as a rambler, (to
use his own words) I took a snatch where I could get it, nay more, I
railed at marriage downright, and in a publick auditory when I did
interpret that sixth Satire of Juvenal, out of Plutarch and Seneca, I
did heap up all the dicteries [or sayings] I could against women; but
now recant with Stesichorus, I sing a Palinode, I approve of marriage,
I am glad I am a married man, I am heartily glad I have a wife, so
sweet a wife, so noble a wife, so young, so chaste a wife, so loving a
wife, and I do wish and desire all other men to marry, and especially
Scholars; that as of old Marcia did by Hortensius, Terentia by Tullius,
Calphurnia to Plinius, Pudentilla to Apuleius, hold the candle whilst
their husbands did meditate and write, so theirs may do to them, and
as my dear Camilla doth to me. Let other men be averse, rail then and
scoff at women, and say what they can to the contrary, a single man is
an happy man, &c., but this is a toy,

    Reject not in your prime sweet love and mirth;   (HORACE)

these men are too distrustful and much to blame, to use such speeches,

Forbear to blame on womankind
The guilt that in one girl you find. (HORACE)

They must not condemn all for some. As there be many bad, there be some good wives; as some be vicious, some be virtuous: read what Solomon hath said in their praises, and Siracides. " Blessed is the man that hath a virtuous wife, for the number of his days shall be double. A virtuous woman rejoiceth her husband, and she shall fulfil the years of his life in peace. A good wife is a good portion, an help, a pillar of rest."

Who takes a wife, hath brother and sister too. (APHRANIUS)

He that hath no wife wandereth to and fro mourning. Women are the sole, only joy, and comfort of a man's life, born for the use and pleasure of men, and the founding of a family.

> *Joy of the human race, solace in life,*
> *By night caressing, and by day the object*
> *Of pleasant care, the strong desire of men,*
> *The hope of lads.* (LOECHAEUS)

A wife is a young man's Mistress, a middle age's companion, an old man's Nurse: sharer of joys and sorrows, a prop, an help, &c.

> *Man's best possession is a loving wife,*
> *She tempers anger and diverts all strife.* (EURIPIDES)

There is no joy, no comfort, no sweetness, no pleasure in the world like to that of a good wife. With what harmony, saith our Latin Homer, a loving wife and constant husband lead their lives; she is still the same in sickness and in health, his eye, his hand, his bosom-friend, his partner at all times, his other self, not to be separated by any calamity, but ready to share all sorrow, discontent, and as the Indian women do, live and die with him, nay more, to die presently for him. Admetus, King of Thessaly, when he lay upon his death-bed, was told by Apollo's Oracle, that if he could get any body to die for him, he should live longer yet, but when all refused, his parents, although decrepit, friends and followers, forsook him, Alcestis his wife, though young, most willingly undertook it; what more can be desired or expected? And although on the other side there be an infinite number of bad husbands (I should rail downright against some of them) able to discourage any women; yet there be some good ones again, and those most observant of Marriage Rites. An honest Country-fellow (as Fulgosus relates it) in the kingdom of Naples, at plough by the Sea side, saw his wife carried away by Mauritanian Pirates, he ran after in all haste, up to the chin first, and when he could wade no longer, swam, calling to the Governor

of the ship to deliver his wife, or if he must not have her restored, to
let him follow as a prisoner, for he was resolved to be a Galley-slave,
his drudge, willing to endure any misery, so that he might but enjoy
his dear wife. The Moors, seeing the man's constancy, and relating the
whole matter to their Governor at Tunis, set them both free, and gave
them an honest pension to maintain themselves during their lives. I
could tell many stories to this effect; but put case it often prove otherwise, because marriage is troublesome, wholly therefore to avoid it is
no argument; he that will avoid trouble must avoid the world (Eusebius). Some trouble there is in marriage, I deny not. And if matrimony
be a burden, saith Erasmus, yet there be many things to sweeten it, a
pleasant wife, pretty children, *the chief delight of the sons of men.* And
howsoever, though it were all troubles, it must willingly be undergone
for publick good's sake.

> *Hear me, O my countrymen, saith Susarion,*
> *Women are nought, yet no life without one.* (STOBÆUS)

Say they are evils, yet they are necessary evils, and for our own ends
we must make use of them to have issue, to give pleasure and restore
the race, and to propagate the Church. For to what end is a man born?
why lives he, but to increase the world? and how shall he do that well,
if he do not marry? Saith Nevisanus, matrimony makes us immortal,
and according to Tacitus, 'tis the sole and chief prop of an Empire.

He lives contemptibly through whom none else has life,   (PALINGENIUS)
which Pelopidas objected to Epaminondas, he was an unworthy member of a Common-wealth, that left not a child after him to defend it;
and as Trismegistus to his son Tatius, have no commerce with a single
man: holding belike that a bachelor could not live honestly as he
should; and with Georgius Wicelius, a great Divine and holy man, who
of late by twenty-six arguments commends marriage as a thing most
necessary for all kind of persons, most laudable and fit to be embraced:
and is persuaded withal, that no man can live and die religiously, and
as he ought, without a wife, he is false, an enemy to the Common-wealth,
injurious to himself, destructive to the world, an apostate to nature, a
rebel against Heaven and Earth. Let our wilful, obstinate, and stale
Bachelors ruminate of this. If we could live without wives, as Marcellus
Numidicus said in A. Gellius, we would all want them, but because we
cannot, let all marry, and consult rather to the publick good, than their
own private pleasure or estate. It were an happy thing, as wise Euripides hath it, if we could buy children with gold and silver, and be so
provided, without women's company, but that may not be.

Earth, air, sea, land, eftsoon would come to nought,
The world itself should be to ruin brought.   (SENECA)

Necessity therefore compels us to marry.

But what do I trouble myself, to find arguments to persuade to, or commend marriage? behold a brief abstract of all that which I have said, and much more, succinctly, pithily, pathetically, perspicuously, and elegantly delivered in twelve motives to mitigate the miseries of marriage, by Jacobus de Voragine.

1. Hast thou means? thou hast one to keep and increase it.
2. Hast none? thou hast one to help to get it.
3. Art in prosperity? thine happiness is doubled.
4. Art in adversity? she'll comfort, assist, bear a part of thy burden to make it more tolerable.
5. Art at home? she'll drive away melancholy.
6. Art abroad? she looks after thee going from home, wishes for thee in thine absence, and joyfully welcomes thy return.
7. There's nothing delightsome without society, no society so sweet as matrimony.
8. The band of conjugal love is adamantine.
9. The sweet company of kinsmen increaseth, the number of parents is doubled, of brothers, sisters, nephews.
10. Thou art made a father by a fair and happy issue.
11. Moses curseth the barrenness of matrimony, how much more a single life?
12. If nature escape not punishment, surely thy will shall not avoid it.

All this is true, say you, and who knows it not? but how easy a matter is it to answer these motives, and to make an Antiparody quite opposite unto it? To exercise myself I will essay.

1. Hast thou means? thou hast one to spend it.
2. Hast none? thy beggary is increased.
3. Art in prosperity? thy happiness is ended.
4. Art in adversity? like Job's wife, she'll aggravate thy misery, vex thy soul, make thy burden intolerable.
5. Art at home? she'll scold thee out of doors.
6. Art abroad? If thou be wise, keep thee so, she'll perhaps graft horns in thine absence, scowl on thee coming home.
7. Nothing gives more content than solitariness, no solitariness like this of a single life.
8. The band of marriage is adamantine, no hope of losing it, thou art undone.

9. Thy number increaseth, thou shalt be devoured by thy wife's friends.

10. Thou art made a cornuto by an unchaste wife, and shalt bring up other folks' children instead of thine own.

11. Paul commends marriage, yet he prefers a single life.

12. Is marriage honourable? What an immortal crown belongs to virginity!

So Siracides himself speaks as much as may be for and against women, so doth almost every Philosopher plead for and against, every Poet thus argues the case (though what cares the common man what they say?), so can I conceive peradventure, and so canst thou: when all is said, yet since some be good, some bad, let's put it to the venture. I conclude therefore with Seneca, Why dost thou lie alone, let thy youth and best days to pass away? Marry whilst thou mayest, whilst thou art yet able, yet lusty,

Find her to whom you may say, " Thou art my only pleasure,"   (OVID) make thy choice, and that freely, forthwith, make no delay, but take thy fortune as it falls. 'Tis true,

> *Unhappy he who lights on a bad wife,*
> *Happy he who obtains a good one.*   (EURIPIDES)

'Tis an hazard both ways I confess, to live single, or to marry; it may be bad, it may be good; as it is a cross and calamity on the one side, so 'tis a sweet delight, an incomparable happiness, a blessed estate, a most unspeakable benefit, a sole content on the other; 'tis all in the proof. Be not then so wayward, so covetous, so distrustful, so curious and nice, but let's all marry, lie in mutual warm embrace. Take me to thee, and thee to me, to morrow is St. Valentine's day, let's keep it Holiday for Cupid's sake, for that great God Love's sake, for Hymen's sake, and celebrate Venus' Vigil with our Ancestors for company together, singing as they did,

To-morrow let him love who ne'er loved yet,
Nor let him who e'er loved before forget,
'Tis tuneful spring, the world's new-born in spring
It is love's season, birds then pairing sing,
'Tis then the woods renew their annual green.   (PERVIGILIUM VENERIS)

Let him that is averse from marriage read more in Barbarus, Lemnius, P. Godefridus, Nevisanus, Alex. ab Alexandro, Tunstall, Erasmus' tracts In Praise of Matrimony, &c., and I doubt not but in the end he will rest satisfied, recant with Beroaldus, do penance for his former folly, singing some penitential ditties, desire to be reconciled to the

Deity of this great God Love, go a pilgrimage to his Shrine, offer to his Image, sacrifice upon his altar, and be as willing at last to embrace marriage as the rest. There will not be found, I hope, no, not in that severe family of Stoicks, who shall refuse to submit his grave beard, and supercilious looks to the clipping of a wife, or disagree from his fellows in this point. For what more willingly (as Varro holds) can a proper man see than a fair wife, a sweet wife, a loving wife? Can the world afford a better sight, sweeter content, a fairer object, a more gracious aspect?

Since then this of marriage is the last and best refuge and cure of Heroical love, all doubts are cleared, and impediments removed; I say again, what remains, but that according to both their desires, they be happily joined, since it cannot otherwise be helped. God send us all good wives, every man his wish in this kind, and me mine!

> And God that all this wyde world hath wrought,
> Send him his love that hath it dere y-bought.

If all parties be pleased, ask their Banns, 'tis a match. Rhodanthe and Dosicles shall go together, Clitiphon and Leucippe, Theagenes and Chariclea, Poliarchus hath his Argenis,* Lysander Calista, (to make up the mask) and Iphis enjoys his Ianthe.

> And Troilus in lust and in quiete
> Is with Creseide, his owne herte swete.

And although they have hardly past the pikes, through many difficulties and delays brought the match about, yet let them take this of Aristænetus (that so marry) for their comfort: after many troubles and cares, the marriages of Lovers are more sweet and pleasant. As we commonly conclude a Comedy with a wedding, and shaking of hands, let's shut up our discourse, and end all with an Epithalamium.

Happiness to bride and groom! God give them joy together! Hymen, lead the wedding home, Hymen Hvmenaeus, come! 'Tis well done, and not without the aid of the gods, 'tis an happy conjunction, a fortunate match, an even couple, they both excel in gifts of body and mind, are both equal in years, youth, vigour, alacrity, she is fair and lovely as Lais or Helena, he as another Cleinias or Alcibiades, —

> *Then modestly go sport and toy,*
> *And let's have every year a boy.*   (CATULLUS)

Go give a sweet smell as Incense, and bring forth flowers as the Lily: that we may say hereafter, Faith, Pamphilus has got a son. In the mean time I say,

* John Barclay's poem of that name.

O gentle youths, go sport yourselves betimes,
Let not the Doves outpass your murmurings,
Or Ivy-clasping arms, or oyster kissings. (GALLIENUS)

And in the morn betime, as those Lacedæmonian Lasses saluted Helena and Menelaus, singing at their windows, and wishing good success, do we at yours:

Good morrow, Master Bridegroom, and Mistress Bride,
Many fair lovely Bairns to you betide!
Let Venus to you mutual love procure,
Let Saturn give you riches to endure.
Long may you sleep in one another's arms,
Inspiring sweet desire, and free from harms. (THEOCRITUS)

Even all your lives long,

The love of Turtles hap to you,
And Ravens' years still to renew. (ERASMUS)

Let the Muses sing, (as he said) the Graces dance, not at their weddings only, but all their days long; so couple their hearts, that no irksomeness or anger ever befall them. Let him never call her other name than my joy, my light, or she call him otherwise than sweet-heart. To this happiness of theirs, let not old age any whit detract, but as their years, so let their mutual love and comfort increase. And when they depart this life,

Because they have so sweetly liv'd together,
Let not one die a day before the other,
He bury her, she him, with even fate,
One hour their souls let jointly separate. (OVID)
O happy both! if that my lines have power,
No time shall ever make your memory fade. (VIRGIL)

And this is enough said of love, subject, as Kornmannus said, to correction by those who know better. Who would more of the remedies of love, let them read Jason Pratensis, Arnoldus, Montaltus, Savanarola, Langius, Valescus, Crimisonus, Alexander Benedictus, Laurentius, Valleriola, the poet Ovid, and our Chaucer, with whom I conclude.

For myne wordes here and every part,
I speak hem alle under correcioun,
Of you that feeling have in love's art,
And put it all in your discrecion,
To increse or maken diminucion,
Of my language, that I you beseech:
But now to purpose of my rather speech.

SECTION —MEMBER

SUBSECTION 1 — *Jealousy, its Equivocations, Name, Definition, Extent, several kinds; of Princes, Parents, Friends. In Beasts, Men: before marriage, as Corrivals; or after, as in this place*

VALESCUS DE TARANTA, Ælian Montaltus, Felix Platerus, Guianerius, put Jealousy for a cause of Melancholy, others for a Symptom; because melancholy persons, amongst these passions and perturbations of the mind, are most obnoxious to it. But methinks for the latitude it hath, and that prerogative above other ordinary Symptoms, it ought to be treated of as a Species apart, being of so great and eminent note, so furious a passion, and almost of as great extent as Love itself, as Benedetto Varchi holds, No Love without a mixture of Jealousy; who's not jealous, loves not. For these causes I will dilate, and treat of it by itself, as a bastard-branch, or kind of Love-Melancholy, which, as Heroical Love goeth commonly before marriage, doth usually follow, torture, and crucify in like sort, deserves therefore to be rectified alike, requires as much care and industry, in setting out the several causes of it, prognosticks and cures. Which I have more willingly done, that he that is or hath been jealous, may see his error as in a glass; he that is not, may learn to detest, avoid it himself, and dispossess others that are any wise affected with it.

Jealousy is described and defined to be a certain suspicion which the Lover hath of the party he chiefly loveth, lest he or she should be enamoured of another: or any eager desire to enjoy some beauty alone, to have it proper to himself only: a fear or doubt, lest any foreigner should participate or share with him in his love. Or (as Scaliger adds) a fear of losing her favour, whom he so earnestly affects. Cardan calls it, a zeal for love, and a kind of envy lest any man should beguile us. Ludovicus Vives defines it in the very same words, or little differing in sense.

There be many other Jealousies, but improperly so called all; as that of Parents, Tutors, Guardians, over their children, friends whom they love, or such as are left to their wardship or protection.

Storax, young master's not returned from supper,
Nor any of the slaves that went to meet him; (TERENCE)
as the old man in the Comedy cried out in passion, and from a solicitous fear and care he had of his adopted son: not of beauty, but lest they should miscarry, do amiss, or any way discredit, disgrace (as Vives

notes) or endanger themselves and us. Ægeus was so solicitous for his son Theseus, (when he went to fight with the Minotaur) of his success, lest he should be foiled; fear always will believe the worst. We are still apt to suspect the worst in such doubtful cases, as many wives in their husbands' absence, fond mothers in their children's, lest if absent they should be misled or sick, and are continually expecting news from them, how they do fare, and what is become of them, they cannot endure to have them long out of their sight. Oh my sweet son! O my dear child! &c. Paul was jealous over the Church of Corinth, as he confesseth, " with a godly jealousy, to present them a pure Virgin to Christ "; and he was afraid still lest, as the Serpent beguiled Eve through his subtilty, so their minds should be corrupted from the simplicity that is in Christ. God himself in some sense is said to be jealous, " I am a jealous God, and will visit "; so, " Shall thy jealousy burn like fire for ever? " But these are improperly called Jealousies, and by a Metaphor, to shew the care and solicitude they have of them. Although some Jealousies express all the Symptoms of this which we treat of, fear, sorrow, anguish, anxiety, suspicion, hatred, &c., the object only varied. That of some fathers is very eminent to their sons and heirs; for though they love them dearly being children, yet now coming towards man's estate they may not well abide them, the son and heir is commonly sick of the father, and the father again may not well brook his eldest son, they are full of quarrels and enmities. But that of Princes is most notorious, as when they fear corrivals, (if I may so call them), successors, emulators, subjects, or such as they have offended. Impatience ever goes with power; they are still suspicious, lest their authority should be diminished, as one observes; and as Commines hath it, it cannot be expressed what slender causes they have of their grief and suspicion, a secret disease that commonly lurks and breeds in Princes' families. Sometimes it is for their honour only, as that of Adrian the Emperor, that killed all his emulators. Saul envied David: Domitian Agricola, because he did excel him, obscure his honour as he thought, eclipse his fame. Juno turned Prœtus' daughters into Kine, for that they contended with her for beauty; Cyparissæ, King Etocles' children, were envied of the Goddesses for their excellent good parts, and dancing amongst the rest, saith Constantine.* & for that cause flung down head-long from heaven, and buried in a pit, but the earth took pity of them, and brought out cypress trees to preserve their memories. Niobe, Arachne, and Marsyas can testify as much. But it is most grievous when it is for a kingdom itself, or matters of commodity, it produceth lamentable

* In his Husbandry.

effects, especially amongst Tyrants, and such as are more feared than beloved of their subjects, that get and keep their sovereignty by force, and fear, as Phalaris, Dionysius, Periander held theirs. For though fear, cowardice, and jealousy, in Plutarch's opinion, be the common causes of tyranny, as in Nero, Caligula, Tiberius, yet most take them to be symptoms. For what slave, what hang-man (as Bodine well expresseth this passion) can so cruelly torture a condemned person, as this fear and suspicion? Fear of death, infamy, torments, are those furies and vultures that vex and disquiet tyrants, and torture them day and night, with perpetual terrors and affrights, envy, suspicion, fear, desire of revenge, and a thousand such disagreeing perturbations, turn and affright the soul out of the hinges of health, and more grievously wound and pierce, than those cruel masters can exasperate and vex their prentices or servants, with clubs, whips, chains, and tortures. Many terrible examples we have in this kind. amongst the Turks especially, many jealous outrages; Selimus killed Cornutus his youngest brother, five of his Nephews, Mustapha Bassa, and divers others. Bajazet, the second Turk, jealous of the valour and greatness of Achmet Bassa, caused him to be slain. Solyman the Magnificent murdered his own Son Mustapha; and 'tis an ordinary thing amongst them to make away their brothers, or any competitors, at the first coming to the Crown: 'tis all the solemnity they use at their fathers' funerals. What mad pranks in his jealous fury did Herod of old commit in Jewry, when he massacred all the children of a year old! Valens the Emperor in Constantinople, when as he left no man alive of quality in his kingdom that had his name begun with Theo; Theodoti, Theognosti, Theodosii, Theoduli, &c., they went all to their long home, because a wizard told him that name should succeed in his Empire! And what furious designs hath John Basilius,* that Muscovian tyrant, practised of late! It is a wonder to read that strange suspicion, which Suetonius reports of Claudius Cæsar and of Domitian, they were afraid of every man they saw; and which Herodian [reports] of Antoninus and Geta, those two jealous brothers, the one could not endure so much as the other's servants, but made away him, his chiefest followers, and all that belonged to him, or were his well-wishers. Maximinus, perceiving himself to be odious to most men, because he was come to that height of honour out of base beginnings, and suspecting his mean parentage would be objected to him, caused all the Senators that were nobly descended to be slain in a jealous humour, turned all the servants of Alexander his predecessor out of doors, and slew many of them, because they lamented their master's death, suspecting them to be traitors

* Ivan the Terrible.

for the love they bare to him. When Alexander in his fury had made
Clitus his dear friend to be put to death, and saw now (saith Curtius)
an alienation in his subjects' hearts, none durst talk with him, he began
to be jealous of himself, lest they should attempt as much on him, and
said, they lived like so many wild beasts in a wilderness, one afraid of
another. Our modern stories afford us many notable examples. Henry
the Third of France, jealous of Henry of Lorraine, Duke of Guise,
Anno 1588, caused him to be murdered in his own chamber. Lewis
the Eleventh was so suspicious, he durst not trust his children, every
man about him he suspected for a traitor: many strange tricks Commines telleth of him. How jealous was our Henry the Fourth of
King Richard the Second, so long as he lived, after he was deposed! and
of his own son Henry, in his later days! which the Prince well perceiving, came to visit his father in his sickness, in a watchet velvet gown,
full of oilet [or eyelet] holes, and with needles sticking in them, (as an
emblem of jealousy) and so pacified his suspicious father, after some
speeches and protestations, which he had used to that purpose. Perpetual imprisonment, as that of Robert Duke of Normandy, in the
days of Henry the First, forbidding of marriage to some persons, with
such like edicts and prohibitions, are ordinary in all states. In a word
(as he [R. Tofte in his Blason of Jealousy] said) three things cause
Jealousy, a mighty state, a rich treasure, a fair wife; or where there is
a crackt title, much tyranny, and many exactions. In our state, as being
freed from all these fears and miseries, we may be most secure and
happy under the reign of our fortunate Prince.

> *His fortune hath indebted him to none,*
> *But to all his people universally;*
> *And not to them but for their love alone,*
> *Which they account as placèd worthily.*
> *He is so set, he hath no cause to be*
> *Jealous, or dreadful of disloyalty;*
> *The pedestal whereon his greatness stands,*
> *Is held of all our hearts, and all our hands.*   (DANIEL)

But I rove, I confess. These equivocations, Jealousies, and many such,
which crucify the souls of men, are not here properly meant, or in this
distinction of ours included, but that alone which is for beauty, tending
to love, and wherein they can brook no corrival, or endure any participation: and this Jealousy belongs as well to brute beasts, as men. Some
creatures, saith Vives, Swans, Doves, Cocks, Bulls, &c., are jealous as
well as men, and as much moved, for fear of communion.

In Venus' cause what mighty battles make
Your raving bulls, and stirs for their herd's sake:
And harts and bucks, that are so timorous,
Will fight and roar, if once they be but jealous.   (SENECA)

In Bulls, Horses, Goats, this is most apparently discerned; Bulls especially, he will not admit another Bull to feed in the same pasture, saith
Oppian: which Stephanus Bathorius, late king of Poland, used as an
Impress, with that motto, A kingdom admits not of two kings. R. T., in
his Blazon of Jealousy, telleth a story of a Swan about Windsor; that
finding a strange Cock with his mate, did swim I know not how many
miles after to kill him, and when he had done so, came back and killed
his hen: a certain truth, he saith, done upon Thames, as many Water-
men, and neighbour Gentlemen can tell. They keep their faith; for my
part, I do believe it may be true; for Swans have ever been branded
with that Epithet of Jealousy.

> The jealous swanne against his death that singeth,
> And eke the owle that of death bode bringeth.

Some say as much of Elephants, that they are more jealous than any
other creatures whatsoever; and those old Egyptians, as Pierius informeth us, express in their Hieroglyphicks the passion of Jealousy by
a Camel; because that fearing the worst still about matters of Venery,
he loves solitudes, that he may enjoy his pleasure alone, and he will
quarrel and fight with whosoever comes next, man or beast, in his
jealous fits. I have read as much of Crocodiles; and if Peter Martyr's
authority be authentick, you shall have a strange tale to that purpose
confidently related. Another story of the jealousy of dogs, see in Hieronymus Fabricius.

But this furious passion is most eminent in men, and is as well
amongst Bachelors, as married men. If it appear amongst Bachelors,
we commonly call them rivals or corrivals, a metaphor derived from a
River; for as a River, saith Acron and Donatus, divides a common
ground betwixt two men, and both participate of it; so is a woman
indifferent betwixt two suitors, both likely to enjoy her; and thence
comes this emulation, which breaks out many times into tempestuous
storms, and produceth lamentable effects, murder itself, with much
cruelty, many single combats. They cannot endure the least injury
done unto them before their Mistress, and in her defence will bite off
one another's noses; they are most impatient of any flout, disgrace,
least emulation or participation in that kind. Memmius bites the arm
of Largus. Memmius the Roman (as Tully tells the story), being cor-

rival with Largus at Terracina, bit him by the arm, which fact of his was so famous, that it afterwards grew to a proverb in those parts. Phædria could not abide his corrival Thraso; for when Parmeno demanded, whether he would command him any more service: No more (saith he) but to speak in his behalf, and to drive away his corrival if he could. Constantine, in the eleventh book of his husbandry, chapter 11, hath a pleasant tale of the Pine-tree: she was once a fair Maid, whom Phineus and Boreas, two corrivals, dearly sought; but jealous Boreas broke her neck, &c. And in his 18th chapter he telleth another tale of Mars, that in his jealousy slew Adonis. Petronius calleth this passion a furious emulation; and their symptoms are well expressed by Sir Geoffrey Chaucer in his first Canterbury tale. It will make the nearest and dearest friends fall out; they will endure all other things to be common, goods, lands, monies, participate of each other's pleasures, and take in good part any disgraces, injuries in another kind: but as Propertius well describes it in an Elegy of his, in this they will suffer nothing, have no corrivals.

> *Stab me with sword, or poison strong*
> *Give me to work my bane:*
> *So thou court not my lass, so thou*
> *From Mistress mine refrain.*
> *Command myself, my body, purse,*
> *As thine own goods take all,*
> *And as my ever dearest friend,*
> *I ever use thee shall.*
> *O spare my Love, to have alone*
> *Her to myself I crave,*
> *Nay, Jove himself I'll not endure*
> *My Rival for to have.*   (In R. T.)

This Jealousy which I am to treat of, is that which belongs to married men, in respect of their own wives; to whose estate, as no sweetness, pleasure, happiness, can be compared in the world, if they live quietly and lovingly together; so if they disagree or be jealous, those bitter pills of sorrow and grief, disastrous mischiefs, mischances, tortures, gripings, discontents, are not to be separated from them. A most violent passion it is where it taketh place, an unspeakable torment, a hellish torture, an infernal plague, as Ariosto calls it, a fury, a continual fever, full of suspicion, fear and sorrow, a martyrdom, a mirth-marring monster. " The sorrow and grief of heart of one woman jealous of another, is heavier than death," as Peninnah did Hannah, " vex her and upbraid her sore." 'Tis a main vexation, a most intolerable burden, a corrosive to all content, a frenzy, a madness itself, as Benedetto Varchi proves out of that select Sonnet of Giovanni de la Casa, that reverend Lord, as he styles him.

SUBSECTION 2 — *Causes of Jealousy. Who are most apt. Idleness, Melancholy, Impotency, long Absence, Beauty, Wantonness, naught themselves. Allurements from time, place, persons, bad usage, Causes*

ASTROLOGERS make the stars a cause or sign of this bitter passion, and out of every man's Horoscope will give a probable conjecture whether he will be jealous or no, and at what time, by direction of the significators to their several promissors: their Aphorisms are to be read in Albubator, Pontanus, Scheiner, Junctine, &c. Bodine ascribes a great cause to the country or clime, and discourseth largely there of this subject, saying, that Southern men are more hot, lascivious, and jealous, than such as live in the North; they can hardly contain themselves in those hotter climes, but are most subject to prodigious lusts. Leo Afer telleth incredible things almost of the lust and jealousy of his Countrymen of Africa, and especially such as live about Carthage, and so doth every Geographer of them in Asia, Turkey, Spaniards, Italians. Germany hath not so many drunkards, England Tobacconists, France Dancers, Holland Mariners, as Italy alone hath jealous husbands. And in Italy some account them of Piacenza more jealous than the rest. In Germany, France, Britain, Scandia, Poland, Muscovy, they are not so troubled with this feral malady, although Damianus à Goes, which I do much wonder at, in his Topography of Lapland, and Herbastein of Russia, against the stream of all other Geographers, would fasten it upon those Northern inhabitants. Altomarus, Poggius, and Munster in his description of Baden, reports that men and women of all sorts go commonly into the Baths together, without all suspicion, the name of Jealousy (saith Munster) is not so much as once heard of among them. In Friesland the women kiss him they drink to, and are kissed again of those they pledge. The virgins in Holland go hand in hand with young men from home, glide on the Ice, such is their harmless liberty, and lodge together abroad without suspicion, which rash Sansovinus, an Italian, makes it a great sign of unchastity. In France, upon small acquaintance, it is usual to court other men's wives, to come to their houses, and accompany them arm in arm in the streets, without imputation. In the most Northern Countries young men and maids familiarly dance together, men and their wives, which, Siena only excepted. Italians may not abide. The Greeks on the other side have their private baths for men and women, where they must not come near, not so much as see one another: and as Bodine observes, the Italians could never endure this, or a Spaniard, the very conceit of it would make him mad: and for that cause they lock up their women, and will not suffer them to be near men, so much as in the Church, but with a partition between. He telleth moreover, how that, when he was Embassador in England, he heard Mendoza the Spanish Legate finding fault with it as a filthy custom for men and women to sit promiscuously in Churches together: but Dr. Dale, the Master of the Requests, told him again, that it was indeed a filthy custom in Spain, where they could not contain themselves from lascivious thoughts in their holy places, but not with us. Baronius in his Annals, out of Eusebius, taxeth Licinius the Emperor for a decree of his made to this effect, that men might not enter the church at the same time with women; for being prodigiously naught [that is, naughty] himself, he so esteemed others. But we are far from any such strange conceits, and will permit our wives and daughters to go to the Tavern with a friend, as Aubanus saith, innocently enough, and suspect nothing, to kiss coming and going, as Erasmus writes in one of his Epistles, which they cannot endure. England is a paradise for women, and hell for horses: Italy a paradise for horses, hell for women, as the diverb goes. Some make a question whether this headstrong passion rage more in women than men, as Montaigne. But sure it is more outrageous in women, as all other melancholy is, by reason of the weakness of their sex. Scaliger concludes against women: Besides their inconstancy, treachery, suspicion, dissimulation, superstition, pride (for all women are by nature proud), desire of sovereignty, if they be great women (he gives instance in Juno) bitterness and jealousy are the most remarkable affections.

> *Tiger, boar, bear, viper, lioness,*
> *A woman's fury cannot express.*   (OVID)

Some say red-headed women, pale-coloured, black-eyed, and of a shrill voice, are most subject to jealousy.

> *High colour in a woman choler shows,*
> *Naught are they, peevish, proud, malicious;*
> *But worst of all, red, shrill, and jealous.*   (R. T.)

Comparisons are odious. I neither parallel them with others, nor debase them any more: men and women are both bad, and too subject to this pernicious infirmity. It is most part a symptom and cause of Melancholy, as Plater and Valescus teach us: melancholy men are apt to be jealous, and jealous apt to be melancholy.

> Pale jealousy, child of insatiate love,
> Of heart-sick thoughts with melancholy bred,
> A hell-tormenting fear no faith can move,
> By discontent with deadly poison fed;
> With heedless youth and error vainly led:
> A mortal plague, a virtue-drowning flood,
> A hellish fire not quenchèd but with blood.   (DRAYTON)

If idleness concur with melancholy, such persons are most apt to be jealous; 'tis Nevisanus' note, An idle woman is presumed to be lascivious, and often jealous. A woman left alone to think, thinks ill; and 'tis not unlikely, for they have no other business to trouble their heads with.

More particular causes be these which follow. Impotency first, when a man is not able of himself to perform those dues which he ought unto his wife: for though he be an honest liver, hurt no man, yet Trebatius the Lawyer may make a question, whether he give every one their own; and therefore when he takes notice of his wants, and perceives her to be more craving, clamorous, unsatiable and prone to lust, than is fit, he begins presently to suspect, that wherein he is defective, she will satisfy herself, she will be pleased by some other means. Cornelius Gallus hath elegantly expressed this humour in an Epigram to his Lycoris:

> She now seeks other youths and other loves,
> Calls me a worn-out, good-for-naught old man.

For this cause is most evident in old men, that are cold and dry by nature, and married to those full of juice, to young wanton wives, with old doting Janivere in Chaucer, they begin to mistrust all is not well.

> ——————— She was yong, and he was olde,
> And therefore he feared to be a cuckolde.

And how should it otherwise be? Old age is a disease of itself, loathsome, full of suspicion and fear; when it is at best, unable, unfit for such matters. As welcome to a young woman as snow in harvest, saith Nevisanus; marry a lusty Maid, and she will surely graft horns on thy head. All women are slippery, often unfaithful to their husbands (as Æneas Sylvius seconds him) but to old men most treacherous: they had rather lie with a corse, than such a one. Youths hate, women despise him. On the other side, many men, saith Hieronymus, are suspicious of their wives, if they be lightly given, but old folks above the rest. Insomuch that she did not complain without a cause, in Apuleius, of an old bald bedridden knave she had to her goodman: Poor woman as I am,

what shall I do? I have an old grim sire to my husband, as bald as a
coot. as little and as unable as a child, a bedful of bones, he keeps all
the doors barred and lockt upon me, woe is me, what shall I do? He
was jealous, and she made him a cuckold for keeping her up: suspicion
without a cause, hard usage, is able of itself to make a woman fly out,
that was otherwise honest, bad usage aggravates the matter. As Nevisanus holds, when a woman thinks her husband watcheth her, she
will sooner offend; they sin openly, all shame is gone, rough handling
makes them worse: as the good wife of Bath in Chaucer brags,

> In his owene grece I made him frye,
> For angre and for verray jealousye.

Of two extremes, this of hard usage is the worst. 'Tis a great fault (for
some men are uxorious) to be too fond of their wives, to dote on them
as Senior Deliro on his Fallace, to be too effeminate. or as some do, to
be sick for their wives, breed children for them, and like the Tiberini
lie in for them, as some birds hatch eggs by turns, they do all women's
offices: Cælius Rhodiginus makes mention of a fellow out of Seneca,
that was so besotted on his wife, he could not endure a moment out of
her company, he wore her scarf when he went abroad next his heart,
and would never drink but in that cup she began first. We have many
such fondlings that are their wives' pack-horses and slaves, (as the
Comical Poet hath it, there's no greater misery to a man than to let his
wife domineer), to carry her muff, dog, and fan, let her wear the
breeches, lay out, spend and do what she will, go and come, whither,
when she will, they give consent.

> Here take my muff, and do you hear, good man;
> Now give me Pearl, and carry you my fan, &c.   (CHALONER)

Many brave and worthy men have trespassed in this kind, and many
noble Senators and soldiers (as Pliny notes) have lost their honour in
being uxorious, so sottishly over-ruled by their wives; and therefore
Cato in Plutarch made a bitter jest on his fellow Citizens, the Romans,
we govern all the world abroad, and our wives at home rule us. These
offend in one extreme; but too hard and too severe, are far more offensive on the other. As just a cause may be long absence of either party,
when they must of necessity be much from home, as Lawyers, Physicians. Mariners, by their professions: or otherwise make frivolous impertinent journeys, tarry long abroad to no purpose, lie out, and are
gadding still, upon small occasions, it must needs yield matter of suspicion, when they use their wives unkindly in the mean time. and never
tarry at home, it cannot choose but engender some such conceit.

If thou be absent long, thy wife then thinks,
Th' art drunk, at ease, or with some pretty minx,
'Tis well with thee, or else beloved of some,
Whilst she, poor soul, doth fare full ill at home.   (TERENCE)

Hippocrates the Physician had a smack of this disease; for when he was to go from home as far as Abdera, and some other remote cities of Greece, he writ to his friend Dionysius (if at least those Epistles be his) to oversee his wife in his absence, (as Apollo set a Raven to watch his Coronis) although she lived in his house with her father and mother, whom he knew would have a care of her; yet that would not satisfy his jealousy, he would have his special friend Dionysius to dwell in his house with her all the time of his peregrination, and to observe her behaviour, how she carried herself in her husband's absence, and that she did not lust after other men: for a woman had need to have an overseer to keep her honest: they are bad by nature, and lightly given all, and if they be not curbed in time, as an unproined tree, they will be full of wild branches, and degenerate of a sudden. Especially in their husband's absence. Though one Lucretia were trusty, and one Penelope, yet Clytæmnestra made Agamemnon cuckold; and no question there be too many of her conditions. If their husbands tarry too long abroad upon unnecessary business, well they may suspect: or if they run one way, their wives at home will fly out another, tit for tat. Or if present, and give them not that content which they ought, (at first unwelcome, soon hateful, the nights in which nothing is accomplished but sleeping), they cannot endure to lie alone, or to fast long. Peter Godefridus, in his second book of Love, and sixth chapter, hath a story out of S. Anthony's life, of a Gentleman, who, by that good man's advice, would not meddle with his wife in the Passion Week, but for his pains she set a pair of horns on his head. Such another he hath out of Abstemius, one persuaded a new married man to forbear the three first nights, and he should all his life time after be fortunate in cattle, but his impatient wife would not tarry so long: well he might speed in cattle, but not in children. Such a tale hath Heinsius of an impotent and slack scholar, a mere student, and a friend of his, that, seeing by chance a fine damsel sing and dance, would needs marry her; the match was soon made, for he was young and rich, of good family, smooth of body, skilled in many arts, like that Apollo in Apuleius. The first night, having liberally taken his liquor (as in that country they do) my fine scholar was so fusled that he no sooner was laid in bed, but he fell fast asleep, never waked till morning, and then much abashed, when the fair morn with purple hue 'gan shine, he made an excuse, I know not what, out of Hippocrates of Cos, &c., and for that time it went current; but when as afterward he did not play the man as he should do, she fell in league with a good fellow, and whilst he sat up late at his study about those Criticisms, mending some hard places in Festus or Pollus, came cold to bed, and would tell her still what he had done, she did not much regard what he said, &c. She would have another matter mended much rather, which he did not perceive was corrupt: thus he continued at his study late, she at her sport elsewhere, enjoying festive nights, hating all scholars for his sake. till at length he began to suspect, and turned a little yellow, as well he might; for it was his own fault; and if men be jealous in such cases (as oft it falls out) the mends is in their own hands, they must thank themselves. Who will pity them, saith Neander, or be much offended with such wives, if they deceive and cornute those that cozened them first? A Lawyer's wife in Aristænetus, because her husband was negligent in his business, slack in his bed-labours, threatened to cornute him: and did not stick to tell Philinna, one of her gossips, as much, and that aloud for him to hear: If he follow other men's matters, and leave his own, I'll have an Orator shall plead my cause. I care not if he know it.

A fourth eminent cause of jealousy may be this, when he that is deformed, and, as Pindar says of Vulcan, without natural graces, hirsute, ragged, yet virtuously given, will marry some fair nice piece. or light housewife, begins to misdoubt (as well he may) she doth not affect him. Beauty and honesty have ever been at odds. Abraham was jealous of his wife, because she was fair: so was Vulcan of his Venus, when he made her creaking shoes, saith Philostratus, that he might hear by them when she stirred, which Mars was not well pleased with. Good cause had Vulcan to do as he did, for she was no honester than she should be. Your fine faces have commonly this fault, and it is hard to find; saith Francis Philelphus in an Epistle to Saxola his friend, a rich man honest, a proper woman not proud or unchaste. Can she be fair and honest too?

Oft has the serpent lain 'neath colored grass,

Beauteous seeming, oft has an evil will

Found purchasers without the husband's knowledge. (HORACE)

He that marries a wife that is snowt fair [or fair-looking] alone, let him look, saith Barbarus, for no better success than Vulcan had with Venus, or Claudius with Messalina. And 'tis impossible almost in such cases the wife should contain, or the good man not be jealous: for when he is so defective, weak, ill proportioned, unpleasing in those parts which women most affect, and she most absolutely fair and able on the other side, if she be not very virtuously given, how can she love him? and although she be not fair, yet if he admire her, and think her so, in his conceit she is absolute, he holds it impossible for any man living not to dote as he doth, to look on her, and not lust, not to covet, and if he be in company with her, not to lay siege to her honesty: or else out of a deep apprehension of his infirmities, deformities, and other men's good parts, out of his own little worth and desert, he distrusts himself (for what is jealousy but distrust?) he suspects she cannot affect him, or be not so kind and loving as she should, she certainly loves some other man better than himself.

Nevisanus will have barrenness to be a main cause of Jealousy. If her husband cannot play the man, some other shall, they will leave no remedies unassayed, and thereupon the good man grows jealous; I could give an instance, but be it as it is.

I find this reason given by some men, because they have been formerly naught themselves, they think they may be so served by others, they turned up trump before the cards were shuffled, they shall have therefore like for like.

> *Wretch as I was, I taught her bad to be,*
> *And now mine own sly tricks are put on me.*   (TIBULLUS)

As the saying is, ill dispositions cause ill suspicions.

> *There is none jealous, I durst pawn my life,*
> *But he that hath defil'd another's wife,*
> *And for that he himself hath gone astray,*
> *He straightway thinks his wife will tread that way.*   (WITHER)

To these two above named causes, or incendiaries of this rage, I may very well annex those circumstances of time, place, persons, by which it ebbs and flows, the fuel of this fury, as Vives truly observes; and such like accidents or occasions, proceeding from the parties themselves, or others, which much aggravate and intend this suspicious humour. For many men are so lasciviously given, either out of a depraved nature, or too much liberty, which they do assume unto themselves, by reason of their greatness, in that they are Noblemen (for license to sin and company in the sinning are great motives) though their own wives be never so fair, noble, virtuous, honest, wise, able, and well given, they must have change.

> *Who being match'd to wives most virtuous,*
> *Noble and fair, fly out lascivious.*   (MARULLUS)

What's granted is not wanted, that which is ordinary is unpleasant. Nero (saith Tacitus) abhorred Octavia his own wife, a noble virtuous Lady, and loved Acte, a base quean in respect. Cerinthus rejected Sulpicia, a nobleman's daughter, and courted a poor servant maid. 'Tis more pleasure to reap in strange fields, for that stolen waters be more pleasant: or, as Vitellius the Emperor was wont to say, the most delightful loves are those that are most dangerous, like stolen Venison, still the sweetest is that love, which is most difficultly attained: they like better to hunt by stealth in another man's walk, than to have the fairest course that may be at game of their own.

> *As Sun and Moon in Heaven change their course,*
> *So they change loves, though often to the worse.*   (PROPERTIUS)

Or that some fair object so forcibly moves them, they cannot contain themselves, be it heard or seen, they will be at it. Nessus the Centaur, was by agreement to carry Hercules and his wife over the River Evenus; no sooner had he set Deianira on the other side, but he would have offered violence unto her, leaving Hercules to swim over as he could: and though her husband was a spectator, yet would he not desist till Hercules with a poisoned arrow shot him to death. Neptune saw by chance that Thessalian Tyro, Enipeus' wife, he forthwith in the fury of his lust counterfeited her husband's habit, and made him cuckold. Tarquin heard Collatine commend his wife, and was so far enraged, that in midst of the night to her he went. Theseus stole Ariadne, ravished that Trœzenian Anaxo, Antiope, and, now being old, Helena, a girl not yet ready for an husband. Great men are most part thus affected all, as an horse they neigh, saith Jeremiah, after their neighbour's wives, and if they be in company with other women, though in their own wives' presence, they must be courting and dallying with them. Juno in Lucian, complains of Jupiter, that he was still kissing Ganymede before her face, which did not a little offend her: and besides, he was a counterfeit Amphitryo, a bull, a swan, a golden shower, and played many such bad pranks, too long, too shameful, to relate.

Or that they care little for their own Ladies, and fear no Laws, they dare freely keep whores at their wives' noses. 'Tis too frequent with noblemen to be dishonest; as he [Seneca] said long since, piety, chastity, and such like virtues are for private men; not to be much looked after in great Courts: and which Suetonius said of the good Princes of his time, they might be all engraven in one Ring, we may truly hold of chaste potentates of our age. For great personages will familiarly run out in this kind, and yield occasion of offence. Montaigne in his Essays gives instances in Cæsar, Mahomet the Turk, that sacked Constantinople, and Ladislaus King of Naples, that besieged Florence: great men, and great soldiers, are commonly great ————— &c., 'tis approved, they are good doers. Mars and Venus are equally balanced in their actions.

> *A dove within a head-piece made her nest,*
> *'Twixt Mars and Venus see an interest.*   (PETRONIUS)

Especially if they be bald, for bald men have ever been suspicious (read more in Aristotle), as Galba, Otho, Domitian, and remarkable Cæsar amongst the rest. Citizens, look to your wives, we are bringing a bald adulterer *; besides, this bald Cæsar, saith Curio in Suetonius, was husband to all women; he made love to Eunoe, Queen of Mauritania, to Cleopatra, to Postumia, wife to Servius Sulpicius, to Lollia, wife to Gabinius, to Tertulla of Crassus, and to Mucia, Pompey's wife, and I know not how many besides: and well he might, for if all be true that I have read, he had a license to lie with whom he list. Among the other honors decreed to Cæsar (as Suetonius and Dion relate) was the right to couple with any woman he pleased. Every private History will yield such variety of instances: otherwise good, wise, discreet men, virtuous and valiant, but too faulty in this. Priam had fifty sons, but seventeen alone lawfully begotten. Philippus Bonus left fourteen bastards. Laurence Medices a good Prince and a wise, but, saith Machiavel, prodigiously lascivious. None so valiant as Castruccius Castrucanus, but as the said author hath it, none so incontinent as he was. And 'tis not only predominant in Grandees, this fault: but if you will take a great man's testimony, 'tis familiar with every base soldier in France, (and elsewhere I think). This vice (saith mine Author) is so common with us in France, that he is of no account, a mere coward, not worthy the name of a soldier, that is not a notorious whoremaster. In Italy he is not a gentleman, that besides his wife hath not a Courtesan and a mistress. 'Tis no marvel then, if poor women in such cases be jealous, when they shall see themselves manifestly neglected, contemned, loathed, unkindly used: their disloyal husbands to entertain others in their rooms, and many times to court Ladies to their faces: other men's wives to wear their jewels: how shall a poor woman in such a case moderate her passion?

> *How felt you then, Dido, beholding this?*   (VIRGIL)

How, on the other side, shall a poor man contain himself from this feral malady, when he shall see so manifest signs of his wife's inconstancy? when as, like Milo's wife, she dotes upon every young man she sees, or as Martial's Sota, deserts her husband and follows Clitus. Though her husband be proper and tall, fair and lovely to behold, able

* The song sung by Cæsar's soldiers on the occasion of his Gallic triumph.

to give contentment to any one woman, yet she will taste of the forbidden fruit: Juvenal's Iberina to an hair, she is as well pleased with
one eye as one man. If a young gallant come by chance into her presence, a Fastidius Brisk, that can wear his clothes well in fashion, with a
lock, gingling spur, a feather, that can cringe, and withal compliment,
court a Gentlewoman, she raves upon him. O what a lovely proper man
he was, another Hector, an Alexander, a goodly man, a demi-god, how
sweetly he carried himself, with how comely a grace, such were his eyes,
his hands, his air, how neatly he did wear his clothes!

> *What gallant mien, how stout of spirit and arms!*   (VIRGIL)

how bravely did he discourse, ride, sing, and dance, &c. and then she
begins to loathe her husband, repugnant to his kiss, to hate him and his
filthy beard, his goatish complexion, as Doris said of Polyphemus, he is
a rammy fulsome fellow, a goblin-faced fellow, he smells, he stinks, he
belches onions and garlic, how like a dizzard, a fool, an ass he looks, how
like a clown he behaves himself! she will not come near him by her
good will, but wholly rejects him, as Venus did her fuliginous Vulcan at
last,

> *No god will have him at his board, no goddess in her bed.*   (VIRGIL)

So did Lucretia, a Lady of Siena, after she had but seen Euryalus,
thought but of him when she returned home, she would not hold her
eyes off him in his presence,

> *So noble was his air and grace of mien,*   (VIRGIL)

and in his absence could think of none but him, she loathed her husband
forthwith, might not abide him.

> *All against the laws of matrimony,*
> *She did abhor her husband's phis'nomy,*

and sought all opportunity to see her sweetheart again. Now when the
good man shall observe his wife so lightly given, to be so free, and
familiar with every gallant, her immodesty and wantonness, (as Camerarius notes) it must needs yield matter of suspicion to him, when she
still pranks up herself beyond her means and fortunes, makes impertinent journeys, unnecessary visitations, stays out so long, with such and
such companions, so frequently goes to plays, masks, feasts, and all
publick meetings, shall use such immodest gestures, free speeches, and
withal shew some distaste of her own husband; how can he choose,
though he were another Socrates, but be suspicious, and instantly jealous?

> *She'll force him to transgress Socratic bounds.*   (CHALONER)

More especially when he shall take notice of their more secret and sly

tricks, which to cornute their husbands they commonly use, (while
you're at the games, she's making game of you), they pretend love,
honour, chastity, and seem to respect them before all men living, saints
in shew, so cunningly can they dissemble, they will not so much as look
upon another man in his presence, so chaste, so religious, and so devout,
they cannot endure the name or sight of a quean, an harlot, out upon
her! and in their outward carriage are most loving and officious, will
kiss their husband, and hang about his neck, (dear husband, sweet husband) and with a composed countenance, salute him, especially when
he comes home, or if he go from home, weep, sigh, lament, and take
upon them to be sick and swoon, (like Jocundo's wife in Ariosto, when
her husband was to depart) and yet arrant, &c. they care not for him,

> Aye me, the thought (quoth she) makes me so 'fraid,
> That scarce the breath abideth in my breast;
> Peace, my sweet love and wife, Jocundo said,
> And weeps as fast, and comforts her his best, &c.
> All this might not assuage the woman's pain,
> Needs must I die before you come again,
> Nor how to keep my life I can devise,
> The doleful days and nights I shall sustain,
> From meat my mouth, from sleep will keep mine eyes, &c.
> That very night that went before the morrow,
> That he had pointed surely to depart,
> Jocundo's wife was sick, and swoon'd for sorrow,
> Amid his arms, so heavy was her heart.

And yet for all these counterfeit tears and protestations, Jocundo coming back in all haste for a jewel he had forgot,

> His chaste and yoke-fellow he found
> Yok'd with a knave, all honesty neglected,
> The adulterer sleeping very sound,
> Yet by his face was easily detected:
> A beggar's brat bred by him from his cradle,
> And now was riding on his master's saddle.

Thus can they cunningly counterfeit. as Platina describes their customs,
kiss their husbands whom they had rather see hanging on a Gallows,
and swear they love him dearer than their own lives, whose soul they
would not ransom for their little dogs. Many of them seem to be precise
and holy forsooth, and will go to such a Church, to hear such a good
man by all means, an excellent man. when 'tis for no other intent (as he
follows it) than to see and to be seen, to observe what fashions are in

use, to meet some Pandar, Bawd, Monk, Friar, or to entice some good fellow. For they persuade themselves, as Nevisanus shews, that it is neither sin nor shame to lie with a Lord or a parish Priest, if he be a proper man, and though she kneel often, and pray devoutly, 'tis (saith Platina) not for her husband's welfare, or children's good, or any friend, but for her sweetheart's return, her Pandar's health. If her husband would have her go, she feigns herself sick, her head aches, and she can not stir : but if her Paramour ask as much, she is for him in all seasons, at all hours of the night. In the kingdom of Malabar, and about Goa in the East-Indies, the women are so subtile, that with a certain drink they give them to drive away cares as they say, they will make them sleep for twenty-four hours, or so intoxicate them that they can remember nought of that they saw done, or heard, and by washing of their feet, restore them again, and so make their husbands cuckolds to their faces. Some are ill disposed at all times, to all persons they like, others more wary to some few, at such and such seasons, as Augusta Livia, she takes no passenger unless the ship is full [that is, only dallied with lovers when already pregnant by her husband]. But as he said,

> No pen could write, no tongue attain to tell,
> By force of eloquence, or help of art,
> Of women's treacheries the hundredth part.   (ARIOSTO)

Both, to say truth, are often faulty ; men and women give just occasions in this humour of discontent, aggravate and yield matter of suspicion : but most part of the chief causes proceed from other adventitious accidents and circumstances, though the parties be free, and both well given themselves. The undiscreet carriage of some lascivious gallant (and on the other hand of some light woman) by his often frequenting of an house, bold unseemly gestures, may make a breach, and by his over familiarity, if he be inclined to yellowness, colour him quite out. If he be poor, basely born, saith Benedetto Varchi, and otherwise unhandsome, he suspects him the less, but if a proper man, such as was Alcibiades in Greece, and Castruccius Castrucanus in Italy, well descended, commendable for his good parts, he taketh on the more, and watcheth his doings. Theodosius the Emperor gave his wife Eudocia a golden apple, when he was a suitor to her, which she long after bestowed upon a young gallant in the Court, of her especial acquaintance. The Emperor, espying this apple in his hand, suspected forthwith, more than was, his wife's dishonesty, banished him the Court, and from that day following forbare to accompany her any more. A rich merchant had a fair wife ; according to his custom he went to travel ; in his absence a good fellow tempted his wife: she denied him, yet he, dying a little after, gave her a legacy for the love he bore her. At his return her jealous husband, because she had got more by land than he had done at Sea, turned her away upon suspicion.

Now when those other circumstances of time and place, opportunity and importunity, shall concur, what will they not effect?

Fair opportunity can win the coyest she that is,
So wisely he takes time, as he'll be sure he will not miss:
Then he that loves her gamesome vein, and tempers toys with art,
Brings love that swimmeth in her eyes, to dive into her heart.

As at Plays, Masks, great feasts and banquets, one singles out his wife to dance, another courts her in his presence, a third tempts her, a fourth insinuates with a pleasing compliment, a sweet smile, ingratiates himself with an amphibological [or equivocal] speech; as that merry companion in the Satirist did to his Glycerium, sitting by her, and paddling palms and pinching fingers;

Take what you will from my garden-close,
If you'll give me what in your garden grows;

with many such, &c., and then, as he [Chaucer] saith,

𝕾𝔥𝔢 𝔪𝔞𝔶 𝔫𝔬 𝔴𝔥𝔭𝔩𝔢 𝔦𝔫 𝔠𝔥𝔞𝔰𝔱𝔦𝔱𝔢𝔢 𝔞𝔟𝔭𝔡𝔢,
𝕿𝔥𝔞𝔱 𝔦𝔰 𝔞𝔰𝔰𝔞𝔦𝔩𝔩𝔢𝔡 𝔲𝔭𝔬𝔫 𝔢𝔟𝔢𝔯𝔭 𝔰𝔭𝔡𝔢.

For after a great feast,

In wine a woman knows not her own husband. (PROPERTIUS)

Noah (saith Hierome) shewed his nakedness in his drunkenness, which for six hundred years he had covered in soberness. Lot lay with his daughters in his drink, as Cinyras with Myrrha,

For what does love in drink scruple to do? (JUVENAL)

The most continent may be overcome, or if otherwise they keep bad company, they are modest of themselves, and dare not offend, confirmed by others, grow impudent, and confident, and get an ill habit.

One violates her bed for gain, another
Seduces other wives to have companions
In guilt. (EURIPIDES)

Or if they dwell in suspected places, as in an infamous Inn, near some Stews, near Monks, Friars, Nevisanus adds, where be many tempters and solicitors, idle persons, that frequent their companies, it may give just cause of suspicion. Martial of old inveighed against them that counterfeited a disease to go to the Bath, for so, many times,

Penelope comes back an unchaste Helen.

Æneas Sylvius puts in a caveat against Princes' Courts, because there be so many brave Suitors to tempt, &c. If you leave her in such a place, you shall likely find her in company you like not, either they come to her, or she is gone to them. Kornmannus makes a doubting jest in his lascivious Country, How much discount on the chastity of a virgin to whom Scholars have frequent approach? And Baldus, the Lawyer, scoffs on, when a Scholar talks with a maid, or another man's wife in private, it is presumed he saith not a Pater Noster. Or if I shall see a Monk or a Friar climb up by a ladder at midnight into a Virgin's or Widow's chamber-window, I shall hardly think he then goes to administer the Sacraments, or to take her Confession. These are the ordinary causes of jealousy, which are intended or remitted, as the circumstances vary.

MEMBER 2

Symptoms of Jealousy, fear, sorrow, suspicion, strange actions, gestures, outrages, locking up, oaths, trials, laws, &c.

OF all passions, as I have already proved, Love is most violent, and of those bitter potions which this Love Melancholy affords, this bastard Jealousy is the greatest, as appears by those prodigious Symptoms which it hath, and that it produceth. For besides Fear and Sorrow, which is common to all Melancholy, anxiety of mind, suspicion, aggravation, restless thoughts, paleness, meagreness, neglect of business, and the like, these men are farther yet misaffected, and in an higher strain. 'Tis a more vehement passion, a more furious perturbation, a bitter pain, a fire, a pernicious curiosity, a gall corrupting the honey of our life, madness, vertigo, plague, hell, they are more than ordinarily disquieted, they lose the blessing of peace of mind, as Chrysostom observes; and though they be rich, keep sumptuous tables, be nobly allied, yet they are most miserable, they are more than ordinarily discontent, more sad, more than ordinarily suspicious. Jealousy, saith Vives, begets unquietness in the mind night and day: he hunts after every word he hears, every whisper, and amplifies it to himself (as all melancholy men do in other matters) with a most unjust calumny of others, he misinterprets every thing is said or done, most apt to mistake or misconster, he pries into every corner, follows close, observes to an hair. 'Tis proper to Jealousy so to do,

> *Pale hag, infernal fury, pleasure's smart,*
> *Envy's observer, prying in every part.* (DANIEL)

Besides those strange gestures of staring, frowning, grinning, rolling of eyes, menacing, ghastly looks, broken pace, interrupt, precipitate, half-turns. He will sometimes sigh, weep, sob for anger,

Such thunder-storms in sooth pour down their showers,

swear and belie, slander any man, curse, threaten, brawl, scold, fight; and sometimes again flatter, and speak fair, ask forgiveness, kiss and coll, condemn his rashness and folly, vow, protest and swear he will never do so again; and then eftsoons, impatient as he is, rave, roar, and lay about him like a mad man, thump her sides, drag her about perchance, drive her out of doors, send her home, he will be divorced forthwith, she is a whore, &c., by and by with all submiss compliment intreat her fair, and bring her in again, he loves her dearly, she is his sweet, most kind, and loving wife, he will not change, not leave her for a Kingdom; so he continues off and on, as the toy takes him, the object moves him, but most part brawling, fretting, unquiet he is, accusing and suspecting not strangers only, but Brothers and Sisters, Father and Mother, nearest and dearest friends. He thinks with those Italians,

Who doth it not in the family
Is one who doth it never or seldomly.

And through fear conceives unto himself things almost incredible and impossible to be effected. As an Heron when she fishes, still prying on all sides, or as a Cat doth a Mouse, his eye is never off hers; he gloats on him, on her, accurately observing on whom she looks, who looks at her, what she saith, doth, at dinner, at supper, sitting, walking, at home, abroad, he is the same, still inquiring, mandering [or crying for her], gazing, listening, affrighted with every small object; why did she smile, why did she pity him, commend him? why did she drink twice to such a man? why did she offer to kiss, to dance? &c., a whore, a whore, an arrant whore! All this he confesseth in the Poet,

Each thing affrights me, I do fear,
Ah pardon me my fear,
I doubt a man is hid within
The clothes that thou dost wear.　(PROPERTIUS)

Is't not a man in woman's apparel? is not somebody in that great chest, or behind the door, or hangings, or in some of those barrels? May not a man steal in at the window with a ladder of ropes, or come down the chimney, have a false key, or get in when he is asleep? If a Mouse do but stir, or the wind blow, a casement clatter, that's the villain, there he is; by his good will no man shall see her, salute her, speak with her, she shall not go forth of his sight, so much as to do her needs. Argus did not so keep his Cow, that watchful Dragon the Golden fleece, or Cerberus the coming in of Hell, as he keeps his wife. If a dear friend or near kinsman come as guest to his house, to visit him, he will never let him be out of his own sight and company, lest peradventure, &c. If the necessity of his business be such that he must go from home, he doth either lock her up, or commit her with a deal of injunctions and protestations to some trusty friends, him and her he sets and bribes to oversee: one servant is set in his absence to watch another, and all to observe his wife, and yet all this will not serve, though his business be very urgent, he will, when he is half way, come back again in all post haste, rise from supper, or at midnight, and be gone, and sometimes leave his business undone, and as a stranger court his own wife in some disguised habit. Though there be no danger at all, no cause of suspicion, she live in such a place, where Messalina herself could not be dishonest if she would, yet he suspects her as much as if she were in a bawdy house, some Prince's Court, or in a common Inn, where all comers might have free access. He calls her on a sudden all to naught, she is a strumpet, a light-housewife, a bitch, an arrant whore. No persuasion, no protestation, can divert this passion, nothing can ease him, secure or give him satisfaction. It is most strange to report, what outrageous acts by men and women have been committed in this kind: by women especially, that will run after their husbands into all places and companies, as Jovianus Pontanus' wife did by him, follow him whithersoever he went, it matters not, or upon what business, raving, like Juno in the Tragedy, miscalling, cursing, swearing, and mistrusting every one she sees. Gomesius, in his third Book of the life and deeds of Francis Ximenes, sometime Archbishop of Toledo, hath a strange story of that incredible jealousy of Joan Queen of Spain, wife to King Philip, mother of Ferdinand and Charles the Fifth, Emperors; when her husband Philip, either for that he was tired with his wife's jealousy, or had some great business, went into the Low Countries, she was so impatient and melancholy upon his departure, that she would scarce eat her meat, or converse with any man; and though she were with child, the season of the year very bad, the wind against her, in all haste she would to sea after him. Neither Isabella her Queen Mother, the Archbishop, or any other friend, could persuade her to the contrary, but she would after him. When she was now come into the Low Countries, and kindly entertained by her husband, she could not contain herself, but in a rage ran upon a yellow-hair'd wench, with whom she suspected her husband to be naught, cut off her hair, did beat her black and blue, and so dragged her about. It is an ordinary thing for women in such cases to scrat the faces, slit the noses, of such as they suspect; as Henry the Second's importune [or cruel] Juno did by Rosamond at Woodstock: for she complains in a modern Poet, she scarce spake,

> But flies with eager fury to my face,
> Offering me most unwomanly disgrace.
> Look how a tigress, &c.
> So fell she on me in outrageous wise,
> As could disdain and jealousy devise.   (DANIEL)

Or if it be so they dare not, or cannot execute any such tyrannical injustice, they will miscall, rail and revile, bear them deadly hate and malice, as Tacitus observes, the hatred of a jealous woman is inseparable against such as she suspects.

> Winds, weapons, flames make not such hurly-burly,
> As raving women turn all topsy-turvy.   (SENECA)

So did Agrippina by Lollia and Calpurnia in the days of Claudius. But women are sufficiently curbed in such cases, the rage of men is more eminent, and frequently put in practice. See but with what rigour those jealous husbands tyrannize over their poor wives. In Greece, Spain, Italy, Turkey, Africa, Asia, and generally over all those hot Countries, your women are your land, to be ploughed at your will; Mahomet in his Alcoran gives this power to men; your wives are as your land, till them, use them, intreat them fair or foul, as you will yourselves.

> I' faith, women live under hard conditions,   (PLAUTUS)

they lock them still in their houses, which are as so many prisons to them, will suffer nobody to come at them, or their wives to be seen abroad. They must not so much as look out. And if they be great persons, they have Eunuchs to keep them, as the Grand Seignior among the Turks, the Sophies of Persia, those Tartarian Mogors, and Kings of China. Saith Riccius, they geld innumerable infants to this purpose; the King of China maintains 10,000 Eunuchs in his family to keep his wives. The Xeriffes of Barbary keep their Courtesans in such strict manner, that if any man come but in sight of them, he dies for it; and if they chance to see a man, and do not instantly cry out, though from their windows, they must be put to death. The Turks have I know not how many black deformed Eunuchs (for the white serve for other ministeries) to this purpose sent commonly from Egypt, deprived in their childhood of all their privities, and brought up in the Seraglio at Constantinople, to keep their wives: which are so penned up they may not confer with any living man, or converse with younger women, have a Cucumber or Carrot sent in to them for their diet, but sliced, for fear,

———— &c., and so live, and are left alone to their unchaste thoughts all the days of their lives. The vulgar sort of women, if at any time they come abroad, which is very seldom, to visit one another, or to go to their Baths, are so covered, that no man can see them, as the Matrons were in old Rome, carried in a litter or chair, so Dion and Seneca record: they all walk veil'd, which Alexander ab Alexandro relates of the Parthians, which, with Andreas Tiraquellus his Commentator. I rather think should be understood of Persians. I have not yet said all, they do not only lock them up, but lock up their private parts: hear what Bembus relates, in book 6 of his Venetian History, of those inhabitants that dwell about Quiloa in Africa. The Lusitanians, he saith, border upon certain tribes who sew up the parts of female infants at birth, leaving a way for the urine, and when they grow up, give them in marriage thus sewn up, so that it is the husband's first business to cut apart the fettered nether lips of the maiden. In some parts of Greece at this day, like those old Jews, they will not believe their wives are honest, without seeing the sheet stained from the first night; our countryman Sands, in his Peregrination, saith, it is severely observed in Zacynthus, or, Zante; and Leo Afer in his time at Fez, in Africa, they will not credit virginity without seeing the bloody napkin, otherwise she is sent back shamed to her parents. Those sheets are publickly shewed by their Parents, and kept as a sign of incorrupt Virginity. The Jews of old examined their maids as to the condition of the membrane called Hymen, which Laurentius in his Anatomy, and others, copiously confute: 'tis no sufficient trial, they contend. And yet others again defend it, Gaspar Bartholinus, Pinæus of Paris, Albertus Magnus, &c., and think they speak too much in favour of women. Ludovicus Boncialus asserts that that natural constriction of the labia, in which they would have virginity to consist, can be brought about by astringent medicines; and if they have been deflowered, wise women (he says) thus befool us. Alsarius Crucius Genuensis says the same. So Avicenna, &c. An old bawdy nurse in Aristænetus (like that Spanish Cœlestina, who made women of five thousand virgins, and by her art restored as many women to virginity), when a fair maid of her acquaintance wept & made her moan to her, how she had been deflowered, and now ready to be married, was afraid it would be perceived, comfortably replied, Fear not, daughter, I'll teach thee a trick to help it. But this is aside from our path. To what end are all those Astrological questions, whether a virgin, whether chaste, whether a woman? and such strange absurd trials in Albertus Magnus, &c., by stones, perfumes, to make them piss, and confess ?

know not what in their sleep; some jealous brain was the first founder of them.

And to what passion may we ascribe those severe laws against jealousy, adulterers, as amongst the Hebrews, amongst the Egyptians (read Bohemus of the Carthaginians, of Turks), amongst the Athenians of old. Italians at this day, wherein they are to be severely punished, cut in pieces, burned, buried alive, with several expurgations [or trials of virtue], &c., are they not as so many symptoms of incredible jealousy? we may say the same of those Vestal Virgins that fetched water in a sieve, as Tatia did in Rome, in the year 800 from the founding of the city, before the Senators; and Æmilia, innocent virgin, that ran over hot irons, as Emma, Edward the Confessor's mother, did, the King himself being a spectator, with the like. We read in Nicephorus that Cunegunda, the wife of Henricus Bavarus, Emperor, suspected of adultery, trod upon red hot coulters, and had no harm: such another story we find in Regino; in Aventinus and Sigonius, of Charles the Third, and his wife Richarda, in the year 887, that was so purged with hot irons. Pausanias saith that he was once an eye-witness of such a miracle at Diana's Temple, a maid without any harm at all walked upon burning coals. Pius the Second, in his description of Europe, relates as much, that it was commonly practised at Diana's Temple, for women to go barefoot over hot coals, to try their honesties. Plinius, Solinus, and many writers, make mention of Feronia's Temple, and Dionysius Halicarnasseus of Memnon's statue, which were used to this purpose; Tatius of Pan his Cave (much like old S. Wilfrid's needle in Yorkshire), wherein they did use to try maids, whether they were honest * : when Leucippe went in, a sweet sound was heard. Austin relates many such examples, all which Lavater contends to be done by the illusion of Devils; though Thomas ascribes it to good Angels. Some, saith Austin, compel their wives to swear they be honest, as if perjury were a lesser sin than adultery; some consult Oracles, as Pheron that blind King of Egypt. Others reward, as those old Romans use to do; if a woman were contented with one man, she had a crown of Chastity bestowed on her. When all this will not serve, saith Alexander Gaguinus, the Muscovites, if they suspect their wives, will beat them till they confess; and if that will not avail, like those wild Irish, be divorced at their pleasures, or

---

* " Within the Church. St. Wilfrid's Needle was in our grandfather's remembrance very famous. A narrow hole this was in the Crypts, or close vaulted room under the ground, whereby women's honesty was tried. For such as were chaste did easily pass through, but as many as had played false were miraculously, I know not how, held fast, and could not creep through." — Camden's Britannia.

else knock them on the heads, as the old Gauls have done in former ages. Of this Tyranny of Jealousy, read more in Parthenius, Camerarius, Cælia's Epistles, Tho. Chaloner, Ariosto, Felix Platerus, &c.

MEMBER 3

Prognosticks of Jealousy, Despair, Madness, to make away themselves and others

THOSE which are jealous, most part, if they be not otherwise relieved, proceed from suspicion to hatred, from hatred to frenzy, madness, injury, murder, and despair.

> *A plague by whose most damnable effect,*
> *Divers in deep despair to die have sought,*
> *By which a man to madness near is brought,*
> *As well with causeless as with just suspect.*   (ARIOSTO)

In their madness many times, saith Vives, they make away themselves, and others. Which induceth Cyprian to call it a fruitful mischief, the seminary of offences, and fountain of murders. Tragical examples are too common in this kind, both new and old, in all ages, as of Cephalus and Procris, Pheron of Egypt, Tereus, Atreus, and Thyestes. Alexander Pheræus was murdered of his wife, on suspicion of keeping a mistress, Tully saith. Antoninus Verus was so made away by Lucilla; Demetrius, the son of Antigonus, and Nicanor, by their wives; Hercules poisoned by Deianira, Cæcinna murdered by Vespasian, Justina a Roman Lady by her husband. Amestris, Xerxes' wife, because she found her husband's cloak in Masistes his house, cut off Masistes his wife's paps, and gave them to the dogs, flayed her besides, and cut off her ears, lips, tongue, and slit the nose of Artaynta her daughter. Our late writers are full of such outrages.

Paulus Æmilius, in his History of France, hath a Tragical story of Chilpericus the First his death, made away by Frédégonde his Queen. In a jealous humour he came from hunting, and stole behind his wife, as she was dressing and combing her head in the Sun, gave her a familiar touch with his wand, which she mistaking for her lover, said, Ah, Landre, a good Knight should strike before, and not behind: but when she saw herself betrayed by his presence, she instantly took order to make him away. Hierome Osorius, in the eleventh book of the deeds of Emanuel, King of Portugal, to this effect hath a Tragical Narration of

one Ferdinandus Calderia, that wounded Gotherinus, a noble Country-
man of his, at Goa in the East Indies, and cut off one of his legs, for
that he looked, as he thought, too familiarly upon his wife, which was
afterwards a cause of many quarrels, and much bloodshed. Guianerius
speaks of a silly jealous fellow, that seeing his child new born, included
in a kell, thought sure a Franciscan, that used to come to his house, was
the father of it, it was so like the Friar's Cowl, and thereupon threatened the Friar to kill him: Fulgosus, of a woman in Narbonne, that cut
off her husband's privities in the night, because she thought he played
false with her. The story of Jonuses Bassa, and fair Manto his wife, is
well known to such as have read the Turkish History, and that of Joan
of Spain, of which I treated in my former Section. Her jealousy, saith
Gomesius, was cause of both their deaths: King Philip died for grief a
little after, as Martian his Physician gave it out, and she for her part,
after a melancholy discontented life, misspent in lurking holes and
corners, made an end of her miseries. Felix Plater, in the first book of
his Observations, hath many such instances, of a Physician of his acquaintance, that was first mad through jealousy, and afterwards desperate; of a Merchant that killed his wife in the same humour, and after
precipitated himself [from a window]; of a Doctor of Law, that cut
off his man's nose: of a Painter's wife in Basil, in the year 1600, that
was mother of nine children, and had been 27 years married, yet afterwards jealous, and so impatient, that she became desperate, and would
neither eat nor drink in her own house, for fear her husband should
poison her. 'Tis a common sign this; for when once the humours are
stirred, and the imagination misaffected, it will vary itself in divers
forms; and many such absurd symptoms will accompany even madness
itself. Sckenkius hath an example of a jealous woman, that by this
means had many fits of the mother: and in his first book, of some that
through jealousy ran mad: of a Baker that gelded himself to try his
wife's honesty, &c. Such examples are too common.

MEMBER 4

SUBSECTION 1 — *Cure of Jealousy: by avoiding occasions, not to be
idle: of good counsel: to contemn it, not to watch or lock them up:
to dissemble it, &c.*

As of all other Melancholy, some doubt whether this malady may be
cured or no, they think 'tis like the Gout, or Switzers, whom we com-

monly call Walloons, those hired Soldiers, if once they take possession
of a Castle they can never be got out.

> *This is that cruel wound, against whose smart*
> *No liquor's force prevails, or any plaster,*
> *No skill of stars, no depth of magick art,*
> *Devisèd by that great clerk Zoroaster;*
> *A wound that so infects the soul and heart,*
> *As all our sense and reason it doth master:*
> *A wound whose pang and torment is so durable,*
> *As it may rightly callèd be incurable.*   (ARIOSTO)

Yet what I have formerly said of other Melancholy, I will say again,
it may be cured, or mitigated at least, by some contrary passion, good
counsel and persuasion, if it be withstood in the beginning, maturely
resisted, and as those Ancients hold, the nails of it be pared before
they grow too long. No better means to resist or repel it, than by avoiding idleness, to be still seriously busied about some matters of impor-
tance, to drive out those vain fears, foolish fantasies, and irksome suspicions out of his head, and then to be persuaded by his judicious
friends, to give ear to their good counsel and advice, and wisely to consider, how much he discredits himself, his friends, dishonours his children,
disgraceth his family, publisheth his shame, and as a Trumpeter of his
own misery, divulgeth, macerates, grieves himself and others; what an
argument of weakness it is, how absurd a thing in its own nature, how
ridiculous, how brutish a passion, how sottish, how odious; for as
Hierome well hath it, others hate him, and at last he hates himself for
it; how hare-brain a disease, mad and furious! If he will but hear them
speak, no doubt he may be cured. Joan, Queen of Spain, of whom I
have formerly spoken, under pretence of changing air, was sent to
Complutum, or Alcala de Henares, where Ximenes the Archbishop of
Toledo then lived, that by his good counsel (as for the present she was)
she might be eased. For a disease of the soul, if concealed, tortures and
overturns it, and by no physick can sooner be removed than by a discreet man's comfortable speeches. I will not here insert any consolatory
sentences to this purpose, or forestall any man's invention, but leave it
every one to dilate and amplify as he shall think fit in his own judgement: let him advise with Siracides. *Be not jealous over the wife of*
thy bosom; read that comfortable and pithy speech to this purpose of
Ximenes in the Author himself, as it is recorded by Gomesius: consult
with Chaloner, or Cælia in her Epistles, &c. Only this I will add, that
if it be considered aright, which causeth this jealous passion, be it just

or unjust, whether with or without cause, true or false, it ought not so heinously to be taken; 'tis no such real or capital matter, that it should make so deep a wound. 'Tis a blow that hurts not, an insensible smart, grounded many times upon false suspicion alone, and so fostered by a sinister conceit. If she be not dishonest, he troubles and macerates himself without a cause; or put case, which is the worst, he be a cuckold, it cannot be helped, the more he stirs in it, the more he aggravates his own misery. How much better were it in such a case to dissemble, or contemn it! why should that be feared, which cannot be redressed? Saith Vives, many women when they see there is no remedy, have been pacified; and shall men be more jealous than women? 'Tis some comfort in such a case to have companions,

'Tis a relief to have companions in misery.

Who can say he is free? who can assure himself he is not one already, or secure himself as to the future? If it were his case alone, it were hard; but being as it is almost a common calamity, 'tis not so grievously to be taken. If a man have a lock, which every man's key will open, as well as his own, why should he think to keep it private to himself? In some Countries they make nothing of it, saith Leo Afer, in many parts of Africa (if she be past fourteen) there's not a Nobleman that marries a maid, or that hath a chaste wife; 'tis so common; as the Moon gives horns once a month to the world, do they to their husbands at least. And 'tis most part true which that Caledonian Lady, Argentocoxus a British Prince his wife, told Julia Augusta, when she took her up for dishonesty, We Britons are naught at least with some few choice men of the better sort, but you Romans lie with every base knave, you are a company of common whores. Severus the Emperor in his time made laws for the restraint of this vice; and as Dion Nicæus relates in his life, three thousand cuckold-makers, or as Philo calls them, false coiners, and clippers of nature's money, were summoned into the Court at once. And yet, the Miller sees not all the water that goes by his mill: no doubt, but as in our days, these were of the Commonalty, all the great ones were not so much as called in question for it. Martial's Epigram, I suppose, might have been generally applied in those licentious times, thy goods, lands, money, wits, are thine own, but, neighbour Candidus, your wife is common. Husband and Cuckold in that age, it seems, were reciprocal terms; the Emperors themselves did wear Actæon's badge; how many Cæsars might I reckon up together, and what a catalogue of cornuted Kings and Princes in every story! Agamemnon, Menelaus, Philip of Greece, Ptolemæus of Egypt, Lucullus, Cæsar, Pompeius,

Cato. Augustus, Antonius, Antoninus, &c., that wore fair plumes of Bull's feathers in their crests. The bravest Soldiers and most Heroical spirits could not avoid it. They have been active and passive in this business, they have either given or taken horns. King Arthur, whom we call one of the Nine Worthies, for all his great valour, was unworthily served by Mordred one of his Round-Table Knights: and Guithera, or Helena Alba, his fair wife, as Leland interprets it, was an arrant honest woman. Saith mine Author, I could willingly wink at a fair Lady's faults, but that I am bound by the laws of History to tell the truth: against his will, God knows, did he write it, and so do I repeat it. I speak not of our times all this while, we have good, honest, virtuous men and women, whom fame, zeal, fear of God, Religion and superstition contains; and yet for all that, we have too many Knights of this order, so dubbed by their wives, many good women abused by dissolute husbands. In some places, and such persons, you may as soon enjoin them to carry water in a sieve, as to keep themselves honest. What shall a man do now in such a case? What remedy is to be had? How shall he be eased? By suing a divorce? that is hard to be effected: if not rightfully, then carefully, they carry the matter so cunningly, that though it be as common as Simony, as clear and as manifest as the nose in a man's face, yet it cannot be evidently proved, or they likely taken in the fact: they will have a knave Gallus to watch, or with that Roman Sulpicia, all made fast and sure,

> Lest he should see her now, not as before
> With fine Cadurcian linen covered o'er,
> But lying naked with her paramour.

She will hardly be surprised by her husband, be he never so wary. Much better then to put it up, the more he strives in it, the more he shall divulge his own shame; make a virtue of necessity, and conceal it. Yea, but the world takes notice of it, 'tis in every man's mouth: let them talk their pleasure, of whom speak they not in this sense? From the highest to the lowest, they are thus censured all: there is no remedy then but patience. It may be 'tis his own fault, and he hath no reason to complain, 'tis tit for tat, she is bad, he is worse. Bethink thyself, hast thou not done as much for some of thy neighbours? why dost thou require that of thy wife, which thou wilt not perform thyself? Thou rangest like a Town Bull, why art thou so incensed if she tread awry?

> Be it that some woman break chaste wedlock's laws,
> And leaves her husband and becomes unchaste:
> Yet commonly it is not without cause,
> She sees her man in sin her goods to waste,

She feels that he his love from her withdraws,
And hath on some perhaps less worthy placed,
Who strike with sword, the scabbard them may strike,
And sure love craveth love, like asketh like.　(ARIOSTO)

She will ever study, saith Nevisanus, to pay back equally, she will quit it if she can. And therefore, as well adviseth Siracides, teach her not an evil lesson against thyself, which as Jansenius, Lyranus, on this text, and Carthusianus interpret, is no otherwise to be understood, then that she do thee not a mischief. I do not excuse her in accusing thee; but if both be naught, mend thyself first; for as the old saying is, A good husband makes a good wife.

Yea, but thou repliest, 'Tis not the like reason betwixt man and woman, through her fault my children are bastards, I may not endure it, let her scowl, brawl, and spend, I care not, so she be honest, I could easily bear it; but this I cannot, I may not, I will not; my faith, my fame, mine eye must not be touched, as the diverb is. I say the same of my wife, touch all, use all, take all but this. I acknowledge that of Seneca to be true, there is no sweet content in the possession of any good thing, without a companion, this only excepted, I say, This. And why this? Even this which thou so much abhorrest, it may be for thy progeny's good, better be any man's son than thine, to be begot of base Irus, poor Seius, or mean Mævius, the Town Swineherd's, a Shepherd's son: and well is he that, like Hercules, he hath any two fathers; for thou thyself hast peradventure more diseases than an horse, more infirmities of body and mind, a canker'd soul, crabbed conditions; make the worst of it, as it is incurable, so it is insensible. But art thou sure it is so? The fellow attends to your business? doth he so indeed? It may be thou art over suspicious, and without a cause, as some are: if it be born at eight months, or like him, and him they fondly suspect, he got it; if she speak or laugh familiarly with such or such men, then presently she is naught with them, such is thy weakness: whereas charity, or a well-disposed mind, would interpret all unto the best. S. Francis, by chance, seeing a Friar familiarly kissing another man's wife, was so far from misconceiving it, that he presently kneeled down, and thanked God there was so much charity left: but they, on the other side, will ascribe nothing to natural causes, indulge nothing to familiarity, mutual society, friendship; but out of a sinister suspicion, presently lock them close, watch them, thinking by those means to prevent all such inconveniences, that's the way to help it; whereas by such tricks they do aggravate the mischief.

'Tis but in vain to watch that which will away.

None can be kept resisting for her part ;
Though body be kept close, within her heart
Advoutry lurks, t' exclude it there's no art.   (OVID)

Argus with an hundred eyes cannot keep her, these love alone many a time evaded, as in Ariosto.

If all our hairs were eyes, yet sure, they said,
We husbands of our wives should be betrayed.

Hierome holds, to what end is all your custody? A dishonest woman cannot be kept, an honest woman ought not to be kept, necessity is a keeper not to be trusted. That which many covet, can hardly be preserved, as Salisburiensis thinks. I am of Æneas Sylvius' mind. Those jealous Italians do very ill to lock up their wives ; for women are of such a disposition, they will most covet that which is denied most, and offend least when they have free liberty to trespass. It is in vain to lock her up if she be dishonest; and as our great Mr. Aristotle calls it, too tyrannical a task, most unfit : for when she perceives her husband observes her and suspects, she sins more freely, saith Nevisanus. She is exasperated, seeks by all means to vindicate herself, and will therefore offend, because she is unjustly suspected. The best course then is to let them have their own wills, give them free liberty, without any keeping.

In vain our friends from this do us dehort,
For beauty will be where is most resort.   (DANIEL)

If she be honest, as Lucretia to Collatinus, Laodamia to Protesilaus, Penelope to her Ulysses, she will so continue her honour, good name, credit,

Ulysses shall my only husband be.   (OVID)

And as Phocion's wife in Plutarch, called her husband her wealth, treasure, world, joy, delight, orb and sphere, she will hers. The vow she made unto her good man, love, virtue, religion, zeal, are better keepers than all those locks, Eunuchs, prisons ; she will not be moved.

First I desire the earth to swallow me,
Before I violate mine honesty,
Or thunder from above drive me to hell,
With those pale ghosts, and ugly nights to dwell.

                            (VIRGIL)

She is resolv'd with Dido to be chaste; though her husband be false, she will be true : and as Octavia writ to her Antony :

These walls that here do keep me out of sight,
Shall keep me all unspotted unto thee,

And testify that I will do thee right,
I'll never stain thine house, though thou shame me. (DANIEL)

Turn her loose to all those Tarquins and Satyrs, she will not be tempted. In the time of Valence the Emperor, saith St. Austin, one Archidamus, a Consul of Antioch, offered an hundred pound of gold to a fair young wife, and besides to set her husband free, who was then a dark prisoner, to be his concubine for a single night; but the chaste matron would not accept of it. When one commended Theano's fine arm to his fellows, she took him up short, Sir, 'tis not common; she is wholly reserved to her husband. Bilia had an old man to her spouse, and his breath stunk, so that no body could abide it abroad, coming home one day, he reprehended his wife, because she did not tell him of it: she vowed unto him she had told him, but that she thought every man's breath had been as strong as his. Tigranes and Armenia his Lady were invited to supper by King Cyrus: when they came home, Tigranes asked his wife, how she liked Cyrus, and what she did especially commend in him? she swore she did not observe him; when he replied again, what then she did observe, whom she looked on? She made answer, her husband that said he would die for her sake. Such are the properties and conditions of good women: and if she be well given, she will so carry herself; if otherwise she be naught, use all the means thou canst, she will be naught. Not the wish, but the lover, is lacking; she hath so many lies, excuses, as an hare hath muses, [or loopholes], tricks, Pandars, Bawds, shifts to deceive, 'tis to no purpose to keep her up, or to reclaim her by hard usage. Fair means peradventure may do somewhat.

Indulgence all the better restraint may prove. (OVID)

Men and women are both in a predicament in this behalf, so sooner won, and better pacified. They will be led, not driven; though she be as arrant a scold as Xanthippe, as cruel as Medea, as clamorous as Hecuba, as lustful as Messalina, by such means (if at all) she may be reformed. Many patient Grizels by their obsequiousness in this kind, have reclaimed their husbands from their wandering lusts. In Nova Francia and Turkey (as Leah, Rachel, and Sarah did to Abraham and Jacob) they bring their fairest damsels to their husbands' beds; Livia seconded the lustful appetites of Augustus: Stratonice, wife to King Deiotarus, did not only bring Electra, a fair maid, to her goodman's bed, but brought up the children begot on her, as carefully as if they had been her own. Tertius Æmilius' wife, Cornelia's mother, perceiving her husband's intemperance, dissimulated the matter, made much of the maid, and would take no notice of it. A new married man, when a pick-thank friend of his, to curry favour, had shewed him his wife familiar in private with a young gallant, courting and dallying, &c., Tush, said he, let him do his worst, I dare trust my wife, though I dare not trust him. The best remedy then is by fair means; if that will not take place, to dissemble it, as I say, or turn it off with a jest: hear Guevara's advice in this case, either take in jest or ignore in silence; for if you take exceptions at every thing your wife doth, Solomon's wisdom, Hercules' valour, Homer's learning, Socrates' patience, Argus' vigilancy will not serve [your] turn. Therefore a less mischief, Nevisanus holds, to dissimulate, to be a buyer of cradles, as the proverb is, than to be too solicitous. A good fellow when his wife was brought to bed before her time, bought half a dozen of Cradles beforehand for so many children, as if his wife should continue to bear children at every two months. Pertinax the Emperor, when one told him a Fiddler was too familiar with his Empress, made no reckoning of it. And when that Macedonian Philip was upbraided with his wife's dishonesty, a Conqueror of Kingdoms could not tame his wife, (for she thrust him out of doors) he made a jest of it. Saith Nevisanus, wise men bear their horns in their hearts, fools on their foreheads. Eumenes, King of Pergamus, was at deadly feud with Perseus of Macedonia, insomuch that Perseus, hearing of a journey he was to take to Delphi, set a company of soldiers to intercept him in his passage; they did it accordingly, and as they supposed, left him stoned to death. The news of this fact was brought instantly to Pergamus; Attalus, Eumenes' brother, proclaimed himself King forthwith, took possession of the Crown, and married Stratonice the Queen. But by and by, when contrary news was brought, that King Eumenes was alive, and now coming to the City, he laid by his Crown, left his wife, as a private man went to meet him, and congratulated his return. Eumenes, though he knew all particulars passed, yet dissembling the matter, kindly embraced his brother, and took his wife into his favour again, as if no such matter had been heard of or done. Jocundo, in Ariosto, found his wife in bed with a knave, both asleep, went his ways, and would not so much as wake them, much less reprove them for it. An honest fellow finding in like sort his wife had played false at Tables, and borne a man too many, drew his dagger, and swore if he had not been his very friend, he would have killed him. Another hearing one had done that for him, which no man desires to be done by a Deputy, followed him in a rage with his sword drawn, and having overtaken him, laid adultery to his charge; the offender hotly pursued, confessed it was true, with which confession he was satisfied, and so left him, swearing, that if he had denied it. he would not have put it up. How much better is it to do thus. than to macerate himself, impatiently to rave and rage, to enter an Action (as Arnoldus Tillius did in the Court of Toulouse, against Martin Guerre his fellow-soldier. for that he counterfeited his habit, and was too familiar with his wife) so to divulge his own shame, and to remain for ever a Cuckold on record! How much better be Cornelius Tacitus, than Publicus Cornutus, to condemn in such cases, or take no notice of it! Saith Erasmus, better be a wittol, and put it up, than to trouble himself to no purpose. And though he will not nod for everybody, be an ass. as he is an ox. yet to wink at it, as many do, is not amiss at some times, in some cases, to some parties, if it be for his commodity, or some great man's sake, his Land-Lord, Patron, Benefactor (as Galba the Roman, saith Plutarch, did by Mæcenas, and Phayllus of Argos did by King Philip, when he promised him an office, on that condition he might lie with his wife) and so to let it pass; it never troubles me. said Amphitruo, to be cornuted by Jupiter; let it not molest thee then; be friends with her; let it, I say, make no breach of love betwixt you. Howsoever, the best way is to contemn it, which Henry the Second, King of France, advised a Courtier of his, jealous of his wife, and complaining of her unchasteness, to reject it, and comfort himself; for he that suspects his wife's incontinence, and fears the Pope's curse, shall never live a merry hour, or sleep a quiet night: no remedy but patience. When all is done, according to that counsel of Nevisanus, if it may not be helped, it must be endured. 'Tis Sophocles' advice, keep it to thyself, and which Chrysostom calls a domestic gymnasium, and a school of Philosophy, put it up. There is no other cure, but time to wear it out, the remedy for injuries is forgetting, as if they had drunk a draught of Lethe in Trophonius' den. To conclude, age will bereave her of it, time and patience must end it.

> The mind's affections Patience will appease,
> It passions kills, and healeth each disease.   (R. T.)

SUBSECTION 2 — *By prevention before, or after marriage, Plato's community, marry a Courtesan, Philters, Stews, to marry one equal in years, fortunes, of a good family, education, good place, to use them well, &c.*

OF such medicines as conduce to the cure of this malady, I have sufficiently treated; there be some good remedies remaining, by way of prevention, precautions, or admonitions, which, if rightly practised, may do much good. Plato, in his Common-wealth, to prevent this mischief belike, would have all things common, wives and children all as one: and which Cæsar in his Commentaries observed of those old Britons, that first inhabited this Land, they had ten or twelve wives allotted to such a family, or promiscuously to be used by so many men: not one to one, as with us, or four, five or six to one, as in Turkey. The Nicholaites, a Sect that sprung, saith Austin, from Nicholas the Deacon, would have women indifferent; and the cause of this filthy sect was Nicholas the Deacon's jealousy, for which, when he was condemned, to purge himself of his offence, he broached his heresy that it was lawful to lie with one another's wives, and for any man to lie with his: like to those Anabaptists in Munster, that would consort with other men's wives as the spirit moved them: or as Mahomet, the seducing Prophet, would needs use women as he list himself, to beget Prophets; 205, their Alcoran saith, were in love with him, and he as able as forty men. Amongst the old Carthaginians, as Bohemus relates out of Sabellicus, the King of the Country lay with the bride the first night, and once in a year they went promiscuously altogether. Munster ascribes the beginning of this brutish custom (unjustly) to one Picardus, a French-man, that invented a new sect of Adamites, to go naked as Adam did, and to use promiscuous venery at set times. When the priest repeated that of Genesis, " Increase and multiply," out went the candles in the place where they met, and without all respect of age, persons, conditions, catch that catch may, every man took her came next, &c. Some fasten this on those ancient Bohemians and Russians: others on the inhabitants of Mambrium, in the Lucerne valley in Piedmont; and, as I read, it was practised in Scotland amongst Christians themselves, until King Malcolm's time, the King or the Lord of the Town had their maidenheads. In some parts of India in our age, and those Icelanders, as amongst the Babylonians of old, they will prostitute their wives and daughters (which Chalcocondylas, a Greek modern writer, for want of better intelligence, puts upon us Britons) to such travellers or sea-faring men, as come amongst them by chance, to shew how far they were from this feral vice of Jealousy, and how little they esteemed it. The Kings of Calicut, as Lod. Vertomannus relates, will not touch their wives, till one of their Biarmi or high Priests have lain first with them, to sanctify their wombs. But those Essenes and Montanists, two strange sects of old, were in another extreme, they would not marry at all, or have any society with women, because of their intemperance they held them all to be naught [or naughty]. Nevisanus the Lawyer, would have him that is inclined to this malady, to prevent the worst, marry a quean, take a whore, so that at least he should not be deceived, knowing her to be what she was, as he might not the others. A fornicator in Seneca constuprated two wenches in a night; for satisfaction the one desired to hang him, the other to marry him. Hieronymus, King of Syracuse in Sicily, espoused himself to Peitho, keeper of the Stews; and Ptolemy took Thais a common Whore to be his wife, had two sons, Leontiscus and Lagus, by her, and one daughter Irene: 'tis therefore no such unlikely thing. A Citizen of Eugubine gelded himself to try his wife's honesty, and to be freed from jealousy: so did a Baker in Basil, to the same intent. But of all other precedents in this kind, that of Combabus is most memorable: who to prevent his Master's suspicion, for he was a beautiful young man, and sent by Seleucus his Lord and King, with Stratonice the Queen, to conduct her into Syria, fearing the worst, gelded himself before he went, and left his genitals behind him in a box sealed up. His Mistress by the way fell in love with him, but he not yielding to her, was accused to Seleucus of incontinency (as that Bellerophon was in like case, falsely traduced by Sthenobœa, to King Prœtus her husband, when she could not persuade him to bed with her) and that by her, and was therefore at his coming home cast into prison: the day of hearing appointed, he was sufficiently cleared and acquitted by shewing his privities, which to the admiration of the beholders he had formerly cut off. The Lydians used to geld women whom they suspected, saith Leonicus, as well as men. To this purpose Saint Francis, because he used to confess women in private, to prevent suspicion, and prove himself a Maid, stripped himself before the Bishop of Assisi and others: and Friar Leonard for the same cause went through Viterbo in Italy without any garments.

Our Pseudo-Catholicks, to help these inconveniences which proceed from Jealousy, to keep themselves and their wives honest, make severe Laws; against adultery, present death; and withal [for] fornication, a venial sin, as a sink to convey that furious and swift stream of concupiscence, they appoint and permit stews, those punks and pleasant sinners, the more to secure their wives in all populous Cities, for they hold them as necessary as Churches; and howsoever unlawful, yet to avoid a greater mischief to be tolerated in policy, as usury, for the hardness of men's hearts; and for this end they have whole Colleges of Courtesans in their Towns and Cities. Of Cato's mind belike, that would have his servants familiar with some such feminine creatures, to avoid worse mischiefs in his house, and made allowance for it. They hold it unpossible for idle persons, young, rich, and lusty, so many servants, Monks, Friars, to live honest, too tyrannical a burden to compel them to be chaste, and most unfit to suffer poor men, younger brothers and soldiers at all to marry, as also diseased persons, votaries, priests, servants. Therefore as well to keep and ease the one as the other, they tolerate and wink at these kind of Brothel-houses and Stews. Many probable arguments they have to prove the lawfulness, the necessity, and a toleration of them, as of usury; and without question in policy they are not to be contra-dicted: but altogether in Religion. Others prescribe philters, spells, charms to keep men and women honest. In order that a woman may not admit any man but her husband: Take the gall-bladder of a goat, and the fat, dry it, heat it in oil, &c., and she'll love none other but you. In Alexis, Porta, &c., you will find much more, and more absurd than these, as in Rhasis, to keep a woman from admitting others than her husband, and make her love him only, &c. But these are most part Pagan, impious, irreligious, absurd, and ridiculous devices.

The best means to avoid these and like inconveniences, are, to take away the causes and occasions. To this purpose Varro writ the Menip-pean Satire, but it is lost. Patricius prescribes four rules to be observed in choosing of a wife (which whoso will may read); Fonseca the Span-iard sets down six special cautions for men, four for women; Sam. Neander out of Shonbernerus, five for men, five for women; Anthony Guevara many good lessons; Cleobulus two alone,* others otherwise; as first to make a good choice in marriage, to invite Christ to their wedding, and which Saint Ambrose adviseth, and to pray to him for her, not to be too rash and precipitate in his election, to run upon the first he meets, or dote on every snowt-fair piece he sees, but to choose her as much by his ears as eyes, to be well advised whom he takes, of what age, &c. and cautelous [or cautious] in his proceeding.

An old man should not marry a young woman, or a young woman an old man,

> *Old and young cattle plough not well together!*   (OVID)

such matches must needs minister a perpetual cause of suspicion, and be distasteful to each other.

> *Night-crows on tombs, owl sits on carcass dead,*
> *So lies a wench with Sophocles in bed.*   (ALCIATI)

For Sophocles, as Athenæus describes him, was a very old man, as cold as January, a bed-fellow of bones, and doted yet upon Archippe a young Courtesan, than which nothing can be more odious. An old man is a most unwelcome guest to a young wench, unable, unfit:

---

* Neither be too easy when alone with her, nor scold her too much in the presence of others. — Burton's note.

Maidens shun their embrace ; abhorrent they
    To Venus, Love, and Hymen. (PONTANUS)

And as in like case a good fellow that had but a peck of corn weekly to
grind, yet would needs build a new Mill for it, found his error eftsoons,
for either he must let his Mill lie waste, pull it quite down, or let others
grind at it: so these men, &c.

Seneca therefore disallows all such unseasonable matches, for that
frequency in nuptial matters will be a curse. And as Tully farther inveighs, 'tis unfit for any, but ugly and filthy in old age. Amorousness in
the old is unseemly, one of the three things God hateth. Plutarch rails
downright at such kind of marriages, which are attempted by old men,
who, already impotent in body, and laid waste by their pleasures, can sin
only in fancy, and makes a question whether in some cases it be tolerable at least for such a man to marry.

    Lust that desires the deed but lacks the power, (JUVENAL)

that is now past those venerous exercises, " as a gelded man lies with a
Virgin and sighs," and now complains with him in Petronius, he is quite
done, though once an Achilles in the fields of love.

    Late a match for any maid,
    I contended not ingloriously. (HORACE)

But the question is, whether he may delight himself as those Priapeian
Popes, which in their decrepit age lay commonly between two wenches
every night, touching and handling their beauties, whether he may pleasure himself thus far ; and as many doting Sires still do to their own
shame, their children's undoing, and their families' confusion: he abhors it, it must be avoided as a Bedlam-master, and not obeyed.

    ——— *Alecto herself*
    Holds the torch at such nuptials, and Hymen wails sadly,

the Devil himself makes such matches. Levinus Lemnius reckons up
three things which generally disturb the peace of marriage : the first is
when they marry intempestive or unseasonably, as many mortal men
marry precipitately and inconsiderately, when they are effete and old:
The second, when they marry unequally for fortunes and birth: The
third, when a sick impotent person weds one that is sound ; the nuptial hopes are frustrate: many dislikes instantly follow. Many doting
dizzards, it may not be denied, as Plutarch confesseth, recreate themselves with such obsolete, unseasonable and filthy remedies (so he calls
them) with a remembrance of their former pleasures, against nature
they stir up their dead flesh ; but an old lecher is abominable ; Nevisanus holds, a woman that marries a third time may be presumed to be
no honester than she should. Of them both, thus Ambrose concludes in

his comment upon Luke, they that are coupled together, not to get children, but to satisfy their lust, are not husbands, but fornicators, with whom St. Austin consents: matrimony without hope of children, is not a wedding but a jumbling or coupling together. In a word (except they wed for mutual society, help, and comfort, one of another, in which respects, though Tiberius deny it, without question old folks may well marry) for sometimes a man hath most need of a wife, according to Puccius, when he hath no need of a wife; otherwise it is most odious, when an old Acherontick dizzard, that hath one foot in his grave, shall flicker after a lusty young wench that is blythe and bonny,

> ———— *Lusty as the sparrow in spring,*
> *Or the snow-white ring-dove.* (PONTANUS)

What can be more detestable?

> *Thou old goat, hoary lecher, naughty man,*
> *With stinking breath, art thou in love?*
> *Must thou be slavering? she spews to see*
> *Thy filthy face, it doth so move.* (PLAUTUS)

Yet as some will, it is much more tolerable for an old man to marry a young woman (Our Lady's match they call it) for she'll be a woman tomorrow, as he said in Tully. Cato the Roman, Critobulus in Xenophon, Traquellus of late, Julius Scaliger, &c., and many famous precedents we have in that kind; but not to the contrary; 'tis not fit for an ancient woman to match with a young man. For as Varro will, when an old woman sports, she makes sport for death, 'tis Charon's match between Cascus and Casca, and the Devil himself is surely well pleased with it. And therefore, as the Poet inveighs, thou old Vetustilla, bed-ridden quean, that art now skin and bones,

> *Thou hast three hairs, four teeth, a breast*
> *Like grasshopper, an emmet's crest,*
> *A skin more rugged than thy coat,*
> *And dugs like spider's web to boot.* (MARTIAL)

Must thou marry a youth again? And yet they would marry any number of husbands; howsoever it is, as Apuleius gives out of his Meroe, a pestilent match, abominable, and not to be endured. In such case, how can they otherwise choose but be jealous? how should they agree one with another? This inequality is not in years only, but in birth, fortunes, conditions, and all good qualities,

> *If you would marry fitly, wed your equal.* (OVID)

'Tis my counsel, saith Anthony Guevara, to choose such a one. Let a Citizen match with a Citizen, a Gentleman with a Gentlewoman: he that observes not this precept (saith he) instead of a fair wife, shall have a fury, for a fit son-in-law a mere fiend, &c. Examples are too frequent.

Another main caution fit to be observed, is this, that though they be equal in years, birth, fortunes, and other conditions, yet they do not omit virtue and good education, which Musonius and Antipater so much inculcate in Stobæus.

> *Parental virtue is a splendid dowry,*
> *And chastity, that shrinks from others' arms*
> *And never breaks its compact.* (HORACE)

If as Plutarch adviseth, one must eat a bushel of salt with him before he choose his friend, what care should be had in choosing a wife, his second self, how solicitous should he be to know her qualities and behaviour! and when he is assured of them, not to prefer birth, fortune, beauty, before bringing up, and good conditions. Coquage, god of Cuckolds, as one [Rabelais] merrily said, accompanies the goddess Jealousy, both follow the fairest, by Jupiter's appointment, and they sacrifice to them together: beauty and honesty seldom agree; straight personages have often crooked manners; fair faces, foul vices; good complexions, ill conditions. Beauty (saith Chrysostom) is full of treachery and suspicion: he that hath a fair wife, cannot have a worse mischief, and yet most covet it, as if nothing else in marriage but that and wealth were to be respected. Francis Sforza, Duke of Milan, was so curious in this behalf, that he would not marry the Duke of Mantua's daughter, except he might see her naked first: which Lycurgus appointed in his Laws, and More in his Utopian Commonwealth approves. In Italy, as a traveller observes, if a man have three or four daughters, or more, and they prove fair, they are married eftsoons: if deformed, they change their lovely names of Lucia, Cynthia, Camæna, call them Dorothy, Ursula, Bridget, and so put them into Monasteries, as if none were fit for marriage but such as are eminently fair: but these are erroneous tenents: a modest Virgin well conditioned, to such a fair snout * piece, is much to be preferred. If thou wilt avoid them, take away all causes of suspicion and jealousy, marry a coarse piece, fetch her from Cassandra's Temple, which was wont in Italy to be a Sanctuary of all deformed Maids, and so thou shalt be sure that no man will make thee cuckold, but for spite. A Citizen of Byzantium in Thrace, had a filthy dowdy, deformed slut to his wife, and finding her in bed with another man, cried out as one amazed: O thou wretch! what necessity brought thee hither? as well he might; for who can affect such a one? But this is warily to be under-

* Snout, or snowt, good-looking.

stood, most offend in another extreme, they prefer wealth before beauty, and so she be rich, they care not how she look; but these are all out as faulty as the rest. Consider your wife's looks, as Sarisburiensis adviseth, that you may not despise her when you see other women, as that Knight in Chaucer, that was married to an old woman,

And al day after hidde him as an owle.
So wo was him, his wyf looked so foule.

Have a care of thy wife's complexion, lest whilst thou seest another, thou loathest her, she prove jealous, thou naught,

Though thy wife be ugly, thy maid beautiful,
Yet from the maid abstain.

I can perhaps give instance. It is a misery to possess that which no man likes: on the other side, what many love is not easily guarded. And as the bragging soldier vaunted in the Comedy, 'tis a great misery to be too handsome. Scipio did never so hardly besiege Carthage, as these young gallants will beset thine house, one with wit or person, another with wealth, &c. If she be fair, saith Guazzo, she will be suspected howsoever. Both extremes are naught, the one is soon beloved, the other loves: one is hardly kept, because proud and arrogant, the other not worth keeping; what is to be done in this case? Ennius in Menelippe adviseth thee as a friend to take one of a middle size, neither too fair nor too foul,

Not the fairest but the chastest doth me please,   (MARULLUS)

with old Cato, though fit, let her beauty be, neither too choice nor too mean, between both. This I approve; but of the other two I resolve with Sarisburiensis, both rich alike, endowed alike, I had rather marry a fair one, and put it to the hazard, than be troubled with a blowze; but do thou as thou wilt, I speak only of myself.

Howsoever, I would advise thee thus much, be she fair or foul, to choose a wife out of a good kindred, parentage, well brought up, in an honest place. He that marries a wife out of a suspected Inn or Alehouse, buys a horse in Smithfield, and hires a servant in Paul's, as the diverb is, shall likely have a jade to his horse, a knave for his man, an arrant honest woman to his wife. Saith Nevisanus, such a mother, such a daughter; cat to her kind. If the mother be dishonest, in all likelihood the daughter will take after her in all good qualities; think you not Pasiphae will bring forth a bull-loving daughter? If the dam trot, the foal will not amble. My last caution is, that a woman do not bestow herself upon a fool, or an apparent melancholy person; jealousy is a symptom of that disease, and fools have no moderation. Justina, a Roman Lady, was much persecuted, and after made away by her jealous husband, she caused and enjoined this Epitaph, as a caveat to others, to be engraven on her tomb.

Learn parents all, and by Justina's case,
Your children to no dizzards for to place.

After marriage, I can give no better admonitions than to use their wives well, and which a friend of mine told me that was a married man. I will tell you as good cheap, saith Nicostratus in Stobæus, to avoid future strife, and for quietness' sake, when you are in bed take heed of your wives' flattering speeches overnight, and curtain sermons in the morning. Let them do their endeavour likewise to maintain them to their means, which Patricius ingeminates, and let them have liberty with discretion, as time and place requires : many women turn queans by compulsion, as Nevisanus observes, because their husbands are so hard, and keep them so short in diet and apparel, poverty and hunger, want of means, makes them dishonest, or bad usage ; their churlish behaviour forceth them to fly out, or bad examples, they do it to cry quittance. In the other extreme some are too liberal, as the proverb is, they make a rod for their own tails, as Candaules did to Gyges in Herodotus, commend his wife's beauty himself, and besides would needs have him see her naked. Whilst they give their wives too much liberty to gad abroad, and bountiful allowance, they are accessory to their own miseries ; as Plautus jibes, they have deformed souls, and by their painting and colours procure their husband's hate, especially,

The wretched husband's lips are smeared with paint. (JUVENAL)
Besides, their wives (as Basil notes) impudently thrust themselves into other men's companies, and by their undecent wanton carriage provoke and tempt the spectators. Virtuous women should keep house ; and 'twas well performed and ordered by the Greeks, that a matron should not be seen in publick without her husband to speak for her ; which made Phidias belike at Elis paint Venus treading on a Tortoise, a symbol of women's silence and house-keeping. For a woman abroad and alone is like a Deer broke out of a Park, whom every hunter follows ; and besides in such places she cannot so well vindicate herself, but as that virgin Dinah " going for to see the daughters of the land," lost her virginity, she may be defiled and overtaken on a sudden.

Poor helpless does, what are we but a prey? (MARTIAL)
And therefore I know not what Philosopher he was, that would have women come but thrice abroad all their time, to be baptized, married, and buried ; but he was too strait-laced. Let them have their liberty in good sort, and go in good sort ; as a good fellow said, so that they look

not twenty years younger abroad than they do at home; they be not spruce, neat, Angels abroad, beasts, dowdies, sluts at home; but seek by all means to please and give content to their husbands; to be quiet above all things, obedient, silent and patient; if they be incensed, angry, chide a little, their wives must not cample [or answer back] again, but take it in good part. An honest woman, I cannot now tell where she dwelt, but by report an honest woman she was, hearing one of her gossips by chance complaining of her husband's impatience, told her an excellent remedy for it, and gave her withal a glass of water, which when he brawled she should hold still in her mouth, and that as often as he chid: she did so two or three times with good success, and at length seeing her neighbour, gave her great thanks for it, and would needs know the ingredients, she told her in brief what it was, fair water, and no more: for it was not the water, but her silence which performed the cure. Let every froward woman imitate this example, and be quiet within doors, and (as M. Aurelius prescribes) a necessary caution it is to be observed of all good matrons that love their credits, to come little abroad, but follow their work at home, look to their household affairs and private business, be sober, thrifty, wary, circumspect, modest, and compose themselves to live to their husbands' means, as a good housewife should do.

One who delights in the distaff, and beguiles
The hours of labor with a song; her duties
Take on an air of virtuous loveliness
When with her maids she's busy at wheel and spindle.   (CHALONER)

Howsoever 'tis good to keep them private, not in prison;

> *Whoever guards his wife with bolts and bars*
> *May be a learned man, but's sure a fool!*   (MENANDER)

Read more of this subject in Arnisæus, Cyprian, Tertullian, Bossus, Godefridus, Levinus Lemnius, Barbarus, Franciscus Patricius, Fonseca, Sam. Neander, &c.

These cautions concern him; and if by those or his own discretion otherwise he cannot moderate himself, his friends must not be wanting by their wisdom, if it be possible, to give the party grieved satisfaction, to prevent and remove the occasions, objects, if it may be to secure him. If it be one alone, or many, to consider whom he suspects, or at what times, in what places he is most incensed, in what companies. Nevisanus makes a question whether a young Physician ought to be admitted in case of sickness, into a new married man's house, to administer a julip, a syrup, or some such physick. The Persians of old would not suffer a young Physician to come amongst women. Apollonides of Cos made Artaxerxes

cuckold, and was after buried alive for it. A gaoler in Aristænetus had a
fine young gentleman to his prisoner; in commiseration of his youth and
person he let him loose, to enjoy the liberty of the prison, but he unkindly made him a Cornuto. Menelaus gave good welcome to Paris a
stranger, his whole house and family were at his command, but he un-
gently stole away his beloved wife. The like measure was offered to Agis,
king of Lacedæmon, by Alcibiades an exile, for his good entertainment,
He was too familiar with Timæa his wife, begetting a child of her, called
Leotychides; and bragging moreover, when he came home to Athens,
that he had a son should be King of the Lacedæmonians. If such objects
were removed, no doubt but the parties might easily be satisfied, or that
they could use them gently, and intreat them well, not to revile them,
scoff at, hate them, as in such cases commonly they do; 'tis an inhuman
infirmity, a miserable vexation, and they should not add grief to grief,
nor aggravate their misery, but seek to please, and by all means give
them content, by good counsel, removing such offensive objects, or by
mediation of some discreet friends. In old Rome there was a Temple
erected by the Matrons to that Viriplaca Dea; another to Venus Verti-
cordia, whither (if any difference happened betwixt man and wife) they
did instantly resort: there they did offer sacrifice, a white Hart, Plutarch
records, without the gall (some say the like of Juno's Temple) and make
their prayers for conjugal peace: before some indifferent arbitrators and
friends, the matter was heard betwixt man and wife, and commonly
composed. In our times we want no sacred Churches, or good men, to end
such Controversies, if use were made of them. Some say, that precious
stone called Beryllus, others a Diamond, hath excellent virtue, to recon-
cile men and wives, to maintain unity and love; you may try this when
you will, and as you see cause. If none of all these means and cautions
will take place, I know not what remedy to prescribe, or whither such
persons may go for ease, except they can get into the same Turkey
Paradise, where they shall have as many fair wives as they will themselves, with clear eyes, and such as look on none but their own husbands,
no fear, no danger of being Cuckolds; or else I would have them observe that strict rule of Alphonsus, to marry a deaf and dumb man to a
blind woman. If this will not help, let them, to prevent the worst, consult
with an Astrologer, and see whether the Significators in her Horoscope
agree with his, that they be not in signs and parts that betoken hateful
looks and domineering, but mutually loving and dutiful, otherwise (as
they hold) there will be intolerable enmities between them: or else get
him the Seal of Venus, a Characteristical Seal stamped in the day and

hour of Venus, when she is fortunate, with such and such set words and charms, which Villanovanus and Leo Suavius prescribe, from the magick Seals of Solomon, Hermes, Raguel, &c., with many such, which Alexis, Albertus, and some of our Natural Magicians put upon us: in order that a woman may not be able to commit adultery with any one, take a lock of her hair, &c., and he shall surely be gracious in all women's eyes, and never suspect or disagree with his own wife, so long as he wears it. If this course be not approved, and other remedies may not be had, they must in the last place sue for a divorce: but that is somewhat difficult to effect, and not all out so fit. For as Felisacus urgeth, if that law of Constantine the great, or that of Theodosius and Valentinian, concerning divorce, were in use in our times, we should have almost no married couples left. Try therefore those former remedies: or as Tertullian reports of Democritus, that put out his eyes because he could not look on a woman without lust, and was much troubled to see that which he might not enjoy; let him make himself blind, and so he shall avoid that care and molestation of watching his wife. One other sovereign remedy I could repeat, an especial Antidote against Jealousy, an excellent cure; but I am not now disposed to tell it, not that like a covetous Empirick, I conceal it for any gain, but some other reasons, I am not willing to publish it; if you be very desirous to know it, when I meet you next, I will peradventure tell you what it is in your ear. This is the best counsel I can give; which he that hath need of, as occasion serves, may apply unto himself. In the meantime,

> *Ye gods, avert from earth the pest!*   (VIRGIL)

As the Proverb is, from Heresy, Jealousy, and Frenzy, good Lord, deliver us.

SECTION 4   MEMBER 1

SUBSECTION 1 — *Religious Melancholy. Its object God; what his beauty is; how it allureth. The parts and parties affected*

THAT there is such a distinct species of Love-Melancholy, no man hath ever yet doubted; but whether this subdivision of Religious Melancholy be warrantable, it may be controverted.

> *Lead on, ye Muses, nor desert me now*
> *Mid-journey, where no footsteps go before,*
> *Nor wheel-tracks marking out a way for me.*   (GROTIUS)

I have no pattern to follow, as in some of the rest, no man to imitate. No Physician hath as yet distinctly written of it, as of the other; all acknowledge it a most notable symptom, some a cause, but few a species or kind. Aretæus, Alexander, Rhasis. Avicenna, and most of our late Writers, as Gordonius, Fuchsius, Plater, Bruel. Montaltus, &c., repeat it as a symptom. Some seem to be inspired of the Holy Ghost, some take upon them to be Prophets. some are addicted to new opinions, some foretell strange things concerning the state of the world, Anti-Christ, saith Gordonius. Some will prophesy of the end of the World to a day almost, and the fall of the Antichrist, as they have been addicted or brought up; for so melancholy works with them. as Laurentius holds. If they have been precisely given, all their meditations tend that way, and in conclusion produce strange effects, the humour imprints symptoms according to their several inclinations and conditions. which makes Guianerius and Felix Plater, put too much devotion, blind zeal, fear of eternal punishment, and that last judgment. for a cause of those Enthusiasticks and desperate persons; but some do not obscurely make a distinct species of it, dividing Love-Melancholy into that whose object is women; & into the other, whose object is God. Plato, in the Banquet, makes mention of two distinct Furies; and amongst our Neotericks, Hercules de Saxoniâ doth expressly treat of it in a distinct species. Love-Melancholy (saith he) is twofold; the first is that (to which peradventure some will not vouchsafe this name or species of Melancholy) affection of those which put God for their object, and are altogether about prayer, fasting, &c., the other about women. Peter Forestus in his Observations delivereth as much in the same words: and Felix Platerus, 'tis a frequent disease; and they have a ground of what they say, forth of Aretæus and Plato. Aretæus an old Author, doth so divide Love-Melancholy, and derives this second from the first, which comes by inspiration or otherwise. Plato in his Phædrus hath these words, Apollo's Priests at Delphi, and at Dodona, in their fury do many pretty feats, and benefit the Greeks, but never in their right wits. He makes them all mad, as well he might; and he that shall but consider that superstition of old, those prodigious effects of it (as in its place I will shew the several furies of our Seers, Pythonesses, Sibyls, Enthusiasts, Pseudo-prophets, Hereticks and Schismaticks in these our latter ages) shall instantly confess, that all the world again cannot afford so much matter of madness, so many stupid symptoms, as superstition, heresy, schism hath brought out: that this species alone may be parallel'd to all the former, hath a greater latitude, and more miraculous effects; that it more besots and infatuates men, than any other above named whatsoever, doth more harm, works more disquietness to mankind, and hath more crucified the souls of mortal men (such hath been the Devil's craft) than wars, plagues, sicknesses, dearth, famine, and all the rest.

Give me but a little leave, and I will set before your eyes in brief a stupend, vast, infinite Ocean of incredible madness and folly: a Sea full of shelves and rocks, sands, gulfs, Euripuses, and contrary tides, full of fearful monsters, uncouth shapes, roaring waves, tempests, and Siren calms, Halcyonian Seas, unspeakable misery, such Comedies and Tragedies, such absurd and ridiculous, feral and lamentable fits, that I know not whether they are more to be pitied or derided, or may be believed, but that we daily see the same still practised in our days, fresh examples, new news, fresh objects of misery and madness in this kind, that are still represented unto us, abroad, at home, in the midst of us, in our bosoms.

But before I can come to treat of these several errors and obliquities, their causes, symptoms, affections, &c., I must say something necessarily of the object of this love, God himself, what this love is, how it allureth, whence it proceeds, and (which is the cause of all our miseries) how we mistake, wander, and swerve from it.

Amongst all those Divine Attributes that God doth vindicate to himself, Eternity, Omnipotency, Immutability, Wisdom, Majesty, Justice, Mercy, &c., his Beauty is not the least. One thing, saith David, have I desired of the Lord, and that I will still desire, to behold the beauty of the Lord. And out of Sion, which is the perfection of beauty, God hath shined. All other creatures are fair, I confess, and many other objects do much enamour us, a fair house, a fair horse, a comely person. I am amazed, saith Austin, when I look up to Heaven, and behold the beauty of the Stars; the beauty of Angels, Principalities, Powers, who can express it? who can sufficiently commend, or set out this beauty which appears in us? so fair a body, so fair a face, eyes, nose, cheeks, chin, brows, all fair and lovely to behold, besides the beauty of the soul, which cannot be discerned. If we so labour, and be so much affected, with the comeliness of creatures, how should we be ravished with that admirable lustre of God himself? — If ordinary beauty have such a prerogative and power, and what is amiable and fair, to draw the eyes and ears, hearts and affections, of all spectators unto it, to move, win, entice, allure: how shall this divine form ravish our souls, which is the fountain and quintessence of all beauty? If Heaven be so fair, the Sun so fair, how much fairer shall he be that made them fair? For by the greatness and beauty of the creatures, proportionally the maker of them is seen. If there be such pleasure in beholding a beautiful person alone, and, as a plausible Sermon, he so much affect us, what shall this beauty of God himself, that is infinitely fairer than all creatures, men, angels? &c. All other beauties are night itself, mere darkness, to this our inexplicable, incomprehensible, unspeakable, eternal, infinite, admirable, and divine beauty.

This lustre, a beauty of all things the most beautiful, this beauty and splendour of the divine Majesty, is it that draws all creatures to it, to seek it, love, admire, and adore it; and those Heathens, Pagans, Philosophers, out of those reliques they have yet left of God's Image, are so far forth incensed, as not only to acknowledge a God, but, though after their own inventions, to stand in admiration of his bounty, goodness, to adore and seek him; the magnificence and structure of the world itself, and beauty of all his creatures, his goodness, providence, protection, enforceth them to love him, seek him. fear him, though a wrong way to adore him: but for us that are Christians, Regenerate, that are his Adopted sons, Illuminated by his Word, having the eyes of our hearts and understandings opened; how fairly doth he offer and expose himself! Austin saith, he wooes us by his beauty, gifts, promises, to come unto him; the whole Scripture is a message, an exhortation, a love-letter to this purpose, to incite us, and invite us, God's Epistle, as Gregory calls it, to his creatures. He sets out his Son and his Church in that Epithalamium, or mystical Song of Solomon, to enamour us the more, comparing his head to *fine gold, his locks curled, and black as a Raven,* ———— *his eyes like doves on rivers of waters, washed with milk; his lips as lilies, dropping down pure juice; his hands as rings of gold set with Chrysolite:* ———— and his Church to *a vineyard, a garden enclosed, a fountain of living waters, an orchard of Pomegranates, with sweet scents of saffron, spike, calamus and cinnamon, and all the trees of incense, as the chief spices; the fairest amongst women, no spot in her, his sister, his Spouse, undefiled, the only daughter of her mother, dear unto her, fair as the Moon, pure as the Sun, looking out as the morning;* ———— that by these figures, that glass, these spiritual eyes of contemplation, we might perceive some resemblance of his beauty, the love betwixt his Church and him. And so in the 45th Psalm, this beauty of his Church is compared to *a Queen in a vesture of gold of Ophir, embroidered raiment of needlework,* that the King might take pleasure in her beauty. To incense us further yet, John in his Apocalypse, makes a description of that heavenly Jerusalem, the beauty of it, and in it the maker of it; likening it to a city of pure gold, like unto clear glass, shining and garnished with all manner of precious stones, having no need of Sun or Moon: for the Lamb is the light of it, the glory of God doth illuminate it: to give us to understand the infinite glory, beauty and happiness of it. Not that it is no fairer than these creatures to which it is compared, but that this vision of his, this lustre of his divine majesty, cannot otherwise be expressed to our apprehensions, *no tongue can tell, no heart can conceive it,* as Paul saith. Moses himself, when he desired to see God in his glory, was answered, that he might not endure it, no man could see his face and live. A strong object overcometh the sight, according to that axiom in Philosophy: if thou canst not endure the Sun beams, how canst thou endure that fulgor and brightness of him that made the Sun? The Sun itself, and all that we can imagine, are but shadows of it, 'tis a surpassing vision, as Austin calls it, the quintessence of beauty this, which far exceeds the beauty of Heavens, Sun and Moon, Stars, Angels, gold and silver, woods, fair fields, and whatsoever is pleasant to behold. All those other beauties fail, vary, are subject to corruption, to loathing; but this is an immortal vision, a divine beauty, an immortal love, an indefatigable love and beauty, with sight of which we shall never be tired, nor wearied, but still the more we see the more we shall covet him. For as one saith, where this vision is, there is absolute beauty: and where is that beauty, from the same fountain comes all pleasure and happiness; neither can beauty, pleasure, happiness, be separated from his vision or sight, or his vision from beauty, pleasure, happiness. In this life we have but a glimpse of this beauty and happiness: we shall hereafter, as John saith, see him as he is: thine eyes, as Isaiah promiseth, shall behold the King in his glory, then shall we be perfectly enamoured, have a full fruition of it, desire, behold and love him alone as the most amiable and fairest object, or chiefest good.

This likewise should we now have done, had not our will been corrupted; and as we are enjoined to love God with all our heart, and all our soul: for to that end were we born, to love this object, as Melancthon discourseth, and to enjoy it. And him our will would have loved and sought alone as our principal good, and all other good things for God's sake: and nature, as she proceeded from it, would have sought this fountain; but in this infirmity of human nature this order is disturbed, our love is corrupt: and a man is like that monster in Plato, composed of a Scylla, a lion, and a man. We are carried away headlong with the torrent of our affections: the world and that infinite variety of pleasing objects in it, do so allure and enamour us, that we cannot so much as look towards God, seek him, or think on him as we should: we cannot, saith

Austin, we cannot contain ourselves from them, their sweetness is so pleasing to us. Marriage, saith Gualter, detains many, a thing in itself laudable, good and necessary, but many deceived and carried away with the blind love of it, have quite laid aside the love of God, and desire of his glory. Meat and drink hath overcome as many, whilst they rather strive to please, satisfy their guts and belly, than to serve God and nature. Some are so busied about merchandise to get money, they lose their own souls, whiles covetously carried: and with an unsatiable desire of gain, they forget God; as much we may say of honour, leagues, friendships, health, wealth, and all other profits or pleasures in this life whatsoever. In this world there be so many beautiful objects, splendours and brightness of gold, majesty of glory, assistance of friends, fair promises, smooth words, victories, triumphs, and such an infinite company of pleasing beauties to allure us, and draw us from God, that we cannot look after him. And this is it which Christ himself, those Prophets and Apostles, so much thundered against. 1 John, 2: 15, dehorts us from: *Love not the world, nor the things that are in the world: if any man love the world, the love of the Father is not in him. For all that is in the world, as the lust of the flesh, the lust of the eyes, and pride of life, is not of the Father, but of the world: and the world passeth away, and the lust thereof; but he that fulfilleth the will of God abideth for ever. No man,* saith our Saviour, *can serve two masters,* but he must love the one and hate the other, Austin well infers: and this is that which all the fathers inculcate. He cannot (Austin admonisheth) be God's friend, that is delighted with the pleasures of the world: make clean thine heart, purify thine heart, if thou wilt see this beauty, prepare thyself for it. It is the eye of contemplation, by which we must behold it, the wing of meditation which lifts us up and rears our souls with the motion of our hearts, and sweetness of contemplation: so saith Gregory, cited by Bonaventure. And as Philo Judæus seconds him, He that loves God will soar aloft and take him wings; and leaving the earth fly up to Heaven, wander with Sun and Moon, Stars, and that heavenly troop, God himself being his guide. If we desire to see him, we must lay aside all vain objects, which detain us and dazzle our eyes, and as Ficinus adviseth us, get us solar eyes, spectacles as they that look on the Sun: to see this divine beauty, lay aside all material objects, all sense, and then thou shalt see him as he is. Thou covetous wretch, as Austin expostulates, why dost thou stand gaping on this dross, muck-hills, filthy excrements? behold a far fairer object, God himself wooes thee; behold him, enjoy him, he is sick for love. He invites thee to his sight, to come into his fair Garden, to eat and drink with him, to be merry with him, to enjoy his presence for ever. Wisdom cries out in the streets, besides the gates, in the top of high places, before the City, at the entry of the door, and bids them give ear to her instruction, which is better than gold or precious stones: no pleasures can be compared to it: leave all then and follow her. In Ficinus' words, I exhort and beseech you, that you would embrace and follow this divine love with all your hearts and abilities, by all offices and endeavours make this so loving God propitious unto you. For whom alone, saith Plotinus, we must forsake the Kingdoms and Empires of the whole earth, Sea, Land, and Air, if we desire to be engrafted into him, leave all and follow him.

Now forasmuch as this love of God is an habit infused of God, as Thomas holds, by which a man is inclined to love God above all, and his neighbour as himself, we must pray to God that he will open our eyes, make clear our hearts, that we may be capable of his glorious rays, and perform those duties that he requires of us, *to love God above all, and our neighbour as ourself*, to keep his commandments. *In this we know,* saith John, *we love the children of God, when we love God and keep his commandments. ———— This is the love of God, that we keep his commandments; he that loveth not, knoweth not God, for God is love, ———— and he that dwelleth in love, dwelleth in God, and God in him,* for love presupposeth knowledge, faith, hope, and unites us to God himself, as Leon Hebræus delivereth unto us, and is accompanied with the fear of God, humility, meekness, patience, all those virtues, and charity itself. For if we love God, we shall love our neighbour, and perform the duties which are required at our hands, to which we are exhorted. We shall not be envious or puffed up, or boast, disdain, think evil, or be provoked to anger, but suffer all things; endeavour to keep the unity of the Spirit in the bond of peace; forbear one another, forgive one another, clothe the naked, visit the sick, and perform all those works of mercy, which Clemens Alexandrinus calls the extent and complement of Love; and that not for fear or worldly respects, but for the love of God himself. This we shall do if we be truly enamoured; but we come short in both, we neither love God nor our neighbour as we should. Our love in spiritual things is too defective, in worldly things too excessive, there is a jar in both. We love the world too much; God too little, our neighbour not at all, or for our own ends.

The mob judges of friendships by their use.   (OVID)

The chief thing we respect is our commodity: and what we do, is for fear of worldly punishment, for vain-glory, praise of men, fashion, and such by-respects, not for God's sake. We neither know God aright, nor seek, love, or worship him as we should. And for these defects, we involve ourselves into a multitude of errors, we swerve from this true love and worship of God: which is a cause unto us of unspeakable miseries; running into both extremes, we become fools, madmen, without sense, as now in the next place I will shew you.

The parties affected are innumerable almost, and scattered over the face of the earth, far and near, and so have been in all precedent ages, from the beginning of the world to these times, of all sorts and conditions. For method's sake I will reduce them to a twofold division, according to those two extremes of Excess and Defect, Impiety and Superstition, Idolatry and Atheism. Not that there is any excess of divine worship or love of God; that cannot be, we cannot love God too much, or do our duty as we ought, as Papists hold, or have any perfection in this life, much less supererogate; when we have all done, we are unprofitable servants. But because we do go astray, are zealous without knowledge, and too solicitous about that which is not necessary, busying ourselves about impertinent, needless, idle, & vain ceremonies, to please the populace, as the Jews did about sacrifices, oblations, offerings, incense, new Moons, feasts, &c., but as Isaiah taxeth them, Who required this at your hands? We have too great opinion of our own worth, that we can satisfy the Law; and do more than is required at our hands, by performing those Evangelical Counsels, and such works of supererogation, merit for others, which Bellarmine, Gregory de Valentia, all their Jesuits and champions defend, that if God should deal in rigour with them, some of their Franciscans and Dominicans are so pure, that nothing could be objected to them. Some of us again are too dear, as we think, more divine and sanctified than others, of a better metal, greater gifts, and with that proud Pharisee, contemn others in respect of ourselves, we are better Christians, better learned, choice spirits, inspired, know more, have special revelation, perceive God's secrets, and thereupon presume, say and do many times which is not fitting to be said or done. Of this number are all superstitious Idolaters, Ethnicks, Mahometans, Jews, Hereticks, Enthusiasts, Divinators, Prophets, Sectaries, and Schismaticks. Zanchius reduceth such infidels to four chief sects; but I will insist and follow mine own intended method: all which, with many other curious persons, Monks, Hermits, &c. may be ranged in this extreme, and fight under this superstitious banner, with those rude Idiots, and infinite swarms of people that are seduced by them. In the other extreme or in defect, march those impious Epicures, Libertines, Atheists, Hypocrites, Infidels, worldly, secure, impenitent, unthankful, and carnal-minded

men that attribute all to natural causes, that will acknowledge no supreme power; that have cauterized consciences, or live in a reprobate
sense: or such desperate persons as are too distrustful of his mercies. Of
these there be many subdivisions, divers degrees of madness and folly,
some more than other. as shall be shewed in the symptoms: and yet all
miserably out, perplexed, doting, and beside themselves for religion's
sake. For as Zanchius well distinguished, and all the world knows, Religion is twofold, true or false; False is that vain superstition of Idolaters, such as were of old, Greeks, Romans, present Mahometans, &c.
Foolish fear of the gods, Tully could term it; or as Zanchius defines it,
when false gods, or that God is falsely worshipped. And 'tis a miserable
plague, a torture of the Soul, a mere madness, a religious madness,
Meteran calls it, or as Seneca, a frantick error; or as Austin, a furious
disease of the Soul; a quintessence of madness; for he that is superstitious can never be quiet. 'Tis proper to man alone; to him alone pride,
avarice, superstition, saith Pliny; which wrings his soul for the present
and to come: the greatest misery belongs to mankind, a perpetual servitude, a slavery, a fear born of fear, an heavy yoke, the seal of damnation,
an intolerable burthen. They that are superstitious, are still fearing,
suspecting, vexing themselves with auguries, prodigies, false tales,
dreams, idle, vain works, unprofitable labours, as Boterus observes, they
are driven hither and thither by their troubled minds, enemies to God
and to themselves. In a word, as Seneca concludes, superstition destroys,
but true Religion honours God. True Religion, where the true God is
truly worshipped, is the way to Heaven, the mother of all virtues, Love,
Fear, Devotion, Obedience, Knowledge, &c. It rears the dejected Soul of
man, and amidst so many cares, miseries, persecutions, which this world
affords, it is a sole ease, an unspeakable comfort, a sweet reposal, a light
yoke, an anchor, and an Haven. It adds courage, boldness, and begets
generous spirits: although tyrants rage, persecute, and that bloudy
Lictor or Serjeant be ready to martyr them, either sacrifice or die, (as
in those persecutions of the primitive Church, it was put in practise, as
you may read in Eusebius, and others) though enemies be now ready to
invade, and all in an uproar, though heaven should fall on his head, he
would not be dismayed. But as a good Christian prince once made answer to a menacing Turk, he easily scorns the wicked host of men, who is
safe in the protection of God: or as Phalaris writ to Alexander in a
wrong cause, he nor any other enemy could terrify him, for that he
trusted in God.

If God be with us, who can be against us? In all calamities, persecutions whatsoever, as David did, he will sing with him, The Lord is my rock, my fortress, my strength, my refuge, the tower and horn of my salvation, &c. In all troubles and adversities, God is my hope and help, still ready to be found, I will not therefore fear, &c., 'tis a fear expelling fear: he hath peace of conscience, and is full of hope, which is (saith Austin) the life of this our mortal life, hope of immortality, the sole comfort of our misery: otherwise as Paul saith, we of all others were most wretched, but this makes us happy, counterpoising our hearts in all misery: superstition torments, and is from the Devil, the author of lies; but this is from God himself, as Lucian that Antiochian Priest made his divine confession in Eusebius, God is the author of our Religion himself, his word is our rule, a lanthorn to us, dictated by the holy Ghost, he plays upon our hearts as so many harp-strings, and we are his Temples, he dwelleth in us, and we in him.

The part affected of superstition, is the brain, heart, will, understanding, soul itself, and all the faculties of it, all is mad, and dotes. Now for the extent, as I say, the world itself is the subject of it, (to omit that grand sin of Atheism) all times have been misaffected, past, present. There is not one that doth good, no not one, from the Prophet to the Priest, &c. A lamentable thing it is to consider, how many myriads of men this Idolatry and Superstition (for that comprehends all) hath infatuated in all ages, besotted by this blind zeal, which is Religion's Ape, Religion's Bastard, Religion's shadow, false glass. For where God hath a Temple, the Devil will have a chapel: where God hath sacrifices, the Devil will have his oblations; where God hath ceremonies, the Devil will have his traditions; where there is any Religion, the Devil will plant superstition; and 'tis a pitiful sight to behold and read, what tortures, miseries it hath procured, what slaughter of souls it hath made, how it raged amongst those old Persians, Syrians, Egyptians, Greeks, Romans, Tuscans, Gauls, Germans, Britons, &c. Saith Pliny (speaking of Superstition), the Britons are so stupendly superstitious in their ceremonies, that they go beyond those Persians. He that shall but read in Pausanias alone, those Gods, Temples, Altars, Idols, Statues, so curiously made, with such infinite cost and charge, amongst those old Greeks, such multitudes of them, and frequent varieties, as Gerbelius truly observes, may stand amazed, and never enough wonder at it; and thank God withal, that by the light of the Gospel, we are so happily freed from that slavish Idolatry in these our days. But heretofore almost in all Countries, in all places, superstition hath blinded the hearts of men. In all ages, what a small portion hath the true Church ever been!

The Devil divides the world's empire with God.

The Patriarchs and their families, the Israelites, a handful in respect [or comparison], Christ and his Apostles, and not all of them neither. Into what traits hath it been compinged, a little flock! how hath superstition on the other side dilated herself, error, ignorance, barbarism, folly, madness, deceived, triumphed, and insulted over the most wise, discreet, and understanding men! Philosophers, Dynasts, Monarchs, all were involved and over-shadowed in this mist, in more than Cimmerian darkness. So much doth superstition deprave ignorant minds and even lead astray the souls of the wise. At this present, how small a party is truly religious! How little in respect! Divide the world into six parts, and one, or not so much, is Christians; Idolaters and Mahometans possess almost Asia, Africa, America, Magellanica. The Kings of China, great Cham, Siam, and Bornaye, Pegu, Deccan, Narsinga, Japan, &c., are Gentiles, Idolaters, and many other petty Princes in Asia, Monomotopa, Congo, and I know not how many Negro Princes in Africa, all Terra Australis Incognita, most of America Pagans, differing all in their several superstitions; and yet all Idolaters. The Mahometans extend themselves over the great Turk's dominions in Europe, Africa, Asia, to the Xeriffes in Barbary, and his territories in Fez, Sus, Morocco, &c. The Tartar, the great Mogor, the Sophy of Persia, with most of their dominions and subjects, are at this day Mahometans. See how the Devil rageth! Those at odds, or differing among themselves, some for Alli, some Enbocar, for Acmar, and Ozimen, those four Doctors, Mahomet's successors, and are subdivided into seventy-two inferior sects, as Leo Afer reports. The Jews, as a company of vagabonds, are scattered over all parts; whose story, present estate, progress from time to time, is fully set down by Mr. Thomas Jackson, Doctor of Divinity, in his comment on the Creed. A fifth part of the world, and hardly that, now professeth Christ, but so inlarded & interlaced with several superstitions, that there is scarce a sound part to be found, or any agreement amongst them.

Presbyter John, in Africa, Lord of those Abyssines, or Æthiopians, is by his profession a Christian, but so different from us, with such new absurdities and ceremonies, such liberty, such a mixture of Idolatry and Paganism, that they keep little more than a bare title of Christianity. They suffer Polygamy, Circumcision, stupend fastings, divorce as they will themselves, &c., and as the Papists call on the Virgin Mary, so do they on Thomas Didymus, before Christ. The Greek or Eastern Church is rent from this of the West, and as they have four chief Patriarchs, so have they four subdivisions, besides those Nestorians, Jacobins, Syrians, Armenians, Georgians, &c., scattered over Asia Minor, Syria, Egypt, &c., Greece, Valachia, Circassia, Bulgary, Bosnia, Albania, Illyricum, Slavonia, Croatia, Thrace, Servia, Rascia, and a sprinkling amongst the Tartars. The Russians, Muscovites, and most of that Great Duke's [Czar's] subjects, are part of the Greek Church, and still Christians: but as one saith, in process of time they have added so many superstitions, they be rather semi-Christians than otherwise. That which remains is the Western Church with us in Europe, but so eclipsed with several schisms, heresies and superstitions, that one knows not where to find it. The Papists have Italy, Spain, Savoy, part of Germany, France, Poland, and a sprinkling in the rest of Europe. In America they hold all that which Spaniards inhabit, Hispania Nova, Castella Aurea, Peru, &c. In the East Indies, the Philippinæ, some small holds about Goa, Malacca, Zelan, Ormus, &c., which the Portuguese got not long since, and those land-leaping [or wandering] Jesuits have essayed in China, Japan, as appears by their yearly letters; in Africa they have Melinda, Quiloa, Mombaze, &c., and some few towns, they drive out one superstition with another. Poland is a receptacle of all religions, where Samisetans, Socinians, Photinians (now protected in Transylvania and Poland), Arians, Anabaptists are to be found, as well as in some German Cities. Scandia is Christian, but Damianus A-Goes the Portugal Knight complains, so mixt with Magick, Pagan Rites and Ceremonies, they may be as well counted Idolaters: what Tacitus formerly said of a like nation, is verified in them, a people subject to superstition, contrary to religion. And some of them as about Lapland and the Pilapians, the Devil's possession to this day, a miserable people (saith mine Author), and which is to be admired and pitied, if any of them be baptized, which the Kings of Sweden much labour, they die within seven or nine days after, and for that cause they will hardly be brought to Christianity, but worship still the Devil, who daily appears to them. In their Idolatrous courses, they rejoice in and worship the Gods of the country, &c. Yet are they [that is, they still are] very superstitious, like our wild Irish. Though they of the better note, the Kings of Denmark & Sweden themselves, that govern them, be Lutherans; the remnant are Calvinists, Lutherans, in Germany equally mixt. And yet the emperor himself, dukes of Lorraine, Bavaria, and the Princes Electors, are most part professed Papists. And though some part of France and Ireland, Great Britain, half the cantons in Switzerland, and the Low Countries, be Calvinists, more defecate [or purified], than the rest, yet at odds amongst themselves, not free from superstition. And which Brochard, the monk, in his description of the Holy Land, after he had censured the Greek church, and showed their errors, concluded at last, I say God grant there be no fopperies in our church. As a dam of water stopped in one place breaks out into another, so doth superstition. I say nothing of Anabaptists, Socinians, Brownists, Barrowists, Familists, &c. There is superstition in our prayers, often in our hearing of sermons, bitter contentions, invectives, persecutions, strange conceits, besides diversity of opinions, schisms, factions, &c. But as the Lord said to Eliphaz the Temanite, and his two friends, *his wrath was kindled against them, for they had not spoken of him things that were right*, we may justly of these Schismaticks and Hereticks, how wise soever in their own conceits, they speak not, they think not, they write not well of God, and as they ought. And therefore, as Erasmus concludes to Dorpius, what shall we wish them, but a sound mind, and a good Physician? But more of their differences, paradoxes, opinions, mad pranks, in the Symptoms: I now hasten to the Causes.

SUBSECTION 2 — *Causes of Religious Melancholy. From the Devil by miracles, apparitions, oracles. His instruments or factors, Politicians, Priests, Impostors, Hereticks, blind guides. In them simplicity, fear, blind zeal, ignorance, solitariness, curiosity, pride, vain-glory, presumption, &c. His engines, fasting, solitariness, hope, fear, &c.*

WE are taught in holy Scripture, that *the Devil rangeth abroad like a roaring Lion, still seeking whom he may devour:* and as in several shapes, so by several engines and devices, he goeth about to seduce us; sometimes he transforms himself into an Angel of Light; and is so cunning, that he is able, if it were possible, to deceive the very Elect. He will be worshipped as God himself, and is so adored by the Heathen, and esteemed. And in imitation of that divine power, as Eusebius observes, to abuse or emulate God's glory, as Dandinus adds, he will have all homage, sacrifices, oblations, and whatsoever else belongs to the worship of God, to be done likewise unto him, he will be like God, and by this means infatuates the world, deludes, entraps, and destroys many a thousand souls. Sometimes by dreams, visions (as God to Moses by familiar conference), the Devil in several shapes talks with them: in the Indies it is common, and in China nothing so familiar as apparitions, inspirations, oracles, by terrifying them with false prodigies, counterfeit miracles, sending storms, tempests, diseases, plagues (as of old in Athens there was Apollo Alexicacus, Apollo the bringer of pestilence and driver away of evils), raising wars, seditions by spectrums, troubling their consciences, driving them to despair, terrors of mind, intolerable pains; by promises, rewards, benefits, and fair means, he raiseth such an opinion of his Deity and greatness, that they dare not do otherwise than adore him, do as he will have them, they dare not offend him. And to compel them more to stand in awe of him, he sends and cures diseases, disquiets their spirits (as Cyprian saith), torments and terrifies their souls, to make them adore him: and all his study, all his endeavour is to divert them from true religion to superstition: and because he is damned himself, and in an error, he would have all the world participate of his errors, and be damned with him. The first mover, therefore, of all superstition, is the Devil, that great enemy of mankind, the principal agent, who in a thousand several shapes, after diverse fashions, with several engines, illusions, and by several names hath deceived the inhabitants of the earth, in several places and countries, still rejoicing at their falls. All the world over before Christ's time, he freely domineered, and held the souls of men in most slavish subjection (saith Eusebius) in diverse forms, ceremonies, and sacrifices, till Christ's coming, as if those Devils of the Air had shared the earth amongst them, which the Platonists held for gods (we are the sport of the gods), and were our governors and keepers. In several places, they had several rites, orders, names, of which read Wierus, Strozius, Cicogna, and others; Adonided amongst the Syrians: Adramelech amongst the Capernaites, Asiniæ amongst the Emathites: Astarte with the Sidonians; Astaroth with the Palestines; Dagon with the Philistines; Tartary with the Hanæi; Milcom amongst the Ammonites: Bel amongst the Babylonians; Beelzebub and Baal with the Samaritans and Moabites; Apis, Isis, and Osiris amongst the Egyptians; Apollo Pythius at Delphi, Colophon, Ancyra, Cumæ, Erythræ; Jupiter in Crete, Venus at Cyprus, Juno at Carthage, Æsculapius at Epidaurus, Diana at Ephesus, Pallas at Athens, &c. And even in these our days, both in the East and West Indies, in Tartary, China, Japan, &c., what strange Idols, in what prodigious forms, with what absurd ceremonies are they adored? What strange sacraments, like ours of Baptism and the Lord's Supper, what goodly Temples, Priests, Sacrifices, they had in America, when the Spaniards first landed there, let Acosta the Jesuit relate, and how the Devil imitated the Ark and the children of Israel's coming out of Egypt; with many such. For as Lipsius well discourseth out of the doctrine of the Stoicks, now and of old, they [that is, the Devils] still and most especially desire to be adored by men. See but what Vertomannus, Marco Polo, Lerius, Benzo, P. Martyr in his Ocean Decades, Acosta. and Mat. Riccius in his Christian Campaign in China, relate. Eusebius wonders how that wise City of Athens, and flourishing Kingdoms of Greece, should be so besotted; and we in our times, how those witty China's [Chinese], so perspicacious in all other things, should be so gulled, so tortured with superstition, so blind, as to worship stocks and stones. But it is no marvel, when we see all out as great effects amongst Christians themselves; how are those Anabaptists, Arians, and Papists above the rest, miserably infatuated! Mars, Jupiter, Apollo, and Æsculapius, have resigned their interest, names, and offices to S. George,

O greatest master of war, by our youths worshipped
As though he were Mars himself! (MANTUAN)

S. Christopher, and a company of fictitious Saints, Venus [hath resigned hers] to the Lady of Loretto. And as those old Romans had several distinct gods, for divers offices, persons, places, so have they Saints, as Lavater well observes out of Lactantius, the name only being changed, 'tis the same spirit or Devil that deludes them still. The manner how, as I say, is by rewards, promises, terrors, affrights, punishments: in a word, fair and foul means, Hope and Fear. How often hath Jupiter, Apollo, Bacchus, and the rest, sent plagues in Greece and Italy, because their sacrifices were neglected!

Many misfortunes have the slighted Gods
Imposed on poor Hesperia, (OVID)

to terrify them, to rouse them up, and the like: see but Livy, Dionysus Halicarnasseus, Thucydides, Pausanias, Philostratus, Polybius, before the battle of Cannæ, prodigies, signs and wonders abounded, both publickly in the temple and privately. Œneus reigned in Ætolia, and because he did not sacrifice to Diana with his other gods (see more in Libanius his Diana), she sent a wild boar, to spoil both men and country, which was afterwards killed by Meleager. So Plutarch in the Life of Lucullus relates, how Mithridates, King of Pontus, at the siege of Cizicum, with all his Navy was overthrown by Proserpina, for neglecting of her holy-day. She appeared in a vision to Aristagoras in the night: Tomorrow, she said, I will cause a contest between a Libyan and a Pontick minstrel; and the day following, this Enigma was understood; for with a great South-wind which came from Libya, she quite overwhelmed Mithridates' army. What prodigies and miracles, dreams, visions, predictions, apparitions, oracles, have been of old at Delphi, Dodona, Trophonius' Den, at Thebes, and Lebadea, of Jupiter Ammon in Egypt, Amphiarus in Attica, &c.; what strange cures performed by Apollo and

Æsculapius! Juno's image and that of Fortune spake, Castor and Pollux fought in person for the Romans against Hannibal's army, as Pallas, Mars, Juno, Venus, for Greeks and Trojans, &c. Amongst our Pseudo-Catholicks, nothing so familiar as such miracles; how many cures done by our Lady of Loretto, at Sichem! of old at our S. Thomas' Shrine, &c. S. Sabine was seen to fight for Arnulphus, Duke of Spoleto. S. George fought in person for John, the Bastard of Portugal, against the Castil-ians; S. James for the Spaniards in America. In the battle of Bannock-burn, where Edward the Second, our English King, was foiled by the Scots, S. Philanus' arm was seen to fight (if Hector Boethius doth not impose), that was before shut up in a silver capcase; another time, in the same author, S. Magnus fought for them. Now for visions, revela-tions, miracles, not only out of the Legend, out of purgatory, but every day comes news from the Indies, and at home, read the Jesuits' Letters, Ribadineira, Thurselinus, Acosta, Lippomannus, Xaverius, Ignatius' Lives, &c., and tell me what difference?

His ordinary instruments or factors which he useth, as God himself did good Kings, Lawful Magistrates, patriarchs, prophets, to the es-tablishing of his Church, are Politicians, Statesmen, Priests, Hereticks, blind guides, Impostors, pseudo-Prophets, to propagate his superstition. And first to begin with Politicians, it hath ever been a principal axiom with them, to maintain religion, or superstition, which they determine of, alter and vary upon all occasions, as to them seems best, they make Religion mere policy, a cloak, a human invention; to rule the vulgar with, as Tacitus and Tully hold. Austin censures Scævola saying and acknowledging, that it was a fit thing cities should be deceived by re-ligion, according to the diverb, If the world will be gulled, let it be gulled, 'tis good howsoever to keep it in subjection. 'Tis that Aristotle and Plato inculcate in their Politicks, Religion neglected brings plagues to the city, opens a gap to all naughtiness. 'Tis that which all our late Politicians ingeminate; Cromerus, Boterus, Clapmarius, Arneseus, Cap-tain Machiavel will have a prince by all means to counterfeit religion, to be superstitious in shew at least, to seem to be devout, frequent holy exercises, honour divines, love the Church, affect priests, as Numa, Ly-curgus, and such law-makers were, and did, not that they had faith, but that it was an easy way to keep power, to keep people in obedience. Though truly, as Cardan writes, the Christian law is the law of piety, justice, faith, simplicity, &c. But this error of his, Innocentius Jentilet-tus, a French Lawyer, and Thomas Bozius, in his book On the Downfall of Peoples and Kings, have copiously confuted. Many Politicians, I dare not deny, maintain Religion as a true means, and sincerely speak of it without hypocrisy, are truly zealous and religious themselves. Justice and Religion are the two chief props and supporters of a well-governed commonwealth; but most of them are but Machiavellians, counterfeits only for political ends: for kingship only (which Campanella in his Triumph of Atheism observes), as amongst our modern Turks, as knowing the greatest dominion is that over men's minds; and that as Sabellicus delivers, A man without Religion is like a horse without a bridle. No better way to curb than superstition, to terrify men's consciences, and to keep them in awe: they make new laws, statutes, invent new religions, ceremonies, as so many stalking-horses, to their own ends. If a religion be false, only let it be supposed to be true, and it will tame fierce minds, restrain desires, and make loyal subjects. Therefore (saith Polybius of Lycurgus) did he maintain ceremonies, not that he was superstitious himself, but that he perceived mortal men more apt to embrace Paradoxes than aught else, and durst attempt no evil things for fear of the gods. This was Zamolxis' stratagem amongst the Thracians. Numa's plot, when he said he had conference with the Nymph Ægeria, and that of Sertorius with an Hart; to get more credit to their Decrees, by deriving them from the gods; or else they did all by divine instinct, which Nicholas Damascen well observes of Lycurgus, Solon, and Minos, they had their laws dictated, by Jupiter himself. So Mahomet referred his new laws to the Angel Gabriel, by whose direction he gave out they were made. Caligula in Dion feigned himself to be familiar with Castor and Pollux, and many such, which kept those Romans under (who, as Machiavel proves, were most superstitious): and did curb the people more by this means, than by force of arms, or severity of human laws. Only the common people were deceived (saith Vaninus, speaking of Religion), your Grandees and Philosophers had no such conceit [or notion], save to establish and maintain their power, which had not been possible without the pretext of religion; and many thousands in all ages have ever held as much, Philosophers especially, they knew these things were fables, but they were silent for fear of Laws, &c. To this end that Syrian Pherecydes, Pythagoras his Master, broached in the East amongst the Heathens first the immortality of the Soul, as Trismegistus did in Egypt, with a many of feigned Gods. Those French and British Druids in the West first taught, saith Cæsar, that souls did not die, but after death went from one to another, that so they might encourage them to virtue. 'Twas for a politick end, and to this purpose the old Poets feigned those Elysian fields, their Æcus, Minos, and Rhadamanthus, their infernal Judges, and those Stygian lakes, fiery Phlegethons, Pluto's Kingdom, and variety of torments after death. Those that had done well went to the Elysian fields, but evil-doers to Cocytus, and to that burning lake of Hell, with fire and brimstone for ever to be tormented. 'Tis this which Plato labours for in his Phædo, and in the third book of his Republick. The Turks in their Alcoran, when they set down rewards and several punishments for every particular virtue and vice, when they persuade men, that they that die in battle shall go directly to Heaven, but wicked livers to eternal torment, and all of all sorts (much like our Papistical Purgatory), for a set time shall be tortured in their graves, as appears by that tract which John Baptista Alfaqui, that Mauritanian Priest, now turned Christian, hath written in his confutation of the Alcoran. After a man's death two black Angels, Nunquir and Nequir (so they call them) come to him to his grave and punish him for his precedent sins; if he lived well, they torture him the less: if ill, they incessantly punish him to the day of judgment. The thought of this crucifies them all their lives long, and makes them spend their days in fasting and prayer, lest these evils should come to pass, &c. A Tartar Prince, saith Marco Polo, called the Old Man of the Mountain, the better to establish his government amongst his subjects, and to keep them in awe, found a convenient place in a pleasant valley, environed with hills, in which he made a delicious Park full of odoriferous flowers and fruits, and a Palace of all worldly contents that could possibly be devised, Music, Pictures, variety of meats, &c., and chose out a certain young man, whom with a soporiferous potion he so benumbed, that he perceived nothing: and so fast asleep as he was, caused him to be conveyed into this fair Garden; where after he had lived awhile in all such pleasures a sensual man could desire, he cast him into a sleep again, and brought him forth, that when he awaked he might tell others he had been in Paradise. The like he did for Hell, and by this means brought his people to subjection. Because Heaven and Hell are mentioned in the Scriptures, and to be believed necessary by Christians: so cunningly can the Devil and his Ministers, in imitation of true Religion, counterfeit and forge the like, to circumvent and delude his superstitious followers. Many such tricks and impostures are acted by Politicians, in China especially, but with what effect I will discourse in the Symptoms.

Next to Politicians, if I may distinguish them, are some of our Priests, (who make Religion Policy) if not far beyond them, for they domineer over Princes and Statesmen themselves. One saith, they tyrannize over men's consciences more than any other torments whatsoever, partly for their commodity and gain; since (as Postellus holds) their livelihood, that corruption of all religions, is at stake; for sovereignty, credit, to maintain their state and reputation, out of Ambition and Avarice, which are their chief supporters. What have they not made the common people believe? Impossibilities in nature, incredible things; what devices, traditions, ceremonies, have they not invented in all ages to keep men in obedience, to enrich themselves? For their enrichment have men's minds been overcome with superstition, as Livy saith. Those Egyptian Priests of old got all the sovereignty into their hands, and knowing, as Curtius insinuates, the common people will sooner obey Priests than Captains, and nothing so forcible as superstition, or better than blind zeal to rule a multitude; have so terrified and gulled them, that it is incredible to relate. All nations almost have been besotted in this kind; amongst our Britons and old Gauls the Druids: Magi in Persia; Philosophers in Greece; Chaldæans amongst the Oriental; Brachmanni in India; Gymnosophists in Æthiopia; the Turditani in Spain; Augurs in Rome, have insulted; Apollo's Priests in Greece, Phæbades and Pythonissæ, by their oracles and phantasms; Amphiaraus and his companions; now Mahometan and Pagan Priests, what can they not effect? How do they not infatuate the world? Scaliger writes of the Mahometan Priests, so cunningly can they gull the commons in all places and Countries. But above all others, that High Priest of Rome, the dam of that monstrous and superstitious brood, the bull-bellowing Pope, which now rageth in the West, that three-headed Cerberus, hath played his part. Whose religion at this day is mere policy, a state wholly composed of superstition and wit, and needs nothing but wit and superstition to maintain it, that useth Colleges and religious houses to as good purpose as Forts and Castles, and doth more at this day by a company of scribbling Parasites, fiery-spirited Friars, Zealous Anchorites, hypocritical Confessors, and those Prætorian soldiers, his Janissary Jesuits, that dissociable society, as Langius terms it, the last effort of the Devil and the very excrement of time, that now stand in the fore-front of the battle, will have a monopoly of, and engross all other learning, but domineer in Divinity, and fight alone almost (for the rest are but his dromedaries and asses), than ever he could have done by garrisons and armies. What power of Prince, or penal Law, be it never so strict, could enforce men to do that which for conscience' sake they will voluntarily undergo? As to fast from all flesh, abstain from marriage, rise to their prayers at midnight, whip themselves, with stupend fasting and penance, abandon the world, wilful poverty, perform canonical and blind obedience, to prostrate their goods, fortunes, bodies, lives, and offer up themselves at their Superior's feet, at his command? What so powerful an engine as superstition? Which they right well perceiving, are of no religion at all themselves. For truly (as Calvin rightly suspects, [and as] the tenor and practice of their life proves) the first of the secrets of these theologians, by which they rule, and in chief, is that they hold there is no God, as Leo X. did, Hildebrand the Magician, Alexander VI., Julius II., mere atheists, and which the common proverb amongst them approves, the worst Christians of Italy are the Romans, of the Romans the Priests are wildest, the lewdest Priests are preferred to be Cardinals, and the baddest man amongst the Cardinals is chosen to be Pope, that is an epicure, as most part the Popes are, Infidels and Lucianists, for so they think and believe; and what is said of Christ to be fables and impostures, of Heaven and Hell, day of Judgment, Paradise, Immortality of the soul, are all dreams, toys, and old wives' tales. Yet as so many whetstones to make other tools cut, but cut not themselves, though they be of no religion at all, they will make others most devout and superstitious, by promises and threats, compel, enforce from, and lead them by the nose like so many bears in a line; when as their end is not to propagate the church, advance God's kingdom, seek His glory or common good, but to enrich themselves, to enlarge their territories, to domineer and compel them to stand in awe, to live in subjection to the See of Rome. For what otherwise care they? Since the world wishes to be gulled, let it be gulled, 'tis fit it should be so. And for which Austin cites Varro to maintain his Roman religion, we may better apply to them: some things are true, some false, which for their own ends they will not have the gullish commonalty take notice of. As well may witness their intolerable covetousness, strange forgeries, fopperies, fooleries, unrighteous subtilties, impostures, illusion, new doctrines, paradoxes, traditions, false miracles, which they have still forged to enthrall, circumvent, and subjugate them, to maintain their own estates. One while by Bulls, Pardons, Indulgences, and their doctrine of good works; that they be meritorious, hope of Heaven, by that means they have so fleeced the commonalty, and spurred on this free superstitious horse, that he runs himself blind, and is an Ass to carry burdens. They have so amplified Peter's patrimony, that from a poor Bishop he is become King of Kings. Lord of Lords, a Demi-god, as his Canonists make him (Felinus and the rest) above God himself. And for his wealth and temporalities, is not inferior to many Kings; his Cardinals Princes' companions; and in every Kingdom almost. Abbots, Priors, Monks, Friars, &c., and his Clergy have engrossed a third part, half, in some places all, into their hands. Three Princes Electors in Germany Bishops; besides Magdeburg, Spires, Salzburg, Bremen, Bamberg, &c. In France, as Bodine gives us to understand, their revenues are twelve millions, and three hundred thousand livres; and of twelve parts of the revenues in France, the Church possesseth seven. The Jesuits, a new sect begun in this age, have, as Midendropius and Pelargus reckon up, three or four hundred Colleges in Europe, and more revenues than many Princes. In France, as Arnoldus proves, in thirty years they have got £200,000 annually. I say nothing of the rest of their orders. We have had in England, as Armachanus demonstrates, above thirty thousand Friars at once, and, as Speed collects out of Leland and others, almost 600 religious houses, and near two hundred thousand pound in revenues of the old rent belonging to them, besides Images of Gold, Silver, Plate, furniture, goods and ornaments, as Weever calculates, and esteems them at the dissolution of the Abbies, worth a million of gold. How many Towns in every Kingdom hath superstition enriched! What a deal of money by musty reliques, Images, Idolatry, have their Mass-Priests engrossed, and what sums have they scraped by their other tricks! Loretto in Italy, Walsingham in England, in those days, where everything shines with gold, saith Erasmus, S. Thomas's shrine, &c., may witness. Delphi, so renowned of old in Greece for Apollo's oracle, Delos, a general meeting-place and market-town defended only by religion, Dodona, whose fame and wealth were sustained by religion, were not so rich, so famous. If they can get but a relic of some Saint, the Virgin Mary's picture, Idols, or the like, that City is for ever made, it needs no other maintenance. Now if any of these their impostures or juggling tricks be controverted, or called in question: if a magnanimous or zealous Luther, an heroical Luther, as Dithmarus calls him, dare touch the monks' bellies, all is in a combustion, all is in an uproar: Demetrius and his associates are ready to pull him in pieces, to keep up their trades, " Great is Diana of the Ephesians ": with a mighty shout of two hours long they will roar and not be pacified.

Now for their authority, what by auricular confession, satisfaction, penance, Peter's keys, thunderings, excommunications, &c., roaring bulls, this High Priest of Rome, shaking his Gorgon's head, hath so terrified the soul of many a silly man, insulted over Majesty itself, and swaggered generally over all Europe for many ages, and still doth to some, holding them as yet in slavish subjection, as never tyrannising Spaniards did by their poor Negroes, or Turks by their galley-slaves. The Bishop of Rome (saith Stapleton, a parasite of his) hath done that

without arms, which those Roman Emperors could never achieve with
forty legions of soldiers, deposed kings, and crowned them again with
his foot, made friends, and corrected at his pleasure, &c. 'Tis a wonder,
saith Machiavel, what slavery King Henry the Second endured for the
death of Thomas à Becket, what things he was enjoined by the Pope,
and how he submitted himself to do that which in our times a private
man would not endure, and all through superstition. Henry the Fourth,
deposed of his Empire, stood barefooted with his wife at the gates of
Canossa. Frederick the Emperor was trodden on by Alexander the Third.
Another held Adrian's stirrup. King John kissed the knees of Pandulph
the Pope's Legate, &c. What made so many thousand Christians travel
from France, Britain, &c., into the Holy Land, spend such huge sums
of money, go a pilgrimage so familiarly to Jerusalem, to creep and
crouch, but slavish superstition? What makes them so freely venture
their lives, to leave their native Countries, to go seek martyrdom in the
Indies, but superstition? to be assassinates, to meet death, murder
Kings, but a false persuasion of merit, of canonical or blind obedience
which they instil into them, and animate them by strange illusions, hope
of being Martyrs and Saints? Such pretty feats can the Devil work by
Priests, and so well for their own advantage can they play their parts.
And if it were not yet enough, by Priests and Politicians to delude mankind, and crucify the souls of men, he hath more actors in his Tragedy,
more irons in the fire, another Scene of Hereticks, factious, ambitious
wits, insolent spirits, Schismaticks, Impostors, false Prophets, blind
guides, that out of pride, singularity, vain-glory, blind zeal, cause much
more madness yet, set all in an uproar by their new doctrines, paradoxes,
figments, crotchets, make new divisions, subdivisions, new sects, oppose
one superstition to another, one Kingdom to another, commit Prince and
subjects, brother against brother, father against son, to the ruin and
destruction of a Commonwealth, to the disturbance of peace, and to make
a general confusion of all estates. How did those Arians rage of old!
How many did they circumvent! Those Pelagians, Manichees, &c., their
names alone would make a just volume. How many silly souls have Impostors still deluded, drawn away, and quite alienated from Christ!
Lucian's Alexander, Simon Magus, whose statue was to be seen and
adored in Rome, saith Justin Martyr, after his decease, Apollonius
Tyanæus, Cynops, Eumo, who by counterfeiting some new ceremonies
and juggling tricks of that Dea Syria, by spitting fire, and the like, got
an army together of 40,000 men, and did much harm: with Eudo de
Stellis, of whom Nubrigensis speaks, that in King Stephen's days imi-

tated most of Christ's miracles, fed I know not how many people in the wilderness, and built castles in the air, &c., to the seducing of multitudes of poor souls. In Franconia, 1476, a base illiterate fellow took upon him to be a prophet, and preach, John Beheim by name, a neatherd at Nicholhausen, he seduced 30,000 persons, and was taken by the commonalty to be a most holy man, come from Heaven. Tradesmen left their shops, women their distaffs, servants ran from their Masters, children from their Parents, scholars left their Tutors, all to hear him, some for novelty, some for zeal. He was burnt at last by the Bishop of Wartzburg, and so he and his heresy vanished together. How many such Impostors, false Prophets, have lived in every King's reign? what Chronicle will not afford such examples! that as so many false lights, have led men out of the way, terrified some, deluded others, that are apt to be carried about with the blast of every wind, a rude inconstant multitude, a silly company of poor souls, that follow all, and are cluttered together like so many pebbles in a tide. What prodigious follies, madness, vexations, persecutions, absurdities, impossibilities, these impostors, hereticks, &c., have thrust upon the world, what strange effects shall be shewed in the Symptoms.

Now the means by which, or advantages the Devil and his infernal Ministers take, so to delude and disquiet the world with such idle ceremonies, false doctrines, superstitious fopperies, are from themselves, innate fear, ignorance, simplicity, Hope and Fear, those two battering Cannons and principal Engines, with their objects, reward and punishment, Purgatory, the Limbo of the Fathers, &c., which now more than ever tyrannise; for what province is free from Atheism, Superstition, Idolatry, Schism, Heresy, Impiety, their factors and followers? Thence they proceed, and from that same decayed image of God, which is yet remaining in us.

> *God gave to man alone to stand erect*
> *And gaze on heaven.* (OVID)

Our own conscience doth dictate so much unto us, we know there is a God, and Nature doth inform us. No tribe so barbarous (saith Tully) but that they believe in a God; not Scythia, nor Greece, nor the Hyperboreans doubt that, (as Maximus Tyrius the Platonist farther adds) let him dwell where he will, in what coast soever, there is no Nation so barbarous, that is not persuaded there is a God. It is a wonder to read [in the missionary Acosta] of that infinite superstition amongst the Indians in this kind, of their tenents in America, for there they superstitiously worship plants, animals, mountains, &c., which they love or fear (some few places excepted, as he grants, that had no God at all). So the Heavens declare the glory of God, and the Firmament declareth his handiwork. Every creature will evince it; every blade of grass testifies to the presence of God. They know it in spite of themselves, as the said Tyrius proceeds, will or nill, they must acknowledge it. The Philosophers, Socrates, Plato, Plotinus, Pythagoras, Trismegistus. Seneca, Epictetus, those Magi, Druids, &c., went as far as they could by the light of Nature; writ many things well of the nature of God, but they had but a confused light, a glimpse. As he that walks by Moonshine in a wood, they groped in the dark; they had a gross knowledge, as he in Euripides,

> *O God, whatever thou art, whether the Sky,*
> *Or the Earth, or somewhat else,*

and that of Aristotle, Being of Beings, pity me! And so of the immortality of the Soul, and future happiness. Pythagoras (saith Hierom) imagined the immortality of the soul, Democritus believed it not, in the consolatory discourse on his condemnation which Socrates argued in his cell; India, Persia, the Goths, played the philosopher. So some said this, some that, as they conceived themselves, which the Devil perceiving, led them farther out (as Lemnius observes) and made them worship him as their God with stocks and stones, and torture themselves to their own destruction, as he thought fit himself, inspired his Priests and Ministers with lies and fictions to prosecute the same, which they for their own ends were as willing to undergo, taking advantage of their simplicity, fear and ignorance. For the common people are as a flock of sheep, a rude, illiterate rout, void many times of common sense, a mere beast, a many-headed beast, will go whithersoever they are led: as you lead a ram over a gap by the horns, all the rest will follow, they will do as they see others do, and as their Prince will have them, let him be of what Religion he will, they are for him. Now for those Idolaters, Maxentius and Licinius, then for Constantine a Christian. Who denies Christ perisheth miserably, the cry goes, for two hours' space, who does not worship Christ is an enemy of the Emperor, louder than ever; and by and by Idolaters again under that Apostate Julianus; all Arrians under Constantius, good Catholicks again under Jovinian. And little difference there is between the discretion of men and children in this case, especially of old folks and women, as Cardan discourseth, when as they are tossed with fear and superstition, and with other men's folly and dishonesty. So that I may say their ignorance is a cause of their superstition, a symptom, and madness itself:

> *Their prayers are cause and punishment at once.*

Their own fear, folly, stupidity, to be deplored Lethargy, is that which gives occasion to the other, and pulls their miseries on their own heads. For in all these Religions and Superstitions, amongst our Idolaters, you shall still find that the parties first affected, are silly, rude, ignorant people, old folks, that are naturally prone to superstition, weak women, or some poor rude illiterate persons, that are apt to be wrought upon, and gulled in this kind, prone without either examination or due consideration (for they take up Religion a trust [or on trust], as at Mercers they do their wares) to believe any thing. And the best means they have to broach first or to maintain it when they have done, is to keep them still in ignorance : for Ignorance is the mother of devotion, as all the world knows, and these times can amply witness. This hath been the Devil's practice, and his infernal Ministers in all ages : not as our Saviour, by a few silly Fishermen, to confound the wisdom of the world, to save Publicans and Sinners, but to make advantage of their ignorance, to convert them and their associates, and that they may better effect what they intend, they begin, as I say, with poor, stupid, illiterate persons. So Mahomet did when he published his Alcoran, which is a piece of work (saith Bredenbachius) full of nonsense, barbarism, confusion without rhyme, reason, or any good composition, first published to a company of rude rusticks, hog-rubbers, that had no discretion, judgment, art, or understanding, and is so still maintained. For it is a part of their policy to let no man comment, dare to dispute or call in question to this day any part of it, be it never so absurd, incredible, ridiculous, fabulous as it is, it must be believed implicitly upon pain of death, no man must dare to contradict it, God and the Emperor, &c. What else do our Papists but, by keeping the people in ignorance, vent and broach all their new ceremonies and traditions, when they conceal the Scripture, read it in Latin, and to some few alone, feeding the slavish people in the mean time with tales out of Legends, and such like fabulous narrations ? Whom do they begin with but collapsed Ladies, some few tradesmen, superstitious old folks, illiterate persons, weak women, discontent, rude, silly companions, or sooner circumvent ? So do all our schismaticks and hereticks. Marcus and Valentinian, hereticks in Irenæus, seduced first I know not how many women, and made them believe they were Prophets. Friar Cornelius of Dort seduced a company of silly women. What are all our Anabaptists, Brownists, Barrowists, Familists, but a company of rude, illiterate, capricious base fellows ? What are most of our Papists, but stupid, ignorant and blind Bayards ? How should they otherwise be, when as they are brought up, and kept still in darkness ? If their Pastors (saith Lavater) had done their duties, and instructed their flocks as they ought, in the Principles of Christian Religion, or had not forbidden them the reading of Scriptures, they had not been as they are. But being so misled all their lives in superstition, and carried hood-winked like Hawks, how can they prove otherwise than blind Idiots, and superstitious Asses? What shall we expect else at their hands? Neither is it sufficient to keep them blind, and in Cimmerian darkness, but withal, as a Schoolmaster doth by his boys, to make them follow their books, sometimes by good hope, promises and encouragements, but most of all by fear, strict discipline, severity, threats and punishment, do they collogue and sooth up their silly Auditors, and so bring them into a fool's paradise. Do well, thou shalt be crowned; but for the most part by threats, terrors and affrights, they tyrannize and terrify their distressed souls: knowing that fear alone is the sole and only means to keep men in obedience, according to that Hemistich of Petronius, the fear of some divine and supreme powers, keeps men in obedience, makes the people do their duties: they play upon their consciences; which was practised of old in Egypt by their Priests; when there was an Eclipse, they made the people believe God was angry, great miseries were to come; they take all opportunities of natural causes, to delude the people's senses, and with fearful tales out of purgatory, feigned apparitions, earthquakes in Japan or China, tragical examples of Devils, possessions, obsessions, false miracles, counterfeit visions, &c. They do so insult over, and restrain them, never Hobby [or Falcon] so dared [or fascinated] a Lark, that they will not offend the least tradition, tread, or scarce look awry. Good God, Lavater exclaims, how many men have been miserably afflicted by this fiction of purgatory!

To these advantages of Hope and Fear, ignorance and simplicity, he hath several engines, traps, devices, to batter and enthrall, omitting no opportunities, according to men's several inclinations, abilities, to circumvent and humour them, to maintain his superstitions; sometimes to stupify, besot them; sometimes again by oppositions, factions, to set all at odds, and in an uproar; sometimes he infects one man, and makes him a principal agent; sometimes whole Cities, Countries. If of meaner sort, by stupidity, canonical obedience, blind zeal, &c. If of better note, by pride, ambition, popularity, vain-glory. If of the Clergy and more eminent, of better parts than the rest, more learned, eloquent, he puffs them up with a vain conceit of their own worth, they begin to swell and scorn all the world in respect of themselves, and thereupon turn hereticks, schismaticks, broach new doctrines, frame new crochets, and the like; or else out of too much learning become mad, or out of curiosity they will search into God's secrets, and eat of the forbidden fruit; or out of presumption of their holiness and good gifts, inspirations. become Prophets, Enthusiasts, and what not? or else if they be displeased, discontent, and have not (as they suppose) preferment to their worth, have some disgrace, repulse, neglected, or not esteemed, as they fondly value themselves, or out of emulation, they begin presently to rage and rave, embroil Heaven and Earth, they become so impatient in an instant, that the whole Kingdom cannot contain them, they will set all in a combustion, all at variance, to be revenged of their adversaries.

Donatus, when he saw Cæcilian preferred before him in the Bishoprick of Carthage, turned heretick, and so did Arius, because Alexander was advanced: we have examples at home, and too many experiments of such persons. If they be laymen of better note, the same engines of pride, ambition, emulation and jealousy take place, they will be gods themselves: Alexander after his victories in India, became so insolent, he would be adored for a god: and those Roman Emperors came to that height of madness they must have Temples built to them, sacrifices to their deities, Divus Augustus, D. Claudius, D. Adrianus: Heliogabalus put out that Vestal fire at Rome, expelled the Virgins, and banished all other Religions all over the world, and would be the sole God himself. Our Turks, China Kings, great Chams, and Mogors, do little less, assuming divine and bombast titles to themselves; the meaner sort are too credulous, and led with blind zeal, blind obedience, to prosecute and maintain whatsoever their sottish leaders shall propose, what they in pride and singularity, revenge, vain glory, ambition, spleen, for gain, shall rashly maintain and broach, their disciples make a matter of conscience, of hell and damnation, if they do it not, and will rather forsake wives, children, house and home, lands, goods, fortunes, life itself, than omit or abjure the least tittle of it, and to advance the common cause, undergo any miseries, turn traitors, assassinates, pseudo-martyrs, with full assurance and hope of reward in that other world, that they shall certainly merit by it, win heaven, be canonized for Saints.

Now when they are truly possessed with blind zeal, and misled with superstition, he hath many other baits to inveigle and infatuate them farther yet, to make them quite mortified and mad, and that under colour of perfection, to merit by penance, going woolward, whipping, alms, fasting, &c. In the year 1320, there was a Sect of whippers in Germany, that to the astonishment of the beholders, lashed, and cruelly tortured themselves. I could give many other instances of each particular. But these works so done are meritorious (" meritorious works performed ") for themselves & others, to make them macerate and consume their bodies, the counterfeit of virtue, those Evangelical counsels are propounded, as our Pseudo-Catholicks call them, canonical obedience, wilful poverty, vows of chastity, monkery, and a solitary life, which extend almost to all religions and superstitions, to Turks, Chinese, Gentiles, Abyssinians, Greeks, Latins, and all Countries. Amongst the rest, fasting, contemplation, solitariness, are as it were certain rams by which the devil doth batter and work upon the strongest constitutions. Saith Peter Forestus some by fasting overmuch, and divine meditations, are overcome. Not that fasting is a thing of itself to be discommended, for it is an excellent means to keep the body in subjection, a preparative to devotion, the physick of the soul, by which chaste thoughts are engendered, true zeal, a divine spirit, whence wholsome counsels do proceed, concupiscence is restrained, vicious and predominant lusts and humours are expelled. The Fathers are very much in commendation of it, and, as Calvin notes, sometimes immoderate. The mother of health, key of heaven, a spiritual wing to erear us, the chariot of the holy Ghost, banner of faith, &c. And 'tis true they say of it, if it be moderately and seasonably used, by such parties as Moses, Elias, Daniel, Christ, and as his Apostles made use of it; but when by this means they will supererogate, and as Erasmus well taxeth, Heaven is too small a reward for it; they make choice of times and meats, buy and sell their merits, attribute more to them than to the ten commandments, and count it a greater sin to eat meat in Lent than to kill a man, and as one saith, respect roast fish more than Christ crucified, salmon more than Solomon, have Christ on their lips and Epicurus in their heart; when some counterfeit, and some attribute more to such works of theirs than to Christ's death and passion; the devil sets in a foot, strangely deludes them, and by that means makes them to overthrow the temperature of their bodies, and hazard their souls. Never any strange illusions of devils amongst hermits, Anachorites, never any visions, phantasms, apparitions, Enthusiasms, Prophets, any revelations, but immoderate fasting, bad diet, sickness, melancholy, solitariness, or some such things were the precedent causes, the forerunners or concomitants of them. The best opportunity and sole occasion the Devil takes to delude them. Marcilius Cognatus hath many stories to this purpose, of such as after long fasting have been seduced by devils: and 'tis a miraculous thing to relate (as Cardan writes) what strange accidents proceed from fasting; dreams, superstition, contempt of torments, desire of death, prophesies, paradoxes, madness; fasting naturally prepares men to these things. Monks, Anachorites, and the like, after much emptiness become melancholy, vertiginous, they think they hear strange noises, confer with Hobgoblins, Devils, rivell up their bodies, and (whilst we harass the enemy, saith Gregory, we slay those we love) they become bare Skeletons, skin and bones; abstaining from meats, they consume their own flesh. Hilarion, as Hierome reports in his life, and Athanasius of Antonius, was so bare with fasting, that the skin did scarce stick to the bones; for want of vapours he could not sleep, and for want of sleep became idle-headed, heard every night infants cry, oxen low, wolves howl, lions roar (as he thought), clattering of chains, strange voices, and the like illusions of devils. Such symptoms are common to those that fast long, are solitary, given to contemplation, over much solitariness and meditation. Not that these things (as I said of fasting) are to be discommended of themselves, but very behoveful in some cases and good: sobriety and contemplation join our souls to God, as that heathen Porphyry can tell us. Ecstasis is a taste of future happiness, by which we are united unto God, a divine melancholy, a spiritual wing, Bonaventure terms it, to lift us up to heaven: but as it is abused, a mere dotage, madness, a cause and symptom of Religious Melancholy. If you shall at any time see (saith Guianerius) a Religious person over-superstitious, too solitary, or much given to fasting, that man will certainly be melancholy, thou mayst boldly say it, he will be so. P. Forestus hath almost the same words, and Cardan, solitariness, fasting, and that melancholy humour, are the causes of all Hermits' illusions. Lavater puts solitariness a main cause of such spectrums and apparitions; none, saith he, so melancholy as Monks and Hermits, the devil's bath melancholy, none so subject to visions and dotage in this kind, as such as live solitary lives, they hear and act strange things in their dotage. Polydore Virgil holds that those prophesies, and Monks' revelations, Nuns' dreams, which they suppose come from God, do proceed wholly by the Devil's means: and so those Enthusiasts, Anabaptists, pseudo-Prophets from the same cause. Fracastorius will have all your Pythonisses, Sibyls, and pseudo-Prophets to be mere melancholy; so doth Wierus prove, and Arculanus, that melancholy is a sole cause, and the Devil together, with fasting and solitariness, of such Sibylline prophesies, if there were ever such, which with Casaubon and others I justly except at; for it is not likely that the Spirit of God should ever reveal such manifest revelations and predictions of Christ to those Pythonisses, Apollo's witches, priests, the Devil's ministers, (they were no better), and conceal them from his own prophets; for these Sibyls set down all particular circumstances of Christ's coming, and many other future accidents, far more perspicuous and plain than ever any prophet did. But howsoever there be no Phœbades or Sibyls, I am assured there be other Enthusiasts, prophets, Fortune Tellers, Magi, (of which read Jo. Boissardus, who hath laboriously collected them into a great volume of late, with elegant pictures, and epitomized their lives) &c., ever have been in all ages, and still proceeding from those causes, who relate their visions, dream of the future, prophetize, and agitated by such madness, think that the Holy Spirit is imparted to them. That which is written of Saint Francis' five wounds, and other such monastical effects, of him and others, may justly be referred to this our Melancholy; and that which Matthew Paris relates of the Monk of Evesham, who saw heaven and hell in a vision; of Sir Owen, that went down into Saint Patrick's Purgatory in King Stephen's days, and saw as much: Walsingham of him that was shewed as much by Saint Julian, Beda reports of King Sebba that saw strange visions; and Stumphius, a cobbler of Basil, 1520, that beheld rare apparitions at Augsburg in Germany. Alexander ab Alexandro [tells] of an Enthusiastical prisoner, (all out as probable as that of Eris the son of Armenius, in Plato's tenth dialogue of his Republic, that revived again ten days after he was killed in a battle, and told strange wonders, like those tales Ulysses related to Alcinous in Homer, or Lucian's True Story itself) was still after much solitariness, fasting, or long sickness, when their brains were addle, and their bellies as empty of meat as their heads of wit. Florilegus hath many such examples, one of Saint Guthlac of Croyland that fought with Devils, but still after long fasting, over-much solitariness, the Devil persuaded him therefore to fast, as Moses and Elias did, the better to delude him. In the same Author is recorded Carolus Magnus' vision, in the year 185, or ecstasis, wherein he saw heaven and hell after much fasting and meditation. So did the Devil of old with Apollo's priests. Amphiaraus, and his fellows, those Egyptians, still enjoin long fasting before he would give any Oracles, three days' abstinence from food and wine before they gave any answers, as Volateran records; and Strabo describes Charon's den, in the way betwixt Tralles and Nysa, whither the Priests led sick and fanatick men: but nothing performed without long fasting, no good to be done. That scoffing Lucian conducts his Menippus to hell by the directions of that Chaldæan Mithrobarzanes, but after long fasting, and such like idle preparation. Which the Jesuits right well perceiving of what force this fasting and solitary meditation is to alter men's minds, when they would

make a man mad, ravish him, improve him beyond himself, to undertake some great business of moment, to kill a King or the like, they
bring him into a melancholy dark chamber, where he shall see no light
for many days together, no company, little meat, ghastly pictures of
Devils all about him, and leave him to lie as he will himself, on the bare
floor in this chamber of meditation, as they call it, on his back, side,
belly, till by this strange usage they make him quite mad and beside
himself. And then after some ten days, as they find him animated and
resolved, they make use of him. The Devil hath many such factors,
many such engines, which what effect they produce, you shall hear in
these following Symptoms.

SUBSECTION 3 — *Symptoms general, love to their own sect, hate of all
other Religions, obstinacy, peevishness, ready to undergo any danger or cross for it; Martyrs, blind zeal, blind obedience, fastings,
vows, belief of incredibilities, impossibilities: Particular of Gentiles, Mahometans, Jews, Christians; and in them, Hereticks old
and new, Schismaticks, Schoolmen, Prophets, Enthusiasts, &c.*

IN attempting to speak of these Symptoms, shall I laugh with Democritus, or weep with Heraclitus? they are so ridiculous and absurd on the
one side, so lamentable and tragical on the other; a mixt Scene offers
itself, so full of errors, and a promiscuous variety of objects, that I
know not in what strain to represent it. When I think of that Turkish
Paradise, those Jewish fables, and pontificial rites, those pagan superstitions, their sacrifices, and ceremonies, as to make images of all matter,
and adore them when they have done, to see them kiss the pyx, creep
to the cross, &c., I cannot choose but laugh with Democritus: but when
I see them whip and torture themselves, grind their souls for toys and
trifles, desperate, and now ready to die, I cannot choose but weep with
Heraclitus. When I see a Priest say mass, with all those apish gestures,
murmurings, &c., read the customs of the Jews' Synagogue, or Mahometan Mosque, I must needs laugh at their folly, who can restrain his
laughter? but when I see them make matters of conscience of such toys
and trifles, to adore the Devil, to endanger their souls, to offer their
children to their Idols, &c., I must needs condole their misery. When I
see two superstitious Orders contend, tooth and nail, with such have
and hold, of goats' wool trifles, some write such great Volumes to no
purpose, take so much pains to so small effect, their Satires, invectives,
apologies, dull and gross fictions; when I see grave learned men rail
and scold like butter-women, methinks 'tis pretty sport, and fit for

Calphurnius and Democritus to laugh at. But when I see so much bloud spilt, so many murders and massacres, so many cruel battles fought, &c., 'tis a fitter subject for Heraclitus to lament. As Merlin when he sat by the lake side with Vortigern, and had seen the white and red dragon fight, before he began to interpret or to speak, fell a weeping, and then proceeded to declare to the King what it meant; I should first pity and bewail this misery of human kind with some passionate preface, wishing mine eyes a fountain of tears, as Jeremy did, and then to my task. For it is that great torture, that infernal plague of mortal man, superstition, of all pests the most pestilential, and able of itself alone to stand in opposition to all other plagues, miseries, and calamities whatsoever; far more cruel, more pestiferous, more grievous, more general, more violent, of a greater extent. Other fears and sorrows, grievances of body and mind, are troublesome for the time; but this is for ever, eternal damnation, hell itself, a plague, a fire: an inundation hurts one Province alone, and the loss may be recovered; but this superstition involves all the world almost, and can never be remedied. Sickness and sorrows come and go, but a superstitious soul hath no rest; superstition can give the soul no peace, no quietness. True Religion and Superstition are quite opposite, as Lactantius describes, the one erears, the other dejects; the one is an easy yoke, the other an intolerable burden, an absolute tyranny; the one a sure anchor, an haven; the other a tempestuous Ocean; the one makes, the other mars; the one is wisdom, the other is folly, madness, indiscretion; the one unfeigned, the other a counterfeit; the one a diligent observer, the other an ape; one leads to heaven, the other to hell. But these differences will more evidently appear by their particular symptoms. What Religion is, and of what parts it doth consist, every Catechism will tell you, what Symptoms it hath, and what effects it produceth: but for their superstitions, no tongue can tell them, no pen express, they are so many, so diverse, so uncertain, so unconstant, and so different from themselves. One saith, there be as many superstitions in the world, as there be stars in heaven, or devils themselves that are the first founders of them: with such ridiculous, absurd symptoms and signs, so many several rites, ceremonies, torments and vexations accompanying, as may well express and beseem the devil to be the author and maintainer of them. I will only point at some of them, the lion's toe-nail, guess at the rest, and those of the chief kinds of superstition, which beside us Christians now domineer and crucify the world, Gentiles, Mahometans, Jews, &c.

Of these symptoms some be general, sòme particular to each private sect: general to all, are, an extraordinary love and affection they bear and shew to such as are of their own sect, and more than Vatinian hate to such as are opposite in Religion, as they call it, or disagree from them in their superstitious rites, blind zeal, (which is as much a symptom as a cause,) vain fears, blind obedience, needless works, incredibilities, impossibilities, monstrous rites and ceremonies, wilfulness, blindness, obstinacy, &c. For the first, which is love and hate, as Montanus saith, no greater concord, no greater discord than that which proceeds from Religion. It is incredible to relate, did not our daily experience evince it, what factions, (as Rich. Dinoth writes), have been of late for matters of Religion in France, and what hurly burlies all over Europe for these many years. There is nothing so intemperately sweeps man along as an accepted opinion as to salvation; for it, forsooth, all nations are wont to sacrifice their bodies and souls, and bind themselves together in strictest bond of poverty. We are all brethren in Christ, servants of one Lord, members of one body, and therefore are or should be at least dearly beloved, inseparably allied in the greatest bond of love and familiarity, united partakers not only of the same cross, but coadjutors, comforters, helpers, at all times, upon all occasions: as they did in the primitive Church, they sold their patrimonies, and laid them at the Apostles' feet, and many such memorable examples of mutual love we have had under the ten general persecutions, many since. Examples on the other side of discord none like, as our Saviour saith, he came therefore into the world to set father against son, &c. In imitation of whom the Devil belike (superstition is still Religion's ape, as in all other things, so in this) doth so combine and glue together his superstitious followers in love and affection, that they will live and die together: and what an innate hatred hath he still inspired to any other superstition opposite! How those old Romans were affected, those ten persecutions may be a witness, and that cruel executioner in Eusebius, sacrifice or die. No greater hate, more continuate, bitter faction, wars, persecution in all ages, than for matters of Religion, no such feral opposition, father against son, mother against daughter, husband against wife, City against City, Kingdom against Kingdom: as of old at Tentyra and Ombos:

> *Immortal hate it breeds, a wound past cure*
> *And fury to the commons still to endure:*
> *Because one City t' other's gods as vain*
> *Deride, and his alone as good maintain.*   (JUVENAL)

The Turks at this day count no better of us than of dogs, so they commonly call us Giaours, infidels, miscreants, make that their main quarrel and cause of Christian persecution. If he will turn Turk, he shall be entertained as a brother, and had in good esteem, a Mussulman or a believer, which is a greater tie to them than any affinity or consanguinity. The Jews stick together like so many burrs, but as for the rest whom they call Gentiles, they do hate and abhor, they cannot endure their Messias should be a common Saviour to us all, and rather as Luther writes, than they that now scoff at them, curse them, persecute and revile them, shall be coheirs and brethren with them, or have any part of fellowship with their Messias, they would crucify their Messias ten times over and God himself, his Angels, and all his creatures, if it were possible, though they endure a thousand hells for it. Such is their malice towards us. Now for Papists, what in a common cause for the advancement of their Religion they will endure, our Traitors and Pseudo-Catholicks will declare unto us; and how bitter on the other side to their adversaries, how violently bent, let those Marian times record, as those miserable slaughters at Merindol and Cabriers, the Spanish Inquisition, the Duke of Alva's tyranny in the Low Countries, the French Massacres and Civil Wars.

So great the evils that religion prompts. (LUCRETIUS)

Not there only, but all over Europe, we read of bloody battles, racks and wheels, seditions, factions, oppositions, standards facing standards, eagles matching eagles, and spear threatening spear, invectives and contentions. They had rather shake hands with a Jew, Turk, or as the Spaniards do, suffer Moors to live amongst them, and Jews, than Protestants; my name (saith Luther) is more odious to them than any thief or murderer. So it is with all hereticks and schismaticks whatsoever: and none so passionate, violent in their tenents, opinions, obstinate, wilful, refractory, peevish, factious, singular and stiff in defence of them; they do not only persecute and hate, but pity all other Religions, account them damned, blind, as if they alone were the true Church, they are the true heirs, have the fee simple of heaven by a peculiar donation, 'tis entailed on them and their posterities, their doctrine sound, they alone are to be saved. The Jews at this day are so incomprehensibly proud and churlish, saith Luther, that they alone wish to be saved, they alone wish to be lords of the world. And, as Buxtorfius adds, so ignorant and self-willed withal, that amongst their most understanding Rabbins you shall find nought but gross dotage, horrible hardness of heart, and stupend obstinacy, in all their actions, opinions, conversations: and yet so zealous withal, that no man living can be more, and vindicate themselves for the elect people of God. 'Tis so with all other superstitious sects, Mahometans, Gentiles in China, and Tartary; our ignorant Papists, Anabaptists, Separatists, and peculiar Churches of Amsterdam, they alone, and none but they can be saved. Zealous (as Paul saith) without knowledge, they will endure any misery, any trouble, suffer and do that which the Sun-beams will not endure to see, driven on by religious fury, all extremities, losses and dangers, take any pains, fast, pray, vow chastity, wilful poverty, forsake all and follow their Idols, die a thousand deaths, as some Jews did to Pilate's soldiers, in like case, thrusting forward their bared throats, and clearly showing (as Josephus hath it) that dearer than life to them was the observance of their country's law. Rather than abjure, or deny the least particle of that Religion which their Fathers profess, and they themselves have been brought up in, be it never so absurd, ridiculous, they will embrace it, and without further enquiry or examination of the truth, though it be prodigiously false, they will believe it: they will take much more pains to go to hell, than we shall do to heaven. Single out the most ignorant of them, convince his understanding, shew him his errors, grossness, and absurdities of his sect, he will not be persuaded. As those Pagans told the Jesuits in Japan, they would do as their fore-fathers have done; and with Ratholde the Frisian Prince, go to hell for company, if most of their friends went thither: they will not be moved, no persuasion, no torture can stir them. So that Papists cannot brag of their vows, poverty, obedience, orders, merits, martyrdoms, fastings, alms, good works, pilgrimages: much and more than all this, I shall shew you, is, and hath been done by these superstitious Gentiles, Pagans, Idolaters and Jews: their blind zeal and idolatrous superstition in all kinds is much at one; little or no difference, and it is hard to say which is the greatest, which is the grossest. For if a man shall duly consider those superstitious rites amongst the Ethnicks in Japan, the Bannians in Guzerat, the Chinese idolaters, Americans of old, in Mexico especially, Mahometan priests, he shall find the same government almost, the same orders and ceremonies, or so like, that they may seem all apparently to be derived from some heathen spirit, and the Roman Hierarchy no better than the rest. In a word, this is common to all superstition, there is nothing so mad and absurd, so ridiculous, impossible, incredible, which they will not believe, observe, and diligently perform as much as in them lies; nothing so monstrous to conceive, or intolerable to put in practice, so cruel to suffer,

which they will not willingly undertake. So powerful a thing is superstition! O Egypt (as Trismegistus exclaims) thy religion is fables, and
such as posterity will not believe. I know that in true Religion itself
many mysteries are so apprehended alone by faith, as that of the
Trinity, which Turks especially deride, Christ's Incarnation, resurrection of the body at the last day, that should be believed (saith Tertullian) for the very reason that it is incredible, &c., many miracles not
to be controverted or disputed of. True wisdom lieth in wonder, not
inquiry, saith Gerhardus; and in matters divine (as a good Father informs us) some things are to be believed, embraced, followed with all
submission and obedience, some again admired [or wondered at].
Though Julian the Apostate scoff at Christians in this point, saying
that the Christian Creed is like the Pythagorean dictum, we make our
will and understanding too slavishly subject to our faith, without
farther examination of the truth; yet, as Saint Gregory truly answers,
our Creed is of a higher excellence, and much more divine; and, as
Thomas will, to one who gives pious thought, reasons are always at hand,
proving credibility in supernatural mysteries; we do absolutely believe
it, and upon good reasons, for, as Gregory well informeth us, that faith
hath no merit, is not worth the name of faith, that will not apprehend
without a certain demonstration: we must and will believe God's word;
and if we be mistaken or err in our general belief, as Richardus de
Sancto Victore vows he will say to Christ himself at the day of judgement, Lord, if we be deceived, thou alone hast deceived us: thus we
plead. But for the rest I will not justify that pontifical transubstantia-
tion, that which Mahometans and Jews justly except at, as Campanella
confesseth, 'tis a most difficult dogma, nor can anything be found more
exposed to the blasphemies of hereticks or the foolish mockeries of
politicians. They hold it impossible, that God should be eaten in bread;
and besides they scoff at it, Behold a people feeding on its God, says
a certain Marius; flies and worms mock at this God, while devouring
and defiling him; he is exposed to fire and water, and robbers steal from
him; they cast his golden pyx on the ground, yet this God does not defend himself: how can it be that he be found whole in each of the
particles of the Host, the same single body, be in so many places, in
the sky, in the earth, &c. But he that shall read the Turks' Alcoran, the
Jews' Talmud, and Papists' Golden Legend, in the mean time will swear
that such gross fictions, fables, vain traditions, prodigious paradoxes and
ceremonies, could never proceed from any other spirit, than that of
the devil himself, which is the Author of confusion and lies; and won-

der withal how such wise men as have been of the Jews, such learned understanding men as Averroes, Avicenna, or those Heathen Philosophers, could ever be persuaded to believe, or subscribe to the least part of them: not detect the fraud: but that as Vanninus answers, they durst not speak for fear of the law. But I will descend to particulars: read their several symptoms and then guess.

Of such symptoms as properly belong to superstition, or that irreligious Religion, I may say as of the rest, some are ridiculous, some again feral to relate. Of those ridiculous, there can be no better testimony than the multitude of their gods, those absurd names, actions, offices they put upon them, their feasts, holy days, sacrifices, adorations, and the like. The Egyptians that pretended so great antiquity, 300 Kings before Amasis: and as Mela writes, 13,000 years from the beginning of their Chronicles, that bragg'd so much of their knowledge of old, for they invented Arithmetick, Astronomy, Geometry: of their wealth and power, that vaunted of 20,000 Cities: yet at the same time their Idolatry and superstition was most gross: they worshipped, as Diodorus Siculus records, Sun and Moon under the name of Isis and Osiris, and after, such men as were beneficial to them, or any creature that did them good. In the city of Bubastis they adored Cats, saith Herodotus, Ibises and Storks, an Ox (saith Pliny), Leeks and Onions, Macrobius,
You, O Egypt, worship leeks and onions.   (PRUDENTIUS)
Scoffing Lucian in his True History, which, as he confesseth himself, was not persuasively written as a truth, but in Comical fashion to glance at the monstrous fictions, and gross absurdities of writers and nations, to deride without doubt this prodigious Egyptian Idolatry, feigns this story of himself; that when he had seen the Elysian fields, and was now coming away, Rhadamanthus gave him a Mallow root, and bade him pray to that when he was in any peril or extremity; which he did accordingly; for when he came to Hydramardia in the Island of treacherous women, he made his prayers to his root, and was instantly delivered. The Syrians, Chaldæans, had as many proper Gods of their own invention; see the said Lucian, Mornay, Guliel. Stuckius, Peter Faber, Selden, Purchas' Pilgrimage, Rosinus of the Romans, and Lilius Giraldus of the Greeks. The Romans borrowed from all, besides their own gods which were of greater & lesser kinds, as Varro holds, certain and uncertain; some celestial select and great ones, others Indigetes [or home-made Gods], half-Gods, Lares [or House-Gods], Lemures [or Sprites], Dioscuri [Castor and Pollux, to swear by], Soters [Saviours, or Deliverers], Parastas [Pillars, or Under-Officers], tutelary deities

amongst the Greeks: gods of all sorts, for all functions; some for the Land, some for Sea; some for Heaven, some for Hell; some for passions, diseases, some for birth, some for weddings, husbandry, woods, waters, gardens, orchards, &c. All actions and offices, Peace, Quiet, Health, Liberty, Happiness, Energy, Readiness for Love, Encouragement, Pan, Sylvanus, Priapus, Flora, Cloacina [Goddess of Sewers], Stercutius [God of Muck], Febris [Goddess of Fevers], Pallor [God of Fear], Invidia [Goddess of Hatred], Protervia [Goddess of Shamelessness], Risus [God of Mirth], Angerona [Goddess of Melancholy], Volupia [Goddess of Pleasure], Vacuna [Goddess of Leisure], Viriplaca [Appeaser of Husbands], Veneranda [Goddess of Reverence], Pales [God of Shepherds], Neptune, Doris [Sea-gods], Kings, Emperors, valiant men that had done any good offices for them, they did likewise canonize and adore for Gods, and it was usually done, among the ancients, as Jac. Boissardus well observes, and the Devil was still ready to second their intents, he crept into their temples, statues, tombs, altars, and was ready to give oracles, cure diseases, do miracles, &c., as by Jupiter, Æsculapius, Tiresias, Apollo, Mopsus, Amphiaraus, &c., Gods and Demi-gods. For so they were Demi-gods, some mediators between Gods and men, as Max. Tyrius, the Platonist, maintains and justifies in many words. When a good man dies, his body is buried, but his soul becomes forthwith a Demi-god, nothing disparaged with malignity of air, or variety of forms, rejoiceth, exults and sees that perfect beauty with his eyes. Now being deified, in commiseration he helps his poor friends here on earth, his kindred and allies, informs, succours, &c., punisheth those that are bad, and do amiss, as a good Genius to protect and govern mortal men appointed by the gods, so they will have it, ordaining some for provinces, some for private men, some for one office, some for another. Hector and Achilles assist Soldiers to this day, Æsculapius all sick men, the Dioscuri Seafaring men, &c., and sometimes upon occasion they shew themselves. The Dioscuri, Hercules and Æsculapius, he saw himself (or the devil in their likeness) not when sleeping but wide awake. So far Tyrius. And not good men only do they thus adore, but tyrants, monsters, devils, (as Stuckius inveighs) Neros, Domitians, Heliogables, beastly women, and arrant whores, amongst the rest. For all intents, places, creatures, they assign gods; to buildings, dwellings, baths, and horses, saith Prudentius. Cuna for cradles, Diverra for sweeping houses, Nodina knots, Prema, Premunda, Hymen, Hymenæus, for weddings; Comus the God of good fellows, gods of silence, of comfort, Hebe, goddess of youth; Mena of the monthly flow of women, &c., male and female gods, of all ages, sexes, and dimensions, with beards, without beards, married, unmarried, begot, not born at all, but as Minerva start out of Jupiter's head. Hesiodus reckons up at least 30,000 gods, Varro 300 Jupiters. As Jeremy told them, their gods were to the multitude of Cities.

> *Whatever heavens, sea, and land begat,*
> *Hills, seas and rivers, God was this and that.*

And which was most absurd, they made gods upon such ridiculous occasions; As children make babies (so saith Mornay) their Poets make Gods, worship them in temples, exhibit them in theatres, as Lactantiuś scoffs. Saturn, a man (gelded, himself), did eat his own children, a cruel tyrant driven out of his kingdom by his son Jupiter, as good a God as himself, a wicked lascivious paltry King of Crete, of whose rapes, lusts, murders, villanies, a whole volume is too little to relate. Venus, a notorious strumpet, as common as a barber's chair, Mars', Adonis', Anchises' whore, is a great she-goddess as well as the rest, as much renowned by their Poets; with many such: and these gods so fabulously and foolishly made, celebrated in Ceremonies, Hymns and Canticles; their errors, (as Eusebius well taxeth) weddings, mirth and mournings, loves, angers, and quarrelling they did celebrate in Hymns, and sing of in their ordinary songs, as it were publishing their villanies. But see more of their originals. When Romulus was made away by the sedition of the senators, to pacify the people, Julius Proculus gave out that Romulus was taken up by Jupiter into Heaven, and therefore to be ever after adored for a God amongst the Romans. Syrophanes of Egypt had one only son, whom he dearly loved, he erected his statue in his house, which his servants did adorn with crowns and garlands, to pacify their master's wrath when he was angry, so by little and little he was adored for a god. This did Semiramis for her husband Belus, and Adrian the Emperor by his minion Antinous. Flora was a rich harlot in Rome, and for that she made the Common-wealth her heir, her birthday was solemnized long after; and to make it a more plausible holiday, they made her Goddess of flowers, and sacrificed to her amongst the rest. The matrons of Rome, as Dionysius Halicarnasseus relates, because at their entreaty Coriolanus desisted from his Wars, consecrated a Church to Woman's Luck; and Venus Barbata [or Barber'd] had a temple erected, for that somewhat was amiss about [her] hair, and so the rest. The Citizens of Alabanda, a small town in Asia Minor, to curry favour with the Romans (who then warred in Greece with Perseus of Macedon, and were formidable to these parts) consecrated a temple to the City of Rome, and made her a goddess, with annual games and sacrifices: so a town of houses was deified, with shameful flattery of the one side to give, and intolerable arrogance on the other to accept, upon so vile and absurd an occasion. Tully writes to Atticus, that his daughter Tulliola might be made a goddess, and adored as Juno and Minerva, and as well she deserved it. Their Holydays and adorations were all out as ridiculous; those Lupercalia of Pan, Floralia of Flora, [those of] Bona Dea, Anna Perenna, Saturnalia, &c., as how they were celebrated, with what lascivious and wanton gestures, bald ceremonies, by what bawdy Priests, how they hang their noses over the smoke of sacrifices, saith Lucian, and lick blood like flies that was spilled about the altars. Their carved Idols, gilt Images of wood, iron, ivory, silver, brass, stone, a log of wood, &c., were most absurd, as being their own workmanship; for, as Seneca notes, they worship gods of wood and despise those who made them, they adore work, contemn the workman; and as Tertullian follows it, had it not been for men, they had never been gods, but blocks still, and stupid statues, in which mice, swallows, birds made their nests, spiders their webs, and in their very mouths laid their excrements. Those Images I say were all out as gross, as the shapes in which they did represent them: Jupiter with a ram's head, Mercury a dog's, Pan like a goat, Hecate with three heads, one with a beard, another without; see more in Carterius and Verdurius of their monstrous forms and ugly pictures: and which was absurder yet, they told them these Images came from heaven, as that of Minerva in her temple at Athens, which they believe came from the sky, saith Pausanias. They formed some like Storks, Apes, Bulls, and yet seriously believed; and that which was impious, and abominable, they made their Gods notorious whoremasters, incestuous Sodomites, (as commonly they were all, as well as Jupiter, Mars, Apollo, Mercury, Neptune, &c.), thieves, slaves, drudges, (for Apollo and Neptune made tiles in Phrygia,) kept sheep, Hercules emptied stables, Vulcan a black-smith, unfit to dwell upon the earth for their villanies, much less in heaven, as Mornay well saith, and yet they gave them out to be such; so weak and brutish, some to whine, lament, and roar, as Isis for her son and Cynocephalus, as also all her weeping Priests; Mars in Homer to be wounded, vexed; Venus run away crying, and the like; than which what can be more ridiculous? Is it not absurd you should lament over that you adore, or adore that you lament over (which Minucius objects); if gods, why, weep? if mortal, why worship? ———— that it is no marvel if Lucian, that adamantine persecutor of superstition, and Pliny could so scoff at them and their horrible Idolatry as they did: if Diagoras took Hercules' Image, and put it under his pot to seeth his pottage, which was, as he said, his 13th Labour. But see more of their fopperies in Cyprian, Chrysostom, Arnobius, Austin, Theodoretus, Clemens Alexandrinus, Minucius Felix, Eusebius, Lactantius, Stuckius, &c. Lamentable, tragical, and fearful those symptoms are, that they should be so far forth affrighted with their fictitious Gods, as to spend the goods, lives, fortunes, precious time, best days in their honour, to sacrifice unto them, to their inestimable loss, such Hecatombs, so many thousand Sheep, Oxen, with gilded horns, Goats, as Crœsus King of Lydia, Marcus Julianus, surnamed, for much sacrifice, Victimarius, & Tauricremus, and the rest of the Roman Emperors usually did with such labour and cost: and not Emperors only and great ones, for the common good, were at this charge, but private men for their ordinary occasions. Pythagoras offered an hundred Oxen for the invention of a Geometrical Problem, and it was an ordinary thing to sacrifice in Lucian's time, a heifer for their good health, four Oxen for wealth, an hundred for a Kingdom, nine Bulls for their safe return from Troy to Pylos, &c. Every God almost hath a peculiar sacrifice, the Sun horses, Vulcan fire, Diana a white hart, Venus a turtle, Ceres an hog, Proserpina a black lamb, Neptune a bull, (read more in Stuckius at large) besides sheep, cocks, corals, frankincense, to their undoings, as if their gods were affected with blood or smoke. And surely (saith he) if one should but repeat the fopperies of mortal men, in their sacrifices, feasts, worshipping their Gods, their rites and ceremonies, what they think of them, of their diet, houses, orders, &c., what prayers and vows they make: if one should but observe their absurdity and madness, he would burst out a laughing, and pity their folly. For what can be more absurd than their ordinary prayers, petitions, requests, sacrifices, oracles, devotions? of which we have a taste in Maximus Tyrius, Plato's second Alcibiades, Persius, Juvenal, there likewise exploded; Lactantius, as if their Gods were an hungry, athirst, in the dark, they light candles, offer meat and drink. And what so base as to reveal their counsels and give oracles out of the bowels and excremental parts of beasts? sordid Gods, Varro truly calls them therefore, and well he might. I say nothing of their magnificent and sumptuous temples, those majestical structures. To the roof of Apollo Didymæus' Temple, the Branchidian, as Strabo writes, a thousand oaks did not suffice. Who can relate the glorious splendour, and stupend magnificence, the sumptuous building of Diana at Ephesus, Jupiter Ammon's Temple in Africa, the Pantheon at Rome, the Capitol,

the Serapeum at Alexandria, Apollo's Temple at Daphne in the Suburbs of Antioch. The great Temple at Mexico, so richly adorned, and
so capacious (for 10,000 men might stand in it at once) that fair Pantheon of Cusco, described by Acosta in his Indian History, which
eclipses both Jews and Christians. There were in old Jerusalem, as
some write, 408 Synagogues; but new Cairo reckons up (if Radzivilius
may be believed) 6800 meskites [or mosques], Fessa 400, whereof 50
are most magnificent, like Saint Paul's in London. Helena built 300 fair
churches in the holy Land, but one Bassa hath built 400 meskites. The
Mahometans have 1000 Monks in a Monastery: the like saith Acosta of
Americans; Riccius of the Chinese, for men and women, fairly built;
and more richly endowed some of them than Arras in Artois, Fulda in
Germany, or Saint Edmundsbury in England with us: who can describe
those curious and costly Statues, Idols, Images, so frequently mentioned
in Pausanias? I conceal their donaries, pendants, other offerings, presents,
to these their fictitious Gods daily consecrated. Alexander the son of
Amyntas, King of Macedonia, sent two statues of pure gold to Apollo at
Delphi. Crœsus King of Lydia dedicated an hundred golden Tiles in the
same place, with a golden Altar: no man came empty-handed to their
Shrines. But these are base offerings in respect; they offered men themselves alive. The Leucadians, as Strabo writes, sacrificed every year a
man, to pacify their Gods, to be thrown down from a mountain, and they
did voluntarily undergo it. The tribe of Decius did so sacrifice to the
Infernal Deities, Curtius did leap into the gulf. Were they not all
strangely deluded to go so far to their Oracles, to be so gulled by them,
both in war and peace, as Polybius relates (which their Augurs, Priests,
Vestal Virgins can witness) to be so superstitious, that they would
rather lose goods and lives, than omit any ceremonies, or offend their
Heathen Gods? Nicias that generous and valiant Captain of the Greeks,
overthrew the Athenian Navy, by reason of his too much superstition,
because the Augurs told him it was ominous to set sail from the Haven
of Syracuse whilst the Moon was eclipsed, he tarried so long, till his
enemies besieged him, he and all his Army was overthrown. The Parthians of old were so sottish in this kind, they would rather lose a victory, nay, lose their own lives, than fight in the night, 'twas against their
Religion. The Jews would make no resistance on the Sabbath, when
Pompey besieged Jerusalem; and some Jewish Christians in Africa, set
upon by the Goths, suffered themselves upon the same occasion to be
utterly vanquished. The superstition of the Dibrenses, a bordering
Town in Epirus, besieged by the Turks, is miraculous almost to re-

port. Because a dead dog was flung into the only Fountain which the City had, they would die of thirst all, rather than drink of that unclean water,* and yield up the City upon any conditions. Though the Prætor and chief Citizens began to drink first, using all good persuasions, their superstition was such, no saying would serve, they must all forthwith die, or yield up the City. I myself (saith Barletius) scarcely dare credit so great a superstition, or attribute a cause so trivial to so great a matter; the story was too ridiculous, he was ashamed to report it, because he thought no body would believe it. It is stupend to relate what strange effects this Idolatry and superstition hath brought forth in these latter years in the Indies, and those bordering parts: in what feral shapes the Devil is adored, lest he should do them harm, as they say; for in the mountains betwixt Scanderoon and Aleppo at this day, there are dwelling a certain kind of people called Coords, coming of the race of the ancient Parthians, who worship the Devil, and allege this reason in so doing; God is a good man, and will do no harm, but the Devil is bad, and must be pleased, lest he hurt them. It is wonderful to tell how the devil deludes them, how he terrifies them, how they offer men, and women sacrifices unto him, an hundred at once, as they did infants in Crete to Saturn of old, the finest children, like Agamemnon's Iphigenia, &c. At Mexico, when the Spaniards first overcame them, they daily sacrificed the hearts of men yet living, 20,000 in a year (Acosta saith), to their Idols made of flour and men's blood, and every year six thousand infants of both sexes; and as prodigious to relate, how they bury their wives with husbands deceased, 'tis fearful to report, and harder to believe,

The widows even vie with one another

Who shall die first; they are ashamed to live,   (PROPERTIUS)
and burn them alive, best goods, servants, horses, when a grandee dies, 12,000 at once amongst the Tartars, when a great Cham departs, or an Emperor in America: how they plague themselves, which abstain from all that hath life, like those old Pythagoreans, with immoderate fasting, as the Bannians about Surat, they of China, that for superstition's sake never eat flesh nor fish all their lives, never marry, but live in deserts and by-places, and some pray to their Idols 24 hours together, without any intermission, biting off their tongues when they have done, for devotion's sake. Some again are brought to that madness by their superstitious Priests, (that tell them such vain stories of immortality, and the joys of heaven in that other life) that many thousands volun-

---

* They were of the Greek church. — Burton's note.

tarily break their own necks, as Cleombrotus Ambraciotes' Auditors of old, precipitate themselves, that they may participate of that unspeakable happiness in the other world. One poisons, another strangleth himself; and the King of China had done as much, deluded with this vain hope, had he not been detained by his servant. But who can sufficiently tell of their several superstitions, vexations, follies, torments? I may conclude with Possevinus, Religion makes wild beasts civil, superstition makes wise men beasts and fools; and the discreetest that are, if they give way to it, are no better than dizzards; nay more, if that of Plotinus be true, that's the drift of religion, to make us like him whom we worship: what shall be the end of Idolaters, but to degenerate into stocks and stones? of such as worship these Heathen gods, for such gods are a kind of Devils, but to become devils themselves? 'Tis therefore a most perilous and dangerous error of all others, as Plutarch holds, a pestilent, a troublesome passion, that utterly undoeth men. Unhappy superstition, Pliny calls it, death takes away life, but not superstition. Impious and ignorant are far more happy than they which are superstitious, no torture like to it, none so continuate, so general, so destructive, so violent.

In this superstitious row, Jews for antiquity may go next to Gentiles; what of old they have done, what Idolatries they have committed in their groves and high places, what their Pharisees, Sadducees, Scribes, Essenes, and such sectaries have maintained, I will not so much as mention: for the present, I presume, no Nation under Heaven can be more sottish, ignorant, blind, superstitious, wilful, obstinate and peevish, tiring themselves with vain ceremonies to no purpose; he that shall but read their Rabbins' ridiculous Comments, their strange interpretation of Scriptures, their absurd ceremonies, fables, childish tales, which they steadfastly believe, will think they be scarce rational creatures; their foolish customs, when they rise in the morning, and how they prepare themselves to prayer, to meat, with what superstitious washings, how to their Sabbath, to their other feasts, weddings, burials, &c. Last of all, the expectation of their Messias, and those figments, miracles, vain pomp that shall attend him, as how he shall terrify the Gentiles, and overcome them by new diseases; how Michael the Arch-Angel shall sound his trumpet, how he shall gather all the scattered Jews into the Holy Land, and there make them a great banquet, wherein shall be all the birds, beasts, fishes, that ever God made; a cup of wine that grew in Paradise, and that hath been kept in Adam's cellar ever since. At the first course shall be served in that great Ox, *that every day feeds on a thousand hills,* that great Leviathan, and a great bird, that laid an egg so big, that by chance tumbling out of the nest, it knocked down 300 tall Cedars, and breaking as it fell, drowned 160 villages: this bird stood up to the knees in the Sea, and the Sea was so deep, that a hatchet would not fall to the bottom in seven years: of their Messias' wives and children (every King of the world shall send him one of his daughters to be his wife, because it is written, " King's daughters shall attend on him ") : Adam and Eve, &c., and that one stupend fiction among the rest : when a Roman Prince asked of Rabbi Jehosua ben Hanania, why the Jews' God was compared to a Lion; he made answer, he compared himself to no ordinary Lion, but to one in the wood Ela, which when he desired to see, the Rabbin prayed to God he might, and forthwith the Lion set forward. But when he was 400 miles from Rome, he so roared, that all the great-bellied women in Rome made aborts, the City walls fell down, and when he came an hundred miles nearer, and roared the second time, their teeth fell out of their heads, the Emperor himself fell down dead, and so the Lion went back. With an infinite number of such lies and forgeries, which they verily believe, feed themselves with vain hope, and in the mean time will by no persuasions be diverted, but still crucify their souls with a company of idle ceremonies, live like slaves and vagabonds, will not be relieved or reconciled.

Mahometans are a compound of Gentiles, Jews, and Christians, and so absurd in their ceremonies, as if they had taken that which is most sottish out of every one of them, full of idle fables in their superstitious law, their Alcoran itself a gallimaufry of lies, tales, ceremonies, traditions, precepts, stole from other sects, and confusedly heaped up to delude a company of rude and barbarous clowns. As how birds, beasts, stones, saluted Mahomet when he came from Mecca, the Moon came down from Heaven to visit him, how God sent for him, spake to him, &c., with a company of stupend figments of the Angels, Sun, Moon, and Stars, &c. Of the day of judgment, and three sounds to prepare to it, which must last 50,000 years, of Paradise, which wholly consists in wenching and feasting, and what is written about flocks [for provender], herds in Paradise, is so ridiculous, that Virgil, Dante, Lucian, nor any Poet can be more fabulous. Their Rites and Ceremonies are most vain and superstitious, Wine and Swine's-flesh are utterly forbidden by their Law, they must pray five times a day, and still towards the South; wash before and after all their bodies over, with many such. For fasting, vows, religious orders, peregrinations, they go far beyond any Papists, they fast a month together many times, and must not eat a bit till

Sun be set. Their Kalenders, Dervises, and Torlachers, [or idle Vaga-bonds] &c., are more abstemious some of them, than Carthusians, Franciscans, Anachorites, forsake all, live solitary, fare hard, go naked, &c. Their Pilgrimages are as far as to the River Ganges (which the Gentiles of those Tracts likewise do) to wash themselves, for that River, as they hold, hath a sovereign virtue to purge them of all sins, and no man can be saved that hath not been washed in it. For which reason they come far and near from the Indies; and infinite numbers yearly resort to it. Others go as far as Mecca to Mahomet's Tomb, which journey is both miraculous and meritorious. The ceremonies of flinging stones to stone the Devil, of eating a Camel at Cairo by the way; their fastings, their running till they sweat, their long prayers, Mahomet's Temple, Tomb, and building of it, would ask a whole volume to dilate; and for their pains taken in this holy Pilgrimage, all their sins are for-given, and they reputed for so many Saints. And divers of them with hot bricks, when they return, will put out their eyes, that they never after see any profane thing, bite out their tongues, &c. They look for their Prophet Mahomet, as Jews do for their Messias. Read more of their Customs, Rites, Ceremonies, in Lonicerus, Bredenbachius, Leo Afer, Busbequius, Sabellicus, Purchas, Theodorus Bibliander, &c. Many foolish Ceremonies you shall find in them; and which is most to be lamented, the people are generally so curious in observing of them, that if the least Circumstance be omitted, they think they shall be damned, 'tis an irremissible offence, and can hardly be forgiven. I kept in my house amongst my followers (saith Busbequius, sometime the Turk's Orator in Constantinople) a Turkey boy, that by chance did eat shell-fish, a meat forbidden by their Law, but the next day when he knew what he had done, he was not only sick to cast and vomit, but very much troubled in mind, would weep and grieve many days after, torment himself for his foul offence. Another Turk, being to drink a cup of wine in his Cellar, first made a huge noise, and filthy faces, to warn his soul, as he said, that it should not be guilty of that foul fact which he was to commit. With such toys as these are men kept in awe, and so cowed, that they dare not resist, or offend the least circumstance of their Law, for conscience sake, misled by superstition, which no human edict otherwise, no force of arms, could have enforced.

In the last place are Pseudo-Christians, in describing of whose super-stitious symptoms, as a mixture of the rest, I may say that which S. Benedict once saw in a vision, one Devil in the market-place, but ten in a Monastery, because there was more work; in populous Cities,

they would swear and for-swear, lie, falsify, deceive fast enough of
themselves, one Devil could circumvent a thousand; but in their religious houses, a thousand Devils could scarce tempt one silly Monk.
All the principal Devils, I think, busy themselves in subverting Christians; Jews, Gentiles, and Mahometans are out of the fold, and need
no such attendance, they make no resistance, for he troubleth not to
scourge those whom he possesseth in peace, they are his own already;
but Christians have that shield of Faith, sword of the spirit to resist,
and must have a great deal of battery before they can be overcome.
That the Devil is most busy amongst us that are of the true Church,
appears by those several Oppositions, Heresies, Schisms, which in all
ages he hath raised to subvert it, and in that of Rome especially,
wherein Antichrist himself now sits and plays his prize. This mystery
of iniquity began to work even in the Apostles' time, many Antichrists
and Hereticks were abroad, many sprung up since, many now present,
and will be to the world's end, to dementate men's minds, to seduce
and captivate their souls. Their symptoms I know not how better to
express, than in that twofold division, of such as lead, and are led.
Such as lead are Hereticks, Schismaticks, false Prophets, Impostors,
and their Ministers: they have some common symptoms, some peculiar.
Common, as madness, folly, pride, insolency, arrogancy, singularity,
peevishness, obstinacy, impudence, scorn, and contempt of all other
sects:

Not bound to swear as any one master dictates. (HORACE)

They will approve of nought but what they first invent themselves, no
interpretation good, but what their infallible spirit dictates: none shall
be second best, no not third, they are only wise, only learned in the
truth, all damned but they and their followers; saith Tertullian, they
make a slaughter of Scriptures, and turn it, as a nose of wax, to their
own ends. So irrefragable, in the mean time, that what they have once
said, they must and will maintain, in whole Tomes, duplications, tripli-
cations, never yield to death, so self-conceited, say what you can. As
Bernard (erroneously some say) speaks of P. Aliardus, all the Fathers
may say this, I say that. Though all the Fathers, Councils, the whole
world contradict it, they care not, they are all one: and as Gregory well
notes of such as are vertiginous, they think all turns round and moves,
all err; when as the error is wholly in their own brains. Magallianus the
Jesuit in his Comment on the first of Timothy, and Alphonsus de Castro,
give two more eminent notes, or probable conjectures to know such
men by (they might have taken themselves by the noses when they said

it), First, they affect novelties and toys, and prefer falsehood before truth; Secondly, they care not what they say, that which rashness and folly hath brought out, pride afterward, peevishness and contumacy shall maintain to the last gasp. Peculiar symptoms are prodigious paradoxes, new doctrines, vain phantasms, which are many and divers, as they themselves. Nicholaites of old would have wives in common: Montanists will not marry at all, nor Tatians, forbidding all flesh, Severians wine; Adamians go naked, because Adam did so in Paradise, and some bare-foot all their lives, because God bid Moses so to do, and Isaiah was bid put off his shoes: Manichees hold that Pythagorean transmigration of souls from men to beasts; the Circumcelliones in Africa with a mad cruelty made away themselves, some by fire, water, breaking their necks, and seduced others to do the like, threatening some if they did not, with a thousand such; as you may read in Austin, (for there were fourscore and eleven Heresies in his time, besides Schisms and smaller factions) Epiphanius, Alphonsus de Castro, Danæus, Gab. Prateolus, &c. Of Prophets, Enthusiasts & Impostors, our Ecclesiastical stories afford many examples: of Eliases and Christs, as our Eudo de Stellis, a Briton in King Stephen's time, that went invisible, translated himself from one to another in a moment, fed thousands with good cheer in the wilderness, and many such; nothing so common as miracles, visions, revelations, prophecies. Now what these brain-sick Hereticks once broach, and Impostors set on foot, be it never so absurd, false, and prodigious, the common people will follow and believe. It will run along like Murrain in cattle, scab in sheep, as Jovianus Pontanus said: as he that is bitten with a mad dog bites others, and all in the end become mad; either out of affection of novelty, simplicity, blind zeal, hope and fear, the giddy-headed multitude will embrace it, and without farther examination approve it.

But these are old, these things that we complain of, they belong to the past. In our days we have a new scene of superstitious Impostors and Hereticks, a new company of Actors, of Antichrists, that great Antichrist himself: a rope * of Popes, that by their greatness and authority bear down all before them: who from that time they proclaimed themselves universal Bishops, to establish their own Kingdom, sovereignty, greatness, and to enrich themselves, brought in such a company of human traditions, Purgatory, the Limbo of the Fathers, of Infants, and all that subterranean Geography, Mass, adoration of Saints, alms,

* Rope, a Middle English form of " roop," noisy, blustering lot; but perhaps here a string or chain.

fastings, bulls, indulgencies, Orders, Friars, Images, Shrines, musty
Reliques, Excommunications, confessions, satisfactions, blind obedi-
ences, vows, pilgrimages, peregrinations, with many such curious toys,
intricate subtilties, gross errors, obscure questions, to vindicate the
better, and set a gloss upon them, that the light of the Gospel was quite
eclipsed, darkness over all, the Scriptures concealed, legends brought in,
religion banished, hypocritical superstition exalted, and the Church
itself obscured and persecuted: Christ and his members crucified more,
saith Benzo, by a few Necromantical, Atheistical Popes, than ever it
was by Julian the Apostate, Porphyry the Platonist, Celsus the Physician, Libanius the Sophister; by those Heathen Emperors, Hunns,
Goths, and Vandals. What each of them did, by what means, at what
times, by what support, superstition climbed to this height, traditions
increased, and Antichrist himself came to his estate, let Magdeburgenses, Kemnisius, Osiander, Bale, Mornay, Fox, Usher, and many others
relate. In the mean time he that shall but see their profane Rites and
foolish Customs, how superstitiously kept, how strictly observed, their
multitude of Saints, Images, that rabble of Romish Deities, for Trades,
Professions, Diseases, Persons, Offices, Countries, Places; St. George for
England; St. Denis, for France; Patrick, Ireland; Andrew, Scotland;
Jago, Spain, &c.; Gregory for Students; Luke for Painters; Cosmas and
Damian for Philosophers; Crispin, Shoe-makers; Katherine, Spinners,
&c.; Anthony for Pigs; Gallus, Geese; Wenceslaus, Sheep; Pelagius,
Oxen; Sebastian, the plague; Valentine, falling-sickness; Apollonia,
tooth-ache; Petronella, for agues; and the Virgin Mary, for sea and
land, for all parties, offices: he that shall observe these things, their
Shrines, Images, Oblations, Pendants, Adorations, Pilgrimages they
make to them, what creeping to Crosses, our Lady of Loretto's rich
Gowns, her Donaries, the cost bestowed on Images, and number of
suitors; S. Nicholas Burge in France; our S. Thomas' Shrine of old at
Canterbury; those Reliques at Rome, Jerusalem, Genoa, Lyons, Prato,
S. Denis; and how many thousands come yearly to offer to them, with
what cost, trouble, anxiety, superstition (for forty several Masses are
daily said in some of their Churches, and they rise at all hours of the
night to Mass, come bare-foot, &c.) how they spend themselves, times,
goods, lives, fortunes, in such ridiculous observations; their tales and
figments, false miracles, buying and selling of pardons, indulgences for
forty thousand years to come, their processions on set days, their strict
fastings, monks, anchorites, friar mendicants, Franciscans, Carthusians,
&c. Their Vigils and Fasts, their Ceremonies at Christmas, Shrovetide,

Candlemas, Palm-Sunday, S. Blase, S. Martin, S. Nicholas' day: their adorations, exorcisms, &c. will think all those Grecian, Pagan, Mahometan superstitions, gods, Idols, and Ceremonies, the Name, Time and Place, habit only altered, to have degenerated into Christians. Whilst they prefer Traditions before Scriptures; those Evangelical Councils, poverty, obedience, vows, alms, fasting, supererogations, before God's Commandments; their own Ordinances instead of his Precepts, and keep them in ignorance, blindness, they have brought the common people into such a case by their cunning conveyances, strict discipline, and servile education, that upon pain of damnation they dare not break the least ceremony, tradition, edict: hold it a greater sin to eat a bit of meat in Lent than kill a man: their consciences are so terrified, that they are ready to despair if a small ceremony be omitted; and will accuse their own Father, Mother, Brother, Sister, nearest and dearest friends, of heresy, if they do not as they do, will be their chief executioners, and help first to bring a fagot to burn them. What mulct, what penance soever is enjoined, they dare not but do it, tumble with S. Francis in the mire amongst hogs, if they be appointed, go woolward,* whip themselves, build Hospitals, Abbies, &c., go to the East or West-Indies, kill a King, or run upon a sword point: they perform all, without any muttering or hesitation, believe all.

> *As children think their babies live to be,*
> *Do they these brazen images they see.* (LUCILIUS)

And whilst the ruder sort are so carried headlong with blind zeal, are so gulled and tortured by their superstitions, their own too credulous simplicity and ignorance, their Epicurean Popes and Hypocritical Cardinals laugh in their sleeves, and are merry in their chambers with their Punks, they do indulge their genius, and make much of themselves. The middle sort, some for private gain, hope of Ecclesiastical preferment, (who taught the parrot to chirp his good-morning?) popularity, base flattery, must and will believe all their paradoxes and absurd tenents, without exception, and as obstinately maintain and put in practice all their traditions and Idolatrous ceremonies, (for their Religion is half a Trade) to the death; they will defend all, the Golden Legend itself, with all the lies and tales in it: as that of S. George, S. Christopher, S. Winifred, S. Denis, &c. It is a wonder to see how Nich. Harpsfield, that pharisaical Impostor, amongst the rest, puzzles himself to vindicate that ridiculous fable of S. Ursula, and the eleven thousand Virgins, as when they lived, how they came to Cologne, by whom mar-

* Wear wool next the skin for penance, like haircloth.

tyred. &c., though he can say nothing for it, yet he must and will approve it: Ursula with her companions ennobled (he saith) this age, whose history I would were as clear and certain as it is certain and clear in my mind that she is a happy virgin in heaven with her companions. They must and will (I say) either out of blind zeal believe, vary their compass with the rest, as the latitude of Religion varies, apply themselves to the times and seasons, and for fear and flattery are content to subscribe and do all that in them lies to maintain and defend their present government, and slavish religious School-men, Canonists, Jesuits, Friars, Priests. Orators, Sophisters, luxuriant wits, who either for that they had nothing else to do, knew not otherwise how to busy themselves in those idle times, for the Church then had few or no open adversaries, or better to defend their lies, fictions, miracles, transubstantiations, traditions, Popes' Pardons, Purgatories, Masses, impossibilities, &c., with glorious shews, fair pretences, big words, and plausible wits, have coined a thousand idle questions, nice distinctions, subtilties, Obs and Sols [Objections and Solutions], such tropological, allegorical expositions, to salve all appearances, objections, such quirks and quiddities, Quodlibetaries, as Bale saith of Ferribrigge and Strode, instances, ampliations, decrees, glosses, canons, that instead of sound Commentaries, good Preachers, are come in a company of mad sophisters, firstly and secondly fellows, Sectaries, Canonists, Sorbonists [Doctors of the Sorbonne], Minorites [Franciscan Friars], with a rabble of idle controversies and questions, Whether the Pope be God, or like to God? whether each shares the nature of Christ? Whether it be as possible for God to be an Humble-Bee, or a Gourd, as a man? Whether he can produce respect without a foundation or term, make a Whore a Virgin? Fetch Trajan's soul from hell, and how? with a rabble of questions about hell fire: whether it be a greater sin to kill a man, or to clout shoes upon a Sunday? Whether God can make another God like unto himself? Such, saith Kemnisius, are most of your School-men (mere Alchemists), 200 Commentators on Peter Lombard; (Pitsius reckons up 180 English Commentators alone, on the matter of the sentences); Scotists, Thomists, Reals, Nominals, &c., and so perhaps that of Saint Austin may be verified, the unlearn'd get heaven while the learn'd go down to hell. Thus they continued in such error, blindness, decrees, sophisms, superstitions; idle ceremonies and traditions were the sum of their new-coined holiness and religion, and by these knaveries and stratagems they were able to involve multitudes, to deceive the most sanctified souls, and if it were possible the very Elect. In the mean time the true Church, as wine and water mixt, lay hid and obscure to speak of till Luther's time, who began upon a sudden to defecate, [or purge], and, as another Sun, to drive away those foggy mists of superstition, to restore it to that purity of the Primitive Church. And after him many good and godly men, divine spirits, have done their endeavours, and still do.

> *And what their ignorance esteem'd so holy,*
> *Our wiser ages do account as folly.*   (DANIEL)

But see the Devil, that will never suffer the Church to be quiet or at rest: no garden so well tilled, but some noxious weeds grow up in it; no wheat, but it hath some tares; we have a mad giddy company of Precisians, Schismaticks, and some Hereticks, even in our bosoms in another extreme,

> *Fools run from one extreme into another,*   (HORACE)

that out of too much zeal in opposition to Antichrist, human traditions, those Romish rites and superstitions, will quite demolish all, they will admit of no ceremonies at all, no fasting days, no Cross in Baptism, no kneeling at Communion, no Church-musick, &c., no Bishop's-Courts, no Church-government, rail at all our Church-discipline, will not hold their tongues, and all for the peace of thee, O Sion. No not so much as Degrees will some of them tolerate, or Universities, all human learning ('tis the Devil's Sewer), hoods, habits, cap and surplice, such as are things indifferent in themselves, and wholly for ornament, decency, or distinction sake, they abhor, hate and snuff at, as a stone-horse [stallion] when he meets a Bear: they make matters of conscience of them, and will rather forsake their livings, than subscribe to them. They will admit of no holy-days, or honest recreations, as of hawking, hunting, &c., no Churches, no bells some of them, because Papists use them: no discipline, no ceremonies but what they invent themselves: no interpretations of Scriptures, no Comments of Fathers, no Councils, but such as their own phantastical spirits dictate, or right reason, as Socinians, by which spirit misled, many times they broach as prodigious paradoxes as Papists themselves. Some of them turn Prophets, have secret revelations, will be of privy council with God himself, and know all his secrets, hold the Holy Spirit by the hair, obstinate asses that they are. A company of giddy heads will take upon them to define how many shall be saved, and who damned in a parish, where they shall sit in Heaven, interpret Apocalypses (precipitate and giddy-pated Commentators, one calls them, as well he might) and those hidden mysteries to private persons, times, places, as their own spirit informs them, private revelations shall suggest, and precisely set down when the world shall come to an end, what year, what month, what day. Some of them again have such strong faith, so presumptuous, they will go into infected houses, expel devils, and fast forty days, as Christ himself did; some call God and his Attributes into question, as Vorstius and Socinus, some Princes, Civil Magistrates, and their authorities, as Anabaptists, will do all their own private spirit dictates, and nothing else. Brownists, Barrowists, Familists, and those Amsterdamian sects and sectaries, are led all by so many private spirits. It is a wonder to reveal what passages Sleidan relates in his Commentaries, of Cretink, Knipperdoling, and their associates, those mad men of Munster in Germany; what strange Enthusiasms, sottish Revelations they had, how absurdly they carried themselves, deluded others; and as profane Machiavel in his Political Disputations holds of Christian Religion in general, it doth enervate, debilitate, take away men's spirits and courage from them, makes men more simple, breeds nothing so courageous Soldiers as that Roman: we may say of these peculiar sects, their Religion takes away not spirits only, but wit and judgment, and deprives them of their understanding: for some of them are so far gone with their private Enthusiasms and Revelations, that they are quite mad, out of their wits.

What greater madness can there be, than for a man to take upon him to be God, as some do? to be the Holy Ghost, Elias, and what not? In Poland, 1518, in the Reign of King Sigismund, one said he was Christ, and got him twelve Apostles, came to judge the world, and strangely deluded the Commons. One David George, an illiterate Painter, not many years since, did as much in Holland, took upon him to be the Messias, and had many followers. Benedictus Victorinus Faventinus writes as much of one Honorius, that thought he was not only inspired as a Prophet, but that he was a God himself, and had familiar conference * with God and his Angels. Lavater hath a story of one John Sartorius, that thought he was the Prophet Elias, and of divers others that had conference with Angels, were Saints, Prophets; Wierus makes mention of a Prophet of Groningen that said he was God the Father; of an Italian and Spanish Prophet that held as much. We need not rove so far abroad, we have familiar examples at home; Hacket that said he was Christ, Coppinger and Arthington, his disciples: Burchet and Hovatus, burned at Norwich. We are never likely seven years together without some such new Prophets, that have several inspirations, some to convert the Jews, some fast forty days, go with Daniel to the Lion's

* Hen. Nicholas, at Leyden, 1580, such a one. — Burton's note.

den; some foretell strange things, some for one thing, some for another. Great Precisians of mean conditions and very illiterate, most part by a preposterous zeal, fasting, meditation, melancholy, are brought into these gross errors and inconveniences. Of these men I may conclude generally, that howsoever they may seem to be discreet, and men of understanding in other matters, discourse well, they have a diseased imagination, they are like comets, round in all places but only where they blaze, otherwise sane, they have impregnable wits many of them, and discreet otherwise, but in this their madness and folly breaks out beyond measure. They are certainly far gone with melancholy, if not quite mad, and have more need of physick than many a man that keeps his bed, more need of Hellebore than those that are in Bedlam.

SUBSECTION 4 — *Prognosticks of Religious Melancholy*

You may guess at the Prognosticks by the Symptoms. What can these signs foretell otherwise than folly, dotage, madness, gross ignorance, despair, obstinacy, a reprobate sense, a bad end? What else can superstition, heresy produce, but wars, tumults, uproars, torture of souls, and despair, a desolate land, as Jeremy teacheth, when they commit Idolaatry, and walk after their own ways? how should it be otherwise with them? What can they expect but *blasting, famine, dearth,* and all the plagues of Egypt, as Amos denounceth; to be led into captivity? If our hopes be frustrate, *we sow much, and bring in little, eat, and have not enough, drink, and are not filled, clothe, and be not warm,* &c.; *we look for much, and it comes to little, whence is it? His house was waste, they came to their own houses, therefore the Heaven staid his dew, the Earth his fruit.* Because we are superstitious, irreligious, we do not serve God as we ought, all these plagues and miseries come upon us; what can we look for else but mutual wars, slaughters, fearful ends in this life, and in the life to come eternal damnation? What is it that hath caused so many feral battles to be fought, so much Christian blood shed, but superstition? That Spanish Inquisition, Racks, Wheels, Tortures, Torments, whence do they proceed? from superstition. Bodine the Frenchman accounts Englishmen Barbarians for their civil wars: but let him but read those Pharsalian fields fought of late in France for Religion, their Massacres, wherein by their own relations in four and twenty years I know not how many millions have been consumed, whole Families and Cities, and he shall find ours to have been but velitations [or skirishes] to theirs. But it hath ever been the custom of Hereticks and Idolaters, when they are plagued for their sins, and God's just judgments come upon them, not to acknowledge any fault in themselves, but still impute it unto others. In Cyprian's time it was much controverted betwixt him and Demetrius an Idolater, who should be the cause of those present calamities. Demetrius laid all the fault on Christians (and so they did ever in the primitive Church, as appears by the first book of Arnobius) that there were not such ordinary showers in Winter, the ripening heat in Summer, no seasonable Springs, fruitful Autumns, no Marble Mines in the Mountains, less gold and silver than of old; that husbandmen, sea-men, soldiers, all were scanted, justice, friendship, skill in Arts, all was decayed, and that through Christians' default, and all their other miseries from them, because they did not worship their gods. But Cyprian retorts all upon him again, as appears by his Tract against him. 'Tis true, the world is miserably tormented and shaken with wars, dearth, famine, fire, inundations, plagues, and many feral diseases rage amongst us, but not as thou complainest, that we do not worship your Gods, but because you are Idolaters, and do not serve the true God, neither seek him, nor fear him as you ought. Our Papists object as much to us, and account us hereticks, we them; the Turks esteem of both as Infidels, and we them as a company of Pagans, Jews against all; when indeed there is a general fault in us all, and something in the very best, which may justly deserve God's wrath, and pull these miseries upon our heads. I will say nothing here of those vain cares, torments, needless works, penance, pilgrimages, pseudo-martyrdom, &c. We heap upon ourselves unnecessary troubles, observations; we punish our bodies, as in Turkey (saith Busbequius) one did, that was much affected with Musick, and to hear Boys sing, but very superstitious; an old Sibyl coming to his house, or an holy woman (as that place yields many) took him down for it, and told him, that in that other world he should suffer for it; thereupon he flung his rich and costly Instruments which he had bedeckt with Jewels, all at once into the fire. He was served in silver plate, and had goodly household-stuff: a little after another religious man reprehended him in like sort, and from thenceforth he was served in earthen vessels. Last of all, a decree came forth, because Turks might not drink wine themselves, that neither Jew nor Christian then living in Constantinople might drink any wine at all. In like sort amongst Papists, fasting at first was generally proposed as a good thing; after, from such meats at set times, and then last of all so rigourously proposed, to bind the consciences upon pain of damnation. First Friday, saith Erasmus, then Saturday, and Wednesday now is in danger of a fast. And for such like toys some so miserably afflict themselves, to despair, and death itself, rather than offend, and think themselves good Christians in it, when as indeed they are superstitious Jews. So saith Leonardus Fuchsius, a great Physician in his time. We are tortured in Germany with these Popish edicts, our bodies so taken down, our goods so diminished, that if God had not sent Luther, a worthy man, in time to redress these mischiefs, we should have eaten hay with our horses before this. As in fasting, so in all other superstitious edicts, we crucify one another without a cause, barring ourselves of many good and lawful things, honest disports, pleasures and recreations; for wherefore did God create them but for our use? Feasts, mirth, musick, hawking, hunting, singing, dancing, &c. God not only ministers to our necessities but sheweth his love by providing for our pleasures also, as Seneca notes, God would have it so. And as Plato gives out, the gods, in commiseration of human estate, sent Apollo, Bacchus, and the Muses, to be merry with mortals, to sing and dance with us. So that he that will not rejoice and enjoy himself, making good use of such things as are lawfully permitted, is not temperate, as he will, but superstitious. *There is nothing better for a man, than that he should eat and drink, and that he should make his Soul enjoy good in his labour.* And as one said of hawking and hunting, I say of all honest recreations, God hath therefore indulged them to refresh, ease, solace and comfort us. But we are some of us too stern, too rigid, too precise, too grossly superstitious, and whilst we make a conscience of every toy, with touch not, taste not, &c., as those Pythagoreans of old, and some Indians now that will eat no flesh, or suffer any living creature to be killed, the Bannians about Guzerat; we tyrannize over our brother's soul, lose the right use of many good gifts, honest sports, games and pleasant recreations, punish ourselves without a cause, lose our liberties, and sometimes our lives. In the year 1270, at Magdeburg in Germany, a Jew fell into a Privy upon a Saturday, and without help could not possibly get out; he called to his fellows for succour, but they denied it, because it was their Sabbath, it was not permitted to do any work; the Bishop hearing of it the next day forbade him to be pulled out because it was our Sunday: in the mean time the wretch died before Monday. We have myriads of examples in this kind amongst those rigid Sabbatarians, and therefore not without good cause, Seneca calls it, as well he might, an intolerable perturbation, that causeth such dire events, folly, madness, sickness, despair, death of body and soul, and hell itself.

SUBSECTION 5 — *Cure of Religious Melancholy*

To purge the world of Idolatry and superstition, will require some monster-taming Hercules, a divine Æsculapius, or Christ himself to come in his own person, to reign a thousand years on earth before the end, as the Millenaries [those who expect the Millenium] will have him. They are generally so refractory, self-conceited, obstinate, so firmly addicted to that religion in which they have been bred and brought up, that no persuasion, no terror, no persecution can divert them. The consideration of which hath induced many commonwealths to suffer them to enjoy their consciences as they will themselves. A toleration of Jews is in most Provinces of Europe: in Asia they have their Synagogues: Spaniards permit Moors to live amongst them: the Mogullians, Gentiles: the Turks, all religions. In Europe, Poland and Amsterdam are the common Sanctuaries. Some are of opinion, that no man ought to be compelled for conscience sake, but let him be of what religion he will, he may be saved, as Cornelius was formerly accepted, Jew, Turk, Anabaptists, &c. If he be an honest man, live soberly and civilly in his profession, (Volkelius, Crellius, and the rest of the Socinians, that now nestle themselves about Cracow and Rakow in Poland, have renewed this opinion) serve his own God, with that fear and reverence as he ought. Let each state keep its own religion (saith Lælius) and let us keep ours; Tully thought fit every city should be free in this behalf, adore their own tutelary and local gods, as Symmachus calls them. Isocrates adviseth Demonicus, when he came to a strange city, to worship by all means the Gods of the place: which Cæcilius labours, and would have every nation keep their own ceremonies, worship their peculiar gods, which Pomponius Mela reports of the Africans, they worship their own gods according to their own ordination. For why should any one nation, as he there pleads, challenge that universality of God (this God of theirs, whom they neither display nor see, wandering about, forsooth, and everywhere present, inquiring into the habits, deeds, and hidden thoughts of all, &c.), as Christians do? Let every Province enjoy their liberty in this behalf, worship one God, or all, as they will, and are informed [inspired to do]. The Romans built Altars to the Gods of Asia, Libya, to unknown and wandering Gods: others otherwise, &c.; Plinius Secundus, as appears by his Epistle to Trajan, would not have the Christians so persecuted, and in some time of the reign of Maximin, as we find it registered in Eusebius, there was a decree made to this purpose, *Let no one be compelled against his will to worship any particular God,* and by Constantine in the 19th year of his reign, as Baronius informeth us, *Let no man shew arrogance against another, what each man chooseth, that let him do;* new gods, new lawgivers, new Priests will have new ceremonies, customs and religions, to which every wise man as a good Formalist should accommodate himself.

> *Saturn is dead, his laws have perished with him:*
> *Obey now Jupiter, who rules the world.* (OVID)

The said Constantine the Emperor, as Eusebius writes, flung down and demolished all the heathen gods, silver, gold statues, altars, Images and temples, and turned them all to Christian Churches (hostile to the popular memorials, he exposed them to ridicule); the Turk now converts them again to Mahometan Meskites [or Mosques]. The like Edict came forth in the reign of Arcadius and Honorius. Symmachus the Orator, in his days, to procure a general toleration, used this argument, Because God is immense and infinite, and his nature cannot perfectly be known, it is convenient he should be as diversely worshipped, as every man shall perceive or understand. It was impossible, he thought, for one religion to be universal: you see that one small Province can hardly be ruled by one law civil or spiritual; and how shall so many distinct and vast Empires of the world be united into one? It never was, never will be. Besides, if there be infinite planetary and firmamental worlds, as some will, there be infinite Geniuses or commanding Spirits belonging to each of them: and so in consequence (for they will be all adored) infinite religions. And therefore let every Territory keep their proper rites and ceremonies, as their tutelary gods will, so Tyrius calls them, and according to the quarter they hold, their own institutions, revelations, orders, Oracles, which they dictate to from time to time, or teach their Priests or Ministers. This tenent was stiffly maintained in Turkey not long since, as you may read in the third Epistle of Busbequius, that all those should participate of eternal happiness, that lived an holy and innocent life, what religion soever they professed: Rustan Bassa was a great Patron of it; though Mahomet himself was sent as the sword of virtue, to enforce all, as he writes in his Alcoran, to follow him. Some again will approve of this for Jews, Gentiles, Infidels, that are out of the fold, they can be content to give them all respect and favour, but by no means to such as are within the precincts of our own Church, and called Christians, to no Hereticks, Schismaticks, or the like; let the Spanish Inquisition, that fourth Fury, speak of some of them, the civil wars and Massacres in France, our Marian times. Magallianus the Jesuit will not admit of conference with an heretick, but severity and rigour to be used. one should not argue with them, but set up pillories for them : and Theodosius is commended in Nicephorus, that he put all Hereticks to silence. Bernard will have club law, fire and sword for Hereticks, compel them, stop their mouths, not with disputations, or refute them with reasons, but with fists; and this is their ordinary practice. Another company are as mild, on the other side, to avoid all heart-burning, and contentious wars and uproars, they would have a general toleration in every kingdom, no mulct at all, no man for religion or conscience be put to death, which Thuanus the French Historian much favours: our late Socinians defend; Vaticanus against Calvin, in a large Treatise in behalf of Servetus, vindicates; Castalio, &c., Martin Bellius, and his companions, maintained this opinion not long since in France, whose error is confuted by Beza in a just Volume. The medium is best, and that which Paul prescribes: " If any man shall fall by occasion, to restore such a one with the spirit of meekness, by all fair means, gentle admonitions " : but if that will not take place, after a second admonition shun the heretick, he must be excommunicate, as Paul did by Hymenæus, delivered over to Satan. A wound that cannot be cured, must be cut away (saith Ovid). As Hippocrates said in Physick, I may well say in Divinity, the fire cures what the sword cannot. For the vulgar, restrain them by laws, mulcts, burn their books, forbid their conventicles: for when the cause is taken away, the effect will soon cease. Now for Prophets, dreamers, and such rude silly fellows, that through fasting, too much meditation, preciseness, or by Melancholy are distempered: the best means to reduce them to a sound mind is to alter their course of life, and with conference, threats, promises, persuasions, to intermix Physick. Hercules de Saxoniâ had such a Prophet committed to his charge in Venice, that thought he was Elias, and would fast as he did: he dressed a fellow in Angel's attire, that said he came from heaven to bring him divine food, and by that means staid his fast, administered his Physick: so by the mediation of this forged Angel he was cured. Rhasis, an Arabian, speaks of a fellow that in like case complained to him, and desired his help: I asked him (saith he) what the matter was, he replied, I am continually meditating of Heaven and Hell, and methinks I see and talk with fiery spirits, smell brimstone, &c., and am so carried away with these conceits, that I can neither eat, nor sleep, nor go about my business: I cured him (saith Rhasis) partly by persuasion, partly by Physick, and so have I done by many others. We have frequently such Prophets and dreamers amongst us, whom we persecute with fire and fagot: I think the most compendious cure for some of them at least, had been in Bedlam. But enough of this.

MEMBER 2

SUBSECTION 1 — *Religious Melancholy in defect; Parties affected, Epicures, Atheists, Hypocrites, worldly secure, Carnalists, all impious persons, impenitent sinners, &c.*

IN that other extreme, or defect of this love of God, knowledge. faith, fear, hope, &c., are such as err both in doctrine and manners, Sadducees, Herodians, Libertines, Politicians; all manner of Atheists, Epicures, Infidels, that are secure, in a reprobate sense, fear not God at all, and such are too distrustful and timorous, as desperate persons be. That grand sin of Atheism or Impiety, Melancthon calls it, monstrous Melancholy; or poisoned Melancholy. A company of Cyclops or Giants, that war with the gods, as the Poets feigned, Antipodes to Christians, that scoff at all Religion, at God himself, deny him and all his attributes, his wisdom, power, providence. his mercy and judgment.

> *That there are ghosts, and an infernal realm,*
> *A ferry, black frogs in the Stygian whirlpool,*
> *And thousands passing over at a time,*
> *Not even boys believe.* (JUVENAL)

That there is either Heaven or Hell, resurrection of the dead, pain, happiness, or world to come, let he who likes believe; for their parts, they esteem them as so many Poet's tales, Bugbears; Lucian's Alexander, Moses, Mahomet, and Christ, are all as one in their Creed. When those bloody wars in France for matters of Religion (saith Richard Dinoth) were so violently pursued betwixt Huguenots and Papists, there was a company of good fellows laughed them all to scorn, for being such superstitious fools, to lose their lives and fortunes, accounting faith, religion, immortality of the soul, mere fopperies and illusions. Such loose Atheistical spirits are too predominant in all Kingdoms. Let them contend, pray, tremble, trouble themselves that will, for their parts, they fear neither God nor Devil; but with that Cyclops in Euripides,

> *They fear no God but one,*
> *They sacrifice to none,*
> *But belly, and him adore,*
> *For Gods they know no more.*

Their God is their belly, as Paul saith; satiety their goddess:

   Their palate is their only reason for living.   (JUVENAL)

The Idol which they worship and adore is their Mistress, with him in Plautus, they had rather have her favour than the Gods'. Satan is their guide, the flesh is their instructor, Hypocrisy their Counsellor, Vanity their fellow-soldier, their Will their law, Ambition their Captain, Custom their Rule: temerity, boldness, impudence their Art, toys their trading, damnation their end. All their endeavours are to satisfy their lust and appetite, how to please their Genius, and to be merry for the present,

   Eat, drink, and love; no pleasure after death.

The same condition is of men and of beasts; as the one dieth, so dieth the other; the world goes round,

   Day follows day, and full moons haste to wane.   (HORACE)

They did eat and drink of old, marry, bury, bought, sold, planted, built, and will do still. *Our life is short and tedious, and in the death of a man there is no recovery, neither was any man known that hath returned from the grave: for we are born at all adventure, and we shall be hereafter as though we had never been; for the breath is as smoke in our nostrils, &c., and the spirit vanisheth as the soft Air. Come let us enjoy the pleasures that are present, let us cheerfully use the creatures as in youth, let us fill ourselves with costly wine and ointments, let not the flower of our life pass by us, let us crown ourselves with Rose-buds, before they are withered, &c.* Lesbia mine, let's live and love. *Come let us take our fill of love, and pleasure in dalliance, for this is our portion, this is our lot.*

   Time flies with noiseless foot, and we grow old.   (OVID)

For the rest of Heaven and Hell, let children and superstitious fools believe it: for their parts they are so far from trembling at the dreadful day of judgment, that they wish with Nero, let it come in their times: so secure, so desperate, so immoderate in lust and pleasure, so prone to revenge, that as Paterculus said of some Caitiffs in his time in Rome, it shall not be so wickedly attempted, but as desperately performed, whate'er they take in hand. Were it not for God's restraining grace, fear and shame, temporal punishment, and their own infamy, they would Lycaon-like exenterate, as so many Cannibals eat up, or [as] Cadmus' soldiers, consume one another. These are most impious, and commonly professed Atheists, that never use the name of God, but to swear by it: that express nought else but Epicurism in their carriage or hypocrisy; with Pentheus, they neglect and contemn these rites and religious ceremonies of the Gods, they will be Gods themselves, or at least companions of the Gods.

> *Cæsar divides the world's empire with Jove.*

Apries an Egyptian tyrant, grew, saith Herodotus, to that height of pride, insolency and impiety, to that contempt of God and men, that he held his Kingdom so sure, neither God nor men could take it from him. A certain blasphemous King of Spain (as Lansius reports) made an edict, that no subject of his, for ten years' space, should believe in, call on, or worship any god. And as Jovius relates of Mahomet the Second, that sacked Constantinople, he so behaved himself, that he believed neither Christ nor Mahomet, and thence it came to pass, that he kept his word and promise no further than for his advantage, neither did he care to commit [care if he committed] any offence to satisfy his lust. I could say the like of many Princes, many private men (our stories are full of them) in times past, this present age, that love, fear, obey, and perform all civil duties, as they shall find them expedient or behoveful to their own ends; which Tacitus reports of some Germans, they need not pray, fear, hope, for they are secure to their thinking, both from God and men. Bulco Opiliensis, sometime Duke of Silesia, was such a one to an hair, he lived (saith Æneas Sylvius) at Uratislavia, and was so mad to satisfy his lust, that he believed neither Heaven nor Hell, or that the soul was immortal, but married wives, and turned them up as he thought fit, did murder and mischief, and what he list himself. This Duke hath too many followers in our days: say what you can, dehort, exhort, persuade to the contrary, they are no more moved,

> *Than were a pillar of flint or Marpesian cliff,* (VIRGIL)

than so many stocks and stones; tell them of Heaven and Hell, 'tis to no purpose, 'tis washing a mudbrick; they answer, as Ataliba, that Indian Prince, did Friar Vincent, when he brought him a book, and told him all the mysteries of salvation, Heaven and Hell were contained in it: he looked upon it, and said he saw no such matter, asking withal how he knew it: they will but scoff at it, or wholly reject it. Petronius in Tacitus, when he was now by Nero's command bleeding to death, instead of good counsel and divine meditations, he made his friends sing him bawdy verses, and scurrile songs. Let them take Heaven, Paradise, and that future happiness that will, it is good being here: there is no talking to such, no hope of their conversion, they are in a reprobate sense, mere carnalists, fleshy-minded men, which howsoever they may be applauded in this life by some few Parasites, and held for worldly wise men, they seem to me (saith Melancthon) to be as mad as Hercules was, when he raved and killed his wife and children. A milder sort of these Atheistical spirits there are that profess Religion, but timidly and hesitantly, tempted thereunto out of that horrible consideration of diversity of Religions, which are and have been in the world (which argument Campanella both urgeth and answers), besides the covetousness, imposture and knavery of Priests which (as Postellus observes) makes people believe less in religion, and those religions some of them so fantastical, exorbitant, so violently maintained with equal constancy and assurance; whence they infer, that if there be so many religious sects, and denied by the rest, why may they not be all false? or why should this or that be preferred before the rest? The Scepticks urge this, and amongst others it is the conclusion of Sextus Empiricus: after many Philosophical arguments and reasons for and against, that there are Gods, and again that there are no Gods, he so concludes, when there are so many contradictions, one only can be true, as Tully likewise disputes: Christians say they alone worship the true God, pity all other sects, lament their case; and yet those old Greeks and Romans that worshipped the Devil, as the Chinese do now, their own gods; as Julian the Apostate, Cæcilius in Minucius, Celsus and Porphyry the Philosopher object; and as Machiavel contends, were much more noble, generous, victorious, had a more flourishing Commonwealth, better Cities, better Soldiers, better Scholars, better Wits. Their Gods often overcame our Gods, did as many miracles, &c., Saint Cyril, Arnobius, Minucius, with many other ancients, of late Lessius, Mornay, Grotius, Savanarola, well defend; but Zanchius, Campanella, Marinus Marcennus, Bozius, and Gentilettus answer all their Atheistical arguments at large. But this again troubles many, as of old, wicked men generally thrive, professed Atheists thrive.

> *There are no Gods, Heavens are toys,*
> *Segius in public justifies;*
> *Because that whilst he thus denies*
> *Their Deities, he better thrives.*   (MARTIAL)

This is a prime Argument: and most part your most sincere, upright, honest, and good men are depressed. *The race is not to the swift, nor the battle to the strong, nor yet bread to the wise, favour nor riches to men of understanding, but time and chance comes to all.* There was a great plague in Athens (as Thucydides relates) in which at last every man with great licentiousness did what he list, not caring at all for God's or men's Laws. Neither the fear of God, nor Laws of men (saith he) awed any man, because the plague swept all away alike, good and bad; they thence concluded, it was alike to worship or not worship the Gods, since they perished all alike. Some cavil and make doubts of Scripture itself, it cannot stand with God's mercy, that so many should be damned, so many bad, so few good, such have and hold about Religions, all stiff on their side, factious alike, thrive alike, and yet bitterly persecuting and damning each other. It cannot stand with God's goodness, protection and providence (as Saint Chrysostom in the dialect of such discontented persons) to see and suffer one man to be lame, another mad, a third poor and miserable all the days of his life, a fourth grievously tormented with sickness and aches to his last hour. Are these signs and works of God's providence, to let one man be deaf, another dumb? A poor honest fellow lives in disgrace, woe and want, wretched he is; when as a wicked Caitiff abounds in superfluity of wealth, keeps whores, parasites, and what he will himself. Do you hear this, Jupiter? Collecting many such things, they weave a tissue of reproaches against God's providence. Thus they mutter and object (see the rest of their Arguments in Marcennus, and in Campanella, amply confuted), with many such vain cavils, well known, not worthy the recapitulation or answering, whatsoever they pretend, they are meantime of little or no Religion.

Couzin-germans to these men are many of our great Philosophers and Deists, who, though they be more temperate in this life, give many good moral precepts, honest, upright, and sober in their conversation, yet in effect they are the same (accounting no man a good Scholar that is not an Atheist) too much learning makes them mad. Whiles they attribute all to natural causes, contingence of all things, as Melancthon calls them, a peevish Generation of men, that misled by Philosophy, and the Devil's suggestion, their own innate blindness, deny God as much as the rest, hold all Religion a fiction, opposite to Reason and Philosophy, though for fear of Magistrates, saith Vaninus, they durst not publickly profess it. Ask one of them of what Religion he is, he scoffingly replies, a Philosopher, a Galenist, an Averroist, and with Rabelais a Physician, a Peripatetick, an Epicure. In spiritual things God must demonstrate all to sense, leave a pawn with them, or else seek some other creditor. They will acknowledge nature and fortune, yet not God: though in effect they grant both: for as Scaliger defines, Nature signifies God's ordinary power; or as Calvin writes, Nature is God's order, and so things extraordinary may be called unnatural: Fortune his unrevealed will; and so we call things changeable that are beside reason and expectation. To this purpose Minucius, and Seneca well discourseth with them. They do not understand what they say; what is Nature but God?

Call him what thou wilt, Nature, Jupiter, he hath as many Names as
Offices. It comes all to one pass, God is the fountain of all, the first
Giver and Preserver, from whom all things depend. God is all in all,
God is everywhere, in every place. And yet this Seneca that could confute and blame them, is all out as much to be blamed and confuted
himself, as mad himself; for he holds to Stoick Fate, that inevitable
necessity, in the other extreme, as those Chaldæan Astrologers of old
did, against whom the Prophet Jeremiah so often thunders, and those
Heathen Mathematicians, Nigidius Figulus, Magicians, and Pricilian-
ists, whom S. Austin so eagerly confutes, those Arabian questionaries,
Nine Judges, Albumazar, Dorotheus, &c., and our Countryman Estu-
idus, that take upon them to define out of those great conjunctions of
Stars, with Ptolomæus, the periods of Kingdoms, or Religions, of all
future Accidents, Wars, Plagues, Schisms, Heresies, and what not? all
from Stars, and such things, saith Maginus, which God hath reserved
to himself and his Angels, they will take upon them to fore-tell, as if
Stars were immediate, inevitable causes of all future accidents. Cæsar
Vaninus,* in his Book, is more free, copious & open in the explication
of this Astrological Tenent of Ptolemy, than any of our modern Writers,
Cardan excepted, a true Disciple of his Master Pomponatius; according
to the doctrine of Peripateticks, he refers all Apparitions, Prodigies,
Miracles, Oracles, Accidents, Alterations of Religions, Kingdoms, &c.,
(for which he is soundly lashed by Marinus Marcennus, as well he
deserves), to natural causes (for spirits he will not acknowledge), to
that light, motion, influences of Heavens and Stars, and to the Intelligences that move the Orbs. Intelligences do all: and after a long Discourse of Miracles done of old, If Devils can do these things, why not
the Intelligences of the heavenly bodies? And as these great Conjunctions, Aspects of Planets, begin or end, vary, are vertical and predominant, so have Religions, Rites, Ceremonies and Kingdoms their beginning, progress, periods: with Cities, Kings, Religions, and individual
men, these things are true and plain, as Aristotle seems to imply, and
daily experience teaches to the reader of history; for what was more
sacred and illustrious, by Gentile law, than Jupiter? what now more
vile and execrable? Thus the celestial bodies set up religions for mortal
benefits, and when the influence ceases, so doth the law, &c. And because, according to their Tenents, the world is eternal, intelligences

---

* Cæsar Vaninus (or Lucilio Vanini), an Italian free-thinker, was condemned as an
atheist, had his tongue cut out, and was strangled at the stake, his body being burned
to ashes, in 1619. His book was The Secrets of Nature (Paris, 1616).

eternal, influence of the Stars eternal, Kingdoms, Religions, Alterations shall be likewise eternal, and run round after many Ages; again great Achilles shall be sent against Troy; religions and their ceremonies shall be born again; human affairs relapse into the same track, there is nothing that was not of old time and shall not be again, saith Vaninus, the same in kind but not in person, as in Plato. These (saith mine Author), these are the Decrees of Peripateticks, which though I recite, as I am a Christian I detest and hate. Thus Peripateticks, and Astrologians held in former times, and to this effect of old in Rome, saith Dionysus Halicarnasseus, when those Meteors and Prodigies appeared in the Air, after the banishment of Coriolanus, men were diversely affected, some said they were God's just judgments for the execution of that good man, some referred all to natural causes, some to the Stars, some thought they came by chance, some by necessity decreed from the beginning, and could not be altered. The last two Opinions of Necessity and Chance were, it seems, of greater note than the rest.

All human things some do ascribe to Fortune,
And think this world without a governor,
That seasons come and go spontaneously. (JUVENAL)

For the first of Chance, as Sallust likewise informeth us, those old Romans generally received. They supposed Fortune alone gave Kingdoms and Empires, Wealth, Honours, Offices; and that for two causes, first, because every wicked, base, unworthy wretch was preferred, rich, potent, &c. Secondly, because of their uncertainty, though never so good, scarce any one enjoyed them long: but after they began upon better advice to think otherwise, that every man made his own fortune. The last of Necessity was Seneca's tenent, that God was so tied to second causes, to that inexorable necessity, that he could alter nothing of that which was once decreed; thus 'twas fated, it cannot be altered, God hath once said it, and it must for ever stand good, no prayers, no threats, nor power, nor thunder itself can alter it. Zeno, Chrysippus, and those other Stoicks, as you may read in Tully, A. Gellius, &c., maintained as much. In all ages, there have been such, that either deny God in all, or in part; some deride him, they could have made a better world, and rule it more orderly themselves, blaspheme him, derogate at their pleasure from him. 'Twas so in Plato's times, Some say there be no gods, others, that they care not for men, a middle sort grant both. If there's no God, whence comes good? If there is a God, whence evil? So Cotta argues in Tully, why made he not all good, or at least tenders not the welfare of such as are good? As the woman told Alexander, if he be not

at leisure to hear Causes, and redress them, why doth he reign? Sextus
Empiricus hath many such Arguments. Thus perverse men cavil. So
it will ever be, some of all sorts, good, bad, indifferent, true, false,
zealous, Ambidexters [or people who would keep in with both parties],
Neutralists, lukewarm Libertines, Atheists, &c. They will see these religious Sectaries agree amongst themselves, be reconciled all, before
they will participate with, or believe any. They think in the mean time
(which Celsus objects, and whom Origen confutes) we Christians adore
a person put to death, with no more reason than the barbarous Getæ
worshipped Zamolxis, the Cilicians Mopsus, the Thebans Amphiaraus,
and the Lebadeans Trophonius; one religion is as true as another, new-
fangled devices, all for human respects; great witted Aristotle's works
are as much authentical to them, as Scriptures, subtil Seneca's Epistles
as Canonical as Saint Paul's, Pindar's Odes as good as the Prophet
David's Psalms, Epictetus' Enchiridion equivalent to wise Solomon's
Proverbs. They do openly and boldly speak this and more, some of
them, in all places and companies. Claudius the Emperor was angry
with Heaven, because it thundered, and challenged Jupiter into the
field; with what madness! saith Seneca; he thought Jupiter could not
hurt him, but he could hurt Jupiter. Diagoras, Demonax, Epicurus,
Pliny, Lucian, Lucretius,

> And Mezentius, the despiser of the Gods,   (VIRGIL)

professed Atheists all in their times: though not simple Atheists neither,
as Cicogna proves, they scoffed only at those Pagan gods, their plurality,
base and fictitious Offices. Gilbertus Cognatus labours much, and so
doth Erasmus, to vindicate Lucian from scandal, and there be those
that apologize for Epicurus; but all in vain, Lucian scoffs at all, Epicurus he denies all, and Lucretius his Scholar defends him in it;

> When human kind was drenched in superstition,
> With ghastly looks aloft, which frighted mortal men, &c.

He alone, as another Hercules, did vindicate the world from that Monster. Uncle Pliny, in express words denies the Immortality of the Soul.
Seneca doth little less, or rather more. Some Greek Commentators
would put as much upon Job, that he should deny the resurrection, &c.,
whom Pineda copiously confutes. Aristotle is hardly censured of some,
both Divines and Philosophers. S. Justin, Gregory Nazianzen, Theodoretus, Origen, Pomponatius justifies in his Tract (so styled at least)
on the Immortality of the Soul, Scaliger (who would forswear himself
at any time, saith Patritius, in defence of his great Master Aristotle),
and Dandinus, acknowledge as much. Averroes oppugns all spirits and

supreme powers; of late Brunus (unhappy Brunus, Kepler calls him),
Machiavel, Cæsar Vaninus lately burned at Toulouse in France, and
Peter Aretine, have publickly maintained such Atheistical Paradoxes,
with that Italian Boccaccio, with his Fable of three Rings, &c., from
which he infers it cannot be known which is the true religion, Jewish,
Mahometan, or Christian, since they have the same signs, &c. Marinus
Marcennus suspects Cardan for his Subtilties, Campanella, and Char-
ron's Book of Wisdom, with some other Tracts, to savour of Atheism:
but amongst the rest that pestilent Book of the Three Impostors of the
World, which you cannot read (he says) without horror, and the
Cymbal of the World, in four dialogues, written by Perier in the year
1538, printed at Paris, &c. And as there have been in all ages such
blasphemous spirits, so there have not been wanting their Patrons, Pro-
tectors, Disciples and Adherents. Never so many Atheists in Italy and
Germany, saith Colerus, as in this age: the like complaint Marcennus
makes in France, 50,000 in that one City of Paris. Frederick the Emperor, as Matthew Paris records (I use his own words), is reported to
have said: Although it may not be told, three Prestidigitators, Moses,
Christ, and Mahomet, in order that they might rule the world, befooled
all the people living in their times. (Henry the Landgrave of Hesse
heard him speak it.) If the Princes of the Empire (he said) would follow my teaching, I would lay out a much better way of believing and
living.

To these professed Atheists we may well add that impious and carnal
crew of worldly-minded men, impenitent sinners, that go to Hell in a
lethargy, or in a dream, who though they be professed Christians, yet
they will make a conscience of nothing they do, they have cauterized
consciences, and are indeed in a reprobate sense, *past all feeling, have
given themselves over to wantonness, to work all manner of unclean-
ness even with greediness.* They do know there is a God, a day of Judgment to come, and yet for all that, as Hugo saith, they are as merry for
all the sorrow, as if they had escaped all dangers, and were in Heaven
already.

> *He put all fears under our feet, and death,*
> *The debt we all must pay, and Acheron's roar.* (VIRGIL)

Those rude idiots and ignorant persons, that neglect and contemn the
means of their salvation, may march on with these, but above all others,
those Herodian temporizing States-men, politick Machiavelians and
Hypocrites, that make a show of Religion, but in their hearts laugh at
it. A pretended sanctity is a double iniquity; they are in a double fault,

that fashion themselves to this world, which Paul forbids, and like Mercury the Planet, are good with good, bad with bad. When they are at Rome, they do there as they see done, Puritans with Puritans, Papists with Papists, all things to all men, Formalists, Ambidexters, luke-warm Laodiceans. All their study is to please, and their god is their commodity, their labour to satisfy their lusts, and their endeavours to their own ends. Whatsoever they pretend. or in publick seem to do, *With the fool, in their hearts, they say there is no God.*

You, sir, what think you about Jupiter? (PERSIUS)

" Their words are as soft as oil, but bitterness is in their hearts," like Alexander the Sixth, so cunning dissemblers, that what they think, they never speak. Many of them are so close, you can hardly discern it, or take any just exceptions at them; they are not factious, oppressors, as most are, no bribers, no simoniacal Contractors, no such ambitious, lascivious persons, as some others are, no drunkards, they rise sober, and go sober to bed, plain dealing, upright honest men, they do wrong to no man, and are so reputed in the world's esteem at least, very zeal-ous in Religion, very charitable, meek, humble, peace-makers, keep all duties, very devout, honest, well spoken of, beloved of all men: but he that knows better how to judge, he that examines the heart, saith they are Hypocrites, they are not sound within. As it is with Writers oftentimes, more holiness is in the Book, than in the Author of it: So 'tis with them; many come to Church with great Bibles, whom Cardan said, he could not choose but laugh at, and will now and then read Austin, frequent Sermons, and yet professed Usurers, mere Gripes, all their life is Epicurism and Atheism, come to Church all day, and lie with a Courtesan at night.

Pretend to be Curii, and live like bacchanals. (JUVENAL)

They have Esau's hands, and Jacob's voice; yea, and many of those holy Friars, sanctified men, saith Hierom, conceal a bandit within their robes. They are wolves in sheep's clothing, fair without, and most foul within. Oft-times under a mourning weed lies lust itself, and horrible vices under a poor coat. But who can examine all those kinds of Hypo-crites, or dive into their hearts? If we may guess at the tree by the fruit, never so many as in these days; shew me a plain dealing true honest man; shame and honesty and fear are fled. He that shall but look into their lives, and see such enormous vices, men so immoderate in lust, unspeakable in malice, furious in their rage, flattering and dissembling (all for their own ends) will surely think they are not truly religious, but of an obdurate heart, most part in a reprobate sense, as in this Age.

But let them carry it as they will for the present, dissemble as they can, a time will come when they shall be called to an account, their melancholy is at hand, they pull a plague and curse upon their own heads. Besides all such as blaspheme, contemn, neglect God, or scoff at him, as the Poets feign of Salmoneus, that would in derision imitate Jupiter's Thunder, he was precipitated for his pains, so shall they certainly rue it in the end (they spit on themselves, who spit at the sky), their doom's at hand, and Hell is ready to receive them.

Some are of Opinion, that it is in vain to dispute with such Atheistical spirits in the mean time, 'tis not the best way to reclaim them. Atheism, Idolatry, Heresy, Hypocrisy, though they have one common root, that is indulgence to corrupt affection, yet their growth is different, they have divers symptoms, occasions, and must have several cures and remedies. 'Tis true, some deny there is any God, some confess, yet believe it not; a third sort confess and believe, but will not live after his Laws, Worship and obey him: others allow God and Gods subordinate, but not one God, no such general God, but several Topick [or Local] Gods for several places, and those not to persecute one another for any differences, as Socinus will, but rather love and cherish.

To describe them in particular, to produce their Arguments and reasons, would require a just volume, I refer them therefore that expect a more ample satisfaction, to those subtil and elaborate Treatises, devout and famous Tracts of our learned Divines (Schoolmen amongst the rest, and Casuists) that have abundance of reasons to prove there is a God, the immortality of the soul, &c., out of the strength of wit and Philosophy bring irrefragable Arguments to such as are ingenious and well disposed; at the least, answer all cavils and objections to confute their folly and madness, and to reduce them, if possible, to a better mind; though to small purpose many times. Amongst others consult with Julius Cæsar Lagalla, Professor of Philosophy in Rome, who hath written a large Volume of late to confute Atheists; of the Immortality of the Soul, Hierome, Montanus, Lelius Vincentius of the same subject; Thomas Giaminus, and Franciscus Collius, a famous Doctor of the Ambrosian College in Milan. Bishop Fotherby in his Atheomastix, Doctor Dove, Doctor Jackson, Abernethy, Corderoy, have written well of this subject in our mother tongue: in Latin, Colerus, Zanchius, Palearius, Illyricus, Philippus, Faber, Faventinus, &c. But above all, the most copious confuter of Atheists, is Marinus Marcennus in his Commentaries on Genesis: with Campanella's Atheism Triumphant. He sets down at large the causes of this brutish passion (seventeen in number

I take it) answers all their Arguments and Sophisms, which he reduceth to twenty-six heads, proving withal his own Assertion; There is a
God, such a God, the true and sole God, by five and thirty reasons. His
Colophon [or Conclusion] is how to resist and repress Atheism, and to
that purpose he adds four especial means or ways, which whoso will
may profitably peruse.

SUBSECTION 2 — *Despair. Despairs, Equivocations, Definitions, Parties
and Parts affected*

THERE be many kinds of desperation, whereof some be holy, some unholy, as one [Abernethy] distinguisheth; that unholy he defines out of
Tully to be a sickness of the soul without any hope or expectation of
amendment: which commonly succeeds fear; for whilst evil is expected,
we fear; but when it is certain, we despair. According to Thomas, it is
a restraint from the thing desired, for some impossibility supposed.
Because they cannot obtain what they would, they become desperate,
and many times either yield to the passion by death itself, or else attempt impossibilities, not to be performed by men. In some cases this
desperate humour is not much to be discommended, as in Wars it is a
cause many times of extraordinary valour; as Josephus, L. Danæus,
and many Politicians hold. It makes them improve their worth beyond
itself, and a forlorn impotent Company become Conquerors in a moment.

One safety to the vanquished — not to seek it.   (VIRGIL)

In such courses when they see no remedy, but that they must either kill
or be killed, they take courage, and oftentimes beyond all hope vindicate themselves. Fifteen thousand Locrians fought against a hundred
thousand Crotonians, and seeing now no way but one, they must all
die, thought they would not depart unrevenged, and thereupon desperately giving an assault, conquered their Enemies. Nor was there other
cause of the victory, (saith Justin mine Author) than their desperation. William the Conqueror, when he first landed in England, sent back
his ships, that his soldiers might have no hope of retiring back. Bodine
excuseth his Countrymen's overthrow at that famous Battle at Agincourt, in Henry the Fifth his time (which, saith Froissart, no History can parallel almost, wherein one handful of English-men overthrew a Royal Army of French-men) with this refuge of despair, a few
desperate fellows being compassed in by their Enemies, past all hope of
life, fought like so many Devils; and gives a caution, that no soldiers
hereafter set upon desperate persons, which after Frontinus and Vige-

tius, Guicciardini likewise admonisheth, not to stop an enemy that is
going his way. Many such kinds there are of desperation, when men are
past hope of obtaining any suit, or in despair of better fortune; despair
makes the monk, as the saying is, and desperation causeth death itself;
how many thousands in such distress have made away themselves, and
many others! For he that cares not for his own, is Master of another
man's life. A Tuscan Sooth-sayer, as Paterculus tells the story, perceiving himself and Fulvius Flaccus his dear friend, now both carried to
prison by Opimius, and in despair of pardon, seeing the young man
weep, said, do as I do; and with that knockt out his brains against the
door-cheek, as he was entering into Prison, and so desperately died. But
these are equivocal, unproper. When I speak of despair, saith Zanchius,
I speak not of every kind, but of that alone which concerns God. It
is opposite to hope, and a most pernicious sin, wherewith the Devil
seeks to entrap men. Musculus makes four kinds of Desperation, of
God, ourselves, our Neighbour, or any thing to be done; but this division of his may be reduced easily to the former: all kinds are opposite
to hope, that sweet Moderator of Passions, as Simonides calls it; I do
not mean that vain hope which phantastical fellows feign to themselves,
which according to Aristotle is a waking dream; but this Divine hope
which proceeds from confidence, and is an Anchor to a floating soul;
hope drives the farmer; even in our temporal affairs, hope revives us,
but in spiritual it further animateth; and were it not for hope, " we of
all others were the most miserable," as Paul saith, in this life; were it
not for hope, the heart would break; " for though they be punished in
the sight of men," yet is their hope " full of immortality," yet doth
it not so rear, as Despair doth deject; this violent and sour passion of
Despair, is of all perturbations most grievous, as Patricius holds. Some
divide it into final and temporal; final is incurable, which befalleth
Reprobates; temporal is a rejection of hope and comfort for a time,
which may befall the best of God's children, and it commonly proceeds
" from weakness of Faith," as in David, when he was oppressed, he
cried out, " O Lord, thou hast forsaken me," but this [is] for a time.
This ebbs and flows with hope and fear; it is a grievous sin howsoever:
although some kind of Despair be not amiss, when, saith Zanchius, we
despair of our own means, and rely wholly upon God: but that species
is not here meant. This pernicious kind of desperation is the subject
of our Discourse, the murderer of the soul, as Austin terms it, a fearful passion, wherein the party oppressed thinks he can get no ease but
by death, and is fully resolved to offer violence unto himself, so sens-

ible of his burthen, and impatient of his cross, that he hopes by death alone to be freed of his calamity (though it prove otherwise) and chooseth with Job, "rather to be strangled and die than to be in his bonds." The part affected is the whole soul, and all the faculties of it; there is a privation of joy, hope, trust, confidence, of present and future good, and in their place succeed fear, sorrow, &c., as in the Symptoms shall be shewed. The heart is grieved, the conscience wounded, and the mind eclipsed with black fumes arising from those perpetual terrors.

SUBSECTION 3 — *Causes of Despair, the Devil, Melancholy, Meditation, Distrust, weakness of Faith, rigid Ministers, Misunderstanding Scriptures, guilty-consciences, &c.*

THE principal agent and procurer of this mischief is the Devil; those whom God forsakes, the Devil, by his permission, lays hold on. Sometimes he persecutes them with that worm of conscience, as he did Judas, Saul, and others. The Poets call it Nemesís, but it is indeed God's just judgment, late but great, he strikes home at last, and setteth upon them *as a thief in the night.* This temporary passion made David cry out, *Lord, rebuke me not in thine anger, neither chasten me in thine heavy displeasure; for thine arrows have lit upon me, &c. There is nothing sound in my flesh, because of thine anger.* Again, *I roar for the very grief of my heart;* and *My God, my God, why hast thou forsaken me, and art so far from my health, and the words of my crying? I am like to water poured out, my bones are out of joint, mine heart is like wax, that is molten in the midst of my bowels.* So Psalms 88, 15th and 16th verses, and Psalm 102. *I am in misery, at the point of death, from my youth I suffer thy terrors, doubting for my life; thine indignations have gone over me, and thy fear hath cut me off.* Job doth often complain in this kind; and those God doth not assist, the Devil is ready to try and torment, *still seeking whom he may devour.* If he find them merry, saith Gregory, he tempts them forthwith to some dissolute act; if pensive and sad, to a desperate end. Sometimes by fair means, sometimes again by foul, as he perceives men severally inclined. His ordinary engine by which he produceth this effect, is the melancholy humour itself, which is the Devil's bath; and as in Saul, those evil spirits get in, as it were, and take possession of us. Black choler is a shoeing-horn, a bait to allure them, insomuch that many writers make melancholy an ordinary cause, and a symptom of despair, for that such men are most apt by reason of their ill-disposed temper, to distrust, fear, grieve, mistake, and amplify whatsoever they preposterously conceive, or falsely apprehend. A scrupulous conscience comes of a natural defect, a melancholy habit (saith Navarrus). The body works upon the mind, by obfuscating the spirits and corrupted instruments, which Perkins illustrates by simile of an Artificer, that hath a bad tool, his skill is good, ability correspondent, by reason of ill tools his work must needs be lame and unperfect. But melancholy and despair, though often, do not always concur; there is much difference; melancholy fears without a cause, this upon great occasion; melancholy is caused by fear and grief, but this torment procures them all extremity of bitterness; much melancholy is without affliction of conscience, as Bright and Perkins illustrate by four reasons; and yet melancholy alone again may be sometimes a sufficient cause of this terror of conscience. Felix Plater so found it in his observations, they think they are not predestinate, God hath forsaken them; and yet otherwise very zealous and religious; and 'tis common to be seen, melancholy for fear of God's judgment and hell fire, drives men to desperation; fear and sorrow, if they be immoderate, end often with it. Intolerable pain and anguish, long sickness, captivity, misery, loss of goods, loss of friends, and those lesser griefs, do sometimes effect it, or such dismal accidents. Saith Marcennus, if they be not eased forthwith, they doubt whether there be any God, they rave, curse, and are desperately mad, because good men are oppressed, wicked men flourish, they have not as they think to their desert, and through impatience of calamities are so misaffected. Democritus put out his eyes, because he could not abide to see wicked men prosper, and was therefore ready to make away himself, as A. Gellius writes of him. Felix Plater hath a memorable example in this kind, of a Painter's wife in Basil, that was melancholy for her son's death, and for melancholy became desperate, she thought God would not pardon her sins, and for four months, still raved, that she was in hell fire, already damned. When the humour is stirred up, every small object aggravates and incenseth it, as the parties are addicted. The same Author hath an example of a merchant-man, that for the loss of a little wheat, which he had over-long kept, was troubled in conscience, for that he had not sold it sooner, or given it to the poor, yet a good Scholar and a great Divine; no persuasion would serve to the contrary, but that for this fact he was damned; in other matters very judicious and discreet. Solitariness, much fasting, divine meditations, and contemplations of God's judgments, most part accompany this melancholy, and are main causes, as Navarrus holds; to converse with such kind of persons so troubled, is sufficient occasion of trouble to some men. Many (saith P. Forestus) through long fasting, serious meditations of heavenly things. fall into such fits; and, as Lemnius adds, if they be solitary given, superstitious, precise, or very devout: seldom shall you find a Merchant, a Soldier, an Inn-keeper, a Bawd, an Host, an Usurer so troubled in mind, they have cheverel [kid-leather] consciences that will stretch, they are seldom moved in this kind or molested: young men and middle age are more wild, & less apprehensive; but old folks, most part, & such as are timorous, are religiously given. Peter Forestus hath a fearful example of a Minister, that through precise fasting in Lent, and overmuch meditation, contracted this mischief, and in the end became desperate. thought he saw devils in his chamber, and that he could not be saved: he smelled nothing, as he said, but fire and brimstone, was already in hell, and would ask them still, if they did not smell as much. I told him he was melancholy, but he laughed me to scorn, and replied, that he saw devils, talked with them in good earnest, would spit in my face, and ask me if I did not smell brimstone, but at last he was by him cured. Such another story I find in Plater. A poor fellow had done some foul offence, and for fourteen days would eat no meat, in the end became desperate, the Divines about him could not ease him, but so he died. Continual meditation of God's judgments troubles many. Many, for fear of the judgment to come, saith Guatinerius, and their uncertainty, are desperate. David himself complains that God's judgments terrified his Soul: " My flesh trembleth for fear of thee, and I am afraid of thy judgments." That day (saith Hierome) I tremble as often as I think of it. The terrible meditation of hell-fire, and eternal punishment, much torments a sinful silly soul. What's a thousand years to eternity? There mourning, tears, eternal sorrow; death undying, end without end: a finger burnt by chance we may not endure, the pain is so grievous, we may not abide an hour, a night is intolerable; and what shall this unspeakable fire then be that burns for ever, innumerable infinite millions of years! O eternity!

Eternity, that word, that tremendous word,
More threatening than all the artillery of heaven, —
Eternity, that word, without end or beginning, &c.
No torments can affright us that time will end;
Eternity, eternity, fills and inflames the heart;
This it is that daily augments our sufferings,
And multiplies our heart-burnings an hundred-fold. (DREXELIUS)

This meditation terrifies these poor distressed souls, especially if their bodies be predisposed by melancholy, they religiously given, and have tender consciences, every small object affrights them, the very inconsiderate reading of Scripture itself, and misinterpretation of some places of it as *Many are called, few are chosen. Not every one that saith Lord. Fear not, little flock. He that stands, let him take heed lest he fall. Work out your salvation with fear and trembling. That night two shall be in a bed, one received, the other left. Straight is the way that leads to Heaven, and few there are that enter therein.* The parable of the seed, and of the sower, *some fell on barren ground, some was choked. Whom he hath predestinated, he hath chosen. He will have mercy on whom he will have mercy. So then it is not of him that willeth, nor of him that runneth, but of God that sheweth mercy.* These and the like places terrify the souls of many; election, predestination, reprobation, preposterously conceived, offend divers, with a deal of foolish presumption, curiosity, needless speculation, contemplation, solicitude, wherein they trouble and puzzle themselves about those questions of grace, freewill, perseverance, God's secrets; they will know more than is revealed by God in his word, human capacity, or ignorance can apprehend, and too importunate inquiry after that which is revealed: mysteries, ceremonies, observation of Sabbaths, laws, duties, &c., with many such which the Casuists discuss, and School-men broach, which divers mistake, misconstrue, misapply to themselves, to their own undoing, and so fall into this gulf. They doubt of their Election, how they shall know it, by what signs. And so far forth, saith Luther, with such nice points, torture and crucify themselves, that they are almost mad, and all they get by it is this, they lay open a gap to the Devil by Desperation to carry them to Hell. But the greatest harm of all proceeds from those thundering Ministers, a most frequent cause they are of this malady: and do more harm in the Church (saith Erasmus) than they that flatter; great danger on both sides, the one lulls them asleep in carnal security, the other drives them to despair. Whereas S. Bernard well adviseth, We should not meddle with the one without the other, nor speak of judgment without mercy; the one alone brings Desperation, the other Security. But these men are wholly for judgment, of a rigid disposition themselves, there is no mercy with them, no salvation, no balsam for their diseased souls, they can speak of nothing but reprobation, hell-fire, & damnation, as they did, Luke, 11 :46, *lade men with burdens grievous to be borne, which they themselves touch not with a finger.* 'Tis familiar with our Papists to terrify men's souls with purgatory, tales, visions, apparitions, to daunt even the most generous spirits, to require charity, as Brentius observes, of others, bounty, meekness, love, patience, when they themselves breathe out nought but lust, envy, covetousness. They teach others to fast, give alms, do penance, and crucify their mind with superstitious observations, bread and water, hair-cloths, whips, and the like, when they themselves have all the dainties the world can afford, lie on a down bed with a Courtesan in their arms. Alas, what we endure for Christ, as he [Leo Decimus] said; what a cruel tyranny is this, so to insult over, and terrify men's souls! Our indiscreet Pastors many of them come not far behind, whilst in their ordinary Sermons they speak so much of election, predestination, reprobation from the beginning of the world, subtraction of grace, præterition, voluntary permission, &c., by what signs and tokens they shall discern and try themselves, whether they be God's true children elect, or reprobate, predestinate, &c., with such scrupulous points, they still aggravate sin, thunder out God's judgments without respect, intempestively rail at, and pronounce them damned in all auditories, for giving so much to sports and honest recreations, making every small fault and thing indifferent an irremissible offence, they so rent, tear, and wound men's consciences, that they are almost mad, and at their wits' ends.

These bitter potions (saith Erasmus) are still in their mouths, nothing but gall and horror, and a mad noise, they make all their auditors desperate, many are wounded by this means, and they commonly that are most devout and precise, have been formerly presumptuous, and certain of their salvation; they that have tender consciences, that follow Sermons, frequent Lectures, that have indeed least cause, they are most apt to mistake, and fall into these miseries. I have heard some complain of Parsons' Resolution, and other books of like nature (good otherwise) they are too tragical, too much dejecting men, aggravating offences; great care and choice, much discretion is required in this kind.

The last and greatest cause of this malady, is our own conscience, sense of our sins, and God's anger justly deserved, a guilty conscience for some foul offence formerly committed.

" *Wretched Orestes, what is wasting you?* "

" *Conscience, for I am conscious of ill deeds.*"   (EURIPIDES)

A good conscience is a continual feast, but a galled conscience is as great a torment as can possibly happen, a still baking oven, (so Pierius in his Hieroglyph, compares it) another hell. Our conscience, which is a great ledger book, wherein are written all our offences, a register to lay them up, (which those Egyptians in their Hieroglyphicks expressed by a mill, as well for the continuance as for the torture of it) grinds our souls with the remembrance of some precedent sins, makes us reflect upon, accuse and condemn our own selves. " Sin lies at door," &c. I know there be many other causes assigned by Zanchius, Musculus, and the rest; as incredulity, infidelity, presumption, ignorance, blindness, ingratitude, discontent, those five grand miseries in Aristotle, ignominy, need, sickness, enmity, death, &c., but this of conscience is the greatest, like an ulcer continually festering in the body, this scrupulous conscience (as Peter Forestus calls it) which tortures so many, that either out of a deep apprehension of their unworthiness, and consideration of their own dissolute life, accuse themselves, and aggravate every small offence, when there is no such cause, misdoubting in the mean time God's mercies, they fall into these inconveniences. The Poets call them Furies, but it is the conscience alone which is a thousand witnesses to accuse us,

Night and day they carry this witness in the breast. (JUVENAL)

A continual testor to give in evidence, to empanel a Jury to examine us, to cry guilty, a persecutor with hue and cry to follow, an apparitor to summon us, a bailiff to carry us, a Serjeant to arrest, an Attorney to plead against us, a gaoler to torment, a Judge to condemn, still accusing, denouncing, torturing and molesting. And as the statue of Juno in that holy city near Euphrates in Assyria will look still towards you, sit where you will in her temple, she stares full upon you, if you go by, she follows with her eye, in all sites, places, conventicles, actions, our conscience will be still ready to accuse us. After many pleasant days, and fortunate adventures, merry tides, this conscience at last doth arrest us. Well he may escape temporal punishment, bribe a corrupt judge, and avoid the censure of law, and flourish for a time; for who ever saw (saith Chrysostom) a covetous man troubled in mind when he is telling of his money, an adulterer mourn with his mistress in his arms? we are then drunk with pleasure, and perceive nothing: yet as the prodigal Son had dainty fare, sweet musick at first, merry company, jovial entertainment, but a cruel reckoning in the end, as bitter as wormwood, a fearful visitation commonly follows. And the devil that then told thee that it was a light sin, or no sin at all, now aggravates on the other side, and telleth thee that it is a most irremissible offence, as he did by Cain and Judas, to bring them to despair; every small circumstance before neglected and contemned, will now amplify itself, rise up in judgment and accuse, the dust of their shoes, dumb creatures, as to Lucian's tyrant the bed and candle, did bear witness, to torment their souls for their sins past. Tragical examples in this kind are too familiar and common: Adrian, Galba,

Nero, Otho, Vitellius, Caracalla, were in such horror of conscience for their offences committed, murders, rapes, extortions, injuries, that they were weary of their lives, and could get no body to kill them. Kenneth III., King of Scotland, when he had murdered his Nephew Malcolm, King Duff's son, Prince of Cumberland, and with counterfeit tears and protestations dissembled the matter a long time, at last his conscience accused him, his unquiet soul could not rest day or night, he was terrified with fearful dreams, visions, and so miserably tormented all his life. It is strange to read what Commines hath written of Lewis the XI., that French King, of Charles the VIII., of Alphonso King of Naples, in the fury of his passion how he came into Sicily, and what pranks he played. Guicciardini, a man most unapt to believe lies, relates how that Ferdinand his father's ghost, who before had died for grief, came and told him that he could not resist the French King, he thought every man cried France, France; the reason of it (saith Commines) was because he was a vile tyrant, a murderer, an oppressor of his subjects, he bought up all commodities, and sold them at his own price, sold Abbies to Jews and Falconers; both Ferdinand his father, and he himself, never made conscience of any committed sin; and to conclude, saith he, it was impossible to do worse than they did. Why were Pausanias, the Spartan Tyrant, Nero, Otho, Galba, so persecuted with spirits in every house they came, but for their murders which they had committed? Why doth the devil haunt many men's houses after their deaths, appear to them living, and take possession of their habitations, as it were, of their palaces, but because of their several villanies? Why had Richard the III. such fearful dreams, saith Polydore, but for his frequent murders? Why was Herod so tortured in his mind? because he had made away Mariamne his wife. Why was Theodoricus the King of the Goths so suspicious, and so affrighted with a fish-head alone, but that he had murdered Symmachus, and Boethius his son-in-law, those worthy Romans? (Cœlius). See more in Plutarch. Yea, and sometimes God himself hath a hand in it, to shew his power, humiliate, exercise, and to try their faith, (divine temptation Perkins calls it) to punish them for their sins. God the avenger, as David terms him, his wrath is apprehended of a guilty soul, as by Saul and Judas, which the Poets expressed by Adrastea, or Nemesis:

> That you may do no evil, Nemesis
> Pursues and dogs the footsteps of ill-doers.

And she is, as Ammianus describes her, the Queen of causes, and moderator of things, now she pulls down the proud, now she rears and encourageth those that are good; he gives instance in his Eusebius; Nicephorus in Maximin and Julian. Fearful examples of God's just judgment, wrath and vengeance, are to be found in all histories, of some that have been eaten to death with Rats and Mice, as Popelius the Second, King of Poland, in the year 830, his wife and children: the like story is of Hatto Archbishop of Mentz, in the year 969, so devoured by these vermin, which howsoever Serrarius the Jesuit impugns by 22 arguments, Trithemius, Munster, Magdeburgenses, and many others relate for a truth. Such another example I find in Giraldus Cambrensis, and where not?

And yet for all these terrors of conscience, affrighting punishments which are so frequent, or whatsoever else may cause or aggravate this fearful malady in other Religions, I see no reason at all why a Papist at any time should despair, or be troubled for his sins; for let him be never so dissolute a Caitiff, so notorious a villain, so monstrous a sinner, out of that Treasure of Indulgences and merits of which the Pope is Dispensator, he may have free pardon, and plenary remission of all his sins. There be so many general pardons for ages to come, 40,000 years to come, so many Jubilees, so frequent Gaol-deliveries out of Purgatory for all souls now living, or after dissolution of the body so many particular Masses daily said in several Churches, so many Altars consecrated to this purpose, that if a man have either money or friends, or will take any pains to come to such an Altar, hear a Mass, say so many Pater-nosters, undergo such and such penance, he cannot do amiss, it is impossible his mind should be troubled, or he have any scruple to molest him. Besides that Sale of Indulgences, which was first published to get money in the days of Leo Decimus, that sharking Pope, and since divulged to the same ends, sets down such easy rates and dispensations for all offences, for perjury, murder, incest, adultery, &c., for so many groschens or dollars (able to invite any man to sin, and provoke him to offend, methinks, that otherwise would not) such comfortable remission, so gentle and parable [procurable] a pardon, so ready at hand, with so small cost and suit obtained, that I cannot see how he that hath any friends amongst them (as I say) or money in his purse, or will at least to ease himself, can any way miscarry or be misaffected, how he should be desperate, in danger of damnation, or troubled in mind. Their ghostly Fathers can so readily apply remedies, so cunningly string and unstring, wind and unwind their devotions, play upon their consciences with plausible speeches, and terrible threats, for their best advantage settle and remove, erect with such facility and deject, let in and out, that I cannot perceive how any man amongst them should much or often labour of this disease, or finally miscarry. The causes above named must more frequently therefore take hold in others.

Subsection 4 — *Symptoms of Despair, Fear, Sorrow, Suspicion, Anxiety, Horror of conscience, fearful dreams and visions*

As Shoe-makers do when they bring home shoes, still cry, Leather is dearer and dearer; may I justly say of those melancholy Symptoms, these of Despair are most violent, tragical and grievous, far beyond the rest, not to be expressed, but negatively, as it is privation of all happiness, not to be endured: *for a wounded spirit who can bear?* What therefore Timanthes did in his picture of Iphigenia, now ready to be sacrificed, when he had painted Calchas mourning, Ulysses sad, but most sorrowful Menelaus, and shewed all his art in expressing variety of affections, he covered the maid's father, Agamemnon's head, with a veil, and left it to every spectator to conceive what he would himself; for that true passion and sorrow in the highest degree, such as his was, could not by any art be deciphered. What he did in his picture, I will do in describing the Symptoms of Despair; imagine what thou canst, fear, sorrow, furies, grief, pain, terror, anger, dismal, ghastly, tedious, irksome, &c., it is not sufficient, it comes far short, no tongue can tell, no heart conceive it. 'Tis an Epitome of hell, an extract, a quintessence, a compound, a mixture of all feral maladies, tyrannical tortures, plagues and perplexities. There is no sickness, almost, but Physick provideth a remedy for it; to every sore Chirurgery will provide a salve: friendship helps poverty; hope of liberty easeth imprisonment; suit and favour revoke banishment; authority and time wear away reproach: but what Physick, what Chirurgery, what wealth, favour, authority can relieve, bear out, assuage, or expel a troubled conscience? A quiet mind cureth all them, but all they cannot comfort a distressed soul: who can put to silence the voice of desperation? All that is single in other melancholy, horrible, dire, pestilent, cruel, relentless, concur in this, it is more than melancholy in the highest degree; a burning fever of the soul; so mad, saith Jacchinus, by this misery; fear, sorrow, and despair he puts for ordinary symptoms of Melancholy. They are in great pain and horror of mind, distraction of soul, restless, full of continual fears, cares, torments, anxieties, they can neither eat, drink, nor sleep for them, take no rest,

> *Neither at bed nor yet at board,*
> *Will any rest despair afford.* (JUVENAL)

Fear takes away their content, and dries the blood. wasteth the marrow, alters their countenance, even in their greatest delights, singing, dancing, dalliance, they are still (saith Lemnius) tortured in their souls. It consumes them to nought, *I am like a Pelican in the wilderness* (saith David of himself, temporally afflicted) *an Owl because of thine indignation. My heart trembleth within me, and the terrors of death have come upon me; fear and trembling are come upon me,* &c., *at death's door. Their soul abhors all manner of meats.* Their sleep is (if it be any) unquiet, subject to fearful dreams and terrors. Peter in his bonds slept secure, for he knew God protected him; and Tully makes it an Argument of Roscius Amerinus' innocency, that he killed not his Father, because he so securely slept. Those Martyrs in the Primitive Church were most cheerful and merry in the midst of their persecutions; but it is far otherwise with these men, tossed in a Sea, and that continually without rest or intermission, they can think of nought that is pleasant, their conscience will not let them be quiet, in perpetual fear, anxiety, if they be not yet apprehended, they are in doubt still they shall be ready to betray themselves, as Cain did, he thinks every man will kill him; *and roar for the grief of heart,* as David did, as Job did. *Wherefore is light given to him that is in misery, and life to them that have heavy hearts? Which long for death, and if it come not, search it more than treasures, and rejoice when they can find the grave.* They are generally weary of their lives, a trembling heart they have, a sorrowful mind, and little or no rest. Fears, terrors, and affrights in all places, at all times and seasons. As Wierus writes, they refuse many of them meat and drink, can not rest, aggravating still and supposing grievous offences, where there are none. God's heavy wrath is kindled in their souls, and notwithstanding their continual prayers and supplications to Christ Jesus, they have no release or ease at all, but a most intolerable torment, and insufferable anguish of conscience, and that makes them through impatience, to murmur against God many times, to rave, to blaspheme, turn Atheists, and seek to offer violence to themselves. *In the morning they wish for evening, and for morning in the evening, for the sight of their eyes which they see, and fear of hearts.* Marinus Marcennus in his Comment on Genesis, makes mention of a desperate friend of his, whom amongst others he came to visit, and exhort to patience, that broke out into most blasphemous Atheistical speeches, too fearful to relate, when they wished him to trust in God. Who is this God, (he saith) that I should serve him? What will it profit me, if I pray to him? If he be present, why does he not succor me? Why does he not set me free, who am destroyed by imprisonment, fasting, squalor, filth? What have I done? Far be from me such a God! Another of his acquaintance brake out into like Atheistical blasphemies upon his Wife's death, raved, cursed, said and did he car'd not what. And so, for the most part, it is with them all, many of them in their extremity think they hear and see visions, outcries, confer with Devils, that they are tormented, possessed, and in hell fire, already damned, quite forsaken of God, they have no sense or feeling of mercy, or grace, hope of salvation, their sentence of condemnation is already past, and not to be revoked, the Devil will certainly have them. Never was any living creature in such torment before, in such a miserable estate, in such distress of mind, no hope, no faith, past cure, reprobate, continually tempted to make away themselves: Something talks with them, they spit fire and brimstone, they cannot but blaspheme, they cannot repent, believe, or think a good thought, so far carried, said Felix Plater, that they are compelled against their will to harbour impious thoughts, to blaspheme against God, to the committing of many horrible deeds, to laying violent hands upon themselves, &c., and in their distracted fits, and desperate humours, to offer violence to others, their familiar and dear friends sometimes, or to mere strangers, upon very small or no occasion: for he that cares not for his own is master of another man's life. They think evil against their wills: that which they abhor themselves, they must needs think, do, and speak. He gives instance in a Patient of his, that when he would pray, had such evil thoughts still suggested to him, and wicked meditations. Another instance he hath, of a woman that was often tempted to curse God, to blaspheme and kill herself. Sometimes the Devil (as they say) stands without and talks with them; sometimes he is within them, as they think, and there speaks and talks, as to such as are possessed: so Apollodorus, in Plutarch, thought his heart spake within him. There is a most memorable example of Francis Spira an Advocate of Padua, in the year 1545, that being desperate, by no counsel of learned men could be comforted; he felt (as he said) the pains of hell in his soul, in all other things he discoursed aright, but in this most mad. Frismelica, Bullovat, and some other excellent Physicians, could neither make him eat, drink, or sleep, no persuasion could ease him. Never pleaded any man so well for himself, as this man did against himself, and so he desperately died. Scrimger, a Lawyer, hath written his life. Cardinal Cresence died so likewise desperate at Verona, still he thought a black dog followed him to his death-bed, no man could drive the dog away (Sleidan). Whilst I was writing this Treatise, saith Montaltus, a Nun came to me for help, well for all other matters, but troubled in conscience for five years last past;

she is almost mad, and not able to resist, thinks she hath offended God, and is certainly damned. Felix Plater hath store of instances of such as thought themselves damned, forsaken of God, &c. One amongst the rest, that durst not go to Church, or come near the Rhine, for fear to make away himself, because then he was most especially tempted. These, and such like symptoms, are intended and remitted, as the malady itself is more or less; some will hear good counsel, some will not; some desire help, some reject all, and will not be eased.

SUBSECTION 5 — *Prognosticks of Despair, Atheism, Blasphemy, violent death, &c.*

MOST part, these kind of persons make away themselves, some are mad, blaspheme, curse, deny God, but most offer violence to their own persons, and sometimes to others. " A wounded spirit who can bear? " as Cain, Saul, Ahitophel, Judas, blasphemed and died. Bede saith, Pilate died desperate, eight years after Christ. Felix Plater hath collected many examples. A Merchant's wife that was long troubled with such temptations, in the night rose from her bed, and out of the window broke her neck into the street: another drowned himself, desperate as he was, in the Rhine; some cut their throats, many hang themselves. But this needs no illustration. It is controverted by some, whether a man so offering violence to himself, dying desperate, may be saved, aye or no? If they die so obstinately and suddenly, that they cannot so much as wish for mercy, the worst is to be suspected, because they die impenitent. If their death had been a little more lingering, wherein they might have some leisure in their hearts to cry for mercy, charity may judge the best; divers have been recovered out of a very act of hanging and drowning themselves, and so brought to a sound mind, they have been very penitent, much abhorred their former fact, confessed that they have repented in an instant, and cried for mercy in their hearts. If a man put desperate hands upon himself, by occasion of madness or melancholy, if he have given testimony before of his Regeneration, in regard he doth this not so much out of his will, as from the violence of his malady, we must make the best construction of it, as Turks do, that think all fools and mad men go directly to heaven.

SUBSECTION 6 — *Cure of Despair by Physick, good counsel, comforts, &c.*

EXPERIENCE teacheth us, that though many die obstinate and wilful in this malady, yet multitudes again are able to resist and overcome, seek for help, and find comfort, are taken from the chops of Hell, and out of

the Devil's paws, though they have by obligation given themselves to
him. Some out of their own strength, and God's assistance, *though he
kill me* (saith Job) *yet will I trust in him,* out of good counsel, advice,
and Physick. Bellovacus cured a Monk, by altering his habit, and course
of life: Plater many by Physick alone. But for the most part they must
concur: and they take a wrong course, that think to overcome this feral
passion by sole Physick; and they are as much out, that think to work
this effect by good advice alone, though both be forcible in themselves,
yet they must go hand in hand to this disease:

> *Each requires the other's aid.*   (HORACE)

For Physick, the like course is to be taken with this, as in other Melancholy: diet, air, exercise, all those passions and perturbations of the
mind, &c., are to be rectified by the same means. They must not be left
solitary, or to themselves, never idle, never out of company. Counsel,
good comfort is to be applied, as they shall see the parties inclined, or
to the causes, whether it be loss, fear, grief, discontent, or some such
feral accident, a guilty conscience, or otherwise by frequent meditation,
too grievous an apprehension, and consideration of his former life; by
hearing, reading of Scriptures, good Divines, good advice and conference, applying God's Word to their distressed souls, it must be corrected
and counter-poised. Many excellent Exhortations, parænetical Discourses are extant to this purpose, for such as are any way troubled in
mind: Perkins, Greenham, Hayward, Bright, Abernethy, Bolton, Culmannus, Hemmingius, Cœlius Secundus, Nicholas Laurentius, are copious in this subject: Azorius, Navarrus, Sayrus, &c., and such as have
written cases of Conscience amongst our Pontificial Writers. But because these men's works are not to all parties at hand, so parable [pro-
curable] at all times, I will for the benefit and ease of such as are afflicted, at the request of some friends,* recollect out of their voluminous
Treatises, some few such comfortable speeches, exhortations, arguments, advice, tending to this subject, and out of God's Word, knowing,
as Culmannus saith upon the like occasion, how unavailable and vain
men's counsels are, to comfort an afflicted conscience, except God's
Word concur and be annexed, from which comes life, ease, repentance,
&c. Presupposing first that which Beza, Greenham, Perkins, Bolton,
give in charge, the parties to whom counsel is given be sufficiently prepared, humbled for their sins, fit for comfort, confessed, tried how they
are more or less afflicted, how they stand affected, or capable of good

---

* My brother. George Burton, Mr. James Whitehall, rector of Checkley, in Staf-
fordshire. my quondam chambers fellow, and late student in Christ Church, Oxon.
— Burton's note

advice, before any remedies be applied. To such therefore as are so throughly searched and examined, I address this following Discourse.

Two main Antidotes, Hemmingius observes, opposite to Despair, good Hope out of God's Word, to be embraced; perverse Security and Presumption from the Devil's treachery, to be rejected; one saves, the other kills, destroys the soul, saith Austin, and doth as much harm as Despair itself. Navarrus the Casuist reckons up ten special cures: 1. God. 2. Physick. 3. Avoiding such Objects as have caused it. 4. Submission of himself to other men's judgments. 5. Answer of all Objections, &c. All which Cajetan, Gerson, Sayrus, repeat and approve out of Emanuel Roderiques. Greenham prescribes six special rules, Culmannus 7 : 1. To acknowledge all help comes from God. 2. That the cause of their present misery is sin. 3. To repent and be heartily sorry for their sins. 4. To pray earnestly to God they may be eased. 5. To expect and implore the prayers of the Church, and good men's advice. 6. Physick. 7. To commend themselves to God, and rely upon his mercy: others otherwise, but all to this effect. But forasmuch as most men in this malady are spiritually sick, void of reason almost, over-borne by their miseries, and too deep an apprehension of their sins, they cannot apply themselves to good counsel, pray, believe, repent, we must, as much as in us lies, occur and help their peculiar infirmities, according to their several Causes and Symptoms, as we shall find them distressed and complain.

The main matter which terrifies and torments most that are troubled in mind, is the enormity of their offences, the intolerable burthen of their sins, God's heavy wrath and displeasure so deeply apprehended, that they account themselves Reprobates, quite forsaken of God, already damned, past all hope of grace, uncapable of mercy, slaves of sin, and their offences so great, they cannot be forgiven. But these men must know, there is no sin so heinous, which is not pardonable in itself; no crime so great, but by God's mercy it may be forgiven. *Where sin aboundeth, grace aboundeth much more.* And what the Lord said unto Paul in his extremity, *My grace is sufficient for thee, for my power is made perfect through weakness;* concerns every man in like case. His promises are made indefinite to all Believers, generally spoken to all, touching remission of sins, that are truly penitent, grieved for their offences, and desire to be reconciled; *I came not to call the righteous, but sinners to repentance,* that is, such as are truly touched in conscience for their sins. Again, *Come unto me all ye that are heavy laden, and I will ease you. At what time soever a sinner shall repent him of his sins from the bottom of his heart, I will blot out all his wickedness out of my remembrance, saith the Lord. I, even I, am he that put away thine iniquity for mine own sake, and will not remember thy sins. As a father* (saith David) *hath compassion on his children, so hath the Lord compassion on them that fear him.* And will receive them again as the Prodigal Son was entertained. If they shall so come with tears in their eyes, and a penitent heart. When the sinner repents, then God relents. *The Lord is full of compassion and mercy, slow to anger, of great kindness. He will not always chide, neither keep his anger for ever. As high as the heaven is above the earth, so great is his mercy towards them that fear him. As far as the East is from the West, so far hath he removed our sins from us.* Though Cain cry out in the anguish of his soul, *my punishment is greater than I can bear,* 'tis not so: Thou liest, Cain (saith Austin), God's mercy is greater than thy sins. *His mercy is above all his works,* able to satisfy for all men's sins, a ransom for all. His mercy is a panacea, a balsam for an afflicted soul, a sovereign Medicine, an Alexipharmacum for all sin, a charm for the Devil; his mercy was great to Solomon, to Manasses, to Peter, great to all Offenders, and whosoever thou art, it may be so to thee. For why should God bid us pray (as Austin infers), *Deliver us from all evil,* if he did not intend to help us? He therefore that doubts of the remission of his sins, denies God's mercy, and doth him injury, saith Austin. Yea, but thou repliest, I am a notorious sinner, mine offences are not so great as infinite. Hear Fulgentius, God's invincible goodness cannot be overcome by sin, his infinite mercy cannot be terminated by any: the multitude of his mercy is equivalent to his magnitude. Hear Chrysostom, Thy malice may be measured, but God's mercy cannot be defined; thy malice is circumscribed, his mercy is infinite. As a drop of water is to the Sea, so are thy misdeeds to his mercy; nay, there is no such proportion to be given; for the Sea, though great, it may be measured, but God's mercy cannot be circumscribed. Whatsoever thy sins be then in quantity, or quality, multitude, or magnitude, fear them not, distrust not. I speak not this, saith Chrysostom, to make thee secure and negligent, but to cheer thee up. Yea, but thou urgest again, I have little comfort of this which is said, it concerns me not: 'tis to no purpose for me to repent, and to do worse than ever I did before, to persevere in sin, and to return to my lusts, as a Dog to his vomit, or a Swine to the mire: to what end is it to ask forgiveness of my sins, and yet daily to sin again and again, to do evil out of an habit? I daily and hourly offend in thought, word, and deed, in a relapse by mine own weakness and wilfulness: my good protecting Angel is gone, I am fallen from that I was, or would be, worse and worse, my latter end is worse than my beginning. Saith Chrysostom, If thou daily offend, daily repent: if twice, thrice, an hundred, an hundred thousand times, twice, thrice, an hundred thousand times repent. As they do by an old house that is out of repair, still mend some part or other; so do by thy soul, still reform some vice, repair it by repentance, call to him for grace, and thou shalt have it; *for we are freely justified by his grace.* If thine enemy repent, as our Saviour enjoined Peter, forgive him seventy seven times; and why shouldest thou think God will not forgive thee? Why should the enormity of thy sins trouble thee? God can do it, he will do it. My conscience (saith Anselm) dictates to me, that I deserve damnation, my repentance will not suffice for satisfaction; but thy mercy, O Lord, quite overcomes all my transgressions. The gods once (as the Poets feign) with a gold chain would pull Jupiter out of Heaven, but all they together could not stir him, and yet he could draw and turn them as he would himself; maugre all the force and fury of these infernal fiends, and crying sins, his grace is sufficient. Confer the debt and the payment; Christ and Adam; sin and the cure of it; the disease and the medicine; confer the sick man to the Physician, and thou shalt soon perceive that his power is infinitely beyond it. God is better able, as Bernard informeth us, to help, than sin to do us hurt; Christ is better able to save, than the Devil to destroy. If he be a skilful Physician, as Fulgentius adds, he can cure all diseases; if merciful, he will. His goodness is not absolute and perfect, if it be not able to overcome all malice. Submit thyself unto him, as Saint Austin adviseth, he knoweth best what he doth; and be not so much pleased when he sustains thee, as patient when he corrects thee; he is Omnipotent, and can cure all diseases when he sees his own time. He looks down from Heaven upon Earth, that he may hear *the mourning of prisoners, and deliver the children of death. And though our sins be as red as scarlet, he can make them as white as snow.* Doubt not of this, or ask how it shall be done; he is all-sufficient that promiseth; saith Chrysostom, he that made a fair world of nought, can do this and much more for his part: do thou only believe, trust in him, rely on him, be penitent, and heartily sorry for thy sins. Repentance is a sovereign remedy for all sins, a spiritual wing to erear us, a charm for our miseries, a protecting Amulet to expel sin's venom, an attractive loadstone to draw God's mercy and graces unto us. Sin made the breach, repentance must help it; howsoever thine offence came, by error, sloth, obstinacy, ignorance, this is the sole means to be relieved. Hence comes our hope of safety, by this alone sinners are saved, God is provoked to mercy. This unlooseth all that is bound, enlighteneth darkness, mends that is broken, puts life to that which was desperately dying: makes no respect

of offences, or of persons. This doth not repel a fornicator, reject a
drunkard, resist a proud fellow, turn away an idolater, but entertains
all, communicates itself to all. Who persecuted the Church more than
Paul, offended more than Peter? and yet by repentance (saith Chrysolo-
gus) they got both the magistery of Holiness. The Prodigal Son went
far, but by Repentance he came home at last. This alone will turn a
Wolf into a Sheep, make a Publican a Preacher, turn a Thorn into an
Olive, make a deboist [debauched] fellow Religious, a Blasphemer sing
Hallelujah, make Alexander the Copper-smith truly devout, make a
Devil a Saint. And him that polluted his mouth with calumnies, lying,
swearing, and filthy tunes and tones, to purge his throat with divine
Psalms. Repentance will effect prodigious cures, make a stupend meta-
morphosis. An Hawk came into the Ark, and went out again an Hawk;
a Lion came in, went out a Lion; a Bear, a Bear; a Wolf, a Wolf; but if
an Hawk come into this sacred Temple of Repentance, he will go forth
a Dove (saith Chrysostom), a Wolf go out a Sheep, a Lion a Lamb.
This gives sight to the blind, legs to the lame, cures all diseases, confers
grace, expels vice, inserts virtue, comforts and fortifies the soul. Shall
I say, let thy sin be what it will, do but repent, it is sufficient?

Who's sorry that he sinned is almost innocent. (SENECA)
'Tis true indeed, and all-sufficient this, they do confess, if they could
repent, but they are obdurate, they have cauterized consciences, they
are in a reprobate sense, they cannot think a good thought, they cannot
hope for grace, pray, believe, repent, or be sorry for their sins, they find
no grief for sin in themselves, but rather a delight, no groaning of
spirit, but are carried head-long to their own destruction, *heaping wrath
to themselves against the day of wrath.* 'Tis a grievous case this, I do
yield, and yet not to be despaired; God of his bounty and mercy calls
all to repentance. Thou mayest be called at length, restored, taken to
his grace, as the Thief upon the Cross at the last hour, as Mary Magda-
lene, and many other sinners have been, that were buried in sin. God
(saith Fulgentius) is delighted in the conversion of a sinner, he sets no
time; deferring of time, or grievousness of sin, do not prejudicate his
grace, things past and to come are all one to him, as present, 'tis never
too late to repent. This Heaven of Repentance is still open for all distressed souls; and howsoever as yet no signs appear, thou mayest repent
in good time. Hear a comfortable speech of St. Austin, Whatsoever thou
shalt do, how great a sinner soever, thou art yet living; if God would
not help thee, he would surely take thee away; but in sparing thy life,
he gives thee leisure, and invites thee to repentance. Howsoever as yet,

I say. thou perceivest no fruit, no feeling, findest no likelihood of it in thyself, patiently abide the Lord's good leisure, despair not, or think thou art a Reprobate; he came to call sinners to repentance, of which number thou art one; he came to call thee, and in his time will surely call thee. And although as yet thou hast no inclination to pray, to repent, thy Faith be cold and dead, and thou wholly averse from all divine functions, yet it may revive, as Trees are dead in Winter, but flourish in the Spring; these Virtues may lie hid in thee for the present, yet hereafter shew themselves, and peradventure already bud, howsoever thou dost not perceive it. 'Tis Satan's policy to plead against, suppress and aggravate, to conceal those sparks of Faith in thee. Thou dost not believe, thou sayest, yet thou wouldest believe if thou couldest, 'tis thy desire to believe; then pray, *Lord help mine unbelief;* and hereafter thou shalt certainly believe: *It shall be given to him that thirsteth.* Thou canst not yet repent, hereafter thou shalt; a black cloud of sin as yet obnubilates thy soul, terrifies thy conscience, but this cloud may conceive a Rain-bow at the last, and be quite dissipated by repentance. Be of good cheer; a child is rational in power, not in act; and so art thou penitent in affection, though not yet in action. 'Tis thy desire to please God, to be heartily sorry; comfort thyself, no time is over-past, 'tis never too late. A desire to repent, is repentance itself, though not in nature, yet in God's acceptance; a willing mind is sufficient. *Blessed are they that hunger and thirst after Righteousness.* He that is destitute of God's Grace, and wisheth for it, shall have it. " The Lord (saith David) will hear the desire of the poor," that is, of such as are in distress of body and mind. 'Tis true, thou canst not as yet grieve for thy sin, thou hast no feeling of Faith, I yield; yet canst thou grieve thou dost not grieve? It troubles thee, I am sure, thine heart should be so impenitent and hard, thou wouldest have it otherwise; 'tis thy desire to grieve, to repent and believe. Thou lovest God's children and Saints in the mean time, hatest them not, persecutest them not, but rather wishest thyself a true Professor, to be as they are, as thou thyself hast been heretofore; which is an evident token thou art in no such desperate case. 'Tis a good sign of thy conversion, thy sins are pardonable, thou art, or shalt surely be reconciled. *The Lord is near them that are of a contrite heart.* A true desire of mercy in the want of mercy, is mercy itself; a desire of grace in the want of grace, is grace itself; a constant and earnest desire to believe, repent, and to be reconciled to God, if it be in a touched heart, is an acceptation of God, a reconciliation, Faith and Repentance itself. For it is not thy Faith and Repentance, as Chrysostom truly teacheth, that is vailable, but God's mercy that is annexed to it, he accepts the will for the deed. So that I conclude, to feel in ourselves the want of grace. and to be grieved for it, is grace itself. I am troubled with fear my sins are not forgiven, Careless objects: but Bradford answers, they are; for God hath given thee a penitent and believing heart, that is, an heart which desireth to repent and believe; for such a one is taken of him (he accepting the will for the deed) for a truly penitent and believing heart.

All this is true, thou repliest, but yet it concerns not thee, 'tis verified in ordinary offenders, in common sins, but thine are of an higher strain, even against the Holy Ghost himself, irremissible sins, sins of the first magnitude, written with a pen of Iron, engraven with the point of a Diamond. Thou art worse than a Pagan, Infidel, Jew, or Turk, for thou art an Apostate and more, thou hast voluntarily blasphemed, renounced God and all Religion, thou art worse than Judas himself, or they that crucified Christ: for they did offend out of ignorance, but thou hast thought in thine heart there is no God. Thou hast given thy soul to the Devil, as Witches and Conjurers do, explicitly and implicitly, by compact, band, and obligation (a desperate, a fearful case) to satisfy thy lust, or to be revenged of thine enemies, thou didst never pray, come to Church, hear, read, or do any divine duties with any devotion, but for formality and fashion sake, with a kind of reluctancy, 'twas troublesome and painful to thee to perform any such thing, against thy will. Thou never mad'st any conscience of lying, swearing, bearing false witness, murder, adultery, bribery, oppression, theft, drunkenness, idolatry, but hast ever done all duties for fear of punishment, as they were most advantageous, and to thine own ends, and committed all such notorious sins, with an extraordinary delight, hating that thou shouldest love, and loving that thou shouldest hate. Instead of Faith, fear, and love of God, repentance, &c. blasphemous thoughts have been ever harboured in his mind, even against God himself, the blessed Trinity: the Scripture false, rude, harsh, immethodical: Heaven, hell, resurrection, mere toys and fables, incredible, impossible, absurd, vain, ill contrived; Religion, Policy, an human invention, to keep men in obedience, or for profit, invented by Priests and Law-givers to that purpose. If there be any such supreme power he takes no notice of our doings, hears not our prayers, regardeth them not, will not, cannot help, or else he is partial, an excepter of persons, author of sin, a cruel, a destructive God, to create our souls, and destinate them to eternal damnation, to make us worse than our dogs and horses, why doth he not govern things better, protect good men, root out wicked livers? why do they prosper and flourish? as she raved in the tragedy,

> *Strumpets dwell in the sky,*

there they shine,

> *And Perseus hath his golden stars.*

Where is his providence? how appears it?

> *In a marble tomb Licinius lies, Cato in a mean one;*
> *And Pompey has none at all. Who says there are gods?*

Why doth he suffer Turks to overcome Christians, the enemy to triumph over his Church, Paganism to domineer in all places as it doth, heresies to multiply, such enormities to be committed, and so many such bloody wars, murders, massacres, plagues, feral diseases? why doth he not make us all good, able, sound? why makes he venomous creatures, rocks, sands, deserts, this earth itself the muckhill of the world, a prison, an house of correction?

> *When we say Jove reigns, we speak not the truth,* (LUCAN)

with many such horrible and execrable conceits, not fit to be uttered; terrible things about religion, horrible things about God. They cannot some of them but think evil, they are compelled, willy nilly, to blaspheme, especially when they come to Church and pray, read, &c., such foul and prodigious suggestions come into their hearts.

These are abominable, unspeakable offences, and most opposite to God, foul and impious temptations, yet in this case, he or they that shall be tempted and so affected, must know, that no man living is free from such thoughts in part, or at some times, the most divine spirits have been so tempted in some sort, evil custom, omission of holy exercises, ill company, idleness, solitariness, melancholy, or depraved nature, and the Devil is still ready to corrupt, trouble, and divert our souls, to suggest such blasphemous thoughts into our phantasies, ungodly, profane, monstrous and wicked conceits. If they come from Satan, they are more speedy, fearful and violent, the parties cannot avoid them: they are more frequent, I say, and monstrous when they come; for the Devil he is a spirit, and hath means and opportunity to mingle himself with our spirits, and sometimes more slily, sometimes more abruptly, and openly, to suggest such devilish thoughts into our hearts; he insults and domineers in Melancholy distempered phantasies, and persons especially: Melancholy is, as Serapio holds, the Devil's bath, and invites him to come to it. As a sick man frets, raves in his fits, speaks and doth he knows not what, the Devil violently compels such crazed souls, to think such damned thoughts against their wills, they cannot but do it; sometimes more continuate, or by fits, he takes his advantage, as the subject is less able to resist, he aggravates, extenuates, affirms, denies, damns, confounds the spirits, troubles heart, brain, humors, organs, senses, and wholly domineers in their imaginations. If they proceed from themselves, such thoughts, they are remiss and moderate, not so violent and monstrous, not so frequent. The Devil commonly suggests things opposite to nature, opposite to God and his word, impious, absurd, such as a man would never of himself, or could not conceive, they strike terror and horror into the party's own heart. For if he or they be asked, whether they do approve of such like thoughts or no? they answer (and their own souls truly dictate as much) they abhor them as Hell, and the Devil himself, they would fain think otherwise if they could: he hath thought otherwise, and with all his soul desires so to think again: he doth resist, and hath some good motions intermixt now and then: so that such blasphemous, impious, unclean thoughts, are not his own, but the Devil's; they proceed not from him, but from a crazed phantasy, distempered humours, black fumes which offend his brain: they are thy crosses, the Devil's sins, and he shall answer for them, he doth enforce thee to do that which thou dost abhor, and didst never give consent to: and although he hath sometimes so slily set upon thee, and so far prevailed, as to make thee in some sort to assent to, to delight in such wicked thoughts, yet they have not proceeded from a confirmed will in thee, but are of that nature which thou dost afterwards reject and abhor. Therefore be not overmuch troubled and dismayed with such kind of suggestions, at least if they please thee not, because they are not thy personal sins, for which thou shalt incur the wrath of God, or his displeasure: contemn, neglect them, let them go as they come, strive not too violently, or trouble thyself too much, but as our Saviour said to Satan in like case, say thou, *Avoid, Satan,* I detest thee and them. Saith Austin, as Satan labours to suggest, so must we strive not to give consent, and it will be sufficient: the more anxious and solicitous thou art, the more perplexed, the more thou shalt otherwise be troubled, and intangled. Besides, they must know this, all so molested and distempered, that, although these be most execrable and grievous sins, they are pardonable yet, through God's mercy and goodness they may be forgiven, if they be penitent and sorry for them. Paul himself confesseth, *He did not the good he would do, but the evil which he would not do; 'tis not I, but sin that dwelleth in me.* 'Tis not thou, but Satan's suggestions, his craft and subtilty, his malice. Comfort thyself then, if thou be penitent and grieved, or desirous to be so, these heinous sins shall not be laid to thy charge; God's mercy is above all sins, which if thou do not finally contemn, without doubt thou shalt be saved. No man sins against the Holy Ghost, but he that wilfully and finally renounceth Christ, and contemneth him and his word to the last, without which there is no salvation, from which grievous sin, God of his infinite mercy deliver us. Take hold of this to be thy comfort, and meditate withal on God's word, labour to pray, to repent, to be renewed in mind, *keep thine heart with all diligence. Resist the Devil, and he will fly from thee*, pour out thy soul unto the Lord with sorrowful Hannah; *pray continually*, as Paul enjoins, and as David did, *meditate on his Law day and night*.

Yea, but this meditation is that that mars all. and mistaken, makes many men far worse, misconceiving all they read or hear, to their own overthrow; the more they search and read Scriptures, or divine Treatises, the more they puzzle themselves, as a bird in a net, the more they are intangled and precipitated into this preposterous gulf. Many are called, but few are chosen, with such like places of Scripture misinterpreted, strike them with horror, they doubt presently whether they be of this number or no: God's eternal decree of predestination, absolute reprobation, and such fatal tables [decrees] they form to their own ruin, and impinge upon this rock of despair. How shall they be assured of their salvation, by what signs? If the righteous scarcely be saved, where shall the ungodly and sinners appear? Who knows, saith Solomon, whether he be elect? This grinds their souls, how shall they discern they are not reprobates? But I say again, how shall they discern they are? From the Devil can be no certainty, for he is a liar from the beginning: if he suggest any such thing, as too frequently he doth, reject him as a deceiver, an enemy of human kind, dispute not with him, give no credit to him, obstinately refuse him, as S. Anthony did in the wilderness, whom the Devil set upon in several shapes, or as the Collier did, so do thou by him. For when the Devil tempted him with the weakness of his faith, and told him, he could not be saved, as being ignorant in the principles of Religion; and urged him moreover to know what he believed, what he thought of such and such points and Mysteries: the Collier told him, he believed as the Church did; but what (said the Devil again) doth the Church believe? as I do (saith the Collier) and what's that thou believest? as the Church doth, &c., when the Devil could get no other answer, he left him. If Satan summon thee to answer, send him to Christ: he is thy liberty, thy protector against cruel death, raging sin, that roaring Lion; he is thy righteousness, thy Saviour, and

thy life. Though he [Satan] say, thou art not of the number of the
Elect, a Reprobate, forsaken of God, hold thine own still,

Be this our wall of brass, (HORACE)

let this be as a Bulwark, a Brazen Wall to defend thee, stay thyself in
that certainty of faith; let that be thy comfort. Christ will protect thee,
vindicate thee, thou art one of his flock, he will triumph over the Law,
vanquish Death, overcome the Devil, and destroy Hell. If he say thou
art none of the Elect, no Believer, reject him, defy him, thou hast
thought otherwise, and mayest so be resolved again; comfort thyself;
this persuasion cannot come from the Devil, and much less can it be
grounded from thyself; men are liars, and why shouldest thou distrust?
A denying Peter, a persecuting Paul, an adulterous cruel David, have
been received; an Apostate Solomon may be converted; no sin at all but
impenitency can give testimony of final reprobation. Why shouldest thou
then distrust, misdoubt thyself, upon what ground, what suspicion? This
opinion alone of particularity? Against that, and for the certainty of
Election and salvation on the other side, see God's good will toward men,
hear how generally his grace is proposed to him, and him, and them,
each man in particular, and to all. *God wills that all men be saved, and
come to the knowledge of the truth.* 'Tis an universal promise, *God sent
not his Son into the world, to condemn the world, but that through him
the world might be saved.* He then that acknowledgeth himself a man
in the world, must likewise acknowledge, he is of that number that is to
be saved: *I will not the death of a sinner, but that he repent and live.*
But thou art a sinner, therefore he will not thy death. *This is the will
of him that sent me, that every man that believeth in the Son, should
have everlasting life. He would have no man perish, but all come to
repentance.* Besides, remission of sins is to be preached, not to a few,
but universally to all men. *Go therefore and tell all Nations, baptizing
them, &c. Go into all the world, and preach the Gospel to every creature.* Now there cannot be contradictory wills in God; he will have all
saved, and not all, how can this stand together? be secure then, believe,
trust in him, hope well, and be saved. Yea, that's the main matter, how
shall I believe, or discern my security, from carnal presumption? my
faith is weak and faint, I want those signs and fruits of Sanctification,
sorrow for sin, thirsting for Grace, groanings of the Spirit, love of Christians as Christians, avoiding occasion of sin, endeavour of new obedience, charity, love of God, perseverance. Though these signs be lan-
guishing in thee, and not seated in thine heart, thou must not therefore
be dejected or terrified; the effects of faith and the Spirit are not yet

so fully felt in thee: conclude not therefore thou art a Reprobate, or doubt of thine Election, because the Elect themselves are without them, before their conversion. Thou mayest in the Lord's good time be converted: some are called at the eleventh hour. Use, I say, the means of thy conversion, expect the Lord's leisure, if not yet called, pray thou mayest be, or at least wish and desire thou mayest be.

Notwithstanding all this which might be said to this effect, to ease their afflicted minds, what comfort our best Divines can afford in this case, Zanchius, Beza, &c., this furious curiosity, needless speculation, fruitless meditation about election, reprobation, free-will, grace, such places of Scripture preposterously conceived, torment still, and crucify the souls of too many, and set all the world together by the ears. To avoid which inconveniences, and to settle their distressed minds, to mitigate those divine Aphorisms (though in another extreme somewhat) our late Arminians have revived that plausible doctrine of universal grace, which many Fathers, our late Lutherans and modern Papists do still maintain, that we have free-will of our selves, and that grace is common to all that will believe. Some again, though less orthodoxal, will have a far greater part saved, than shall be damned (as Cælius Secundus stiffly maintains in his Book, or some Impostor under his name). He calls that other Tenent of special Election and Reprobation, a prejudicate, envious, and malicious opinion, apt to draw all men to desperation. *Many are called, few chosen,* &c. He opposeth some opposite parts of Scripture to it, " Christ came into the world to save sinners," &c. And four especial Arguments he produceth, one from God's power. If more be damned than saved, he erroneously concludes, the Devil hath the greatest Sovereignty; for what is power but to protect? and Majesty consists in multitude. If the Devil have the greater part, where is his mercy? where is his power? Where is his greatness? where his goodness? He proceeds, We account him a murderer that is accessary only, or doth not help when he can; which may not be supposed of God without great offence, because he may do what he will, and is otherwise accessary, and the author of sin. The nature of good is to be communicated, God is good, and will not then be contracted in his goodness; for how is he the Father of mercy and comfort, if his good concern but a few? O envious and unthankful men to think otherwise! Why should we pray to God that are Gentiles, and thank him for his mercies and benefits, that hath damned us all innocuous for Adam's offence, one man's offence, one small offence, eating of an Apple? why should we acknowledge him for our Governor, that hath wholly neglected the salvation of our souls, contemned us, and sent no Prophets or Instructors to teach us, as he hath done to the Hebrews? So Julian the Apostate objects. Why should these Christians (Cælius urgeth) reject us, and appropriate God unto themselves. But to return to our forged Cælius. At last he comes to that, he will have those saved that never heard of, or believed in Christ, from ignorance, with the Pelagians, and proves it out of Origen and others. They (saith Origen) that never heard God's word, are to be excused for their ignorance: we may not think God will be so hard, angry, cruel or unjust as to condemn any man without a hearing. They alone (he holds) are in the state of damnation that refuse Christ's mercy and grace, when it is offered. Many worthy Greeks and Romans, good moral honest men, that kept the Law of Nature, did to others as they would be done to themselves, are as certainly saved, he concludes, as they were that lived uprightly before the Law of Moses. They were acceptable in God's sight, as Job was, the Magi, the Queen of Sheba, Darius of Persia, Socrates, Aristides, Cato, Curius, Tully, Seneca, and many other Philosophers, upright livers, no matter of what Religion, as Cornelius, out of any Nation, so that he live honestly, call on God, trust in him, fear him, he shall be saved. This Opinion was formerly maintained by the Valentinian and Basilidian Hereticks, revived of late in Turkey, of which sect Rustan Bassa was Patron, defended by Galeatius Martius, and some antient Fathers, and of later times favoured by Erasmus, by Zuinglius, whose Tenent Bullinger vindicates, and Gualter approves in a just Apology with many Arguments. There be many Jesuits that follow these Calvinists in this behalf, Franciscus Buchsius Moguntinus, Andradius, many schoolmen, that are verily persuaded, that those good works of the Gentiles did so far please God, that they might deserve eternal life, and be saved in the end. Sesellius, and Benedictus Justinianus in his Comment on the first of the Romans, Mathias Ditmarsh the Politician, with many others, hold a mediocrity, they may be not unworthy of salvation, but they will not absolutely decree it. Hofmannus, a Lutheran Professor of Helmstadt, and many of his Followers, with most of our Church, and Papists, are stiff against it. Franciscus Collius hath fully censured all Opinions, and amply dilated this question, which who so will, may peruse. But to return to my Author, his Conclusion is, that not only wicked Livers, Blasphemers, Reprobates, and such as reject God's grace, but that the Devils themselves shall be saved at last, as Origen long since delivered in his works, and our late Socinians defend, Ostorodius, Smaltius, &c. Those terms of all and for ever in Scripture, are not eternal, but only denote a longer time, which by many Examples they prove. The world shall end like a Comedy, and we shall meet at last in Heaven, and live in bliss altogether; or else in conclusion, fade away into nothing. For how can he be merciful that shall condemn any creature to eternal unspeakable punishment, for one small temporary fault, all posterity, so many myriads, for one and another man's offence: how have you sheep offended? But these absurd paradoxes are exploded by our Church, we teach otherwise. That this vocation, predestination, election, reprobation, was not " out of the corrupt mass," * " faith having been foreseen," as some of our Arminians [believe], or " because of works foreseen," as some of our Papists [believe], nor because of a " passing over " [of the non-elect by God], but [it was] God's absolute decree before the creation of the world (as many of our Church hold), ['t] was from the beginning, before the foundation of the world was laid, or man created (or from Adam's fall, as others will, it is man as fallen who is the object of reprobation); with the perseverance of saints, we must be certain of our salvation, we may fall, but not finally, which our Arminians will not admit. According to his immutable, eternal, just decree and counsel of saving men and Angels, God calls all, and would have all to be saved according to the efficacy of vocation: all are invited, but only the elect apprehended: the rest that are unbelieving, impenitent, whom God in his just judgment leaves to be punished for their sins, are in a reprobate sense; yet we must not determine who are such, condemn ourselves, or others, because we have an universal invitation; all are commanded to believe, and we

* " Out of the corrupt mass " refers to the disputed question: Did predestination precede the fall, or did God predestine some out of the corrupt mass (of mankind as fallen) — that is, did predestination follow the fall? The Arminians taught the second, Burton here asserts the first. " Faith having been foreseen ": the Arminians taught that God foresaw faith in some, and on that ground they were predestined; this Burton denies. " Or because of works foreknown ": the Catholics taught that God predestined those in whom he foresaw good works. " Nor because of a passing over ": some taught that the non-elect were not definitely so predestined, but that God simply passed them over. " It is man as fallen who is the object of reprobation " : the decree is subsequent and not antecedent to the fall. " The perseverance of the saints " : those whom God has elected cannot finally fall away from grace, although they may have lapses; this doctrine the Arminians rejected, and said that even the saints might finally fall away. Burton's argument is, if we are elect, we *must* be certain of our salvation finally, even if we have lapses. It is this certainty which Burton argues they will not admit. The following sentences are somewhat inconsistent: as the invitation is general, and God alone knows whom of them who accept or seem to accept it He has really elected, we need not assume that we are non-elect because we have not the certainty of which he speaks above. (This note is due to the kindness of the Rev. A. E. Garvie, of the Divinity School of the University of London.)

know not how soon or late before our end we may be received. I might
have said more of this subject; but forasmuch as it is a forbidden question, and in the Preface or Declaration to the Articles of the Church,
printed 1633, to avoid factions and altercations, we that are University Divines especially, are prohibited all curious search, to print or
preach, or draw the Article aside by our own sense and Comments,
upon pain of Ecclesiastical censure, I will surcease, and conclude with
Erasmus of such controversies: Let who will dispute, I think that the
laws of our ancestors should be received with reverence, and religiously
observ'd, as coming from God; nor is it safe or pious to invent or spread
evil suspicion as to the public authority. And should any Tyranny exist,
if unlikely to drive men into wickedness, 'tis better to endure it than
resist it by sedition.

But to my former task. The last main torture and trouble of a distressed mind, is, not so much this doubt of Election, and that the promises of grace are smothered and extinct in them, nay quite blotted out,
as they suppose, but withal God's heavy wrath, a most intolerable pain
and grief of heart seizeth on them: to their thinking they are already
damned, they suffer the pains of Hell, and more than possibly can be
expressed, they smell brimstone, talk familiarly with Devils, hear and
see Chimeras, prodigious, uncouth shapes, Bears, Owls, Anticks, black
dogs, fiends, hideous out-cries, fearful noises, shrieks, lamentable complaints, they are possessed, and through impatience they roar and howl,
curse, blaspheme, deny God, call his power in question, abjure Religion,
and are still ready to offer violence unto themselves, by hanging, drowning, &c. Never any miserable wretch from the beginning of the world,
was in such a woful case. To such persons I oppose God's mercy, and his
justice; the judgments of God are mysterious, not unjust; his secret
counsel, and just judgment, by which he spares some, and sore afflicts
others again in this life: his judgment is to be adored, trembled at, not
to be searched or enquired after by mortal men: he hath reasons reserved to himself, which our frailty cannot apprehend. He may punish
all, if he will, and that justly for sin; in that he doth it in some, is to
make a way for his mercy that they repent and be saved, to heal them,
to try them, exercise their patience, and make them call upon him, to
confess their sins, and pray unto him, as David did, *Righteous art thou,
O Lord, and just are thy judgments.* As the poor Publican, *Lord have
mercy upon me a miserable sinner.* To put confidence, and have an assured hope in him, as Job had, *Though he kill me, I will trust in him.*
Saith Austin, kill, cut in pieces, burn my body (O Lord) to save my

soul. A small sickness, one lash of affliction, a little misery, many times, will more humiliate a man, sooner convert, bring him home to know himself, than all those parænetical discourses, the whole Theory of Philosophy, Law, Physick and Divinity, or a world of instances and examples. So that this, which they take to be such an insupportable plague, is an evident sign of God's mercy and justice, of his love and goodness: had they not thus been undone, they had finally been undone. Many a carnal man is lulled asleep in perverse security, foolish presumption, is stupified in his sins, and hath no feeling at all of them: *I have sinned* (he saith) *and what evil shall come unto me?* and *tush, how shall God know it?* And so in a reprobate sense goes down to Hell.

But here, God pulls them by the ear, by affliction, he will bring them to Heaven and Happiness; *Blessed are they that mourn, for they shall be comforted,* a blessed and an happy state, if considered aright, it is, to be so troubled. *It is good for me that I have been afflicted, Before I was afflicted I went astray, but now I keep thy word, Tribulation works patience, patience hope,* and by such like crosses and calamities we are driven from the stake of security. So that affliction is a School or Academy, wherein the best Scholars are prepared to the Commencements of the Deity. And though it be most troublesome and grievous for the time, yet know this, it comes by God's permission and providence, he is a spectator of thy groans and tears, still present with thee, the very hairs of thy head are numbered, not one of them can fall to the ground, without the express will of God: he will not suffer thee to be tempted above measure, he corrects us all, the Lord will not quench the smoking flax, or break the bruised reed; saith Austin, He suffers thee to be tempted for thy good. And as a Mother doth handle her child sick and weak, not reject it, but with all tenderness observe and keep it, so doth God by us, not forsake us in our miseries, or relinquish us for our imperfections, but with all piety and compassion, support and receive us; whom he loves, he loves to the end. Whom he hath elected, those he hath called, justified, sanctified, and glorified. Think not then thou hast lost the Spirit, that thou art forsaken of God, be not overcome with heaviness of heart, but as David said, *I will not fear, though I walk in the shadows of death.* We must all go, not from delights to delights, but from the Cross to the Crown, by Hell to Heaven, as the old Romans put Virtue's Temple in the way to that of Honour: we must endure sorrow and misery in this life. 'Tis no new thing this, God's best servants and dearest children have been so visited and tried. Christ in the Garden cried out, *My God, my God, why hast thou forsaken me?* his

son by nature, as thou art by adoption and grace. Job in his anguish
said, *The arrows of the Almighty God were in him, his terrors fought
against him, the venom drank up his spirit.* He saith, *God was his
enemy, writ bitter things against him, hated him.* His heavy wrath had
so seized on his soul. David complains, *His eyes were eaten up, sunk
into his head; his moisture became as the drought in Summer, his flesh
was consumed, his bones vexed:* yet neither Job nor David did finally
despair. Job would not leave his hold, but still trusted in him, acknowledging him to be his good God. *The Lord gives, the Lord takes, blessed
be the name of the Lord. Behold I am vile, I abhor myself, repent in
dust and ashes.* David humbled himself, and upon his confession received mercy. Faith, hope, repentance, are the sovereign cures and
remedies, the sole comforts in this case; confess, humble thyself, repent,
it is sufficient. Saith Chrysostom, the King of Nineveh's sackcloth and
ashes did that which his Purple Robes and Crown could not effect;
Turn to him, he will turn to thee; the Lord is near those that are of a
contrite heart, and will save such as be afflicted in spirit. *He came to
the lost sheep of Israel.* He is at all times ready to assist. He never rejects a penitent sinner; though he have come to the full height of iniquity, wallowed and delighted in sin; yet if he will forsake his former
ways, he will receive him. Saith Austin, speaking for God, I will spare
him, because he hath not spared himself; I will pardon him, because he
doth acknowledge his offence; let it be never so enormous a sin, *his
grace is sufficient.* Despair not then, faint not at all, be not dejected,
but rely on God, call on him in thy trouble, and he will hear thee, he
will assist, help, and deliver thee. *Draw near to him, and He will draw
near to thee.* Lazarus was poor, and full of boils, and yet still he relied
upon God, Abraham did hope beyond hope.

Thou exceptest, these were chief men, divine spirits, beloved of God,
especially respected; but I am a contemptible and forlorn wretch, forsaken of God, and left to the merciless fury of evil spirits. I cannot hope,
pray, repent, &c. How often shall I say it! thou mayest perform all
these duties, Christian-offices, and be restored in good time. A sick man
loseth his appetite, strength and ability, his disease prevaileth so far,
that all his faculties are spent, hand and foot perform not their duties,
his eyes are dim, hearing dull, tongue distastes things of pleasant relish,
yet nature lies hid, recovereth again, and expelleth all those feculent
matters by vomit, sweat, or some such like evacuations. Thou art spiritually sick, thine heart is heavy, thy mind distressed, thou mayest happily recover again, expel those dismal passions of fear and grief; God

did not suffer thee to be tempted above measure; whom he loves (I say) he loves to the end; hope the best. David in his misery prayed to the Lord, remembering how he had formerly dealt with him; and with that meditation of God's mercy confirmed his Faith, and pacified his own tumultuous heart in his greatest agony. *O my soul, why art thou so disquieted within me*, &c. Thy soul is eclipsed for a time, I yield, as the Sun is shadowed by a cloud; no doubt but those gracious beams of God's mercy will shine upon thee again, as they have formerly done: those embers of Faith, Hope and Repentance, now buried in ashes, will flame out afresh, and be fully revived. Want of Faith, no feeling of grace for the present, are not fit directions; we must live by Faith, not by feeling; 'tis the beginning of grace to wish for grace: we must expect and tarry David, a man after God's own heart, was so troubled himself; *Awake, why sleepest thou? O Lord, arise, cast me not off; wherefore hidest thou thy face, and forgettest mine affliction and oppression? My soul is bowed down to the dust. Arise, redeem us*, &c. He prayed long before he was heard, endured much before he was relieved. He complains, *I am weary of crying, and my throat is dry, mine eyes fail, whilst I wait on the Lord*, and yet he perseveres. Be not dismayed, thou shalt be respected at last. God often works by contrarieties, he first kills, and then makes alive, he woundeth first, and then healeth, he makes man sow in tears, that he may reap in joy; 'tis God's method: he that is so visited, must with patience endure and rest satisfied for the present. The Paschal Lamb was eaten with sour herbs; we shall feel no sweetness of his blood, till we first feel the smart of our sins. Thy pains are great, intolerable for the time; thou art destitute of grace and comfort, stay the Lord's leisure, he will not (I say) suffer thee to be tempted above what thou art able to bear, but will give an issue to temptation. He works all for the best to them that love God. Doubt not of thine election, it is an immutable decree; a mark never to be defaced; you have been otherwise, you may and shall be. And for your present affliction, hope the best, it will shortly end. *He is present with his servants in their affliction. Great are the troubles of the righteous, but the Lord delivereth them out of all. Our light affliction, which is but for a moment, worketh in us an eternal weight of glory. Not answerable to that glory which is to come; though now in heaviness, you shall rejoice.*

Now last of all to those external impediments, terrible objects, which they hear and see many times, Devils, Bugbears, and Mormoluches [or Hobgoblins], noisome smells, &c. These may come, as I have formerly declared in my precedent discourse of the Symptoms of Melancholy, from inward causes: as a concave glass reflects solid bodies, a troubled brain for want of sleep, nutriment, and by reason of that agitation of spirits to which Hercules de Saxoniâ attributes all Symptoms almost, may reflect and shew prodigious shapes, as our vain fear and crazed phantasy shall suggest and feign, as many silly weak women and children in the dark, sick folks, and frantick for want of repast and sleep, suppose they see that they see not: many times such terriculaments [things which produce fright] may proceed from natural causes, and all other senses may be deluded. Besides, as I have said, this humour is the Devil's Bath, by reason of the distemper of humours, and infirm Organs in us: he may so possess us inwardly to molest us, as he did Saul and others, by God's permission; he is Prince of the Air, and can transform himself into several shapes, delude all our senses for a time, but his power is determined [limited]; he may terrify us, but not hurt: *God hath given his Angels charge over us. He is a wall round about his people.* There be those that prescribe Physick in such cases, 'tis God's instrument, and not unfit. The Devil works by mediation of humours, and mixt diseases must have mixt remedies. Levinus Lemnius is very copious in this subject, besides that chief remedy of confidence in God, prayer, hearty repentance, &c., of which, for your comfort and instruction, read Lavater, Wierus, and others, and that Christian armour which Paul prescribes; he sets down certain Amulets, herbs, and precious stones, which have marvellous virtues all, to drive away Devils and their illusions. Sapphires, Chrysolites, Carbuncles, &c., which have the marvellous virtue of keeping off ghosts, goblins, nightmares, spirits of the air, if faith can be put in the records of the antients. Of herbs, he reckons us Pennyroyal, Rue, Mint, Angelica, Piony: Richard Argentine adds hypericon or S. John's wort, which by a divine virtue drives away Devils, and is therefore called Expeller of Demons; all which rightly used, by their suffitus [or fumigation] expel Devils themselves, and all devilish illusions. Anthony Musa, the Emperor Augustus his Physician, approves of Betony to this purpose; the antients used therefore to plant it in Church-yards, because it was held to be an holy herb, and good against fearful visions, did secure such places it grew in, and sanctified those persons that carried it about them. Mattiolus says the same. Others commend accurate musick; so Saul was helped by David's harp. Fires to be made in such rooms where spirits haunt, good store of lights to be set up, odours, perfumes, and suffumigations, as the Angel taught Tobias,* of brimstone and bitumen, thus [or frankincense], myrrh, briony-root, with many such simples which Wecker hath col-

* Tobit, vi.

lected. Take of sulphur one drachm, boiled again in white vine water, that the sulphur may be diluted; let it be given to the patient: for diseases are devils (saith Richard Argentine). Vigetus hath a far larger receipt to this purpose, which the said Wecker cites out of Wierus. Take sulphur, wine, bitumen, opoponax, gambanum, castor oil, &c. Why sweet perfumes, fires and so many lights should be used in such places, Ernestus Burgravius, Lamps of Life and Death, and Fortunius Lycetus assigns this cause, because good spirits are well pleased with, but evil abhor them, And therefore those old Gentiles, present Mahometans, and Papists, have continual lamps burning in their Churches all day, and all night, lights at funerals, and in their graves; burning lamps of molten gold, for many ages to endure (saith Lazius) lest Devils harm the body, lights ever burning, as those Vestal Virgins, Pythonisses maintained heretofore, with many such, of which read Tostatus, Thyreus, Pictorius, see more in them. Cardan would have the party affected wink altogether in such a case, if he see ought that offends him, or cut the Air with a sword in such places they walk and abide; shoot a pistol at them, for being aerial bodies (as Cælius Rhodiginus, Tertullian, Origen, Psellas, and many hold) if strucken, they feel pain. Papists commonly enjoin and apply crosses, holy-water, sanctified beads, Amulets, musick, ringing of bells, for to that end are they consecrated, and by them baptized, Characters, counterfeit relicks, so many Masses, Peregrinations, oblations, adjurations, and what not? Alexander Albertinus à Rocha, Petrus Thyreus, and Hieronymus Mengus, with many other Pontificial writers, prescribe and set down several forms of exorcisms, as well to houses possessed with Devils, as to demoniacal persons; but I am of Lemnius' mind, 'tis but a mere mockage, a counterfeit charm, to no purpose, they are fopperies and fictions, as that absurd story * is amongst the rest, of a penitent woman seduced by a Magician in France, at S. Bawn, exorcised by Domphius, Michaelis, and a company of circumventing Friars. If any man (saith Lemnius) will attempt such a thing, without all those juggling circumstances, Astrological elections of time, place, prodigious habits, fustian, big, sesquipedal words, spells, crosses, characters, which exorcists ordinarily use. let him follow the example of Peter and John, that without any ambitious swelling terms, cured a lame man, *In the name of Jesus Christ rise and walk.* His Name alone is the best and only charm against all such diabolical illusions; so doth Origen advise, and so Chrysostom, This will be your staff, this your impregnable tower, this your armour. Saith S. Austin, many men will desire my counsel and opinion, what's to be

---

* Done into English by W. B., 1613. — Burton's note. [See W. B. in Index.]

done in this behalf? I can say no more, they with true faith. which
worketh through love, let them fly to God alone for help. Athanasius
prescribes as a present charm against Devils, the beginning of the 67th
Psalm, *Hear my voice, O God, in my prayer: preserve my life from fear
of the enemy,* &c. But the best remedy is to fly to God. to call on him,
hope. pray, trust, rely on him, to commit ourselves wholly to him. What
the practice of the Primitive Church was in this behalf, and the way of
expelling Devils, read Wierus at large.

Last of all: if the party affected shall certainly know this malady to
have proceeded from too much fasting, meditation, precise life. contemplation of God's judgments (for the Devil deceives many by such
means) in that other extreme he circumvents Melancholy itself. reading some Books, Treatises, hearing rigid Preachers, &c. If he shall perceive that it hath begun first from some great loss, grievous accident,
disaster, seeing others in like case, or any such terrible object. let him
speedily remove the cause, which to the cure of this disease Navarrus so
much commends, turn away his thoughts from the painful subject, by
all opposite means, art, and industry, let him ease the soul by all honest
recreations, refresh and recreate his distressed soul; let him direct his
thoughts, by himself and other of his friends. Let him read no more
such tracts or subjects, hear no more such fearful tones, avoid such
companies, and by all means open himself, submit himself to the advice
of good Physicians, and Divines, which is a relief in uneasiness, as he
calls it, hear them speak to whom the Lord hath given the tongue of
the learned, to be able to minister a word to him that is weary, whose
words are as flagons of wine. Let him not be obstinate, head-strong,
peevish, wilful, self-conceited (as in this malady they are) but give ear
to good advice, be ruled and persuaded; and no doubt but such good
counsel may prove as prosperous to his soul, as the Angel was to Peter,
that opened the Iron-gates, loosed his bands, brought him out of prison,
and delivered him from bodily thraldom; they may ease his afflicted
mind, relieve his wounded soul, and take him out of the jaws of Hell
itself. I can say no more, or give better advice to such as are any way
distressed in this kind, than what I have given and said. Only take this
for a corollary and conclusion, as thou tenderest thine own welfare in
this, and all other melancholy, thy good health of body and mind,
observe this short Precept, give not way to solitariness and idleness.
Be not solitary, be not idle.

HOPE, YE MISERABLE,
YE HAPPY, TAKE HEED

Dost thou wish to be free from doubt? dost desire to escape uncertainty? be penitent, then, while still sound, of wholesome mind; being so, thou art safe, I tell thee, because thou hast been penitent whilst thou mightest have been sinning: so saith Austin.

FINIS

APPENDIX I

THE CONCLUSION OF THE AUTHOR
TO THE READER

[This, which appeared at the end of the first edition, was not reprinted in any subsequent issue. Much of it was later transferred to the prefatory " Democritus to the Reader." But we have deemed it of sufficient interest to warrant republication.]

THE last section shall be mine, to cut the strings of Democritus' visor, to unmask and show him as he is.

Why will you thus a mighty vase intend,

If in a worthless bowl your labors end? (HORACE)

Democritus began as a Prologue in this Tragi-comedy, but why doth the author end, and act the Epilogue in his own name? I intended at first to have concealed myself, but second thoughts, &c. For some reasons I have altered mine intent, and am willing to subscribe.

On me! on me! Here am I who did the deed:

Turn your eyes on me, O Reader, my work you read.

If ought be otherwise than it should be, since I have now put myself upon the stage, I must undergo and abide the censure of it, the die is cast, and I may not escape it. It is most true, the style proclaims the man, our style bewrayes us, and as hunters find their game by the trace, so is a man descried by his writings. I have laid myself open (I know it) in this Treatise, and shall be censured I doubt not, yet this is some comfort: our censures are as various as our palates. If I be taxed, exploded by some, I shall happily be as much approved and commended by others. It was Democritus' fortune, at once laughed at and admired, and 'tis the common doom of all writers: I seek not to be commended; nor am I indeed so very ugly, I would not be vilified. I fear good men's censures: the tongues of servants you may despise: as the barking of a dog I securely contemne the malicious and scurrile obloquies, flouts, calumnies of those railers and detractors: I scorn the rest. I am none of the best of you. I am none of the meanest; howsoever, I am now come to retract some part of that which I have writ —

When I peruse this tract which I have writ,

I am abash't, and much I hold unfit. (OVID)

973

I could wish it otherwise, expunged, and to this end I have annexed this Apologetical Appendix, to crave pardon for that which is amiss. I do suspect some precedent passages have been distastefull, as too Satyricall & bitter: some again as too Comical, homely, broad, or lightly spoken. For the first, I grant that of Tacitus to be true: a bitter jest leaves a sting behind it; and as an honourable & worthy man observes: They fear a Satyrist's wit, and he their memories (Sr. Fr. Bacon). I might therefore suspect, but I hope I have wronged no man. And though for this I have Apologized already, yet in Medea's words:

> And in my last words this I do desire,
> That what in passion I have said or ire;
> May be forgotten and a better mind,
> Be had of us hereafter as you find.

To the other of lightness, I make answer. — To the pure all things are pure, and as Augusta Livia sometimes said: A naked man to a modest woman is no otherwise than a picture. *Bad heart, bad disposition; Evil to him who evil thinks*. If in thy censure it be too light, I advise thee, as Lipsius did his reader for some places of Plautus: If they like thee not let them pass; or oppose that which is good to that which is bad, reject not therefore all. But, to invert that verse of Martial and apply it to my present use, which Jerome Wolfius did to his Translation of Suidas:

Some is bad, some indifferent, some good; I have inserted some things more homely or light, which I would request every man to interpret to the best, — and conclude in Scaliger's words to Cardan: If thou didst know me well, thou wouldst not only pardon these witticisms of mine, but would even consider it unworthy that so kindly a soul as I should find it necessary to avert even the slightest suspicion. But this likewise I have formerly excused withall those harsh compositions, Tautological repetitions, perturbations of tenses and numbers &c. I should indeed (had I wisely done) observed that precept of the poet: Let it be withheld up to the ninth year, and have taken more care; or as Alexander the Physician would have done by lapis lazuli, 50 times washed before it be used; I should have perused, corrected and amended this Tract, but I had not that happy leasure, no amanuenses, assistants; and was enforced as a Bear doth her whelps, to bring forth this confused lump, and had not space to lick it into form, as she doth her young ones; but even so to publish it, as it was written at first, once for all, in an extemporanean style, whatever came uppermost, as I do commonly all other exercises, standing on one leg, as he

made verses out of a confused company of notes; I poured forth whatever my genius dictated, and writ with as small deliberation as I do
ordinarily speak. So that as a river runs precipitate & swift, & sometimes dull and slow; now direct, now winding about; now deep, then
shallow; now muddy, then clear; now broad, then narrow, doth my
style flow, now more serious, then light, now more elaborate or remiss,
Comical, Satyrical, as the present subject required, or as at that time
I was affected. And if thou vouchsafe to read this Treatise, it shall seem
no otherwise to thee than the way to an ordinary traveller: sometimes
fair, sometimes foul, here Champion, there inclosed; barren in one
place, better soil in another; by woods, groves, hills, dales, plains, &c.
I shall lead thee over high mountains, & through dangerous valleys, &
dewy meadows, & plowed fields, through variety of objects, that which
thou shalt like and dislike.

For the matter itself or method, if it be faulty, consider I pray you
that of Columella: No one is perfect, or made perfect by zeal alone, no
man can observe all, much is defective, and may be justly taxed, altered
in Galen, Aristotle, and the very best. He is a good huntsman (one
observes) can catch some, not all. I have done mine indeavor. Besides,
I dwell not in these humane studies, or Physick, they are no part of
my profession, I do not draw this furrow, sweat in this field, I am but
a stranger, a smatterer in them, here and there I pull a flower. And I do
easily grant, if a rigid censurer should criticise on this which I have
writ, he should not find three faults, as Scaliger in Terence, but 300,
even as many as he hath done in Cardan's subtilties, or Borocius on
Sacro-Boscus. If ought be amiss, I require friendly admonition, no
bitter invective, otherwise as in ordinary controversies, we may contend, and likely misuse one another, but to what purpose? we are
both scholars, say Arcadians both, and adepts in part-singing. If we do
wrangle, what shall we get by it? trouble and wrong ourselves, make
sport for others.

When all is done, it may be, that which thou so much reprehendest
and in thy judgement dost so much condemn, is not faulty, not to be
condemned: So many men so many minds; I like it, so doth he, thou
dost not; is it therefore unfit, absurd and ridiculous? Every man
abounds in his own sense, and one man cannot express what every man
thinks, or please all. It is the common humour; to discommend that
which they dislike themselves; if ought be omitted, added, if he say not
point blank, as they would have it, he is an idiot, an ass, a nobody. An
easy matter it is to find fault, to censure, vilify, detract from others, a

thing of nothing when it is done; and who could not have done as much?

As for the end of the present Discourse. I refer you to that which hath been formerly said. In the mean time, if any man shall say: Physician Heal thyself, or, as in *Wisdom* (17.8) it was objected to those Wizards: — They that promised to drive away fear and trouble from the sick person, were sick for fear, and worthy to be laughed at. I reply with Sulpitius: They that cure others, cannot well prescribe Physick to themselves.

It now remains that I make thankful remembrance of such friends to whom I have been beholden for their approbation, or troubled in perusing several parts, or all of this Treatise. For I did impart it to some of our worthiest Physicians, whose approbations I had for matters of Physick, and to some Divines, and others of better note in our University, as well as to my more private Collegiate friends, whose censures when I had passed, and that with good encouragement to proceed, I was the bolder to hasten it, with the permission of the Higher authorities, to the Press. I will name no man, or prefix, as the custom is, any Encomiastick verses, which I thank my friends have been offered, lest if either whole or part should be misliked, I should prejudice their judgement, I acknowledge myself much beholding and bound to them: if ought be amiss, I take it wholly to myself, and say again:

> *On me! On me! Here am I who did the deed,*
> *Turn your tongues 'gainst me O scoffers,*
> *You naught approved: mine the faulty screed.*

But I am overtroublesome, I will conclude, if first I may request a favourable censure of such faults as are omitted in the Press. The Copy (as I have said) was once written and in haste, I could not always be there myself; or I had been still present. The Miller sees not all the water goes by his mill. Besides many letters mistaken, misplaced, added, omitted, as i for y, or a for e, or o, false points, &c. which are in some copies only, not throughout: (To point at each particular of which were to pick out the seeds of a foul bushel of corn) some of the chiefest, as thou shalt find them corrected, I desire thee to take notice of. My translations are sometimes rather Paraphrases, and that only taken which was to my purpose; quotations are often inserted in the text, which make the style more harsh, or in the Margin as it happened. Greek Authors, Plato, Plutarch, Athenaus, &c. I have cited out of their interpreters, because the Original was not so ready &c. I have indeed mingled Sacred with profane, but I hope not profaned; and in repetition of Authors' names, not according to Chronology, ranked them willy nilly; sometimes Neotericks, before Ancients, as my memory suggested.

These are the things which I thought good to mention in this Epilogue, the consideration of which I leave to thy favorable censure, and with all submissiveness, as I ought, my self and these my labours to a friendly Reader. Farewell & be kind.

From my Study in Christ Church, Oxon. December 5, 1620.

ROBERT BURTON

APPENDIX II

THE DATE OF BURTON'S BIRTH AS CALCULATED FROM HIS NATIVITY

[The date of Burton's birth has previously been uncertain. His elder brother, William, in his Description of Lincolnshire, gave it as Feb. 8, 1578 (Julian style, now called 1578–9). The nativity, or horoscope, above the bust in Christ Church cathedral, gives the date as Feb. 8, 1576 (now called 1576–7 *). But a nativity in Burton's own handwriting has recently come to light, and has been printed in the Proceedings of the Oxford Bibliographical Society, Vol. I, Part III, 1925, from which it is reproduced in this volume. We have asked Dr. Florian Cajori, professor of the history of mathematics at the University of California, to calculate, if possible, the date of Burton's birth from the astronomical data furnished in the nativity itself. This he has done, as described in the letter following, and the question may now be regarded as settled.]

Berkeley, Calif., Sept. 9, '27.

My dear Sir:

I find that the positions of Jupiter and Saturn in Burton's horoscope indicate the year 1577 as the date of Burton's birth.

Horoscope computation is usually arduous, but in this case I was able to get the desired result easily by the comparison of different horoscopes. In Burton's horoscope Jupiter appears in the " house " having the initial line Leo 24° 20′, and the final line Libra 28° 46′ (?). The question arises, " Is Jupiter in Virgo or in Libra? " Being written down nearer to Virgo, the reading should be " Virgo 9° 59′." That this mode of interpretation is correct can be verified by reference to the Introduction to Astrology, by William Lilly, edited by Zadkiel, London, 1913, pp. 156 and 157, and many other places. In Burton's horoscope, Saturn appears in Capricorn 9° 58′.

* Perhaps it should be explained that the Gregorian calendar, introduced into Catholic countries in 1582, was not adopted in England till 1752; and not only was there a discrepancy of ten days, in the 16th c., between the two calendars, so that Feb. 8 in the Julian style would be equal to Feb. 18 in the Gregorian style, but also the legal New Year began in England on March 25, so that the year 1576 extended through the following March 24, including February of what we should now call 1577. This is the meaning of the date Feb. 8, 1576–7.

I chose the planets Jupiter and Saturn, rather than others, because they are furthest from the sun and therefore least affected, in their apparent positions in the Zodiac, by the motion of the earth. Jupiter completes an orbital revolution in 11.862 years, Saturn in 29.46 years. Taking the planet Jupiter, I compared Burton's horoscope with that of Edward VI. (Oct. 11, 1537), where Jupiter appears in Taurus, 18° 41'. In passing from Taurus 18° 41' through the intervening signs of Gemini, Cancer, and Leo, the number of degrees in the Zodiac is 11° 19' + 30° + 30° + 30° + 9° 59' = 111° 18'. The difference in time between the two horoscopes, taking 1577 as the year of Burton's birth, is 39.32 years. In that time Jupiter swept in the Zodiac over a number of degrees, x, as indicated by the following proportions: 11.862 : 39.32 = 360° : x = 1193.3°. This indicates that Jupiter made, in 39.32 years, three orbital revolutions and 113° 18' over. Taking the year 1578, that difference is 143° 42'; taking 1576, the difference is 83°. It follows, therefore, that the year 1577 is the one in which Burton was born. His horoscope writing indicates either 1576 or 1578. The date Feb. 8, 1576 agrees with the date Feb. 8, 1577, provided we interpret (as we may) Feb. 8, 1576 to mean " Feb. 8, 1576–77," by which we understand " Feb. 8 of the legal year 1576, which began the preceding March and ended March 1577." *

I copy the results of my computations with Jupiter and Saturn, in the comparison of horoscopes, —

Edward VI.	*Burton*	*Computed difference*	
Oct. 11, 1537 —	Feb. 8, 1576:	Jupiter, 82° 54';	Saturn, 108° 12'
" " "	" " 1577:	" 113° 18';	" 120° 27'
" " "	" " 1578:	" 143° 42';	" 132° 42'
	Horoscope difference Jupiter, 111° 18';		Saturn, 113° 5'

Death of Charles I.	*Burton*	*Computed difference*	
Jan. 30, 1648–49 —	Feb. 8, 1576:	Jupiter, 55° ;	Saturn, 171° 36'
" " " "	" " 1577:	" 24° 24';	" 159° 30'
" " " "	" " 1578:	" −6° ;	" 147° 24'
	Horoscope difference Jupiter, 28° 55';		Saturn, 149° 27'

Goethe	*Burton*	*Computed difference*	
Aug. 28, 1749 —	Feb. 8, 1576:	Jupiter, 228° ;	Saturn, 39° 24'
" " "	" " 1577:	" 198° ;	" 51° 30'
" " "	" " 1578:	" 168° ;	" 63° 36'
	Horoscope difference Jupiter, 196° 12';		Saturn, 54° 54'

* See footnote on the Julian and Gregorian year, p. 978.

American Independence	Burton	Computed difference			
Jul. 4, 1776 —	Feb. 8, 1576:	Jupiter, 38°	;	Saturn,	71° 24′
" " "	" " 1577:	" 68° 18′;		"	83° 48′
" " "	" " 1578:	" 98°	;	"	96° 12′

Horoscope difference Jupiter, 64° 01′; Saturn, 85° 8′

The Jupiter data point conclusively to 1577 as the year of Burton's birth. The Saturn data point to the same conclusion, but less convincingly, as was to be expected from the fact that Saturn moves over only 12° of the Zodiac in a year, and has a greater eccentricity of orbit than Jupiter.

FLORIAN CAJORI

APPENDIX III

A NOTE ON EMENDATIONS AND ERRATA

First, those places in the text of the 6th edition where the meaning is obscure or the grammar incorrect, and a correct text can be restored from an earlier edition: Page 100 * — " The Pope is more than a man, as his parats make him "; as Prof. Bensly has pointed out, the early editions read " parasites." Page 122 — " Alexander Tertullianus " has been corrected to " Alexander Trallianus." Page 264 — Of the scholar: " Like an ass, he wears out his time for provender, and can shew a stum rod, . . . an old torn gown " &c.; in all previous editions it is " stumpe rod," which, as Shilleto suggests, is probably a schoolmaster's rod worn by long use to a stump; perhaps we should print " stump rod," but we have merely restored the old reading with its archaic final " e." Page 330 — " Physicians, that study to cure diseases, catch them themselves, will be sick, and appropriate all symptoms they find related of others to their own persons." We restore the reading of the 4th and 5th editions, " Physicians, that studying " &c. Page 364 — Of magical deceptions: " But most part it is in the brain that deceives them." We follow earlier editions in reading " But most part is in the brain," — though this is not quite clear; perhaps the correct reading would be " But most part it is the brain that deceives them." Page 408 — " Whether . . . that hungry Spaniard's discovery . . . be as true as . . . his of Utopia, or his of Lucinia." From the 1st edition we restore " Lusinia," the name of John Barclay's imaginary country in his political allegory, Argenis. Page 723 — Of secret love, it is said that by its symptoms " it may be described "; from the 4th edition we restore " described." Page 758 — Concerning a company of young men and maids: " they might all three sing and dance "; again thanks is due to Prof. Bensly for finding in the earlier editions the correct reading, " all there." Page 785 — If the lover be a judge of female beauty, " he shall find many faults in Physiognomy, and ill colour; if form, one side of the face likely bigger than the other," &c.; the 3d edition supplies the correct reading, " ill colour,

* The quotation following the page-number represents, in every case, the unemended text, followed by the emendation.

ill form." Page 802 — " Oftentimes they may and will not, 'tis their own foolish proceedings that mars all "; earlier editions read " proceeding." Page 812 — Of the chastity of monks: " I am of Tertullian's opinion, few can continue but by compulsion." Earlier editions give us " few can contain." Page 817 — " behold a brief abstract of all that which I have said, . . . elegantly delivered in twelve motions to mitigate the miseries of marriage "; but a little below we are told " how easy it is to answer these motives," and the earlier editions give us " motives " instead of " motions " in the first passage as well. Page 832 — " He that marries a wife that is snowy fair alone "; as Prof. Bensly has pointed out, " snowt fair " is the correct reading.

Second are corrections of the text of the 6th edition, as reprinted by Shilleto, which have been made in other reprints of the 6th and 7th editions; they have been newly compared with the texts of the early editions, but not with the 1651-2 edition, and some of them may concern typographical errors which have crept into the Shilleto text: Page 401 — " the same is incalculcated by Crato "; it should be " inculcated." Page 624 — " Leon Hebræus, in his first dialogue, educeth them all to these three "; it should be " reduceth." Page 669 — " Wherefore did that royal Virgin in Apuleius, when she fled from the thieves' den, made such an Apostrophe to her Ass on whom she rode "; it should be " make such an Apostrophe." Page 733 — " For fire, saith Xenophon, burns them alone that stands near it "; " stand near it " is correct. Page 829 — Of the jealousy of elderly husbands: " Insomuch that she did not complain without cause, in Apuleius, of an old bald bedridded knave she had to her goodman." " Bedridden " is the right reading. Page 896 — Of wicked Jesuits who would persuade some one to assassinate a king: " they bring him into a melancholy dark chamber, . . . till by his strange usage they make him quite mad "; it should be " by this strange usage." Page 898 — " no greater concord, no greater discord then that which proceeds from Religion "; by the 5th edition, this and other " thens " have become " thans " (and we have used the modern spelling generally without referring in every case to earlier editions). Page 913 — " Of Prophets, Enthusians and Impostors "; " Enthusians " is a term which some will regret to lose, but it should be " Enthusiasts." Page 915 — " It is a wonder to see now Nich. Harpsfield . . . puzzles himself "; " to see how " is the correct reading. Page 960 — Of Christian consolation: " let his be as a Bulwark, a Brazen Wall to defend thee "; the correct reading is " let this be." Page 962 — " Galeatius, Martius " is rightly one man, "Galeatius Martius" (though here other reprints leave out Martius and the next ten words).

In looking up "set tippling" in the sentence, page 103, which reads in Shilleto's text, "When our countrymen sacrificed to their goddess Vacuna, and set tippling by their Vacunal fires," we found an interesting variation in the first edition: "When our Countrimen set turning an apple with a pot of ale and a toste by their Vacunal fires." Too bad the apple, ale, and toast were lost in Burton's subsequent revisions: But "set tippling" has become "sate tippling" by the 3d edition; we print "sat tippling."

Next are emendations not based on the text of any early edition, but which we take to be corrections of fairly obvious typographical errors: Page 37 — "When Socrates had taken great pains to find out a wise man, . . . he concludes all men were fools"; we print "he concluded." Page 69 — We supply the necessary "I" before "love and honour in the mean time all good laws." Page 100 — "I must needs except Lipsius and the Pope, and expunge their name out of the catalogue of fools." We print "names." Page 103 — "to say and do what them list"; we print "what they list." Page 416 — "Is it from Topick stars"; we print "Tropick stars," which has a definite meaning and fits the context. Page 508 — "good men have wealth that we should not think it evil; and bad men that they should not rely on or hold it so good"; we print "and bad men that we should not rely on or hold it so good." Page 511 — In the first line of Burton's translation of Lucretius: "men still attending fears"; we print "men's still attending fears." Page 681 — "a round black eye is the best, the Son of Beauty"; we print "Sun of Beauty." Page 736 — "and if thou werst not so indeed"; we print "wert." Page 808 — "If she have fortunes of her own, let her make a man"; "make" might be defended on several grounds, but the context, with its "take him for a husband" a few lines below, persuades us that this is merely a typographical error, and we print "take a man." Page 858 — We believe that "stout fair" is a misprint for "snout fair"; we print "snowt-fair," as on page 832.

There are some corrections of proper names — though we do not mention all the cases in which we have given a more familiar or a corrected spelling, as Marco Polo for M. Polus, Fuchsius for Fuschius, &c. Page 262 — "S. Bernard rode all day long by the Lemnian Lake"; we print "Lake Leman." Page 451 — "Cl. Bruxer's Philosophy Game"; Prof. Bensly having identified him for us, we print "Claude Boissiere's."

Page 948 — " Springer a Lawyer "; again following Prof. Bensly's identification, we print " Scrimger, a Lawyer."

Finally there are a few instances where we have arbitrarily made some slight change for the sake of greater intelligibility: Page 18 — " libraries and shops are full of our putid papers "; we print " putrid," which means the same and is more familiar. Page 22 — " not regarding what, but who write ": we print " who writes." Page 529 — " 'tis a fortune which some indefinitely prefer "; " indefinitely " here means " infinitely," and we print it so.

We also note here the following errata: On page 71, " grievances, which must disturb a body politick " was corrected by earlier editions to " much disturb," and then, by some editorial oversight, changed back again to " must disturb," as the 6th edition wrongly has it. On page 579, we should doubtless have translated the Greek " Zeus " and printed " that proud Jupiter Menecrates," as Burton has it on pages 258 and 382. It was doubtless unnecessary, on page 504, to alter " Adrian the Fourth Pope " into " Pope Adrian the Fourth "; a comma after Fourth, as in Shilleto's text, would have served the turn. Alterations of punctuation, and the general omission of titles of books from the text, are dealt with in our editorial preface. The very broad editorial privileges of omission there claimed with regard to Burton's long and repetitive lists of names was only once taken liberal advantage of, on page 579, in the omission of Amatus Lusitanus, Godefridus Stegius, and Hollerius, before " and all our Herbalists." And we confess an error on page 160, where " Alexander " should read " Alexander ab Alexandro." The discovery of further errors we must now leave to others.

INDEX

divers in their makinges so they do varie in their colours. some have a colour of a darke baye. others bee of an Ashe colour. commonly they bee of a Greene colour, and with blacke spottes, such spottes as the cattes of Algallia have, of a sadde gray colour, al which are finely compounded of certeyne thynne skales, or rindes. one uppon another. lyke to the skales of an Onion.... It is a light stone and easy to be scraped or cutte, lyke to Alabaster. because it is soft; if it bee long in the water, it dissolveth.... It is given in Pouder, and they say that it doth the same effect by chewing of it, or holding of it in the Mouth: for after it is taken, it dooth provoke sweate and dooth expell the Venome.... This stone dooth profit much to them that be sad and melancholike, the Emperour tooke it many times for thys effect."), 563, 593, 594 note

Biarmannus, denying the reality of witchcraft, 174, 176; denying that the devil has carnal relations with women, 648

Biarmi, high priests who sanctify the wombs of the wives of the kings of Calicut, 856

Biarmia, 558

Bibliander, Theodore (Swiss writer, 16th c.), on the Mahometans, 911

Biesius, Nicolas (Dutch phys., poet & philos., 16th c.), 284

Bilia, who took it for granted that all men had bad breaths like her husband (the story is St. Jerome's example of a truly modest wife), 853

Blancanus, Josephus (Jesuit, auth. Echometria, also a bk. Explaining the Mathematical Places of Aristotle, and one On the Fabric of the World), 365, 409, 412, 421, 426

Blasius (comparative anatomist, 17th c., auth. Anatomical Observations in regard to Man, Monkey, Horse, &c., pub. Amsterdam), 289

Blason of Jealousy (Robert Tofte's translation or adaptation of Varchi's poem: the Blason was a 16th c. French mode of descriptive poetry in which there was continual praise or vituperation of the subject, a kind popularized by Clément

Marot: for further references, see Tofte), 825

Bleskenius, Dithmarus, see Dithmarus Bleskenius

Blondus, Flavius (Ital. histor., 15th c., auth. Italy Described), 75

Blood, 128

Blood-letting, 582, 583, 584

Boccaccio, 449, 718, 753, 933

Boccalinus (Trajano Boccalini. Ital. satirist, 16th–17th c., auth. Parnassian Justice, transl. after Burton's death into English as The Politicke Touchstone), 81, 290

Boccaris (Bocchoris, Egyptian king, XXIV. dynasty), 498

Bocerus, (Johann Boedeker or Bocker. German historian & poet, 16th c.), 448

Boderius, Thomas, 390

Bodine (Jean Bodin, French political philosopher, 16th c., auth. The Devil-Mania of Sorcerers, 1580: though liberal in political opinions, he believed in the reality of witchcraft; auth. also of a bk. on political science; visitor to England on a diplomatic mission, 1581), 66, 91, 123, 124, 159, 160, 163, 166, 167, 174, 176, 177, 178, 184, 206, &c.

Bodley, Sir Thomas (founder of the Bodleian library, Oxford), 457, 458

Boethius (Boetius, Roman statesman, philos., & Christian, 5th–6th c.; auth., while in prison awaiting death. of the celebrated Consolation of Philosophy, transl. by Alfred into Anglo-Saxon, into Eng. by Chaucer, Lydgate, & Queen Elizabeth), 66, 138, 239, 491, 492, 526, 631, 783, 813

Boethius, Hector (Hector Boece, or Boyce, Scottish histor., 15th–16th c., auth. History of Scotland, 1527), 168, 179, 188, 202, 411, 431, 558, 648, 881

Bohemus, see Aubanus

Boissardus, Jacobus (Jean Jacques Boissard, French antiquary & Latin poet, 16th c., auth. bks. on magic & sorcery, apparitions, divination, &c., also a Topography of Rome, 1597–1602), on news from the absent through familiar spirits, 160; examples of magical feats, 167; spirits consulted by princes, 173; on "stick-frees," 177–8; dotage, 363; sorcerers, 382; picture galleries, 454;

ERRATA

Page ix (Introduction)
Line 9 should read: "had gone into *eight* when Dr. Johnson's famous"
Line 22: "1811" is probably wrong: it is more likely the edition of 1800 to which Lamb referred, that being the year in which Coleridge suggested to him the writing of his imitation of Burton's Anatomy. However several octavo reprints had appeared prior to the publication of Lamb's essay, *Detached Thoughts on Books and Reading,* where he raised the complaint. The edition read by Keats was that of 1813.

Page 600 (prose)
Line 25: *Randoletius* should read— *Rondoletius.*

Page 628 (the footnote)
Line 1: the first name should read, Julius Cæsar Scaliger.
Line 5: "Bordone" should read *Burdone.*
Line 6: "Bordone" should read *Burdone.*
—the point being that Gaspar Scioppius, in his book (published in 1607), made a wretched pun on the word *Burdon,—Burdonis* being the Latin equivalent of "from a mule."

ADDITIONS AND CORRECTIONS TO INDEX

Page 986
Afer, Leo (Traveller and historian, 16th c., auth. Description of Africa.), 207, 300, 302, 456, 656, 844, 849, 876, 911.

Page 990
Atwater, B. should read.—*Atwater, William* (Bishop Eng. ch. 16th c.).

Page 996
Burton, George (Robert's brother), 950 note.

Page 997
Line 2 should read: Bensly's articles in Notes & Queries,

Page 1009
Faventinus should have been entered as: Victorius Benedictus Faven-

tinus Empiric phys. 1481-1561: wrote De curandis morbis, important in Burton's study of melancholia.

Page 1009
Fienus, should read: Fienus, Thomas.

Page 1011
Add to "Gemma, Cornelius" (*16th c. Astrol. and phys.*)

Page 1013 (second column)
Hildesheim. Change to: Hildesheim, Franciscus (Germ. Med. writer, 16th & 17th cent., from whose "De cerebri et capitis morbis internis Spicilegia." Frankfurt, 1612, Burton so often quotes).

Page 1014
Jason Pratensis. Change "Dutch" to *Swiss:* His book, "De cerebri Morbis" (Basle, 1549), is often quoted by Burton.

Page 1016
On this page are two entries of "*Laurentius.*" There should be but one, viz.: Laurentius Andre du Laurens, auth. "De Morbis Melancholicis tractabus, 1599; phys. to Henry IV., and great anatomist. Died at Paris in 1609.

Page 1016
Leon the Hebrew (Don Judah Abravanel [1565-1630], auth. "Dialoghi di Amore," Rome 1535), 612, 618, 621, 622, 644, 872.

Page 1018
Melanelius, Matthias Theodorus (16th cent. phys. auth. "De Melancholia ex Galeni, Rufi, etc. 1540).

Page 1020
Montaltus, Ælianus. Should be Montaltus, Ælianus. Portuguese phys. died at Tours, 1616. His book on mental pathology, "Archipathologia," Paris 1614, was one of Burton's most useful source-books.

Page 1020
Montanus. Should read: Montanus, John Bapt. Veronese phys. & poet, 1498-1551, called "the second Galen"; his *Consultations,* Basle, 1563, contain a large section devoted to melancholy.

Page 1023
 Picatrix. Celebrated medieval book
  of magic; prob. 12th or 13th cent.
  compilation. Never printed, but
  widely circulated in Ms. form.
Page 1023
 Platerus is same as *Plater* above,
  viz.: Felix Plater.
Page 1026
 Rondoletius, Guillame (referred to
  by Rabelais under the name of
  "Rondibilis"; he was one of the

first scientific zoologists; 1509-
 1566).
Page 1026
 Roeslin, Helisaeus; Eliseo Roeslin;
  Germ. phys. and astron. 16th c.
  His "Theoria Nova cœlestium
  Meteorum"—Strassburg, 1578—, is
  referred to by Burton. 420, 421,
  422, 427, 428.
Page 1029
 Thuanus. Jacques August De Thou.
  (French hist. 1553-1617.)